Flash® Builder™ 4 and Flex® 4 Bible

Flash® Builder™ 4 and Flex® 4 Bible

David Gassner

Wiley Publishing, Inc.

Flash® Builder™ 4 and Flex® 4 Bible

Published by
Wiley Publishing, Inc.
10475 Crosspoint Boulevard
Indianapolis, IN 46256
www.wiley.com

Copyright © 2010 by Wiley Publishing, Inc., Indianapolis, Indiana

Published by Wiley Publishing, Inc., Indianapolis, Indiana

Published simultaneously in Canada

ISBN: 978-0-470-48895-9

Manufactured in the United States of America

10 9 8 7 6 5 4 3 2 1

For general information on our other products and services or to obtain technical support, please contact our Customer Care Department within the U.S. at (877) 762-2974, outside the U.S. at (317) 572-3993 or fax (317) 572-4002.

Library of Congress Control Number: 2010922565

For Jackie

About the Author

David Gassner is president of Bardo Technical Services, an Adobe training partner in Seattle, Washington, and serves as Content Manager for Developer Titles for lynda.com. As an author for lynda.com, he has recorded video training titles on Flex, AIR, ColdFusion, Dreamweaver, and ASP. NET. He holds Adobe developer and instructor certifications in Flex, ColdFusion, Flash, and Dreamweaver, is an Adobe Master Instructor, and has been a regular speaker at Allaire, Macromedia, and Adobe conferences.

David earned a BA from Pitzer College in Claremont, California (his home town), and an MFA from the Professional Theatre Training Program at U.C. San Diego. In his copious free time (and putting his MFA to good use), he is an active director and actor in Seattle's live theater scene. He shares his home with his wonderful wife, Jackie (Go Mets!), and he receives occasional visits from his thoroughly adult kids, Thad, Jason, and Jenny.

Credits

Senior Acquisitions Editor
Stephanie McComb

Executive Editor
Jody Lefevere

Project Editor
Katharine Dvorak

Technical Editor
Drew Falkman

Copy Editor
Lauren Kennedy

Editorial Director
Robyn Siesky

Business Manager
Amy Knies

Senior Marketing Manager
Sandy Smith

Vice President and Executive Group Publisher
Richard Swadley

Vice President and Executive Publisher
Barry Pruett

Project Coordinator
Patrick Redmond

Graphics and Production Specialists
Nikki Gately
Amy Hassos
Joyce Haughey

Quality Control Technicians
Laura Albert
John Greenough
Melanie Hoffman
Lindsay Littrell
Lauren Mandelbaum

Proofreading
Christine Sabooni

Indexing
BIM Indexing & Proofreading Services

Media Development Project Manager
Laura Moss

Media Development Assistant Project Manager
Jenny Swisher

Media Development Associate Producer
Shawn Patrick

Contents at a Glance

Preface xxiii
Acknowledgments xxvii

Part I: Flex Fundamentals 1
Chapter 1: About Flex 4 3
Chapter 2: Using Flash Builder 4 31
Chapter 3: Building a Basic Flex Application 73
Chapter 4: Understanding the Anatomy of a Flex Application 99
Chapter 5: Using Bindings and Components 135
Chapter 6: Debugging Flex Applications...167
Chapter 7: Working with Events...207

Part II: Designing Flex Applications 247
Chapter 8: Using Flex Visual Controls..249
Chapter 9: Working with Text 287
Chapter 10: Using Layout Containers 311
Chapter 11: Using Cascading Style Sheets......................................341
Chapter 12: Controlling Animation and Working with Drag and Drop....371
Chapter 13: Managing View States...399
Chapter 14: Declaring Graphics with MXML and FXG 419
Chapter 15: Skinning Spark Components 443
Chapter 16: Managing Application Navigation 469
Chapter 17: Working with Pop-up Windows 503

Part III: Working with Data...............................531
Chapter 18: Modeling and Managing Data......................................533
Chapter 19: Using List Controls...571
Chapter 20: Using Advanced List Controls 603
Chapter 21: Using the Flex Charting Controls 647
Chapter 22: Working with Data Entry Forms 675
Chapter 23: Working with HTTPService and XML 707
Chapter 24: Managing XML with E4X 749

Part IV: Integrating Flex Applications with Application Servers 775

Chapter 25: Working with SOAP-Based Web Services 777
Chapter 26: Integrating Flex Applications with BlazeDS and Java 807
Chapter 27: Using the Message Service with BlazeDS 849
Chapter 28: Integrating Flex Applications with ColdFusion 873
Chapter 29: Integrating Flex Applications with PHP 911

Part V: Additional Subjects 939

Chapter 30: Localizing Flex 4 Applications 941
Chapter 31: Deploying Desktop Applications with Adobe AIR 955

Index 983

Contents

Preface xxiii

Acknowledgments xxvii

Part I: Flex Fundamentals   1

Chapter 1: About Flex 4 3

Learning the Fundamentals of Flex 4
    Getting to know Flex applications.......................................4
    Flex versus Flash development..8
    Flex and object-oriented programming 11
Understanding Adobe Flash Player 18
    Learning a little Adobe Flash Player history........................19
    Understanding Flash Player penetration statistics 21
    Using the debug version of Flash Player 21
    Flash Player installation..22
Flex 4 Development Tools 26
    Understanding Flash Builder 4 26
    Using the Flex 4 SDK 26
Getting Help 29
Summary 29

Chapter 2: Using Flash Builder 4 31

Getting Flash Builder 31
Installing Flash Builder 4 32
    Installing Flash Builder with the stand-alone configuration 32
Getting to Know Eclipse Features..36
    The Eclipse workspace 37
    Configuring Eclipse 43
Using Flash Builder..45
    Creating a Flex project 45
    Understanding Flash Builder's user interface 49
Getting Help 55
    Exploring the Help contents...55
    Searching for Help terms...56
    Using dynamic help 57

Contents

Searching for Code...58
    Using Eclipse search tools 58
    Using Flash Builder code model search tools...........................60
Generating Code 64
    Generating getter and setter methods 64
    Generating event handlers 66
Integrating Flash Builder with Flash Professional CS5.................66
Summary 71

Chapter 3: Building a Basic Flex Application......................73

Creating a "Hello World" Application 74
    Switching workspaces 74
    Creating the project...75
    Saying hello...78
Understanding the html-template Folder 81
    The HTML wrapper template 82
    History management files 87
Deploying the Application 88
    Creating a release build 88
    Testing the release build..90
    Deploying the release build 91
    Integrating an application into an existing Web page 91
    Integrating Flex applications with Dreamweaver 93
Summary 97

Chapter 4: Understanding the Anatomy of a Flex Application 99

MXML and ActionScript 3 101
Understanding MXML 104
    MXML is XML!...104
    MXML and containership...110
    MXML and nonvisual classes..112
Understanding ActionScript 3 114
    ActionScript syntax 114
    Declaring variables 114
    Conditional statements..117
    Looping..119
Combining MXML and ActionScript 120
    Using the <fx:Script> element 120
    Using external ActionScript files...120
    Managing ActionScript code with Flash Builder 124
Using the Application Component 128
    Passing application parameters..130
    Controlling application dimensions..130
    Setting the layout property 131
Summary 134

Chapter 5: Using Bindings and Components 135

Using Binding Expressions...136
    Shorthand MXML binding expressions..136
    Using <fx:Binding>..137
    Making expressions bindable...137
Using MXML Components..139
    Creating MXML components...139
    Instantiating MXML components 144
Adding Properties and Methods to Components...149
    Component properties 150
    Component methods...152
Using Component Libraries..155
    Creating component libraries...155
    Using component libraries..159
Creating Flash-based Components..161
Summary...165

Chapter 6: Debugging Flex Applications 167

Debugging Basics..168
    The debug version of the application...169
    Running an application in debug mode..169
Using trace() and the Logging API...172
    Using the trace() function...172
    Using the Logging API..175
Using Breakpoints...180
    Setting and clearing breakpoints 180
    Setting and removing breakpoints in an MXML or ActionScript editor.............180
    Setting conditional breakpoints...181
    Using the Breakpoints view...183
    Using breakpoints in a debugging session 185
    Inspecting variables and expressions 187
    Controlling application execution with the Debug view 192
Profiling Flex Applications..194
Using the Network Monitor..196
    Configuring a Flex project for use with ColdFusion 197
    Tracing network traffic...201
Summary...206

Chapter 7: Working with Events 207

The Flex Event Architecture..208
Handling Events in MXML..210
    Declaring event listeners in MXML...210
    Working with event objects..213

Contents

Handling Events with addEventListener() 223
    Setting up an event listener 223
    Using event name constants 226
    Removing an event listener.. 227
Using Event Bubbling 227
Using Custom Events.. 230
    Declaring custom events... 231
    Dispatching custom events.. 233
    Handling custom events 235
Using Custom Event Classes 237
    Creating the ActionScript class... 238
    Dispatching a custom event class... 242
    Handling an event that uses a custom event class............................... 244
Summary 246

Part II: Designing Flex Applications   247

Chapter 8: Using Flex Visual Controls 249

Instantiating and Customizing Controls.. 250
    Instantiating controls with MXML and ActionScript............................. 250
    Setting control properties and styles.. 251
    Understanding UIComponent and GraphicElement 251
Using Spark Text Controls 253
    Using text control properties 254
    Text entry controls 259
Using Layout Controls 263
    The HRule and VRule controls 263
    The Spacer control 265
Using Button Controls 266
    The Button control 266
    The LinkButton control... 268
    The CheckBox control... 268
    The RadioButton controls... 269
Other Data Entry Controls 271
    The NumericStepper control 272
    Date controls.. 273
    The ColorPicker control 275
Using Interactive Controls... 277
    The ScrollBar controls 277
    The Slider controls 279
Using the Image and BitmapImage Controls 281
    Resizing images 283
    Embedding images 284
    Changing images at runtime... 285
Summary 286

Chapter 9: Working with Text. 287

Using Advanced Text Layout 288
  Presenting richly formatted text...288
  Presenting text in columns 292
  Using bidirectional text 292
Controlling Fonts with Cascading Style Sheets...294
  Selecting fonts 295
  Using device fonts..296
  Using embedded fonts...297
Manipulating Text...303
Formatting Text Values 305
  Creating formatter objects 305
  Setting formatter properties...306
  Using formatters in binding expressions...307
  Using formatters in static methods 308
Summary 310

Chapter 10: Using Layout Containers 311

Using MX Basic Containers 312
  Using vertical and horizontal layout containers 312
  Using the Canvas container 315
  Using MX container styles..317
Using Spark Group Components 319
  Using the Group component 320
  Using VGroup and HGroup 321
  Using the Spark BorderContainer 323
Using Panel Containers 325
  Panel properties 326
  Using the MX ControlBar container..328
  Using Spark panels with control bars 329
Using Constraint-Based Layout 330
  Positioning components in Design mode..331
  Using constraint properties 332
Sizing Containers and Controls..333
  Content-based sizing...333
  Absolute sizing..334
  Percentage sizing...334
  Constraint-based sizing...335
Creating a Scrolling Region 337
Summary 339

Contents

Chapter 11: Using Cascading Style Sheets **341**

About Cascading Style Sheets..341

What Is a Style Sheet? 343

Using Inline Style Declarations...344

Declaring Style Sheets with <fx:Style>..345

Using Style Selectors 346

    Using type selectors...346

    Using descendant selectors...350

    Using style name selectors..351

    Using ID selectors 352

    Using the global selector 352

Using Embedded Style Sheets 353

Using External Style Sheets 356

    Creating a blank style sheet 356

    Exporting existing styles..359

Using Compiled Style Sheets 363

    Compiling style sheets..363

    Loading compiled style sheets 363

Controlling Styles with ActionScript 366

    Setting and getting style information 366

    Modifying style selectors at runtime 367

Summary 370

**Chapter 12: Controlling Animation and
Working with Drag and Drop** **371**

Using Effects 372

    Declaring and playing effect classes 373

    Declaring effects in ActionScript...375

    Using the new Spark effects..377

    Using composite effects 383

    Using easing classes..387

Using Drag-and-Drop Operations 388

    Implementing drag-and-drop with List controls..389

    Implementing custom drag-and-drop operations 391

Summary 398

Chapter 13: Managing View States **399**

Understanding View States...400

Defining View States in Design View..401

    Creating a new state 401

    Defining a view state's overrides 404

Switching View States at Runtime 406

Declaring View States in MXML...407

    Adding and removing components..408

    Overriding properties, styles, and event handlers.......................................409

Contents

Managing View States in Components 412

Using Transitions 414

    Declaring a transition 414

    Using Parallel and Sequence effects in transitions 415

Summary 418

Chapter 14: Declaring Graphics with MXML and FXG 419

Declaring Vector Graphics in MXML 420

    Drawing lines and shapes 420

    Adding visual effects 425

Using FXG Files 432

    Creating FXG graphics with Creative Suite software 432

    Using FXG files in Flex applications 439

Summary 442

Chapter 15: Skinning Spark Components 443

Creating and Using Spark Custom Skins 444

    Skinning a Spark application 444

    Binding a custom skin to a Spark component 451

Skinning Other Spark Components 455

    Creating a new skin 455

    Assigning custom skins with CSS 461

    Customizing the skin 462

Summary 467

Chapter 16: Managing Application Navigation 469

Understanding Classic Web Navigation 470

Understanding Flex Navigation 471

Using Navigator Containers 471

    Declaring a ViewStack in MXML 472

    Using custom components in a navigator container 472

    Creating a ViewStack in Design mode 473

    Working with navigator containers in ActionScript 477

    Managing creation policy 482

    Managing navigator container dimensions 484

Using Navigator Bar Containers 484

    Using a data collection as a dataProvider 485

    Handling navigator bar events 487

    Using a ViewStack as a dataProvider 487

    Managing navigator bar presentation 488

Using Menu Controls 491

    Menu data providers 492

    Handling menu events 493

    Using the Menu control 494

    Using the MenuBar control 495

Contents

Using Other Navigator Containers 497

    The TabNavigator container 498

    The Accordion container 500

    TabNavigator and Accordion keyboard shortcuts 501

Summary 502

Chapter 17: Working with Pop-up Windows **503**

Using the Alert Class 504

    Presenting pop-up windows with Alert.show() 504

    Controlling Alert window modality 504

    Managing Alert window buttons 506

    Handling Alert window events 508

    Using a custom graphical icon 509

    Using CSS selectors with the Alert class 512

Using the PopUpMenuButton Control 514

    Creating a data provider 514

    Handling events 515

Using the PopUpButton control 517

    Declaring the pop-up window 518

    Handling events and managing pop-up behavior 518

Working with Custom Pop-up Windows 521

    Defining a custom pop-up window 521

    Managing custom pop-up windows with the PopUpManager class 524

Summary 530

Part III: Working with Data   **531**

Chapter 18: Modeling and Managing Data **533**

Creating a Data Model 534

    Using the <fx:Model> element 535

Using Value Objects 539

    Using the New ActionScript Class wizard 540

    Value object class syntax 541

    Instantiating value object classes 549

Using Data Collections 552

    Declaring an ArrayCollection 553

    Setting a data collection object's source property 554

    Accessing data at runtime 555

    Managing data at runtime 556

    Using data cursors 562

Summary 569

Chapter 19: Using List Controls **571**

Using Data Providers 574

    Using hard-coded data providers 575

    Using dynamic data providers 577

Controlling List Item Labels 579
    Using the labelField property 579
    Using the labelFunction property 582
List Control Events and Properties 584
Handling User Data Selections 585
    Using the change event 585
    Using the selectedItem property 585
    Using the selectedIndex property 587
    Selecting complex data objects 588
Using Custom Item Renderers..590
    Using drop-in item renderers 591
    Using inline renderers and editors..593
    Using component item renderers 597
    Customizing Spark item renderers with view states............................600
Summary 602

Chapter 20: Using Advanced List Controls 603

Using ComboBox and DropDownList Controls..603
    Using the prompt property..604
    Using the ComboBox control 605
    Selecting complex data objects with ActionScript................................607
    Using the Spark ButtonBar control 611
Using the DataGrid Control 613
    Customizing the DataGrid display..614
    Displaying custom labels in DataGrid column cells 619
Advanced Item Renderers and Editors 622
    Using the dataChange event 623
    Using Spark item renderers 626
    Using item editors 627
Using List Controls with Horizontal and Tile Layout....................................635
Using the AdvancedDataGrid Control 641
    Hierarchical data display 641
    Grouping flat data 644
Summary 646

Chapter 21: Using the Flex Charting Controls 647

Understanding Flex's Types of Charts 648
Declaring Chart Controls 650
Setting Chart Properties and Styles..652
    Using pie charts 652
    Using financial charts..663
    Using bar, column, line, and area charts..666
Summary 673

Contents

Chapter 22: Working with Data Entry Forms **675**

Using the Form Container..676
    Using the FormHeading control 678
    Using the FormItem container...680
    Setting a default button 681
Using Custom Form Components...683
    Creating a custom Form component 683
    Adding controls to a Form component..685
Validating Data Entry...687
    Creating a validator object..688
    Controlling validation with trigger events..688
    Controlling validation with ActionScript 691
    Controlling validation rules and error messages 695
Sharing Data with the Application..697
    Modeling Form data with a value object..697
    Dispatching a custom event...699
Summary 705

Chapter 23: Working with HTTPService and XML **707**

Using RPC and REST Architectures..708
    Understanding the Representational State Transfer architecture 708
    Understanding the Remote Procedure Call architecture..709
Creating Data-Centric Applications with Flash Builder 4...710
    Creating and managing data connections 710
    Defining a return data type..714
    Binding returned data to visual controls..719
Declaring and Configuring HTTPService Objects...722
    Creating an HTTPService object 722
    Essential HTTPService properties..723
Sending and Receiving Data...727
    Understanding asynchronous communications 727
    Handling HTTPService responses..727
    Working with CallResponder and AsyncToken 736
    Working with ItemResponder and AsyncToken 739
Working with Value Objects...741
Passing Parameters to Server Pages..744
    Using named parameters...744
    Using bound parameters...745
Handling Cross-Domain Policy Issues..746
Summary 748

Chapter 24: Managing XML with E4X **749**

Using XML Classes...750
  Creating an XML object...751
  Using the XMLList class...754
  Using the XMLListCollection class..755
Using E4X Expressions..756
  Extracting data from XML objects 758
  Modifying data in XML objects...765
Working with Namespaces 770
Summary 774

**Part IV: Integrating Flex Applications
with Application Servers   775**

Chapter 25: Working with SOAP-Based Web Services **777**

Understanding SOAP..778
Understanding WSDL..780
Using the WebService Component...783
  Installing ColdFusion 783
  Creating a WebService object 784
  Handling Web service results 786
  Passing parameters to Web service operations...........................796
Using Web Service Data Connections 798
  Defining a data connection...799
  Managing Web service data connections 801
Summary 805

Chapter 26: Integrating Flex Applications with BlazeDS and Java **807**

Using BlazeDS...808
  Understanding supported platforms..808
  Getting started with BlazeDS 809
Creating Flex Projects for Use with BlazeDS.................................814
Using the Proxy Service 817
  Configuring the Proxy Service...817
  Using the default destination...818
  Using named destinations 822
Using the Remoting Service..824
  Creating and exposing Java classes 825
  Configuring Remoting Service destinations 828
Using the RemoteObject Component...830
  Instantiating the RemoteObject component................................830
  Calling remote methods 830
  Handling RemoteObject results...831
  Passing arguments to remote methods......................................838

Contents

Passing data between ActionScript and Java 840
Using value object classes..841
Working with BlazeDS Data Connections in Flash Builder 4.................................845
Enabling RDS with BlazeDS...846
Defining BlazeDS data connections 847
Summary 848

Chapter 27: Using the Message Service with BlazeDS 849

Understanding the Message Service...850
Configuring Messaging on the Server..851
Configuring channels for messaging..851
Configuring messaging adaptors and destinations 854
Creating a Flex Messaging Application...856
Creating a Flex project 856
Sending messages...857
Receiving and processing messages 858
Sending and Receiving Complex Data...862
Filtering Messages on the Server 865
Using the selector property 865
Using subtopics..866
Tracing Messaging Traffic 871
Summary 872

Chapter 28: Integrating Flex Applications with ColdFusion 873

Understanding Flash Remoting and ColdFusion 874
Creating a Flex project for use with ColdFusion...875
Configuring Flash Remoting on the server..877
Creating ColdFusion Components for Flex 878
Using CFCs with the RemoteObject Component...880
Setting the source property 881
Creating a RemoteObject instance 881
Calling CFC functions..882
Handling CFC Function Results..883
Using binding expressions..883
Using the result event..884
Handling results from multiple CFC functions 888
Passing Arguments to CFC Functions 891
Using explicit arguments...891
Using bound arguments 892
Using named arguments..892
Using Value Object Classes 894
Creating a ColdFusion value object 894
Creating an ActionScript value object..895
Returning value objects from ColdFusion to Flex..896

Receiving value objects from ColdFusion 897
Passing value object arguments to CFC functions 899
Working with RemoteObject Faults 900
Handling the fault event 900
Generating custom exceptions from a CFC function 901
Working with Data Connections in Flash Builder 903
Calling ColdFusion 9 Services 905
Configuring ColdFusion security 905
Using ColdFusion 9 client-side service components 907
Summary 910

Chapter 29: Integrating Flex Applications with PHP 911

Installing PHP 912
Installing WampServer on Windows 913
Managing WampServer 914
Installing MAMP on Mac OS X 916
Managing MAMP servers 917
Creating a Flex Project for Use with PHP 919
Using PHP with HTTPService and XML 922
Using the PHP SimpleXML extension 922
Retrieving XML data with HTTPService 923
Using PHP and Remoting with Zend AMF 924
Installing Zend AMF 925
Creating a service class in PHP 927
Calling a PHP class with RemoteObject 928
Returning complex data from Zend AMF 929
Understanding ActionScript to PHP data serialization 932
Using PHP Data Connections in Flash Builder 932
Defining data connections 932
Generating a service based on a database table structure 935
Summary 938

Part V: Additional Subjects   939

Chapter 30: Localizing Flex 4 Applications 941

Using Locales to Select Application Resources 941
Changing locales at compile time 943
Changing locales at runtime 944
Using Custom Resource Bundles 947
Creating resource bundles at runtime 947
Using external resource bundles 950
Summary 954

Contents

Chapter 31: Deploying Desktop Applications with Adobe AIR 955

Understanding AIR Architecture 956
Installing Adobe AIR..958
    Downloading the AIR installer...958
    Installing and uninstalling AIR on Windows 958
    Installing and uninstalling AIR on Mac OS X..959
Creating a Flex Desktop Application 960
    Creating a Flex desktop application project..960
    Using the application descriptor file 963
    Packaging a release version of an AIR application......................................967
    Installing AIR applications..969
    Uninstalling AIR applications 971
Flex Application Tips and Tricks with AIR...971
    Debugging AIR applications in Flash Builder...972
    Working with HTML-based content..973
    Using the WindowedApplication component..977
    Creating Remoting channels at runtime...978
A Conclusion about Adobe AIR...980
Summary 981

Index 983

Preface

When Macromedia first released Flash MX in 2002, the product was branded as the new way to build Rich Internet Applications (known by the acronym RIA). The term was invented at Macromedia to describe a new class of applications that would offer the benefits of being connected to the Internet, including access to various types of Web-based services, but would solve many of the nagging issues that had been inherent in browser-based applications since the mid-1990s. Using Flash Player to host graphically rich applications delivered as Flash documents would address issues such as the ongoing differences between Web browsers in implementation of Cascading Style Sheets (CSS) and JavaScript. And because such applications would be able to leverage Flash Player's original strengths, including animation and delivery of rich media (audio and video) to the desktop, the applications could be both functional and visually compelling.

The first push into the new frontier of RIAs met with mixed success. Many applications built and delivered with Flash MX and ColdFusion MX (Macromedia's recommended middleware application server software at the time) were very impressive. Perhaps the best known of this class is the iHotelier hotel reservations application, which is still used by many large hotels around the world. The application presents customers with a Flash-based interface they can use to find and reserve hotel rooms from a visually intuitive single-screen interface. A customer can input information and get a nearly instantaneous response without having to navigate the multi-page interface of classic HTML-based Web applications.

Meanwhile, developers who were creating these applications were madly pulling their hair out. Building data-centric applications in Flash meant that they were working with a binary source file, making it difficult to integrate with source control systems. At the time, ActionScript wasn't particularly object-oriented (although this part of the situation improved drastically with the release of ActionScript 2 in Flash MX 2004), and there was no enforcement of code placement standards. Its loose data typing and lack of strong compile-time error checking or debugging tools led to phenomena such as "silent failure" — the moment when something that's supposed to happen doesn't, and no information is offered as to the reason.

In large multi-developer environments, figuring out where to put the code in a Flash document was a significant part of the application planning process, because the product wasn't really designed for application development. And the ActionScript editor built into Flash gave experienced developers fits. Java developers, in particular, were used to sophisticated code editors, and working in Flash slowed their productivity and increased their frustration.

Flex 1 was Macromedia's first response to these issues. Released initially as a server-based product, Flex was designed to let enterprise application developers use a workflow they were accustomed to. Flex Builder 1, built on top of the Dreamweaver code base, was a first stab at providing a better code editor and was included for those organizations that purchased a server license. Issues remained, but developers who were accustomed to building applications in source code were able to use their usual workflows, and multiple developers could collaborate more easily because Flex applications were built as source code files that could be shared.

Flex 2 went further with the delivery of ActionScript 3, a true object-oriented language. The Flex 2 SDK was free, and Flex Builder 2 was the first version of the integrated development environment (IDE) delivered as an Eclipse plug-in. The IDE's licensing changed to a per-developer model, identical to the model used by other successful developer tools. For enterprise application developers, the situation got better and better.

Flex 3 offered developers the ability not only to build better Web-based applications but also to deliver desktop applications using Adobe AIR (formerly known as the Adobe Integrated Runtime). Anything you could do in Flex 3 on the Web, you could also do in Flex 3 on the desktop. The Flex 3 SDK added new visual controls, such as the `AdvancedDataGrid`, that were licensed as part of Flex Builder 3 Professional (now known in Flash Builder 4 as the Premiere edition). And Flex Builder 3 added debugging features, such as the Flex Profiler, that improved developer productivity.

With Flex 4, Adobe introduces a new way of implementing visual designs. The new Spark component set includes a radically redesigned *component skinning* architecture that combines the ease of MXML-based programming with the power of Flash Player's visual rendering capabilities. Flex 4 applications can take advantage of the new features of Flash Player 10, including the Flash Text Engine (FTE) and Text Layout Framework (TLF) that enable complex text presentation, and 3D animations. The newly renamed Flash Builder 4 (formerly known as Flex Builder) is now positioned as the ActionScript editing product of choice for both Flex and Flash developers. Flash Builder 4 includes new code refactoring and formatting features and the Network Monitor debugging tool that traces network traffic when a Flex application communicates with an application server at runtime.

This book offers a comprehensive overview of Flex 4 application development. Detailed explanations of building applications using the Flex 4 SDK are combined with explorations of how to integrate applications with the most popular Web service architectures and application servers. The book is not designed as a replacement for the Flash Builder and Flex 4 documentation (which at last count included multiple publications and more than 2,000 pages). Instead, it offers a combination of references, tutorials, and tips for building and delivering Flex application to the Web and the desktop and takes you through learning Flex in a natural sequence.

For those who like to listen as they learn, check out my video training titles at lynda.com (`www.lynda.com`), including training on Flash Builder 4 and Flex 4, Adobe AIR, ColdFusion, and Dreamweaver.

Getting the Most Out of This Book

Most chapters are accompanied by sample Flex applications and other source code that you can download from the Wiley.com Web site at `www.wiley.com/go/flex4`. Each chapter's sample files are independent from other chapters, so if you want to jump to a particular subject, you don't first have to go through the sample code for all the preceding chapters.

Many of the files from the Web site are delivered as Flex Project archive files. A Flex Project archive, also known as an FXP file, is a new format introduced in Flash Builder 4. It's a file with the extension of `.fxp`, and it contains everything you need to import an existing project into Flash Builder. It's portable between operating systems, so you can import the file into any version of Flash Builder 4, whether on Windows or Mac OS X. It's also the format that's exported by Flash Catalyst, a new product from Adobe Systems that enables graphic designers to create interactive prototypes of Flex applications without having to know MXML and ActionScript.

If you're using the free Flex SDK (rather than Flash Builder), you can still use the Flex Project archive files. Just rename them with a file extension of `.zip` and then extract them to a folder somewhere on your system. Following current best-practice recommendations, the project's application source code files are always in a subfolder of the archive root named `src`.

For chapters that deal with application servers such as BlazeDS, ColdFusion, or PHP, you'll need to download and install that software to run the sample applications from the Web site. Each relevant chapter includes the URL from which the software can be downloaded and complete installation instructions. For these chapters, you typically are instructed to create a Flex project from scratch and then extract files from a ZIP file from the Web site into the project (rather than importing a Flex Project archive file).

Finally, you can let me know about issues you find in the book or offer suggestions for subjects you'd like to see covered in a future edition. Visit `www.bardotech.com/flexbible` to ask questions and offer feedback.

Using the Book's Icons

The following margin icons help you get the most out of this book:

Note
Notes highlight useful information that you should take into consideration. ∎

Tip
Tips provide additional bits of advice that make particular features quicker or easier to use. ∎

Caution

Cautions warn you of potential problems before you make a mistake. ■

New Feature

The New Feature icon highlights features that are new to Flex. ■

Cross-Reference

Watch for the Cross-Ref icon to learn where in another chapter you can go to find more information on a particular topic. ■

On the Web

This icon points you toward related files on the book's Web site, www.wiley.com/go/flex4. ■

Web Resource

The Web Resource icon directs you to other materials available online. ■

Acknowledgments

It's a truism, and it's also true, that no book of any length can be completed without the support and sufferance of family, friends, and colleagues. While this book is a revision of the first edition, *Flex 3 Bible*, the extent of the changes that Adobe Systems introduced in the Flex 4 SDK and Flash Builder 4 have made the book new again.

First, I'd like to thank the great folks at Wiley Publishing who always took my calls. Stephanie McComb and Katharine Dvorak were always willing to hear the newest idea and help me figure out what was next. And Drew Falkman, fellow Flex instructor at Bardo Tech and aspiring screenwriter, ferreted out the technical issues without regard for my sensitive side.

The Adobe Certified Instructors who join me at Bardo Technical Services in teaching Adobe Flex to the world have taught me more about Flex than just about anyone. Thanks to Simeon Bateman, Drew Falkman (again), Alex Hearnz, and Jeanette Stallons.

Neil Salkind, Katrina Bevan, and Stacey Barone at Studio B relieved me of having to worry about the business details.

Since early in this century, I've worked as a technical trainer and courseware developer with an extraordinary crew, the Adobe instructional development team members who have moved from Allaire to Macromedia to Adobe and never lost their stride: Matt Boles, Robert Crooks, Sue Hove, Deborah Prewitt, James Talbot, and Leo Schuman. Some have moved on to other adventures, but their mark on the Flex educational world has been significant.

Members of the Adobe Flex product management team, including Matt Chotin and Tim Buntel, pointed me in the right direction more times than they know. Jeff Vroom of the LiveCycle Data Services and BlazeDS development team humbled himself to be my teaching assistant at a couple of Adobe conferences and is more the master of this material than I.

And finally, for my family who dealt with me deciding to do this again: my kids, Thad, Jason, and Jenny, and my extraordinary wife and best friend in the whole world, Jackie.

Part I

Flex Fundamentals

IN THIS PART

Chapter 1
About Flex 4

Chapter 2
Using Flash Builder 4

Chapter 3
Building a Basic Flex Application

Chapter 4
Understanding the Anatomy
of a Flex Application

Chapter 5
Using Bindings and Components

Chapter 6
Debugging Flex Applications

Chapter 7
Working with Events

About Flex 4

Flex 4 is the most recent version of a platform for developing and deploying software applications that run on top of Adobe Flash Player for the Web and Adobe AIR for the desktop. While such tools have existed for many years, the most recent set from Adobe Systems enables programmers with object-oriented backgrounds to become productive very quickly using the skills they already have learned in other programming languages and platforms.

Since the release of Flex 2, the Flex development environment has encouraged a development workflow similar to that used in desktop development environments such as Visual Studio, Delphi, and JBuilder. The developer writes source code and compiles an application locally and then, for applications designed for deployment from the Web, uploads the finished application to a Web server for access by the user. That isn't how Flex started, however.

Flex was originally released by Macromedia as a server-based application deployment and hosting platform. In the early versions of the Flex product line, an MXML/ActionScript compiler was included in a Java-based Web application hosted on a Java Enterprise Edition (JEE) server. Application source code was stored on the server. When a user made a request to the server, the application was compiled "on request" and delivered to the user's browser, and hosted by the Flash Player.

This server-based compilation and application deployment model is still available in a component now known as the Flex Web Tier Compiler. But the version of the compiler that's delivered in the Web Tier Compiler isn't always the same as the one that's included in both the Flex 4 Software Developers Kit (SDK) and the newly renamed Flash Builder 4. And most developers find it simpler to use the primary "local compilation" development model.

IN THIS CHAPTER

Understanding the fundamentals of Flex

Getting to know Flex applications

Developing in Flex versus Flash

Using Flex with object-oriented programming

Understanding the Flash Player

Learning the history of the Flash Player

Making the most of Flex 4 development tools

Getting help

In this chapter, I describe the nature of Flex applications, the relationship between Flex applications and Adobe Flash Player, and how Flex leverages the nearly ubiquitous distribution of Flash Player on multiple operating systems. I also describe how Flex applications can be packaged for deployment as desktop applications using Adobe AIR.

Learning the Fundamentals of Flex

The Flex product line enables developers to deploy applications that run on Flash Player as Web applications and on Adobe AIR as native desktop applications. The compiled applications that you create with Flex are in the same format as those produced by the Adobe Flash authoring environment (such as Adobe Flash CS4), but the process of creating the applications is very different.

Getting to know Flex applications

A Flex application is built as a Flash-based software presentation that you create with the Flex 4 SDK. Most Flex developers create their applications using the Flash Builder 4 integrated development environment product line (formerly named Flex Builder). And a new product from Adobe, Flash Catalyst, helps to bridge the gap between developers who use Flash Builder and designers who use Photoshop or Illustrator to create application designs.

One major difference between the Flex SDK and Flash Builder is that the SDK on its own is free and mostly open source, while Flash Builder is available only through a license that you purchase from Adobe Systems. But in addition to the Flex SDK that's at the core of Flash Builder, the complete development environment includes many tools that will make your application development more productive and less error-prone than working with the SDK and another editing environment.

Web Resource

The release version of the Flex SDK is bundled with Flash Builder 4, but you can download and use more recent builds of the SDK from Adobe's open-source Web site at `http://opensource.adobe.com/wiki/display/flexsdk/Flex+SDK`**.** ∎

Flash Builder 4 Premium (the more complete and expensive of the available Flash Builder editions) also includes a set of components known as the Data Visualization components that aren't licensed in the open-source Flex SDK. The Data Visualization components include the charting components for presenting data as interactive visual charts and a couple of advanced interactive data-centric components called the `AdvancedDataGrid` and `OlapDataGrid` that present relational data with groups, summaries, multicolumn sorting, and other advanced features.

Note

The Flex Data Visualization components were available as a separately licensed product in the Flex 2 product line. With the release of Flex 3, they became available only as part of the Flex Builder 3 Professional license. The license model for the data visualization components has stayed the same in Flash Builder 4 Premium. ∎

Flex as Open Source

In February 2008, Adobe Systems released the Flex SDK as an open-source project, licensed under the Mozilla Public License (MPL), version 1.1. This license enables you to modify and extend source code and to distribute components of the code (or the entire SDK). You must make any changes that you make to the ActionScript files that are part of the Flex SDK available to other developers. This does not affect your own proprietary code. You still own the MXML and ActionScript code you write for your own applications. To get a copy of the MPL, visit www.mozilla.org/MPL/.

As described previously, not all components in the Flex SDK are available in the open-source package. Some components, such as the Flex charting components and the advanced data presentation controls, are available only through commercial licenses. Also, Flash Builder is available only through a license that you purchase from Adobe.

The open-source Flex SDK is managed through the Web site at http://opensource.adobe.com/wiki/display/flexsdk/. Additional information and ongoing discussions of the Flex open-source project are available at these Web sites:

- http://flex.org/
- http://forums.adobe.com/community/opensource/flexsdk/general

Flex programming languages

Flex applications are written using three programming languages — ActionScript 3, MXML, and FXG (Flash XML Graphics):

- **ActionScript 3.** The most recent version of the ActionScript language to evolve in the Flash authoring environment over the lifetime of the product. A complete object-oriented language, ActionScript 3 is based on the ECMAScript Edition 4 draft language specification. It includes most of the elements of object-oriented languages, including class definition syntax, class package structuring, strong data typing of variables, and class inheritance.

- **MXML.** A pure XML-based markup language that is used to define a Flex application and many of its components. Most of the elements in MXML correspond to an ActionScript 3 class that's delivered as part of the Flex class library.

- **FXG.** A new XML-based language that enables you to represent graphic objects as XML markup. The new Adobe Flash Catalyst application generates projects that describe functional applications and their graphic presentations in a combination of MXML, FXG, and ActionScript. You can then develop these projects further in Flash Builder 4. MXML includes many vector graphic drawing tags that enable you to declare low-level graphic objects in your Flex applications. These tags are designed to follow the FXG markup language's syntax and element and attribute names. You can also treat complete FXG files as graphical images.

New Feature

FXG (Flash XML Graphics) was created by Adobe as a language that represents graphical objects in a Flex application. Its capabilities closely follow the rendering model of Adobe Flash Player 10. There are many similarities between FXG and SVG (Scalable Vector Graphics), another XML language that represents graphics that's been available for many years. In fact, the Adobe development team first considered using SVG, but decided to create a new language because the existing SVG didn't match how graphics are rendered in Flash Player. Many Adobe Creative Suite products are able to export graphics as FXG markup, including Photoshop, Illustrator, and Fireworks. ■

When you compile a Flex application, your MXML code is rewritten in the background into pure ActionScript 3. MXML can be described as a "convenience language" for ActionScript 3 that makes it easier and faster to write your applications than if you had to code completely in ActionScript.

Note

Beginning with Flash CS3 Professional, ActionScript 3 also is used in the Flash authoring environment for logical code, creating class definitions, and other programming tasks. Unlike Flex, which uses only version 3 of ActionScript, you can create Flash documents in Flash that use older versions of the language, such as ActionScript 2. ■

The diagram in Figure 1.1 describes the relationship between the Flex SDK's command-line compiler, Flex Builder, the MXML and ActionScript programming languages, and the Flash Player and AIR.

MXML versus ActionScript 3

You can use MXML and ActionScript interchangeably in many situations. MXML is commonly used to declare visual layout of an application and many objects, but it's frequently your choice as a developer as to when to use each language.

In these examples, I'm declaring an instance of an ActionScript class named Label and setting some *properties* and *styles*. The Label class is part of the Flex 4 class library that's included with both the Flex SDK and Flash Builder 4. Its purpose is to present simple text in a Flex application.

New Feature

The Label control used in these examples is a member of a new component collection named the Spark components. (Controls and containers used in Flex 2 and 3 are now known as the MX components.) The Spark Label and two other new controls named RichText and RichEditableText are designed to replace the MX Label and Text controls. ■

Declaring objects in MXML

The Label control is represented in MXML as a tag named <s:Label/>. To create an instance of the Label control using MXML and set its text property to a value of Hello from MXML, declare the tag and set the property as an EXtensible Markup Language (XML) attribute. The following example also sets the fontWeight and fontSize styles to affect the control's appearance.

```
<s:Label id="myMXMLText" text="Hello from MXML"
    fontSize="18" fontWeight="bold"/>
```

FIGURE 1.1

The Flex SDK and Flash Builder both compile source code in MXML and ActionScript, producing executable applications that are hosted by the Flash Player on the Web or the AIR on the desktop.

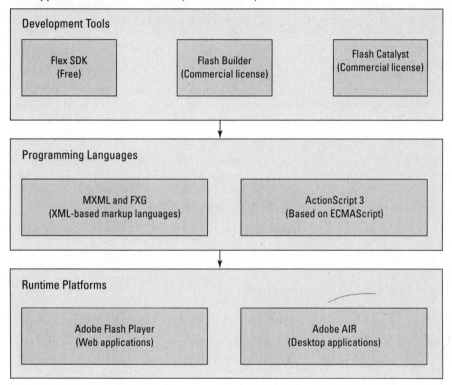

Cross-Reference

The XML namespace prefix s: refers to the new Spark namespace that's declared at the top of all new Flex 4 applications:

```
xmlns:s="library://ns.adobe.com/flex/spark"
```

I describe this and other new Flex 4 namespaces in Chapter 4. ■

Declaring objects in ActionScript 3

You can instantiate and add Label and other controls to the application's layout using ActionScript 3. When using this coding model, you first declare the object as a variable. If you want the reference to the object to persist, you declare it outside of any functions. You then instantiate the object using the class's constructor method and set its properties and styles, and add the object to the application's content group so it becomes visible.

You can set the control's properties and styles anytime after creating the object:

```
import mx.events.FlexEvent;
import spark.components.Label;
protected var myActionScriptText:Label;
protected function creationCompleteHandler(event:FlexEvent):void
{
  myActionScriptText = new Label();
  myActionScriptText.text = "Hello from ActionScript";
  myActionScriptText.setStyle("fontSize", 18);
  myActionScriptText.setStyle("fontWeight", "bold");
  this.contentGroup.addElement(myActionScriptText);
}
```

The preceding ActionScript code accomplishes exactly the same steps as the MXML code in the first example. Notice that it takes many lines of ActionScript, some inside a custom function, to replace the MXML declaration. This difference in the amount of code needed to accomplish any particular task is one of the reasons MXML exists. MXML can significantly reduce the amount of code in your application without compromising its features or performance.

New Feature

The new Flex 4 `Application` container referenced with the `<s:Application>` tag places its child objects in a `Group`, which is addressed by the container's `contentGroup` property. This new `Application` container is also a member of the new Spark component collection. ∎

Note

Assuming that the previous ActionScript code is in a main application file, the prefix `this` in the method call `this.contentGroup.addElement()` refers to the application itself. If the same code were in an MXML component or ActionScript class, `this` would refer to the current instance of that component or class. ∎

Flex versus Flash development

The line separating the terms *Flex* and *Flash* has changed over the years. As I described previously, Flex originally referred to the entire product line: the class library, compilers, development tool, and server environment. The original Flex server is now named LiveCycle Data Services, and the development tool formerly known as Flex Builder is now named Flash Builder, because it's used to create and edit ActionScript code by both Flash and Flex developers. In this discussion, I use the term Flash to refer to the visual authoring environment known as Flash Professional, and not the recently renamed Flash Builder. And I use the term Flex to refer primarily to the Flex 4 SDK.

Developers tend to use Flex instead of Flash when they want to create software applications that have these characteristics:

- Projects built by multi-developer teams
- High level of interactivity with the user

- Use of dynamic data with application servers such as ColdFusion, PHP, or JEE
- Highly scaled applications in terms of the number of views, or screens, from which the user can select

In contrast, developers tend to use Flash when they are creating documents with these characteristics:

- Documents whose main purpose is to present visual animation
- Marketing presentations
- Hosting of Web-based video

Many applications that are built in Flash can be built in Flex, and vice versa. Your choice of development tools is frequently driven by your background and existing skill set.

Developing in Flash

As I described earlier, developers who use Flash are frequently focused on presenting animation, hosting video, and the like. Flash is generally considered superior for animation work because of its use of a timeline to control presentations over a designated period of time. Flash supports a variety of animation techniques that make use of the timeline, including:

- Frame by frame animation
- Motion tweening
- Shape tweening
- Inverse kinematics

Flash also enables you to create animations using pure ActionScript code, but that approach also can be used in Flex. If you come from a graphic design background and are used to thinking visually, you will appreciate the precision and visual feedback that the Flash development environment provides.

The format of the primary source document used in Flash, the FLA file, is binary rather than text-based. As a result, it doesn't work well in multi-developer environments, where source-code management systems are commonly use to manage code. You can't easily *diff*, or discover differences between, different versions of a binary file. In these environments, it's common to move as much ActionScript code to external text-based files as possible, even when a project's primary format is built in Flash. In Flash CS5 Professional and Flash Builder 4, Adobe has now made it much easier to move between the products. And starting with Creative Suite 5, Flash Builder 4 is now included with the Web Premium software bundle that also includes Dreamweaver, Fireworks, and other Web-based development tools.

Developing in Flex

Developers who use Flex to build applications frequently have a background in some other programming language. Presentations can be created and made useful in Flash without any programming, but a Flex application is almost entirely code-based. Animations are created entirely through ActionScript, because neither the Flex SDK nor Flash Builder has a timeline as part of their development toolkits.

Flex also has superior tools for handling large-scale applications that have dozens or hundreds of views, or screens. Flash CS3 had a screen document feature, but the feature didn't receive the development attention from Adobe that would have been required to make it a compelling architectural choice for these "enterprise" applications. The feature was removed in Flash CS4.

Finally, Flex applications are built in source code, which is stored in text files. These text files are easy to manage in source-code control applications such as Subversion. As a result, multi-developer teams who are dependent on these management tools find Flex development to be a natural fit to the way they already work.

Flash Builder's design view feature has become increasingly friendly and useful to graphic designers, but it isn't always intuitive to a designer who's used to "real" graphic design tools like Adobe's Photoshop, Illustrator, and Fireworks. The introduction of Adobe Flash Catalyst, a new graphic design application that supports creation of graphically rich compositions for Flex applications, now enables graphic designers to participate as full partners in Flex application development.

Table 1.1 describes some of the core differences between Flex and Flash development.

TABLE 1.1

Differences Between Flex and Flash Development

Task	Flex	Flash
Animation	Flex uses ActionScript classes called Effects to define and play animations. There is no timeline.	The Flash timeline allows animation frame-by-frame or tweening, and also supports programmatic animation with ActionScript.
Working with data	Flex has multiple tools for working with data and application servers, including the RPC components (HTTPService, WebService, and RemoteObject). It is also a natural fit for use with LiveCycle Data Services.	Flash can communicate with the same application servers as Flex, but its programming tools aren't as intuitive or robust.
Design	Flash Builder has a design view for WYSIWYG (What You See Is What You Get) application layout but doesn't have visual tools for creating graphic objects from scratch. The new Adobe Flash Catalyst enables designers to import compositions from PhotoShop and Illustrator and transform them into Flex applications that can be developed further in Flash Builder.	Flash has very good graphic design tools, although not as complete a toolkit as Illustrator. However, it has excellent tools for importing and using graphics created in Photoshop and Illustrator.

Task	Flex	Flash
Programming languages	Flex 4 and Flash Builder 4 support ActionScript 3 and MXML for component definition and instantiation, and FXG to declare low-level graphics.	Flash Professional CS4 supports all versions of ActionScript (but only one version per Flash document) but does not support MXML.
Code management	Flex applications are created as source code in text files, which are completely compatible with source-code management systems.	Flash documents are binary, which presents problems when building applications in multi-developer environments that require source-code management tools.

Note

Flash-based applications built for desktop deployment with Adobe AIR can be created in either Flash Builder with the Flex SDK or in Flash Professional. AIR applications can be created from any compiled Flash document or from HTML-based content. ▪

Flex and object-oriented programming

Flex application development is especially compelling for developers who are already acquainted with object-oriented programming (OOP) methodologies. Object-oriented programming is a set of software development techniques that involve the use of software "objects" to control the behavior of a software application.

OOP brings many benefits to software development projects, including:

- Consistent structure in application architectures
- Enforcement of contracts between different modules in an application
- Easier detection and correction of software defects
- Tools that support separation of functionality in an application's various modules

You'll find no magic bullets in software development: You can create an application that's difficult to maintain and at risk of collapsing under its own weight in an OOP language just as easily as you can create one that primarily uses procedural programming. But a good understanding of OOP principles can contribute enormously to a successful software development project.

And because ActionScript 3 is a completely object-oriented language, it serves Flex developers well to understand the basic concepts of OOP and how they're implemented in Flex development.

OOP is commonly supported by use techniques known as modularity, encapsulation, inheritance, and polymorphism.

Modularity

Modularity means that an application should be built in small pieces, or modules. For example, an application that collects data from a user should be broken into modules, each of which has a particular purpose. The code that presents a data entry form, and the code that processes the data after it has been collected, should be stored in distinct and separate code modules. This results in highly maintainable and robust applications, where changes in one module don't automatically affect behavior in another module.

The opposite of modularity is *monolithic*. In monolithic applications such as the example in Listing 1.1, all the code and behavior of an application are defined in a single source-code file. These applications tend to be highly "brittle," meaning that changes in one section of the application run a high risk of breaking functionality in other areas. Such applications are sometimes referred to as *spaghetti code* because they tend to have code of very different purposes wrapped around each other.

LISTING 1.1

A monolithic Flex application

```
<?xml version="1.0" encoding="utf-8"?>
<s:Application xmlns:fx="http://ns.adobe.com/mxml/2009"
  xmlns:s="library://ns.adobe.com/flex/spark"
  xmlns:mx="library://ns.adobe.com/flex/mx">
  <fx:Script>
    <![CDATA[
      import mx.collections.ArrayCollection;
      [Bindable]
      private var myData:ArrayCollection;
      ...additional ActionScript code...
    ]]>
  </fx:Script>
  <s:VGroup>
    <mx:DataGrid dataProvider="{myData}">
      <mx:columns>
        <mx:DataGridColumn/>
        <mx:DataGridColumn/>
        <mx:DataGridColumn/>
      </mx:columns>
    </mx:DataGrid>
    <mx:Form>
      <mx:FormItem label="First Name:">
        <s:TextInput id="fnameInput"/>
      </mx:FormItem>
      <mx:FormItem label="Last Name:">
        <s:TextInput id="lnameInput"/>
      </mx:FormItem>
      <mx:FormItem label="Address:">
```

```
      <s:TextInput id="addressInput"/>
    </mx:FormItem>
  </mx:Form>
 </s:VGroup>
</s:Application>
```

In the previous application, all the application's functionality is mixed together: data modeling, data collection, and logical scripting. Although the application might work, making changes without introducing bugs will be difficult, especially for a multi-developer team trying to work together on the application without constantly disrupting each other's work.

A modular application such as the version in Listing 1.2 breaks up functionality into modules, each of which handles one part of the application's requirements. This architecture is easier to maintain because the programmer knows immediately which module requires changes for any particular feature.

LISTING 1.2

A modular Flex application

```
<?xml version="1.0" encoding="utf-8"?>
<s:Application xmlns:fx="http://ns.adobe.com/mxml/2009"
  xmlns:s="library://ns.adobe.com/flex/spark"
  xmlns:valueObjects="valueObjects.*"
  xmlns:views="views.*"
  xmlns:forms="forms.*">
  <fx:Script source="scriptFunctions.as"/>
  <valueObjects:AValueObject id="vo"/>
  <views:ADataGrid id="grid"/>
  <forms:AForm id="form"/>
</s:Application>
```

Flex implements modularity through the use of MXML components and ActionScript classes that together implement the bulk of an application's functionality.

Encapsulation

Encapsulation means that a software object should hide as much of its internal implementation from the rest of the application as possible, and should expose its functionality only through publicly documented *members* of the object. A class definition that's properly encapsulated exposes and documents these object members to enable the application to set properties, call methods, handle events, and refer to constants. The documentation of the object members is known as the application programming interface (API) of the class.

In the Flex class library, class members include:

- **Constants.** Properties whose values never change.
- **Events.** Messages the object can send to the rest of the application to share information about the user's actions and/or data it wants to share.
- **Methods.** Functions you can call to execute certain actions of the object.
- **Properties.** Data stored within the object.
- **Skin Parts.** A part of a Spark component that displays a part of the component and can be modified in a custom skin.
- **Skin States.** A view state that a component reacts to by displaying, hiding, or changing parts of the component's visual presentation.
- **Styles.** Visual characteristics of an object that determine its appearance.

In Flex, encapsulation is fully implemented in ActionScript 3. Each member that you define in a class can be marked using an access modifier to indicate whether the particular method or property is `public`, `private`, `protected`, or `internal`. A `public` method, for example, enables any part of the application to execute functionality that's encapsulated within the class, without the programmer who's calling the method having to know the details of how the action is actually executed.

For example, imagine a class that knows how to display a video in the Flash Player and allows the developer to start, stop, and pause the video, and control the video's audio volume. The code that executes these functions will have to know a lot about how video is handled in Flash and the particular calls that will need to be made to make the audio louder or softer. The API of the class, however, could be extremely simple, including methods to execute each of these actions with very simple calls from the main application, like this:

```
public class VideoPlayer()
{
  public function VideoPlayer(videoFile:String):void
  { ... call video libraries to load a video ... }
  public function start():void
  { ... call video libraries to play the video ... }
  public function stop():void
  { ... call video libraries to stop the video ... }
  public function setVolume(volume:int):void
  { ... call video libraries to reset the volume ... }
}
```

The application that instantiates and uses the class wouldn't need to know any of the details; it just needs to know how to call the methods:

```
var myVideoPlayer:VideoPlayer = new VideoPlayer("myvideo.flv");
myVideoPlayer.start();
myVideoPlayer.setVolume(1);
```

We say, then, that the `VideoPlayer` class *encapsulates* complex behavior, hiding the details of the implementation from the rest of the application.

Inheritance

Inheritance refers to the capability of any class to extend any other class and thereby inherit that class's properties, methods, and so on. An inheritance model enables you to define classes with certain members (properties, methods, and so on) and then to share those members with the classes that extend them.

In an inheritance relationship, the class that already has the capabilities you want to inherit is called the *superclass, base class,* or *parent class.* The class that extends that class is known as the *subclass, derived class,* or *child class.* Unified Modeling Language (UML) is a standardized visual language for visually describing class relationships and structures. In this book, I frequently use UML diagrams such as the example shown in Figure 1.2 to describe how a class is built or its relationship to other classes.

FIGURE 1.2

This is an example of a UML diagram that describes a relationship between a base and a derived class.

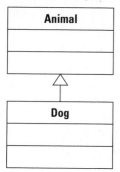

One class can extend a class that in turn extends another. UML diagrams can be extended to describe these relationships as well. The UML diagram shown in Figure 1.3 describes a three-tier inheritance relationship between a superclass named `Animal` and subclasses named `Dog` and `Poodle`.

In Figure 1.2, methods of the superclass `Animal` are inherited by the subclass `Dog`. `Dog` has additional methods and properties that aren't shared with its superclass and that can override the superclass's existing methods with its own implementations. The same relationship exists between `Dog` and `Poodle`.

Because all versions of `Animal` sleep in the same way, calling `Dog.sleep()` or `Poodle.sleep()` actually calls the version of the method implemented in `Animal`. But because `Dog` has its own `eat()` method, calling `Dog.eat()` or `Poodle.eat()` calls that version of the method. And finally, because all dogs bark in a different way, calling `Poodle.bark()` calls a unique version of the `bark()` method that's implemented in that particular class.

FIGURE 1.3

This diagram describes a three-part inheritance relationship.

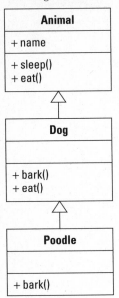

Inheritance enables you to grow an application over time, creating new subclasses as the need for differing functionality becomes apparent.

In Flex, the ActionScript inheritance model enables you to create extended versions of the components included in the Flex class library without modifying the original versions. Then, if an upgraded version of the original class is delivered by Adobe, a simple recompilation of the application that uses the extended class will automatically receive the upgraded features.

Polymorphism

Polymorphism means that you can write methods that accept arguments, or *parameters*, data typed as instances of a superclass, but then pass an instance of a subclass to the same method. Because all subclasses that extend a particular superclass share the same set of methods, properties, and other object members, the method that expects an instance of the superclass also can accept instances of the subclass and know that those methods can be called safely.

Polymorphism also can be used with a programming model known as an *interface*. An interface is essentially an abstract class that can't be directly instantiated. Its purpose is to define a set of methods and other object members and to describe how those methods should be written. But in an interface such as the one shown in Figure 1.4, the method isn't actually implemented; it only describes the arguments and return data types that any particular method should have.

FIGURE 1.4

This UML diagram describes the relationship between an interface and an implementing class.

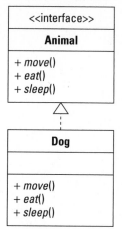

A class "implements" an interface by creating concrete versions of the interface's methods that actually do something. As with the relationship between super- and subclasses, a method might be written that accepts an instance of the interface as an argument. At runtime, you actually pass an instance of the implementing class.

For example, you might decide that `Animal` should be abstract; that is, you would never create an instance of an Animal, only of a particular species. The following code describes the interface:

```
public interface Animal
{
  public function sleep()
  {}
}
```

The interface doesn't actually implement these methods. Its purpose is to define the method names and structures. A class that implements the interface might look like this:

```
public class Dog implements Animal
{
  public function sleep()
  { ... actual code to make the dog sleep ... }
  public function bark()
  { ... actual code to make the dog bark ... }
}
```

Notice that a class that implements an interface can add other methods that the interface doesn't require. This approach is sometimes known as *contract-based programming*. The interface constitutes a contract between the method that expects a particular set of methods and the object that implements those methods.

Flex supports polymorphism both through the relationship between superclasses and subclasses and through creation and implementation of interfaces in ActionScript 3.

Understanding Adobe Flash Player

Flex applications are executed at runtime by Adobe Flash Player or by Adobe AIR. In either case, they start as applications compiled to the SWF file format.

When you deploy a Flex application through the Web, it's downloaded from a Web server at runtime as a result of a request from a Web browser. The browser starts Adobe Flash Player, which in turn runs the application.

Adobe AIR includes Flash Player as one of its critical components. Other components include a Web browser kernel to execute HTML (Hypertext Markup Language), CSS (Cascading Style Sheets), and JavaScript, and APIs for local file access and persistent data storage. The version of Flash Player that's included with AIR is the same as the one that runs on users' systems as a Web browser plug-in or ActiveX control. As a result, any functionality that you include in a Flex application should work the same regardless of whether the application is deployed to the Web or the desktop.

The diagram shown in Figure 1.5 describes the architectural difference between Flash Player's deployment in a Web browser versus AIR.

FIGURE 1.5

Flash Player installed with a Web browser versus AIR

Web deployment model

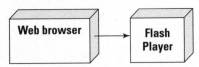

Flash Player called as ActiveX or plug-in

Desktop deployment model

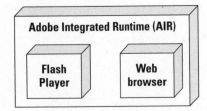

Flash Player and Web browser
integrated into runtime

Learning a little Adobe Flash Player history

FutureWave Software originally created a product called Future Splash Animator, which in turn evolved from a product called SmartSketch. The player for the animations was Java-based and was the ancestor of the current Adobe Flash Player. After its purchase by Macromedia, the product was renamed and released in 1996 as Macromedia Flash 1.0.

The product went through a steady evolution, starting with basic Web animation and eventually becoming a full-featured programming environment with rich media (video and audio) hosting capabilities.

During its time with Macromedia, Flash (the authoring tool) was packaged as part the Studio bundle and was integrated with other Studio products such as Dreamweaver and Fireworks. Macromedia positioned Flash MX and MX 2004 as development environments for what the company began to call *rich internet applications* (RIAs). Although the development environment that was Flash never fully satisfied the requirements of application developers (see the discussion of issues that are commonly encountered in Flash when developing true applications in the section on Flex versus Flash development in this chapter), Flash Player continued to grow in its capability to host the finished applications, however they were built.

After Adobe Systems purchased Macromedia, Flash became a part of the Adobe Creative Suite 3 (CS3) product bundles. Along with this rebundling came increased integration with other Creative Suite products such as Illustrator and Photoshop. Other Adobe products such as After Effects and Premiere include new export features that enable their video-based output files to be integrated into Flash-based presentations. First introduced with Flash Professional CS4 in 2008, Flash Player 10 offers many new features, along with improved runtime performance.

Table 1.2 describes the major milestones in the history of Adobe Flash Player.

TABLE 1.2

Flash Player History

Version	Year	New Features
Macromedia Flash Player 1	1996	Basic Web animation
Macromedia Flash Player 2	1997	Vector graphics; some bitmap support; some audio support; object library
Macromedia Flash Player 3	1998	The movieclip element; alpha transparency, MP3 compression; stand-alone player; JavaScript plug-in integration
Macromedia Flash Player 4	1999	Advanced ActionScript; internal variables; the input field object; streaming MP3
Macromedia Flash Player 5	2000	ActionScript 1.0; XML support; Smartclips (a component-based architecture); HTML 1.0 text formatting

continued

TABLE 1.2   (continued)

Version	Year	New Features
Macromedia Flash Player 6	2002	Flash remoting for integration with application servers; screen reader support; Sorenson Sparc video codec
Macromedia Flash Player 7	2003	Streaming audio and video; ActionScript 2; first version associated with Flex
Macromedia Flash Player 8	2005	Graphical user interface (GIF) and portable network graphic (PNG) loading; ON VP6 video codec; faster performance; visual filters including blur and drop shadow; file upload and download; improved text rendering; new security features
Adobe Flash Player 9	2006	ActionScript 3; faster performance; E4X XML parsing; binary sockets; regular expressions
Adobe Flash Player 9 Update 3 (version 9.0.28)	2007	H.264 video; hardware-accelerated full-screen video playback
Adobe Flash Player 10	2008	3D effects; custom filters and effects; advanced text rendering; dynamic sound generation; vector data type; dynamic streaming; Speex audio codec; enhanced file upload and download APIs; color correction
Adobe Flash Player 10.1	2010	The first release as part of the Open Screen Project. First version on cell phones to support ActionScript 3. HTTP Streaming, advanced video delivery.

Each new product bundling and relationship has increased the capabilities of Flash Player. As a result, the most recent version of Flash Player as of this writing (version 10.1) has all the features I've described:

- Web-based animation
- Object-oriented programming with ActionScript 3
- Rich media hosting and delivery

Note

In addition to the version of Flash Player that's delivered for conventional computers, Macromedia and Adobe have released Flash Lite for hosting Flash content on devices such as cell phones and PDAs (Personal Digital Assistants). Beginning with Flash CS5 Professional, Adobe Systems Flash Player 10.1 will work on most small devices such as cell phones and support ActionScript 3. In addition, Flash CS5 will enable you to compile Flash presentations as native iPhone applications.

The Flex development team isn't far behind. The Flex Mobile SDK will enable you to create applications for mobile deployment using the Flex application architecture. For more information on this effort, visit the Flex Mobile Web page: http://labs.adobe.com/technologies/flex/mobile/. ■

Understanding Flash Player penetration statistics

One of the attractions of Flash Player is its nearly ubiquitous penetration rate in the Web. Each new version of Flash Player has achieved a faster rate of installation growth than each version before it; version 9 is no different. As of December 2009 (according to statistics published on Adobe's Web site), the penetration rate for Flash Player versions 7, 8, and 9 was 98 percent or greater (including in emerging markets), and Flash Player 10 already had a penetration rate of 93 percent or greater. Of course, these rates change periodically; for the most recent Flash Player penetration rates, visit:

```
www.adobe.com/products/player_census/flashplayer/
```

Penetration rates are important to organizations that are deciding whether to build applications in Flex, because the availability of Flash Player 10 (required to run the most recently published Flex applications and Flash documents) determines whether a Flex application will open cleanly or require the user to install or upgrade the Player prior to running the application. If a user needs to install the Flash Player, however, there are many ways to get the job done.

Using the debug version of Flash Player

The *debug* version of Flash Player differs from the production version in a number of ways. As I describe in the following section, you can install the debug version of the Flash Player from installers that are provided with Flex Builder 4 and the Flex 4 SDK.

The debug version of Flash Player includes these features:

- Integration with fdb, the command-line debugger that's included with the Flex SDK
- Capability to process and report logging messages issued with the trace() function
- Integration with Flash Builder debugging tools such as breakpoints
- Other debugging tools

To ensure that you're running the Flash Debug Player, navigate to this Web page in any browser that you think has the Flash Player installed:

```
www.adobe.com/go/tn_19245
```

As shown in Figure 1.6, you should see a Flash document that tells you which version of the Flash Player is currently installed. When you load this document with the Flash Debug Player, it displays a message indicating that you have the Content Debugger Player. This tool also tells you whether you're running the ActiveX or Plugin Player and which version.

FIGURE 1.6

Discovering your Flash Player version

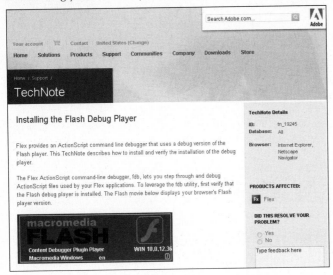

Flash Player installation

As of this writing, Flash Player 10 is available for these operating systems:

- Windows
- Mac OS X
- Linux
- Solaris

For up-to-date information about current operating system support, including minimum browser and hardware requirements, visit this Web page:

    www.adobe.com/products/flashplayer/systemreqs/

Flash Player can be installed on a user's computer system in a variety of ways:

- As an integrated Web browser plug-in
- As a stand-alone application
- As part of Adobe AIR

Note

Regardless of how you install Flash Player, users who install Flash Player must have administrative access to their computer. On Microsoft Windows, this means that you must be logged in as an administrator. On Mac OS X, you must have an administrator password available during the installation. ■

Uninstalling Flash Player

Before installing Flash Player, make sure any existing installations have been removed. The process for uninstalling Flash Player differs from one operating system to another, but in all cases you must close any browser windows before trying to uninstall the Flash Player.

On Windows XP, use operating system's standard tools for uninstalling any software: the Control Panel's Add or Remove Programs feature on Windows XP or Windows Vista's Uninstall or change a program screen (shown in Figure 1.7).

On Mac OS X, use the uninstaller application that's available for download from this Web page:

        www.adobe.com/go/tn_14157

FIGURE 1.7

Windows Vista's Uninstall or change a program feature, listing both the plug-in and ActiveX versions of the Flash Player

Flash Player 10 ActiveX and plug-in versions

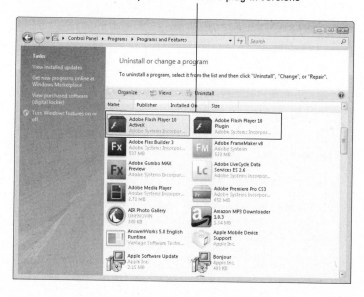

Installation with Flash Builder

When you install Flash Builder 4, the debug version of Flash Player is installed automatically. To ensure that this part of the installation succeeds, make sure that you've closed any browser windows before you start the installation. If the installation detects open browser windows, it prompts you to close those windows before continuing the installation process.

Using Flash Builder installation files

If you need to reinstall the debug version of the Flash Player, you should use the version that's included with Flash Builder or the Flex SDK. If you've installed Flash Builder, you can find the installation files in a subfolder within the Flash Builder installation folder. On Windows, the default folder is named:

```
C:\Program Files\Adobe\Flash Builder 4\Player\Win
```

This folder has three files:

- **Install Flash Player 10 Plugin.exe.** The plug-in version for Firefox, Safari, and other browsers.
- **Install Flash Player 10ActiveX.exe.** The ActiveX control for Internet Explorer.
- **FlashPlayer.exe.** The stand-alone player (does not require installation — just run it!).

Installing Flash Player from the Web

You also can get the Flash Player from the Adobe Web site. Select a download location, depending on whether you want the production or debug version of the player.

Downloading the production Flash Player

End users who want to run Flex applications and other Flash-based content can download the Flash Player installer from this Web page:

```
http://get.adobe.com/flashplayer/
```

When you see the page shown in Figure 1.8, you should see a link to download the Flash Player that's appropriate for your operating system and browser.

Caution

The version of Flash Player that you download from this page is the production version, rather than the debug version. If you have the production version installed, you can test your applications, but you can't take advantage of debugging tools such as tracing, breakpoints, and expressions evaluation. ∎

Tip

The Flash Player Download Center might include a link to download the Google toolbar or other content. You do not have to download and install this unrelated content to get all the features of the Flash Player. ■

FIGURE 1.8

Downloading Flash Player from Adobe.com

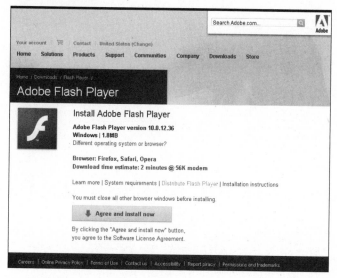

Downloading the debug version of Flash Player

You can download the debug version of Flash Player from this Web page:

        www.adobe.com/support/flashplayer/downloads.html

As shown in Figure 1.9, you should see links for all versions of Flash Player, including both debug and production versions, for a variety of operating systems and browsers.

Tip

You might find an even more recent version of the Flash Player on the Adobe Labs Web page at http:// labs.adobe.com. Adobe Labs hosts projects that are still in development, but that are far enough along that Adobe is sharing the current code with the community. ■

FIGURE 1.9

The Adobe Flash Player Support Center

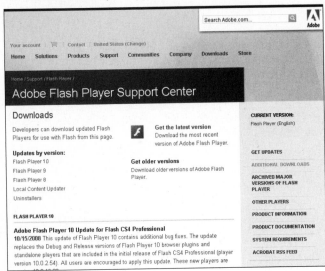

Flex 4 Development Tools

Flex developers have many development tools to choose from: Flash Builder 4, the Flex 4 SDK, and Flash Catalyst.

Understanding Flash Builder 4

Flash Builder 4, formerly known as Flex Builder, is an *integrated development environment* (IDE) for building Flex applications. This is the tool that most developers use to build Flex applications. I describe Flash Builder 4 in detail in Chapter 2.

Using the Flex 4 SDK

The Flex class library and command-line tools you need to build Flex applications are completely free. As long as you don't need to use Flash Builder or certain components that require a license, you can download the Flex SDK from Adobe and build and deploy as many applications as you want. The obvious benefit is the cost. The drawback to this approach is that you'll have to select a text editor, such as Emacs or a version of Eclipse without the Flash Builder plug-in that doesn't have the specific support for Flex application development that you get with Flash Builder.

You can download the most recent version of the Flex 4 SDK from this Web page:

```
http://opensource.adobe.com/wiki/display/flexsdk/Download+Flex+4
```

The SDK is delivered in a zipped archive file that can be extracted to any platform.

The SDK includes most of the class library you use to build Flex applications. The following components, however, require a license for deployment:

- Flex Data Visualization components, including charting and other advanced visual controls
- Application profiling tools

As shown in Figure 1.10, if you decide to use the Data Visualization components without a license, any instances of the components are displayed in your application with a watermark, indicating that you are using an evaluation version of the component.

A watermarked charting component

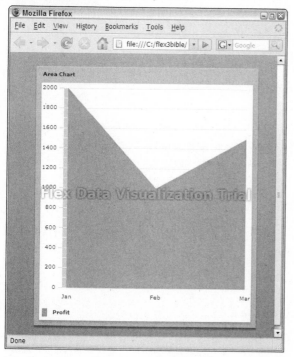

In addition to the Flex class library, the Flex 4 SDK includes these command-line tools:

- **adl.** The AIR debug application launcher.
- **adt.** The AIR developer tool.

- **acompc.** The AIR component compiler.
- **amxmlc.** The AIR application compiler.
- **asdoc.** A tool to extract documentation from ActionScript classes and generate HTML file sets known as *ASDocs*.
- **compc.** A compiler for building component libraries, Runtime Shared Libraries (RSLs), and theme files.
- **fcsh.** The Flex Compiler Shell, which you can use to execute multiple compilation tasks without the overhead of having to launch a new Java Virtual Machine (JVM) for each task.
- **fdb.** A debugger to debug applications.
- **mxmlc.** A compiler for building Flex applications.
- **optimizer.** A tool for reducing ActionScript compiled file size and creating a "release version" of an application, component, or RSL.

Detailed information about how to use each of these command-line tools is available in Adobe's documentation.

Using MXMLC, the command-line compiler

To compile a Flex application with mxmlc, the command-line compiler, it's a good idea to add the location of the Flex 4 SDK bin directory to your system's path. This enables you to run the compiler and other tools from any folder without having to include the entire path in each command.

Tip

When you install Flash Builder 4 on Microsoft Windows, the installer provides a menu choice that opens a command window and adds all directories containing Flex 4 components to the current path. To use this tool, choose All Programs ⇨ Adobe ⇨ Adobe Flex 4 SDK Command Prompt from the Windows Start menu. ∎

To compile an application from the command line, switch to the folder that contains your main application file:

```
cd /flex4bible/myfiles
```

Assuming this directory contained a file called HelloWorld.mxml, to compile the application, you would run this command:

```
mxmlc HelloWorld.mxml
```

After compilation is complete, your directory will contain a new file called HelloWorld.swf. This is the compiled application that you deploy to your Web server.

Tip

The command-line compiler has many options for tuning your application. For complete details on how to use the compiler, see the Adobe documentation. ∎

Getting Help

Documentation for Flash Builder 4 and Flex 4 is available from the Adobe Web site at:

```
http://help.adobe.com/en_US/Flex/4.0/UsingFlashBuilder/index.html
```

The most current version of the ActionScript 3.0 Language Reference in for the Flex 4 SDK is available at:

```
http://help.adobe.com/en_US/Flex/4.0/langref/
```

The documentation also is delivered in the new Adobe Community Help application with Flash Builder 4. I describe how to explore and use this version of the documentation in Chapter 2.

Summary

In this chapter, I gave an introduction to the world of application development with Adobe Flex. You learned the following:

- Flex applications are built as source code and compiled into Flash documents.

- Flex applications are built in three programming languages: MXML, FXG, and ActionScript.

- Flex applications can be run as Web applications with Adobe Flash Player, delivered through a Web browser.

- Flex applications also can be run as cross-operating system native desktop applications, hosted by the Adobe AIR.

- The Flex 4 SDK is free and available as an open-source project that's managed by Adobe Systems.

- Flash Builder 4 is a commercial integrated development environment for building Flex applications.

- Flash Catalyst is a new application that enables graphic designers to create working prototypes of graphically rich Flex applications and define graphical skins for Flex components.

- Flex developers tend to have a background in object-oriented software development, but anyone who's willing to invest the time can become proficient in Flex application development.

Using Flash Builder 4

Flash Builder 4 is Adobe's preferred development tool for building applications with the Flex 4 SDK. Flash Builder is available for both Windows and Mac OS X.

Although you can develop and deploy Flex applications to the Web or the desktop with the free Flex SDK, Flash Builder is a worthwhile investment that can increase developer productivity, reduce bugs, speed up coding, and generally make the process of developing a Flex application much more enjoyable.

New Feature

As I described in Chapter 1, Flash Builder was named Flex Builder in releases prior to version 4. It's been renamed by Adobe to position it as the preferred programmer's editor for all Flash Player programming, whether by Flash or Flex developers. ■

Getting Flash Builder

You can get Flash Builder from Adobe as a free limited-time trial, or you can purchase a license. Two licenses currently are available for Flash Builder 4:

- **Flash Builder 4 Standard Edition.** This license includes everything you need to build basic Flex applications for the desktop and the Web, but it does not include a license for the Flex Data Visualization components or certain other advanced development and testing tools.

IN THIS CHAPTER

Getting and installing Flash Builder 4

Installing Flash Builder as an Eclipse plug-in

Getting to know Flash Builder features

Using views and perspectives

Using workspaces and projects

Creating a Flex project

Using the Help system

Searching for and refactoring code

Using Flash Builder 4 new features

Integrating Flash Builder 4 and Flash Professional CS5

- **Flash Builder 4 Premium Edition.** This license includes the Flash Builder Standard Edition feature set and adds the Data Visualization components including charting controls and the `AdvancedDataGrid` and `OLAPDataGrid`. The Flash Builder Premium license also includes the Flex Profiler and the Flex Test Automation framework, which you can use along with HP QuickTest Professional (formerly Mercury QuickTest) to perform automated client testing on a Flex application.

Installing Flash Builder 4

Adobe offers versions of Flash Builder for Windows and Mac OS X. Regardless of which operating system you select, Flash Builder can be installed in two ways:

- As a stand-alone installation that includes everything you need
- As a plug-in on top of an existing installation of Eclipse

Regardless of which installation option you select, Flash Builder runs as a plug-in, or an integrated component, of another software product called Eclipse. So, before installing Flash Builder, it's important to understand the nature of Eclipse first.

Note

When you select the stand-alone configuration, Flash Builder 4 is installed with Eclipse 3.5.1. The plug-in installation requires Eclipse version 3.4 or later. On Mac OS X, the Eclipse installation must be the Carbon version; in the initial release of Flash Builder 4, the Cocoa version is not supported. ■

New Feature

Eclipse 3.5.1 includes a new user interface for performing updates and installation of plug-ins, a new Markers view that integrates problems, bookmarks and tasks, improved text search, and many other new features. ■

Installing Flash Builder with the stand-alone configuration

The stand-alone installation of Flash Builder includes everything you need to get started building Flex applications. The installation includes these components in a single integrated package:

- The Java Runtime Environment (JRE) when installing on Windows
- The Eclipse workbench
- Two versions of the Flex SDK (versions 3.4 and 4.0)
- The Flash Builder plug-in
- The debug version of Flash Player 10

Tip

On Windows, both the ActiveX version of Flash Player for Internet Explorer and the plug-in version for all other browsers are installed. Before starting the installation, close any browser windows to allow the installation of Flash Player to complete successfully. ■

Running the stand-alone installer

Start the installer and navigate through the first few screens. When prompted for the installation folder, select the location where you want to install the product. At the end of the installation process, review the Install Options screen (shown in Figure 2.1) and then complete the installation.

FIGURE 2.1

The Install Options screen

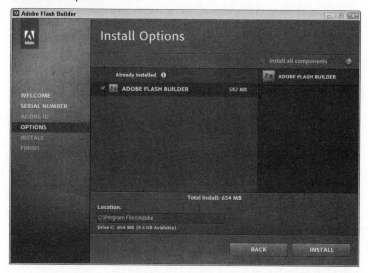

Eclipse is an open-source software product that serves as a platform for building and deploying application development tools. Eclipse was originally developed by IBM as a Java integrated development environment. The software was then donated to the Eclipse Foundation, which describes itself as a "not-for-profit, member supported corporation." The purpose of the Eclipse Foundation is to organize and support ongoing development of Eclipse and related software. You can visit the Eclipse Foundation online at www.eclipse.org.

Eclipse is described as a *workbench*. It serves as a platform for many software products, each of which is typically devoted to development in a particular language or platform. These individual products are known as *plug-ins*. An Eclipse installation can host as many plug-ins as you like, for as many different programming languages as you work in. This enables you to do your development work in a single development environment and easily switch among Java, Flex, ColdFusion, XML, and any other languages for which you've installed the appropriate plug-ins.

Hundreds of plug-ins are available for the Eclipse workbench. Table 2.1 describes some Eclipse plug-ins that are commonly used by Flex application developers.

Getting Eclipse

When you install Flash Builder with the stand-alone installation option, you get a complete copy of Eclipse 3.5.1 as part of the installation. If you want to install Flash Builder using the plug-in installation option, you first need to download and install an Eclipse distribution.

TABLE 2.1

Eclipse Plug-ins for Flex Developers

Plug-in	Description	Available from
Java Development Tools (JDT)	The most commonly used Eclipse-based Java development integrated development environment (IDE); includes a Java editor with code editing, generation, debugging, and analysis tools	`www.eclipse.org/jdt`
Web Tools Project	A set of tools for developing Web and Java Enterprise Edition (EE) applications	`www.eclipse.org/webtools`
CFEclipse	An open-source, freely licensed plug-in for ColdFusion developers	`www.cfeclipse.org`
ColdFusion Builder	A new Eclipse plug-in from Adobe Systems for ColdFusion developers that supports the new features of ColdFusion 9	`www.adobe.com/coldfusion`

Preparing to install Eclipse

Before installing an Eclipse distribution, you need to have the JRE installed on your computer.

Mac OS X developers already have the JRE installed as part of the operating system's default configuration. Windows developers should check for an existing JRE and install it if it isn't found.

You can download and install the most recent JRE from `http://java.sun.com/javase/downloads/index.jsp`. Just follow the prompts to install the JRE, and you'll be ready to install Eclipse.

Eclipse Licensing

Eclipse is licensed under the Eclipse Public License version 1.0 (EPL). This license enables you to freely download, install, and use Eclipse on as many computers as you like. The license is structured so that plug-ins that are created by software companies, nonprofit organizations, or individuals can be distributed under open-source licenses (as with the Java Development Tools or CFEclipse) or sold as commercial products (as with Flash Builder).

Selecting an Eclipse distribution

Many prepackaged distributions of Eclipse are available. The basic product includes just the workbench and enables you to completely customize your installation. Other distributions include various combinations of plug-ins and configurations for common development scenarios.

Table 2.2 describes some of the common Eclipse distributions.

TABLE 2.2

Eclipse Distributions

Plug-in	Description	Available from
Eclipse IDE for Java Developers	Includes the JDT, a source-code management client, EXtensible Markup Language (XML) editor, and other useful tools	`www.eclipse.org/downloads`
Eclipse IDE for Java EE Developers	All listed in the previous entry, plus Mylyn, for integration with Bugzilla, Trac, and JIRA (server environments for source-code management)	`www.eclipse.org/downloads`
Eclipse Classic	Includes the JDT, plus tools for developers who want to create their own Eclipse plug-ins	`www.eclipse.org/downloads`
Web Tools Platform All-in-One	Includes text and graphics editors for a variety of languages and platforms; enables certain features of Flash Builder for generating Java server-side code	`www.eclipse.org/webtools`

Installing Eclipse

Eclipse distributions are typically delivered as compressed archive files without formal setup applications.

Eclipse on Windows

On Windows, the Eclipse distribution is in the ZIP archive format. You install Eclipse on Windows simply by extracting the archive to any folder on your system.

For example, if you select the most recent Eclipse IDE for J2EE Developers on Windows, the installation file will be named `eclipse-jee-ganymede-SR2-win32.zip`. Extract the ZIP file to any folder on disk, such as `C:\eclipse`.

To start Eclipse on Windows, run `eclipse.exe` from the Eclipse folder.

Eclipse on Mac OS X

On Mac OS X, the Eclipse distribution is in an archive format known as tarball. You install Eclipse on Mac OS X by extracting the archive to any folder on your system. Extract the archive file to any folder on disk, such as the Applications folder on your hard disk.

After installing Eclipse on Mac OS X, locate the Eclipse icon `Eclipse` in the Eclipse folder. Select the icon and press ⌘+O or double-click on the icon to start Eclipse.

Installing the Flash Builder plug-in

To install Flash Builder as a plug-in on top of your existing Eclipse installation, use the appropriate installation application for your operating system.

The Flash Builder plug-in installation is self-explanatory. Just follow the prompts to complete the installation, and then start up your copy of Eclipse. Along the way, you'll be asked whether you want to install a full copy of Eclipse as a preview or install the plug-in into an existing Eclipse installation.

Getting to Know Eclipse Features

The Flash Builder feature set combines the capabilities of the Eclipse workbench with customized tools that increase Flex application development productivity. Figure 2.2 shows the default Flash Builder layout the first time you open it after installation. In this section, I describe the basic tools of Eclipse: workspaces, projects, views, editors, and perspectives.

FIGURE 2.2

Flash Builder in the default Flash perspective

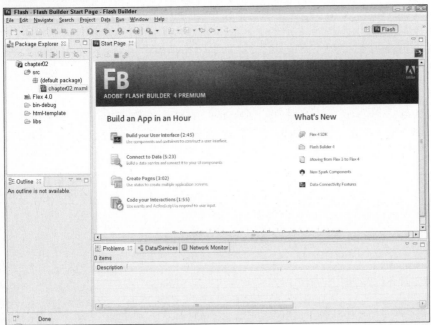

The Eclipse workspace

An Eclipse workspace consists of a collection of development projects, plus configuration settings for both the built-in Eclipse features and certain customized features that are part of Flash Builder.

When Eclipse first starts up, you're prompted to select a workspace. The default workspace folder will differ based on whether you're using Flash Builder's stand-alone configuration or the plug-in, but the location is your personal folder. Table 2.3 lists the specific locations you'll see for different operating systems.

TABLE 2.3

Default Workspace Locations by Operating System

Operating System	Default Workspace Location
Windows XP	`C:\Documents and Settings\[username]\ My Documents\Flash Builder 4`
Windows Vista and Windows 7	`C:\Users\[username]\Documents\Flash Builder 4`
Mac OS X	`/Users/[username]/Documents/Flash Builder 4`

The most visible and important purpose of an Eclipse workspace is to serve as a table of contents for a set of projects. The workspace, however, does more; it maintains all the information you need to manage your projects, including configuration settings for Eclipse, Flash Builder, and other plug-ins you might have installed.

Choose File ➪ Switch Workspace from the Eclipse menu to switch workspaces. Workspaces you've used previously may be displayed on the menu; if the workspace you want is available, just select it.

To select a different workspace (whether new or one that already exists), select Other from the submenu. As shown in Figure 2.3, type the name of the workspace folder or use the folder browsing tool to select it. If you type the name of a folder that doesn't yet exist, it is created for you.

Tip

You can optionally choose to copy settings for the current workspace to the new workspace by opening the Copy Settings section and selecting one or both of the available options. ∎

When you select a new workspace, Eclipse automatically restarts to allow any file or folder locks to be released.

FIGURE 2.3

This dialog box asks for a new workspace location.

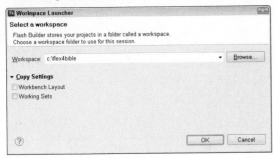

Eclipse projects

An Eclipse project contains all the resources needed for a particular application or group of related applications. A basic Eclipse project contains only a reference to a particular root folder. Most projects you create will be for a particular programming language or platform and will be associated with a particular Eclipse plug-in such as Flash Builder, CFEclipse, the JDT, or others.

Note

A single project can be referenced in multiple workspaces. ■

Because the project creation process can vary widely for various plug-ins, I describe the details of Flex project creation in a later section.

Eclipse views

An Eclipse view is a user interface panel that serves a specific function. Some of the views you use in Flash Builder are part of the Eclipse workbench and are common to all Eclipse plug-ins. For example, the Problems view, which displays current compilation errors and warnings, is used in most plug-ins. Other views are unique to Flash Builder and are useful only in the context of Flex application development.

To open a view that currently isn't displayed on the screen, choose Window ➪ Other Views. As shown in Figure 2.4, all views from all installed plug-ins are available.

New Feature

Eclipse 3.5.1 has a Markers view that presents information about various markers in your source code, including Problems, Tasks, Bookmarks, and Breakpoints. You can't add new tasks, breakpoints, or bookmarks from this view, but you can double-click to navigate to existing markers. Choose Window ➪ Other Views, and then choose General ➪ Markers to open the Markers view. ■

Each view can be used in either docked or detached mode. Docking positions for views include the top, bottom, left, and right of the workspace window.

FIGURE 2.4

You can select from all views from all installed plug-ins in this dialog box.

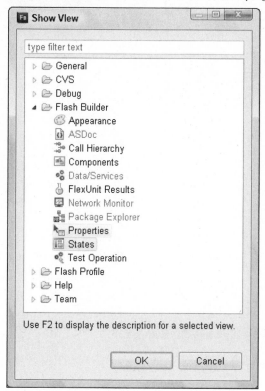

To move a docked view, follow these steps:

1. **Click and drag the view's tab.**

2. **Move the view until the cursor displays a black line indicating where the view will be docked.**

3. **Release the mouse button to drop the view in its new location.**

Figure 2.5 shows the process of docking a view.

As shown in Figure 2.6, to detach a view, right-click the view's tab (Ctrl+click on the Mac) and select Detached from the context menu. After a view has been detached, it can be moved anywhere on your screen, including to a second monitor you use in spanned mode.

FIGURE 2.5

Docking a view

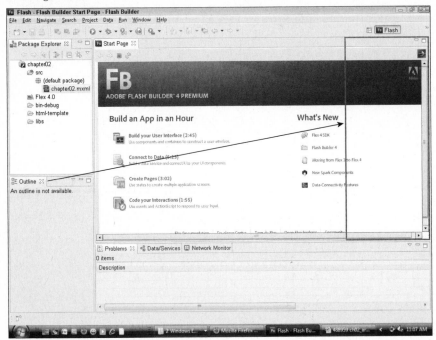

FIGURE 2.6

Detaching a view

Tip

To maximize a view to full screen, double-click the view's tab. Double-clicking the tab again restores it to its original size. When a view is displayed in full screen, a set of buttons to the left of the view includes a Restore button at the top that also restores it to its original size. ■

Eclipse editors

An editor is special kind of view that's designed to support development for a particular programming language. The basic Eclipse installation includes a text editor you can use to edit any text file. Each plug-in adds its own unique editors. For example, the Flash Builder plug-in includes editors for MXML and ActionScript files.

The editor is placed in the center of the workspace window and cannot be detached. To open multiple editors on a single file, right-click the editor tab and select New Editor. As shown in Figure 2.7, the same file is opened again in a separate editor view. You can then drag the new editor and redock it in a new location. When you have multiple editors open in this way, any changes you make in one of the editors are immediately reflected in the others. In Flash Builder, this enables you to have one editor open in Design view and the other open in Source view simultaneously.

FIGURE 2.7

Multiple editors open to a single source file

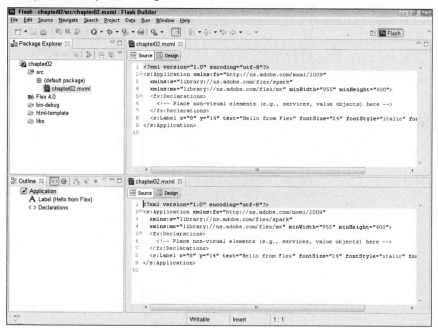

Eclipse perspectives

An Eclipse *perspective* is a particular arrangement of views. Each plug-in typically includes one or more predefined perspectives. For example, Flash Builder 4 includes these perspectives:

- Flash

- Flash Debug
- Flash Profile

When you install Flash Builder with the stand-alone configuration, the default perspective is Flash. You can select a different perspective in two ways:

- From the Eclipse menu, choose Window ➪ Perspective and select a perspective.
- As shown in Figure 2.8, use the Perspective selection tool in the upper-right corner of the workspace window.

FIGURE 2.8

Selecting a perspective from the perspective selection tool

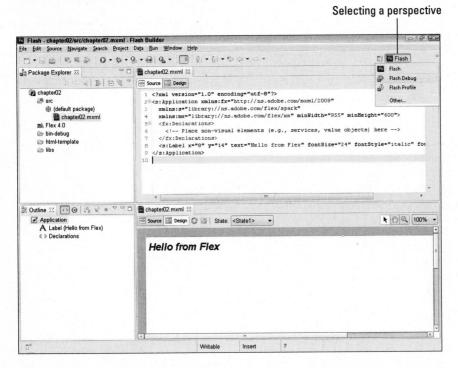

Tip

After customizing the layout of views within a perspective, you can save the new layout to a custom perspective that you can then select as needed. To create your own custom perspective, choose Window ➪ Perspective ➪ Save Perspective As from the Flash Builder menu and give the custom perspective a descriptive name that's easy to remember. ∎

Tip

The keyboard shortcut Ctrl+F8 (Windows) or ⌘+F8 (Mac) enables you to select a perspective without reaching for the mouse. ■

Configuring Eclipse

Most configuration options for Eclipse are available from the Preferences dialog box. Choose Window ➪ Preferences from the Eclipse menu to open the dialog box shown in Figure 2.9.

You can change configurations that are common to all Eclipse plug-ins in the General section of the Preferences dialog box. Some preferences that you might want to customize are deeply buried in the tree of options. I describe some of the preferences that are frequently used, but I also encourage you to explore this area of the product.

Changing fonts

You can configure the font that's used to present text in the MXML, ActionScript, and text editors in the General section of the Preferences dialog box.

FIGURE 2.9

The Eclipse Preferences dialog box

To find this setting in the Preferences dialog box (shown in Figure 2.10), follow these steps:

1. Choose Window ➪ Preferences to open the Preferences dialog box.
2. Choose General ➪ Appearance ➪ Colors and Fonts from the tree control on the left.

3. In the Colors and Fonts configuration tree on the right, choose Basic ⇨ Text Font.

4. Click the Change button, and select the font from the font selection dialog box that appears.

5. After selecting a font, click OK to return to the Preferences dialog box, and click OK again to save your changes.

Selecting a Web browser

When you test a Flex Web application, you run the application in Flash Player, hosted by a Web browser of your choice. Flash Builder uses the Eclipse Web Browser configuration option. By default, this option uses your system browser (the same browser that's used when you navigate to a URL from an e-mail client or other link on your system).

Using the Eclipse Preferences dialog box, you can override this setting and select a specific Web browser. With the Preferences dialog box open, choose General ⇨ Web Browser from the tree of configuration options. As shown in Figure 2.11, you see a list of available browsers. The default selection tells Eclipse to use the system default browser. Select the browser you prefer, and click OK to save your changes. The next time you run or debug a Flex application, it opens in the browser you selected.

Many other configuration options are available, but most are useful or relevant only when working with a particular kind of file or application. I describe these options at other points in the book.

FIGURE 2.10

Selecting a text font

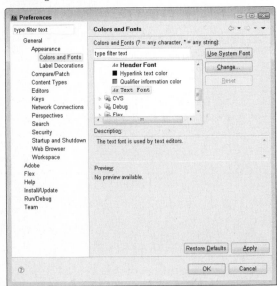

FIGURE 2.11

Selecting a Web browser

Using Flash Builder

Flash Builder has a common set of tools that you use to create and test Flex applications, whether it's installed with the stand-alone or plug-in configuration. In this section, I describe the most common tasks related to Flex application development: creating a Flex project and finding Help resources.

Creating a Flex project

An Eclipse project is a collection of applications and their associated resources. When using Flash Builder, you should create your project as a resource known as a *Flex project*. In addition to standard Eclipse project settings, a Flex project contains many configuration options that are designed specifically for Flex developers.

Choose File ➪ New ➪ Flex Project from the Flash Builder menu to create a new Flex project.

In the New Flex Project wizard's first screen, shown in Figure 2.12, provide the following information:

- **Project name.** This should be created using letters, numbers, and the _ (underscore) symbol. While in certain cases you can include spaces or other special characters, it's generally not recommended.

- **Project location.** This can be anywhere on your disk. The default location is a folder named just like the project, placed under the workspace folder, but you don't have to put it there. This is where the project configuration and primary source-code files, and possibly compiled applications, are stored.
- **Application type.** This is set to either *Web application* or *Desktop application*.
  - Selecting Web application causes the application to be delivered through the browser and run in Flash Player.
  - Selecting Desktop application creates an application that installs for use with Adobe AIR and runs as a native application on the user's desktop.

Note

Flash Builder does not enable you to create a single Flex project whose applications can be deployed on either Flash Player or AIR. Each project must specify one and only one of these deployment options. Flash Builder can share resources between multiple projects so that each project is created as a shell for a particular deployment option, and the bulk of an application's resources are maintained in a third project known as a Flex Library Project, which compiles to a sharable SWC file. ■

New Feature

In Flash Builder 4, you can convert a project that was originally created for the Web to a desktop application that's deployed with Adobe AIR. Right-click on the project in the Project Navigator view and choose Add/ Change Project Type ⇨ Convert to Desktop/Adobe AIR Project. You'll need to make any required code changes to the project, such as changing the root element of the main application file to use the WindowedApplication **component, but you won't need to recreate the project from scratch. ■**

- **Flex SDK version.** This is set to the default SDK (currently "Flex 4.0") or a specific version of the SDK.
  - Flex 4.0 projects use the new Spark components but can also use the older Halo components. They also implement new view state management syntax and other language features of the newer SDK.
  - Flex 3.4 projects don't have access to the new Spark components and use the older view state management syntax.
- **Server technology.** These application servers are directly supported by Flash Builder:
  - ASP.NET
  - ColdFusion
  - J2EE (also known as Java EE or simply JEE)
  - PHP

  When you select J2EE as your server technology, you can then select either Adobe LiveCycle Data Services ES or the open-source product BlazeDS.

FIGURE 2.12

This is the first screen in the New Flex Project wizard.

Note

When you select ColdFusion as your server technology, you're also prompted to select LiveCycle Data Services ES, BlazeDS, or ColdFusion Flash Remoting as a communications option. In ColdFusion 9, BlazeDS is installed automatically with the ColdFusion server. See Adobe's ColdFusion support Web site at www.adobe.com/support/coldfusion for more information. ■

New Feature

In Flex Builder 3, you had to install and test the application server before you created the Flex project because you couldn't change the project's associated server technology later. Flash Builder 4 enables you to switch to a different application server for an existing project. Choose Project ➪ Properties ➪ Flex Server, select an application server, and configure it for use with the current project. ■

For this section, I'll assume you've set the application server type to None. (For options specific to particular application servers, see Chapter 24 through Chapter 29.)

The next screen of the Flex Project wizard asks you to provide the *Compiled Flex application location*, also known as the *Output folder*. The default is a subfolder of the project root named *bin-debug*. This folder contains a compiled version of the application, which you'll use for debugging and testing. The production version of the application is created in a separate step after the project has been created.

Tip

When you create a project without an associated application server, the output folder is created as a subfolder of the project root. For Web applications, you then test the application by loading it into the browser from the local file system. For projects that do use an application server, the output folder is created within the document root folder of the testing Web server, and the application is loaded from the server with an HTTP request. ∎

The last screen of the Flex Project wizard, shown in Figure 2.13, asks for this information, as follows:

- **Main source folder.** This is where you place the .mxml and .as source-code files that constitute your application source. Your application .mxml files are placed in this folder. You can also create subfolders of the Main source folder to contain component and class files. These subfolders are known as *packages*.

- **Main application file.** This is the name of your first application. The filename defaults to the name of the project, plus the required .mxml file extension. During compilation, this becomes an ActionScript class definition, so you must follow the class naming requirements: You can only use letters, numbers, and underscores, and the filename must start with an alphabetical character (A–Z). A single project can contain more than one application, but you can create only a single application during project creation. Other applications have to be created after the project is open.

- **Output folder URL.** For Web applications, the Output folder URL is the Web address you'll use to test the application in a Web browser. This option appears only when you're creating a Flex project for Web applications. By leaving this option blank in a Web project that doesn't use an application server, you indicate that you want to run or debug the application by loading the compiled application from the hard disk. Using this default configuration has the advantage of not requiring a Web server for testing (similar to loading a Hypertext Markup Language [HTML] Web page into the browser from the local disk).

- **Application ID.** For desktop applications deployed with Adobe AIR, the Application ID is a unique identifier assigned to your application. This option appears only when you are creating a Flex project for desktop applications.

Note

In Flex Builder 2, the source-code root folder defaulted to the project root folder. Starting with Flex Builder 3, the recommended main source-code root folder is now a subfolder of the project named src. ∎

Note

The first part of the application filename (the part before the file extension of .mxml) becomes an ActionScript class name during the compilation process. This is why you must follow class naming conventions when you name your application file. An ActionScript class name can include letters, numbers, the $ symbol, and the _ (underscore) symbol but must begin with a letter, the $ symbol, or the _ (underscore) symbol; you can't start a class or application filename with a number. ∎

To accept your project configurations, click the Finish button to create the Flex project and the main application file.

FIGURE 2.13

This dialog box asks for the main source folder, main application filename, and output folder URL when you are creating a Web application.

Understanding Flash Builder's user interface

Flash Builder 4 adds unique tools to Eclipse to facilitate Flex application development. These tools include Editors and Views. In this section, I describe them.

The MXML editor

Flash Builder includes two editors you can use when creating your Flex applications The MXML editor is used to work with MXML files, whether they represent application files or custom components.

When you open an MXML file that's associated with a currently open project, the file is always opened in the MXML editor. This editor has two different modes: Source mode and Design mode. Whether the file opens initially in Design or Source mode depends on what mode you've used most recently on other files.

As shown in Figure 2.14, you select whether you want to use Source or Design mode by clicking one of the buttons at the top of the MXML editor.

FIGURE 2.14

Source mode and Design mode selection buttons

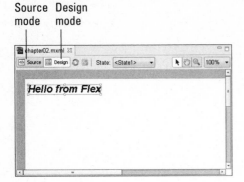

Tip

You can toggle between Source view and Design view with the keyboard shortcut Ctrl+~ on both Windows and Mac OS X. ∎

The ActionScript editor

The ActionScript editor is designed for editing files that contain pure ActionScript code. This editor is useful whether you're a Flex developer or a Flash developer, because both products now can use the latest version of the ActionScript programming language.

When you open an AS file, the file is opened in the ActionScript editor, as shown in Figure 2.15. Both the MXML and ActionScript editors include these features to make coding faster and more productive:

- Language color-coding
- Auto-import of external ActionScript classes
- Auto-completion of MXML tags and attributes
- Auto-completion of variable symbol names
- Code hinting for function arguments and class members
- Intelligent language search for symbols and their declarations
- Easy linking to consumed components and classes

New Feature

Flash Builder 4 has a new Correct Indentation feature that enables you to automatically format your code. To use it, first select the section of ActionScript or MXML code you want to format, then select Source ⇨ Correct Indentation from the Flash Builder menu. For a shortcut, press Ctrl+A (Windows) or ⌘+A (Mac) to select all of the current code file, and then press Ctrl+I (Windows) or ⌘+I (Mac) to automatically indent the selected code.

You can configure how indentation is managed in Flash Builder's workspace preferences. Select Window ⇨ Preferences from the Flash Builder menu, and then select Flash Builder ⇨ Indentation in the category list. Preferences are available in the primary Indentation screen, and also in its nested ActionScript and MXML screens. ∎

FIGURE 2.15

The ActionScript editor

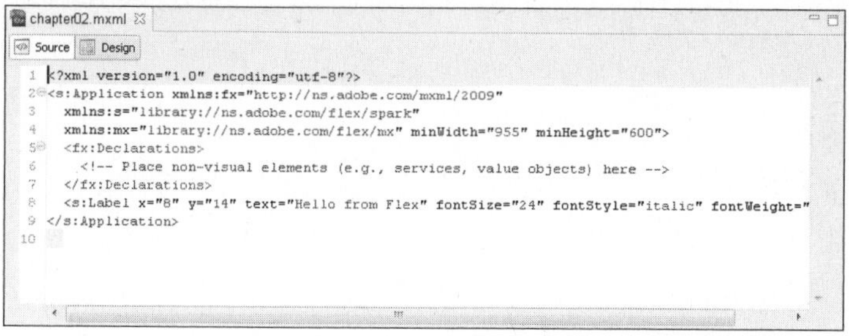

```
chapter02.mxml ⊠
<//> Source   Design
1  <?xml version="1.0" encoding="utf-8"?>
2  <s:Application xmlns:fx="http://ns.adobe.com/mxml/2009"
3    xmlns:s="library://ns.adobe.com/flex/spark"
4    xmlns:mx="library://ns.adobe.com/flex/mx" minWidth="955" minHeight="600">
5    <fx:Declarations>
6      <!-- Place non-visual elements (e.g., services, value objects) here -->
7    </fx:Declarations>
8    <s:Label x="8" y="14" text="Hello from Flex" fontSize="24" fontStyle="italic" fontWeight="
9  </s:Application>
10
```

Flash Builder views

Flash Builder 4 includes custom views that serve particular purposes.

Package Explorer view

The Package Explorer view, shown in Figure 2.16, replaces the Flex Navigator view that was used in Flex Builder 3. The new view displays a tree of folders, files, and code packages and enables you to locate and open any project resource, but adds a listing of properties and methods you declare in your MXML and ActionScript code. This view is displayed by default in both the Flash and the Flash Debug perspectives. When using any of Flash Builder's perspectives, you can open the view by choosing Window ➪ Package Explorer from the Eclipse menu.

FIGURE 2.16

The Package Explorer view

```
Package Explorer ⊠
▲ chapter02
  ▲ src
    ▲ (default package)
      ▲ HelloWorld.mxml
        ▲ HelloWorld
            ◇ aProperty : String
            ◇ aMethod() : void
      mypackage
    ▷ package2
  ▷ Flex 4.0
  ▷ bin-debug
  ▷ bin-release
  ▷ html-template
    libs
```

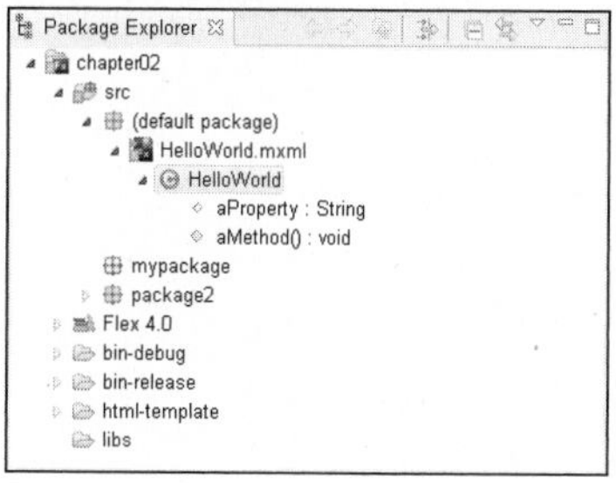

Tip

Notice in Figure 2.16 that the Package Explorer view displays not just the application and class files, but also drills down to display a component's methods and properties. You can double-click any property or method to jump to that part of a component or class's source code. ■

You can create new project resources directly within the Package Explorer view by right-clicking on a PC (or Ctrl+clicking on the Mac) any project folder or package. From the context menu that appears, select the type of resource you want to create.

The Package Explorer view can display code packages using one of two presentation styles:

- **Hierarchical.** The hierarchical presentation (the default) displays packages in a tree control, in a visual style similar to that used to present a directory structure.

- **Flat.** The flat presentation shows all code packages as siblings and does not assume a parent-child relationship between packages.

Figure 2.17 shows the different package presentation styles.

FIGURE 2.17

The Package Explorer view's two presentation styles: hierarchical (left) and flat (right)

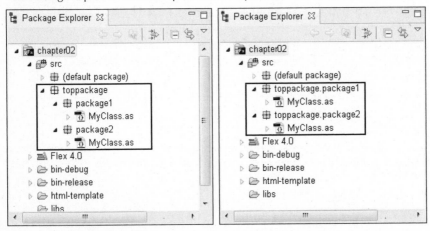

Hierarchical presentation   Flat presentation

Follow these steps to switch between package presentation styles:

1. **Click the View Menu button on the Package Explorer toolbar.** This button appears as a downward-pointing arrow.

2. **Choose Package Presentation ⇨ Flat to switch to flat presentation, or choose Package Presentation ⇨ Hierarchical to switch back to the default presentation.**

Outline view

The Outline view, shown in Figure 2.18, displays a tree of the objects that have been declared in an MXML or ActionScript file. This view is displayed by default only in the Flash perspective. Choose Window ➪ Outline from the Eclipse menu to open this view in any other perspective.

The Outline view enables you to easily locate code representing any declared variable or object, whether the object has been declared in MXML or ActionScript.

To locate code representing any variable or object using the Outline view, click the object in the view. The cursor in the current editor then jumps to that part of the code and selects the code that declares the object.

FIGURE 2.18

The Outline view

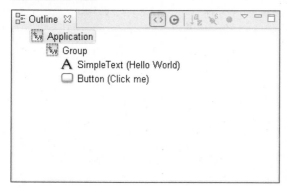

Tip

When an MXML editor has focus, the default Outline view shows only those objects that are declared in MXML code. To see properties and methods that are declared inside a <Script> section, click the Show class view button in the Outline view's toolbar. ■

Problems view

The Problems view, shown in Figure 2.19, displays current compilation errors and warnings. When your code contains a bug, the Problems view shows you these details:

- The description of the problem (an error message)
- The resource containing the problem (a source-code file)
- The path of the resource (the folder containing the problem file)
- The location of the problem (the line number)
- The type of problem

New Feature

In Eclipse 3.5.1, warnings and errors are displayed in groups in a tree presentation. You must click the group's tree icon to see its compiler messages. ■

Double-click a problem in the Problems view to jump to the problem code. If the file containing the problem isn't currently open, Flash Builder opens the file and places the cursor in the appropriate editor.

FIGURE 2.19

The Problems view

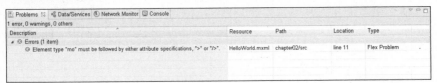

Tip

Keep only those projects open that you're currently working on. If you have the Build Automatically feature turned on (the default setting), Flash Builder recompiles all open projects whenever any source file in any of the projects has been modified and saved.

If you have any remaining errors or warnings in projects you have open but aren't using, it slows Flash Builder's compilation process and keeps those errors and warnings in the Problems view until you fix them or close the project. ■

Design views

These views are used only when an MXML editor is in Design view:

- The Properties view enables you to set object properties through a simple user interface and generates the appropriate MXML code to represent your selections.
- The Appearance view allows you to edit some key styles of your MXML objects.
- The Components view enables you to drag and drop common user interface components, including Containers and Controls, into your application.
- The States view enables you to manage alternate view states through Design view and generates code to represent the new states.

Debugging views

These views are primarily used when debugging a Flex application:

- The Console view displays tracing information and other detailed debugging messages.
- The Debug view contains controls for stepping through code, terminating a debugging session, and resuming a debugging session.

- The Variables view displays the values of all pre-declared variables that are currently in scope while application execution is stopped on a breakpoint.

- The Breakpoints view enables you to manage your breakpoints.

- The Expressions view enables you to evaluate and inspect arbitrary ActionScript expressions while application execution is stopped on a breakpoint.

- The Network Monitor allows you to monitor and introspect remote service calls.

New Feature

The new Network Monitor view enables you to monitor HTTP traffic sent between the Flex application and an application server at runtime. ∎

Cross-Reference

Debugging views are described in greater detail in Chapter 6. ∎

Getting Help

The documentation for the Flex development platform is delivered as part of the Flash Builder installation. You can access the documentation in a variety of ways:

- Explore the Help contents

- Search for specific terms

- Use context-sensitive Help

Exploring the Help contents

In Flash Builder, you can get to the Help contents, shown in Figure 2.20, by choosing Help ➪ Flash Builder Help.

New Feature

In Flash Builder 4, the online help content is displayed in a new application named Adobe Community Help. This is a desktop application that hosts both help content authored by Adobe and links to content provided by third-party documentation resources. ∎

The initial help screen contains links for all the Flex documentation. The main documentation for Flash Builder is under Using Flash Builder 4. Under this heading, you'll find these links (among others):

- About Flash Builder

- Flash Builder Workbench

- Working with data in Flash Builder

- Extending services for data-centric development

- ActionScript 3.0 Reference

Each link takes you to a section of the help content that describes that aspect of Flex development.

FIGURE 2.20

The Help Contents screen

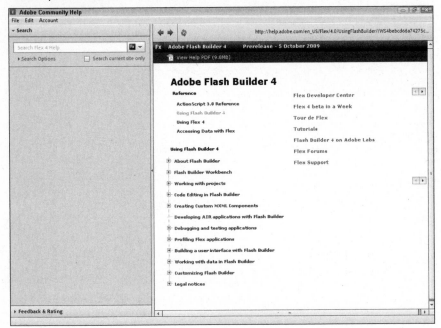

Searching for Help terms

The Adobe Community Help application enables you to search for any terms you need to find. To search for a Help term, follow these steps:

1. **Choose Help ⇨ Flash Builder Help from the Flash Builder menu.**

2. **Click in the Search input box and type a term.**

3. **Press Enter or Return.**

A successful search displays links to pages that contain your terms (see Figure 2.21). Click any link to display the help content. The page is displayed in a separate pane of the Help window.

Tip

When help content is displayed in the Adobe Community Help application, it's hosted either on the Adobe Web site or locally on your hard disk. When working with local content, the content is hosted by a local http server. you may find that the first content page you open takes some time as the server starts up in the background. After it's started, though, it stays open for the duration of your Eclipse session. ■

FIGURE 2.21

Searching in the Help window

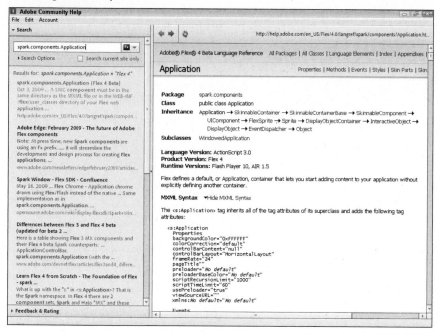

Using dynamic help

The dynamic help feature enables you to find Help content related to the code you're currently editing. For example, suppose you're working with the DataGrid component and want to find out what properties, methods, or events are available. You can easily jump to a Help topic related to that component and display the information in the Adobe Community Help application.

To display dynamic help in Adobe Community Help, follow these steps:

1. **Place the cursor anywhere in the class type declaration or MXML tag for which you want help.**

2. **Press Shift+F2.**

The Help topic should be correctly selected and displayed in a separate Help window.

Note

When you place the cursor in an ActionScript class name or MXML tag for which Flash Builder has API documentation and press Shift+F2 to open the Help application, the first help item listed is usually the API documentation for that class. ■

Searching for Code

Flash Builder and Eclipse have a number of tools that enable you to search for and locate code. Two of the tools are part of the Eclipse workbench, and a third is part of the Flash Builder plug-in.

Using Eclipse search tools

Eclipse has two tools that enable you to search for code: Find/Replace and Find in Files. The first is designed to locate code one file at a time; the second can search for code in multiple files.

Using Find/Replace

You use the Find/Replace dialog box, shown in Figure 2.22, to search for code in the currently opened file. This dialog box is available only in an MXML editor that's currently open in Source view. Choose Edit ➪ Find/Replace (keyboard shortcut Ctrl+F [Windows] or ⌘+F [MAC]) from the Flash Builder menu to open this dialog box.

FIGURE 2.22

The Find/Replace dialog box

Tip

After you execute a Find operation with the Find/Replace dialog box, you can repeat the operation with the menu choices Find Next and Find Previous on the Flash Builder Edit menu. The keyboard shortcuts for these operations in the stand-alone version of Flash Builder are Ctrl+K for Find Next and Ctrl+Shift+K for Find Previous. By default, the Find operation searches forward from the current cursor location. To search the entire file, place the cursor at the top of the file before opening the Find/Replace dialog box. Alternatively, you can choose to search backwards from the current cursor location. ■

Using Find in Files

The Find in Files dialog box, shown in Figure 2.23, also known as the File Search tool, enables you to search across multiple files in a project, directory, or workspace. It has many options that enable you to fine-tune your search. Choose Search ⇨ Find in Files from the Flash Builder menu to open this dialog box, or if you are using the Flash Builder Eclipse plug-in you can find this option under Search ⇨ File.

FIGURE 2.23

The Find in Files (File Search) dialog box

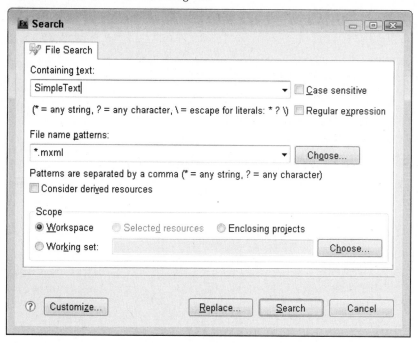

To use this tool, make these selections:

- Set the Containing text field to the string you want to find.
- Select case sensitivity and whether you're searching with a regular expression.
- Set the filename patterns field to indicate what kind of files you want to search. For example, if you want to limit your search to ActionScript files and classes, set this value to `*.as`. You can click the Choose button to select one or more file extensions to search.
- Set the Scope to the Workspace, Selected resources, or Enclosing projects.

Click the Search button to execute the operation. Results are displayed in a Search view that contains links to all found resources, as shown in Figure 2.24.

The Search view, presenting found resources

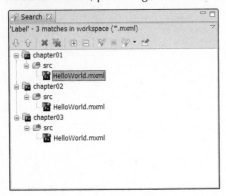

Using Flash Builder code model search tools

Flash Builder includes new search tools that are based on the code model. With these tools you can

- Search for object references
- Search for object declarations
- Refactor code

Searching for references

If you know where a variable or object's declaration is located, you can use the code model tools to locate all the object's references:

1. **In an MXML or ActionScript editor, place the cursor anywhere in the variable declaration.**

2. **Choose Search ➪ References from the Flash Builder menu.** Alternatively, you can right-click the variable declaration and choose References from the context menu.

3. **Select the scope of the search from these options:**
   - Workspace
   - Project
   - File

The results of the search are displayed in the Search view.

Searching for a declaration

If you know where a variable or object is used, you can use the code model tools to locate the object's original declaration:

1. **In an MXML or ActionScript editor, place the cursor anywhere in the variable reference.**

2. **Choose Search ⇨ Declarations from the Flash Builder menu.** Alternatively, you can right-click the variable declaration and select Declarations from the context menu.

3. **Select the scope of the search from these options:**

   - Workspace

   - Project

   - File

The results of the search are displayed in the Search view.

Flex Builder 3 added a new option called Mark Occurrences. This feature causes any variable name or type reference to be highlighted wherever it occurs in the source-code file you're editing. For example, if you place the cursor in an `<s: Label>` declaration, all `<s:Label>` declarations in the current file are highlighted. Similarly, if you place the cursor in a variable such as `myVar`, all references or declarations of that variable are highlighted.

New Feature

In Flash Builder 4, Mark Occurrences is selected by default when you create a new workspace. ∎

As shown in Figure 2.25, you can toggle this feature on and off from the Flash Builder toolbar by clicking the icon with the image of a highlighter pen.

FIGURE 2.25

The toggle button for Mark Occurrences

Refactoring variable names

When you refactor code, you globally rename object references or types. This is very different from a global search-and-replace operation that's based on string values. In a global search and replace, you can make a mess if you accidentally find substrings that are part of something else. With code refactoring, the search is based on internal references that are known to the Flex compiler and Flash Builder's code modeling tools.

To globally rename a variable with the code refactoring tool, follow these steps:

1. **Place the cursor in any of the variable's reference or declarations.**

2. **Choose Source ⇨ Refactor ⇨ Rename from the Flash Builder menu.** (Or you can right-click in the variable and choose Refactor ⇨ Rename from the context menu, or press the keyboard shortcut Ctrl+Alt+R.)

3. **In the Rename Variable dialog box, shown in Figure 2.26, enter the new variable name.** You can preview refactoring changes by clicking the dialog box's Preview button. The preview dialog box, shown in Figure 2.27, displays the Original and Refactored source code.

4. **Click OK to accept the changes and globally rename the variable.**

FIGURE 2.26

The Rename Variable dialog box

FIGURE 2.27

Previewing refactoring changes

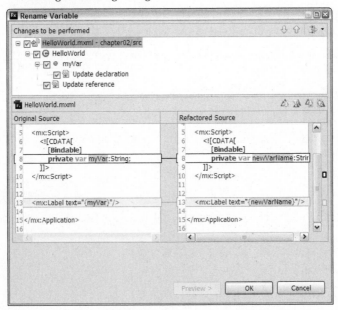

Refactoring source-code files

Renaming ActionScript and MXML files also is considered a refactoring operation, because these files represent ActionScript types that must be maintained consistently throughout a project.

To refactor a file, just rename the file in the Package Explorer view:

1. **Select a file, and press F2 (Windows) or Return (Mac), or right-click and select Rename from the context menu.**

2. **In the Rename Class dialog box, enter a new filename.**

3. **Optionally preview the changes.**

4. **Click OK to accept the changes.**

Any references to the changed file are updated through the current project, including the class declaration and constructor name.

Note

If you rename an ActionScript class file from the Package Explorer view, the class declaration and constructor method (if it exists) within the file are updated to match the filename. ∎

Moving existing source-code files

Flash Builder 4 adds the capability to move source-code files to new packages. This feature works with both MXML components and ActionScript classes.

New Feature

The capability to refactor an application or project for changes in a class or component's physical location was added in Flash Builder 4. ∎

You can move a class or component from either the Package Explorer view or from within the source code.

In the Package Explorer, click the class you want to move, then choose File ➪ Move. (You can also right-click on the class and select Move from the context menu.) As shown in Figure 2.28, a dialog box prompts you for the new location.

Select a new folder location and click Preview to preview the source-code changes, or click OK to complete the Move operation.

To execute the same refactoring operation in an ActionScript class's source code, right-click on the class name, then choose Refactor ➪ Move from the context menu. The same dialog appears to allow you to preview or complete the refactoring operation.

Note

When you move an ActionScript class file to a new package, the class file itself is refactored with an updated package name, and existing references to the class are updated through the current project. ∎

Note

If you move an ActionScript class from one folder to another by dragging it within the Package view, or you rename a package, the package declaration within the class files is updated by the code refactoring engine. ■

FIGURE 2.28

Moving a class or component

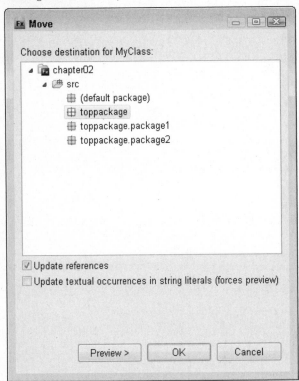

Generating Code

Flash Builder 4 includes many features that enable you to generate and modify your application code. Some of these features have been part of the product since version 2, while others are new to Flash Builder 4.

Generating getter and setter methods

ActionScript 3 has always supported the use of getter and setter methods to provide access to a class's private properties, but previous versions of Flash Builder didn't do anything to help developers build the required code.

New Feature

Getter and setter method generation is a new feature of Flash Builder 4. ■

You can now declare a public property and then use Flash Builder to convert it to a private property, supported by the required methods. Try this:

1. **Create a new ActionScript class.**

2. **Declare a public property named** `myVar` **data typed as a** `String`. The ActionScript class might start looking like this:

```
package
{
  public class MyClass
  {
    public var myVar:String;
  }
}
```

3. **Place the cursor anywhere in the variable name.**

4. **Choose Source ⇨ Generate Getter/Setter.** As shown in Figure 2.29, a dialog box appears that prompts you for options.

Generating getter and setter methods

5. **Accept all the dialog box's default settings and click OK.**

The `public` property is renamed with an underscore prefix and changed to a `private` property, and the required getter and setter methods are generated. The resulting class now looks like this:

```
package
{
  public class MyClass
  {
    private var _myVar:String;
    public function get myVar():String
    {
      return _myVar;
    }
    public function set myVar(v:String):void
    {
      _myVar = v;
    }
  }
}
```

You don't have to use getters and setters everywhere in your code (public properties do just fine for most purposes), but when you need them, Flash Builder now makes it much easier to build the basic code structure.

Generating event handlers

Flash Builder enables you to define *event handlers* (methods that are called in reaction to an event that's dispatched by your application) as attributes of MXML tags. For example, this Button component calls a method named button1_clickHandler() in reaction to its `click` event:

```
<s:Button label="Click me" click="button1_clickHandler()"/>
```

Flash Builder 4 now can generate both the required event handler function and the code to call it. I describe this feature in Chapter 7.

Integrating Flash Builder with Flash Professional CS5

Flash Builder 4 and Flash Professional CS5 are designed to work together in a number of ways. As Flash developers have become more accustomed to using ActionScript 3 in their presentations, they've yearned for a better code editing experience than the Flash user interface provides. Flash Builder can provide that experience.

Flash presentations that use ActionScript 3 have a Document Class property that you set in the Properties panel. You can create this class (and any other supporting ActionScript classes) in a Flash Professional project in Flash Builder. If you're using Flash Professional CS5, the project will start with information about the movieclip symbols and other addressable objects in the Flash presentation and will provide code hinting, code completion, import statement management, and other features that Flex developers have used for years.

Before creating a Flash Professional project in Flash Builder, first create a Flash presentation in Flash Professional. Flash Builder is able to address Flash presentations that are saved in the traditional binary FLA format or in the new XML-based XFL format.

Follow these steps to create a new Flash presentation:

1. **Open both Flash Builder and Flash Professional CS5 on your desktop.**
2. **Starting in Flash Professional CS5, select File ➪ New from the menu.**
3. **Select ActionScript 3.0 in the New Document dialog box and click OK.**
4. **Save the file in a folder anywhere on disk.**

Caution

Your Flash presentation's filename and the folder in which it's saved should have different names. If they share the same name, Flash Builder won't be able to create the required Flash Professional project. ■

5. **Add a text object to the stage using the text tool and set its type to TLFText.** Assign it an instance name of myText. (If you're working with a previous version of Flash Professional, you can set the type as Dynamic Text.)
6. **Select Window ➪ Components.**
7. **Drag a Button from the User Interface section of the Components panel to the stage.**
8. **Assign the new Button an instance name of myButton.**
9. **Save the file.**

Next, set the new presentation's document class and create a Flash Builder project to manage it:

1. **Open the Properties panel.**
2. **As shown in Figure 2.30, set Class to any class name.** I usually set the class name to the same name as the Flash presentation but without the file extension. For example, I set the document class for FlashPreso.fla as FlashPreso.
3. **Click the pencil icon next to the class name.**
4. **If you see an ActionScript Class Warning dialog box telling you that the class doesn't exist, click OK and then click the pencil icon again.**
5. **In the dialog box that appears next, shown in Figure 2.31, select Flash Builder as your editing application and click OK.**

FIGURE 2.30

Setting a Flash presentation's class name in the Properties panel

FIGURE 2.31

Selecting Flash Builder to edit the document class

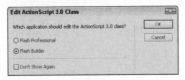

6. **Switch to Flash Builder (it might take focus on its own).** A dialog box appears that asks you to create a new Flash Professional project. The Target File is set automatically to point to the Flash presentation file you started with.

7. **Accept all default settings and click Finish.**

The Flash Professional project is created in Flash Builder with an ActionScript class that's named as you requested assigned in Flash Professional.

Tip

The generated class extends the `Sprite` class and represents the Flash presentation:

```
package
{
  import flash.display.Sprite;
  public class FlashPreso extends Sprite
  {
    public function FlashPreso()
    {
    }
  }
}
```

If you want to manipulate the presentation's timeline from the ActionScript class, change the superclass from `Sprite` to `MovieClip`:

```
package
{
  import flash.display.MovieClip;
  public class FlashPreso extends MovieClip
  {
    public function FlashPreso()
    {
    }
  }
} ∎
```

For each object you want to address in your ActionScript code, add a `public` property declaration in the class declaration (but outside the constructor method). Assign each property a name and type matching the instance name and object type in Flash. Be sure to include any required `import` statements. This version of the class declares `Button` and `TLFTextField` properties to match the Flash presentation's objects:

```
package
{
  import fl.controls.Button;
  import fl.text.TLFTextField;

  import flash.display.MovieClip;
  public class FlashPreso extends MovieClip
  {
    public var myText:TLFTextField;
    public var myButton:Button;
    public function FlashPreso()
    {
    }
  }
}
```

Note

When you save changes to your code, Flash Builder switches over to Flash Professional and checks the names and types of all of your declarations. If your code doesn't match the objects in the presentation, Flash Builder displays compiler errors. ■

You're now ready to add code to manage your application's functionality at runtime. The document class in Listing 2.1 listens for a click event on the button object and responds by changing the text object's display.

A document class that addresses two objects in a Flash presentation

```
package
{
  import fl.text.TLFTextField;
  import fl.controls.Button;

  import flash.display.Sprite;
  import flash.events.MouseEvent;
  public class FlashPreso extends Sprite
  {
    public var myText:TLFTextField;
    public var myButton:Button;
    public function FlashPreso()
    {
      myButton.addEventListener(MouseEvent.CLICK, clickHandler);
    }
    protected function clickHandler(event:MouseEvent):void
    {
      myText.text = "You clicked";
    }
  }
}
```

Note

The Document Class feature was introduced in Flash CS3 Professional and works with all Flash presentations that use ActionScript 3. The steps described in this section can be adapted for use with any of these versions. ■

You can test your Flash presentation from within either Flash Professional or Flash Builder. In either product, select Run ➪ Test Movie from the menu or press Ctrl+Enter (Windows) or ⌘+Enter (Mac). If you start from Flash Builder, Flash Professional takes focus to launch the presentation.

Once you've created a simple document class successfully, you can then add as many ActionScript classes as your presentation requires. And when you set the linkage properties of a movieclip symbol in Flash Professional to a new ActionScript class, you can then jump to Flash Builder to create and edit the class just as you did with the document class.

Summary

In this chapter, I described the nature and behavior of Flash Builder 4. You learned the following:

- Flash Builder 4 is a plug-in designed for use with Eclipse.

- Flash Builder 4 is available for the Windows and Mac OS X operating systems.

- Flash Builder's stand-alone configuration includes everything you need to build Flex applications, including Eclipse 3.5.1.

- Flash Builder's plug-in installation option enables you to install Flash Builder on top of an existing Eclipse installation.

- The Flash Builder plug-in installation requires Eclipse 3.4.

- Flash Builder can be used by both Flex and Flash developers to edit their ActionScript files.

- Flash Builder adds many tools in the form of Views and Editors to Eclipse to make coding faster and more productive.

- Flash Builder includes many valuable code generation, searching, and refactoring tools to make your coding experience more productive.

- Flash Builder 4 and Flash Professional CS5 are designed to work together to create a seamless ActionScript editing experience.

- Many tools that are a part of the Eclipse workbench are critical to effective use of Flash Builder.

Building a Basic Flex Application

In this chapter, I describe how to create and deploy a basic "Hello World" Flex application for the Web. After the application is built, I describe the fundamental nature of a Flex application, including the relationship between the application SWF file and the supporting HTML (Hypertext Markup Language) files. I describe the contents of the HTML "wrapper" file that's generated for you in Flash Builder and its associated JavaScript library file.

Finally, I describe how to deploy the Flex application into a Web site in these ways:

- As a distinct application that opens in its own window
- As an applet that's displayed as part of an existing Web page
- As a desktop application deployed on Adobe AIR

By the end of this chapter, you should have a good sense of what a Flex application is and how it's delivered to the user.

Note

The code samples and screen shots in this chapter assume that you're using Flash Builder 4 to build the application. If you're using the Flex 4 SDK and your own text editor, the steps will be similar, but you won't have access to some of the code completion and other productivity tools I describe. ■

IN THIS CHAPTER

Creating a "Hello World" application

Switching workspaces

Creating a Flex project

Understanding HTML templates

Exporting a release build

Deploying a Flex application on the Web

Integrating Flex applications with Web pages in Dreamweaver CS4

Creating a "Hello World" Application

In all programming languages, your first task is to write a "Hello World" application. The most simple of applications, it typically contains no more than a single line of text output.

Note

Throughout these instructions, I assume that you're using the stand-alone version of Flash Builder. Where the steps are different in the plug-in version, I provide alternative steps in a Tip. ■

Switching workspaces

As described in Chapter 2, your first step is to create a Flex project. The project hosts the application's source code and other assets.

Follow these steps to switch to a new workspace:

1. **Open Flash Builder 4.**

2. **From the menu, choose File ➪ Switch Workspace.**

3. **Select a new folder named flex4bible anywhere on your hard disk and then click OK.** If you're working on Windows, the folder might be C:\flex4bible. On Mac OS X, the folder should be in your home directory; for example, /Users/[username]/Documents/flex4bible.

   After selecting the workspace, you should see Flash Builder close and reopen. The new workspace, shown in Figure 3.1, should display the Flash Builder Start Page and the default Flash perspective. The newly created workspace is empty and contains no projects.

Note

Workspace folders are sometimes created as sibling folders to the projects they reference, rather than parent folders. This is because a workspace contains references to an absolute location on the hard disk and isn't portable. If you change the location of your project folders, you have to re-create the workspace. ■

Tip

You can re-create a workspace from scratch by first closing Flash Builder and then deleting the workspace folder's .metadata subfolder using Windows Explorer or Finder. When you reopen Flash Builder, the workspace data is recreated automatically.

You'll then need to import any existing projects to see them in the Package Explorer view. Choose File ➪ Import to open the Import dialog box. Then choose General ➪ Existing Projects into Workspace. Browse and select the project's root folder. After verifying that your project is visible and has been selected, click Finish. ■

FIGURE 3.1

The default Flash perspective in a new workspace

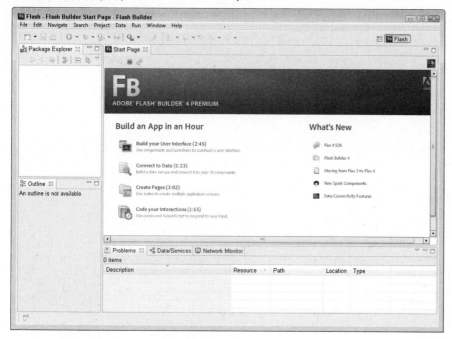

Creating the project

Follow these steps to create a Flex project:

1. From the menu, choose File ➪ New ➪ Flex Project.

Tip

If you're using the plug-in version of Flash Builder, choose File ➪ New ➪ Other. Then from the wizard that appears, choose Flash Builder ➪ Flex Project. ∎

2. **In the first screen, shown in Figure 3.2, enter** chapter03 **as the Project name.**

3. **Confirm the Use default location option under Project location is selected.** The project location defaults to a folder named chapter03 under the workspace folder. For example, on Windows the default folder might be C:\flex4bible\chapter03.

4. **Choose the Web application (runs in Flash Player) option for the Application type.**

5. **Choose the Use default SDK (currently "Flex 4.0") option for the Flex SDK version.**

6. **Select None/Other from the Application server type drop-down menu, and click Next.**

FIGURE 3.2

The first screen of the New Flex Project wizard

7. **On the Configure Output screen, shown in Figure 3.3, accept the Output folder setting of bin-debug.** This is the location of the compiled debug version of the application and its supporting files.

8. **Click Next.**

Note

In Flex Builder 2, the default Output folder was set by default to `bin`, and the folder contained both the debug and the release build of the compiled application. Starting with Flex Builder 3, the Output folder defaults to `bin-debug` to distinguish it from the separate folder you create when you export a release build. ■

9. On the Create a Flex project screen, shown in Figure 3.4, accept these default settings:

- Main source folder: `src`.
- Main application file: `HelloWorld.mxml`.
- Output folder URL: Accept the default setting, leaving it blank.

FIGURE 3.3

The second screen of the New Flex Project wizard

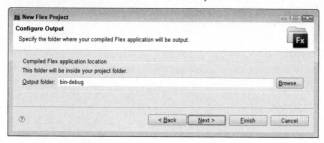

FIGURE 3.4

The third screen of the New Flex Project wizard

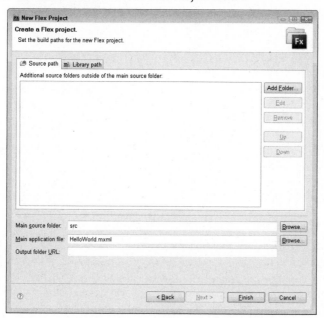

10. **Click Finish to create the project and the main application file.** As shown in Figure 3.5, you should see the main application file appear in the Editor view. If you're working in a completely new workspace, the file should appear in Source mode; that is, you should see the application's source code.

Note

I've added line feeds after each of the starting tags attributes in Figure 3.5 to make it all fit on the screen. ∎

FIGURE 3.5

The new main application file in Source mode

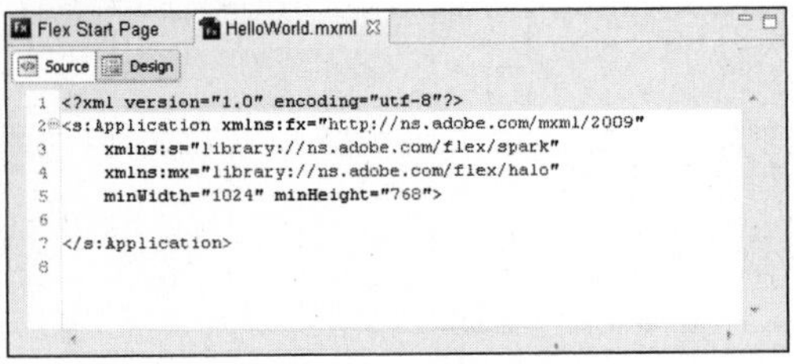

Saying hello

Flex 4 applications use a new architecture for laying out the application's child objects. In Flex 3, the <mx:Application> component had a layout property that was set to a String value of absolute, horizontal, or vertical. In Flex 4, the <s:Application> tag's layout is determined by an instance of a Layout class. You typically set the application's layout property with an <s:layout> tag, wrapped around an instance of the layout class you want to use. The following code sets an application to use vertical layout:

```
<?xml version="1.0" encoding="utf-8"?>
<s:Application xmlns:fx="http://ns.adobe.com/mxml/2009"
  xmlns:s="library://ns.adobe.com/flex/spark"
  xmlns:mx="library://ns.adobe.com/flex/mx"
  minWidth="955" minHeight="600">
  <s:layout>
    <s:VerticalLayout/>
  </s:layout>
</s:Application>
```

The default layout for a Flex 4 application is a scheme known as *basic* layout. This architecture is similar to Flex 3's *absolute* layout, which caused visual objects to retain their positions relative to the application's top-left corner. In your simple application, you'll use vertical layout.

Note

A simple Flex 4 application uses more XML namespaces and MXML child tags than in Flex 3. I describe these in detail in Chapter 4. ∎

Follow these steps to display a simple message in your Flex application:

1. **Make sure your application is displayed in Source mode.**

2. **Delete the minWidth and minHeight attributes from the <s:Application> tag.** This enables the application to automatically resize itself to adjust to the browser's dimensions.

3. **Delete the <fx:Declarations> element and its nested comment.** This element is used to declare nonvisual objects in Flex 4 but isn't required in this simple application.

4. **Place the cursor between the <s:Application> tags.**

5. **Type** `<layout`. As you type, you should see that a window appears (shown in Figure 3.6) that contains a list of proposed properties and objects you can use in this context.

Using code hinting

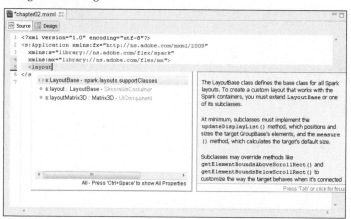

6. **Select s:layout from the list, and then type > to close the tag.** You should see that Flash Builder auto-completes the `<s:layout>` tag:

```
<s:layout>
</s:layout>
```

7. **With the cursor between the <s:layout> tags, type** `<vertical`. Select `s:VerticalLayout` from the list, then complete the tag with XML empty tag syntax:

```
<s:layout>
  <s:VerticalLayout/>
</s:layout>
```

8. **Add a paddingTop setting of 20 and a horizontalAlign setting of center to the <s:Vertical> tag:**

```
<s:VerticalLayout paddingTop="20" horizontalAlign="center"/>
```

New Feature

In Flex 4, the padding, alignment, and gap settings that help to determine automatic layout are now implemented in the `VerticalLayout` and `HorizontalLayout` classes, rather than in containers such as `Application`. Also, these settings are now implemented as properties rather than as styles. ∎

   9. Place the cursor on an empty line of code between the </:layout> end tag and the </s:Application> end tag.

   10. Type <label, then select s:Label from the class list.

   11. Complete the Label object as follows:

```
<s:Label text="Hello World" fontSize="36"/>
```

New Feature

The `<s:Label>` tag in this application creates an instance of the Spark `Label` component. Unlike the older MX version of `Label`, this new control is able to render right-to-left text and take advantage of other new text rendering features in Flash Player 10. There are also new text controls named `RichText` and `RichEditableText`. I describe these controls in Chapter 9. ∎

   12. Check your completed application. The code should look like this:

```
<?xml version="1.0" encoding="utf-8"?>
<s:Application xmlns:fx="http://ns.adobe.com/mxml/2009"
  xmlns:s="library://ns.adobe.com/flex/spark"
  xmlns:mx="library://ns.adobe.com/flex/mx">
  <s:layout>
    <s:VerticalLayout paddingTop="20" horizontalAlign="center"/>
  </s:layout>
  <s:Label text="Hello World" fontSize="36"/>
</s:Application>
```

   13. Choose File ➪ Save to save the file.

   14. **Choose Run ➪ Run HelloWorld to run the application in a browser.** As shown in Figure 3.7, you see that the application opens in a browser window.

FIGURE 3.7

The finished application running in a Web browser

Tip

You also can use the keyboard shortcut Ctrl+F11 (Windows) or ⌘+Shift+F11 (Mac) to run the current application. ■

Understanding the html-template Folder

Each Flex project that's designed for deployment over the Web contains a folder named html-template. This folder contains models for the HTML and supporting files that run your application in the browser. Whenever you save changes to your source code, Flash Builder automatically rebuilds your application using the HTML model file to generate an HTML wrapper. At the same time, it copies the contents of the html-template folder to the output folder that contains the compiled application. Figure 3.8 shows the contents of the html-template folder.

Note

The html-template folder and its contents do not need to be copied to the Web server to deploy the application. These files are used only during the compilation process. ■

FIGURE 3.8

The html-template folder structure

Tip

Flash Builder has a Build Automatically property that causes your applications to be automatically compiled every time you save changes to any source-code file. If you want your applications to be recompiled only when you choose, change the property in Flash Builder by choosing Project ➪ Build Automatically. Use the same menu choice to turn the property back on. ■

During the compilation process, most of the files in the html-template directory are simply copied to the output folder that contains the debug version of the project's applications. The HTML wrapper file that you use at runtime is generated based on a model file in html-template named index.template.html. In addition, any files in the source-code root that aren't either code files built in MXML or ActionScript, or that don't represent embedded assets, such as binary graphical files, are copied, along with their directory structure, to the output folder as well.

Tip

You can choose whether asset files that aren't embedded in the application are copied to the output folder. Choose Project ⇨ Properties, and then select the Flex Compiler category. Under Compiler options, set Copy non-embedded files to output folder to your preferred setting. This setting also affects which files are included in a release build folder for a Web application, or an AIR installer package for desktop applications. ■

The `html-template` directory contains three files and one subfolder:

- **index.template.html.** A model file that is the basis for the generated HTML "wrapper" files that call the application at runtime.

- **swfobject.js.** A JavaScript library containing functions used at runtime to load Flash Player. This file also contains "sniffer" code that can discover whether Flash Player is currently loaded on the user's desktop and, if so, which version.

- **playerProductInstall.swf.** A Flash application that's used to upgrade a user's system when Flash Player 6.65 or higher is installed.

- **The history subfolder.** Contains files to implement the history management feature (for non-IE browsers only):

  - `historyFrame.html` is a model for an HTML page that's loaded into an `<iframe>` in the main page at runtime.

  - `history.js` is a JavaScript library containing functions that are called by `historyFrame.html`.

  - `history.css` contains Cascading Style Sheet (CSS) rules to suppress the visibility of the history frame in the main page.

New Feature

Flash Builder 4 now uses the open-source SWFObject JavaScript library to deploy Flash Player and the application, rather than the proprietary `AC_OE_Tags.js` **file that was used in Flex Builder 3. Documentation and the most recent versions of the SWFObject library are available at** `http://code.google.com/p/swfobject/.` **■**

The HTML wrapper template

The HTML template file, `index.template.html`, contains a combination of these elements:

- HTML code
- Calls to JavaScript functions that are stored in `swfobject.js`
- "History" files that manage the navigation history and deep linking
- Placeholders for values that are passed to the generated version of the file

At compile time, the HTML template is used to generate an HTML "wrapper" file that you deploy to your Web server. In this section, I describe each part of the file and its purpose.

The HTML <head> section

The <head> section of the model HTML file contains links to a set of CSS and JavaScript files. The <title> element contains a variable that's filled in from the Application's pageTitle property:

```
<title>${title}</title>
```

To fill in this value in the generated HTML wrapper page, set the pageTitle property in the <s:Application> start tag:

```
<s:Application xmlns:fx="http://ns.adobe.com/mxml/2009"
  xmlns:s="library://ns.adobe.com/flex/spark"
  xmlns:mx="library://ns.adobe.com/flex/mx"
  pageTitle="Hello World">
```

Next, a CSS declaration eliminates default margins and paddings, and sets the height of the <html> and <body> elements to 100%. The flashContent id selector refers to a <div> element that determines where the application is displayed in the Web page:

```
<style type="text/css" media="screen">
  html, body { height:100%; }
  body { margin:0; padding:0; overflow:hidden; text-align:center; }
  #flashContent { display:none; }
</style>
```

Tip

The overflow setting of hidden means that if the size of Flash Player (or another element in the page) overflows the boundaries of the page, the remainder is hidden. If you want the page to show scrollbars instead, change the value of the overflow style to scroll. ■

A <link> tag incorporates the history.css file from the history folder, and a <script> tag imports the history.js JavaScript library:

```
<link rel="stylesheet" type="text/css" href="history/history.css" />
<script type="text/javascript" src="history/history.js"></script>
```

This <script> element imports the swfobject code library:

```
<script type="text/javascript" src="swfobject.js"></script>
```

Then, another <script> element contains code that evaluates the user's current version of Flash Player and reacts accordingly:

- If the version of Flash Player that's required by your application is present, the application is loaded.

- If the user has at least Flash Player 6,0,65, but not your required version, the Flash application playerProductInstall.swf is loaded to assist the user in upgrading his player software. If any errors are encountered (if the user doesn't have administrative rights to his computer, for example), the Flash-based upgrade installer fails with a useful error message (rather than just hanging and letting the user wonder what happened).

- If Flash Player isn't available, or a version older than 6,0,65 is present, a link to download Flash Player from the Adobe Web site is presented.

This section of the HTML document's JavaScript code defines which version of Flash Player is required for the current application:

```
var swfVersionStr =
"${version_major}.${version_minor}.${version_revision}";
```

The version_major, version_minor, and version_revision parameters can be set in the Flex project's properties:

1. **Choose Project ➪ Properties from the Flash Builder menu.**

2. **In the Properties dialog box, select the Flex Compiler section, as shown in Figure 3.9.**

3. **In the Required Flash Player version option, change the version numbers as needed.**

FIGURE 3.9

Setting the required Flash Player version number

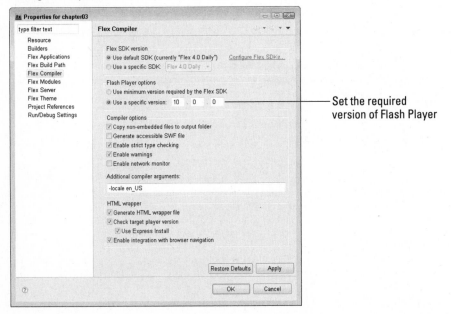

Tip

When you create a new Flex Project in Flash Builder 4, the project's required Flash Player version is determined by the Flex SDK's configuration. This setting is in the SDK folder's `frameworks/flex-config.xml` file, in the `<target-player>` element:

```
<target-player>10.0.0</target-player>
```

If you change the contents of `flex-config.xml`, you should "clean" all projects to force recompilation. Choose Project ➪ Clean, select Clean all projects, and click OK. ∎

The rest of the script completes the version evaluation and runs the application:

```
var xiSwfUrlStr = "playerProductInstall.swf";
var flashvars = {};
var params = {};
params.quality = "high";
params.bgcolor = "${bgcolor}";
params.allowscriptaccess = "sameDomain";
var attributes = {};
attributes.id = "${application}";
attributes.name = "${application}";
attributes.align = "middle";
swfobject.embedSWF(
    "${swf}.swf", "flashContent",
    "${width}", "${height}",
    swfVersionStr, xiSwfUrlStr,
    flashvars, params, attributes);
<!-- JavaScript enabled so display the flashContent div in case it is
    not replaced with a swf object. -->
swfobject.createCSS("#flashContent", "display:block;text-
    align:left;");
```

The call to `swfobject.embedSWF()` dynamically generates HTML code that runs Flash Player and the application at the location of the `<div>` with an id of `flashContent`. The call to `swfobject.createCSS()` hides the remainder of the `<div>` tag's contents so doesn't display if the application runs successfully.

The `<head>` section contains the `<div>` tag with an id of `flashContent`:

```
<div id="flashContent">
  <p>
    To view this page ensure that Adobe Flash Player version
    ${version_major}.${version_minor}.${version_revision} or
    greater is installed.
  </p>
  <a href="http://www.adobe.com/go/getflashplayer">
    <img src="http://www.adobe.com/images/shared/download_buttons/
      get_flash_player.gif" alt="Get Adobe Flash Player" />
  </a>
</div>
```

Its contents are only displayed if the application or the Flash upgrade installer aren't loaded successfully. By default, it displays a text message indicating which version of Flash Player is required and a linked image that takes the user to the Adobe Web site to download the latest version of Flash Player. You can customize this section of the HTML code as desired.

Running the application

When the HTML wrapper file instantiates Flash Player, it passes certain parameters in a `params` object:

```
var params = {};
params.quality = "high";
params.bgcolor = "${bgcolor}";
params.allowscriptaccess = "sameDomain";
```

The `quality` and `allowScriptAccess` parameters have fixed values. The `bgcolor` parameter is set dynamically, as defined in the application's `<s:Application>` tag or in a CSS declaration for the `S|Application` type selector.

Note

The `allowScriptAccess` **property can be set to** `never`, `always`, **or** `sameDomain`. **It controls outbound scripting capabilities from within Flash Player. For more information on the outbound script security model, see the article at** `www.adobe.com/go/tn_16494`. ∎

Using the flashvars parameter

You can pass arbitrary named parameters to the application in the `flashvars` object. The object is defined and then passed into the Flex document. You can add named parameters to the `flashvars` object:

```
var flashvars = {};
var flashvars.param1 = "Some value";
```

These parameters are then available in your Flex application via the application's `parameters` property:

```
trace(this.parameters.param1);
```

The HTML <noscript> section

This `<noscript>` element at the bottom of the page contains code to instantiate Flash Player in browsers that don't support JavaScript:

```
<noscript>
  <object classid="clsid:D27CDB6E-AE6D-11cf-96B8-444553540000"
    width="${width}" height="${height}" id="${application}">
    <param name="movie" value="${swf}.swf" />
    <param name="quality" value="high" />
    <param name="bgcolor" value="${bgcolor}" />
```

```
      <param name="allowScriptAccess" value="sameDomain" />
      <!--[if !IE]>-->
      <object type="application/x-shockwave-flash"
        data="${swf}.swf" width="${width}" height="${height}">
        <param name="quality" value="high" />
        <param name="bgcolor" value="${bgcolor}" />
        <param name="allowScriptAccess" value="sameDomain" />
      <!--<![endif]-->
      <a href="http://www.adobe.com/go/getflashplayer">
        <img src="http://www.adobe.com/images/shared/download_buttons/
            get_flash_player.gif" alt="Get Adobe Flash Player" />
      </a>
      <!--[if !IE]>-->
        </object>
      <!--<![endif]-->
      </object>
   </noscript>
```

This section of code is executed only in browsers that don't support JavaScript at all or where the user has disabled JavaScript through her browser's security settings. This circumstance is rare, but not unheard of, in current browser installations.

The only real drawback to loading Flash Player in this manner is that if the user is working with Microsoft Internet Explorer, loading Flash Player without JavaScript code can result in an odd user experience: To interact with the application, first the user must click the Flash document (the Flex application) or press the spacebar. This is an irritant, but certainly not crippling.

Caution

If you add or change parameters, they must be applied to both the JavaScript and the `embed` and `object` tag versions in the HTML wrapper file. ■

Caution

You can customize this HTML as desired, but you should always do so in the HTML template page, rather than the version that's generated in the output folders. If you customize the generated files directly, they'll just be overwritten the next time you compile the application. ■

History management files

The `html-template` folder contains a subfolder called `history`. This folder contains a set of files called by the HTML wrapper file from an `<iframe>` element that's dynamically written to the browser window by the JavaScript code. Their purpose is to implement a feature known as history management when using a `ViewStack`, `TabNavigator`, or `Accordion` container. This feature enables the user to navigate forward and backward through an application's view state with the Web browser's Forward and Back buttons in Web browsers other than Microsoft Internet Explorer. Another supported feature, deep linking, enables you to construct URL patterns that cause the application to open with a particular state based on the URL request.

If you don't need to use the navigator container history management feature or deep linking, you can cause Flash Builder to stop generating the history files on a per-project basis. Follow these steps to disable history management and deep linking:

1. **In the Package Explorer view, select the project.**

2. **Select Project ⇨ Properties from the Flash Builder menu.**

3. **In the Properties dialog box, choose the Flex Compiler category, and then uncheck the option to Enable integration with Web browsers.**

4. **Click OK to save your changes.** A dialog box warns you that because you changed options for the HTML wrapper, all files in the `html-template` folder will be rewritten and/or deleted.

5. **Click OK to close the dialog box and wait for the project to be rebuilt.**

6. **Look at the html-template folder and the bin-debug folder in the Package Explorer view.** You should see that the `history` subfolder is no longer generated as part of the project's deployment files.

Web Resource

Deep linking was added in Flex 3. More information on deep linking is available on the Web at: `http://livedocs.adobe.com/flex/3/html/help.html?content=deep_linking_2.html` ∎

Deploying the Application

You've created the application, and it runs beautifully in your development and testing environment. Now you want to share the application with your users. This section describes how to create a version of the application that's suitable for public release and make the application available to your audience.

Creating a release build

The version of the application that's created in your output folder, and that you run during the testing and debugging phase of development, is the "debug" version of the application. This compiled SWF file is significantly larger than the version you'll ultimately deploy for your users, because it contains additional internal information that's used only during debugging.

Note

In Flex Builder 2, the debug and release builds of the application were placed in a single output folder. To deploy the application, you copied all files except the HTML and SWF files with the word debug in their file-names to the Web server. Starting with version 3, Flex Builder separates the debug and release builds into separate folders and requires a manual export process for the release build. ∎

To create a release build of a Flex Web application, follow these steps:

1. **From the Flash Builder menu, choose Project ⇨ Export Release Build, or File ⇨ Export ⇨ Release Build.**

2. **In the Export Release Build dialog box, shown in Figure 3.10, make these choices:**

   a. Select the application you want to export.

   b. Indicate whether you want to enable the View Source feature.

   c. Select a folder to which you want to export the release build.

3. **Click Finish to export the release build.**

FIGURE 3.10

The Export Release Build dialog box for a Web application

Note

A release build folder contains only a single application and its supporting files. In contrast, the `bin-debug` folder contains the debug versions of all applications in a project. ∎

After exporting the release build, you should have a new folder containing the compiled application and its supporting files. This version of the application is optimized for delivery to the user. It doesn't contain debug information, and as a result it's significantly smaller than the debug version.

The size of a basic "Hello World" compiled application file with a single `Label` control will be either 98K for the debug version, or 51K for the release build. Clearly, you want your users to be downloading and using the release build.

New Feature

In Flex 4, the ActionScript classes and other elements of the SDK that are shared by all Flex applications are compiled by default into RSL (Runtime Shared Library) files that are separate from the application SWF file. These files, which also have a file extension of `.swf`, are loaded by the application at runtime as their classes are needed. Examples of these files include `framework_4.0.0.12685.swf`, `spark_4.0.0.12685.swf`, and so on. (The specific version number embedded in the filenames changes depending on which version of the Flex 4 SDK the application is compiled with.) When you deploy a Flex 4 Web application, you must copy all of the SWF files in the release folder to the application folder on your Web site.

You can change this behavior in the Framework linkage drop-down menu on the Flex Build Path screen of the project options dialog box. To cause the SDK classes to be compiled into the main application SWF files, set Framework linkage to Merge into code. After saving your changes, select Project ➪ Clean from the Flash Builder menu, then click OK to rebuild the project's applications. The resulting application SWF file will be much larger, but you'll have fewer files to upload to the Web site. ■

Testing the release build

You can test the release build of a Flex Web application by opening its HTML wrapper file in a Web browser. Here's how:

1. **From the Package Explorer view, open the release build folder and locate the HTML wrapper file.** This file has the same name as the application itself, but has a `.html` file extension.

2. **Right-click the HTML file, and choose Open With ➪ Web Browser.**

The application opens in a Web browser nested with an Eclipse editor view, as shown in Figure 3.11.

FIGURE 3.11

Running the release build in a Web Browser editor view

Caution

When you run the release build as described previously, the application always opens from the local file system, rather than from any Web server you might have configured. If you need to test the application with a Web server, you have to manually configure the server, or place your bin-release folder within your Web server's document root folder, then open the file from a Web browser using the appropriate URL. ■

Deploying the release build

To deploy the release build of the application, just upload all files in the release build folder to your Web site using File Transfer Protocol (FTP) or whichever method you typically use to deploy other files to your Web site. These files will include the following:

- The compiled application SWF file
- The SWF files containing framework classes, used by the application as RSL's
- The HTML wrapper file
- The JavaScript library file
- `playerProductInstall.swf`
- The `history` folder
- Any assets added to your application

Then provide the URL of the HTML wrapper page to your users. For example, if the release build of an application named `registration` is uploaded to a subfolder of my Web site, `www.bardotech.com`, and the HTML wrapper file is named `registration.html`, then the deployment URL is this:

```
www.bardotech.com/registration/registration.html
```

Tip

Programmers sometimes make users navigate to a Flex application in a new browser window. The new window then has a fresh "history," which means the browser's Back button is disabled and the user can't accidentally unload the application by trying to go back to a previous screen. The following HTML code would open the application from the home page of my Web site:

```
<a href="registration/registration.html" target="_blank"/> ■
```

Integrating an application into an existing Web page

Some Flex applications are designed to be presented as *applets* (an application that represents only part of a Web page). This is easy to accomplish if you have some working knowledge of HTML. Here's how:

1. **Create a region of a Web page where you want to host the application.** Design it just as you would to host an image, an ActiveX control, or a Java applet. You can use HTML tables or more modern `<div>` tags with CSS to control the size and position of the hosting region.

2. **In the Flex application code, set the <s:Application> tag's height and width to a specific number of pixels that will make the application size match the available space in the Web page.** For example, if you have a `<div>` tag in the hosting page that's 300 pixels high and 200 pixels wide, use this code in the Flex application to size it appropriately:

```
<s:Application xmlns:fx="http://ns.adobe.com/mxml/2009"
   xmlns:s="library://ns.adobe.com/flex/spark"
   xmlns:mx="library://ns.adobe.com/flex/mx"
   height=»300» width=»200»>
```

When the application is compiled, the `height` and `width` settings are passed into the generated HTML file.

3. **Copy the JavaScript includes and initialization code from the <head> section of the generated HTML wrapper file to the <head> section of the hosting HTML page.**

4. **Create a <div> element with an id of flashContent in your Web page where you want to display the application.**

Caution

When you deploy a hosted Flex applet to a Web server, be sure to include all the same files as before: the JavaScript library, history files, and upgrade installer SWF file (`playerProductInstall.swf`). ■

As shown in Figure 3.12, the application will look like a part of the HTML page, but will offer all the dynamic functionality that you've programmed.

FIGURE 3.12

A Flex application running in an HTML file as an applet

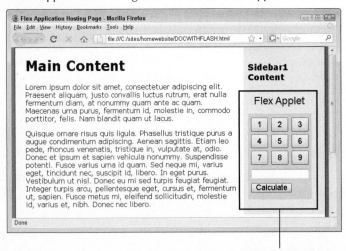

The Flex application

Integrating Flex applications with Dreamweaver

Dreamweaver is the common application of choice for Web site developers who are not necessarily application developers. Because compiled Flex applications are basically Flash documents, though, it's possible to use Dreamweaver's Web page code generation capabilities to import a Flex application into an existing Web page.

Caution

When you integrate a Flex application into a Web page using Dreamweaver, you won't have the integrated history management feature, because Dreamweaver treats the Flex application as a simple SWF file. ■

Note

The steps I describe in this section are the same for all recent versions of Dreamweaver, starting with Dreamweaver MX. The resulting Web page code, however, differs depending on the version. The generated code I describe here is accurate for both Dreamweaver CS4 and Dreamweaver CS5. ■

Follow these steps to integrate a Flex application into a Web page with Dreamweaver CS4:

1. Select Project ➪ Properties from the Flash Builder menu.

2. In the Project properties dialog box, open the Flex Build Path screen.

3. **Set Framework linkage to Merged into code and click OK.** This results in building a single application SWF file that can be integrated into a Web page in Dreamweaver.

4. **In the Flex application code, set the <s:Application> tag's height and width to a specific number of pixels that will make the application size match the available space in the Web page.** For example, if you have a <div> tag in the hosting page that's 150 pixels high and 250 pixels wide, use this code in the Flex application to size it appropriately:

```
<s:Application xmlns:fx="http://ns.adobe.com/mxml/2009"
  xmlns:s="library://ns.adobe.com/flex/spark"
  xmlns:mx="library://ns.adobe.com/flex/mx"
  height=»250» width=150»>
```

5. **Select Project ➪ Export Release Build from the Flash Builder menu.** Follow the remaining prompts to create the application's release build.

6. **Copy the application SWF file from the release build folder into your Dreamweaver site.**

7. **In Dreamweaver, place the cursor in the region where you want the Flex application to appear.**

8. **Choose Insert ➪ Media ➪ SWF from the Dreamweaver menu.** As shown in Figure 3.13, a browsing dialog box prompts you to select a Flash document.

FIGURE 3.13

Selecting a Flex application as a Flash document in Dreamweaver

9. Select the Flex application SWF file.

10. **If prompted for Object Tag Accessibility Attributes, as shown in Figure 3.14, enter the title you want to make available to Web site visitors who use screen reader software.** The application initially is displayed as a gray rectangle, as shown in Figure 3.15.

FIGURE 3.14

Setting accessibility attributes in Dreamweaver

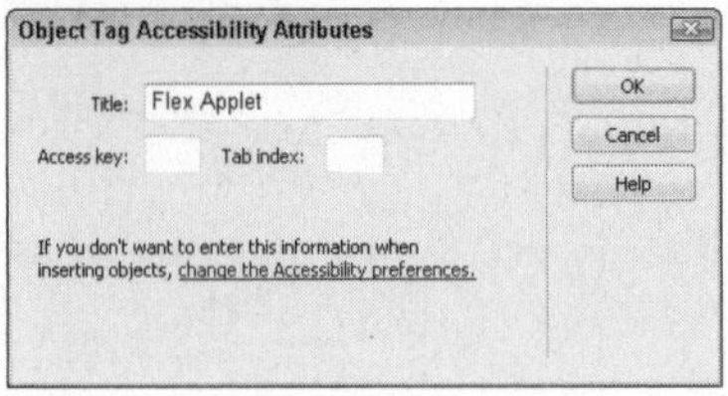

Tip

You can also start the process of inserting a Flash document in Dreamweaver by dragging or selecting the Flash document from the Assets panel, or by pressing the keyboard shortcut Ctrl+Alt+F (Windows) or ⌘+Alt+F (Mac). ■

FIGURE 3.15

The disabled application

11. **With the disabled SWF file selected in Dreamweaver's Design view, click the Play button in the Properties panel (shown in Figure 3.16) to run the application.** You should see the application load in Dreamweaver.

12. **Click the Stop button in the Properties panel to stop previewing the application.**

13. **Choose View ➪ Live View, or click the Live View button on the Document toolbar, to preview the page.** Select it again to exit Live View.

14. **Save the hosting Web page.**

FIGURE 3.16

Click Play to load the application in Dreamweaver.

Click to preview the Flex application

Tip

You can also preview the page, including the Flex application, with Dreamweaver CS4's new Live View feature. ■

Caution

If you have Flash Professional, and you click the Edit button in Dreamweaver's Properties panel, Flash opens and prompts you for a FLA file that contains the SWF file's source. Because the SWF file was created in Flex, there is no such file. You can't edit a Flex application in the Flash authoring environment. ■

As shown in Figure 3.17, when you save the Web page in Dreamweaver CS4 and CS5, a dialog box informs you that files named `swfobject_modified.js` and `expressInstall.swf` have been added to the site. These files serve the same purpose as the `swfobject.js` and `playerProductInstall.swf` files that were generated in Flash Builder and must be deployed to the Web site to ensure that the Flex application is displayed correctly.

FIGURE 3.17

Dreamweaver added the JavaScript library to the site.

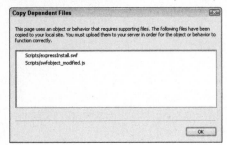

Caution

Dreamweaver is supposed to detect the Flex application's required Flash Player version and generate HTML code that requires that version. It might get it wrong and generate code that looks like this:

```
<param name="swfversion" value="6.0.65.0" />
```

You should modify this code to indicate that the application requires Flash Player 10 or higher:

```
<param name="swfversion" value="10.0.0" /> ■
```

Summary

In this chapter, I described how to use Flash Builder 4 to create and manage simple Flex projects and applications. You learned the following:

- When using Flash Builder, Flex applications are built in Flex projects.

- Flex applications are compiled into SWF files and require additional supporting files when they're deployed.

- The files in the `html-template` folder are used to model generated HTML wrapper files.

- Compiled files in the default `bin-debug` folder are meant for debugging and testing and are significantly larger than the version you deploy to your Web site.

- Flex applications designed for deployment in a Web browser use the open-source SWFObject JavaScript library to dynamically generate HTML code that loads Flash Player and displays your application at runtime.

- You should create a release build of your Flex application for deployment to a Web site.

- A release build folder normally contains the release build of a single application.

- You can integrate a Flex application into an existing Web page by sizing it correctly and copying code from the generated HTML file into the hosting page.

- You can use Dreamweaver CS4 to import and integrate a Flex application into a Web page.

Understanding the Anatomy of a Flex Application

I n this chapter, I describe the basic architecture of a Flex application from the point of view of a developer. In previous chapters, I described the role of Adobe Flash Player in hosting a Flex application at runtime, regardless of whether you use the version of Flash Player that's hosted by a Web browser (a Web application) or the version that's embedded in Adobe AIR (a desktop application).

In either case, Flash Player "plays" the application with a bit of software known as the ActionScript Virtual Machine (AVM). Flash Player 10 (the version that runs Flex 4 applications) includes two versions of the AVM. The first is for older documents and applications built in Flash and Flex 1.x that use ActionScript 1 and 2. The other, newer AVM is for documents and applications that use ActionScript 3.

Note

Flash Player versions 9 and 10 can run either ActionScript 2 or ActionScript 3, but not both simultaneously. A Flash component built with ActionScript 2 that's incorporated into an application built in Flex 2 or higher has its ActionScript code ignored by the Flash Player at runtime. ■

Flash Player is doing the work at runtime, interpreting your ActionScript code and executing the application's functionality. And while a Flex application is typically built in a combination of MXML and ActionScript code, Flash Player understands only compiled ActionScript.

As I described previously, MXML is a façade, or a convenience language, for ActionScript. In this section of the book, I describe the relationship between the two programming languages and explain how a Flex application is architected.

IN THIS CHAPTER

Using Flex programming languages

Understanding MXML and FXG

Understanding XML syntax

Using Flex 4 XML namespaces

Creating application containership with MXML

Understanding ActionScript 3

Combining MXML and ActionScript

Using the MXML and ActionScript editors in Flash Builder 4

Using the new Spark `Application` **component**

Importing FXP Files into Flash Builder

Most of the sample files for this book from the Wiley Web site are delivered in the new FXP (Flex Project) format. FXP files have an .fxp file extension but are really ZIP archive files that contain all of a project's assets and properties. FXP files can be created by either Flash Builder 4 or Adobe's new graphic design application for Flex application development, Flash Catalyst. The exercise file archives for this book were created in Flash Builder.

Follow these steps to import FXP files into a Flash Builder 4 workspace:

1. Choose File ⇨ Import FXP from the Flash Builder menu.

2. In the Import Flex Project dialog box that appears, shown in the following figure, browse and select the FXP file for the current chapter from the Web site files.

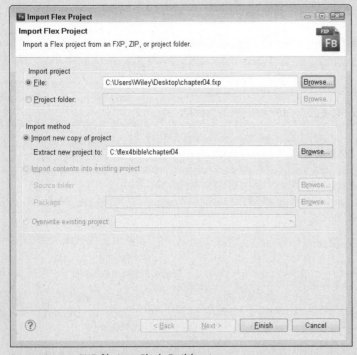

Importing an FXP file into Flash Builder 4

3. Indicate which folder should be the "root" under which the imported project will be created. The default is the workspace folder.

4. Click Finish to import the project.

A project archive includes source code, other application assets, and project property settings. After importing the archive file, you can immediately compile and run any of its applications.

New Feature

The new version of MXML that was introduced with Flex 4 has primitive graphical classes that, when declared with MXML, mimic the syntax of FXG (Flash XML Graphics), Adobe's new XML-based language for describing graphics rendering in Flash Player. For example, this "FXG" code describes a rectangle with a solid blue fill and no stroke:

```
<s:Rect width="200" height="200">
  <s:fill>
    <s:SolidColor color="#0000FF" />
  </s:fill>
</s:Rect>
```

You'll see this sort of markup used in MXML declarations throughout this book. As with other elements of MXML, these graphical elements represent ActionScript classes that are used during compilation. ■

On the Web

To use the sample code for this chapter, import the `chapter04.fxp` Flex project file from the Web site files into your Flash Builder workspace. ■

MXML and ActionScript 3

Three versions of the MXML programming language have been developed by Macromedia and Adobe. In the first version, MXML, which was used in Flex 1.0 and 1.5 applications, was rewritten into ActionScript 2 during the compilation process. In Flex 2 and 3, you use a version of MXML that compiles into ActionScript 3. In Flex 4, the new version of MXML mimics FXG markup to describe low-level graphics. In fact, what appears to be FXG is really just an MXML declaration of an ActionScript class that's translated into ActionScript 3 during compilation just like any other.

You can see how MXML is interpreted into ActionScript by adding a compiler option to your project properties:

1. Select a Flex Project in the Flex Package Explorer view.

2. Choose Project ⇨ Properties from the Flash Builder menu.

3. In the Properties dialog box, select Flex Compiler.

4. As shown in Figure 4.1, you modify the Additional compiler arguments field by adding this argument setting:

   ```
   -keep-generated-actionscript=true
   ```

5. Click OK to save the changes.

6. After the project has been rebuilt, look at the source-code root folder in the Flex Package Explorer view. As shown in Figure 4.2, a new subfolder named `generated` is created that contains many ActionScript files.

Note

Keeping generated classes doesn't have any benefit for your application's functionality or performance. I show the feature only to illustrate how the compiler translates MXML code in the background. ■

FIGURE 4.1

Setting a compiler argument to keep generated ActionScript code

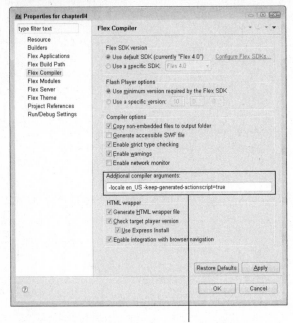

Compiler argument to keep generated ActionScript

FIGURE 4.2

The new generated code subfolder in the project source-code root folder

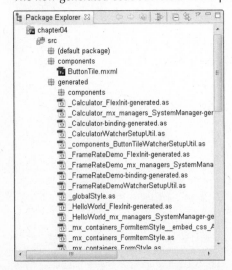

Even a very simple "Hello World" application generates a large number of ActionScript files. Most are boilerplate interpretations of internal ActionScript classes that must be available to the compiler for every Flex application. But look for the file representing your specific application to see how your specific MXML code is interpreted.

If you have a main application file named `HelloWorld.mxml`, you'll find generated ActionScript files named `HelloWorld-generated.as` and `HelloWorld-interface.as` in the project source root's `generated` subfolder. `Helloworld_generated.as` is the primary generated application file. Review this generated code to understand how your MXML code is interpreted.

Consider this simple Hello World application:

```xml
<?xml version="1.0" encoding="utf-8"?>
<s:Application xmlns:fx="http://ns.adobe.com/mxml/2009"
  xmlns:s="library://ns.adobe.com/flex/spark">
  <s:layout>
    <s:VerticalLayout paddingTop="20" horizontalAlign="center"/>
  </s:layout>
  <s:Label text="Hello World" fontSize="36"/>
</s:Application>
```

The following is just part of the generated ActionScript file. The methods set up the application's layout, instantiate its `Label` object, and set its properties and styles:

```actionscript
private function _HelloWorld_VerticalLayout1_c() :
  spark.layouts.VerticalLayout
{
  var temp : spark.layouts.VerticalLayout =
   new spark.layouts.VerticalLayout();
  temp.paddingTop = 20;
  temp.horizontalAlign = "center";
  return temp;
}
private function _HelloWorld_Array1_c() : Array
{
  var temp : Array = [_HelloWorld_Label1_c()];
  return temp;
}
private function _HelloWorld_Label1_c() :
  spark.components.Label
{
  var temp : spark.components.Label =
   new spark.components.Label();
  temp.text = "Hello World";
  temp.setStyle("fontSize", 36);
  return temp;
}
```

It takes a few MXML declarations to handle the work of all that ActionScript code. That's the power of MXML!

Understanding MXML

MXML is a pure XML-based markup language that is a convenience language for ActionScript 3. In this and previous chapters, I've shown examples of how you can accomplish certain tasks in either language, and in most cases the MXML version requires significantly less code.

MXML is XML!

As pure XML, MXML follows all conventions and syntax rules that are common to all such languages, including the following:

- **XML is case sensitive.** All element and attribute names must be declared exactly as they're defined in the language documentation.

- **All tags must have end tags or use empty tag syntax.** For example, the `<Label>` element usually doesn't need an end tag, so it's declared as `<Label/>`. The extra slash character indicates that no end tag is needed.

- **Element tags can't be overlapped.** In Hypertext Markup Language (HTML), you might get away with overlapping element tag containership, such as `<b><i>My Text</b></i>`. In HTML, the browser typically just figures it out and does the right thing. In XML, this sort of markup breaks the hierarchical parent-child relationship between elements that's required for the XML processor to correctly parse the file.

- **Every XML document has a single root element.** In an MXML application file designed for Web deployment, the root element is always `<s:Application>`. For AIR applications, the root element is `<s:WindowedApplication>`. In MXML component files, the root element is whatever existing class you want to extend. But no matter what, you must have a single root element.

- **XML attribute values must be wrapped in quotation marks.** This is another supposed requirement of HTML that you can sometimes ignore in a browser environment. In XML, if you forget the quotation marks around an attribute value, the compiler just gives up and displays an error.

What Does MXML Stand For?

Adobe's documentation doesn't say whether MXML is an acronym or, if it is, what it abbreviates. Whereas most XML-based languages have clear meanings, this one is just, well, MXML. Some developers have guessed that it stands for "Macromedia Extensible Markup Language" because it was invented at Macromedia prior to the company's acquisition by Adobe. Other suggestions include "Multidimensional XML" and "Maximum eXperience Markup Language" (based on Macromedia's old mantra, "Experience Matters").

Adobe isn't saying. So that means you get to make up your own version here. MXML stands for (write in your vote): _____.

Other XML rules are important to understanding the coding requirements of MXML, including the use of CDATA blocks and XML comments, but the bottom line is that MXML is a real XML language. So if a rule is true for XML, it's true for MXML as well.

Using XML as a programming language

Although XML was originally designed to represent data for exchange over the Internet, it isn't the only XML-based language to gain popularity as an application development tool. These languages have been used effectively to build or add functionality to software applications:

- **XSLT (Extensible Stylesheet Language Transformations).** A language that's defined by the World Wide Web Consortium (W3C) and implemented in many products and platforms to transform XML from one "flavor" into another.

- **XUL (XML User Interface Language).** A language for defining application interfaces that's incorporated into the Mozilla Web browser kernel.

- **XAML (Extensible Application Markup Language).** A language developed by Microsoft that's very similar in purpose and design to MXML and used to define applications that run in Microsoft's SilverStream player.

To be productive with an XML-based programming language, it's important to understand some basic XML concepts and how they affect programming techniques. In this section, I describe the concepts of namespaces, reserved characters, and other XML concepts that you might find helpful.

XML namespaces

A namespace in XML gives a language designer a way of defining and binding together element and attribute names into a language that can then be recognized by an XML processor. The string that's used to identify a namespace in XML is known as a *URI Reference*.

Web Resource

The technical description of XML namespaces is available at the W3C's Web site: www.w3.org/TR/REC-xml-names/#sec-namespaces. ■

The Uniform Resource Identifier (URI) that identifies an XML namespace is typically created as a combination of the following:

- A Web address owned by the organization that manages the XML language

- A subdirectory structure indicating the name of the language and, optionally, the year in which the language was defined

The namespace URI for Flex 2 and 3 applications looked like this:

```
www.adobe.com/2006/mxml
```

The new version of MXML that's used in Flex 4 uses three namespaces. The first is required in all MXML files and represents the core language:

```
http://ns.adobe.com/mxml/2009
```

This means that the most recent version of MXML was defined in 2009 by Adobe Systems. In each MXML document's root element, this namespace is declared with a prefix of `fx`. The prefix is then used on all MXML compiler tags — that is, tags that constitute instructions to the Flex compiler, as opposed to representing ActionScript classes. For example, this declaration creates an area where you can add ActionScript code to an MXML file:

```
<fx:Script>
</fx:Script>
```

Flex 4 uses two other critical namespaces. This namespace, associated by default with the s prefix, is used to represent the new Spark components (sometimes known as "Gumbonents" due to Flex 4's public code name of "Gumbo"):

```
library://ns.adobe.com/flex/spark
```

The last namespace, which is associated with the old mx prefix, is used to represent Flex 3 components that are still in use, now known as MX components:

```
library://ns.adobe.com/flex/mx
```

Note

An even older version of the MXML language was used in Flex 1.x. The namespace URI for that version of the language was:

```
www.macromedia.com/2004/mxml
```

The 2004 version of the language is distinguished from the current version by both the domain name (from when Flex was owned by Macromedia) and the year of its definition. ∎

As the first step in the Flex compilation process, the Flex compiler reads the XML markup in the application. If it sees a namespace other than the one it expects, it generates a compiler error.

Caution

An XML namespace URI is case sensitive and must be spelled exactly as indicated in the previous example. Changing even a single character from lowercase to uppercase causes the compiler to fail. Also, even though a namespace URI looks like a Web address, it's really just a simple string. The Flex compiler does not use the URI to make any requests to the Adobe Web site, and you don't need access to the Internet to compile a Flex application. ∎

XML namespace prefixes

A namespace prefix is an arbitrary string that's assigned to a namespace URI as an alias. You optionally define a namespace prefix with the `xmlns` attribute, separated from the prefix by a colon (`:`). Herein lies the key benefit of namespaces: different types of XML can be used in the same document by matching the prefix with an identifier (the URI), and the XML parser can handle each type in its own unique way.

In applications built in Flex 2 and 3, the root element of each MXML file defined a namespace prefix of mx with this syntax:

```
<mx:Application xmlns:mx="http://www.adobe.com/2006/mxml">
</mx:Application>
```

The mx prefix was then used in every declaration of an MXML element, such as the Label:

```
<mx:Label text="Hello World"/>
```

This means that the Label element is a member of the XML language that's defined by the mx prefix's bound URI.

Flex 4 uses three namespaces, each with its own prefix:

```
<s:Application xmlns:fx="http://ns.adobe.com/mxml/2009"
  xmlns:s="library://ns.adobe.com/flex/spark"
  xmlns:mx="library://ns.adobe.com/flex/mx">
</s:Application>
```

In Flex 4, each component or compiler instruction is declared with the element name and the appropriate prefix:

```
<s:Label text="Hello World"/>
```

Note

There are two distinct versions of the Label component: the old MX version and the new Spark version. The new version supports Flash Player 10's advanced text rendering features, while the older version doesn't. You choose which you want with the namespace prefix. ■

Understanding MXML manifests

An MXML manifest is an XML file that maps MXML tags to their equivalent ActionScript classes. The Flex 4 SDK stores its manifest files in the frameworks folder. A master configuration file named flex-config.xml lists the following manifests in its <namespaces> element:

```
<namespaces>
  <namespace>
    <uri>http://ns.adobe.com/mxml/2009</uri>
    <manifest>mxml-2009-manifest.xml</manifest>
  </namespace>
  <namespace>
    <uri>library://ns.adobe.com/flex/spark</uri>
    <manifest>spark-manifest.xml</manifest>
  </namespace>
  <namespace>
    <uri>library://ns.adobe.com/flex/mx</uri>
    <manifest>mx-manifest.xml</manifest>
  </namespace>
  <namespace>
    <uri>http://www.adobe.com/2006/mxml</uri>
    <manifest>mx-manifest.xml</manifest>
  </namespace>
</namespaces>
```

Each manifest file lists the namespace's MXML tags and their equivalent ActionScript classes. The Flex compiler looks up each MXML tag in your application code to find out how to translate it to an ActionScript class. For example, the mx-2009-manifest.xml file lists the core ActionScript data type classes that can be declared in MXML with the fx prefix:

```
<componentPackage>
  <!-- AS3 built-ins -->
  <component id="Array" class="Array" lookupOnly="true"/>
  <component id="Boolean" class="Boolean" lookupOnly="true"/>
  <component id="Class" class="Class" lookupOnly="true"/>
  <component id="Date" class="Date" lookupOnly="true"/>
  <component id="DesignLayer" class="mx.core.DesignLayer"/>
  <component id="Function" class="Function" lookupOnly="true"/>
  <component id="int" class="int" lookupOnly="true"/>
  <component id="Number" class="Number" lookupOnly="true"/>
  <component id="Object" class="Object" lookupOnly="true"/>
  <component id="RegExp" class="RegExp" lookupOnly="true"/>
  <component id="String" class="String" lookupOnly="true"/>
  <component id="uint" class="uint" lookupOnly="true"/>
  <component id="Vector" class="__AS3__.vec.Vector"
    lookupOnly="true"/>
  <component id="XML" class="XML" lookupOnly="true"/>
  <component id="XMLList" class="XMLList" lookupOnly="true"/>
</componentPackage>
```

The spark-manifest.xml file lists the components that can be referenced with the s prefix. Here are just a few of them:

```
<component id="AddAction" class="spark.effects.AddAction"/>
<component id="Animate" class="spark.effects.Animate"/>
<component id="AnimateColor" class="spark.effects.AnimateColor"/>
<component id="AnimateFilter" class="spark.effects.AnimateFilter"/>
<component id="AnimateTransitionShader"
  class="spark.effects.AnimateTransitionShader"/>
<component id="AnimateTransform"
  class="spark.effects.AnimateTransform"/>
<component id="AnimateTransform3D"
  class="spark.effects.AnimateTransform3D"/>
```

Some MXML tags are listed in both the Spark and the MX manifests, but in both cases they represent the same underlying ActionScript class. For example, the RPC components (HTTPService, WebService, and RemoteObject) are members of the mx.rpc.http.mxml package. For convenience, these classes are represented in the manifests for both the Spark and MX component groups. This declaration uses the Spark prefix:

```
<s:HTTPService id="contactService" url="data/contacts.xml"/>
```

And this uses the MX prefix:

```
<mx:HTTPService id="contactService" url="data/contacts.xml"/>
```

Both represent the same ActionScript class.

Using XML child elements

You can declare any property, style, or event handler using XML child element syntax instead of an XML attribute. For example, the two following code snippets are functionally identical.

Version 1 with an attribute:

```
<s:Label text="Hello World"/>
```

Version 2 with a child element:

```
<s:Label >
  <s:text>Hello World</s:text>
<s:Label >
```

The text property of the Label control has the same value in both cases, but the attribute version requires quotation marks around the property value to satisfy the XML requirement that all attribute values must be quoted.

In many cases, deciding which syntax to use is a coin flip; in others, the choice is pretty clear.

Using CDATA blocks

In XML, CDATA blocks are used to protect literal characters from XML processors that would otherwise interpret them as part of the XML markup, rather than the document's content. This is particularly important in Flex when you're trying to create ActionScript code that's nested within an MXML document.

When you create an <fx:Script> section to host some ActionScript code, Flash Builder adds a CDATA block automatically if you follow the right sequence in typing the tag. Try this:

1. **Place the cursor in an MXML application just underneath the <s:Application> start tag.** (The <fx:Script> section can be placed anywhere in the document as long as it's a direct child of the root element, but it's frequently placed in this location.)
2. **Type this string:** <scri. You should see a list of available MXML tags.
3. **Press Enter (Windows) or Return (Mac) to select the <fx:Script> tag.**
4. **Type a closing > character to close the tag.**

You should see that Flash Builder auto-completes the <fx:Script> tag set and creates a CDATA block between the tags:

```
<fx:Script>
  <![CDATA[
  ]]>
</fx:Script>
```

The cursor is placed inside the CDATA block; this is where the ActionScript code should be placed.

The purpose of the CDATA block is to ensure that characters that are considered *reserved* by the XML processor are interpreted as scripting characters, rather than XML markup. XML considers these characters reserved:

```
< > & " '
```

All five characters have clear meanings in both ActionScript and XML, so if you don't protect the code, the XML processor will think, for example, that the < character is part of the tag syntax, rather than meaning "less than" as it does for ActionScript, and you get a parser error when you try to compile.

XML entities

On rare occasions, you'll encounter a situation where a reserved character just has to be placed in an XML structure, and the alternative is to write many lines of ActionScript code. To solve these cases, XML provides the concept of *entities* — strings that are aliases for the characters that XML considers reserved.

These are the entities for the five XML reserved characters. (They may look familiar; they are the same in HTML.)

```
&amp; = & (ampersand)
&lt; = < (less than)
&gt;> = (greater than)
&quot; = " (double quote)
&apos; = ' (apostrophe/single quote)
```

Here's a scenario where this comes in handy. Imagine that you want to set an object's enabled property using a Boolean binding expression. The object should be enabled only when a certain value is less than 0. You might first try the binding like this:

```
<s:Button label="Click Me" enabled="{someValue < 3}"/>
```

This will cause the compiler to fail because according to XML syntax rules, the < character isn't permitted within an attribute value. You can solve this issue in a number of ways, but the one with the least amount of code that also retains the same logic looks like this:

```
<s:Button label="Click Me" enabled="{someValue &lt; 3}"/>
```

The XML processor that's at the core of the Flex compiler accepts this code and translates <, the XML entity, to the literal < character before the ActionScript parser does its part. The code might look odd, but it works.

MXML and containership

You can use MXML to declare both visual and nonvisual objects. When using the markup language to declare visual objects, positioning of code determines both containership and the order of objects in the application's visual presentation.

The Application component can contain both low-level graphics and visual components such as containers and controls. This is the containership in the application in Listing 4.1:

- The Application component contains a primitive graphic rectangle declared with the Rect element, and a Group (the Flex 4 equivalent of a Flex 3 Canvas).
- The Group contains another rectangle and a VGroup (the Flex 4 equivalent of a VBox).
- The VGroup contains three Label controls.

The first rectangle's dimensions are 80% of the application's available size, and the dimensions of the Group are set to 50%; both are centered in the application with the horizontalCenter and verticalCenter constraints. The VGroup is centered in the Group, and sizes itself dynamically based on its contents.

LISTING 4.1

An application containing a graphical skin and a combination of Spark and Halo components

```xml
<?xml version="1.0" encoding="utf-8"?>
<s:Application xmlns:fx="http://ns.adobe.com/mxml/2009"
  xmlns:s="library://ns.adobe.com/flex/spark"
  xmlns:mx="library://ns.adobe.com/flex/mx"
  xmlns:components="components.*">
  <s:Rect width="80%" height="80%"
    horizontalCenter="0" verticalCenter="0">
    <s:fill>
      <s:SolidColor color="#999999"/>
    </s:fill>
  </s:Rect>
  <s:Group width="50%" height="50%"
    horizontalCenter="0" verticalCenter="0">
      <s:Rect width="100%" height="100%">
        <s:fill>
          <mx:SolidColor color="#cccccc"/>
        </s:fill>
      </s:Rect>
      <s:VGroup horizontalCenter="0" verticalCenter="0">
        <s:Label text="This is Label 1"/>
        <s:Label text="This is Label 2"/>
        <s:Label text="This is Label 3"/>
      </s:VGroup>
  </s:Group>
</s:Application>
```

On the Web

The code in Listing 4.1 is available in the Web site files in the chapter04 project's src folder as Containership.mxml. ∎

The application's visual presentation is shown in Figure 4.3.

Both the visual display components and the graphical elements that are nested within a component such as `Application` are considered to be part of the component's *content*. This is the list of visual objects that make up what the user sees at runtime.

Tip

You can add visual objects to a Flex 4 component's content at runtime with ActionScript code. Flex 4 containers have a `contentGroup` object with methods named `addElement()` and `addElementAt()` that are designed for this purpose; another method named `setElementIndex()` enables you to move objects around within the container's display list. ■

FIGURE 4.3

An application with multiple containers, controls, and graphical objects

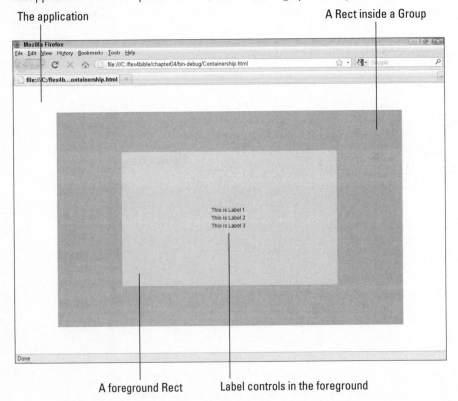

The application   A Rect inside a Group

A foreground Rect   Label controls in the foreground

MXML and nonvisual classes

You also can use MXML to declare nonvisual ActionScript class instances. The following code declares an instance of the `WebService` class that's used to make calls to SOAP-based Web services.

```
<s:WebService id="myService"
  wsdl="http://www.bardotech.com/services/Myservice?wsdl"/>
```

New Feature

In previous versions of Flex, you could declare nonvisual classes anywhere in an MXML document. In Flex 4, you now must wrap these objects inside an `<fx:Declarations>` **element:**

```
<fx:Declarations>
  <s:WebService id="myService"
    wsdl="http://www.bardotech.com/services/Myservice?wsdl"/>
</fx:Declarations>
```
■

These sorts of nonvisual controls are known as *faceless* components, because they don't have visual representation in the application. The `<fx:Declarations>` element must be a direct child element of the MXML file's root element, such as the `<s:Application>` element in a main application file. The following code, for example, is incorrect and would generate the compiler error shown in Figure 4.4:

```
<?xml version="1.0" encoding="utf-8"?>
<s:Application xmlns:fx="http://ns.adobe.com/mxml/2009"
  xmlns:s="library://ns.adobe.com/flex/spark"
  xmlns:mx="library://ns.adobe.com/flex/halo">
  <s:VGroup>
    <fx:Declarations>
      <s:WebService id="myService"
        wsdl="http://www.bardotech.com/services/Myservice?wsdl"/>
    </fx:Declarations>
  </s:VGroup>
</s:Application>
```

FIGURE 4.4

The Problems view displaying a compiler error for incorrectly placed faceless controls

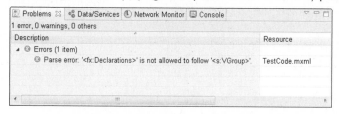

Because `VGroup` is a visual container, it can contain only other visual objects. To fix this problem, move the `<fx:Declarations>` element so that it becomes a direct child of the `<s:Application>` root element.

Understanding ActionScript 3

ActionScript 3 is the most recent version of the programming language that drives both Flash and Flex. ActionScript 3 is an implementation of the ECMAScript 4th Edition recommendation. ECMAScript in turn was originally based on Netscape's JavaScript.

A complete description of ActionScript 3 is beyond the scope of this book, but it's worth an overview of the language's basic syntax.

Web Resource

A formal description of the proposed ECMAScript 4th Edition standard is available in PDF format at www. ecmascript.org/es4/spec/overview.pdf. ∎

Note

In addition to ActionScript 3, subsets of the ECMAScript 4th Edition recommendation also have been implemented in Microsoft's JScript.NET. ∎

ActionScript syntax

ActionScript 3, and the language recommendation on which it's modeled, ECMAScript, share syntax with languages such as C, C++, C#, and Java. Like these languages, ActionScript has these syntactical features:

- All identifiers and keywords are case sensitive.
- Keywords are always lowercase.
- Statements end with a ; (semicolon) character, as in x = 0;.
- Boolean expressions used in conditional clauses are wrapped in parentheses, as in:

  ```
  if (aBoolean) {}
  ```
- {} (brace) characters are used to denote code blocks.

Note

The semicolon character at the end of lines is optional when you code one statement per line but is used nearly universally to improve code readability. ∎

Declaring variables

You declare ActionScript 3 variables with the var keyword:

```
var myVariable:String="Hello World";
```

Note

In JavaScript, as implemented in Web browsers, the var keyword is optional. When you declare a variable inside a function, the variable expires when the function's execution is complete. The lack of the var keyword causes the variable to persist and to be visible to the entire Web page.

In ActionScript 3, the `var` keyword is required for all variable declarations. When you declare a variable inside a function, it's always local to the function. Variables declared outside functions always persist for the lifetime of the component or class. ■

The variable name is usually followed by a data type declaration using what's known as *post-colon* data typing syntax. The following ActionScript code declares a variable named `myStrictVar`, typed as a `String`:

```
var myStrictVar:String;
```

The type declaration isn't required, but if you leave it out the compiler generates a warning. If you want to use a "loose" type declaration that enables the variable to hold values of any type, use the wild card * character after the colon:

```
var myLooseVar:*;
```

Note

The use of post-colon syntax to statically type a variable is the subject of some controversy. This syntax is part of the ECMAScript recommendation and was implemented by Macromedia with the goal of standardization with the rest of the industry. Some Java developers find the syntax odd, because in Java, static data typing is accomplished with the data type before the variable name:

```
public String currentValue;
```

The data typing result is the same, but the syntax is just turned around. ■

Using access modifiers

An *access modifier* is a keyword that defines a class member's visibility to the rest of the application. In code placed outside function declarations, the variable declaration is preceded by an access modifier keyword that determines the variable's visibility to the rest of the application.

Cross-Reference

When you declare a variable outside a function, you're really declaring a property of a component or class. When the code is in the main MXML application file, the property is a member of the `Application` component. I describe this aspect of declaring object members, including how to declare other component members such as functions and constants, in Chapter 5. ■

You can use any one of these access modifiers in a variable declaration placed outside a function:

- **public.** All code throughout an application can access the variable.
- **private.** Only code in the current component or class can access the variable.
- **protected.** Only code in the current component or class, or any its subclasses, can access the variable.
- **internal.** Only code in the current component or class, or any other component or class in the same package, can access the variable.

You use only one access modifier for any particular variable declaration.

Caution

If you don't include an access modifier in a variable declaration placed outside a function, the compiler generates a warning and the access for that member is set to the default of `internal`. In ActionScript 2, the same code would have resulted in a default access of `public` and no compiler warning would have been generated. ■

Declaring variables within functions

Variables declared within functions don't require or accept access modifiers. By declaring the variable within the function, you restrict its visibility and lifetime to the duration of the function itself. This ActionScript code declares a variable within a function:

```
private function myFunction()
{
  var myVar:String;
}
```

Once the function has completed execution, any variables declared within its body expire. The objects they refer to may stay in memory, but Flash Player's automatic garbage collection feature periodically sweeps and destroys any objects that no longer have references. You don't have to deal with this garbage collection in your code.

Initializing variable values

You can set initial values in a variable declaration by adding the assignment operator (a single = character) and the value after the variable name. The following code creates a variable named `myValue` and assigns its initial value at the same time:

```
public var myValue:String = "Hello World!";
```

Note

Variable declarations, including those that declare and set a variable's initial value, can be placed either inside or outside functions. Code that modifies an existing variable's value, however, must be placed inside a function. ■

Using ActionScript operators

ActionScript shares operators with languages such as C, C++, C#, and Java. Table 4.1 lists common mathematical and comparison operators that work in all these languages.

TABLE 4.1

ActionScript 3 Operators

Operator	Purpose	Example

+	Mathematical addition and string concatenation	Addition:
		`var result:Number = 1 + 1;`
		
		Concatenation:
		`var result:String = "Hello " + "World";`

Operator	Purpose	Example
−	Mathematical subtraction	`var result:Number = 20 - 10;`
/	Mathematical division	`var result:Number = 20 / 2;`
*	Mathematical multiplication	`var result:Number = 20 * 2;`
%	Modulus (returns remainder from integer division)	`var result:int = 12 % 5;`
==	Equals	`var is:Boolean=(value1 == value2)`
!=	Assignment	`var value:Number=1;`
>	Greater than	`if (value > 3) {}`
<	Less than	`if (value < 3) {}`
&&	Logical AND	`if (value1 > 3 && value1 < 10) {}`
||	Logical OR	`if (value1 < 3 || value2 > 10) {}`

The language includes many more operators, categorized as Logical, Relational, Assignment, and Bitwise operators. Again, if you have a background in C, Java, or similar languages, you can let that experience be your guide.

Conditional statements

ActionScript uses two types of conditional statements. The more common formulation uses an `if` keyword with a Boolean expression to determine whether code will be executed. You can then optionally add `else` and `else if` clauses to the statement.

A simple `if` statement looks like this:

```
if (some Boolean expression)
{
... do something ...
}
```

For example, if you want to evaluate whether a user has selected a row in a `DataGrid` or `List` control, you might code it like this:

```
if (myDataGrid.selectedIndex != -1)
{
   var myData:Object = myDataGrid.selectedItem;
}
```

The Boolean expression works because `DataGrid` and `List` controls have a `selectedIndex` property that indicates the ordinal position of the currently selected data element. If nothing is selected, this property always returns –1.

You can optionally add `else` and `else if` clauses to an `if` statement like this:

```
if (some Boolean expression)
{
  ... do this!
}
else if (some other expression)
{
  ... do that!
}
else
{
  ... do something else!
}
```

When using these optional clauses, you can have as many else if clauses as you need and a single else clause that is always at the end of the whole code section.

```
private function onLoad():void
{
  if (str == "value1")
  {
    Alert.show("value1");
  }
  else if (str == "value2")
  {
    Alert.show("value2");
  }
  else if (str == "yes")
  {
    Alert.show("something else");
  }
}
```

You can also use switch statements to evaluate a single expression against multiple possible values:

```
switch (some expression)
{
  case value1:
    ... do something ...
    break
  case value2:
    ... do something else ...
  default:
    ... do another thing ...
}
```

Note

In some languages, such as Java, switch statements can only be used to evaluate expressions with particular datatypes, such as primitives (int, double, and so on). In ActionScript 3, the expression you evaluate with a switch statement can be of any data type. ■

You can also use the *ternary* operator to assign a value based on a condition that's either `true` or `false`. Shared by many languages, the ActionScript version of the ternary operator follows C-type syntax, separating the condition from the true result with a question mark, and the `true` result from the `false` result with a colon:

```
var myVar:String = (isTrue ? "It's True" : "It's False");
```

The ternary operator results in a terse version of the following verbose code:

```
var myVar:String;
if (isTrue)
{
  myVar = "It's True";
}
else
{
  myVar = "It's False";
}
```

Looping

Looping constructs look basically the same as in Java, JavaScript, C, and other similar languages. A `for` loop enables you to loop a given number of times.

```
for (var i:int=0; i<10; i++)
{
   ... do this 10 times ...
}
```

The `for` statement establishes a *counter* variable (named `i` in the previous example); in the second part of the expression, it causes the loop to continue as long as `i` is less than 10; and in the third part, it increments the variable's value by 1 each time through the loop.

You also can use a `while` statement to execute a loop:

```
var i:int = 0;
while (i<10)
{
  do this 10 times!
  i++;
}
```

In preceding example, I have used the `while` statement to loop a specific number of times. It also can be used to evaluate any Boolean expression and determine whether to continue the looping process or break out of the loop and continue with the remainder of the code.

Note

In many cases, the choice of a `for` or a `while` loop is a style choice that's completely up to you. ∎

Combining MXML and ActionScript

You can accomplish many tasks with either MXML or ActionScript code, and only a few are restricted to one language or the other. Most Flex applications use both. The main application file is always in MXML, and that file can then contain or refer to ActionScript code in a variety of ways.

Using the <fx:Script> element

You can use the <fx:Script> element to wrap ActionScript code that becomes a part of the application or component that the current MXML file represents. The advantage of including the scripting in the MXML file is that all the code for a particular component is in one place. Disadvantages include:

- Some developers find that mixing declarative (MXML) and programmatic (ActionScript) syntax in a single file can look odd and be a bit confusing.
- Flash Builder provides certain code management tools for ActionScript code that's stored in external files that aren't available in MXML files.

In terms of functionality and application performance, either of these approaches works fine. So it's purely a question of style and preference.

If you decide to include ActionScript in an MXML file, create the <fx:Script> element as a pair of tags wrapped around a CDATA block. Then place your ActionScript code inside the CDATA block:

```
<fx:Script>
  <![CDATA[
    ...scripting goes here...
  ]]>
</fx:Script>
```

Tip

To insert a CDATA block into a source-code file, place the cursor where you want the CDATA to appear, and then choose Source ➪ Insert CDATA Block from the Flash Builder menu. Or use the keyboard shortcut, press Ctrl+Shift+D (Windows) or ⌘+Shift+D (Mac). ∎

Caution

Just as with the <fx;Declarations> element, the <fx:Script> element must be a direct child of the MXML file's root element. ∎

Using external ActionScript files

You can link an MXML file to an external ActionScript file with the source property of the <Script> element. The ActionScript file should have a file extension of .as and can contain as much ActionScript code as you need.

Any code in the external file is compiled as part of the MXML file and the ActionScript class it represents but is executed after objects declared in MXML are instantiated so you can access these objects in your ActionScript code. Because the external file isn't in XML format, you don't need to embed the `<Script>` element or the CDATA block inside the file to protect the code.

Follow these steps to create an external ActionScript file:

1. **Choose File ➪ New ➪ ActionScript File from the Flash Builder menu.** (Don't select ActionScript Class — that's a different sort of file I'll describe in a later chapter.)

2. **In the New ActionScript File dialog box, select the folder in which you want to create the file.** External ActionScript files can go anywhere in the project source-code root folder, because you'll explicitly refer to the file's location when you link to it from an MXML file. I usually place the file in the same folder as the MXML file it's linked to.

3. **Enter the name of the file.** It should have a file extension of `.as`, but the rest of the filename is up to you. For an application named `HelloWorld.mxml`, the matching external ActionScript file would be `helloWorld.as`.

4. **Click Finish to create the file.**

Note

Notice that in this usage, the external ActionScript filename starts with a lowercase character. This doesn't have any technical effect on the code, but it's a way of indicating that it's a simple file containing ActionScript code, as opposed to an ActionScript class (which, by object-oriented programming conventions, has an initial uppercase character). ■

After the file has been created, you link to it from the MXML file with the `<fx:Script>` element and add a `source` property pointing to the external file. The application in Listing 4.2 embeds its ActionScript code in an `<fx:Script>` tag set.

Caution

Any particular `<fx:Script>` element can contain nested ActionScript or use the `source` property to link to an external ActionScript file, but it cannot do both at the same time. You can, however, have as many `<Script>` declarations in a single MXML file as you need. ■

LISTING 4.2

An MXML application with nested ActionScript

```
<?xml version="1.0" encoding="utf-8"?>
<s:Application xmlns:fx="http://ns.adobe.com/mxml/2009"
  xmlns:s="library://ns.adobe.com/flex/spark"
  xmlns:mx="library://ns.adobe.com/flex/mx"
  xmlns:components="components.*">
  <fx:Script>
    <![CDATA[
```

continued

LISTING 4.2   *(continued)*

```
      [Bindable]
      private var currentResult:Number=0;
      [Bindable]
      private var currentInput:String="";

      private function calculateHandler(event:Event):void
      {
        currentResult += Number(currentInput);
        currentInput="";
      }
      private function selectHandler(event:TextEvent):void
      {
        currentInput += event.text;
      }
    ]]>
  </fx:Script>
  <s:Panel title="Calculator" horizontalCenter="0" top="20">
    <s:layout>
      <s:VerticalLayout horizontalAlign="center"/>
    </s:layout>
    <mx:Form>
      <components:ButtonTile id="input"
        select="selectHandler(event)"
        calculate="calculateHandler(event)"/>
      <mx:FormItem label="Entry:">
        <s:TextInput text="{currentInput}" editable="false" width="80"/>
      </mx:FormItem>
      <mx:FormItem label="Total:">
        <s:TextInput text="{currentResult}" editable="false" width="80"/>
      </mx:FormItem>
    </mx:Form>
  </s:Panel>
</s:Application>
```

On the Web

The code in Listing 4.2 is available in the Web site files in the chapter04 project folder as CalculatorWithScript.mxml. ■

Listing 4.3 shows the same application after the ActionScript has been moved to an external file.

LISTING 4.3

MXML application Calculator.mxml with linked ActionScript file

```
<?xml version="1.0" encoding="utf-8"?>
<s:Application xmlns:fx="http://ns.adobe.com/mxml/2009"
```

```
    xmlns:s="library://ns.adobe.com/flex/spark"
    xmlns:mx="library://ns.adobe.com/flex/mx"
    xmlns:components="components.*">
    <fx:Script source="calculator.as"/>
    <s:Panel title="Calculator" horizontalCenter="0" top="20">
      <s:layout>
        <s:VerticalLayout horizontalAlign="center"/>
      </s:layout>
      <mx:Form>
        <components:ButtonTile id="input"
          select="selectHandler(event)"
          calculate="calculateHandler(event)"/>
        <mx:FormItem label="Entry:">
          <s:TextInput text="{currentInput}" editable="false" width="80"/>
        </mx:FormItem>
        <mx:FormItem label="Total:">
          <s:TextInput text="{currentResult}" editable="false" width="80"/>
        </mx:FormItem>
      </mx:Form>
    </s:Panel>
  </s:Application>
```

On the Web

The code in Listing 4.3 is available in the Web site files in the `chapter04` project folder as `Calculator.mxml`. ∎

You have just as much code to manage, but the XML markup is cleaner and easier to read. And, as shown in Listing 4.4, the ActionScript file now contains only the scripting code:

LISTING 4.4

External ActionScript file calculator.as

```
//ActionScript code for Calculator.mxml
[Bindable]
private var currentResult:Number=0;
[Bindable]
private var currentInput:String="";
private function calculateHandler(event:Event):void
{
  currentResult += Number(currentInput);
  currentInput="";
}
private function selectHandler(event:TextEvent):void
{
  currentInput += event.text;
}
```

On the Web

The code in Listing 4.4 is available in the Web site files in the `chapter04` project's `src` folder as `calculator.as`. ∎

Managing ActionScript code with Flash Builder

Whether you're working with MXML or ActionScript, Flash Builder's Outline view enables you to easily find function and variable declarations within the source code. The Outline view appears in the lower-right corner of Flash Builder in the default Flex Development perspective.

Using the Outline view with ActionScript

When working with MXML, the default Outline view displays a tree of MXML elements. As shown in Figure 4.5, the `<fx:Script>` element shows up as a single selectable object.

New Feature

In Flash Builder 4, MXML elements that represent compiler instructions always appear at the bottom of the Outline view, regardless of where they're placed in the actual code. All visual objects appear at the top of the outline. ∎

FIGURE 4.5

Flash Builder's Outline view with the MXML editor

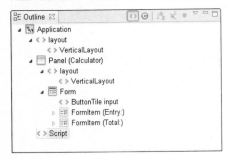

To navigate to a specific function or variable declaration using the Outline view, click the Show class view icon at the top of the view. As shown in Figure 4.6, you're now able to click a declaration and jump to that bit of code.

When using the outline's Class view, you can change the display with these other options that are accessed from buttons at the top of the Outline view:

- **Sort.** Displays variables and functions in alphabetical order.
- **Hide Static Functions and Variables.** Hides variables and functions that are marked with the `static` modifier.
- **Hide Non-Public Members.** Hides variables and functions that aren't marked with the `public` access modifier.

Outline view and the Class view buttons

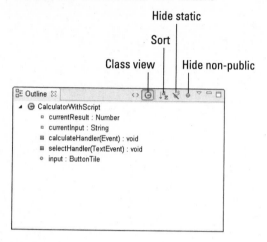

Note

You need to click an item only once in the Outline view to jump to the matching code. ∎

Tip

From any object reference in the ActionScript file, hold down Ctrl (Windows) or ⌘ (Mac) and click the reference to jump to that object's declaration. This works whether the declaration is in the ActionScript file or an external MXML file and for both custom classes and Flex library classes whose source code has been provided by Adobe. ∎

Flash Builder 4 adds a new documentation feature that enables you to quickly get information about an ActionScript class from the Flex SDK. Move the cursor over a component declaration and wait about one second. As shown in Figure 4.7, a documentation window appears. If the available documentation for that component exceeds the height of the window, you can then press F2 to give the window focus. You can then resize or scroll through the window to see all the available documentation.

Managing code in the ActionScript editor

When you store ActionScript code in an external file, Flash Builder provides some additional code management tools.

Code folding

Code folding refers to the capability of the Flash Builder editor to fold, or collapse, certain sections of code and hide them from view. In an MXML editor, code folding is based on the source file's MXML elements. As shown in Figure 4.8, an MXML file displays code folding icons at the beginning of each MXML element. You'll see a folding icon for the `<fx:Script>` tag that enables you to collapse that section of code to a single line.

FIGURE 4.7

Opening API documentation quickly within Flash Builder

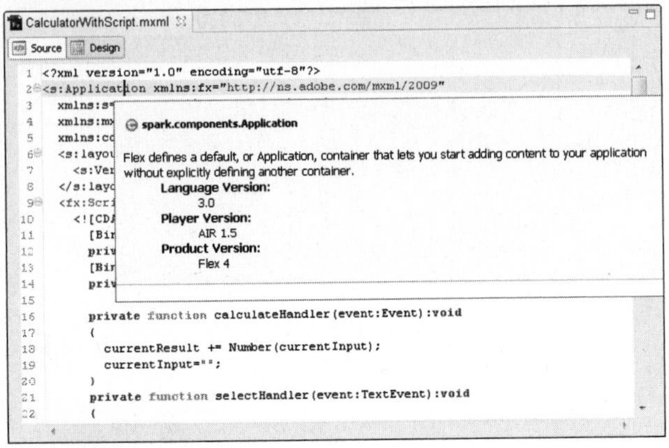

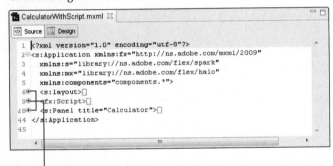

FIGURE 4.8

Code folding icons in an MXML file

Code folding icons

Clicking the icon reduces the MXML element at that line to a single line of displayed code. Then, when you move the cursor over the folding icon, you see a pop-up window showing the first of code in the collapsed section. Clicking the icon again expands it to full display.

In an ActionScript file, because you are using Flash Builder's ActionScript editor, code folding collapses function declarations instead of MXML elements. As shown in Figure 4.9, you can click any function's folding icon and reduce it to a single line of code.

You also can collapse all functions in a file to single-line display:

1. **Right-click in the column of line numbers.**

2. **Choose Folding ⇨ Collapse Functions to reduce all functions to single-line displays.**

Code folding icons in an ActionScript file

```
calculator.as ✕
  1  //ActionScript code for Calculator.mxml
  2  [Bindable]
  3  private var currentResult:Number=0;
  4  [Bindable]
  5  private var currentInput:String="";
  6
  7⊞ private function calculateHandler(event:Event):void
 12⊞ private function selectHandler(event:TextEvent):void
 13
```

Code folding icons

Now all functions are displayed as single lines of code.

And finally, moving the cursor over a folded icon that is in a collapsed state displays the contents of the folded function.

Organizing import statements

An import statement informs the compiler about the location of ActionScript classes it needs to compile in an application or component. Most ActionScript classes must be explicitly imported to be recognized by the compiler. This import statement makes a class named ArrayCollection available to the compiler:

```
import mx.collections.ArrayCollection;
```

In Flash Builder 2, the development environment helped you build an import list by creating import statements for classes you referred to as you typed. But later, if you removed a class reference from the body of the code, the import statement would be left in the file. This doesn't cause any harm to the application (import statements on their own don't add size or functionality to a compiled application), but it could be confusing later when you opened the file and saw import statements that had nothing to do with the code's functionality.

In Flex Builder 3, the ActionScript editor added the capability to organize an ActionScript file's import statements with a simple menu selection or keyboard shortcut. When you organize imports, unused import statements are removed and the ones you need are left in alphabetical order, grouped by package.

Consider this list of import statements:

```
import mx.controls.Alert;
import flash.net.FileFilter;
import flash.net.URLRequest;
import mx.collections.ArrayCollection;
import mx.validators.Validator;
import flash.net.FileReference;
```

To organize this list, choose Source ➪ Organize Imports from the Flash Builder menu. (Or press the keyboard shortcut Ctrl+Shift+O.) After organization, the list now looks like this:

```
import flash.net.FileFilter;
import flash.net.FileReference;
import flash.net.URLRequest;
import mx.controls.Alert;
import mx.validators.Validator;
```

The `import` statement for the unused class is removed, and the remaining statements are alphabetized and grouped by package.

In Flash Builder 4, this feature is now available in MXML files as well. Just as with ActionScript files, you can now use the Organize Imports feature to alphabetize and group import statements and remove unused imports in the `<fx:Script>` sections of your MXML documents.

Using the Application Component

The `Application` component is always declared as the root element of an MXML application file. It represents the top level of the application's containership hierarchy.

New Feature

The Flex 4 `Application` **component is part of the Spark component set. It replaces the** `Application` **container that was used in previous versions of Flex, now known as the** `MX Application` **component. You can still use the MX version if you prefer, but only the new version implements Flex 4's advanced layout architecture and declarative skinning and is compatible with Flex projects created in Flash Catalyst.** ■

The Flex 4 version of the `Application` component is defined as an ActionScript class with the fully qualified name `spark.components.Application`. The `Application` class supports important properties and styles that are not part of other Flex 4 containers. Table 4.2 shows these properties and styles.

TABLE 4.2

Application Properties and Styles

Property	Purpose	Example
pageTitle	A value that's passed through to the HTML wrapper and displayed in place of the ${title} placeholder.	`<s:Application pageTitle="My Flex App"/>`
backgroundColor	A color value stated as a hexadecimal code.	`<s:Application backgroundColor="#FF00FF"/>`

Property	Purpose	Example

controlBarContent	An array of visual objects that are laid out in a skin part named controlBarGroup and typed as a Group. The default skin "docks" the control bar at the top of the screen.	`<s:Application..>`
		`<s:controlBarContent>`
		`... navigation elements...`
		`</s:controlBarContent>`
		`</s:Application>`

frameRate	The number of frames per second at which changes are reflected in Flash Player. The default in Flex is 24 frames/second. This property must be set in MXML.	`<s:Application frameRate="60"/>`
url	A read-only property returning the URL from which the application SWF file was opened.	`var currentURL:String = this.url;`

Tip

You can make typing appear to be smoother in a Flex application by increasing the frameRate. For example, if the cursor is in a TextArea or TextInput control and you hold down a key at 24 frames/second, the effect can be a bit "jumpy." That is, the characters may not appear at an even rate. Setting the frameRate to 60 or 90 frames/second may noticeably improve this "animation." In theory, this could have a negative effect on CPU usage on the client system, but in testing on a modern computer, it's difficult to see a difference. ∎

New Feature

The MX version of the Application component had a static property named application that referenced the application itself. The commonly used expression was Application.application. In Flex 4, this functionality has been moved to a static property named topLevelApplication, in a new class named FlexGlobals. So, the new version of this expression is FlexGlobals.topLevelApplication. As with the Flex 3 version, this expression is defined in the API to return an Object, but the native type matches the application's actual name. So, to create a variable that references an application named HelloWorld, use this syntax:

```
private var myApp:HelloWorld =
    FlexGlobals.topLevelApplication as HelloWorld; ∎
```

Note

The url property refers to the URL from which the application SWF file was loaded. For example, when running the URLDemo.mxml application from the local disk, the browser's URL is displayed as:

```
file:///C:/flex4bible/chapter04/bin-debug/URLDemo.html
```

The url property returns this value:

```
file:///C:/flex4bible/chapter04/bin-debug/URLDemo.swf ∎
```

Passing application parameters

You pass parameters to the application from the browser using a special Flash Player variable named `flashvars`. If you're using the HTML wrapper file that's generated during compilation by Flash Builder 4, the `flashvars` variable is declared as a JavaScript object in the HTML wrapper file JavaScript code. You can add your own parameters by declaring named properties of the `flashvars` object:

```
var flashvars = {};
flashvars.state="New";
```

The `flashvars` object is then passed to Flash Player in the call to `swfobject.embedSWF()`:

```
swfobject.embedSWF(
   "${swf}.swf", "flashContent",
   "${width}", "${height}",
   swfVersionStr, xiSwfUrlStr,
   flashvars, params, attributes);
```

To retrieve these values at runtime, use the `Application` object's `parameters` property. The `parameters` property is a dynamic object that enables you to address its named properties with dot notation, as in:

```
currentState=this.parameters.state;
```

Note

If you're hosting a Web-based Flex application on a dynamic application server such as ColdFusion or PHP, you can generate the `flashvars` variable dynamically. ∎

Controlling application dimensions

The default values for the `Application` component's width and height are both 100 percent. These values are passed to Flash Player through the HTML wrapper file that's generated by Flash Builder. For example, this code:

```
<s:Application xmlns:fx="http://ns.adobe.com/mxml/2009"
   xmlns:s="library://ns.adobe.com/flex/spark"
   xmlns:mx="library://ns.adobe.com/flex/mx"
   width="300" height="200">
</s:Application>
```

results in these values being passed to Flash Player in the generated HTML wrapper page:

```
swfobject.embedSWF(
   "URLDemo.swf", "flashContent",
   "300", "200",
   swfVersionStr, xiSwfUrlStr,
   flashvars, params, attributes);
```

These dimension properties are then passed to the application by Flash Player. In contrast the minWidth and minHeight properties that are set automatically on new applications affect only the Flex application itself, and not the HTML wrapper file.

Setting the layout property

The Application component's layout property controls how its nested visual objects are laid out on the screen.

New Feature

The new Application component is extended from SkinnableContainer, and uses Flex 4's new component layout architecture. In previous versions of Flex, the application's layout property was a simple string with possible values of vertical, horizontal, and absolute. In Flex 4 components, the layout property is set to an instance of a complex object. ■

The layout property is set to an instance of a class that extends a superclass named LayoutBase. These classes and their built-in properties, styles, and methods allow for flexible and portable customization of layout details. The Flex 4 SDK includes these prebuilt layout classes:

- **BasicLayout.** The default. Places objects in the container based on object's positioning properties: x, y, top, bottom, left, right, horizonalCenter, and verticalCenter.

- **HorizontalLayout.** Lays out objects in a single row from left to right.

- **VerticalLayout.** Lays out objects in a single column from top to bottom.

- **TileLayout.** Arranges objects in either rows or columns of equally sized cells. This is designed to replace Flex 3's Tile container.

You typically declare the application's layout property with an MXML child element:

```
<?xml version="1.0" encoding="utf-8"?>
<s:Application xmlns:fx="http://ns.adobe.com/mxml/2009"
  xmlns:s="library://ns.adobe.com/flex/spark"
  xmlns:mx="library://ns.adobe.com/flex/mx">
  <s:layout>
    <s:VerticalLayout/>
  </s:layout>
  ...add visual objects here...
</s:Application>
```

This creates an instance of the VerticalLayout class and assigns it to the application's layout property.

Vertical and horizontal layout

Settings of vertical and horizontal cause the application to lay out its nested visual objects automatically. As shown in Figure 4.10, setting layout to a VerticalLayout object causes objects in the application's display list to appear in a single column.

FIGURE 4.10

An application with vertical layout

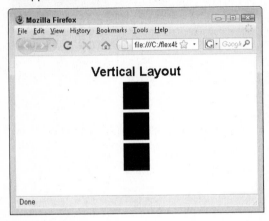

Note

The new `Application` **component doesn't implement the old** `horizontalAlign` **and** `verticalAlign` **styles. These are now implemented as properties of the layout classes. For example,** `HorizontalLayout` **supports** `verticalAlign`, **and** `VerticalLayout` **supports** `horizontalAlign`. **Both of these layout classes support padding properties:** `paddingTop`, `paddingBottom`, `paddingLeft`, **and** `paddingRight`. ■

Figure 4.11 shows what happens when you change the `Application` object's `layout` property to an instance of `HorizontalLayout`. Objects in the display list are laid out in a row from left to right.

FIGURE 4.11

An application with horizontal layout

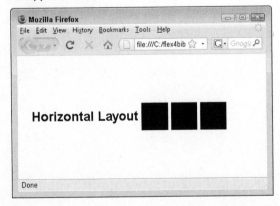

Note

The `HorizontalLayout` and `VerticalLayout` classes require the application to calculate the quantity and size of the nested controls at runtime, and then in a second pass to place them on the screen. This calculation has to be re-executed each time the application is resized (for example, if the user resizes the browser). On slower computers, this process can seem a bit sluggish. One solution to improve client-side performance in this situation is to switch to `BasicLayout`, because the application then doesn't have to do this calculation. ■

Basic layout

An application with basic layout enables each object to be placed in a specific position relative to the top-left corner of the application.

New Feature

In Flex 3, the scheme now known as basic layout was called absolute layout. They have the same meaning, although certain implementation details have changed. ■

As shown in Figure 4.12, basic layout has the additional advantage of being able to overlap objects. When objects have `alpha` settings that enable transparency, as is the case with default settings of the new `Button` component, you can make objects show through each other from back to front.

Note

The z-index, or relative depth, of overlapping visual objects is controlled by their order in the container's display list. When declared in MXML, the last declared object has the highest z-index and overlaps any other objects with which it shares screen space. ■

FIGURE 4.12

An application with `absolute` layout and overlapping

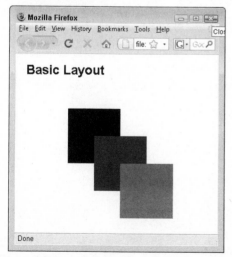

Besides `Application`, these Spark components support the `layout` property:

- `Panel`
- `Group`
- `BorderContainer`
- `Window` (used only in desktop applications deployed with Adobe AIR)
- `WindowedApplication` (used only in desktop applications deployed with Adobe AIR)
- `NavigatorContent` (used to "wrap" Spark components you want to manage in a `ViewStack`)
- `ItemRenderer` (used to render repeated elements in `List` components)

I describe them in detail in Chapter 9.

Summary

In this chapter, I described the basic anatomy of a Flex application. You learned the following:

- MXML and ActionScript 3 are the two programming languages you use for Flex development.
- ActionScript 3 is based on the ECMAScript 4th Edition recommendation.
- ActionScript's syntax is similar to Java, JavaScript, C, C++, and C#.
- MXML is a "convenience" language that compiles into ActionScript.
- MXML is a pure XML-based language.
- FXG is an XML language for describing graphics rendering as implemented in Flash Player 10.
- The Flex 4 SDK includes ActionScript classes that, when declared with MXML, mimic FXG syntax.
- You can combine MXML and ActionScript in a number of ways.
- The new Spark-based `Application` component is the root element in a Flex application designed for Web deployment.
- The `Application` class's layout `property` can be set to instances of classes that extend `LayoutBase`.

Using Bindings and Components

In Chapter 1, I described the object-oriented concept of *modularity* and how dividing an application into small pieces can increase developer productivity and improve long-term maintenance of an application. I also described the concept of *encapsulation* that encourages developers to create application building blocks that hide the details of a feature's implementation from the rest of the application, and only expose tools in the module's public interface that are needed to set and get the module's information and execute its functions.

In this chapter, I describe some of the basic building blocks of a Flex application that can improve its modularity and make it easier to manage over time. I start with a look at binding expressions and describe how they help you easily move data around an application. A binding expression can move data from one object to another at runtime without explicit event handling or ActionScript statements. I describe a couple of binding syntax styles and show when to use each.

This chapter also includes a description of how to create and use custom MXML components in a Flex application. In the last section of this chapter, I describe how to package and manage multiple components and classes in a component library using a Flex Library Project.

On the Web

To use the sample code for this chapter, import the `chapter05.fxp` Flex project file from the Web site files into your Flash Builder workspace. ∎

IN THIS CHAPTER

Using binding expressions

Creating MXML components

Instantiating MXML components

Creating component properties and methods

Creating and using component libraries

Creating Flash-based controls

Using Binding Expressions

As I previously described, a binding expression enables you to move data from one object to another at runtime without having to handle complex events or write lots of ActionScript code.

Tip

Binding expressions represent only one possible approach to managing data within a Flex application. Because they generate automatic event broadcasters and listeners, they can create significant application activity when overused. Sometimes it's best just to assign object properties using ActionScript code. ■

The purpose of a binding is to "listen" for changes to an expression and to "broadcast" the expression's value to an object's property. The expression that returns the value is known in a binding as the *source*. The expression to which you pass the value when it changes is known as the *destination*.

Look at this example of two controls:

```
<s:TextInput id="sourceText" text="some value"/>
<s:Label id="destinationLabel"/>
```

If you want the first control's text property value to be displayed in the second control, you refer to the first as the source and the second as the destination.

Flex supports three binding syntax styles:

- A simple, shorthand MXML-based version that wraps a binding expression in an attribute of an MXML declaration
- A longhand MXML-based version that uses the `<fx:Binding>` tag
- A longhand ActionScript-based version that uses the `mx.binding.utils.BindingUtils` class

Note

The longhand ActionScript-based version of creating a binding has some limitations compared to MXML. While the `BindingUtils` class enables you to create a binding at runtime, it does not support the use of simple ActionScript or ECMAScript for XML (E4X) expressions, and it doesn't have as good a set of error and warning detection as bindings declared in MXML. ■

Shorthand MXML binding expressions

In the shorthand MXML version, you start by assigning an `id`, or unique identifier, to the source control. This becomes the instance name of your object for future reference:

```
<s:TextInput id="sourceText" text="some value"/>
```

In the destination control's declaration, you use an ActionScript expression that refers to the source control's text property, wrapped in `{ }` characters:

```
<s:Label text="{sourceText.text}"/>
```

At runtime, if the source control's `text` property changes, the destination control is updated at the same time.

New Feature

Flex 4 adds new syntax to create two-way bindings between components. In Flex 3, you could implement this sort of two-way transfer of data with redundant coding:

```
<s:TextInput id="input1" text="{input2.text}"/>
<s:TextInput id="input2" text="{input1.text}"/>
```

In Flex 4, you can accomplish the same thing with a single binding expression in just one of the controls. Add the @ character as a prefix to the binding expression, placed before the braces:

```
<s:TextInput id="input1" text="@{input2.text}"/>
<s:TextInput id="input2"/> ■
```

Using <fx:Binding>

The longhand MXML binding syntax uses an `<fx:Binding/>` tag with properties of `source` and `destination` to define the two expressions:

```
<fx:Binding source="sourceText.text"
   destination="destinationText.text"/>
```

The `<fx:Binding>` tag can be used when the destination object is declared in ActionScript code, rather than MXML. Because shorthand syntax works only in the context of an MXML declaration, it just doesn't work for this case.

In the following code, a value entered into a `TextInput` control is passed to a pre-declared variable named `myVar` whenever the user makes a change. That variable's value is then passed to the `Label` control using a shorthand binding expression.

```
<fx:Script>
  <![CDATA[
    [Bindable]
    private var myVar:String
  ]]>
</fx:Script>
<fx:Binding source="myInput.text" destination="myVar"/>
<s:TextInput id="myInput"/>
<s:Label text="{myVar}"/>
```

Tip

You might not use the `<fxBinding>` tag in the simplest Flex applications, but the first time you need to pass a value to an object or expression that's declared in ActionScript, you'll find it a valuable tool. ■

Making expressions bindable

Most object properties in the Flex framework's library are *bindable*, meaning that if the property's value changes at runtime, the new value is *broadcast* to the listening destination object. When you declare your own variables in ActionScript, their values aren't automatically bindable; you have to mark them with a `[Bindable]` metadata tag to indicate that they should share new values with the rest of the application.

Consider this code:

```
<fx:Script>
  <![CDATA[
    private var myVar:String="Hello World";
  ]]>
</fx:Script>
<s:Label id="destinationLabel" text="{myVar}"/>
```

The variable `myVar` shares its value with the `destinationLabel` control at application startup, but because the variable isn't marked as bindable, any changes at runtime won't be passed to the control. In fact, the compiler notices this problem and generates a compiler warning, as shown in Figure 5.1.

FIGURE 5.1

A compiler warning for a binding to a non-bindable expression

To fix this and get rid of the compiler warning, add the `[Bindable]` metadata tag before the variable declaration:

```
<fx:Script>
  <![CDATA[
    [Bindable]
    private var myVar:String="Hello World";
  ]]>
</fx:Script>
<s:Label id="destinationLabel" text="{myVar}"/>
```

The compiler warning disappears, and if the source expression's value changes at runtime, the `Label` control correctly displays the new value.

Tip

The `[Bindable]` metadata tag must be placed immediately before the variable it modifies. If you prefer, you can place both on a single line:

```
[Bindable] private var myVar:String="Hello World"; ■
```

The View in Model-View-Controller

A single Flex application can have dozens or hundreds of "views" — that is, screens or visual representations of data that execute particular functions, collect data, or present information to the user. If you try to implement all these views in a single source-code file, the result can be a mess.

Similarly, the application may need to make calls to remote servers to get data, and implement object structures in application memory in which to hold that data at runtime. In classic model-view-controller application architecture, the parts of the application that make the calls, and the classes that contain, or represent, the data, are known as *model components*.

The *controller* part of the architecture is responsible for receiving and interpreting user input. In Flex, the controller is frequently implemented as a mapping of application events to actions that the application is capable of executing.

You can create view components with either MXML or ActionScript, but for most purposes an MXML component is the simplest approach. And after you create the components, you need a way to share data with them and make them do things. In this chapter, I describe how to build the Flex application's views as MXML components and how to design the components to hold and receive data.

Using MXML Components

As I described in Chapter 1, *modularity* means that you break up an application into pieces that are focused on particular application tasks. A modular application tends to be more stable and maintainable than one that mixes many types of functionality into a single source-code file.

Flex supports the object-oriented concept of modularity through the use of custom MXML components and ActionScript classes. In this section, I describe how to create and incorporate MXML components in a Flex application.

Creating MXML components

Like the application itself, an MXML component is defined in a source-code file with an extension of `.mxml`. At compilation time, an MXML component is rewritten as an ActionScript class where the name of the class matches the first part of the component's filename. For example, if you create a file named `MyComponent.mxml`, the resulting ActionScript class is named `MyComponent`.

Tip

I strongly recommend that you create components in subfolders of the project source root folder, rather than the source folder itself. This enables you to group components by purpose into packages. For example, you might have one folder for forms, another for `DataGrid` and `List` components (data-aware components), a third for navigational tools, and so on. The names of the folders are up to you but should follow ActionScript naming conventions: letters, numbers, and underscore characters, always starting with a lowercase alphabetical letter. ■

Tip

Because an MXML component is really an ActionScript class, I recommend that you follow object-oriented naming conventions for class definitions. Specifically this means that component filenames usually start with an initial uppercase character and use mixed-case after that. This is a convention, not a technical requirement, but it's one that most Flex developers follow. ■

Component inheritance

Each MXML component extends, or is derived from, an existing ActionScript class. You indicate which class the current component extends with the MXML file's root element. So a class named `MyComponent.mxml` that extends the `VGroup` container looks like this:

```
<?xml version="1.0" encoding="utf-8"?>
<s:VGroup xmlns:fx="http://ns.adobe.com/mxml/2009"
  xmlns:s="library://ns.adobe.com/flex/spark"
  xmlns:mx="library://ns.adobe.com/flex/mx">
  ...place additional MXML tags here...
</s:VGroup>
```

Caution

Notice that the MXML component file's root element includes the same three namespace and prefix declarations as the main application file. The `http://ns.adobe.com/mxml/2009` namespace is required in all Flex 4 MXML files, and the Spark and MX namespaces are required if you use any of those components. When you create an MXML component using the New MXML Component wizard, all three namespaces are added to the component's root element automatically. ■

The preceding MXML code results in the inheritance relationship described by the Unified Modeling Language (UML) diagram in Figure 5.2.

FIGURE 5.2

The inheritance relationship between `VGroup`, the superclass, and the custom component, the subclass

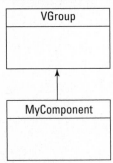

Reverse Domain Package Names

Some developers prefer to create their components and ActionScript classes in a folder structure that includes their organization's domain information and an application identifier. Instead of a simple folder named `forms`, you might have a folder structure named `com/bardotech/myapplication/forms`. Because the folder structure represents a *package* in class management terms, this creates a globally unique identifying system for each group of components. A file named `MyForm.as` in the previous folder is known by its fully qualified name as `com.bardo.tech.myapplication.forms.MyForm`.

Notice that the domain name `bardotech.com` becomes a package structure of `com.bardotech`. This convention of reversing the parts of a domain name in a package structure is described in the documentation for the Java programming language and has been adopted by some Flex developers.

In Java, this practice is strongly encouraged. Because the Java Virtual Machine searches for classes in its classpath at runtime, as well as during compilation, using globally unique class names ensures that if a library of classes with conflicting names just happens to be in your application's classpath, the globally unique package identifier reduces the possibility of class naming conflicts.

In ActionScript, the build path is used only during the compilation process. By the time you run the application, it's already been compiled into the SWF byte code format. The ActionScript Virtual Machine uses only the classes that are compiled into the application, but it doesn't use the build path to search for classes as they're needed at runtime. As a result, this particular reason for the globally unique package name only applies to the world of ActionScript when you incorporate third-party code libraries in the form of SWC files (component libraries) and RSL (Runtime Shared Library) files where you don't control the names of the classes.

You might still want to use these sorts of package names in code libraries that are shared between multiple projects to ensure that compile-time conflicts don't emerge. But for code that's unique to a single application, these deeply nested package names don't have any technical benefit.

Creating a new MXML Component

To create a new MXML component with Flash Builder, first create a folder in the project's source root to contain the component. Then use the New MXML Component wizard to create the component source-code file.

Creating a component folder

To create a component folder, follow these steps:

1. Right-click the project's src folder in the Flex Navigator view.
2. Choose New ➪ Folder.
3. Enter a new folder name of `components`, and click Finish.

Note

Folder names that represent packages, by convention, are usually all lowercase. For example, the folder containing form components should be named `forms`, not `Forms` or `FORMS`. ■

Creating the MXML component

Follow these steps to create the MXML component:

1. **Right-click the new folder in the Package Explorer view.**
2. **Choose New ➪ MXML Component.**
3. **As shown in Figure 5.3, enter the component name** `MyComponent`.

FIGURE 5.3

The New MXML Component wizard

4. **Set Layout to spark.layouts.VerticalLayout.**
5. **Set the value for Based on to spark.components.Panel.**
6. **Accept the default values in the Width and Height settings.**
7. **Click Finish to create the new MXML component.**
8. **If the component opens in Design mode, click the Source button to view the generated code.** It should look like this:

```
<?xml version="1.0" encoding="utf-8"?>
<s:Panel xmlns:fx="http://ns.adobe.com/mxml/2009"
  xmlns:s="library://ns.adobe.com/flex/spark"
  xmlns:mx="library://ns.adobe.com/flex/mx"
  width="400" height="300">
  <s:layout>
    <s:VerticalLayout/>
  </s:layout>
  <fx:Declarations>
```

```
    <!-- Place non-visual elements
       (e.g., services, value objects) here -->
  </fx:Declarations>
</s:Panel>
```

9. Delete the <fx:Declarations> element and its nested comment.

10. Set the <s:Panel> tag's title property to "My Custom Component".

Adding content to the component

To add content to the component, follow these steps:

1. Set the VerticalLayout object's paddingTop and paddingLeft styles set to 20:

```
<s:layout>
  <s:VerticalLayout paddingTop="10" paddingLeft="10"/>
</s:layout>
```

2. Place the cursor inside the <s:Panel> tags, after the <s:layout> element.

3. Add three Label controls with the following code:

```
<s:Label text="These Label objects"/>
<s:Label text="are inside my custom"/>
<s:Label text="component"/>
```

4. Save your changes.

Listing 5.1 shows the completed code for the finished component.

LISTING 5.1

A completed custom component based on the Spark Panel

```
<?xml version="1.0" encoding="utf-8"?>
<s:Panel xmlns:fx="http://ns.adobe.com/mxml/2009"
  xmlns:s="library://ns.adobe.com/flex/spark"
  xmlns:mx="library://ns.adobe.com/flex/mx"
  width="400" height="300"
  title="My Custom Component">
  <s:layout>
    <s:VerticalLayout paddingTop="10" paddingLeft="10"/>
  </s:layout>
  <s:Label text="These Label objects"/>
  <s:Label text="are inside my custom"/>
  <s:Label text="component"/>
</s:Panel>
```

On the Web

The code in Listing 5.1 is available in the Web site files in the chapter05 **project as** components/
MyComponent_Complete.mxml. ∎

Instantiating MXML components

You use MXML components by creating instances of the components in your application. You can instantiate a component using either MXML or ActionScript code.

Instantiating a component with MXML

If the MXML component represents a visual object such as a container or control, it's most commonly instantiated using MXML code. Before an MXML component can be instantiated, you must declare a custom XML namespace prefix that's associated with the folder in which the component's source-code file is stored.

It's best to declare the custom namespace prefix in the MXML file's root element start tag, the value of which contains the folder location of your components (in dot notation) and ends with an asterisk to indicate that all components in this folder are available in this namespace:

```
<s:Application xmlns:fx="http://ns.adobe.com/mxml/2009"
  xmlns:s="library://ns.adobe.com/flex/spark"
  xmlns:mx="library://ns.adobe.com/flex/mx"
  xmlns:components="components.*">
```

You then instantiate the component with standard XML syntax, using the namespace prefix and the component name as an XML element:

```
<components:MyComponent id="comp1"/>
```

Tip

A custom namespace that you declare for a particular folder also serves as an `import` declaration for all classes in that folder. If you need to refer to components or classes in that folder in other parts of the MXML file, a separate `import` statement is not required. ∎

You also can declare the namespace prefix directly within the component instantiation like this:

```
<components:MyComponent id="comp1" xmlns:components="components.*"/>
```

This works, but the namespace prefix is available only for the single component instance. When you place the namespace prefix in the current MXML file's root element, you can then declare multiple instances of any component in the `components` folder.

The namespace prefix is arbitrary; that is, you can name it anything. I recommend, however, that you assign a prefix that's the same as the folder name, as in

```
xmlns:components="components.*"
```

This has two benefits:

- Because the namespace prefix matches the folder name, you'll recognize the component file's location when you look at the code.
- Flash Builder can create the latter version of the namespace declaration for you if you follow a particular sequence in coding the object. I describe this sequence in the next tutorial.

Here's how you create an application that instantiates the custom MXML component:

1. **Create a new MXML application in the current project.** When the application code has been generated, remove the `minHeight` and `minWidth` properties.

2. **Place the cursor between the <s:Application> tags, but after any <fx:Declarations> element that might have been created automatically.**

3. **Type the < character, and then** my, **the first couple of characters in the component name.** (This string is unique enough to display a small number of items in the list of available ActionScript classes.)

   As shown in Figure 5.4, the list of available classes appears and the custom component is displayed.

Tip

If the list of available classes disappears, press Ctrl+spacebar to bring it back. This works in Flash Builder wherever code hinting is available. ■

4. **Press Enter (Windows) or Return (Mac) to select the custom component from the list of available ActionScript classes.** Flash Builder completes the code with the namespace prefix and the component name:

   ```
   <components:MyComponent
   ```

5. **Type /> to complete the tag.** The code should now look like this:

   ```
   <components:MyComponent/>
   ```

FIGURE 5.4

Selecting the custom component using code hinting

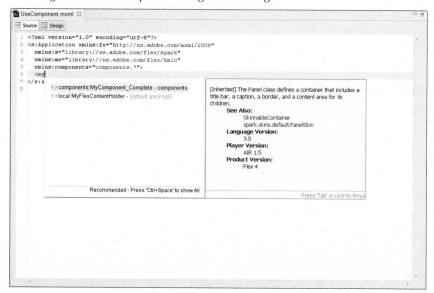

6. **Look at the <s:Application> start tag.** You should see that the `<Application>` tag has been populated with the required namespace prefix to support the selected component. The tag looks like this:

```
<s:Application xmlns:fx="http://ns.adobe.com/mxml/2009"
  xmlns:s="library://ns.adobe.com/flex/spark"
  xmlns:mx="library://ns.adobe.com/flex/mx"
  xmlns:components="components.*">
```

7. **Add a layout property as a child element of the Application.** Set it to a `Vertical` Layout object with `horizontalAlign` set to `center` and `paddingTop` set to 20:

```
<s:layout>
  <s:VerticalLayout horizontalAlign="center" paddingTop="20"/>
</s:layout>
```

8. **Save and run the application.**

Listing 5.2 shows the application's completed code.

LISTING 5.2

An application that includes an instance of a custom component

```
<?xml version="1.0" encoding="utf-8"?>
<s:Application xmlns:fx="http://ns.adobe.com/mxml/2009"
  xmlns:s="library://ns.adobe.com/flex/spark"
  xmlns:mx="library://ns.adobe.com/flex/mx"
  xmlns:components="components.*">
  <s:layout>
    <s:VerticalLayout horizontalAlign="center" paddingTop="20"/>
  </s:layout>
  <components:MyComponent/>
</s:Application>
```

On the Web

The code in Listing 5.2 is available in the Web site files in the `chapter05` **project as** `UseComponent.mxml`. ■

Figure 5.5 shows the application with a single instance of the custom MXML component.

Inserting a custom component instance in Design mode

You also can instantiate the custom component in Design mode by simply dragging it from Flash Builder's Components view:

1. **Click Design to switch to Design mode.**

2. **In the Components view in the lower-left corner of Flash Builder, open the Custom section.** You should see your new custom component.

3. **As shown in Figure 5.6, drag the custom component from the Components view into the application.** The component instance should appear in the application's Design mode.

FIGURE 5.5

An application with an instance of a custom component

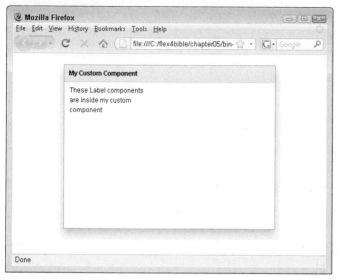

FIGURE 5.6

Dragging a custom component into an application

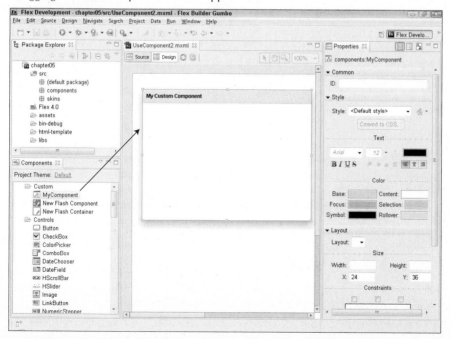

New Feature

In Flex Builder 3, when you dragged a custom component into an application in Design mode and the component package's namespace prefix hadn't been previously defined, Flex Builder created an automatically numbered namespace prefix such `ns1` (for "namespace 1"). It also created the MXML code that instantiates the component using paired tags, instead of the preferred empty tag syntax. The resulting generated code looked like this:

```
<ns1:MyComponent x="100" y="100">
</ns1:MyComponent>
```

This code worked fine, but the namespace wasn't meaningful and didn't match the folder name. In Flash Builder 4, the same action now creates a new namespace prefix that matches the folder name:

```
<components:MyComponent x="100" y="100">
</components:MyComponent> ■
```

Instantiating a component with ActionScript

Because an MXML component is really an ActionScript class definition, you can instantiate the component with pure ActionScript code. As with any pre-built component in the Flex framework, you follow these steps:

1. Create an import statement that refers to the component as a class.

2. Declare a variable with its data type set to the component as a class.

3. Instantiate the component using a no-arguments constructor method call.

4. Add the component instance to the display list of the application's primary content group or another component.

New Feature

In Flex 4, the `Application` component doesn't have a direct display list. Instead, its `contentGroup` property refers to its default group of visual objects. When you declare MXML components as child objects, they're automatically added to the `contentGroup`. When you create a custom skin for the `Application` component, you can control the placement and layout of this content by creating a `Group` in the skin with an id of `contentGroup` (known as the contentGroup skin part). ■

New Feature

In Flex 3, child objects were added to a container programmatically with a method named `addChild()`. In Flex 4, you use a method named `addElement()`, and call it as a member of the `contentGroup` object There are other new methods named `getElementAt()`, `removeElement()`, `removeAllElements()`, `setElementIndex()`, and so on. All components that extend a class named `SkinnableContainer` can use these methods. ■

Listing 5.3 shows the code for an application that creates and displays a single instance of the custom component upon application startup.

LISTING 5.3

Instantiating a custom component with ActionScript

```
<?xml version="1.0" encoding="utf-8"?>
<s:Application xmlns:fx="http://ns.adobe.com/mxml/2009"
  xmlns:s="library://ns.adobe.com/flex/spark"
  xmlns:mx="library://ns.adobe.com/flex/mx"
  creationComplete="app_creationCompleteHandler(event)">
  <fx:Script>
    <![CDATA[
      import components.MyComponent_Complete;
      import mx.events.FlexEvent;

      protected var comp:MyComponent_Complete;
      protected function app_creationCompleteHandler(event:FlexEvent):void
      {
        comp = new MyComponent_Complete();
        comp.x = 100;
        comp.y = 100;
        this.contentGroup.addElement(comp);
      }
    ]]>
  </fx:Script>
</s:Application>
```

On the Web

The code in Listing 5.3 is available in the Web site files in the `chapter05` project as `UseComponentWith AS.mxml`. ∎

Adding Properties and Methods to Components

Components and classes can have *member* objects. A member object is a pre-declared item that's instantiated along with the class. ActionScript classes support these member types:

- **Properties.** Properties hold dynamic data values.
- **Constants.** Constants hold fixed data values.
- **Methods.** Methods execute actions.
- **Events.** Events send messages to other parts of the application.
- **Styles.** Styles control a visual object's presentation.

In this section, I describe how to define properties, constants, and methods in an MXML component.

Component properties

A *property* is a variable that's owned by a class definition. In ActionScript 3, all variables are actually properties of some object. If you declare a variable in an application source file, that variable is actually a property of the application object.

Setting properties

The syntax to declare a property looks like this:

```
[access modifier] var [variable name]:[data type];
```

A `public` property named `currentValue` with a data type of `String` is declared with this code:

```
public var currentValue:String;
```

You can set the property's initial value upon object instantiation with this code:

```
public var currentValue:String = "Default value";
```

Note

In browser-based JavaScript, the `var` keyword is optional and can be used to control a variable's scope: A variable declared in a function with `var` is local to the function, while a variable declared without `var` is global to the current HTML page. In ActionScript, the `var` keyword is always used to mark any variable or property declaration. ■

Cross-Reference

The available access modifiers for variables and properties are described in Chapter 4. ■

Static properties

A *static property* is a value that can be referred to by other parts of the application from the class definition, rather than from an instance of a class. You make a property static by adding the `static` keyword either before or after the access modifier:

```
public static var myStaticVar:String;
```

You then refer to the property using the class name as a prefix:

```
var newValue:String = MyComponent.myStaticVar;
```

Making a property bindable

As I described earlier in this chapter, properties are bindable only if you explicitly mark them with the `[Bindable]` metadata tag. A property that's marked as bindable always broadcasts changes in its value to objects within the component. A property that's also marked as public broadcasts changes to the application or other module that instantiates the component.

In Listing 5.4, a component has a bindable public variable named `valueToDisplay`. A `Label` control within the component displays the property's value.

LISTING 5.4

A component with a bindable public property

```xml
<?xml version="1.0" encoding="utf-8"?>
<s:Group xmlns:fx="http://ns.adobe.com/mxml/2009"
  xmlns:s="library://ns.adobe.com/flex/spark"
  xmlns:mx="library://ns.adobe.com/flex/mx"
  width="400" height="300">
  <fx:Script>
    <![CDATA[
      [Bindable]
      public var valueToDisplay:String;
    ]]>
  </fx:Script>
  <s:Label text="{valueToDisplay}" fontSize="24"/>
</s:Group>
```

On the Web

The code in Listing 5.4 is available in the Web site files in the `chapter05` **project as** `components/CompWithBindableProp.mxml`. ∎

Declaring public properties with MXML tags

You also can declare a property with MXML. For example, this code declares the same `String` property as in the previous example:

```xml
<fx:String id="valueToDisplay"/>
```

A property that's declared in this way is implicitly marked as public and bindable, so the `public` access modifier and the `[Bindable]` metadata tag aren't required.

When you declare a property using MXML, you must wrap the MXML tag inside the `<fx:Declarations>` element. The component in Listing 5.4 could be rewritten in pure MXML as:

```xml
<?xml version="1.0" encoding="utf-8"?>
<s:Group xmlns:fx="http://ns.adobe.com/mxml/2009"
  xmlns:s="library://ns.adobe.com/flex/spark">
  <fx:Declarations>
    <fx:String id="mxmlVar"/>
  </fx:Declarations>
  <s:Label text="{mxmlVar}"/>
</s:Group>
```

Passing data to a component property

You can pass data to a component property with either dot syntax in ActionScript or MXML property declarations. To pass data using an MXML property declaration, declare the property as an XML attribute of the object declaration and set the value with either a literal value or a binding expression.

This is an example of passing a literal value:

```
<components:MyComponent valueToDisplay="Hello World"/>
```

This is an example of using a binding expression:

```
<components:MyComponent valueToDisplay="{aBindableValue}"/>
```

In either case, the value is passed to the public property. And because that property is marked as bindable within the component, its new value is then passed to any control or expression that's bound to it.

Using constants

A *constant* is a property whose value is set at the time of declaration and never changes. Common uses of constants in ActionScript include:

- **Aliases for literal values within components that are referred to multiple times in a component or class's implementation.** For example, this private constant represents the literal string "All Products":

```
private const ALLPRODUCTS:String="All Products";
```

- **Aliases for properties of objects that are used externally.** For example, custom event classes frequently have static public constants whose values are names of custom events for which the current event class is used:

```
public static const SELECTED:String="selected";
```

Note

By object-oriented convention, constant identifiers are spelled in all uppercase, as in SELECTED. This distinguishes them in your code from property identifiers, which are spelled with an initial lowercase character and optional mixed case thereafter. ∎

Note

Because a constant's value never changes, it doesn't make sense to make it bindable. In fact, if you mark a constant declaration with the [Bindable] metadata tag, a compiler error results. ∎

Component methods

A *method* is a function that belongs to a class or component definition. The dictionary meaning of the word "method" is "a way of doing something, especially a systematic way." This makes sense in the context of class definitions; a method defines how a class accomplishes a particular task.

Depending on your background with various programming languages, you might think of a method as a *function* or a *subroutine*. In fact, methods are marked in ActionScript with the function keyword.

Defining methods

Use this syntax to define a method in a component:

```
[access modifier] function [methodName](
[argument declarations] ):[data type]
{
}
```

A sample method might look like this:

```
public function getValue():String
{
   return someValue;
}
```

As with properties, methods are marked with one of the four access modifiers that are also used with properties: public, private, protected and internal.

As with properties, if you don't include an access modifier with a method declaration, the access defaults to internal.

The code in Listing 5.5 creates a component with two public properties named firstName and lastName and one public method named getFullName() that returns a concatenated string. The component also contains two Label controls that display the current values of the two properties.

LISTING 5.5

A component with a public method

```
<?xml version="1.0" encoding="utf-8"?>
<s:Panel xmlns:fx="http://ns.adobe.com/mxml/2009"
  xmlns:s="library://ns.adobe.com/flex/spark"
  xmlns:mx="library://ns.adobe.com/flex/mx"
  width="200" height="150">
  <s:layout>
    <s:VerticalLayout paddingLeft="10" paddingTop="10"/>
  </s:layout>
  <fx:Script>
    <![CDATA[
      [Bindable]
      public var firstName:String;
      [Bindable]
      public var lastName:String
      public function getFullName():String
      {
        return firstName + " " + lastName;
      }
    ]]>
  </fx:Script>
  <s:Label text="First Name: {firstName}"/>
  <s:Label text="Last Name: {lastName}"/>
</s:Group>
```

On the Web

The code in Listing 5.5 is available in the Web site files in the `chapter05` project's `components` package as `CompWithPublicMethod.mxml`. ∎

Calling component methods

You call component methods with either ActionScript statements or binding expressions. Listing 5.6 shows an application that uses the component in Listing 5.5 and displays the concatenated value returned from the component's public method.

LISTING 5.6

An application calling a component method in a binding expression

```
<?xml version="1.0" encoding="utf-8"?>
<s:Application xmlns:fx="http://ns.adobe.com/mxml/2009"
  xmlns:s="library://ns.adobe.com/flex/spark"
  xmlns:mx="library://ns.adobe.com/flex/mx"
  xmlns:components="components.*">
  <s:layout>
    <s:VerticalLayout horizontalAlign="center" paddingTop="20" gap="20"/>
  </s:layout>
  <components:CompWithPublicMethod
    id="myComp"
    firstName="Peter"
    lastName="Programmer"/>
  <s:Label text="Value from component method: {myComp.getFullName()}"/>
</s:Application>
```

On the Web

The code in Listing 5.6 is available in the Web site files in the `chapter05` project as `UseComponentWith Method.mxml`. ∎

When you call a component method without any arguments in a binding expression, it executes only upon initial object construction (for example, upon application startup). This syntax doesn't have an implicit mechanism to tell the Flex framework that the method should be called again:

```
<s:Label text="{myComp.getFullName()}"/>
```

However, it's a simple matter to call the function with an ActionScript statement. In Listing 5.7, the component's property values are passed in with expressions that bind to visual controls in the application, and the application calls the component's `getFullName()` method to retrieve and display the resulting concatenated value.

LISTING 5.7

Calling a component method with an ActionScript statement

```
<?xml version="1.0" encoding="utf-8"?>
<s:Application xmlns:fx="http://ns.adobe.com/mxml/2009"
  xmlns:s="library://ns.adobe.com/flex/spark"
  xmlns:mx="library://ns.adobe.com/flex/mx"
  xmlns:components="components.*">
  <s:layout>
    <s:VerticalLayout horizontalAlign="center" paddingTop="20"/>
  </s:layout>
  <components:CompWithPublicMethod id="myComp"
    firstName="{firstNameInput.text}"
    lastName="{lastNameInput.text}"/>
  <s:TextInput id="firstNameInput"/>
  <s:TextInput id="lastNameInput"/>
  <s:Label id="fullNameOutput"/>
  <s:Button label="Get Full Name"
    click="fullNameOutput.text=myComp.getFullName()"/>
</s:Application>
```

On the Web

The code in Listing 5.7 is available in the Web site files in the `chapter05` project's `src` folder in the default package as `CallComponentMethodWithAS.mxml`. ∎

Using Component Libraries

A component library is an archive file in ZIP format that has a file extension of `.swc`. Component libraries that are compatible with Flex applications can be created with these tools:

- Flash CS3 or CS4
- The Flex SDK's `compc` command-line component compiler
- A Flex Library Project created and managed in Flash Builder

In this section, I describe how to create and use a component library in Flash Builder with a Flex Library Project.

Creating component libraries

A Flex Library Project is designed to create a component library: an archive file that contains pre-compiled ActionScript classes and other assets. Unlike a Flex Project, which contains complete applications, a Flex Library Project contains only the building blocks of an application. Its purpose is to create component library files that contain pre-built ActionScript code and related assets that can be dropped into a Flex application for immediate use.

Creating a library project

Follow these steps to create a Library Project in Flash Builder:

1. Choose File ⇨ New ⇨ Flex Library Project from the Flash Builder menu.

Tip

If you're using the plug-in version of Flash Builder, choose File ⇨ New ⇨ Other from the Eclipse menu. Then choose Flash Builder ⇨ Flex Library Project from the wizard dialog box. ■

2. In the New Flex Library Project wizard, shown in Figure 5.7, provide a Project name, select the Use default location option, and indicate whether Adobe AIR libraries should be included.

FIGURE 5.7

The first screen of the New Flex Library Project wizard

3. Click Next.

4. In the next screen, shown in Figure 5.8, accept the default locations for the Main source folder and Output folder.

5. If any assets such as image or XML files should be included with the component library, click the Assets tab and select the files you want to include.

Note

When you first create the Library Project, you may not have assets to add right away. You can easily add assets to the project later through the Project Properties. ■

FIGURE 5.8

The second screen of the New Flex Library Project wizard

6. Click Finish to create the project.

Creating a project's folder structure

As with components that are built in a Flex Project, you create subfolders in a Flex Library Project's source code root folder that represent the packages in which various components are stored. In Flash Builder 4, new component library projects have a default `src` folder that serves as the source-code root. You create your package subfolders created under the source-code root.

Follow these steps to create a component in a Library Project:

1. **If the project doesn't have a package in which to create the component, right-click the src folder project in the Flex Package Explorer view and choose New ⇨ Package.**

2. **In the New Package wizard, shown in Figure 5.9, enter the new folder name and click Finish.**

3. **Right-click the package in which you want to create the component, and choose New ⇨ MXML Component.**

FIGURE 5.9

Creating a project subfolder

4. **Create the component using the same options as in a Flex Project.** Enter the Filename, select which component the custom component is based on, and enter or clear any `width` or `height` properties.

5. **Click Finish to create the component.**

Note

When you create a new folder under the project source-code root folder, it also results in creating a package. ■

After the component has been built, look in the project's output folder (the output folder's default name is `bin`). You'll find a new file with a name consisting of the project name and the `.swc` file extension. For example, a Library Project named `MyCompLibrary` generates a component library file named `MyCompLibrary.swc`.

The SWC file is a compressed archive file in ZIP format. It contains a compiled SWF file named `library.swf` with your components and classes in compiled byte code, and a manifest file in XML format named `catalog.xml` that lists the library's contents. In addition to your custom classes, the SWC file contains references to (but not definitions of) any superclasses, and copies of the component's skinning graphics and other embedded assets.

New Feature

When you export a Flex Project library to the new FXP format, it's saved with a file extension of `.fxpl` instead of `.fxp`. In all other regards, the Flex Project format is the same for Flex Projects and Flex Library Projects. ■

Using component libraries

You incorporate component libraries into Flex applications in two ways:

- Add a component library to a Flex Project's source path.
- Copy the component library into a Flex Project's `libs` folder.

Caution

When using component libraries, you should make sure the library was compiled using a version of the Flex SDK that's compatible with your application. ∎

Adding a component library to a project's build path

Each Flex Project has a *build path* that consists of a list of folders and component libraries whose components and classes are available to the current project. The build path includes a source path of folders in which ActionScript and MXML source code is stored, and a library path that includes compiled component libraries. The build path is set in the project properties dialog box.

Follow these steps to add a component library to a Flex Project's build path:

1. In the Flex Navigator view, select a Flex Project.
2. Choose Project ⇨ Properties from the Flash Builder menu.

Tip

You also can right-click the project in the Flex Navigator view and select Properties from the context menu. ∎

3. Select Flex Build Path in the Project Properties dialog box.
4. As shown in Figure 5.10, click the Library path tab.

The Library path screen enables you to add the component libraries in these ways:

- For Library Projects that are managed in the current Flash Builder workspace, click Add Project. As shown in Figure 5.11, select the Library Project and click OK. All components and classes in the selected Library Project become available to the current Flex Project.
- For component libraries that you've built in another workspace or received from another developer, you can do either of the following:
  - Add a folder containing one or more `.swc` files.
  - Add an individual SWC file to the Flex Project build path.

  In either case, you must ensure that the Flex Library Project is open in Flash Builder before trying to modify the build path of the application's Flex Project.

Using the libs folder

Every new Flex Project has a folder named `libs` that's already a part of the project's source path. To use the `libs` folder, copy a SWC file into the project's `libs` folder, as shown in Figure 5.12. The classes and component in the component library are now immediately available to the Flex Project.

FIGURE 5.10

Setting the Flex Build Path in the Project Properties dialog box

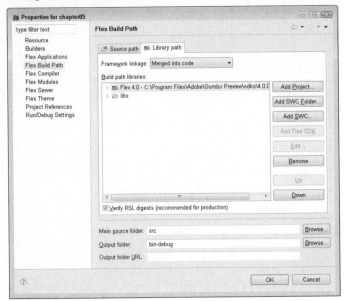

FIGURE 5.11

Adding a Library Project to a Flex Project's Library path

Copied SWC file

Flex project

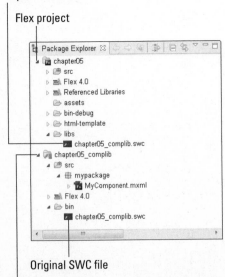

Original SWC file

Flex library project

FIGURE 5.12

A component library in a Flex Project's `libs` folder

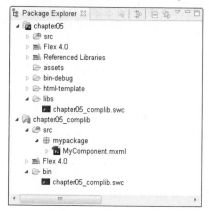

Caution

When you copy a component library file that you created into the `libs` folder, you detach it from the Flex Library project that manages its source code. Each time you modify the library's code, you have to then re-copy the compiled library to the Flex project to make the modified code available. The `libs` folder is most effectively used when you add libraries that you have received from other developers, when you aren't managing the library's source code. ■

Flex Library Projects enable you to easily switch back and forth between shared code that's managed in the library and the application-specific code in your application's project. This can be especially handy when working with desktop and Web applications that share many components but are delivered differently.

Regardless of how you create and use a component library, it's a valuable architecture that enables you to package and manage one or more components for use and reuse in your Flex applications.

Tip

You can't run an MXML application from directly within a Flex library project. During library project development, you should create a Flex project with at least one application that's used to test library project components and classes. ■

Creating Flash-based Components

Flash Builder 4 adds a new feature that enables you to quickly and easily create components in Flash Professional CS5 for use in Flex applications. While previous versions of Flex and Flash have supported creating and using such components, the workflow wasn't particularly easy. Developers had to install extra software and then manually import the resulting components into their Flex projects.

In Flash Builder 4, you start in Design mode. Flash Builder's Components view enables you to add a new Flash component, switches over to Flash Professional to enable you to develop the component's functionality, and then returns to Flash Builder for integration of the component into the application.

Caution

You must have Flash Professional CS5 installed on your system to create new Flash-based components from within Flash Builder 4. ■

Follow these steps to create and use a Flash component:

1. **Create a new Flex application.**

2. **View the application in Design mode.**

3. **Open the Custom section of the Components view.** As shown in Figure 5.13, the Components view has options to add Flash Professional Components and Flash Professional Containers.

4. **Drag the New Flash Professional Component option into the application.** The new component hasn't been implemented yet, but it's temporarily represented by a placeholder graphic, as shown in Figure 5.14.

5. **Make sure the new Flash component is selected in Design mode, and then in the Properties view (see Figure 5.15), click Create in Adobe Flash.** A dialog box, shown in Figure 5.16, appears that prompts you for the new component's Class name and SWC file name.

6. **Set the Class name as desired.**

7. **Set the SWC filename as desired, but ensure that it has a file extension of .swc.**

8. **Click Create.**

FIGURE 5.13

The New Flash Component option in the Components view

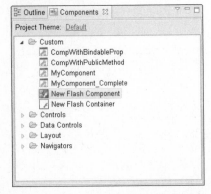

FIGURE 5.14

A new Flash component in Design mode

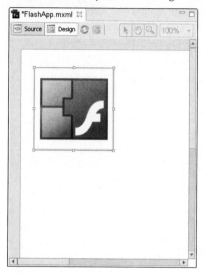

FIGURE 5.15

Properties view for a new Flash component

FIGURE 5.16

Setting the class name and SWC filename

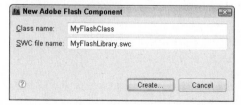

When you complete the wizard, Flash opens on your computer with your new component file open for editing. Here are some tips for working on the component:

- **The Flash component initially has a single layer.** It's a good idea to immediately create a new layer for your custom content.

- **The default layer has a rectangle shape with a light gray (#CCCCCC) fill and a dashed outline stroke.** This shape is optional; you can delete it, but it's useful as a background object to show the size of the Flash component in the hosting Flex application.

- **The Flash component has Publish settings that require Flash Player 10 and ActionScript 3.** You must use ActionScript 3, and not ActionScript 2, to retain compatibility with Flex.

After completing your component, click Done in the Flash interface, shown in Figure 5.17.

FIGURE 5.17

This Flash component uses a Shape tween, a feature of Flash Professional that isn't available in the Flex SDK.

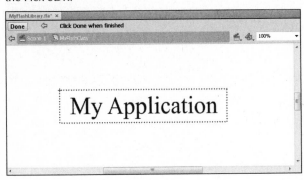

After the Flash component has been exported, return to Flash Builder. A preview of your component should appear in Design mode.

When you create a new Flash component from Flash Builder's Design mode, these new files are created in the project's `assets` folder:

- **An FLA file.** The Flash source file.

- **A SWF file.** A compiled Flash application file. (This file is created as a side effect of the Flash compilation process and doesn't do anything in your application.)

- **A SWC file.** A compiled Flash component library file.

The SWC file is also copied to the project's `libs` folder to make it a part of the project's build path.

On the Web

The `chapter05` project includes an application file named `FlashApp.mxml` that incorporates a Flash component. The source files for the component, `MyFlashLibrary.fla`, `MyFlashLibrary.swf`, and `MyFlashLibrary.swc` are in the project's `assets` folder, and another copy of the component SWC file is in the project's `libs` folder. ■

Tip

To edit the Flash Professional component, select it in Design mode, then click Edit in Flash Professional in the Properties view. Alternatively, you can double-click the component in Design mode. Either way, the component is re-opened in Flash for editing. ■

Summary

In this chapter, I described the use of binding expression and MXML components in developing Flex applications. You learned the following:

- Bindings are used to move data between objects and expressions.

- Bindings can be created with binding expressions or the `<Binding/>` tag.

- A binding creates a broadcaster/listener relationship between two ActionScript expressions.

- You can define two-way bindings between components with streamlined syntax that was introduced in the Flex 4 SDK.

- An MXML component is a building block of a Flex application that encapsulates functionality.

- MXML components are frequently used to create the view modules in a model-view-controller application architecture.

- MXML components are really classes that support properties, methods, and other members of the ActionScript class architecture.

- Component libraries can be used to package and manage components and classes.

- Component libraries are useful for sharing code with multiple projects and applications.

- Flash Builder 4 enables you to easily create Flash-based components that can be integrated into your Flex application. You must have Flash Professional CS5 installed on your computer to use this feature.

Debugging Flex Applications

Flash Builder includes powerful tools that enable you to easily debug and fine-tune your applications. Of course, software without bugs is a mythical beast — at least at the beginning of a software development project. In many cases, the question of whether you complete your application within the time you originally estimate depends on how quickly you can find and fix an application's defects, or bugs.

As with many good integrated development environments, Flash Builder includes a variety of tools to help you find and fix an application's issues and understand what's happening inside the application at runtime, including these tools:

- **The trace() function.** Sends runtime messages to the Flash Builder console and other logging targets.

- **The <s:TraceTarget/> tag.** Defines runtime tracing for network communications.

- **Breakpoints.** Suspends an application's execution and enables you to inspect its internal state at runtime.

- **Variable and expression tools.** Displays the value of various ActionScript expressions while an application is suspended in a breakpoint.

- **Profiling tools.** Enables you to see what's happening at runtime in terms of performance and memory usage.

- **Network Monitor.** Enables you to trace network traffic at runtime between a Flex client application and an application server when exchanging RPC (Remote Procedure Call) requests and responses.

In this chapter, I describe the tools you can use to debug and test your Flex applications.

IN THIS CHAPTER

Understanding debugging basics

Starting a debugging session

Using the trace() function

Using the Logging API

Creating self-logging components

Using breakpoints

Setting breakpoint properties

Inspecting data

Profiling Flex applications

Inspecting network traffic with the Network Monitor

On the Web

To use the sample code for this chapter, import the `chapter06.fxp` **Flex project archive file from the Web site files into your Flash Builder workspace.** ■

Debugging Basics

Debugging simply means that when you run an application, you want special debugging information that helps you find and fix application issues. Debugging with Flex requires the right kind of file and the right kind of runtime environment. Before executing debugging tasks, you need to be sure of three things:

- You are using the debug version of Adobe Flash Player.
- You are using the debug version of the application.
- You are running the application in debug mode.

If you're not sure whether you're running the debugger version of Flash Player, follow these steps to find out:

1. **Navigate to any site that contains Flash content, such as** www.adobe.com.
2. **Move the cursor over the Flash presentation and right-click (or Ctrl+click on Mac OS X).**
3. **Examine the context menu that appears.**

If the menu contains a Debugger menu item, even if it's disabled as shown in Figure 6.1, then you're running the debugger version of Flash Player.

If you don't see the Debugger menu item, you'll need to uninstall Flash Player and then reinstall the correct version before using any of the debugging tools in Flash Builder.

FIGURE 6.1

The Debugger menu item is disabled, but present, indicating that the Flash Player dubugger is running.

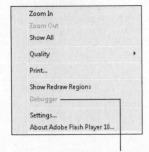

The Debugger menu choice

Cross-Reference

See Chapter 1 for more information on getting and installing different versions of Adobe Flash Player. ■

The debug version of the application

When you create a Flex Project in Flash Builder, the New Flex Project wizard creates an *output* folder in which the debug version of the application and its supporting files are created. As I described in Chapter 3, the application's debug version file size is significantly larger than the release version that you deploy to your Web site or users' desktops because it includes special information and functionality that can be used in a debugging session both by Flash Builder's debugging tools and by the `fdb` command-line debugger.

The default name of the output folder is `bin-debug`. The name of the compiled debug version of the application is the same as the main application source file, but it has the `.swf` file extension.

Tip

In Flex Projects that don't use an application server, the output folder is normally a subfolder of the project's root folder, such as `/bin-debug`. In projects that do use an application server, the `bin-debug` folder is typically created under the document root of the testing Web server and then made accessible in the Flex Package Explorer view through an Eclipse linked folder. ■

Running an application in debug mode

Follow these steps to run an application in debug mode:

1. Open the application you want to debug in Flash Builder.
2. Choose Run ⇨ Debug [application source file] from the Flash Builder menu.

Tip

If you're using the plug-in version of Flash Builder, the Debug menu choice runs the last debugging configuration or enables you to select from a list of configurations. ■

You also can debug an application with the Debug button on the toolbar. This button is next to the Run button and can be used in two ways:

- When you click the Debug button, Flash Builder launches a debug session with the currently displayed application, or the default application if the current file is a component or class source file.

- When you click the arrow on the edge of the Debug button, as shown in Figure 6.2, you see a list of the current project's applications and can select one to debug.

When you debug a Web application, it opens in the browser with the same URL as when you run in standard mode. You can tell that a debug session is running in Flash Builder, though. As shown in Figure 6.3, Flash Builder's Console view appears whenever a debug session starts and displays a debugging message indicating which file is being debugged.

FIGURE 6.2

Launching a debug session

FIGURE 6.3

The Console view during a debug session

The Console view displaying the currently running application file name

Managing the Console view

The Console view in its default state displays text messages without any word wrapping. You can change this behavior through the view's preferences:

1. Choose Window ⇨ Preferences.

2. In the Preferences dialog box, choose Run/Debug ⇨ Console.

3. As shown in Figure 6.4, select the Fixed width console option and set a line length between 80 characters (the default) and 1,000 characters.

4. Change any other options, and click OK.

The Console view now word wraps long lines so you don't have to scroll horizontally to see entire messages.

FIGURE 6.4

The Console view Preferences dialog box

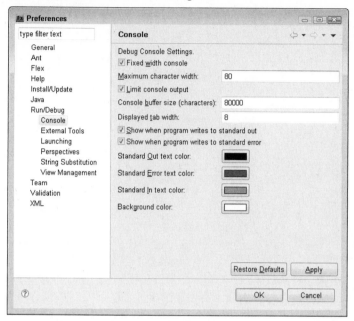

Terminating a debugging session

You should always explicitly terminate a debugging session before trying to run or debug an application again. You can terminate a debugging session in many ways:

- Choose Run ➪ Terminate from the Flash Builder menu.
- As shown in Figure 6.5, click the square red Terminate button in the Console view.
- Click the square red Terminate button in the Debug view (visible in the Flex Debugging perspective).
- Close the browser in which the application is running (for a Web application).
- Close the application (for a desktop application).

Tip

When you terminate a Web application's debugging session from within Flash Builder, the browser sometimes closes automatically, depending on which Web browser and operating system you're using and whether any other tabs or browser windows are open. For example, provided that no other sites are open, Internet Explorer and Firefox on Windows always close automatically. Firefox on the Mac doesn't always close automatically. The fact that this behavior differs from one operating system to another is not a cause for concern. ■

FIGURE 6.5

The Console view's Terminate button

The Terminate button

Using trace() and the Logging API

With Flex, you can generate and send logging messages to Flash Builder and other logging targets at runtime. Tracing is typically useful when you're trying to get runtime information about the following:

- Variable values
- The order of application execution
- Whether various bits of code are being executed as expected

In its simplest use, logging is accomplished through use of the trace() method. More advanced logging techniques are also available through an interface known as the Logging API.

Using the trace() function

The trace() function is *global* to Flash Player; that is, it's always available without your having to reference or import an ActionScript class. The purpose of the trace() function is to send a text message to a logging target. In its simplest form, trace is called with a String value:

```
trace('A tracing message');
```

You also can pass in variables and concatenated expressions that can result in a String:

```
trace("The value of myVariable is " + myVariable);
```

In fact, any object that can serialize to a String can be passed to trace(). In this example, an Array of String values is passed to trace():

```
trace(['hello', 'world']);
```

Because the Array class is automatically serialized as a comma-delimited string, the resulting output message looks like this:

```
hello,world
```

Trace messages in Flash Builder's Console view

When you debug a Flex application with Flash Builder, the value you pass into `trace()` is displayed in Flash Builder's Console view.

Tip

Calls to `trace()` are ignored when you run, rather than debug, an application even though the same debug version of your application is being executed. These calls are also stripped from an application's release version, so you can leave any calls to `trace()` in an application without affecting runtime performance or file size. ∎

Try these steps to see the `trace()` function at work:

1. Create a new Flex application with the following code:

```
<?xml version="1.0" encoding="utf-8"?>
<s:Application xmlns:fx="http://ns.adobe.com/mxml/2009"
  xmlns:s="library://ns.adobe.com/flex/spark"
  xmlns:mx="library://ns.adobe.com/flex/mx">
  <s:layout>
    <s:VerticalLayout horizontalAlign="center" paddingTop="20"/>
  </s:layout>
  <s:Button label="Call Trace" click="trace('Button Clicked')"/>
</s:Application>
```

2. Click Debug, or press F11 (Windows) or ⌘+F11 (Mac), to debug the application.

3. Click Call Trace in the application to call `trace()`.

4. Switch back to Flash Builder, and look at the Console view. As shown in Figure 6.6, you should see the tracing message displayed in the Console view.

FIGURE 6.6

A tracing message in the Console view

Tracing message in the Console view

Sending tracing messages to flashlog.txt

Messages also can be saved to a text file named `flashlog.txt`. The `flashlog.txt` file is created by the debugger version of Flash Player in a particular folder on your system.

Configuring Flash Player with mm.cfg

You configure the use of `flashlog.txt` with another text file named `mm.cfg`. This file contains parameters that control what messages are sent to, and saved in, the file. The location of `mm.cfg` differs by operating system. Table 6.1 shows the location for each operating system that's supported by Flash Player.

Location of mm.cfg

Operating System	Location
Macintosh OS X	/Library/Application Support/Macromedia
Windows 95/98/ME	%HOMEDRIVE%\%HOMEPATH%
Windows 2000 & XP	C:\Documents and Settings\username
Windows Vista & 7	C:\Users\username
Linux	/home/username

To save both error reporting and tracing messages to the `flashlog.txt` file, add these parameters on their own separate lines in `mm.cfg`:

```
ErrorReportingEnable=1
TraceOutputFileEnable=1
```

After these settings have been created, the next time you debug a Flex application or Flash document, the `flashlog.txt` is created automatically. Each time you call `trace()`, the message is saved to the file, in addition to being sent to Flash Builder's Console view.

Location of flashlog.txt

The `flashlog.txt` file is placed in a particular location that differs by operating system. Table 6.2 shows the location of `flashlog.txt` for each operating system on which Flash Player is supported.

Location of flashlog.txt

Operating System	Location
Macintosh OS X	/Users/username/Library/Preferences/Macromedia/Flash Player/Logs
Windows 95/98/ME/2000/XP	C:\Documents and Settings\username\Application Data\Macromedia\Flash Player\Logs
Windows Vista & 7	C:\Users\username\AppData\Roaming\Macromedia\Flash Player\Logs
Linux	/home/username/.macromedia/Flash_Player/Logs

Tip

Both `mm.cfg` and `flashlog.txt` are simple text files and can be viewed and edited with any text editor. ■

Using the Logging API

The Logging API is an advanced architecture that enables you to filter logging messages that are generated by the Flex Framework, and send messages to a logging target of your choice. The Logging API consists of an ActionScript interface named `ILogger`, a class that implements `ILogger` named `LogLogger`, a singleton class named `Log`, and a predefined tracing target class named `TraceTarget`. You can extend the API (application programming interface) by creating your own versions of `ILogger` implementations and tracing targets, but you also can make very good use of the API with just these pre-built components.

Tip

ActionScript 3 enables developers to use interfaces to define the required elements of a class definition. An interface isn't the same thing as a class. For example, it doesn't implement any code in its method definitions, and you can't create an instance of an interface directly. Its purpose is to establish a contract that must be fulfilled by any classes that claim to implement its members.

In the Flex framework, interfaces are always named within an initial uppercase `I`, followed by a descriptive name. For example, the interface named `ILogger` can be described simply as "the Logger interface." ■

Using the Log class

You get started with the Logging API by creating a `Logger` object using the `Log` class's static `getLogger()` method. You can create custom logger objects that are sensitive to particular categories of events, and you can automatically include that category information in logging messages.

The syntax for `getLogger()` is:

```
private var myLogger:ILogger = Log.getLogger("myCategory");
```

The category you pass into `getLogger()` must be a nonblank string. If the category you provide is registered by an existing class that implements `ILogger`, you get an instance of that class. Otherwise, you get an instance of a class named `mx.logging.LogLogger` that implements basic logging functions.

The Logging API supports these levels, in ascending order of panic:

- ALL
- DEBUG
- INFO
- WARN
- ERROR
- FATAL

The Log class implements these methods that enable you to determine whether a logging target has been defined for various logging levels:

- `isDebug():Boolean`
- `isInfo():Boolean`
- `isWarn():Boolean`
- `isError():Boolean`
- `isFatal():Boolean`

Using Logger objects

A logger class implements the `ILogger` interface. The interface includes these methods to send messages to a logging target:

- `debug(message:String, ... rest):void`
- `error(message:String, ... rest):void`
- `fatal(message:String, ... rest):void`
- `info(message:String, ... rest):void`
- `warn(message:String, ... rest):void`
- `log(level:int, message:String, ... rest):void`

After you've created a logger object, you send a logging message with one of the previous methods. Most methods create a message with a specific logging level. For example, to send a message with a level of DEBUG, you call the logger object's `debug()` method:

```
myLogger.debug("My debug message");
```

The debugging levels are defined as constants in a class named `mx.logging.LogEventLevel`. You also can send logging messages with the logger object's `log()` method and explicitly pass in the appropriate level:

```
myLogger.log(LogEventLevel.DEBUG, "My debug message");
```

Tip

The use of the `LogEventLevel` class's constants to select a logging level is considered a best practice. As with event names, any typos in the names of the constants result in compiler errors, as opposed to runtime errors or silent failures that you may encounter when using simple strings. ■

Logging levels are used to filter which messages are handled by various logging targets.

Self-logging components

The Logging API can be used to create a self-logging component. For example, the application in Listing 6.1 is a `Button` component that logs each click event to a logging target.

A self-logging button component

```xml
<?xml version="1.0" encoding="utf-8"?>
<s:Button xmlns:fx="http://ns.adobe.com/mxml/2009"
  xmlns:s="library://ns.adobe.com/flex/spark"
  xmlns:mx="library://ns.adobe.com/flex/mx"
  click="logEvent(event)">
  <fx:Script>
    <![CDATA[
      import mx.logging.Log;
      import mx.logging.ILogger;

      private var myLogger:ILogger = Log.getLogger("buttonEvents");

      private function logEvent(event:MouseEvent):void {
        myLogger.debug("LoggingButton " + event.target.id + " was clicked");
      }
    ]]>
  </fx:Script>
</s:Button>
```

On the Web

The code in Listing 6.1 is available in the Web site files in the `chapter06` project's `debug` package as `LoggingButton.mxml`. ■

Cross-Reference

The code sample in Listing 6.1 uses the Flex event model to handle component events. The event model is described in Chapter 7. ■

Using tracing targets

A tracing target is a class that can receive and process tracing messages. The `TraceTarget` class is included in the Flex Framework and is ideally suited to use in Flex applications.

When you use the `TraceTarget` class, the output of the Logging API behaves just like output you create with the `trace()` method. The messages appear in Flash Builder's Console view and, if you've configured Flash Player as described previously, are saved in `flashlog.txt`.

The `TraceTarget` class supports these properties:

- **fieldSeparator:String.** A string value to separate other values included in a logging message; defaults to a single space character.
- **includeCategory:Boolean.** Indicates whether to include the logging message's category in the logging message.

- **includeDate:Boolean.** Indicates whether to include the current date in the logging message.

- **includeLevel:Boolean.** Indicates whether to include the logging level in the logging message.

- **includeTime:Boolean.** Indicates whether to include the current time in the logging message.

- **level:int.** A logging level that this target will handle; defaults to `LogEventLevel.ALL`.

You can instantiate `TraceTarget` with either MXML or ActionScript. Use this syntax to instantiate the class in its simplest form:

```
<s:TraceTarget/>
```

New Feature

In Flex 4, the `<sTraceTarget/>` element must be placed inside the `<fx:Declarations>` element, along with other nonvisual object declarations:

```
<fx:Declarations>
  <s:TraceTarget/>
</fx:Declarations>  ■
```

Caution

The `Declarations` tag uses the `fx` prefix, because it's a core part of MXML. The `TraceTarget` tag can use either the `mx` or the `s` prefix, because although it's part of the Flex 3 class library, it's registered in the manifests for both the older MX and the new Spark component sets. ■

Tip

The `<s:TraceTarget/>` MXML declaration does not require an `id` property. Unless you need to call its methods or properties directly, the object can be declared anonymously. ■

In its default form, `TraceTarget` becomes a tracing target that handles all logging levels. However, the tracing messages you see include only the messages themselves and none of the other available logging data such as date, time, level, and category. Use this syntax to include all that information and separate the data elements from each other with a | (pipe) character:

```
<s:TraceTarget id="myTarget"
  includeCategory="true"
  includeLevel="true"
  includeDate="true"
  includeTime="true"
  fieldSeparator="|"/>
```

Finally, to make a tracing target display messages only for a particular logging level, use this syntax:

```
<s:TraceTarget id="myTarget"
  includeCategory="true"
  includeLevel="true"
  includeDate="true"
  includeTime="true"
  fieldSeparator="|"
  level="{LogEventLevel.DEBUG}"/>
```

Caution

In the last example, the `LogEventLevel` class would have to be imported before being referenced in the `TraceTarget.level` binding expression:

```
import mx.logging.LogEventLevel; ■
```

The resulting trace output generated by the self-logging button component in Listing 6.1 would look like this:

```
5/17/2009|21:43:44.051|[DEBUG]|buttonEvents|LoggingButton myLoggingButton was
    clicked
```

The application in Listing 6.2 uses the self-logging button and a `TraceTarget` object. The `TraceTarget` object is configured only to handle messages with a logging level of DEBUG and to include all available information in each message.

LISTING 6.2

An application with a self-logging component

```
<?xml version="1.0" encoding="utf-8"?>
<?xml version="1.0" encoding="utf-8"?>
<s:Application xmlns:fx="http://ns.adobe.com/mxml/2009"
  xmlns:s="library://ns.adobe.com/flex/spark"
  xmlns:mx="library://ns.adobe.com/flex/mx"
  xmlns:debug="debug.*">
  <fx:Declarations>
    <s:TraceTarget id="myTarget"
      includeCategory="true"
      includeLevel="true"
      includeDate="true"
      includeTime="true"
      level="{LogEventLevel.DEBUG}"
      fieldSeparator="|"/>
  </fx:Declarations>
  <fx:Script>
    <![CDATA[
      import mx.logging.LogEventLevel;
    ]]>
  </fx:Script>
  <debug:LoggingButton id="myLoggingButton" label="Log Click Event"
    horizontalCenter="0" top="20"/>
</s:Application>
```

On the Web

The code in Listing 6.2 is available in the Web site files in the `chapter06` project folder as `UseLogging Button.mxml`. ■

The Logging API can enable you to build applications that keep you informed about their actions during a debugging session without having to make constant calls to the `trace()` method. With some advanced ActionScript programming, you also can create your own custom logger and tracing target classes.

Using Breakpoints

A breakpoint enables you to suspend application execution at runtime and inspect the application's current state. Once you're in a breakpoint, you can look at variable values, evaluate arbitrary ActionScript expressions, and take other actions that help you figure out what's happening.

Setting and clearing breakpoints

Breakpoints can be set on any line that includes at least one ActionScript statement. For example, this code declares a button component but has no ActionScript code:

```
<s:Button label="Debug"/>
```

If you set a breakpoint on the line containing that MXML declaration and then run the application in debug mode, the breakpoint icon changes to display a little red X to indicate that it will be ignored by the debugger. If you then hover the mouse cursor over the breakpoint while the application is suspended, Flash Builder displays a tooltip saying that you can't put a breakpoint in that location.

If, however, the same MXML declaration includes an event handler that executes some ActionScript code, it becomes a valid target for a breakpoint:

```
<s:Button label="Debug" click="clickHandler()"/>
```

Because this version of the declaration executes an ActionScript statement, placing a breakpoint on that line successfully suspends the application when the user clicks the button.

Setting and removing breakpoints in an MXML or ActionScript editor

You can set or remove a breakpoint in an MXML or ActionScript editor. To do so, perform one of these actions:

- Place the cursor on the line where you want the breakpoint, and press Ctrl+Shift+B (Windows) or ⌘+Shift+B (Mac).
- Double-click the line number in the editor.
- As shown in Figure 6.7, right-click the line number in the editor, and select Toggle Breakpoint.

  As shown in Figure 6.8, the breakpoint appears as a small dot to the left of the line number.

FIGURE 6.7

Right-click a line number to see this context menu, and select Toggle Breakpoint.

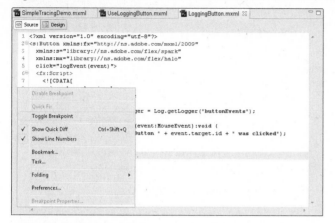

FIGURE 6.8

A Breakpoint represented by a small icon next to a line number

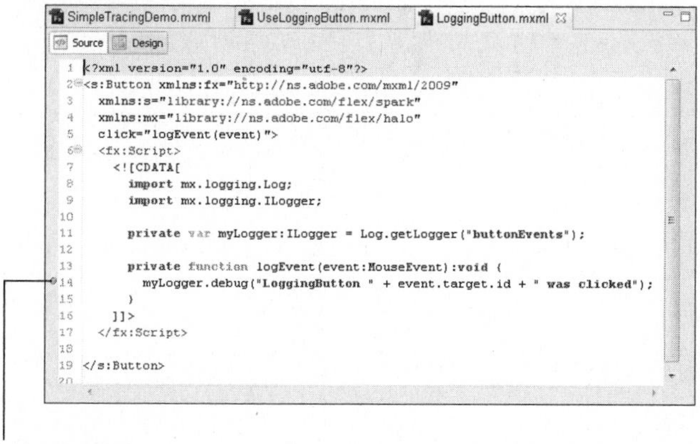

A breakpoint

Setting conditional breakpoints

Each breakpoint has a set of properties you can configure to determine when the breakpoint is triggered.

New Feature

Conditional breakpoints are a new feature of Flash Builder 4. ∎

You can set the following properties on each individual breakpoint:

- **Enabled.** A Boolean value indicating whether the breakpoint will be respected.
- **Hit Count.** A positive integer that indicates you only want to suspend the application when the breakpoint is hit the *nth* time.
- **Enable Condition.** An ActionScript expression. If it's a Boolean expression, it can be used to suspend the application only when the condition is true. Otherwise, use it to suspend the application only when the expression's value changes.

You can set breakpoint properties either from an MXML or ActionScript editor or from the Breakpoints view. Follow these steps:

1. **After creating a breakpoint in an ActionScript or MXML editor, right-click (or Ctrl+click on Mac) on the breakpoint icon next to the line number.**

2. **Select Breakpoint Properties from the context menu.**

3. **As shown in Figure 6.9, set the breakpoint properties.** For example, if you only want to suspend the application when a variable named myVar has a value of 3, select Enable Condition and then type this expression in the text box:

   ```
   myVar==3
   ```

4. **Click OK.**

FIGURE 6.9

The Breakpoint Properties dialog box

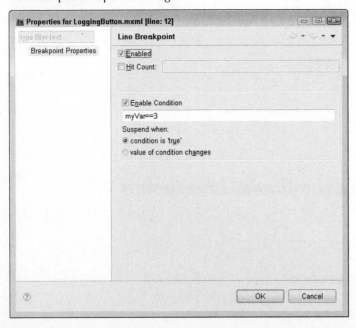

Caution

When setting a conditional breakpoint to be triggered only when a comparison of two values returns true, make sure you use the double-equals (==) comparison operator in the expression, rather than the single-equals (=) assignment operator. ■

Using the Breakpoints view

Flash Builder's Breakpoints view shows you the application's current breakpoints and enables you to add, remove, enable, or disable breakpoints as needed.

The Breakpoints view is displayed in the Flex Debugging perspective. To use the Breakpoints view, follow these steps:

1. **Choose Window ➪ Perspective ➪ Flex Debugging from the Flash Builder menu.**

2. **Click the Breakpoints tab in the upper-right corner of the Flash Builder interface.** The Breakpoints view, shown in Figure 6.10, displays all breakpoints for the current project.

FIGURE 6.10

The Breakpoints view

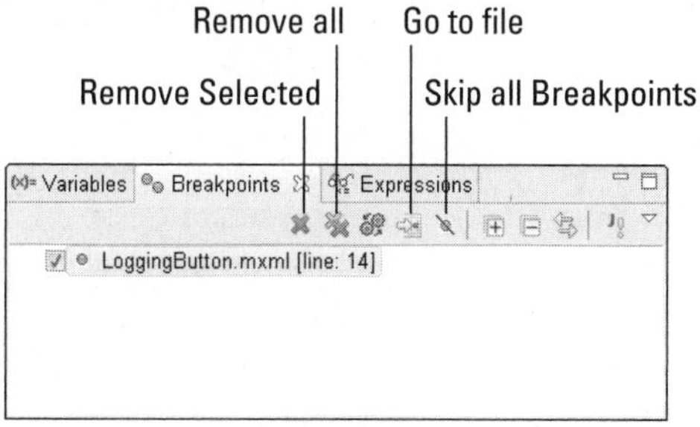

The Breakpoints view includes these tools:

- **Remove.** Removes the currently selected breakpoint.

- **Remove All.** Removes all breakpoints in the current project.

- **Show Breakpoints.** Supported by Selected Target; shows breakpoints only for a selected debug target.

- **Go to File for Breakpoint.** Opens file for current breakpoint and moves cursor to that position.

- **Skip All Breakpoints.** Causes debugging session to ignore breakpoints.

Click the appropriate button to use any of the tools listed previously. The Remove All Breakpoints tool requires you to confirm the operation.

Exporting breakpoints to an external file

The Breakpoints view enables you to export and import breakpoint definitions to external files. A breakpoints file has a file extension of `.bkpt`. Follow these steps to export breakpoints:

1. **Right-click anywhere in the Breakpoints view, and select Export Breakpoints from the context menu.**

2. **In the Export Breakpoints dialog box, shown in Figure 6.11, select the following:**

   - Which breakpoints you want to export

   - The file to which you want to export breakpoints

   - The Overwrite existing file without warning check box (if you want to overwrite your existing file)

FIGURE 6.11

The Export Breakpoints dialog box

3. **Click Finish to create the breakpoints file.**

A breakpoints export file is in XML format. Listing 6.3 shows the contents of a typical breakpoints file.

LISTING 6.3

An exported breakpoints file

```
<?xml version="1.0" encoding="UTF-8"?>
<breakpoints>
  <breakpoint enabled="true" persistant="true" registered="true">
    <resource path="/chapter06/src/debug/LoggingButton.mxml" type="1"/>
    <marker lineNumber="12"
      type="com.adobe.flexbuilder.debug.flash.lineBreakpoint.marker">
      <attrib name="org.eclipse.debug.core.enabled" value="true"/>
      <attrib name="org.eclipse.debug.core.id"
        value="com.adobe.flexbuilder.debug"/>
      <attrib name="message"
        value="Line breakpoint: LoggingButton.mxml [line: 12]"/>
    </marker>
  </breakpoint>
</breakpoints>
```

Importing breakpoints from an external breakpoint file

Follow these steps to import an external breakpoints file:

1. **Right-click anywhere in the Breakpoints view, and select Import Breakpoints from the context menu.**

2. **In the Import Breakpoints dialog box, shown in Figure 6.12, select these options, if appropriate:**

   - Whether you want to update existing breakpoints
   - Whether you want to automatically create breakpoint working sets

3. **Click Finish to import the breakpoints file.**

The breakpoints in the external file are imported and are immediately available in the Breakpoints view.

Using breakpoints in a debugging session

After you've set breakpoints, you can use them during a debugging session by executing the code on which the breakpoints are set.

When an application is running in debug mode and is suspended at a breakpoint, Flash Builder tries to take system focus. If you are not currently using the Flex Debugging perspective, the Confirm Perspective Switch dialog box, shown in Figure 6.13, prompts you to switch to that perspective.

FIGURE 6.12

Importing a breakpoints file

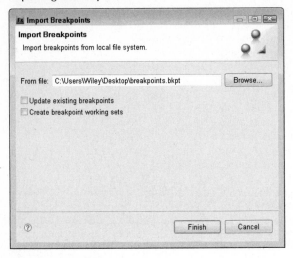

FIGURE 6.13

When a breakpoint has been activated, you're prompted to open the Flex Debugging perspective with the Confirm Perspective Switch dialog box.

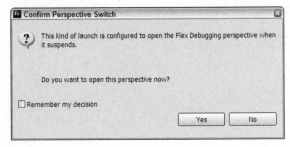

Tip

The Confirm Perspective Switch dialog box has an option that enables you to remember the decision to switch to the Flex Debugging perspective when you encounter a breakpoint. If you select this option, Flash Builder always switches to this perspective automatically in future uses of breakpoints. You can turn this on and off by selecting an option in the Run/Debug section of Flash Builder's Preferences dialog box. ■

After a breakpoint has been activated, Flash Builder shows you the current code execution position with the Debug Current Instruction Pointer, shown in Figure 6.14. If you move the cursor over the pointer icon, you see a pop-up window displaying information about the current line.

FIGURE 6.14

The Debug Current Instruction Pointer and current line information

Inspecting variables and expressions

When a breakpoint is active during a debugging session, Flash Builder enables you to inspect values of variables and objects that are in the application's scope. You can use two views for this purpose:

- The Variables view
- The Expressions view

Using the Variables view

The Variables view displays a tree of declared variables and object properties that are in scope at the point of the current instruction. Information in the Variables view is available only during a breakpoint; when you resume application execution, the Variables view no longer displays data.

The Variables view always has a tree item labeled `this`. The item refers to the application when the currently executing code is in the Application scope, or to the current component or class when the currently executing code is in that scope.

As shown in Figure 6.15, when you click the expansion icon with the + character next to `this`, you see a list of all properties of the application or current object. A tree item representing an object has an `inherited` branch that displays properties declared in the current object's inheritance hierarchy.

Note

Flex Builder 3 added the `inherited` branch to separate properties that are declared within the current class from those declared in its superclasses. ∎

Tip

The Variables tree is recursive; that is, you can click down to any object within the application, and then click the `inherited`⇨`$parent` item under the button and return to the `Application` object. ∎

FIGURE 6.15

The Variables view

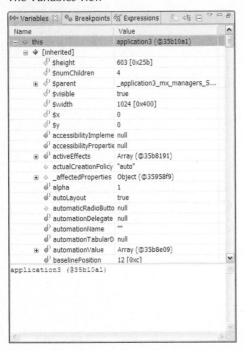

When you place a breakpoint inside a function, the Variables view displays tree items for any variables that are declared within the function. For example, the following code declares a variable named myVar data typed as a Number:

```
private function myFunction():void
{
    var myVar:Number=1;
} //place breakpoint here
```

When you stop code execution with a breakpoint on the function's final line, the resulting Variables view displays the value of myVar as 1, as shown in Figure 6.16.

Setting watchpoints

A *watchpoint* is an instruction to suspend the application at runtime when a particular variable's value changes.

New Feature

Watchpoints are a new feature of Flash Builder 4. ∎

FIGURE 6.16

Displaying a local variable in the Variables view

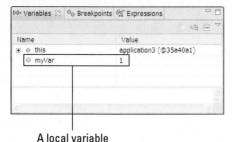

A local variable

You set watchpoints in the Variables view while the application is already suspended. You can set watchpoints on these types of variables:

- A variable set outside any functions as a property of the current application or module
- A property of a complex object declared locally within a function

You cannot set watchpoints on these types of variables:

- Local variables defined within a function
- Implicit getter functions that use the `get` keyword

Caution

Watchpoints are removed when the current debugging session is terminated. If you want to set them again, do so after suspending the application at a breakpoint. ■

The application in Listing 6.4 triggers a breakpoint in one method and changes a variable value in another.

LISTING 6.4

An application that can be used to trigger a watchpoint

```
<?xml version="1.0" encoding="utf-8"?>
<s:Application xmlns:fx="http://ns.adobe.com/mxml/2009"
  xmlns:s="library://ns.adobe.com/flex/spark"
  xmlns:mx="library://ns.adobe.com/flex/mx">
  <s:layout>
    <s:VerticalLayout horizontalAlign="center" paddingTop="20"/>
  </s:layout>
  <fx:Script>
    <![CDATA[
```

continued

LISTING 6.4 *(continued)*

```
    private var xyz:String;
    protected function breakpointButton_clickHandler(
      event:MouseEvent):void
    {
      trace('debug');
    }
    protected function watchpointButton_clickHandler(
      event:MouseEvent):void
    {
      xyz='New Value';
    }
  ]]>
</fx:Script>
<s:Button id="breakpointButton" label="Trigger Breakpoint"
  click="breakpointButton_clickHandler(event)"/>
<s:Button id="watchpointButton" label="Trigger Watchpoint"
  click="watchpointButton_clickHandler(event)"/>
</s:Application>
```

On the Web

The code in Listing 6.4 is available in the Web site files in the `chapter06` project as `UseWatchpoint.mxml`. ∎

Follow these steps to use a watchpoint:

1. Create a breakpoint at a line containing an ActionScript statement, such as the call to trace() in Listing 6.4.

2. Run the application in debug mode and take whatever action is required to trigger the breakpoint.

3. Open the Variables view in the Debugging perspective.

4. Locate the variable you want to watch.

5. Right-click on the variable and select Toggle Watchpoint.

6. Open the Debug view and resume the application.

7. Take an action that results in changing the variable, such as the second function in Listing 6.4.

You should see that Flash Builder suspends the application right after the line of code that changed the variable value. Your changed variable, along with any other changed variables, should be highlighted to yellow in the Variables view.

Tip

If you trigger a watchpoint as a result of inline ActionScript code inside an MXML event listener, such this:

```
click="xyz='New Value'"
```

the next ActionScript statement to be executed might be part of the Flex SDK. In this example, the application would be suspended and the source code file `ButtonBase.as` would be opened, because its event handling code is the next code to be executed. To prevent this, move the code that changes the variable's value to a custom function, and then call the function from the MXML event listener. ■

Using the Expressions view

In many cases, evaluating an arbitrary ActionScript expression is useful. Here are some cases that come to mind:

- An expression that's deeply nested in the Variable view and hard to locate
- A compound expression that executes calculations that aren't pre-declared in the application code

The Expressions view is available in the Flex Debugging perspective and enables you to evaluate these expressions easily. As with the Variables view, information in the Expressions view is available only during a breakpoint; when you resume application execution, the Expressions view no longer displays data.

To use the Expressions view, first click the Expressions tab in the Flex Debugging perspective's upper-right area, shown in Figure 6.17.

FIGURE 6.17

The Expressions tab

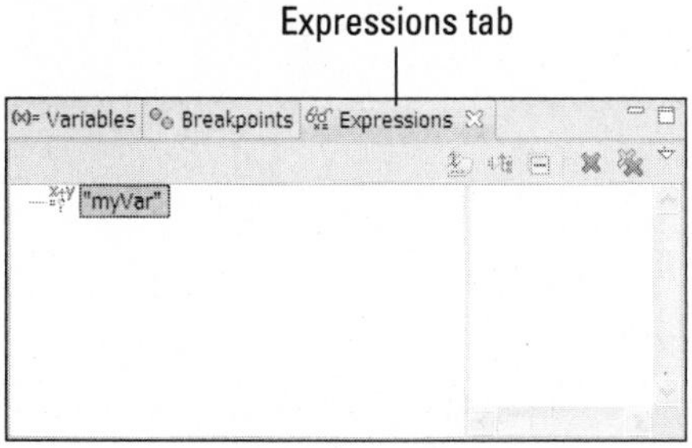

Adding an expression

You can add an expression either in the Expressions view or in the MXML or ActionScript editor that refers to an expression.

To add an expression in the Expressions view, right-click anywhere in the view and select Add Watch Expression from the context menu. Type the expression into the Add Watch Expression dialog box, shown in Figure 6.18.

To add an expression from within an MXML or ActionScript editor, right-click the expression in the code and select Create Watch Expression from the context menu. You should see the expression added to the Expressions view.

Tip

You also can evaluate a pre-coded expression during a breakpoint in an MXML or ActionScript editor by moving the mouse over the expression. A tool tip is displayed showing the expression's name and current value. ∎

Adding a watch expression

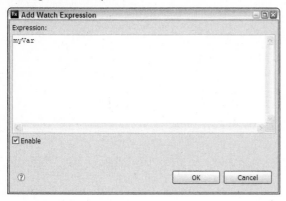

The Expressions view has some limitations in terms of the types of expressions that can be evaluated. Here are some examples:

- You can't include a namespace or a fully qualified package in a class reference.

- You can't use the keyword `super`.

- E4X predicate filtering expressions are not supported, such as `myNode.(@ myAtt='aValue')`.

Tip

If you need to refer to a class by its fully qualified name in a dynamic expression, including its package prefix, use this code:

```
getDefinitionByName("spark.components.Button");
```
∎

Controlling application execution with the Debug view

When a breakpoint is active in a debugging session, Flash Builder's Debug view enables you to step through, resume, or terminate application execution. The Debug view, shown in Figure 6.19, has these tools:

- **Resume.** This tools resumes code execution. If a breakpoint is encountered prior to enabling you to interact with the application, you return to Flash Builder. Otherwise, you can switch back to the application and continue interactions.

- **Suspend.** When an application is running, selecting this tool suspends the application without a predefined breakpoint and enables you to inspect variables and expressions.

- **Terminate.** This tool terminates the debugging session. The Terminate button in the Console view is identical in appearance and function.

- **Disconnect.** This tool disconnects the debugger when debugging remotely.

- **Step Into.** When called with the cursor on a function call, this tool steps into the function call.

- **Step Over.** When called with the cursor on a function call, this tool executes the function and moves to the next line of code.

- **Step Return.** This tool completes the current function and stops at the next line of code after the function has been called.

Tip

When you step through code in Flash Builder, code execution pauses on each ActionScript statement, expression evaluation, and variable declaration. At times you'll find that you even step into the source code of Flex internal library classes, where available. ■

FIGURE 6.19

The Debug view

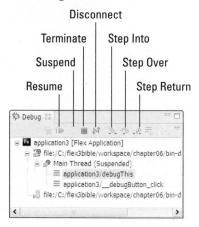

The Debug view tools described previously also are available as menu selections and, in most cases, keyboard shortcuts. For example, to terminate a debugging session, choose Run ➪ Terminate from the Flash Builder menu or press Ctrl+F2 on Windows or ⌘+F2 on Mac OS X. Figure 6.20 shows the Run menu as it appears during a debugging session. Notice that each feature's keyboard shortcut is noted on the menu.

New Feature

Flash Builder 4 adds a new feature named Run to Line. While in a breakpoint, right-click on a line of ActionScript code that you want to run to, then select Run to Line from the context menu. The application resumes and then is suspended again at the line you selected. ■

Flash Builder's Run menu during a debugging session

Profiling Flex Applications

Flash Builder includes tools for profiling Flex applications at runtime, providing valuable information about the frequency and duration of method calls, the size and number of object instances in memory, and overall memory usage.

Note

The Flex profiling tools were added in Flex Builder 3. They are included only with a Flash Builder Premium license. ■

The profiling tools are packaged in a Flash Builder perspective named the Flash Profile perspective (formerly named the Flex Profiling perspective). You can profile an application from the Flash Builder toolbar or menu.

Follow these steps to run an application in profiling mode:

1. **Close any open browser windows.** (If you have a browser window already open, profiling may not start correctly.)

2. **Choose Run ⇨ Profile from the Flash Builder menu and select the application you want to profile.** You also can click the Profile button on the toolbar.

   When a profiling connection has been established, you're prompted for profiling options, as shown in Figure 6.21.

3. **Select options and click Resume.**

4. **Once the application has resumed execution in the browser, execute application functions and switch back to Flash Builder to see how the application is performing internally.**

As shown in Figure 6.22, the Memory Usage view displays a graph showing overall memory usage.

FIGURE 6.21

Selecting profiling options

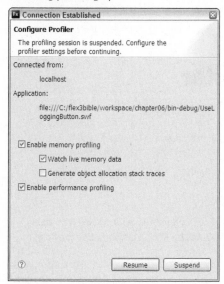

FIGURE 6.22

The Memory Usage view in the Flex Profiling perspective

As shown in Figure 6.23, the Live Objects view displays statistical data about objects in Flash Player memory.

FIGURE 6.23

The Live Objects view in the Flex Profiling perspective

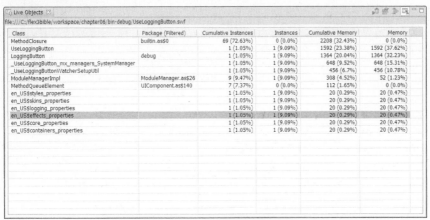

Class	Package (Filtered)	Cumulative Instances	Instances	Cumulative Memory	Memory
MethodClosure	builtin.as$0	69 (72.63%)	0 (0.0%)	2208 (32.43%)	0 (0.0%)
UseLoggingButton		1 (1.05%)	1 (9.09%)	1592 (23.38%)	1592 (37.62%)
LoggingButton	debug	1 (1.05%)	1 (9.09%)	1364 (20.04%)	1364 (32.23%)
_UseLoggingButton_mx_managers_SystemManager		1 (1.05%)	1 (9.09%)	648 (9.52%)	648 (15.31%)
_UseLoggingButtonWatcherSetupUtil		1 (1.05%)	1 (9.09%)	456 (6.7%)	456 (10.78%)
ModuleManagerImpl	ModuleManager.as$26	9 (9.47%)	1 (9.09%)	308 (4.52%)	52 (1.23%)
MethodQueueElement	UIComponent.as$140	7 (7.37%)	0 (0.0%)	112 (1.65%)	0 (0.0%)
en_US$styles_properties		1 (1.05%)	1 (9.09%)	20 (0.29%)	20 (0.47%)
en_US$skins_properties		1 (1.05%)	1 (9.09%)	20 (0.29%)	20 (0.47%)
en_US$logging_properties		1 (1.05%)	1 (9.09%)	20 (0.29%)	20 (0.47%)
en_US$effects_properties		1 (1.05%)	1 (9.09%)	20 (0.29%)	20 (0.47%)
en_US$core_properties		1 (1.05%)	1 (9.09%)	20 (0.29%)	20 (0.47%)
en_US$containers_properties		1 (1.05%)	1 (9.09%)	20 (0.29%)	20 (0.47%)

Using the Network Monitor

Flash Builder 4 includes a new feature called the Network Monitor, which can be used to debug network traffic between a Flex application running from the Web or the desktop that communicates with an application server at runtime. It works with any nonencrypted HTTP request, including those created with Flash Player's URLRequest and the Flex SDK's RPC components (HTTPService, WebService, and RemoteObject).

Note

The Network Monitor does not work with data exchanged over a secure connection with SSL or with data that's managed by the Data Management Service (a service hosted by Adobe LiveCycle Data Services). ■

Developers who've used Flash Remoting since its early days to communicate with application servers such as ColdFusion might remember the NetConnection Debugger, a similar tool that enabled you to trace and inspect network traffic at runtime. The new Network Monitor brings back these capabilities and improves on them. It's tightly integrated into Flash Builder, so you no longer need to start up an extra application to get the debugging information you need.

You can use the Network Monitor to inspect the size and contents of requests and responses sent between the Flex client and the application server and to find out how long the server takes to respond to a request.

Note

In the tutorials in this section, I describe how to use the Network Monitor with ColdFusion and a set of sample Flex applications that communicate with ColdFusion at runtime. ColdFusion provides all of the services that work with Network Monitor: REST-style data exchange with XML, SOAP-based Web services, and AMF (Action

Message Format) with Flash Remoting. If you don't use ColdFusion, you can adapt these tutorials for use with any application server that supports one or more of these protocols. ■

Web Resource

The ColdFusion code for the tutorials in this section is already written and doesn't require a database. It's compatible with both ColdFusion 8 and ColdFusion 9, so if you're an experienced ColdFusion developer, you can use whichever version you already have installed. If you don't already have ColdFusion, you can download and install the developer edition for free from www.adobe.com/products/coldfusion. ■

Cross-Reference

I describe how to integrate Flex applications with HTTPService and XML in Chapter 23, with SOAP-based Web services in Chapter 25, and with ColdFusion in Chapter 28. ■

Configuring a Flex project for use with ColdFusion

The Web site files for this chapter include three applications that you can use to explore the Network Monitor. Each uses one of the Flex SDK's RPC components to communicate with the server and retrieve data.

Configuring a Flex project to use ColdFusion

First I describe how to configure a Flex project for use with ColdFusion. Flash Builder 4 enables you to configure an existing Flex project for use with an application server; this is a new feature that wasn't available with Flex Builder 3.

1. In the Package Explorer view, right-click on the project (Ctrl+click on the Mac) and select Properties from the context menu.

2. In the Properties dialog box, choose Flex Server from the category list, as shown in Figure 6.24.

3. Set the Application server type to ColdFusion with ColdFusion Flash Remoting.

4. Set the ColdFusion installation type to Standalone.

5. Uncheck Use default location for ColdFusion server.

6. **Enter the ColdFusion root folder location.** The default location for ColdFusion 9 on Windows with the most commonly used server configuration is C:\ColdFusion9; on Mac OS X, it's /Applications/ColdFusion9.

Note

The ColdFusion installation I'm using for this tutorial is on Windows and uses ColdFusion's development Web server, listening on port 8500 (the default). If your ColdFusion installation differs, or you're using a different application server, make any necessary adjustments for your application server, ColdFusion version, installation location, operating system, and Web server. If you're using ColdFusion and the Web site files, be sure to name the output folder chapter06 under the Web root folder as indicated, as the Flex and ColdFusion code both assume this relative location for the Web service and Flash Remoting applications. ■

FIGURE 6.24

Configuring the Flex project for use with ColdFusion

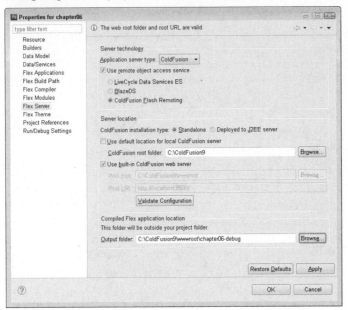

7. **Click Validate Configuration to confirm that Flash Builder is able to connect to ColdFusion.** You should see a message at the top of the dialog box indicating that the Web root folder and root URL are valid. The Compiled Flex application location defaults to a folder named `chapter06-debug` under the ColdFusion Web root folder.

8. **Change the Compiled Flex application location to a folder named chapter06 (that is, remove the –debug suffix from the default setting).**

9. **Click OK to save your changes.**

When you set the Compiled Flex application location (also known as the *output folder*) to a location under the application server's document root folder, the project's nonembedded assets are copied to this folder as well. This includes the XML files and ColdFusion Components (CFCs) that are called from this tutorial's sample Flex applications at runtime.

Testing the Flex applications

Next, follow these steps to open and test each of the sample applications:

1. **Open HTTPServiceDemo.mxml from the project's default package and look at the code.** This application retrieves a static XML file from the server with an instance of the `HTTPService` class and saves its data to an `ArrayCollection` when the `result` event is dispatched:

```
<s:HTTPService id="service" url="data/contacts.xml"
  result="arData = event.result.contacts.row"
  fault="Alert.show(event.fault.faultString,
    event.fault.faultCode)"
  showBusyCursor="true"/>
<s:ArrayCollection id="arData"/>
```

2. **Run the application.** As shown in Figure 6.25, the application has a `DataGrid` and a `Button` control.

3. **Click Get Data in the application.** After a few moments, the data should be displayed in the `DataGrid`.

FIGURE 6.25

The completed application displaying data retrieved from ColdFusion

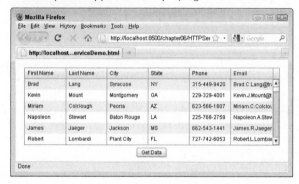

Tip

If the application's remote request fails, return to Flash Builder and select Project ⇨ Clean from the menu. Then click OK in the Clean dialog box. Flash Builder rebuilds the project from scratch and copies the data and CFC files to the server. Then run and test the application again. ■

4. **Close the browser and return to Flash Builder.**

5. **Open WebServiceDemo.mxml and look at the code.** This application retrieves data from the server with a call to a SOAP-based Web service operation, using an instance of the `WebService` class:

```
<s:WebService id="service"
  wsdl="cfc/ContactService.cfc?wsdl"
  result="arData = event.result as ArrayCollection"
  fault="Alert.show(event.fault.faultString,
         event.fault.faultCode)"
  showBusyCursor="true"/>
<s:ArrayCollection id="arData"/>
```

6. **Run the application and click Get Data.** After a few moments, the data should be displayed in the `DataGrid`.

7. **Close the browser and return to Flash Builder.**

8. **Open RemoteObjectDemo.mxml and look at the code.** This application retrieves data from the server with a Flash Remoting call to a ColdFusion Component (CFC) function, using an instance of the `RemoteObject` class:

```
<s:RemoteObject id="service"
  destination="ColdFusion"
  source="chapter06.cfc.ContactService"
  result="arData.source = event.result as Array"
  fault="Alert.show(event.fault.faultString,
          event.fault.faultCode);"
  showBusyCursor="true"/>
<s:ArrayCollection id="arData"/>
<valueObjects:Contact id="dummyVO"/>
```

9. **Run the application and click Get Data.** After a moment, the data should be displayed in the `DataGrid`.

10. **Close the browser and return to Flash Builder.**

Note

The Web service and Flash Remoting applications call the same ColdFusion code on the server. This server-side code opens an XML file and parses it, then delivers the data as an array of value objects in the response:

```
<cfcomponent>
  <cffunction name="getData"
    returntype="chapter06.cfc.Contact[]" access="remote">
    <cfset var contact = "">
    <cfset var contactObj = "">
    <cffile action="read" file="#expandPath('contacts.xml')#"
      variable="contactsStr">
    <cfset contactsXML = xmlParse(contactsStr)>
    <cfset contacts=contactsxml.contacts.row>
    <cfset arData = arrayNew(1)>
    <cfloop from="1" to="#arrayLen(contacts)#" index="i">
      <cfscript>
        contact = contacts[i];
        contactObj =
          createObject("component", "chapter06.cfc.Contact");
        contactObj.contactid = contact.contactid.xmltext;
        contactObj.firstname = contact.firstname.xmltext;
        contactObj.lastname = contact.lastname.xmlText;
        contactObj.streetaddress =
          contact.streetaddress.xmlText;
        contactObj.city = contact.city.xmlText;
        contactObj.state = contact.state.xmlText;
        contactObj.phone = contact.phone.xmlText;
        contactObj.email = contact.email.xmlText;
        arrayAppend(arData, contactObj);
```

```
        </cfscript>
      </cfloop>
      <cfreturn arData>
    </cffunction>
</cfcomponent> ▪
```

Tracing network traffic

Once your application is successfully retrieving data from a server with an RPC component, you can use the Network Monitor to trace and inspect the request and response packets that are exchanged at runtime between the Flex application (the client) and the application server.

To use the Network Monitor, it must be enabled for the current Flex project. It doesn't matter whether you're running the application in normal or debug mode; when enabled, the Network Monitor traces network traffic in either condition.

Enabling the Network Monitor

You enable the Network Monitor from the Network Monitor view. This view is available by default in both the Flash and the Flash Debug perspectives, so you don't necessarily have to switch to the Flash Debug perspective to use the tool.

Follow these steps to enable the Network Monitor for your project:

1. **Open the Network Monitor view.** By default, the Network Monitor is displayed in the tabbed region at the bottom of the Flash Builder interface. If you don't see it, select Window ⇨ Network Monitor from the menu.

   The Network Monitor view displays four icons that take the following actions when clicked (see Figure 6.26):

   - Enable/Disable
   - Suspend
   - Clear
   - Save

2. **Click Enable Monitor.** The icon changes to indicate that clicking it again will disable the monitor when clicked.

FIGURE 6.26

The Network Monitor view

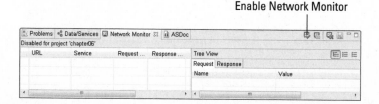

That's it! The Network Monitor will now trace and display your requests and responses when an application requests data with any of the RPC components.

Tracing HTTPRequest data

Follow these steps to run the HTTPRequestDemo application and inspect the requests and responses generated with a static XML file:

1. **Open and run HTTPServiceDemo.mxml.**

2. **When the application appears in the browser, click Get Data.**

3. **Close the browser and return to Flash Builder.**

4. **Look at the Network Monitor view.** The panel on the left shows the most recent server communication (see Figure 6.27), with columns displaying the following information:

   - The URL the request was sent to

   - The data type of the RPC component that sent the request

   - The request and response times

   - The elapsed time in milliseconds

   - The operation (also known as the HTTP method, this value is typically either GET or POST)

FIGURE 6.27

The left panel of the Network Monitor, displaying basic request statistics

5. **Click the request in the left panel to select it, then look at the right panel.** The right panel has buttons that can be used to view request and responses in one of three formats:

   - Tree view displays data as an expandable tree.

   - Raw view displays data in its raw text form.

   - Hex view displays data in binary format.

6. **Click the Response tab in the right panel.**

7. **Click each of the three buttons in the right panel to see the response in the three views.** Figure 6.28 shows the three views of the HTTPService response.

Note

With a large data set, it might take a few seconds to render the raw and hex views. ■

FIGURE 6.28

The three views of a response from the server

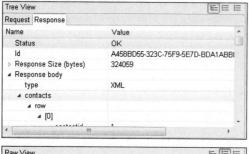

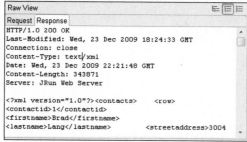

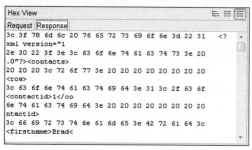

8. Look at the response in Tree View.

9. **Notice the Response Size (bytes).** On my system, the response size is 324,059 bytes, representing the combined size of the raw XML file and the HTTP response header returned from the Web server.

Tracing WebService data

Next you'll run the WebServiceDemo application and inspect the request and response. Follow these steps:

1. Open and run WebServiceDemo.mxml.

2. When the application appears in the browser, click Get Data.

3. **After the data has been retrieved and displayed in the application, close the browser and return to Flash Builder.**

4. **Look at the Network Monitor view.**

5. **Click the WebService request in the left panel to select it.**

6. **In the right panel, click the Response tab.** Notice that the size of Response Size (bytes) is significantly larger than the version returned by HTTPService (52,1538 bytes on my system).

7. **Expand the response tree to show the structure of the returned data.** Notice that the data is returned in the XML-based SOAP format (see Figure 6.29).

A SOAP Web service response, displayed in the Network Monitor

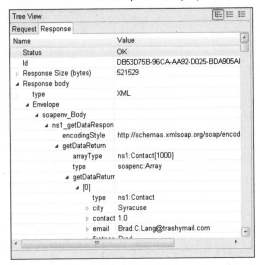

Tracing RemoteObject data

Next, follow these steps to run the RemoteObjectDemo application and inspect the request and response:

1. **Open and run RemoteObjectDemo.mxml.**

2. **When the application appears in the browser, click Get Data.**

3. **After the data has been retrieved and displayed in the application, close the browser open and return to Flash Builder.** In the Network Monitor view, there are two requests listed in the left panel. The first request represents a ping from the client to the server that

the `RemoteObject` class uses to check the server's responsiveness. The second request represents the call to the CFC function `getData()` and has a Service value of RemoteObject.

4. **Click the request with the Service value of Remote Object on the left side of the Network Monitor view.**

5. **In the right panel, click the Response tab as shown in Figure 6.30.** The Response Size (bytes) is significantly smaller than the value for either the HTTPService or the WebService demo (189015 bytes on my system).

FIGURE 6.30

A response from a RemoteObject request shown in the Network Monitor

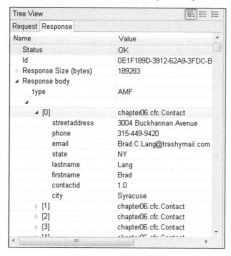

6. **Expand the Response body section until you see the data returned from the server.** Notice that the response body type is AMF, and that the type of the returned data objects is `chapter06.cfc.Contact`, a strongly typed value object class defined on the server as a CFC.

Note

AMF is the binary format used by ColdFusion Flash Remoting and the `RemoteObject` class to exchange data over the Web. The significantly reduced size of the response is a direct result of using this binary format instead of the raw XML used by `HTTPService` or the SOAP format used by `WebService`. ∎

In this demonstration, I evaluated the size of the responses being returned with the RPC components and found that the sizes were dramatically different. As a developer, my conclusion would be (and always is) to use Flash Remoting and the `RemoteObject` class whenever possible to reduce packet size and speed up network communications.

You can also use the Network Monitor to evaluate how long each RPC component takes to retrieve data from the server. In these sample applications, the `WebService` and `RemoteObject` classes call the same server-side code, so comparing their elapsed times would give you meaningful information. Because the `HTTPService` class is simply retrieving a static XML file, its elapsed time is much shorter. Regardless of which RPC component and application server you use, though, I recommend testing each scenario multiple times and taking an average of the results. There are many possible influences with any particular request and response; if you have too little sample data, you might be basing your decisions on results that aren't representative of the real world.

Summary

In this chapter, I described tools that help you debug a Flex application. You learned the following:

- The `trace()` method enables you to send debugging messages to Flash Builder's Console view at runtime.
- The `flashlog.txt` file also receives tracing and error messages when configured with the `mm.cfg` file.
- The locations of `flashlog.txt` and `mm.cfg` differ between operating systems.
- The Logging API enables you to create self-logging components and filter logging messages based on logging level and category.
- Breakpoints enable you to suspend application execution so you can inspect variables and object properties at runtime.
- Flex 4 adds new breakpoint properties that enable you to configure conditional breakpoints.
- The Variables view displays pre-declared variables and object property values when the application is suspended.
- The Expressions view enables you to evaluate arbitrary ActionScript expressions at runtime.
- The Debug view enables you to step through code and otherwise control application execution during a debugging session.
- The new Run to Line command enables you to resume execution and then suspend at a line of your choice without adding another breakpoint.
- The new Network Monitor traces network traffic when using one of the RPC components (`HTTPService`, `WebService`, and `RemoteObject`), enabling you to inspect the size and content of request and response data, and find out the duration of network communications.

Working with Events

F
lex applications are *event-driven*, which means that with the exception of the first phases of application startup, every action is the result of some trigger that causes the action to take place.

Many events are produced by internal functions within the Flex framework that don't necessarily have anything to do with a user's interactions with the application. These are sometimes known as *system* events. Other events, known as *user* events, are designed to inform you of actions taken by the user. These actions, known as user *gestures*, consist of key presses or mouse actions such as moving the mouse or pressing one of its buttons.

Regardless of how an event is generated, you can capture and handle the event in a number of ways. During event handling, you have access to information about the event from a variable known as an *event object*.

And when you need to share information between an application's components, you can create and dispatch your own custom events to move information and data around the application as needed.

This chapter describes the Flex event architecture: how to find out what events occur and when, what data you can get from them, and how to build your own event architecture.

On the Web

To use the sample code for this chapter, import the `chapter07.fxp` **Flex project file from the Web site files into your Flash Builder workspace.** ■

IN THIS CHAPTER

Understanding the Flex event architecture

Using MXML event listeners

Generating event handler functions with Flash Builder 4

Handling events with `addEventListener()`

Declaring and dispatching custom events

Creating and using custom event classes

The Flex Event Architecture

The ActionScript objects you use to build Flex applications communicate with each other and share data by dispatching events. For example, consider a `Button` control that's declared with MXML:

```
<s:Button label="Click Me"/>
```

As an instance of the `spark.components.Button` class, this object supports many properties and methods that are known as the members of the `Button` class. The `Button` class is capable of generating many events. Each of these events also is considered a member of the class.

To find out which events are supported by a particular class, look at the application programming interface (API) documentation for that class. To get to the API documentation quickly in Flash Builder, place the cursor anywhere in the MXML or ActionScript component or class declaration and press Shift+F2 to open the help system and go to the page for that component.

The class's member types are listed at the top of the API documentation. Any class that is capable of generating events displays an `Events` link, as shown in Figure 7.1.

The Events link in the API documentation for the `Button` class

Click here for events documentation

When you click the Events link, the help page navigates to the Events section. As shown in Figure 7.2, you may initially see only a short list of events that are supported by the class or, as in this case, none at all. Any events listed here are defined locally in the current class. The Spark version of the Button class doesn't have any of its own native events; even an event named button Down that was defined locally in the MX version of Button is now derived from a class named ButtonBase.

FIGURE 7.2

The Button class doesn't have any of its own native events.

Click here to see inherited events

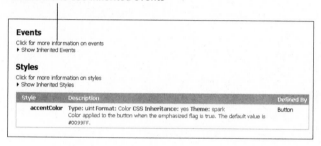

But you also see a Show Inherited Events link that, when clicked, expands the list to include events that are inherited from the current class's inheritance hierarchy. When you click Show Inherited Events, you see all events that are available to the current class. For example, the Button class's most commonly used event is named click. This event is defined in another class named InteractiveObject, one of the Button class's superclasses. This information is available in the documentation, as shown in Figure 7.3.

FIGURE 7.3

The Button's click event is defined in a superclass named InteractiveObject.

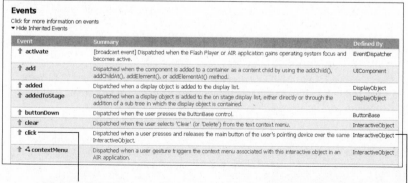

The click event   The superclass that defines the event

Handling Events in MXML

Flex developers can select from one of many strategies for handling events. All events can be handled with:

- Event handlers in MXML object declarations expressed as XML attributes
- The ActionScript addEventListener() method

Some Flex components, such the RPC classes HTTPService, WebService, and RemoteObject, support another event handling strategy using *responder* classes.

The XML-based event handling strategy can be used with objects that are declared in MXML; the other strategies work for any object, whether declared in MXML or ActionScript.

Declaring event listeners in MXML

An MXML event listener uses an XML attribute where the attribute's name matches the name of the event being handled. For example, the Button control's click event uses an XML attribute that's also named click. The value of the XML attribute is an ActionScript statement that causes some action to take place.

Executing a single ActionScript statement in an event handler

If you need to execute a single ActionScript statement for any particular event, you can place the ActionScript code directly in the MXML-based event handler. In the following code, when the user clicks the Button component, the click event is handled and the ActionScript statement in the click XML attribute is executed:

```
<s:Button label="Click Me"
  click="messageLabel.text='You clicked the button'"/>
<s:Label id="messageLabel"/>
```

Tip

Notice in the previous code that the literal string You clicked the button is wrapped in single quotes. This is because the click XML attribute's value (the ActionScript statement) is wrapped in double quotes. In ActionScript, single and double quotes are interchangeable as long as you match them up correctly. ■

Note

In browser-based JavaScript, the Dynamic HTML (DHTML) equivalent of this event architecture uses event names starting with the word "on" and finishing with the actual event. For example, in JavaScript, you'd use this code to handle an onClick event:

```
<input type="button" onClick="doSomething()"/>
```

The result is the same as in MXML: The event handler consists of a markup-based attribute that calls scripting code to be executed upon the event being dispatched. Only the event naming pattern is different. ■

A simple event handling application

Follow these steps to create a simple application that uses an MXML-based event handler:

1. Create a new MXML application with its layout set to VerticalLayout.

2. Add a Label control to the application with its id set to myText.

3. Add a Button component with its label property set to Click Me.

4. Add a click attribute with ActionScript code that changes the Label control's text property to a value of You Clicked!. The completed application's code is shown in Listing 7.1.

5. Run the application, and click the button to see the Label control's text property change.

LISTING 7.1

An application with a simple MXML-based event handler

```
<?xml version="1.0" encoding="utf-8"?>
<s:Application xmlns:fx="http://ns.adobe.com/mxml/2009"
  xmlns:s="library://ns.adobe.com/flex/spark"
  xmlns:mx="library://ns.adobe.com/flex/mx">
  <s:layout>
    <s:VerticalLayout horizontalAlign="center" paddingTop="20"/>
  </s:layout>
  <s:Label id="myText"/>
  <s:Button id="myButton" label="Click me"
    click="myText.text='You clicked the button'"/>
</s:Application>
```

On the Web

The code in Listing 7.1 is available in the Web site files in the `chapter07` project as `SimpleEvent.mxml`. ∎

Handling events with ActionScript functions

When you need to execute more than a single ActionScript statement in response to an event, you should create a custom function. The function enables you to add as much code as you need. The event handler function can be very simple:

```
private function clickHandler():void
{
   ... add ActionScript code here ...
}
```

Now all the code you want to call is wrapped inside `clickHandler()`, so to execute the code, call the function from the object's event handler:

```
<s:Button label="Click Me" click="clickHandler()"/>
```

Tip

You can name your event handler functions anything you like. The convention of naming the function with the word "handler" at the end isn't a technical requirement, but it helps you identify the function's purpose.

If you have more than a single object whose events you need to handle, try naming the event handler functions to identify the event that's being handled and the object that's dispatching the event. For example, if you have two buttons with functions to save or cancel an operation, you might name the event handler functions `save ClickHandler()` and `cancelClickHandler()`. To call the functions you'd then use this code:

```
<s:Button label="Save" click="saveClickHandler()"/>
<s:Button label="Cancel" click="cancelClickHandler()"/>■
```

Using an event handler function

Follow these steps to create an application that uses an event handler function:

1. Create a new application with its `layout` set to `VerticalLayout`.

2. Add a `Label` control with an `id` property set to `myText`.

3. Add an `<fx:Script>` tag set at the top of the application.

4. Within the `<fx:Script>` section, add a private function named `ClickHandler()` that changes the `Label` control's text property to a value of You Clicked!.

5. Add a `Button` component to the application with a label property set to Click Me.

6. In the `Button` component's `click` event handler, call the `ClickHandler()` function. The completed application's code is shown in Listing 7.2.

7. Run the application, and click the button to see the `Label` control's `text` property change.

LISTING 7.2

Using an event handler function

```
<?xml version="1.0" encoding="utf-8"?>
<s:Application xmlns:fx="http://ns.adobe.com/mxml/2009"
  xmlns:s="library://ns.adobe.com/flex/spark"
  xmlns:mx="library://ns.adobe.com/flex/mx">
  <s:layout>
    <s:VerticalLayout horizontalAlign="center" paddingTop="20"/>
  </s:layout>
  <fx:Script>
```

```
<![CDATA[
  private function clickHandler():void
  {
    myText.text='You clicked the button';
  }
]]>
  </fx:Script>
  <s:Label id="myText"/>
    <s:Button id="myButton" label="Click me" click="clickHandler()"/>
</s:Application>
```

On the Web

The code in Listing 7.2 is available in the Web site files in the `chapter07` project as `EventWithFunction.mxml`. ■

Tip

Event handler functions typically return `void`, meaning that their purpose is to take some action but not return any value. When using an MXML-based event handler, this architecture is optional. As described later in this chapter, when setting up an event handler with the `addEventListener()` function, the return datatype of `void` is required. ■

Working with event objects

Every event that's dispatched in the Flex framework creates a variable known as an *event object*. The purpose of an event object is to share information about the nature of the event, including the event's name, the object that dispatched the event, the context of the event, and detailed information that might be useful in understanding what happened.

The event object's variable name

To handle an event and get information from the event object, you typically create an event handler function that's designed to receive the event object as an argument. When the event occurs, you then call the event handler function and pass the event object as its argument. For the duration of an MXML-based event handler, the name of the event object is always the same: `event` (always spelled in lowercase). So, assuming you've created a `clickHandler()` function that's designed to receive an event argument, the syntax of the MXML object declaration becomes this:

```
<s:Button label="Click Me" click="clickHandler(event)"/>
```

Using event object arguments

The event object is always an instance of an ActionScript class named `flash.events.Event` or a subclass of this `Event` class. When you create an event handler function to receive an event object, you can always datatype the argument as the `Event` class:

```
private function clickHandler(event:Event):void
{
  myLabel.text="You clicked the button";
}
```

Tip

All event objects can be handled as the Event class as they're passed into an event handler function, even if their true type is a subclass of the Event class. This convenient shortcut is made possible by ActionScript's support for polymorphism, where objects can be cast, and handled, as their superclass types. As long as you don't need to refer to event object properties that are only implemented in the subclass, such as MouseEvent, typing the event object as Event doesn't have any negative effect on the application's performance or functionality. ■

Generating an event handler function

Flash Builder 4 adds a new feature that generates an event handler function for you. The function name and signature are constructed with this pattern:

```
[objectId]_[eventName]Handler(event:[EventClassName]):void
```

For example, for a control with its id set to myButton, the generated event handler function for the click event would be:

```
myButton_clickHandler(event:MouseEvent):void
```

New Feature

The capability to generate event handler functions is a new feature of Flash Builder 4. ■

Follow these steps to generate an event handler function:

1. **Add an instance of the Button component to an application with an id of myButton and a label of Click me:**

   ```
   <s:Button id="myButton" label="Click me"/>
   ```

2. **Place the cursor before the tag's final characters (/>), and press the spacebar.** You should see a list of the Button component's events, styles, and properties.

3. **Type the first few characters of the event name; for example, type cli to see the click event.**

4. **Press Enter (Windows) or Return (Mac) to select the click event.** As shown in Figure 7.4, Flash Builder shows a Generate Click Handler prompt.

5. **Press Enter (Windows) or Return (Mac) to generate the event handler function.**

FIGURE 7.4

A prompt offering to generate an event handler function

The resulting function is placed inside an `<fx:Script>` tag set. If one already exists, it's placed there; otherwise, an `<fx:Script>` tag set is created. The resulting code looks like this:

```
<fx:Script>
<![CDATA[
    protected function myButton_clickHandler(event:MouseEvent):void
    {
        // TODO Auto-generated method stub
    }
]]>
</fx:Script>
```

Tip

The resulting event handler function has an access modifier of `protected`, meaning the function is available to the current component and any of its derived components. For event handler functions you generate in a custom MXML component, this means that if you create any subcomponents, they'll inherit your custom event handler functions. ▪

Tip

When Flash Builder generates an event handler function, it automatically figures out which event class will be used as the event object. For example, the `Button` component's `click` event generates an instance of `MouseEvent`, while the `creationComplete` event generates an instance of `FlexEvent`. The generated function signature includes correct datatyping of the function argument. Flash Builder also generates any `import` statements that might be required. ▪

You can also generate an event handler function for certain objects in Design mode. For example, follow these steps to generate an event handler for a `Button` object's `click` event:

1. In Design mode, select the Button for which you want to generate the event handler.

2. Look at the Properties view and locate the button next to the On click prompt, shown in Figure 7.5.

Generating an event handler from the Properties view

Click to generate event handler

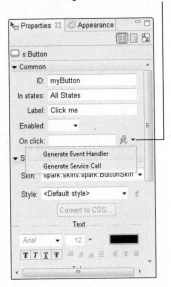

3. **Click the button to see available options.** The list includes:

   - Generate Event Handler
   - Generate Service Call

4. **Select Generate Event Handler.**

Flash Builder switches to Source mode and generates both the event handler in the `<s:Button>` tag and the required event handler function.

Using event object properties

As shown in the Unified Modeling Language (UML) diagram in Figure 7.6, the Event class supports properties and methods that enable you to get information about the event and in some cases control its behavior. (The diagram shows only certain key properties and methods of the Event class. See the class's application programming interface [API] documentation for a complete list.)

These are the key properties of the Event class:

- **type:String.** The name of the event that was dispatched as a String. For example, when the click event is handled, the value of the event object's type property is "click."

- **target:Object.** A reference to the object that dispatched the event. Because the target property points to the object, any of that object's properties are then available with extended dot syntax. For example, a Button component's id property would be available as event.target.id and its label as event.target.label.

UML diagram of the Event class

flash.events.Event
+ type : String + target : Object + currentTarget : Object + bubbles : Boolean + cancelable : Boolean
+ clone() : Object + stopPropagation()

Note

Other key properties of the Event class are described in this chapter's section on event bubbling. ■

When you pass an event object to an event handler function as an argument, you have access to all the event object's properties for the duration of the function. To capture information about the event, use the properties that are of interest:

```
private function clickHandler(event:Event):void
{
  myLabel.text="You clicked the button labeled " +
    event.target.label;
}
```

Tip

When writing code that refers to event.target, you might notice that properties like label that aren't available on all ActionScript classes aren't suggested by Flash Builder code completion tools. This is because the expression event.target is known to the Flex compiler and to Flash Builder as an instance of the ActionScript Object class, and only properties that are implemented in that class will be suggested for auto-completion.

If you know that event.target refers to a Button in the context of a particular event handler function, you can safely refer to the Button class's properties (such as label). The code will compile and execute correctly, even if Flash Builder's code completion isn't able to help you write it. ■

Using event object properties in an application

Follow these steps to create an application that uses event object properties:

1. Create a new application with its layout set to VerticalLayout.

2. Add a Label control with its id property set to myText.

3. Add a Button component to the application with its id set to myButton and its label set to Click Me.

4. After the label setting, type cli and press Ctrl+Space.

5. Press Enter to select the click event.

6. Press Enter again to generate the <fx:Script> block and the new event handler function:

```
<fx:Script>
<![CDATA[
  protected function button1_clickHandler(event:MouseEvent):void
  {
    // TODO Auto-generated method stub
  }
]]>
</fx:Script>
```

7. Remove the TODO comment from the event handler function and add this code to the event handler function to display the event type and the id of the event target:

```
myText.text="The " + event.type +
  " event was dispatched by " + event.target.id;
```

8. Close the <s:Button> tag with the /> string. The Button code should look like this:

```
<s:Button id="myButton" label="Click Me"
  click="myButton_clickHandler(event)"/>
```

The completed application's code is shown in Listing 7.3.

9. Run the application and click the button to see the Label control display the event object's property values.

LISTING 7.3

Using event object properties

```
<?xml version="1.0" encoding="utf-8"?>
<s:Application xmlns:fx="http://ns.adobe.com/mxml/2009"
  xmlns:s="library://ns.adobe.com/flex/spark"
  xmlns:mx="library://ns.adobe.com/flex/mx">
  <fx:Script>
    <![CDATA[
      protected function myButton_clickHandler(event:MouseEvent):void
      {
```

```
      myText.text="The " + event.type +
         " event was dispatched by " + event.target.id;
    }
  ]]>
 </fx:Script>
 <s:layout>
   <s:VerticalLayout horizontalAlign="center" paddingTop="20"/>
 </s:layout>
 <s:Label id="myText"/>
 <s:Button id="myButton" label="Click Me"
   click="myButton_clickHandler(event)"/>
</s:Application>
```

On the Web

The code in Listing 7.3 is available in the Web site files in the `chapter07` project's `src` folder in the default package as `EventObjectProperties.mxml`. ■

Event class inheritance

Event objects are created as specific class types depending on the nature of the event that's dispatched. For example, events having to do with mouse actions are typically instances of a class named `flash.events.MouseEvent`. As shown in the UML diagram in Figure 7.7, `MouseEvent`, `ResultEvent`, `TextEvent`, and dozens of other classes in the Flash and Flex class libraries are directly extended from the `Event` class.

FIGURE 7.7

All event classes are directly extended from the `Event` superclass

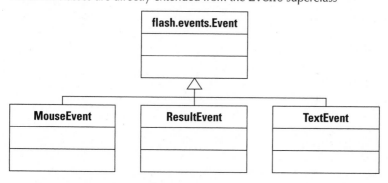

When an event class such as `MouseEvent` extends `Event`, it inherits that superclass's basic properties such as `type` and `target`. The subclass typically defines additional properties that are useful for that particular event. The `MouseEvent` class adds properties to track button state, mouse cursor position, and other useful information. Some of these properties include:

- **altKey:Boolean.** Set to `true` if the Alt key is held down when the event is dispatched; otherwise set to `false`.

- **ctrlKey:Boolean.** Set to `true` if the Ctrl key is held down when the event is dispatched; otherwise set to `false`.

- **shiftKey:Boolean.** Set to `true` if the Shift key is held down when the event is dispatched; otherwise set to `false`.

- **commandKey:Boolean.** Set to `true` if the command key on the Mac is held down when the event is dispatched; otherwise set to `false`. Always set to `false` on Windows.

- **localX:int.** The number of pixels from the left border where the user clicked an object dispatching the event.

- **localY:int.** The number of pixels from the top border where the user clicked an object dispatching the event.

- **stageX:int.** The number of pixels from the left border where the user clicked the *stage* (Flash Player region).

- **stageY:int.** The number of pixels from the top border where the user clicked the stage (Flash Player region).

- **buttonDown:Boolean.** Set to `true` if the primary mouse button is pressed when the event is dispatched; otherwise set to `false`.

Which event class will I get?

To find out what specific class will be dispatched for a particular event, you can use one of these strategies:

- Place your mouse cursor over the event argument in your MXML event handler attribute to display a tooltip hint.

- Debug the application, and inspect the event object in the Variables view.

- Read the API documentation for the class whose event you're handling.

Debugging the event object

Follow these steps to debug the application and inspect the event object:

1. Place a breakpoint in the event handler function on a line of ActionScript code or, if the function is empty, on the line with the function's closing brace:

```
private function clickHandler(event:MouseEvent):void
{
} //place breakpoint here
```

2. Debug the application.

3. Trigger the event that calls the event handler function (for example, by clicking a button).

4. When the breakpoint suspends the application, inspect the function's `event` argument in the Flex Debugging perspective's Variables view.

As shown in Figure 7.8, the Variables view displays the event object's type and all its current property values.

The event object's type displayed in the Variables view

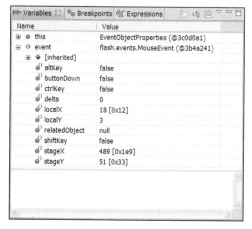

Reading the documentation

Documentation for every event in the Flex SDK includes the type of the event object that will be dispatched when the event occurs. For example, the documentation for the Button class's click event shows that the event object is an instance of flash.events.MouseEvent. To find this information, follow these steps:

1. **Place the cursor in the object declaration in Source view.**

2. **Press F1 to display a list of Help subjects.**

3. **Click the link for the class or component you're using.**

4. **In the API documentation, click the Events link.**

5. **Locate the event you're interested in, and click its link.**

As shown in Figure 7.9, you should see the specific type of the class that will be dispatched for that event.

Handling specific event objects

To capture information that's available only in one of the extended event classes, declare the datatype of an event handler function's event argument as that class. For example, this event handler function expects an instance of MouseEvent:

```
private function clickHandler(event:MouseEvent):void
{
  myLabel.text="You clicked; was the alt key pressed? " +
    event.altKey;
}
```

FIGURE 7.9

Documentation for the `click` event

Property	Value
altKey	true if the Alt key is active (Windows or Linux).
bubbles	true
buttonDown	For click events, this value is always false.
cancelable	false; there is no default behavior to cancel.
commandKey	true on the Mac if the Command key is active; false if it is inactive. Always false on Windows.
controlKey	true if the Ctrl or Control key is active; false if it is inactive.
ctrlKey	true on Windows or Linux if the Ctrl key is active. true on Mac if either the Ctrl key or the Command key is active. Otherwise, false.
currentTarget	The object that is actively processing the Event object with an event listener.
localX	The horizontal coordinate at which the event occurred relative to the containing sprite.
localY	The vertical coordinate at which the event occurred relative to the containing sprite.

The `altKey` property is available only because the `event` argument is declared as the subclass that supports that property. If the `event` argument instead is declared as the `Event` superclass, the `altKey` property isn't recognized by the compiler, and a compiler error results.

The complete application shown in Listing 7.4 is an application that captures a `MouseEvent` and displays the status of the keys on the keyboard at the moment the event is dispatched.

LISTING 7.4

An application that handles a MouseEvent object

```
<?xml version="1.0" encoding="utf-8"?>
<s:Application xmlns:fx="http://ns.adobe.com/mxml/2009"
  xmlns:s="library://ns.adobe.com/flex/spark"
  xmlns:mx="library://ns.adobe.com/flex/mx">
  <s:layout>
    <s:VerticalLayout horizontalAlign="center" paddingTop="20"/>
  </s:layout>
  <fx:Script>
```

```
<![CDATA[
  private function clickHandler(event:MouseEvent):void
  {
    myText.text="The " + event.type +
      " event was dispatched by " + event.target.id;
    altText.text="Alt key pressed: " + event.altKey;
    ctrlText.text="Ctrl key pressed: " + event.ctrlKey;
    shiftText.text="Shift key pressed: " + event.shiftKey;
  }
]]>
</fx:Script>
<s:Label id="myText"/>
<s:Label id="altText"/>
<s:Label id="ctrlText"/>
<s:Label id="shiftText"/>
<s:Button id="myButton" label="Click Me" click="clickHandler(event)"/>
</s:Application>
```

On the Web

The code in Listing 7.4 is available in the Web site files in the `chapter07` **project as** `MouseEventObject Properties.mxml`. ∎

Handling Events with addEventListener()

You also can set up event handlers with a method named `addEventListener()`. This method is defined in an ActionScript class named `EventDispatcher`, which appears in the inheritance hierarchy of every ActionScript class that's able to dispatch events. Stated more briefly, you can call `addEventListener()` from any object that knows how to dispatch an event.

Setting up an event listener

The following MXML code declares a `Button` component with a `click` event handler:

```
<s:Button id="myButton" label="Click Me"
  click="clickHandler(event)"/>
```

The following code uses the `addEventListener()` method instead of the MXML-based event handler to accomplish the same task:

```
myButton.addEventListener("click", clickHandler);
```

The first argument you pass to `addEventListener()` is the name of the event you're listening for. The second argument is the name of the function you want to call when the event is dispatched.

Event Class Inheritance and Polymorphism

The fact that you can define an event handler function to expect either the specific event class, such as `MouseEvent`, or its superclass, such as `Event`, is a reflection of the support for polymorphism in ActionScript's implementation of object-oriented programming. I describe the concept of polymorphism in detail in Chapter 1. Merriam-Webster defines polymorphism as "the quality or state of existing in or assuming different forms." In this case, the different forms the event object takes are its native type (`MouseEvent`) or its superclass type (`Event`).

One reason some developers set an event object to the superclass is because they don't know the event's native class type and don't want to take time to look it up. This sounds lazy, but in many cases the specific properties of the native type just aren't needed in that situation, and using the `Event` superclass makes for faster programming.

You also can use the superclass type to make a function reusable with events that dispatch different native types, again where they don't need the specific properties that are supported by the native types. This is the true purpose of implementing polymorphism in object-oriented languages: to support code that's reusable in many different circumstances.

Caution
Notice that you pass the name of the function as the second argument, not the complete code required to call the function. You're designating which function to call, rather than calling the function immediately. ∎

The object from which you call `addEventListener()` always calls the listener function with the same signature, passing a single argument that's datatyped as the appropriate event class for that event. Event listener functions designed to be used with `addEventListener()` always have the same signature:

```
[access modifier] function [functionName](
  event:[event class data type]):void
{}
```

So a function designed to receive an instance of `MouseEvent` always looks like this:

```
private function clickHandler(event:MouseEvent):void
{
  ... execute event handling code ...
}
```

Tip
The event handler function's access modifier doesn't necessarily have to be `private`. But if the function is only used within the current component, there's no need to further broaden access to the function. ∎

You typically call `addEventListener()` during application startup or initial object construction, where it can replace an MXML-based event handler definition. For example, you might set up your event listeners in a function named `app_creationCompleteHandler()` that's called upon the `Application` component's `creationComplete` event. The application in Listing 7.5 uses this strategy. Notice the following:

- The `clickHandler()` function returns `void`.

- The `app_creationCompleteHandler()` function is called during application startup upon the application's `creationComplete` event.

- The MXML-based declaration of the `Button` component doesn't have a `click` event handler; this would be redundant and in fact would result in the event handler function being called twice.

LISTING 7.5

An application that uses addEventListener()

```
<?xml version="1.0" encoding="utf-8"?>
<s:Application xmlns:fx="http://ns.adobe.com/mxml/2009"
  xmlns:s="library://ns.adobe.com/flex/spark"
  xmlns:mx="library://ns.adobe.com/flex/mx"
  creationComplete="app_creationCompleteHandler(event)">
  <s:layout>
    <s:VerticalLayout horizontalAlign="center" paddingTop="20"/>
  </s:layout>
  <fx:Script>
    <![CDATA[
      import mx.events.FlexEvent;
      protected function app_creationCompleteHandler(event:FlexEvent):void
      {
        myButton.addEventListener(MouseEvent.CLICK, clickHandler);
      }
      protected function clickHandler(event:MouseEvent):void
      {
        myText.text="The " + event.type +
          " event was dispatched by " + event.target.id;
      }
    ]]>
  </fx:Script>
  <s:Label id="myText"/>
  <s:Button id="myButton" label="Click Me"/>
</s:Application>
```

On the Web

The code in Listing 7.5 is available in the Web site files in the `chapter07` project's `src` folder in the default package as `UsingAddEventListener.mxml`. ∎

Using event name constants

Each event class in the Flex framework implements constants that have values equal to the names of events for which the event class is used. For example, the MouseEvent class has many constants that reflect the names of events for which this event class is dispatched (shown with their equivalent values):

- CLICK = "click"
- MOUSE_DOWN = "mouseDown"
- MOUSE_UP = "mouseUp"
- MOUSE_MOVE = "mouseMove"
- RIGHT_CLICK = "rightClick"
- MOUSE_WHEEL = "mouseWheel"

There are more, but you get the picture. You use these constants in calls to addEventListener() instead of phrasing the event name as a literal string. For example, instead of this code:

```
myButton.addEventListener("click", clickHandler);
```

you can use this:

```
myButton.addEventListener(MouseEvent.CLICK, clickHandler);
```

When you use event name constants, you reduce the risk of typing errors in your code. When you use literal strings to indicate which event you want to listen for, it's easy to misspell the name. For example, this code would result in an event listener that will never be triggered, because there is no event named clik:

```
myButton.addEventListener("clik", clickHandler);
```

Because the event name is phrased as a literal string, the compiler has no way of knowing that it's misspelled. Of course, you can make the same mistake with an event name constant:

```
myButton.addEventListener(MouseEvent.CLIK, clickHandler);
```

But in this case, the compiler would complain, telling you that there is no such property or constant as CLIK in the MouseEvent class, and you'd be able to find and fix the error at a much earlier stage of development.

Another advantage of using event name constants comes from Flash Builder's code completion tool. As shown in Figure 7.10, when you type the name of the MouseEvent class and add a period, you see a list of available constants that are members of the class. You can then select the appropriate event name and ensure that it's typed correctly from the beginning.

Tip

When you type the id of an object that dispatches events and then a period, followed by addEventListener(, code completion for the addEventListener() method's first argument displays constants for all events that can be dispatched by the object from which addEventListener() is being called. ■

FIGURE 7.10

Flash Builder's code completion tool with event name constants

Flex Builder's code completion with event name constants

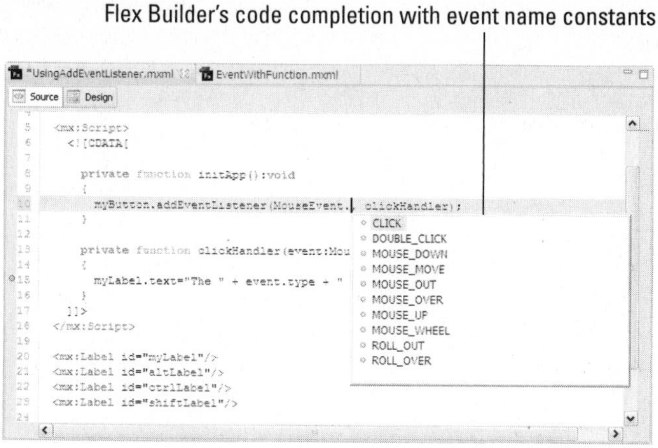

Removing an event listener

You can remove an event listener that was set up with `addEventListener()` with the `removeEventListener()` method. This method also is defined in the `EventDispatcher` class and can be called from any object that dispatches events.

The basic syntax for `removeEventListener()` is the same as `addEventListener()`:

```
myButton.removeEventListener(MouseEvent.CLICK, clickHandler);
```

The `addEventListener()` and `removeEventListener()` methods enable you to add and remove event listeners as needed whenever an application's requirements change logically at runtime.

Using Event Bubbling

Event bubbling refers to the process of dispatching events through multiple levels of inheritance. Consider this application code, which defines a `Button` control inside a `VBox` container:

```
<?xml version="1.0" encoding="utf-8"?>
<s:Application xmlns:fx="http://ns.adobe.com/mxml/2009"
  xmlns:s="library://ns.adobe.com/flex/spark"
  xmlns:mx="library://ns.adobe.com/flex/mx">
  <s:VGroup id="myGroup">
    <s:Button label="Click me" id="myButton"/>
  </s:VGroup>
</s:Application>
```

When the Button component is clicked, it dispatches a click event. All event objects have a Boolean property named bubbles. When this property's value is set to true, as it is by default with the MouseEvent class, the event first is dispatched by the object that was clicked, then by its container, and so on up the display tree until it's dispatched by the application itself.

Each time the event bubbles up another containership level, the event object is received again by the event handler for the current container. But one property is changed: Each event object has a currentTarget property that refers to the object that's currently dispatching the event. This property is changed as the event object bubbles, but the event object's target property continues to reference the object that originally dispatched the event.

You can stop an event from continuing to bubble through the containership hierarchy by calling a method of the event object named stopPropagation():

```
event.stopPropagation();
```

This is sometimes necessary when a common event such as click might otherwise be handled in ways that don't work for your application.

Tip

Another way to stop a visual component from dispatching mouse events is to set its mouseEnabled **property to false.** ■

The application in Listing 7.6 uses a two-level containership hierarchy: a Button inside a VGroup inside an Application. All objects handle the click event and dispatch the event object to a clickHandler() function, where the target and currentTarget are logged. The TextArea control that's used to log the events explicitly handles its own click event and stops that event from bubbling to the container and application.

LISTING 7.6

An application that logs event bubbling

```xml
<?xml version="1.0" encoding="utf-8"?>
<s:Application xmlns:fx="http://ns.adobe.com/mxml/2009"
  xmlns:s="library://ns.adobe.com/flex/spark"
  xmlns:mx="library://ns.adobe.com/flex/mx"
  click="clickHandler(event)">
<s:layout>
  <s:VerticalLayout horizontalAlign="center" paddingTop="20"/>
</s:layout>
<fx:Script>
  <![CDATA[
    protected function clickHandler(event:MouseEvent):void
    {
      eventLog.text += "target=" + event.target.id +
        ", currentTarget=" + event.currentTarget.id + "\n\n";
    }
```

```
      ]]>
   </fx:Script>
   <s:VGroup id="myGroup" left="10" top="10" width="50"
     click="clickHandler(event)">
      <s:Button id="myButton" label="Click me" click="clickHandler(event)"
        horizontalCenter="0"/>
      <s:TextArea id="eventLog"
        height="110" width="300"
        horizontalCenter="0"
        click="event.stopPropagation()"/>
   </s:VGroup>
</s:Application>
```

On the Web

The code in Listing 7.6 is available in the Web site files in the `chapter07` project's `src` folder in the default package as `EventBubbling.mxml`. ■

As shown in Figure 7.11, each time the event is handled, the `target` property always points to the `Button` component, while the `currentTarget` changes with each new call to the event handler function.

FIGURE 7.11

An event bubbling demonstration

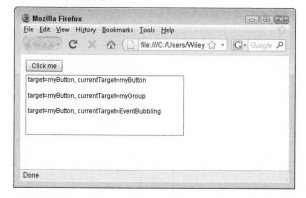

Tip

Event bubbling works only if the parent container declares the event you want to handle. For example, if you try to handle a `change` event from a `ComboBox` in a parent `VBox` in MXML, an error occurs because the compiler says there is no `change` event to listen for. To overcome this limitation, create your own custom component based on the container you want to use, and explicitly declare the selected event as a member of the new version of the container. ■

Using Custom Events

You use custom events to communicate information and data between application components. As I described previously, Flex applications are built with a modular architecture, with functionality divided between multiple components. When a component needs to share information with the rest of the application, it does so by dispatching an event.

The following MXML component displays three choices of Small, Medium, and Large in a group of RadioButton components:

```
<?xml version="1.0" encoding="utf-8"?>
<s:VGroup xmlns:fx="http://ns.adobe.com/mxml/2009"
  xmlns:s="library://ns.adobe.com/flex/spark"
  xmlns:mx="library://ns.adobe.com/flex/mx">
  <fx:Declarations>
     <s:RadioButtonGroup id="sizeGroup"/>
  </fx:Declarations>
  <s:RadioButton value="Small"
    label="Small" groupName="sizeGroup"/>
  <s:RadioButton value="Medium"
    label="Medium" groupName="sizeGroup"/>
  <s:RadioButton value="Large"
    label="Large" groupName="sizeGroup"/>
</s:VGroup>
```

On the Web

The previous code is available in the Web site files in the chapter07 project as components/
SizeSelectorStart.mxml. ∎

New Feature

As with all other nonvisual components, the RadioButtonGroup control must now be declared inside an
<fx:Declarations> tag set. ∎

When the user clicks a radio button to make a selection, the component can share the following information with the rest of the application:

- The user selected something.
- The user selected a particular bit of data.

To share the information, you'll need to follow these steps within the component:

1. Define a custom event that the MXML component is capable of dispatching.
2. Create an event object at runtime.
3. Populate the event object with data.
4. Dispatch the event object.

In the application that instantiates the custom component, you'll follow these steps:

1. **Create an event handler using either an MXML-based event attribute or the addEventListener() method.**

2. **Create a custom event handler function that extracts the data from the dispatched event object.**

Declaring custom events

You declare custom events in a component with the `<fx:Metadata>` tag and a metadata tag named `[Event]`. Start by adding the `<fx:Metadata>` tag set as a child of the component root:

```
<?xml version="1.0" encoding="utf-8"?>
<s:VGroup xmlns:fx="http://ns.adobe.com/mxml/2009"
  xmlns:s="library://ns.adobe.com/flex/spark"
  xmlns:mx="library://ns.adobe.com/flex/mx">
  <fx:Metadata>
  </fx:Metadata>
  ... other controls...
</s:VGroup>
```

Within the `<fx:Metadata>` tag set, add one `[Event]` metadata tag for each custom event you want to declare. The syntax of the `[Event]` metadata tag is:

```
[Event(name="[custom event name]", type="[event object type]")]
```

The `[Event]` metadata tag has these two attributes:

- **name.** A string that identifies your custom event, and can be of any value. Just as the Flex framework uses event names like `click`, `change`, and `mouseMove`, you can select any meaningful string as long as it doesn't contain any spaces or special characters. This value is required.

- **type.** The name of an event class that will be instantiated and dispatched to an event listener. The default is the `flash.events.Event` class.

If you only need to dispatch an event that informs the event listener that the event occurred, and don't need to share specific data, you can use a shorthand form of the `[Event]` tag that omits the `type` attribute:

```
[Event(name="sizeSelected")]
```

If you need to share specific data with the event listener and use a special event class that is designed to contain that data, include the `type` property and refer to the fully qualified event class name:

```
[Event(name="sizeSelected", type="flash.events.TextEvent")]
```

Tip

The `TextEvent` class is a standard part of the Flash SDK and has a `text` property you can use to package and share a simple `String` value. If you only need to share a `String`, it doesn't make sense to create a custom event class — you'd just be reinventing a wheel. ■

Adding an event declaration to a custom component and testing it

Follow these steps to add an event declaration to a custom MXML component:

1. Open components/SizeSelectorStart.mxml from the chapter07 project from the Web site.

2. Add an `<fx:Metadata>` tag set after the starting `<s:VGroup>` tag.

3. Within the `<fx:Metadata>` tag set, declare a custom event named `sizeSelected` that dispatches an event object typed as `flash.events.TextEvent`. The code to declare the event looks like this:

   ```
   <fx:Metadata>
     [Event(name="sizeSelected", type="flash.events.Event")]
   </fx:Metadata>
   ```

4. Save the file.

5. Create a new MXML application named `CustomEventApp.mxml` in the chapter07 project with its layout set to VerticalLayout.

6. Add a custom namespace prefix to the `<s:Application>` tag mapped to the components folder:

   ```
   xmlns:components="components.*"
   ```

7. Place the cursor after the `<s:layout>` tags and declare an instance of the `SizeSelector` component with MXML with id of `selector`.

   ```
   <components:SizeSelector id="selector"/>
   ```

8. Place the cursor after the `SizeSelector` tag name and before the ending `/>` characters.

9. Press the spacebar to see a list of available class members.

10. Type `size` to filter the list. As shown in Figure 7.12, you should see that the list displays the new `sizeSelected` event as a member of the component.

11. Remove the partial event attribute `size` (you learn how to use this attribute in the next section) so you have only the tag declaration with no event listener.

12. Save and run the application.

FIGURE 7.12

A custom event shown in Flash Builder's code completion tool

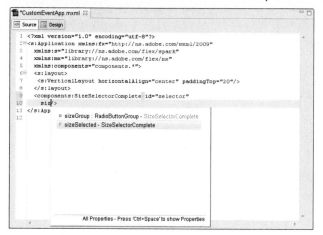

As shown in Figure 7.13, the application displays the component but isn't yet handling the custom event.

FIGURE 7.13

The application with the custom component

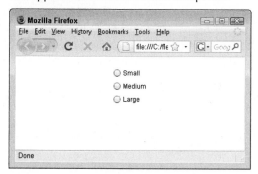

Dispatching custom events

To dispatch a custom event, follow these steps:

1. **Create an instance of the event class you declared as the event type.**

2. **When you instantiate the event object, set its type property as the name of the custom event.** All event classes in the Flex framework have a constructor method that enables you to set the event name as you instantiate the object:

   ```
   var myEvent:Event = new Event("[event name]");
   ```

3. Populate the event object with data, if applicable.

4. Call the component's dispatchEvent() method, and pass the event object as the only argument:

```
dispatchEvent(myEvent);
```

The complete code to dispatch a TextEvent class for an event named sizeChanged looks like this:

```
var e:TextEvent = new TextEvent("sizeChanged");
e.text = "some value I want to share";
dispatchEvent(e);
```

Follow these steps to dispatch an event from the custom component:

1. Reopen components/SizeSelectorStart.mxml from the chapter07 project.

2. Change the [Event] metadata tag's type attribute to flash.events.TextEvent:

```
<Metadata>
  [Event(name="sizeSelected", type="flash.events.TextEvent")]
</Metadata>
```

3. Place the cursor inside the RadioButtonGroup component start tag.

4. Type itemClick and press Enter (Windows) or Return (Mac).

5. When prompted to Generate ItemClick Handler, press Enter (Windows) or Return (Mac) again. You should see that Flash Builder generates an event handler function named sizeGroup_itemClickHandler() with the appropriate event object type, ItemClickEvent.

6. Add this code to the event handler function:

```
var e:TextEvent = new TextEvent("sizeSelected");
e.text = sizeGroup.selection.value as String;
dispatchEvent(e);
```

7. Save the file.

The completed component code is shown in Listing 7.7.

LISTING 7.7

A completed component that dispatches a custom event with data

```
<?xml version="1.0" encoding="utf-8"?>
<s:VGroup xmlns:fx="http://ns.adobe.com/mxml/2009"
  xmlns:s="library://ns.adobe.com/flex/spark"
  xmlns:mx="library://ns.adobe.com/flex/mx">
  <fx:Script>
    <![CDATA[
      import mx.events.ItemClickEvent;
```

```
  protected function sizeGroup_itemClickHandler(
    event:ItemClickEvent):void
  {
    var e:TextEvent = new TextEvent("sizeSelected");
    e.text = sizeGroup.selection.value as String;
    dispatchEvent(e);
  }
]]>
</fx:Script>
<fx:Metadata>
  [Event(name="sizeSelected", type="flash.events.TextEvent")]
</fx:Metadata>
<fx:Declarations>
  <s:RadioButtonGroup id="sizeGroup"
    itemClick="sizeGroup_itemClickHandler(event)"/>
</fx:Declarations>
<s:RadioButton value="Small" label="Small" groupName="sizeGroup"/>
<s:RadioButton value="Medium" label="Medium" groupName="sizeGroup"/>
<s:RadioButton value="Large" label="Large" groupName="sizeGroup"/>
</s:VGroup>
```

On the Web

The code in Listing 7.7 is available in the `chapter07` **project from the Web site as** `components/SizeSelectorComplete.mxml`. ∎

Tip

The `RadioButtonGroup` **component's** `selection.value` **property must be explicitly cast as a** `String`, **because the API declares it as an** `Object` **and the** `String` **type is expected by the** `TextEvent` **class's** text **property.** ∎

Handling custom events

Event handling with custom events looks just like handling events that are predefined by classes in the Flex framework. You can handle a custom event in these two ways:

- With an MXML-based event attribute that executes explicit ActionScript code
- With the `addEventListener()` method

Handling a custom event with MXML

To handle an event with an MXML declaration, add an XML attribute named for the event to the MXML declaration of the object that will dispatch the event. When the event is dispatched, call a custom event handler function and pass the event object as an argument:

```
<components:SizeSelectorStart
  sizeSelected="sizeSelectedHandler(event)"/>
```

Create a custom event handler function that expects the appropriate event class as its event argument:

```
private function sizeSelectedHandler(event:TextEvent):void
{
    ... process event data here ...
}
```

When the event occurs, the event handler function is executed and the data can then be appropriately handled.

Tip

Flash Builder 4 is able to automatically generate event handler functions for custom component instances in the same manner as with the Flex SDK's built-in components. ■

Follow these steps to handle a custom event with an MXML event handler:

1. **Open CustomEventApp.mxml from the chapter07 project.**
2. **Add a `Label` control at the end of the application with an `id` of `sizeMessage`.**
3. **Place the cursor inside the `<components:SizeSelectorStart>` tag, right before the ending `/>` characters.**
4. **Type `size` and press Ctrl+Space (Windows) or ⌘+Space (Mac) to see a list of the component's events, styles, and properties.**
5. **Select the custom `sizeSelected` event.** When prompted with Generated SizeSelected Handler, press Enter (Windows) or Return (Mac) to generate the event handler function:

   ```
   protected function sizeselector1_sizeSelectedHandler(
       event:TextEvent):void
   {
       // TODO Auto-generated method stub
   }
   ```
6. **Within the event handler function, set the `text` property of the `sizeMessage` object to the `text` property of the event object.** The function should now look like this:

   ```
   sizeMessage.text = "You selected " + event.text;
   ```
7. **Save and run the application, and click a radio button.**

When you click a radio button in the custom component, you should see that its value is displayed in the application.

The completed application code is shown in Listing 7.8.

LISTING 7.8

An application that uses a component that dispatches a custom event with data

```
<?xml version="1.0" encoding="utf-8"?>
<s:Application xmlns:fx="http://ns.adobe.com/mxml/2009"
  xmlns:s="library://ns.adobe.com/flex/spark"
  xmlns:mx="library://ns.adobe.com/flex/mx"
  xmlns:components="components.*">
  <fx:Script>
    <![CDATA[
      protected function selector_sizeSelectedHandler(event:TextEvent):void
      {
        sizeMessage.text = "You selected " + event.text;
      }
    ]]>
  </fx:Script>
  <s:layout>
    <s:VerticalLayout horizontalAlign="center" paddingTop="20"/>
  </s:layout>
  <components:SizeSelectorComplete id="selector"
    sizeSelected="selector_sizeSelectedHandler(event)"/>
  <s:Label id="sizeMessage"/>
</s:Application>
```

On the Web

The completed application is available in the Web site files as `CustomEventAppComplete.mxml` **in the** `chapter07` **project.** ■

Using Custom Event Classes

You can use custom event classes when you need to share complex data with the application or other components. For example, a data entry form component might need to share more than a single string value when the user clicks the form's button to indicate that data entry is complete.

An ActionScript class that's designed to be used as an event object has these requirements:

- The custom event class must be extended from `flash.events.Event`.

- The custom event class's constructor method should call the `Event` class's constructor method and pass the name of the event using a virtual method named `super()`.

- Data elements that are wrapped inside the event class are declared as public properties.

- If the event class is designed to bubble upward through the container hierarchy, the custom event class's `bubbles` property must be set to `true`.

- If you plan to "re-dispatch" an event object (that is, pass it to `dispatchEvent()` after receiving it in an event handler function), the custom event class must declare a `clone()` method that overrides the version declared in the superclass `Event`.

Creating the ActionScript class

Custom event classes are designed as ActionScript classes that extend the `Event` class. You can place the custom event class in any folder within a project source root; they're frequently placed in a folder simply named `events`.

Using the New ActionScript Class wizard

Follow these steps to create a custom event class that contains data for a Login form:

1. In the chapter07 project's source root, right-click the events subfolder and select New ⇨ ActionScript class.

2. In the New ActionScript Class wizard, shown in Figure 7.14, enter LoginEvent as the Name of the new class.

FIGURE 7.14

The New ActionScript Class wizard

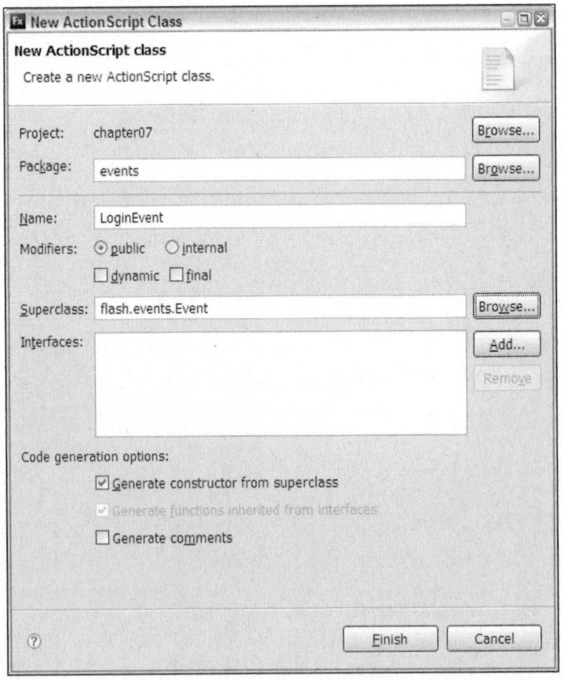

3. Click Browse next to the Superclass text box.

4. In the Superclass dialog box, shown in Figure 7.15, type Event to browse to the flash.events.Event class.

FIGURE 7.15

The Superclass dialog box

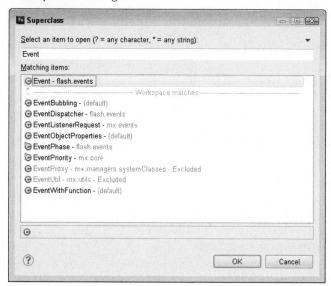

5. Click OK to select the Event class.

6. Select the Generate constructor from superclass option.

7. Click Finish to create the LoginEvent class.

The generated class code should now look like this:

```
package events
{
  import flash.events.Event;
  public class LoginEvent extends Event
  {
    public function LoginEvent(type:String,
      bubbles:Boolean=false, cancelable:Boolean=false)
    {
      super(type, bubbles, cancelable);
    }
  }
}
```

Tip

Notice that the call to the `super()` method passes the `type` (the name of the event), `bubbles` and `cancelable` arguments. The last two properties are marked as optional with default values of `false`. This means that when you create an instance of the `LoginEvent` class, you only need to pass the name of the event if you don't need the `bubbles` or `cancelable` properties set to `true`:

```
var myEvent:LoginEvent = new LoginEvent("myEventName");
```

Declaring public properties

Each data value you want to wrap into the custom event class should be declared as a public property. For example, a data value for the user's password in a login data entry form would be declared as:

```
public var password:String;
```

Follow these steps to add user and password data elements to the custom event class:

1. In the generated LoginEvent.as file, place the cursor inside the class declaration.
2. Declare two public properties named username and password, both datatyped as String:

    ```
    public var username:String;
    public var password:String;
    ```

Declaring event name constants

If you know the name of certain custom events for which the custom event class is designed, you can declare static event name constants that serve the same purpose of such constants as `MouseEvent.CLICK`; they help you accurately code the rest of the application.

For example, if the `LoginEvent` class will be used for a custom event named `login`, you would declare the event name constant with:

```
public static const LOGIN:String="login";
```

When you listen for the event using `addEventListener()`, you can use the constant with this code:

```
myComponent.addEventListener(LoginEvent.LOGIN, loginHandler);
```

Overriding the clone() method

The `Event` class has a method named `clone()` that's used to create a copy of the Event object. As I described previously, the `clone()` method is called when you re-dispatch an event after receiving it in an event handler function.

Caution

When you override a method in ActionScript, you must include the `override` keyword in the method declaration:

```
override public function superMethod():void
{}
```

If you don't include the `override` keyword and the method name matches one that's already declared in the current class's inheritance hierarchy, the compiler generates an error. ■

Keep in mind these rules for overriding the `clone()` method:

- The method must be marked with `override` and `public`.
- The method's return datatype should be `Event`.
- Within the method:
    - Instantiate the current custom event class.
    - Populate the new copy with data from the current copy.
    - Return the new copy.

The `clone()` method for the `LoginEvent` class would look like this:

```
override public function clone():Event
{
  var newEvent:LoginEvent = new LoginEvent(type);
  newEvent.username = username;
  newEvent.password = password;
  return newEvent;
}
```

Notice that the current object's `type` property (the name of the current event) is passed to the new copy of the event object in the constructor method call.

The ActionScript class in Listing 7.9 declares custom properties and event name constants and overrides the superclass's `clone()` method.

LISTING 7.9

A custom event class with properties and event name constants

```
package events
{
  import flash.events.Event;
  public class LoginEventComplete extends Event
  {
    public var username:String;
    public var password:String;
```

continued

LISTING 7.9   *continued*

```
public static const LOGIN:String="login";
public function LoginEventComplete(type:String,
  bubbles:Boolean=false, cancelable:Boolean=false)
{
  super(type, bubbles, cancelable);
}
override public function clone():Event
{
  var newEvent:LoginEvent = new LoginEvent(type);
  newEvent.username = username;
  newEvent.password = password;
  return newEvent;
}
  }
}
```

On the Web

The code in Listing 7.9 is available in the Web site files as `events/LoginEventComplete.as` **in the** `chapter07` **project.** ■

Dispatching a custom event class

When you dispatch a custom event class, follow these steps, which are the same as for pre-built event classes in the Flex framework:

1. **Define a custom event that sets the type as the new custom ActionScript class.**
2. **Create an event object typed as the custom event class at runtime.**
3. **Populate the event object with data.**
4. **Dispatch the event object.**

To declare a custom event named `login` that dispatches an instance of the `LoginEvent` class described previously, the code within the custom Form component would look like this:

```
<fx:Metadata>
  [Event(name="login", type="events.LoginEvent")]
</fx:Metadata>
```

At runtime, you create an instance of the event class, passing the event name into the constructor method:

```
var e:LoginEvent = new LoginEvent("login");
```

Next, populate the event object with data. Assuming you have `TextInput` controls with `id` properties of `userNameInput` and `passwordInput`, the code would be:

```
e.username = userNameInput.text;
e.password = passwordInput.text;
```

Finally, dispatch the event just as you would with one of the pre-built event classes:

```
dispatchEvent(e);
```

Listing 7.10 shows a `Form` component that declares and dispatches a custom event using the custom event class.

LISTING 7.10

A Form component that dispatches a custom event object

```
<?xml version="1.0" encoding="utf-8"?>
<mx:Form xmlns:fx="http://ns.adobe.com/mxml/2009"
  xmlns:s="library://ns.adobe.com/flex/spark"
  xmlns:mx="library://ns.adobe.com/flex/mx">
  <fx:Metadata>
    [Event(name="login", type="events.LoginEventComplete")]
  </fx:Metadata>
  <fx:Script>
    <![CDATA[
      import events.LoginEventComplete;
      private function clickHandler():void
      {
        var e:LoginEventComplete = new LoginEventComplete("login");
        e.username = userNameInput.text;
        e.password = passwordInput.text;
        dispatchEvent(e);
      }
    ]]>
  </fx:Script>
  <mx:FormItem label="User Name:">
    <s:TextInput id="userNameInput"/>
  </mx:FormItem>
  <mx:FormItem label="Password:">
    <s:TextInput id="passwordInput"/>
  </mx:FormItem>
  <mx:FormItem>
    <s:Button label="Log In" click="clickHandler()"/>
  </mx:FormItem>
</mx:Form>
```

On the Web

The code in Listing 7.10 is available in the Web site files as `components/LoginFormComplete.mxml` in the `chapter07` project. ■

Note

The Flex 4 SDK does not include a Spark version of the `Form` container; use the MX version instead. ■

Handling an event that uses a custom event class

You can handle an event that uses a custom event class in two ways — the same as with the Flex framework's pre-built event classes:

- With an MXML-based event handler
- With `addEventListener()`

In either case, you create a custom event handler function that expects an `event` argument typed as your custom event class:

```
private function loginHandler(event:LoginEvent):void
{}
```

Tip

Unlike the event classes in the `flash.events` package, your custom event classes must be imported prior to use:

```
import events.LoginEvent;
```

Flash Builder can create `import` statements for you as you type. For example, as you type the string `LoginEvent` in the event handler function signature, Flash Builder presents a list of classes that match what you've typed. When you select your class, the `import` statement for that class is added at the top of the ActionScript code. ■

Tip

If you don't see the list of available classes, press Ctrl+space to trigger Flash Builder's code completion tool. ■

Within the event handler function, extract data as needed. The complete event handler function might look like this:

```
private function loginHandler(event:LoginEvent):void
{
  messageLabel.text = "You logged as " + event.username +
    " with a password of " + event.password;
}
```

Then, to call the event handler function, use an MXML-based event handler, as in:

```
<components:LoginForm login="loginHandler(event)"/>
```

Or, if you prefer to use addEventListener(), call this code as the application starts up:

```
myForm.addEventListener(LoginEvent.LOGIN, loginHandler);
```

Either way, the loginHandler() function is called and the data is delivered to the application.

Tip

Flash Builder 4 can automatically create an event handler function for custom event objects as well as for objects that are defined in the core Flex SDK. Just be sure you properly defined the event in the component's metadata:

```
<fx:Metadata>
  [Event(name="login", type="events.LoginEventComplete")]
</fx:Metadata> ■
```

The application in Listing 7.11 uses the LoginForm component and listens for its Login event. When the event is dispatched, the application extracts and displays the custom event class properties.

LISTING 7.11

An application using a component with a custom event class

```
<?xml version="1.0" encoding="utf-8"?>
<s:Application xmlns:fx="http://ns.adobe.com/mxml/2009"
  xmlns:s="library://ns.adobe.com/flex/spark"
  xmlns:mx="library://ns.adobe.com/flex/mx"
  xmlns:components="components.*">
  <fx:Script>
    <![CDATA[
      import events.LoginEventComplete;
      private function loginHandler(event:LoginEventComplete):void
      {
        messageLabel.text = "You logged as " + event.username +
          " with a password of " + event.password;
      }
    ]]>
  </fx:Script>
  <s:Panel title="Please Log In" horizontalCenter="0" top="20">
    <components:LoginForm id="myForm" login="loginHandler(event)"/>
    <s:controlBarContent>
      <s:Label id="messageLabel"/>
    </s:controlBarContent>
  </s:Panel>
</s:Application>
```

On the Web

The code in Listing 7.11 is available in the Web site files as `LoginApp.mxml`. ∎

Summary

In this chapter, I described the Flex event architecture and how you can create your own events to share data between application components. You learned the following:

- Flex applications are event-driven.
- Every component that dispatches events includes `EventDispatcher` in its inheritance hierarchy.
- You handle events with either MXML-based event handlers or the `addEvent Listener()` method.
- Event handler functions receive a single `event` argument and return `void`.
- Flash Builder 4 adds the capability to generate event handler functions for all Flex components and events.
- You can declare and dispatch custom events from your custom components.
- You can create custom event classes to store and send data from custom components to the rest of the application.
- To make a custom event class bubble, set its `bubbles` property to `true`.
- Override the `Event` class's `clone()` method if you want to be able to re-dispatch custom event objects from an event handler method.
- You handle custom events and event classes with the same architecture as pre-built classes that are included in the Flex SDK.

Part II

Designing Flex Applications

IN THIS PART

Chapter 8
Using Flex Visual Controls

Chapter 9
Working with Text

Chapter 10
Using Layout Containers

Chapter 11
Using Cascading Style Sheets

Chapter 12
Controlling Animation and
Working with Drag and Drop

Chapter 13
Managing View States

Chapter 14
Declaring Graphics with MXML
and FXG

Chapter 15
Skinning Spark Components

Chapter 16
Managing Application
Navigation

Chapter 17
Working with Pop-up Windows

Using Flex Visual Controls

In previous chapters, I've described various aspects of Flex application development and declared instances of *controls* such as `Label` and `Button`.

Flex uses two types of visual components:

- **Containers.** Visual components that can contain other objects.
- **Controls.** Visual components that display information or provide the application with user interaction capabilities.

In Flex 4, there are two distinct groups of components:

- **Spark.** These components are new to Flex 4. They share a new architecture for *skinning*, or defining the control's visual appearance. The Spark control set also includes a set of controls known as *primitives* that aren't skinnable but give you access to important features of Flash Player 10. These include the controls for rendering vector graphics such as `Rect` and `Ellipse`, and for embedding bitmap graphics such as `BitmapGraphic`.
- **MX.** These components are inherited from the Flex 3 SDK, and many are still used in Flex 4. In some cases, such as the `DataGrid` and its related controls, the MX versions will eventually be replaced by Spark versions as the Flex SDK evolves. In other cases, such as `ViewStack` and other navigation containers, the Spark component set doesn't implement the exact equivalent functionality yet, but Flex 4 adds features that make these components useful in applications that primarily use Spark components.

IN THIS CHAPTER

Understanding Flex controls

Using text controls

Using layout controls

Using button controls

Using interactive controls

Presenting images

A Flex visual control can serve two purposes:

- All visual controls help you create the visual presentation of the application.
- Interactive controls enable the user to provide you with information through data entry and mouse gestures (such as moving the mouse or clicking its buttons).

In this chapter, I describe the nature of Flex visual controls and show the interface and usage of commonly used controls in data entry forms and other visual presentations.

On the Web

To use the sample code for this chapter, import the `chapter08.fxp` **Flex project file from the Web site files into your Flash Builder workspace. The Web site files for this chapter include sample applications for most of the controls described here.** ■

Instantiating and Customizing Controls

As I described previously, a Flex control is really an ActionScript class that can be instantiated either with an MXML tag-based declaration or an ActionScript statement.

To determine the behavior and use of a control, you need to know a control's public interface, or its API (application programming interface). Because a control is written as an ActionScript class, to get information from the control and to be able set its appearance, you need to know the control's members, their requirements, and their behavior. You need to know the control's

- Properties
- Methods
- Events
- Styles
- Effects
- Constants

In Flex 4, controls that implement the new Spark skinning architecture add these new members:

- Skin Parts
- Skin States

This information is available in the Flex API documentation for each framework's included controls.

Instantiating controls with MXML and ActionScript

When you instantiate a control with MXML, it's known as *declarative* instantiation:

```
<s:Button id="myButton" label="Click Me"/>
```

The same code in ActionScript is known as *programmatic* instantiation:

```
import spark.components.Button;
var myButton:Button = new Button();
myButton.label = "Click Me";
this.contentGroup.addElement(myButton);
```

Either way, the result is a visual object that's created in Flash Player memory and displayed in the parent container. The behavior of the object is determined by its API and internal implementation.

Setting control properties and styles

A control's properties and styles can be set in two ways:

- Upon instantiation with MXML attributes
- With ActionScript code

Properties and styles that are set with MXML attributes are done pretty much the same way. This `Label` control has a `text` property and a `color` style:

```
<s:Label id="myLabel"
    text="my text value" color="#ff0000"/>
```

But when you use ActionScript code to reset the object's properties and styles at runtime, the syntax is different. Properties are set with simple dot syntax:

```
myLabel.width = 100;
```

Styles are set with a method named `setStyle()` that takes two arguments: the style name and its new value:

```
myText.setStyle("fontWeight", "bold");
```

Cross-Reference
Styles are described in more detail in Chapter 11, but you need to understand this fundamental difference between properties and styles as you acquaint yourself with the controls that I describe in this chapter. ■

Understanding UIComponent and GraphicElement

As with any other ActionScript class, a control's members are a combination of those that are declared locally in the class and those that are declared in the class's inheritance hierarchy.

Both MX components (the components that are inherited from the Flex 3 SDK) and Spark components are extended from a superclass named `UIComponent`.

MX containers such as `DividedBox` and `ViewStack` can only contain content objects in their display lists that are instances of classes that extend `UIComponent`. In contrast, Spark containers, such as `Group` and `Panel` (the Spark version), can contain any element that implements the `IVisualElement` interface.

Some Spark visual classes, including such as `Rect`, `Ellipse`, and `BitmapImage`, are implemented as *primitives* rather than as components. These primitive elements can still be added to the display list of Spark containers because they're extended from a class named `GraphicalElement` that implements `IVisualElement`. But since they aren't extended from `UIComponent`, they can't be added as direct children of MX containers. For example, if you want to add a `Rect` as a child of an MX `VBox`, you must first wrap it inside a Spark container such as `Group`.

MX and Spark containers also differ in how they add elements to their display list. When you add an element to a Spark container with an MXML declaration, it's actually added to the container's `contentGroup`, an instance of the `Group` container that's known as a *skin part*. To add the component to a group programmatically, you call `contentGroup.addElement()`, or one of its related methods. The `addElement()` method requires an argument referencing an object that implements the `IVisualElement` interface. These include the `UIComponent` and `GraphicElement` classes (and their subclasses), so you can add both components (both MX and Spark) and primitives to any Spark container.

Tip

The `GraphicElement` and `UIComponent` classes share a set of methods and properties that represent the minimum API required for layout and display within a Flex 4 application. These shared methods and properties are defined in the `IVisualElement` interface. ∎

Table 8.1 describes key properties that are declared in the `UIComponent` and `GraphicElement` classes and are inherited by all MX and Spark components.

TABLE 8.1

Key Component Properties

Property	Data Type	Description
enabled	Boolean	Determines whether a component can receive user interactions, and in some cases, whether a "disabled" style will be used in its display.
height	Number	The height of the component in pixels. In MXML, you can also set `height` to a percentage setting such as "100%," but in ActionScript, the percentage would be set through the `percentHeight` property.
Id	String	This becomes the component's instance (variable) name. Each component id within the scope of the application or the current custom component must be unique. The value of the `id` property cannot be reset at runtime. Components that are instantiated in MXML without an `id` property are anonymous and cannot be directly addressed in ActionScript or binding expressions.
maxHeight	Number	The maximum height of the component in pixels.
maxWidth	Number	The maximum width of the component in pixels.
minHeight	Number	The minimum height of the component in pixels.

Property	Data Type	Description
minWidth	Number	The minimum width of the component in pixels.
percentHeight	Number	Percent height relative to the component's parent. This returns a meaningful value only if explicitly set.
percentWidth	Number	The percent width relative to the component's parent. This returns a meaningful value only if explicitly set.
styleName	String	A previously declared Cascading Style Sheets (CSS) style name (sometimes known as a CSS class) whose properties the component inherits.
tooltip	String	A string that appears in a tool tip when the mouse hovers over the component.
visible	Boolean	Whether the control is visible.
width	Number	The width of the control in pixels. In MXML, you also can set width to a percentage setting such as "100%," but in ActionScript, the percentage would be set through the percentWidth property.
x	Number	The number of pixels from the left edge of the control's parent to the left edge of the control. This is meaningful only in a container with absolute layout.
y	Number	The number of pixels from the top edge of the control's parent to the top of the control. This is meaningful only in a container with absolute layout.

Many more component properties are available that are used less frequently than those listed in Table 8.1. See the API documentation for a complete list.

Using Spark Text Controls

The Flex 3 MX components included five controls that were designed to display or accept text entry:

- **Label.** A single-line display control.

- **Text.** A variable-height display control.

- **TextInput.** A single-line data entry control.

- **TextArea.** A variable-height data entry control.

- **RichTextEditor.** A compound data entry control that accepts text and property settings and converts its content to HTML 1.0 code.

Flex 4 replaces the MX text controls with these five Spark text controls:

- **Label.** A new version of the display-only Label control that supports both single-line and word-wrapped display.

- **RichText.** A display-only control that supports single-line and word-wrapped display, and can display richly formatted text including different fonts, colors, sizes, and inline graphics.
- **RichEditableText.** In addition to the functionality of `RichText`, this control supports hyperlinks, scrolling, selecting, and editing, but does not have the "chrome" (borders and backgrounds) of the `TextInput` control.
- **TextInput.** A new version of the `TextInput` control that supports Flash Player 10's new text rendering capabilities.
- **TextArea.** A new version of the `TextArea` control that supports Flash Player 10's new text rendering capabilities.

As with the MX text controls, all of the Spark text controls extend `UIComponent`, so you can add them as children of both MX and Spark containers.

Tip
Adobe recommends that you only use the new Spark text controls in a Flex 4 application. While the old `Label` and `Text` controls still work in most circumstances, they don't support Flash Player 10's new text rendering capabilities. ■

Cross-Reference
For reasons of space, I only describe the details of the new Spark text controls in this book. For a complete description of the MX text controls, see the Flex 3 Bible (Wiley, 2008). ■

Using text control properties

All five Spark text controls support a common set of properties and styles, and each supports certain properties and styles that are unique to that control's functions and requirements.

Using the text property
The `text` property is used to set or get simple string values with all five Spark text controls. As with all properties, its value can be accessed in either MXML or ActionScript.

To set the `text` property in MXML, you can use either an XML text attribute or a nested child `<s:text>` tag set. This `Label` control has its `text` property set through an attribute:

```
<s:Label id="myLabel" text="Hello World"/>
```

This `Label` control has its `text` property set with a nested child element:

```
<s:Label id="myLabel">
  <s:text>Hello World</s:text>
</s:Label>
```

The two preceding `Label` declarations both result in displaying the words "Hello World" on the screen.

To set or get the `text` property in ActionScript, use simple dot syntax:

```
myLabel.text = "A new string";
```

Using the content property

The following Spark text controls support the `content` property:

- `RichText`
- `RichEditableText`
- `TextArea`

The `content` property enables you to define richly formatted text to be displayed by the control. The rich text is displayed by Flash Player using its Text Layout Framework (TLF), which is part of the Flash Text Engine (FTE) that was introduced in Flash Player 10. You can assign a string that contains these tags: `<s:span>`, `<s:div>`, and `<s:p>`. Each tag can be used with common style attributes such as `color`, `fontWeight`, `fontStyle`, and `fontSize`. The following MXML code declares a `RichText` control that contains three paragraphs. The first paragraph is small and normal, the second is larger and bold, and the third is larger and includes mixed text:

```
<s:RichText id="myRichText">
  <s:content>
    <s:p fontSize="10">A small normal paragraph</s:p>
    <s:p fontSize="14" fontWeight="bold">
    A medium bold paragraph</s:p>
    <s:p fontSize="18">A large
    <s:span fontStyle="italic">mixed-text</s:span> paragraph</s:p>
  </s:content>
</s:RichText>
```

Figure 8.1 shows the resulting `RichText` object displaying richly formatted text.

FIGURE 8.1

A `RichText` object displaying richly formatted text

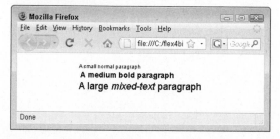

Managing rich text display with the TextFlow class

The MXML markup demonstrated in the preceding section only works during compilation. When the application is compiled, the content property's value is transformed into an instance of the TextFlow class. To manage rich text display at runtime, you create an instance of the TextFlow class using ActionScript code and populate it with data. You then assign the TextFlow object to the text control's textFlow property.

Caution

The content **and** textFlow **properties both represent the rich text that's displayed by one of the Spark text controls. The** content **property should only be used to represent literal rich text that's compiled into the application in an MXML declaration. To set or get rich text with ActionScript code, use the** textFlow **property.** ■

A TextFlow object sits at the top of a tree of child objects that represent the paragraph, span, and div elements specified in the <s:content> element's markup. Each element represents an ActionScript class, as shown here:

- **<s:p>.** Represents a ParagraphElement object.
- **<s:div>.** Represents a DivElement object.
- **<s:span>.** Represents a SpanElement object.

You can compose a TextFlow object at runtime with ActionScript code by creating instances of these objects and adding them to a TextFlow tree. The following example creates a TextFlow object containing a paragraph object with two span objects. The first displays normal text, and the second displays bold text. The code then assigns the resulting object to an existing text control through its textFlow property.

```
import flashx.textLayout.elements.TextFlow;
var textFlow:TextFlow = new TextFlow();
var p:ParagraphElement = new ParagraphElement();
var span:SpanElement = new SpanElement();
span.text = "Hello, ";
p.addChild(span);
span = new SpanElement();
span.setStyle("fontWeight", "bold");
span.text = "World!";
p.addChild(span);
textFlow.addChild(p);
myRichText.textFlow = textFlow;
```

The TextFlow class implements an extensive set of methods and properties that enable you to control rich text display at runtime. For more information, see the class's API documentation.

Looking at the TextFlowUtil class

The Flex 4 SDK's TextFlowUtil class implements export(), importFromText(), and importFromXML() methods that enable you to set and get the value of a Spark text control's textFlow property at runtime. The application in Listing 8.1 declares an XML object and then imports it into the `textFlow` property of a `RichText` control when the first button is clicked. When the second button is clicked, the text equivalent of the `textFlow` property is exported and displayed in a `Label` control:

LISTING 8.1

An application using TextFlowUtil to import rich text XML

```
<?xml version="1.0" encoding="utf-8"?>
<s:Application xmlns:fx="http://ns.adobe.com/mxml/2009"
  xmlns:s="library://ns.adobe.com/flex/spark"
  xmlns:mx="library://ns.adobe.com/flex/mx">
  <fx:Script>
    <![CDATA[
      import flashx.textLayout.formats.WhiteSpaceCollapse;
      import spark.utils.TextFlowUtil;
      protected function button1_clickHandler(event:MouseEvent):void
      {
        var richTextXML:XML =
          <TextFlow xmlns="http://ns.adobe.com/textLayout/2008">
            <p fontSize="10">A small normal paragraph</p>
            <p fontSize="14" fontWeight="bold">
              A medium bold paragraph</p>
            <p fontSize="18">A large
              <span fontStyle="italic">
               mixed-text paragraph</span></p>
          </TextFlow>
        myRichText.textFlow = TextFlowUtil.importFromXML(
          richTextXML, WhiteSpaceCollapse.PRESERVE);
      }
      protected function button2_clickHandler(event:MouseEvent):void
      {
        var xmlText:XML = TextFlowUtil.export(myRichText.textFlow);
        myLabel.text = xmlText.toXMLString();
      }
    ]]>
  </fx:Script>
  <s:layout>
    <s:VerticalLayout horizontalAlign="center" paddingTop="20"/>
  </s:layout>
  <s:HGroup gap="10">
    <s:Button label="Import Rich Text"
      click="button1_clickHandler(event)"/>
    <s:Button label="Export Rich Text"
      click="button2_clickHandler(event)"/>
  </s:HGroup>
  <s:RichText id="myRichText"/>
  <s:Label id="myLabel"/>
</s:Application>
```

On the Web

The code in Listing 8.1 is available in the Web site files in the `chapter08` **project as** `TextFlowXMLDemo.`
`mxml.` ◼

Notice that the root element of the XML data is named `TextFlow`, with this default namespace:

```
http://ns.adobe.com/textLayout/2008
```

The `TextFlowUtil` class enables you to save and retrieve properly formatted text data. You can save the text in a database or, if you're working in a desktop application, an XML file on the local hard disk.

Using the whiteSpaceCollapse style

The `whiteSpaceCollapse` style applies only to rich text set through the `content` property. It has these possible values:

- **collapse.** The default. Collapses, or normalizes, all whitespace within a `content` object. This is similar to how a Web browser reduces tabs, line feeds, and space characters into a single displayed space for display.

- **preserve.** Retains all whitespace characters as literals for display.

In this code, a `RichText` control displays a long text value set through the `htmlText` property:

```
<s:RichText id="myRichText" whiteSpaceCollapse="preserve">
  <s:content>
      <s:p>Some text
      with internal
      line feeds and tabs</s:p>
  </s:content>
</s:RichText>
```

Figure 8.2 shows how the control is displayed with `whiteSpaceCollapse` set to `preserve`. Notice that the extra line feeds and spaces in the code are displayed in the application.

FIGURE 8.2

A `RichText` control with `whiteSpaceCollapse` set to `preserve`

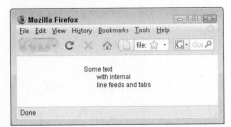

Tip

The `whiteSpaceCollapse` **style is defined for the** `RichText`, `RichEditableText`, **and** `TextArea` **con-trols. Use this property when displaying text (rather than accepting data entry); when you use it with the** `RichEditableText` **or** `TextArea` **controls, it should be paired with an** `editable` **property set to** `false`. ■

Tip

The possible values of the `whiteSpaceCollapse` **style are enumerated as constants in the** `flashx.textLayout.formats.WhiteSpaceCollapse` **class. You can use these constants when setting the style at runtime:**

```
myText.setStyle("whiteSpaceCollapse",
  WhiteSpaceCollapse.PRESERVE);  ■
```

Text entry controls

Flex 4 introduces new versions of the two primary text entry controls: `TextInput` and `TextArea`.

The TextInput control

The `TextInput` control accepts a single line of data entry. This instance of the `TextInput` control is displayed with all default properties and styles:

```
<s:TextInput id="myInput"/>
```

The `TextInput` control doesn't have its own `label` property, so it's commonly combined with a `Label` control and wrapped in an `HGroup` container, or wrapped in a `FormItem` container, which has its own `label` property. When combined with an `HGroup` container and a `Label` control, it looks like this:

```
<s:HGroup verticalAlign="middle">
  <s:Label text="Enter some text:"/>
  <s:TextInput id="myInput"/>
</s:HGroup>
```

As shown in Figure 8.3, the `TextInput` control is displayed as a rectangular region with a default background color of white.

FIGURE 8.3

A simple `TextInput` control

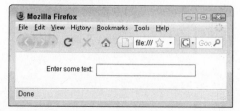

In addition to supporting the `text` and `content` properties I described previously, the `TextInput` and `TextArea` controls define certain properties that are of particular use in controlling data entry. Table 8.2 lists these properties.

TABLE 8.2

TextInput and TextArea Properties

Property	Data Type	Description
displayAsPassword	Boolean	When set to `true`, causes entered characters to be displayed as "*" characters. Defaults to `false`.
editable	Boolean	When set to `false`, prevents the control from receiving focus or data entry. Defaults to `true`.
maxChars	Int	The maximum number of characters the control accepts. If you exceed the `maxChars` value, you don't see a visible error message, but the control stops accepting entry.
restrict	String	Determines which characters the user can enter.
selectable	Boolean	Determines whether the control's text can be selected.

The restrict property

The `restrict` property enables you to restrict which characters can be typed into a `TextInput` control. The property's value defaults to `null`, meaning the user can enter any character. Any other value means the user can enter only those characters, or ranges of characters, that are listed.

The `restrict` property accepts either literal individual characters or ranges of characters, with no delimiter between each selection. For example, a `restrict` value of `abc` means you can enter any of the three characters: a, b, or c.

To enter a range of characters, separate the beginning and ending characters of the range with a hyphen. A `restrict` value of `a-z0-9` allows any alphabetical or numeric character.

The `restrict` property is case-sensitive, so if its value is set to `A-Z`, the user can enter only uppercase characters. Any characters that are entered in lowercase are converted to uppercase automatically. To allow alphabetical characters to be entered in either uppercase or lowercase, enter the range twice, as in `A-Za-z`. If you want to include the dash (-) or backslash (\) as permitted characters, you must first use the escape character, the backslash (\).

Tip

When a value is typed into a text control that isn't allowed by the control's `restrict` property, the user doesn't see an error — the typed value is just ignored. ■

Working with selected text

The Spark version of the TextInput control has a selectRange() method that enables you to programmatically select sections of text. The control's read-only selectionAnchorPosition and selectionActivePosition properties enable you to find out what's currently selected.

New Feature

The selectRange() **method and the read-only properties described in this section replace the** selection BeginIndex **and** selectionEndIndex **properties in the MX version of the** TextInput **control.** ■

This function selects all of a TextInput control's text and calls the control's setFocus() method to ensure that it has focus after the function has been executed:

```
private function selectText():void
{
  myInput.selectRange(0, myInput.text.length);
  myInput.setFocus();
}
```

This function determines which text is currently selected and uses the String class's subString() method to get the selected text:

```
private function showSelectedText():void
{
  var beginIndex:int = myInput.selectionAnchorPosition;
  var endIndex:int = myInput.selectionActivePosition;
  var selectedText:String =
    myInput.text.substring(beginIndex, endIndex);
  //return focus to the control and reset its selection
  myInput.setFocus();
  myInput.selectRange(beginIndex, endIndex);
  Alert.show(selectedText, "Selected Text");
}
```

Note

When the TextInput **control loses focus, its selections are lost. The code in the preceding example might be executed as a result of the user having clicked a button, which causes the** TextInput **control to lose focus. The function resets the control's focus and selected range to restore its original state after the function has been executed.** ■

Tip

When using the selection index properties, remember that all indexing in ActionScript is zero based. If selectionAnchorPosition **returns a value of 1, the second character is the first one that's selected.** ■

The TextArea control

The `TextArea` control implements most properties and methods of the `TextInput` control, but it works better when long values are to be entered. Unlike `TextInput`, it allows line feeds and wraps text that is too long to fit on a single line.

The `TextArea` control automatically creates a vertical scrollbar if its `text` or `content` value is too long to be displayed given the control's current size. This `TextArea` control has a specified height and width of 150 pixels each and a `text` value that's long enough to trigger a vertical scrollbar:

```
<s:TextArea id="myTextArea" width="150" height="150">
  <s:text>
  <![CDATA[Lorem ipsum dolor sit amet, consectetuer adipiscing elit.
    Praesent aliquam, justo convallis luctus rutrum, erat nulla
    fermentum diam, at nonummy quam ante ac quam. Maecenas urna
    purus, fermentum id, molestie in, commodo porttitor, felis. Nam
    blandit quam ut lacus. Quisque ornare risus quis ligula.
    ]]>
  </s:text>
</s:TextArea>
```

As shown in Figure 8.4, the `TextArea` displays a vertical scrollbar to accommodate the long text.

Tip

The Spark version of the `TextArea` control implements a `widthInChars` property that enables you to set the control's width based on a number of characters using the control's primary font family and size. It takes the font's em measurement (the width of the letter "M" in pixels) and multiplies it by the value you assign to `widthInChars` to set the `TextArea` control's width in pixels. For example, you would set `widthInChars` to 80 to enable the control to display approximately 80 characters per line. ∎

FIGURE 8.4

A `TextArea` control with a vertical scrollbar

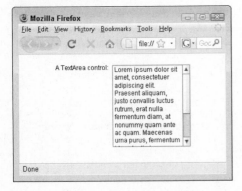

Using Layout Controls

A layout control creates visual output, but it isn't designed to be interactive in same way as a `Button`, `TextInput`, or other such control. These three controls affect layout but don't create any interaction with the user:

- `HRule`. A horizontal rule.
- `VRule`. A vertical rule.
- `Spacer`. An invisible control that can change other components' positions in horizontal or vertical layout.

Note

In the Flex 4 SDK, the MX versions of the layout controls described in this section have not been replaced by Spark versions. ■

The HRule and VRule controls

The `HRule` and `VRule` controls display a single line in the application. `HRule` creates a horizontal line, while `VRule` creates a vertical line. Each displays a primary line called the *stroke* and a secondary line called the *shadow*. You control the stroke and shadow colors and widths separately through distinct style settings.

Both `HRule` and `VRule` support the properties described in Table 8.3 to determine the control's appearance.

TABLE 8.3

HRule and VRule Properties

Property	Data Type	Description	Default
Width	Number	The width of the control	HRule: 100 VRule: 2
Height	Number	The height of the control	HRule: 2 VRule: 100
strokeColor	Uint	The control's stroke line color	0xC4CCCC
strokeWidth	Number	The width of the primary line in pixels	2
shadowColor	Uint	The control's shadow line color	0xEEEEEE

`HRule` and `VRule` objects are typically used to visually separate other visual components. The application in Listing 8.2 displays two Spark `Panel` containers in an application with a vertical layout, separated with the `HRule` control:

LISTING 8.2

An application using HRule

```xml
<?xml version="1.0" encoding="utf-8"?>
<s:Application xmlns:fx="http://ns.adobe.com/mxml/2009"
  xmlns:s="library://ns.adobe.com/flex/spark"
  xmlns:mx="library://ns.adobe.com/flex/mx">
  <s:layout>
    <s:VerticalLayout horizontalAlign="center"
      paddingTop="20" gap="20"/>
  </s:layout>
  <s:Panel id="panel1" title="Panel 1" height="75" width="150">
    <s:Label text="Some text"
      horizontalCenter="0" verticalCenter="0"/>
  </s:Panel>
  <mx:HRule strokeColor="#000000" width="{panel1.width}"/>
  <s:Panel title="Panel 2" height="75" width="150">
    <s:Label text="Some text"
      horizontalCenter="0" verticalCenter="0"/>
  </s:Panel>
</s:Application>
```

On the Web

The code in Listing 8.2 is available in the Web site files in the `chapter08` project as **HRule**Demo.mxml. ■

As shown in Figure 8.5, the HRule appears between the other two controls.

FIGURE 8.5

Two Panel containers separated by the HRule control

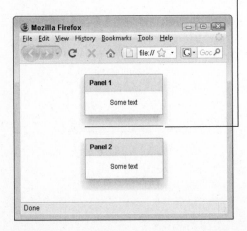

The HRule control

The Spacer control

The Spacer control is invisible and "pushes" other objects in an application or other container that uses vertical or horizontal layout. Its width and height properties, set to Number values, dictate how much additional space they add to the layout.

Tip

The Spacer control isn't useful in containers that use basic layout, because the controls dictate their absolute positions through x and y properties or through constraint-based layout. ■

The application in Listing 8.3 uses a Spacer with a height of 100 pixels to add vertical separation between two Panel containers:

LISTING 8.3

An application using Spacer

```
<?xml version="1.0" encoding="utf-8"?>
<s:Application xmlns:fx="http://ns.adobe.com/mxml/2009"
  xmlns:s="library://ns.adobe.com/flex/spark"
  xmlns:mx="library://ns.adobe.com/flex/mx">
  <s:layout>
    <s:VerticalLayout horizontalAlign="center"
      paddingTop="20" gap="20"/>
  </s:layout>
  <s:Panel id="panel1" title="Panel 1" height="75" width="150">
    <s:Label text="Some text"
      horizontalCenter="0" verticalCenter="0"/>
  </s:Panel>
  <mx:Spacer />
  <s:Panel title="Panel 2" height="75" width="150">
    <s:Label text="Some text"
      horizontalCenter="0" verticalCenter="0"/>
  </s:Panel>
</s:Application>
```

On the Web

The code in Listing 8.3 is available in the Web site files in the chapter08 project as SpacerDemo.mxml. ■

As shown in Figure 8.6, the space between the controls includes both the size of the Spacer and the verticalGap of the application.

FIGURE 8.6

Two controls separated with a `Spacer`

The Spacer control is invisible

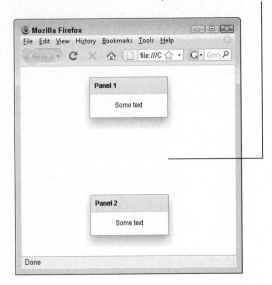

Using Button Controls

These Flex SDK button controls allow interaction with the user:

- `Button`
- `LinkButton`
- `CheckBox`
- `RadioButton`
- `PopupButton`

Tip

In the Flex 4 SDK, the `Button`, `CheckBox`, and `RadioButton` controls have been rewritten as Spark controls. The MX versions of the `LinkButton` and `PopupButton` controls are still used but now support Spark-style skinning using the `LinkButtonSkin` and `PopupButtonSkin` classes. ■

The Button control

The `Button` control is displayed as a rectangular object that can display a label and a graphical icon. It is one of the most commonly used interactive controls, and you typically use event listeners with the `Button` control and call ActionScript in reaction to its `click` event.

This simple `Button` control has a `label` of "Click Me" and a `click` event listener that displays an Alert dialog box:

```
<s:Button label="Click Me" click="Alert.show('You clicked')"/>
```

The MX version of the `Button` control behaves by default as a *command* button to indicate that some action should be executed. To use an MX `Button` as a control that switches between two states, set its `toggle` property to `true`. The MX version of the `Button` control has a `Boolean` property named `selected` that defaults to `false`. When `toggle` is set to `true`, each `click` event causes the `selected` property to switch back and forth between `true` and `false`.

In Flex 4, a new Spark `ToggleButton` control implements the same functionality. As with the MX `Button`, it supports the `selected` property and its appearance changes as the `selected` property switches back and forth between `true` and `false`.

This Spark `ToggleButton` control's `toggle` property is set to `true`. Each time it's clicked, the `selected` property switches between `true` and `false`. The `Label` displays the `selected` property's current value through a binding expression:

```
<s:ToggleButton id="toggleButton"
  label="Toggle Button" toggle="true"/>
<s:Label text="Button selected: {toggleButton.selected}"/>
```

As shown in Figure 8.7, the control's appearance changes depending on the value of its `selected` property. If `selected` is `false`, the control appears as a concave button; if `selected` is `true`, the control's appearance flattens to indicate that it's selected.

FIGURE 8.7

Toggle buttons with the `selected` property set to `true` and `false`

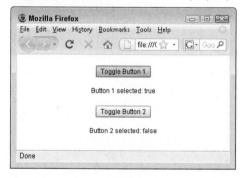

The LinkButton control

The MX LinkButton control performs all the actions of a Button, but it has an appearance and behavior more like a traditional HTML (Hypertext Markup Language) hyperlink. You set its label property to determine the text displayed on its face. Just like the Button control, you typically use an event listener to call ActionScript in reaction to its click event.

```
<mx:LinkButton label="Home" click="Alert.show('You clicked')"/>
```

In its initial state, the LinkButton is transparent and shows only its label and icon (if any). As shown in Figure 8.8, when the cursor hovers over a LinkButton, its background color changes and a mouse cursor shaped as a pointing hand appears.

FIGURE 8.8

The LinkButton with the mouse hovering over it

Tip

The MX LinkButton control extends the MX version of Button, so it supports all of its superclass's properties and methods. Some, however, aren't very useful with the LinkButton. For example, while the toggle property is available with LinkButton, setting it to true doesn't cause any difference in appearance when the user clicks it to set selected to true or false. ■

The CheckBox control

The CheckBox control enables the user to toggle its state to true or false. Just as with the Button control, CheckBox supports the label property. The label appears by default to the right of the icon and is a clickable object; that is, clicking the icon and the label both have the same effect of toggling selected to true or false.

This CheckBox control displays the label "Option selected":

```
<s:CheckBox id="myCheckBox" label="Option selected"/>
```

As shown in Figure 8.9, the CheckBox control's selected property causes an icon shaped as a check mark inside a box to be displayed. When selected is false, the icon appears as an empty box.

FIGURE 8.9

A CheckBox control with its selected property set to true

At runtime, you determine or set whether the control is checked through its selected property:

```
private function myCheckBox_changeHandler(event:Event):void
{
  if (myCheckBox.selected)
  {
    Alert.show("You selected the CheckBox");
  }
  else
  {
    Alert.show("You deselected the CheckBox");
  }
}
```

The RadioButton controls

RadioButton controls are designed to be used together in groups to represent mutually exclusive options. For example, this control represents the value "Small" and has its label set to the same value:

```
<s:RadioButton value="Small" label="Small"/>
```

To group multiple radio buttons, use a control named RadioButtonGroup. This control is a non-visual object and provides a way to group RadioButton controls together so that only one of them can be selected at any given time. The RadioButtonGroup control is assigned an id property. Then each RadioButton joins the group by naming the RadioButtonGroup in its groupName property.

This is a group of mutually exclusive RadioButton controls, because they all share the same groupName property:

```
<fx:Declarations>
  <s:RadioButtonGroup id="buttonGroup"/>
</fx:Declarations>
```

```
<s:RadioButton value="Small" label="Small"
  groupName="buttonGroup"/>
<s:RadioButton value="Medium" label="Medium"
  groupName="buttonGroup"/>
<s:RadioButton value="Large" label="Large"
  groupName="buttonGroup"/>
```

Tip

RadioButtonGroup **is implemented as a nonvisual control rather than a visual container. This gives you the freedom to arrange** RadioButton **controls anywhere on-screen, rather than visually grouped together. In Flex 4, you must declare such objects inside an** <fx:Declarations> **element.** ∎

The application in Listing 8.4 displays a group of RadioButton controls grouped with a RadioButtonGroup. When the user clicks Check Status, a pop-up window created by the Alert class displays the selected value.

LISTING 8.4

An application using a radio button group

```
<?xml version="1.0" encoding="utf-8"?>
<s:Application xmlns:fx="http://ns.adobe.com/mxml/2009"
  xmlns:s="library://ns.adobe.com/flex/spark"
  xmlns:mx="library://ns.adobe.com/flex/mxmx">
  <s:layout>
    <s:VerticalLayout horizontalAlign="center" paddingTop="20"/>
  </s:layout>
  <fx:Script>
    <![CDATA[
      import mx.controls.Alert;
      protected function buttonGroup_changeHandler(event:Event):void
      {
        Alert.show("You selected " + buttonGroup.selectedValue,
          "Radio Button Selected");
      }
    ]]>
  </fx:Script>
  <fx:Declarations>
    <s:RadioButtonGroup id="buttonGroup"
      change="buttonGroup_changeHandler(event)"/>
  </fx:Declarations>
  <s:VGroup>
    <s:RadioButton value="Small" label="Small"
      groupName="buttonGroup" selected="true"/>
    <s:RadioButton value="Medium" label="Medium"
      groupName="buttonGroup"/>
    <s:RadioButton value="Large" label="Large"
```

```
            groupName="buttonGroup"/>
    </s:VGroup>
</s:Application>
```

On the Web

The code in Listing 8.4 is available in the Web site files in the `chapter08` **project as** `RadioButtonDemo.` `mxml.` ■

Figure 8.10 shows the application displaying the resulting `RadioButton` controls and a pop-up window created by the `Alert` class that's displayed when the user clicks a `RadioButton` or otherwise selects a new value.

Tip

The `RadioButtonGroup` **control dispatches the** `change` **event whenever its** `selectedValue` **property changes. It also dispatches an** `itemClick` **event when the user clicks on any of the group's member objects.** ■

FIGURE 8.10

An application with `RadioButton` controls

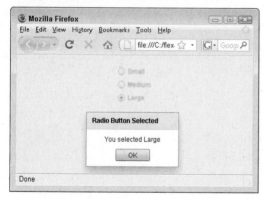

Other Data Entry Controls

The Flex framework includes these other controls that can be used to collect data from the application's user:

- `NumericStepper`
- `DateField`
- `DateChooser`
- `ColorPicker`

271

Each of these controls is designed to support data entry for a particular type of data.

Tip

In the Flex 4 SDK, the `NumericStepper` control has been rewritten as a Spark component. The MX versions of the `DateField`, `DateChooser`, and `ColorPicker` controls are the most recent versions and can be used in Flex 4 applications. ■

The NumericStepper control

The `NumericStepper` is a compound control that's designed for numeric data entry. It includes a `TextInput` control for direct entry and a set of buttons that increment and decrement the control's current value.

The `NumericStepper` doesn't have its own `label` property, so it's typically paired with a `Label` control or wrapped in a `FormItem` container, which has a `label` property. This code declares a simple `NumericStepper` wrapped in an `HGroup` with a `Label`:

```
<s:HGroup>
  <s:Label text="Enter value:"/>
  <s:NumericStepper id="myStepper" value="5"/>
</s:HGroup>
```

As shown in Figure 8.11, the control displays its `value` property, and the user can change it.

FIGURE 8.11

A `NumericStepper` control

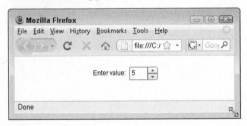

The `NumericStepper` supports these properties that determine its behavior:

- **minimum.** The minimum permitted value; defaults to 0.
- **maximum.** The maximum permitted value; defaults to 10.
- **stepSize.** The amount to increment or decrement when the control's buttons are clicked; defaults to 1.
- **maxChars.** The maximum length of the value that can be directly typed into the control.

This NumericStepper has a minimum value of 5, a maximum value of 25, and a stepSize of 5:

```
<mx:NumericStepper id="myStepper"
   minimum="5" maximum="25" stepSize="5"/>
```

The NumericStepper control's value property is bindable and can be used in a binding expression or ActionScript statement to get the value the user has entered:

```
<s:Label text="You entered: {myStepper.value}"/>
```

Date controls

Two data entry controls are designed to show or select a date value:

- **DateChooser.** Displays a calendar from which the user selects a date.
- **DateField.** Displays a TextInput and a small calendar icon. When either is clicked, a calendar is displayed for date selection.

The DateChooser control

The DateChooser control presents an interactive calendar that displays a month and year and enables the user to do the following:

- Navigate forward and back one month at a time
- Select a single date, multiple dates, or a range of dates with mouse operations

The following code declares a simple DateChooser control:

```
<mx:DateChooser id="myDateChooser"/>
```

The DateChooser control supports Boolean properties named allowMultipleSelection and allowDisjointSelection that respectively enable a user to select multiple and non-contiguous dates. Changing either property causes changes in the control's visual presentation.

As shown in Figure 8.12, the DateChooser is presented as a visual calendar from which the user makes selections.

The DateField control

The DateField control presents the user with an input control and a small calendar icon. By default, when the user clicks either the icon or the input, a calendar control pops up that looks the same as the DateChooser and enables the user to make his selection. However, unlike the DateChooser component, only a single date value can be selected.

FIGURE 8.12

A DateChooser control

The following code declares a simple DateField control:

```
<mx:DateField id="myDateField"/>
```

As shown in Figure 8.13, the DateField is presented as an input control and icon which, when clicked, present a calendar control.

The DateField control has a Boolean property named editable that's set to false by default. When set to true, the user can click into the input area and type a date value.

FIGURE 8.13

A DateField control

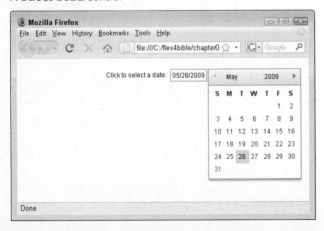

Date entry properties and methods

The DateChooser and DateField controls share a common set of properties that enable you to control their behavior and collect their data. Table 8.4 describes these properties and their capabilities.

TABLE 8.4

Date Entry Control Properties

Property	Data Type	Description	Default
selectedDate	Date	The currently selected date value.	null
showToday	Boolean	Determines whether the current date is highlighted.	true
dayNames	Array	An array of String values used as labels for the day names.	["S", "M", "T", "W", "T", "F", "S"]
minYear	Int	The minimum allowed year.	1900
maxYear	Int	The maximum allowed year.	2100
disabledDays	Array	An array of integer values indicating by zero-based index days that aren't selectable.	[] Setting of [0,6] would disable Sunday and Saturday
disabledRanges	Array of Object	A set of disabled ranges. Each range has named properties of range-Start and rangeEnd typed as Date values.	[]
selectableRange	Object	A selectable range. Requires named properties of rangeStart and rangeEnd typed as Date values.	null

Other useful properties are described in the API documentation for DateField and DateChooser.

The ColorPicker control

The ColorPicker control enables a user of your application to select from one of standard "web-safe" colors. It displays a button and, when clicked, a palette of colors. The currently selected color is represented by the control's selectedColor property, which returns a uint (unsigned integer) value. You can pass the value of the control's selectedColor to any other style or property which expects a color value.

Note

The ColorPicker control has not been rewritten in the Spark component framework for Flex 4. The MX version of the control, however, works fine in Flex 4 applications. ∎

The application in Listing 8.5 displays a `ColorPicker` control. When the user selects a color, a change event is dispatched. The code in the event handler function sets the application's `backgroundColor` style to the color that's selected by the application user:

LISTING 8.5

An application using a color picker

```xml
<?xml version="1.0" encoding="utf-8"?>
<s:Application xmlns:fx="http://ns.adobe.com/mxml/2009"
  xmlns:s="library://ns.adobe.com/flex/spark"
  xmlns:mx="library://ns.adobe.com/flex/mx"
  backgroundColor="#EEEEEE">
  <fx:Script>
    <![CDATA[
      import mx.events.ColorPickerEvent;
      protected function colorPicker_changeHandler(
        event:ColorPickerEvent):void
      {
        this.setStyle("backgroundColor", event.target.selectedColor);
      }
    ]]>
  </fx:Script>
  <s:Panel title="Using the ColorPicker control"
    horizontalCenter="0" top="20" width="300">
    <s:layout>
      <s:HorizontalLayout paddingTop="20" paddingRight="10"
        paddingLeft="20" paddingBottom="10"/>
    </s:layout>
    <s:Label text="Choose an application background color:"/>
    <mx:ColorPicker id="colorPicker" selectedColor="#EEEEEE"
      change="colorPicker_changeHandler(event)"/>
  </s:Panel>
</s:Application>
```

On the Web

The code in Listing 8.5 is available in the Web site files in the `chapter08` **project as** `ColorPickerDemo.mxml.` ■

Figure 8.14 shows the resulting application, with a `ColorPicker` control inside a `Panel`.

FIGURE 8.14

The ColorPicker control

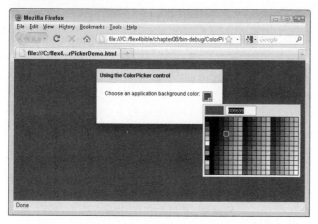

Using Interactive Controls

Beyond the data entry controls I described previously, certain controls are designed for user interaction that can be used in a variety of applications. In this section, I describe the ScrollBar and Slider controls.

The ScrollBar controls

There are two versions of the ScrollBar control:

- **HScrollBar.** For a horizontal scrollbar.
- **VScrollBar.** For a vertical scrollbar.

A ScrollBar control has four graphic elements: a track, a button, and two arrows. The user changes the control's current value by clicking and dragging the button, clicking above or below the button, or clicking one of the arrows. The ScrollBar returns its current value through its scrollPosition property. The scrollPosition property isn't bindable, so typically it handles ScrollBar interactions by listening for the scroll event, which is dispatched each time the position of the button changes.

Cross-Reference

The Flex 4 SDK also includes a new Scroller component that's designed to enable scrolling in Spark containers such as the new version of Panel. I describe how to use the Scroller component in Chapter 10. ■

ScrollBar properties

The new Spark versions of the VScrollBar and HScrollBar controls are extended from the ScrollBar superclass, which implements the properties described in Table 8.5.

TABLE 8.5

ScrollBar Properties

Property	Data Type	Description	Default
Value	Number	The position of the scroll button relative to the top of a VScrollBar or the left of an HScrollBar. This property is bindable.	null
Minimum	Number	The minimum value of scrollPosition.	0
Maximum	Number	The maximum value of scrollPosition.	100
pageSize	Number	Determines delta of change in pixels when user clicks before or after the scroll button.	20

The change event

The change event is dispatched each time the user interacts with the ScrollBar control. Its event object is typed as an event class named mx.events.ScrollEvent, which has a position property containing the new scrollPosition.

In the application in Listing 8.6, the HScrollBar control's new scrollPosition is displayed in a Label control whose text property is changed each time the scroll event is handled:

LISTING 8.6

An application using a scroll bar

```
<?xml version="1.0" encoding="utf-8"?>
<s:Application xmlns:fx="http://ns.adobe.com/mxml/2009"
  xmlns:s="library://ns.adobe.com/flex/spark"
  xmlns:mx="library://ns.adobe.com/flex/mx">
  <s:layout>
    <s:VerticalLayout horizontalAlign="center" paddingTop="20"/>
  </s:layout>
  <fx:Script>
    <![CDATA[
      [Bindable]
      protected var scrollPos:Number;
      protected function myScrollBar_changeHandler(event:Event):void
      {
        scrollPos = event.target.value;
      }
```

```
      ]]>
    </fx:Script>
    <s:Label id="scrollLabel" fontSize="18" fontWeight="bold"
      text="Current scroll position: {scrollPos}"/>
    <s:HScrollBar id="myScrollBar" width="300"
      minimum="0" maximum="300" pageSize="100"
      change="myScrollBar_changeHandler(event)"/>
  </s:Application>
```

On the Web

The code in Listing 8.6 is available in the Web site files in the `chapter08` **project as** `RadioButtonDemo.` `mxml.` ■

Figure 8.15 shows the `HScrollBar` and `Label` controls.

FIGURE 8.15

An `HScrollBar` and a `Label` control displaying its current position

The Slider controls

There are two versions of the `Slider` control:

- **HSlider.** For a horizontal slider.
- **VSlider.** For a vertical slider.

A `Slider` control displays a track and a "thumb" graphic that enables the user to select a value by clicking and dragging the thumb. You allow the slider to select any value within a range or restrict it to selecting values at particular intervals. The control also can display two thumb icons to represent starting and ending values.

The user interacts with the `Slider` control by clicking and dragging the thumb icon or by clicking before or after the thumb. If the user clicks before or after the thumb, the slider slides to the selected position. If the `Slider` has implemented snapping through the `snapInterval` property, the thumb slides to the snapping position that's closest to where the mouse click occurred.

The Slider controls return their current value through the value property. The value property is bindable, so you can handle Slider interactions through either binding expressions or events. Each time the Slider control's value changes, it dispatches the change event.

Slider properties

The VSlider and HSlider are extended from the Slider superclass, which implements the properties described in Table 8.6.

TABLE 8.6

Slider Properties

Property	Data Type	Description	Default
value	Number	The currently selected value of the Slider based on thumb position. Relevant only when thumbCount is 1.	0
minimum	Number	Minimum value of the Slider.	0
maximum	Number	Maximum value of the Slider.	10
snapInterval	Number	When set a value other than 0, enforces snapping to particular intervals between minimum and maximum. If set to 0, sliding is continuous.	0

The application in Listing 8.7 declares a horizontal Slider. Its value is displayed in a Label control through a binding expression.

LISTING 8.7

An application using a slider

```
<?xml version="1.0" encoding="utf-8"?>
<s:Application xmlns:fx="http://ns.adobe.com/mxml/2009"
  xmlns:s="library://ns.adobe.com/flex/spark"
  xmlns:mx="library://ns.adobe.com/flex/mx"
  creationComplete="executeBindings(true)">
  <s:layout>
    <s:VerticalLayout horizontalAlign="center" paddingTop="50"/>
  </s:layout>
  <s:HSlider id="mySlider" width="300"
    minimum="0" maximum="300"
    snapInterval="50"/>
  <s:Label fontSize="18" fontWeight="bold"
    text="Current slider position: {mySlider.value}"/>
</s:Application>
```

On the Web

The code in Listing 8.7 is available in the Web site files in the chapter08 **project as** SliderDemo.mxml. ■

Figure 8.16 shows the resulting application.

FIGURE 8.16

A horizontal slider

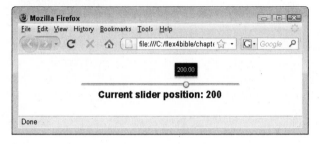

Slider events

The Slider controls also support a set of events that enable you to detect and handle changes to the Slider control's value with ActionScript event handlers. Slider events include the following:

- **change.** Dispatched when the control's value property changes as a result of a user gesture.
- **thumbDrag.** Dispatched when the user drags the thumb icon.
- **thumbPress.** Dispatched when the user presses on the thumb icon with the left mouse button.
- **thumbRelease.** Dispatched when the user releases the thumb icon.

The change event dispatches an event object typed as flash.events.Event, while the thumbDrag, thumbPress, and thumbRelease events dispatch an object typed as spark. events.TrackBaseEvent.

Using the Image and BitmapImage Controls

The Flex SDK presents images with the MX Image and the Spark BitmapImage control. The MX Image control can be used to present images that are downloaded from a server at runtime, loaded from the local hard disk at runtime (for AIR applications only, because Web applications don't have access to the local file system), or embedded in the Flex application. The Spark

BitmapImage control, which is implemented as a *primitive* class (rather than as a component), supports embedding of images but is not able to download images from the Web or load images from the local file system at runtime.

The Image and BitmapImage controls can be declared in either MXML or ActionScript. You determine which image is presented with the source property.

When used to load images at runtime, the MX Image control's source property is set to a full URI (Uniform Resource Identifier) path (subject to Flash Player security restrictions) or a location that's relative to the application location.

Tip

For Web applications, the application location is the Web server and folder from which the application's SWF file is downloaded. For desktop applications, the application location is the folder on the hard disk in which the AIR application is installed. ■

Flash Player and Adobe AIR can load these types of images at runtime:

- JPEG
- GIF
- PNG
- SWF

Tip

SWF files are treated as static images by the Image control, but if the SWF file was built in the Flash authoring environment and incorporates animation, the animation plays successfully in the Flex application. ■

Cross-Reference

For more complex uses of content built in the Flash authoring environment, see the description of creating Flash components in Chapter 5. ■

This code declares an MX Image control that loads a graphic file named flower1.jpg at runtime from an assets subfolder of the application's location folder:

```
<mx:Image source="assets/flower1.jpg"/>
```

Figure 8.17 shows the application displaying the graphic.

You can also load images at runtime by setting the Image control's source property with a binding expression. This Image downloads and displays a new image file each time the value of a bindable variable named selectedImage changes:

```
<mx:Image source="assets/{selectedImage}"/>
```

Notice that the value of the source property combines a literal value containing the location of the file and a binding expression containing the filename.

FIGURE 8.17

An application displaying an image with the `Image` control

Resizing images

The `Image` and `BitmapImage` controls size themselves by default based on the native dimensions of the original graphic image file. For example, if the image is 200 pixels wide by 300 pixels high and you don't declare a specific size, the control sizes itself to those dimensions.

You can resize images at runtime with the `Image` control's `height` and `width` properties. Both properties reflect the image size in pixels. If you set only one of these dimension properties, the `Image` control automatically calculates and resets the other dimension to maintain the image's original aspect ratio (the ratio of width to height). If this size is smaller than the original image, the image will appear smaller, but the entire `Image` control will be larger.

If you set both the height and width and don't exactly match the original aspect ratio, set the control's `maintainAspectRatio` property to `false` to enable it to skew the image:

```
<mx:Image source="graphics/flower1.jpg"
    height="200" width="400"
    maintainAspectRatio="false"/>
```

Figure 8.18 shows the image with explicit `height` and `width` properties and `maintain AspectRatio` set to `false`.

FIGURE 8.18

An image with specific `width` and `height` and `maintainAspectRatio` set to `false`

Embedding images

When you embed an image in a Flex application, you expand the size of the application by the size of the graphic file. At runtime an embedded image is displayed instantly, rather than having to be loaded from the Web or disk; the result is an improvement in perceived application performance, as well as the ability to import SVG (Scalable Vector Graphics) images in your Flex application.

You can embed images in a Flex application in two ways. If you want to embed an image once and always display it in the same location, use this syntax:

```
<s:BitmapImage source="@Embed('graphics/flower1.jpg')"/>
```

Because you're embedding the image in a particular instance of the `Image` control, you can't easily reuse the embedded image elsewhere in the application. If you want an embedded image that can easily be bound to various controls, use the `[Embed]` metadata tag and a `Class` variable declaration inside a Script section:

```
[Embed(source="graphics/flower1.jpg")]
[Bindable]
public var flowerImage:Class;
```

Then set the `BitmapImage` control's `source` property to the variable name using a binding expression:

```
<s:BitmapImage source="{flowerImage}"/>
```

Tip

When you embed images with the `[Embed]` metadata tag, you have the freedom to display the embedded image anywhere in the application. This is the same technique I described earlier when discussing using embedded images as `Button` control icons. ■

New Feature

Flex 4 adds two elements named `<fx:Library>` **and** `<fx:Definition>` **that can be used to define reusable visual elements in an MXML file. The following application defines a graphical element named** `FlowerImage` **based on a** `BitmapImage` **and then presents it twice:**

```
<?xml version="1.0" encoding="utf-8"?>
<s:Application xmlns:fx="http://ns.adobe.com/mxml/2009"
  xmlns:s="library://ns.adobe.com/flex/spark"
  xmlns:mx="library://ns.adobe.com/flex/mx">
  <fx:Library>
    <fx:Definition name="FlowerImage">
      <s:BitmapImage source="@Embed('assets/flower1.jpg')"/>
    </fx:Definition>
  </fx:Library>
  <s:HGroup horizontalCenter="0" top="20" gap="15">
    <fx:FlowerImage/>
    <fx:FlowerImage/>
  </s:HGroup>
</s:Application> ■
```

Changing images at runtime

You can change which image is displayed at runtime in a few different ways. The MX Image control's source property can be reset to a String, indicating the relative location of an image to be loaded at runtime. With both the MX Image and the Spark BitmapImage, you can set source to a variable that references an embedded image. This code embeds two images and switches the source of the Image control to one of the variable references when the button is clicked:

```
<fx:Script>
  <![CDATA[
    [Embed(source="assets/flower1.jpg")]
    [Bindable]
    public var flowerImage1:Class;
    [Embed(source="assets/flower2.jpg")]
    [Bindable]
    public var flowerImage2:Class;
  ]]>
</fx:Script>
<s:BitmapImage id="myImage" source="{flowerImage1}"/>
<s:Button label="Change Image" click="myImage.source=flowerImage2"/>
```

You also can set the source property using a binding expression. This code uses a group of RadioButton controls to enable the user to switch between the two embedded images:

```
<fx:Declarations>
  <s:RadioButtonGroup id="flowerGroup"/>
</fx:Declarations>
<s:BitmapImage source="{flowerGroup.selectedValue}"/>
<s:RadioButton value="{flowerImage1}" label="Image 1"
  groupName="flowerGroup" selected="true"/>
```

```
<s:RadioButton value="{flowerImage2}" label="Image 2"
  groupName="flowerGroup"/>
```

You also can change images at runtime with the MX Image control's load() method. The load() method accepts a single argument that can be either a String for a runtime loaded image or a variable referencing an embedded image. This code shows a Button control with a click event handler that causes a new image to be loaded at runtime:

```
<mx:Image id="myImage" source="assets/flower1.jpg"/>
<s:Button label="Change Picture"
  click="myImage.load('assets/flower2.jpg')"/>
```

Tip

It doesn't matter whether you use the load() method or simply change the value of the source property. Both actions have the same effect on the MX Image control. ▪

Summary

In this chapter, I described the nature of Flex controls and the details of some of the most useful controls in the Flex framework. You learned the following:

- Flex visual components consist of containers and controls.

- A container is a visual component that contains other objects.

- A visual control presents information to the user and can also be interactive.

- Controls can be used for application layout, to display data, and to collect data from the user.

- The new Spark components include these text controls: Label, RichText, RichEditableText, TextInput, and TextArea.

- Layout controls include HRule, VRule, and Spacer.

- Button controls include Button, CheckBox, RadioButton, and PopupButton.

- Other data entry controls include NumericStepper, DateField, DateChooser, and ColorPicker.

- Other interactive controls include HScrollBar, VScrollBar, HSlider, and VSlider.

- The MX Image control displays images that are loaded at runtime or embedded in the Flex application.

- The Spark BitmapImage control is a lighter weight primitive (rather than a complete component) that only works with embedded images.

Working with Text

IN THIS CHAPTER

Using advanced text layout

Controlling fonts

Using device fonts

Embedding fonts

Setting font rotation

Using formatter classes

When you present text in a Flex application, many choices and tools can determine how text is displayed and processed. Text values can be "hard-coded" in an application, retrieved from a data source (such as database on a server), and stored in memory as constants or variables.

When text is presented to the user in visual control, you select many font settings, including the font typeface and its size, weight, and style. In this chapter, I describe the various tools available for text processing and presentation in Flex. I describe these strategies and techniques:

- Using the Flash Text Engine (FTE) to present complex text
- Selecting device fonts for text display that are already installed on the client computer
- Embedding fonts to tightly control text display regardless of the state of the client computer
- Formatting of text values with the `formatter` family of classes

Any discussion of text presentation in Flex must include the use of Cascading Style Sheets (CSS) to select font typefaces and styles, and the use of visual controls that are specifically designed for text presentation, such as the `Label` and `RichText` controls. (Refer to Chapter 8 for a detailed discussion about the use of visual controls and Chapter 11 for more information about CSS.) In this chapter, I describe uses of styles that are specifically designed to control text presentation, and I expand on the use of the `Label` and `RichText` controls in presenting text to the user.

On the Web

To use the sample code for this chapter, import the `chapter09.fxp` **Flex project from the Web site files into your Flash Builder workspace.** ■

Using Advanced Text Layout

Flex 4 applications require Flash Player 10, whether the application is deployed over the Web or on the desktop with Adobe AIR. One of the benefits of this most recent version of Flash Player is its capability to present complex text with an element of the software known as the *Flash Text Engine* (FTE) and the *Text Layout Framework* (TLF).

The FTE supports these features:

- Bidirectional and vertical text layout
- Support for more than 30 alphabets and character sets, including Arabic, Hebrew, Chinese, Japanese, Korean, Thai, Lao, the major writing systems of India, and others
- Advanced typographical control, including kerning, masks, blends, whitespace handling, margins, and indentations
- Display of text across multiple columns

The following new text controls, initially described in Chapter 8, support the features of the FTE and TLF:

- `Label`
- `RichText`
- `RichEditableText`
- `TextInput`
- `TextArea`

The FTE is a set of classes that support complex text presentation. These classes are a part of Flash Player 10 and are available to all Flash documents regardless of whether they're built with the Flex SDK or the Flash authoring environment. The TLF is a separate framework, provided in the set of classes packaged in the component library file `textLayout.swc`. This SWC file is included with the Flex 4 SDK, so its classes are available to all Flex 4 applications.

Presenting richly formatted text

As I previously described in Chapter 8, the `RichText`, `RichEditableText`, and `TextArea` controls support the `content` and `textFlow` properties, which you can use to describe richly formatted text. When you set the `content` property's value with a child element in an MXML declaration, you can include a number of tags that create various layout and visual effects. Each tag is the equivalent of an ActionScript class that's provided as part of the TLF.

Table 9.1 shows the tags you can include in a content string, their ActionScript equivalents.

TABLE 9.1

TLF Tags and Equivalent Classes

Tag	Class	Description
`<s:div>`	`DivElement`	Defines a horizontal block with no implicit vertical white space above or below.
`<s:p>`	`ParagraphElement`	Defines a horizontal block with implicit vertical white space above and below.
`<s:span>`	`SpanElement`	Defines a section of text to which various text styles can be applied.
`<s:a>`	`LinkElement`	Defines a section of text that, when clicked, links to a Uniform Resource Locator (URL).
`<s:img>`	`InlineGraphicElement`	Defines an inline graphic.
`<s:br>`	`BreakElement`	Defines a line feed.
`<s:tab>`	`TabElement`	Defines a tab character.
`<s:tcy>`	`TCYElement`	Causes text to be drawn horizontally within a line that otherwise is laid out vertically.

You declare each of the TLF tags with the Spark XML namespace prefix of `s:`, as shown in the application in Listing 9.1. The application's `RichText` object has its `content` set to display text with mixed font sizes and font faces, and bold and italicized characters.

LISTING 9.1

An application with richly formatted text

```
<?xml version="1.0" encoding="utf-8"?>
<s:Application xmlns:fx="http://ns.adobe.com/mxml/2009"
  xmlns:s="library://ns.adobe.com/flex/spark"
  xmlns:mx="library://ns.adobe.com/flex/mx">
  <s:layout>
    <s:VerticalLayout horizontalAlign="center" paddingTop="20" gap="20"/>
  </s:layout>
  <s:RichText id="myRichText">
    <s:content>
      <s:p fontSize="10" fontFamily="_sans">
        A small normal paragraph in a serif font</s:p>
      <s:p fontSize="14" fontWeight="bold" fontFamily="_serif">
        A medium bold paragraph in a sans serif font</s:p>
      <s:p fontSize="18" fontFamily="_typewriter">A large
        <s:span fontStyle="italic">mixed-text</s:span>
        paragraph in a typewriter font</s:p>
    </s:content>
  </s:RichText>
</s:Application>
```

On the Web

The code in Listing 9.1 is available in the Web site files as `RichTextDemo.mxml` **in the** `chapter09` **project.** ■

Figure 9.1 shows the resulting application. Line feeds and vertical space in the `RichText` object result from the <p> tags, and text is displayed in various font styles based on the `fontWeight`, `fontStyle`, and `fontFamily` attributes.

An application with a `RichText` object

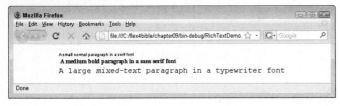

Each of the container elements, including `<s:p>`, `<s:div>`, and `<s:span>`, support many attributes that match identically named styles. These include, but are not limited to:

- `backgroundColor`
- `color`
- `fontFamily`
- `fontSize`
- `fontStyle`
- `fontWeight`
- `lineHeight`
- `lineThrough`
- `textAlign`
- `textDecoration`
- `textIndent`
- `textRotation`
- `whiteSpaceCollapse`

For example, the application in Listing 9.2 defines two paragraphs. Each paragraph has its first line indented 20 pixels and justifies the text to expand and fill the entire line. The first paragraph has a `marginBottom` setting of 10 pixels to add vertical white space between the paragraphs.

LISTING 9.2

An application with content that uses text styles

```
<?xml version="1.0" encoding="utf-8"?>
<s:Application xmlns:fx="http://ns.adobe.com/mxml/2009"
  xmlns:s="library://ns.adobe.com/flex/spark"
  xmlns:mx="library://ns.adobe.com/flex/mx">
  <s:RichText id="myText" width="200" horizontalCenter="0" top="20">
    <s:content>
      <s:p textIndent="20" textAlign="justify">Lorem ipsum dolor sit amet,
      consectetuer adipiscing elit. Praesent aliquam, justo convallis
      luctus rutrum, erat nulla fermentum diam, at nonummy quam ante ac
      quam.</s:p>
      <s:p textIndent="20" textAlign="justify">Maecenas urna purus,
      fermentum id, molestie in, commodo porttitor, felis. Nam blandit quam
      ut lacus. Quisque ornare risus quis ligula.</s:p>
    </s:content>
  </s:RichText>
</s:Application>
```

On the Web

The code in Listing 9.2 is available in the Web site files as `TextIndentDemo.mxml` in the `chapter09` **project.** ■

Figure 9.2 shows the resulting application.

FIGURE 9.2

A `RichText` object that uses text justification and indentation

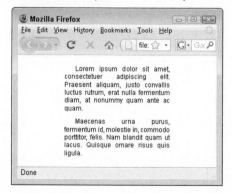

Presenting text in columns

The new text controls support columnar display. Use these properties to define the number and size of the columns and gutters (gaps between the columns):

- `columnCount`. Set to `auto` (the default) or a numeric value from 1 to 50.
- `columnWidth`. Set as a `Number` to indicate the columnar width in pixels.
- `columnGap`. Set as a `Number` to determine the width of the gap between the columns in pixels.

The application in Listing 9.3 presents a `RichText` object with three columns. The text in the control's content property flows from one column to the next.

LISTING 9.3

Displaying text in multiple columns

```
<?xml version="1.0" encoding="utf-8"?>
<s:Application xmlns:fx="http://ns.adobe.com/mxml/2009"
  xmlns:s="library://ns.adobe.com/flex/spark"
  xmlns:mx="library://ns.adobe.com/flex/mx">
<s:RichText id="myTextArea" width="500" height="75"
   columnCount="3" columnWidth="150" columnGap="25"
   horizontalCenter="0" top="20">
   <s:content>
     Lorem ipsum dolor sit amet, consectetuer adipiscing elit.
     Praesent aliquam, justo convallis luctus rutrum, erat
     nulla fermentum diam, at nonummy quam ante ac quam.
     Maecenas urna purus, fermentum id, molestie in,
     commodo porttitor, felis. Nam blandit quam ut lacus.
     Quisque ornare risus quis ligula.
   </s:content>
  </s:RichText>
</s:Application>
```

On the Web

The code in Listing 9.3 is available in the Web site files as `ColumnDemo.mxml` in the `chapter09` project. ∎

Figure 9.3 shows the resulting text layout in multiple columns.

Using bidirectional text

The new Flex 4 text controls support bidirectional text; that is, if you want to present a string that includes both Latin characters and an alphabet that runs right to left, such as Hebrew or Arabic, the text engine will present the text successfully if you set the control's `direction` property to a value of `rtl` (right to left).

The application in Listing 9.4 uses a `RichText` control that displays some text that's a mixture of Latin characters such as those used in English, plus some words in Hebrew.

FIGURE 9.3

A text control laying out text in multiple columns

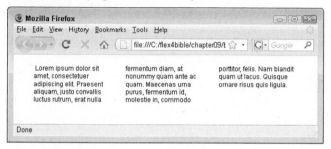

LISTING 9.4

Presenting bidirectional text

```
<?xml version="1.0" encoding="utf-8"?>
<s:Application xmlns:fx="http://ns.adobe.com/mxml/2009"
  xmlns:s="library://ns.adobe.com/flex/spark"
  xmlns:mx="library://ns.adobe.com/flex/mx">
  <s:RichText id="myText" width="200" fontSize="18"
    direction="rtl"  horizontalCenter="0" top="20">
    <s:content>
      <![CDATA[
      ‏.הדלקההו הספדהה תיישעת Lorem Ipsum לש ימלוג טסקט טושט אוה‏
      ]]>
    </s:content>
  </s:RichText>
</s:Application>
```

On the Web

The code in Listing 9.4 is available in the Web site files as `RTLDemo.mxml` in the `chapter09` project. ∎

Figure 9.4 shows the resulting display, successfully mixing the two alphabets.

FIGURE 9.4

A RichText control displaying mixed text

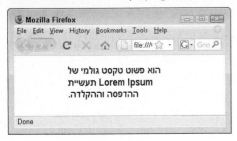

Controlling Fonts with Cascading Style Sheets

Cascading Style Sheets (CSS) constitute one of the most important tools you have for modifying the appearance of text on the screen. In this section, I describe specific styles and their values that you can use to change how Label, RichText, TextInput, or TextArea controls present textual information.

Cross-Reference
I describe more extensive use of CSS in Flex applications in Chapter 11. ■

In Flex 3, some font styles could be used with both device and embedded fonts, while others could be used only with embedded fonts. In Flex 3 applications, you could apply these styles to all fonts:

- fontFamily. Determines the typeface.
- color. Determines the typeface color.
- fontSize. Determines the font size.
- fontWeight. Selects a bold font.
- fontStyle. Selects an italicized font.
- textDecoration. Selects an underlined font.

These styles had an effect only on embedded fonts:

- kerning. Enables adjustments to the horizontal gap between characters.
- fontAntiAliasType. Enables the use of these advanced anti-aliasing styles:
  - fontGridType. Determines whether to measure fonts based on pixels or subpixels.
  - fontThickness. Determines the thickness of font glyph edges.
  - fontSharpness. Determines the sharpness of font glyphs.

In Flex 4, you can apply all font styles to all text, regardless of whether the application is using a device font or an embedded font.

Selecting fonts

You select which typeface you want to use with the `fontFamily` (or `font-family`) style. This `Label` control presents its text in the `Arial` typeface with an inline style declaration:

```
<s:Label fontFamily="Arial" text="Hello World"/>
```

When you declare the `fontFamily` style in an embedded or external style sheet, you can use either the camel-case version of the style name, `fontFamily`, or the hyphenated version, `font-family`. This type selector sets an application's default font for the `Label` and `RichText` controls to `Times New Roman`:

```
<fx:Style>
  @namespace s "library://ns.adobe.com/flex/spark";
  s|Label, s|RichText {
    font-family:"Times New Roman";
  }
</fx:Style>
```

Cross-Reference
I describe the use of namespaces to label type selectors in Flex 4 CSS declarations in Chapter 11. ■

Tip
When you designate a typeface that has spaces in its name, always wrap the font name in quotation marks. If you don't use quotes, the CSS parser removes the spaces from the font name, resulting in a font name Flash Player might not recognize.

For example, a font declared with a name of `Bookman Old Style Bold` without surrounding quotes is transformed internally to `BookmanOldStyleBold` and no longer matches up correctly with its actual font on the client system. ■

Caution
If you misname a typeface in a `fontFamly` declaration, Flash Player renders the unrecognized font as the client system's default `serif` typeface, which is typically **Times Roman**. ■

Two types of fonts can be used in Flex applications:

- **Device fonts.** Typefaces that are installed on the client system.
- **Embedded fonts.** Typefaces that are embedded in a compiled Flex application and delivered to the client system as part of the application SWF file.

Table 9.2 lists the pros and cons of using device versus embedded fonts.

TABLE 9.2

Pros and Cons of Device and Embedded Fonts

	Pros	Cons
Device fonts	Enable you to minimize the size of the compiled Flex application and speed the download of the application during startup (for Web applications) or installation (for desktop applications).	Limited to those fonts that are installed universally, so your graphic design capabilities are limited.
Embedded fonts	Enable you to use any font to which you have access during development. Supports anti-aliasing for smoother font rendering.	Result in a larger compiled application SWF file. If not managed carefully, embedded fonts can result in a "bloated" application file and significantly slow download and installation.

Using device fonts

When you declare a device font, you should declare a list of fonts you'd like to use in order of preference to ensure it looks as close as possible to how you intend it. The last item in the list should be a generic device font name that selects a font based on what's available on the client system.

This CSS declaration sets the fontFamily style as a list with a first preference of Helvetica and a last preference of the generic font family _sans:

```
<fx:Style>
  @namespace s "library://ns.adobe.com/flex/spark";
  s|Label, s|RichText {
    font-family:Helvetica, Arial, "_sans";
  }
</fx:Style>
```

The first choice, Helvetica, is typically available on Mac OS X but not on Windows. If Flash Player doesn't find this font on the client system, it then looks for the second choice, Arial, which is installed by default on both Windows and Mac OS X. The final choice,_sans, refers to the general family of sans serif fonts. If Flash Player doesn't find either of the first two choices, it uses the client system's default font of that family.

Three generic device font names are recognized by Flash Player:

- _sans. Refers to smoother typefaces that are generally selected for their easy readability on computer screens. This family includes such fonts as Arial, Helvetica, and Verdana and is used in this book as the font family for headline text.

- _serif. Refers to typefaces that have nonstructural visual details added to the ends of font lines. This font family includes such fonts as Times Roman (and its variants, such as Times New Roman) and Baskerville and is used in this book as the font family for paragraph text.

- _typewriter. Refers to fixed pitch typefaces that look like they were created on typewriters. This font family includes such fonts as Courier (and its variants, such as Courier New) and Prestige Elite and is used in this book to represent code samples.

Caution

If you designate only a single typeface in a `fontFamily` **declaration and that font doesn't exist on the client system, Flash Player replaces the font as needed. In this case, the application might not appear to the user as originally designed. ■**

Using embedded fonts

When you embed a font in a Flex application, you guarantee that the font will be available to the client system.

Embedded fonts offer great advantages to graphic designers:

- You can strongly "brand" an application's appearance with fonts that are unique to a particular company's design standards.
- Embedded fonts support anti-aliasing, which enables you to control the sharpness of the font to a fine degree.

Embedded fonts have these limitations:

- When you embed a font, the size of the compiled SWF file expands to include the font definition.
- Only TrueType or OpenFace fonts can be embedded directly within Flex applications with simple style declarations or ActionScript metadata tags.

New Feature

In Flex 3, the capability to apply rotation or transparency to a text control was limited to embedded fonts. In Flex 4, you can rotate a text control or set its `alpha` **property to control transparency for both device and embedded fonts. ■**

Note

You can embed other font styles such as PostScript Type 1 or bitmap fonts, but these fonts must first be embedded in a Flash document to vectorize them, and only then can they be embedded in a Flex application. ■

Caution

Fonts that you've downloaded or purchased from a font vendor aren't always licensed for use in a Flash document or Flex application. Check your license for any restrictions on a font's use. ■

Declaring embedded fonts with CSS

You can embed a font with the `@font-face` style selector in an embedded or external style sheet. This selector supports the following style names:

- `src:local`. Selects a font by its system font name. Fonts embedded in this manner can only be used with MX text controls.

- `src:url`. Selects a font by the location and name of the font file. Fonts embedded in this manner can be used by both MX and Spark text controls.

- `fontFamily`. Designates a font name that can be used by the rest of a Flex application to refer to the embedded font.

Each embedded font declaration must include `fontFamily` to create an alias by which the embedded font will be referenced in the rest of the application and either `src:local` or `src:url` to designate the font to embed.

Embedding by font file location

You can embed a font that you haven't installed in your operating system by referring to the font by its file location. You can refer to font files from anywhere in your file system, but for convenience you should copy the font file somewhere in your project and then refer to it with a relative file location.

This `@font-face` declaration embeds a font by its filename and assigns a `fontFamily` of Goudy:

```
@font-face {
  src:url("../fonts/GOUDOS.TTF");
  font-family:"Goudy";
}
```

After the font has been embedded, you can use the `fontFamily` style to use the font in a particular text control with an inline style declaration or in a set of controls with a style selector. This Spark `Label` control uses the embedded font:

```
<s:Label fontFamily="Goudy" text="An embedded font"/>
```

This CSS declaration includes the `@font-face` selector to embed a font, and a type selector that assigns the embedded font to `Label` and `RichText` controls:

```
<fx:Style>
  @namespace s "library://ns.adobe.com/flex/spark";
  @font-face {
    src:url("../fonts/GOUDOS.TTF");
    font-family:"Goudy";
  }
  s|Label, s|RichText {
    font-family: Goudy;
  }
</fx:Style>
```

Embedding font variations

Fonts that support variations in presentation such as bold and italics are delivered as individual font files. When embedding a font by its filename, if the font is defined in multiple files (one for each combination of font weight and style), you must declare each variation with a separate `@font-face` selector. If you set all of a font's selectors with the same `fontFamily`, you can then refer to the individual fonts from an inline style declaration or a style selector by simply referencing the appropriate font family name.

The application in Listing 9.5 uses the Goudy font with all its variations and a set of `Label` controls that use the font in multiple sizes and variations of appearance. The `@font-face` declarations embed all three of a font's available variations and assign the same `fontFamily` to each. The `font-weight` and `font-style` settings in each `@font-face` selector determine when each font file will be used.

LISTING 9.5

An application using an embedded font

```
<?xml version="1.0" encoding="utf-8"?>
<s:Application xmlns:fx="http://ns.adobe.com/mxml/2009"
  xmlns:s="library://ns.adobe.com/flex/spark"
  xmlns:mx="library://ns.adobe.com/flex/mx">
  <s:layout>
    <s:VerticalLayout horizontalAlign="center" paddingTop="20" gap="20"/>
  </s:layout>
  <fx:Style>
    @font-face {
      src:url("../fonts/GOUDOS.ttf");
      font-family:"Goudy";
    }
    @font-face {
      src:url("../fonts/GOUDOSB.ttf");
      font-family:"Goudy";
      font-weight:bold;
    }
    @font-face {
      src:url("../fonts/GOUDOSI.ttf");
      font-family:"Goudy";
      font-style:italic;
    }
  </fx:Style>
  <s:Label id="text1" text="Goudy 18"
    fontFamily="Goudy" fontSize="18"/>
  <s:Label text="Goudy 30"
    fontFamily="Goudy" fontSize="30"/>
  <s:Label text="Goudy 72"
    fontFamily="Goudy" fontSize="72"/>
  <s:Label text="Goudy italic"
    fontFamily="Goudy" fontSize="72" fontStyle="italic"/>
  <s:Label text="Goudy bold"
    fontFamily="Goudy" fontSize="72" fontWeight="bold"/>
</s:Application>
```

On the Web

The code in Listing 9.5 is available in the Web site files as `EmbedFontByFileName.mxml` **in the** `chapter09` **project.** ∎

Figure 9.5 shows the resulting application with Spark `Label` controls displaying text in various sizes and styles.

FIGURE 9.5

An application displaying text in an embedded font

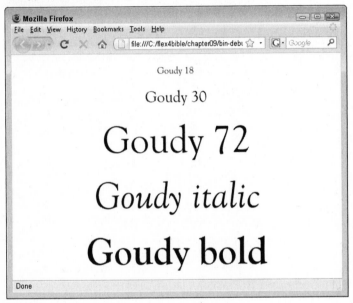

Web Resource

In these examples, I'm using a font named Goudy Old Style, which is included by default with Windows XP and Vista. You can download more specialized fonts from various Web sites, such as `www.1001freefonts.com`. ∎

Embedding ranges of characters in CSS

When you embed a typeface, you significantly increase the size of the compiled Flex application. For example, in the previous example where two font files were embedded in the application, the compiled debug version of the application increased in size from 152,533 bytes to 308,776 bytes, or roughly twice the original size. This is because font definition files contain font outlines for every possible character, frequently including outlines for non-Latin characters that you might never use in your application.

You can restrict which characters of a typeface are embedded in your application by declaring the `unicodeRange` style. This style takes an array of range designators, each starting and ending with a Unicode character in hexadecimal code.

Note

Unicode is a standard for encoding characters on computer systems that uses unique numbers, known as code points, for each character. Flex uses the most common encoding style, where each character description starts with the string U+ and ends with a four-character hexadecimal representation of the code point. For example, the Unicode expression `U+0021` **represents the exclamation point,** `U+005A` **represents an uppercase Z character, and so on.** ■

Web Resource

A PDF document containing a chart of the Basic Latin alphabet in Unicode is available at `http://unicode.org/charts/PDF/U0000.pdf`**. Charts of other character sets are available in PDF format at** `www.unicode.org/charts`**. Complete information about the Unicode standard is available at** `www.unicode.org`**.** ■

The following declaration embeds a broad range of basic Latin Unicode characters that would normally be used in an English language Flex application. The Unicode range of `U+0021`, representing the exclamation point (!), through `U+007E`, representing the tilde (~), includes all uppercase and lowercase alpha characters, numeric characters, and most common punctuation:

```
@font-face
{
  fontFamily: "Goudy";
  src:url("../fonts/GOUDOS.ttf");
  unicodeRange:U+0021-U+007E;
}
```

After adding this `unicodeRange` setting to both embedded fonts in the preceding example, the compiled application in the release build is a bit larger than the application without any embedded fonts, but significantly smaller than the version with both fonts embedded with all their character outlines. The result is an application that downloads and installs more quickly but still has all the text display functionality you need.

For European languages such as French, where an extended Latin alphabet is required, you can add additional ranges of characters that include versions of the Latin alphabet characters with accents and other required annotations. This style declaration embeds both the set of characters known in Unicode as Basic Latin and another set of characters known as Latin Extended A:

```
@font-face
{
  fontFamily: "Goudy";
  src:url("../fonts/GOUDOS.ttf");
  unicodeRange:
    U+0021-U+007E, //Basic Latin
    U+0100-U+017F; //Latin Extended A
}
```

Tip

When declaring fonts with CSS, you can compile the font declarations into an external CSS file as a SWF file. This enables you to load fonts at runtime, potentially assisting with initial application load times. ■

Note

The Flash Builder installation contains a file named `flash-unicode-table.xml` in the `sdks/4.0.0/` `framesworks` folder. This file contains definitions of common Unicode character ranges. The file is not processed with the command-line compiler or Flash Builder, but it can serve as a handy reference to common Unicode ranges. ■

Declaring embedded fonts with ActionScript

You also can embed fonts with the ActionScript `[Embed]` metadata tag by either font location or system name. The `[Embed]` tag must be placed inside an `<fx:Script>` tag set and include either a `source` attribute for fonts embedded by filename or a `systemFont` attribute for fonts embedded by system name.

An `[Embed]` declaration for font embedding requires these attributes:

- `fontName`. Used to select an alias by which the font will be known to the rest of the application.
- `mimeType`. Must always be set to `application/x-font`.

The `[Embed]` tag is always followed by a variable declaration typed as `Class`. This variable is never accessed directly in ActionScript code, so its name can be anything you like. This `[Embed]` tag embeds a font by filename and assigns a `fontName` of `myEmbeddedFont`:

```
[Embed(source='../fonts/MyCustomFont.ttf',
  fontName='myEmbeddedFont',
  mimeType='application/x-font')]
private var font1:Class;
```

Note

The name of the variable declared after the `[Embed]` metadata tag is arbitrary and is only used internally to store the font. It isn't referred to in other ActionScript code, so you can name the variable anything you like. ■

Note

The `[Embed]` metadata tag also supports a `unicodeRange` attribute that can be used to limit which font characters are embedded. ■

Declaring embedded fonts in ActionScript gives you the same benefits as CSS declarations and has the same requirements:

- Each individual font file must be declared separately.
- Each font variation, such as bold or italics, must be declared separately even if the variation isn't stored in a separate file.

Manipulating Text

Both embedded and device fonts can be rotated and include transparency. In addition, device fonts support *anti-aliasing* to render text in clear, high-quality resolution.

You can rotate a text control that uses either a device or an embedded font with the control's `rotation` property. The value of `rotation` defaults to 0 (indicating standard control layout). A positive value from 1 to 180 indicates that the control is rotated clockwise, while a negative value from –1 to –180 causes the control to rotate counterclockwise. Values outside these ranges are added to or subtracted from 360 to get a valid value.

The code in Listing 9.6 embeds a system font and then uses the font in a control that's rotated 90 degrees counterclockwise to turn the control on its side.

LISTING 9.6

A rotated control with an embedded font

```
<?xml version="1.0" encoding="utf-8"?>
<s:Application xmlns:fx="http://ns.adobe.com/mxml/2009"
  xmlns:s="library://ns.adobe.com/flex/spark"
  xmlns:mx="library://ns.adobe.com/flex/mx">
  <fx:Script>
    <![CDATA[
      [Embed(source='../fonts/GOUDOS.ttf',
        fontName='Goudy',
        mimeType='application/x-font')]
      private var font1:Class;
    ]]>
  </fx:Script>
  <s:Label fontFamily="Goudy"
    text="Rotated Text" fontSize="24"
    rotation="45"
    horizontalCenter="0" top="20"/>
</s:Application>
```

On the Web

The code in Listing 9.6 is available in the Web site files as `RotatingFonts.mxml` **in the** `chapter09` **project.** ■

Figure 9.6 shows the resulting application.

You can set the `rotation` property at runtime through bindings or ActionScript statements. The code in Listing 9.7 binds a `Label` control's `rotation` property to a `Slider` control's `value`. As the user manipulates the `Slider`, the `Label` rotates.

FIGURE 9.6

A rotated text control

LISTING 9.7

A Label control with an embedded font, rotating based on a Slider control's value

```xml
<?xml version="1.0" encoding="utf-8"?>
<s:Application xmlns:fx="http://ns.adobe.com/mxml/2009"
  xmlns:s="library://ns.adobe.com/flex/spark"
  xmlns:mx="library://ns.adobe.com/flex/mx">
  <s:layout>
    <s:VerticalLayout horizontalAlign="center" paddingTop="20" gap="20"/>
  </s:layout>
  <fx:Script>
    <![CDATA[
      [Embed(source='../fonts/GOUDOS.ttf',
        fontName='Goudy',
        mimeType='application/x-font')]
      private var font1:Class;
    ]]>
  </fx:Script>
  <s:HSlider id="mySlider"
    width="150"
    minimum="-180" maximum="180" value="0"
    liveDragging="true"/>
  <s:Label fontFamily="Goudy"
    text="Rotated Text" fontSize="24"
    rotation="{mySlider.value}"/>
</s:Application>
```

On the Web

The code in Listing 9.7 is available in the Web site files as `RotatingFontsWithSlider.mxml` **in the** `chapter09` **project.** ∎

Figure 9.7 shows the resulting application, with the control rotated based on the Slider control's current value.

FIGURE 9.7

As the user manipulates the Slider control, the Label control's rotation property is updated based on the binding expression.

Formatting Text Values

The Flex SDK includes a set of formatter classes you can use to return particular types of data values as formatted strings. There are six classes in this group. The Formatter class is the superclass from which all other classes are extended, and the other five classes are designed to format particular types of values.

The formatter classes include the following:

- CurrencyFormatter. Formats numeric values as currencies.
- DateFormatter. Formats date values.
- NumberFormatter. Formats numeric values.
- PhoneFormatter. Formats phone numbers.
- ZipCodeFormatter. Formats zip codes.

Each of the formatter classes has a set of properties that determines the format of the returned string, and a format() method that's used to process a value into a formatted string.

Creating formatter objects

You can create a formatter object with either MXML or ActionScript. As with other ActionScript classes, you use the class name in an MXML declaration:

```
<mx:DateFormatter id="myDateFormatter"/>
```

Caution

The formatter classes are nonvisual components and must be declared within the `<fx:Declarations>` element in Flex 4 applications. Because they're part of the MX component group, you declare them with the `mx` prefix, as in `<mx:CurrencyFormatter>`. If you declare a formatter inside a visual container, a compiler error is generated and the application does not successfully compile. ∎

To create a formatter object in ActionScript, declare and instantiate a variable typed as the appropriate formatter class. Flash Builder should create an import statement for the class; if not, create it manually:

```
import mx.formatters.DateFormatter;
var myDateFormatter:DateFormatter = new DateFormatter();
```

Setting formatter properties

Each formatter class has its own set of properties that determine how it formats strings. The `DateFormatter`, for example, has a single `formatString` property that can be used to create a custom date format. The `formatString` property takes as its value a string consisting of masking tokens, combined with literal strings. Table 9.3 describes the tokens that can be used in a `DateFormatter` object's `formatString` property.

TABLE 9.3

DateFormatter formatString Tokens

Pattern token	Description
YY	Year as a two-digit number.
YYYY	Year as a four-digit number.
M	Month as a one- or two-digit number without padded zeroes.
MM	Month as a two-digit number with padded zero where necessary.
MMM	Month as a short name. Values include "Jan," "Feb," and so on.
MMMM	Month as a long name. Values include "January," "February," and so on.
D	Day in month as a one- or two-digit number without padded zeroes.
DD	Day in month as a two-digit number with a padded zero where necessary.
E	Day in week as a one- or two-digit number without padded zeroes. Sunday is interpreted as 0, Monday as 1, and so on.
EE	Day in week as a two-digit number with a padded zero where necessary.
EEE	Day in week as a short name. Values include "Sun," "Mon," and so on.
EEEE	Day in week as a long name. Values include "Sunday," "Monday," and so on.
A	Returns "AM" for morning, "PM" for afternoon/evening.
J	Hour in day in a 24-hour format.
H	Hour in day in a 12-hour format.
N	Minutes in hour as a one- or two-digit number without a padded zero.

Pattern token	Description
NN	Minutes in hour as a two-digit number with a padded zero where necessary.
S	Seconds in current minute.
SS	Seconds in current minute with a padded zero.

All text used in a `dateFormat` property other than the supported tokens is considered literal text. For example, a `formatString` of "EEEE, MMMM D, YYYY" on the first day of 2008 returns "Tuesday, January 1, 2008." The comma and space characters in the formatting string are returned along with the token replacements.

In contrast, the `CurrencyFormatter` and `NumberFormatter` classes have properties that affect thousand separators and decimal characters, the number of characters after a decimal, the selection and placement of a currency symbol, and numeric rounding. The `ZipCodeFormatter` and `PhoneFormatter` classes have properties that affect the formatting of those values.

Using formatters in binding expressions

You can use a `formatter` class in a binding expression to change how a value is displayed in a text control. Follow these steps:

1. Create the formatter control, and set its formatting properties.

2. Add a text control that displays a value.

3. Set the text control's text property with a binding expression that wraps the value in the formatter control's format() method.

The application in Listing 9.8 uses a `DateFormatter` to format the `selectedDate` property of a `DateChooser` control.

LISTING 9.8

An application using a DateFormatter

```
<?xml version="1.0" encoding="utf-8"?>
<s:Application xmlns:fx="http://ns.adobe.com/mxml/2009"
  xmlns:s="library://ns.adobe.com/flex/spark"
  xmlns:mx="library://ns.adobe.com/flex/mx">
  <s:layout>
    <s:VerticalLayout horizontalAlign="center" paddingTop="20" gap="20"/>
  </s:layout>
  <fx:Declarations>
    <mx:DateFormatter id="myDateFormatter"
      formatString="EEEE, MMMM D, YYYY"/>
  </fx:Declarations>
```

continued

LISTING 9.8 *(continued)*

```
    <mx:DateChooser id="myDateChooser"/>
    <s:Label fontSize="18"
      text="Selected: {myDateFormatter.format(myDateChooser.selectedDate)}"/>
</s:Application>
```

On the Web

The code in Listing 9.8 is available in the Web site files as `DateFormatterDemo.mxml` **in the** `chapter09`
project. ■

Figure 9.8 shows the resulting application with the `Label` control displaying the date value's
formatted string.

FIGURE 9.8

A formatted date value displayed in a `Label` control

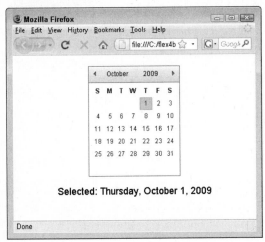

Using formatters in static methods

You may want to use a single formatting rule throughout an application. When you create a
formatter class for each view component in an application, it can become cumbersome to update
all the formatter object's formatting values when they have to be changed.

You can solve this by wrapping a formatter object in a static method that can be called from anywhere in an application. The nature of a static method is that it behaves the same in all circumstances, and it can be called from its class without having to first instantiate the class.

The code in Listing 9.9 shows a class with a static `formatDate()` method. The method accepts a value argument typed as an ActionScript `Object` so that the method can accept either a true date or a string that can be parsed as a date. It then instantiates the `DateFormatter` class local to the function, sets its `formatString` property to control the output, and returns a formatted value.

LISTING 9.9

A utility class with a static method to universally format date values

```
package utilities
{
  import mx.formatters.DateFormatter;
  public class FormatUtil
  {
    public static function dateFormat(value:Object):String
    {
      var df:DateFormatter = new DateFormatter();
      df.formatString = "EEEE, MMMM D, YYYY";
      return df.format(value)
    }
  }
}
```

On the Web

The code in Listing 9.9 is available in the Web site files as `FormatUtil.as` in the `src/utilities` folder of `chapter09` project. ■

To use this static method in an application or component, follow these steps:

1. Declare an import statement for the ActionScript class containing the static method.
2. Wrap the value you want to format in a call to the static method.

The code in Listing 9.10 uses the static method to format the date value.

LISTING 9.10

An application using a static formatting method

```
<?xml version="1.0" encoding="utf-8"?>
<s:Application xmlns:fx="http://ns.adobe.com/mxml/2009"
  xmlns:s="library://ns.adobe.com/flex/spark"
  xmlns:mx="library://ns.adobe.com/flex/mx">
```

continued

LISTING 9.10 *(continued)*

```
<s:layout>
  <s:VerticalLayout horizontalAlign="center" paddingTop="20" gap="20"/>
</s:layout>
<fx:Script>
  <![CDATA[
    import utilities.FormatUtil;
  ]]>
</fx:Script>
<mx:DateChooser id="myDateChooser"/>
<s:Label fontSize="18"
  text="Selected date: {FormatUtil.dateFormat(
    myDateChooser.selectedDate)}"/>
</s:Application>
```

On the Web

The code in Listing 9.10 is available in the Web site files as `DateFormatterWithStaticMethod.mxml` in the `chapter09` project. ■

When you use a static method to wrap formatting functionality, it becomes possible to change formatting rules for the entire application from a single source-code file. The result is an application that's easier to maintain.

Summary

In this chapter, I described how to use device and embedded fonts to determine which typeface is used when displaying text. I also described the use of formatter classes to display values with specific formats. You learned the following:

- You can use device or embedded fonts to display text in various Flex controls.

- Device fonts make the compiled application as small as possible, resulting in faster download and installation.

- Embedded fonts expand graphic design possibilities and provide control for formatting choices such as control rotation and advanced anti-aliasing.

- You can select only certain ranges of characters in an embedded font to minimize the font's impact on the compiled application's size.

- Formatter classes enable you to present various types of values with formatted strings.

- You can declare a formatter object with MXML or ActionScript.

- You can use a formatter in a binding expression or by wrapping it in an ActionScript static method.

Using Layout Containers

Flex has two types of visual components:

- **Containers.** Visual components that can contain other objects.
- **Controls.** Visual components that display information or provide the application with user interaction capabilities.

In Flex 4, you can choose from two sets of containers:

- The MX containers that have been available in previous versions of Flex, such as `Canvas`, `VBox`, and `HBox`.
- The new Spark containers that are designed to work with other Spark components, including `Group`, `VGroup`, `HGroup`, and `BorderContainer`.

Note

Some containers, such as `Panel`, are implemented in both the MX and the Spark component set. You can choose from either version, depending on which component features you need. For example, the MX `Panel` supports use of the `ControlBar` container to add a footer region with horizontal layout to the bottom of the Panel, while the Spark `Panel` supports a `controlBarContent` property that accomplishes the same purpose but enables the use of Spark-based custom skins. Adobe recommends that, whenever possible, you use the Spark containers instead of the MX containers. ■

The layout of a Flex application is determined through a combination of the application's containership hierarchy and the use of *basic* (formerly known as *absolute*) layout tools. Applications are typically designed with a combination of vertical or horizontal flow-style containers that lay out their nested child components automatically and basic layout containers whose nested child components either set their positions with x and y or constraint properties.

IN THIS CHAPTER

Understanding containers

Using MX Box containers

Using Spark Group containers

Using the `BorderContainer`

Using `Panel` **containers**

Using constraint-based layout

Sizing containers and controls

Creating scrollable regions

In this chapter, I describe the prebuilt layout containers in the Flex 4 SDK and how you use them to determine the application's visual appearance.

On the Web

To use the sample code for this chapter, import the `chapter10.fxp` **Flex project archive file from the Web site files into your Flash Builder workspace.** ■

Using MX Basic Containers

Three basic containers included in the MX components implement different layout styles:

- `VBox`. A rectangular area that lays out its nested child objects in a single column from top to bottom. Extends the `Box` container.

- `HBox`. A rectangular area that lays out its nested child objects in a single row from left to right. Extends the `Box` container.

- `Canvas`. A rectangular area that places its nested child objects in specific positions relative to either top/left anchors or constraint-based anchors.

These three containers support the `height` and `width` properties to determine their dimensions. If you don't declare these properties, the containers size themselves automatically to accommodate their child objects.

Note

MX containers support styles for modifying the container's visual presentation, such as those used to define borders and backgrounds. In contrast, Spark containers frequently define their visual presentation through the use of Flash XML Graphics (FXG) based vector graphics. ■

Cross-Reference

The use of FXG graphics is described in Chapter 14. ■

Using vertical and horizontal layout containers

As shown in the Unified Modeling Language (UML) diagram in Figure 10.1, the `VBox` and `HBox` components are extended from a superclass named `Box`.

Tip

While you can use the superclass `Box` **component and set its** `direction` **property to either** `vertical` **or** `horizontal`, **which is the only difference between the subclasses, most often you already know which layout you want and can use the specific subclass.** ■

The `Box`, `VBox`, and `HBox` components place their nested child visual components using two logical passes through the containership. In the first pass, the quantity and size of the nested child objects are collected. In the second pass, the nested objects are placed on the screen. Each time the `Box` component is resized, it re-executes this sizing and placement task.

FIGURE 10.1

The inheritance hierarchy for Box, VBox, and HBox

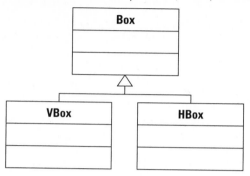

The VBox container

The VBox container behaves like the Application component when its layout is set to vertical: It lays out nested visual components in a single column from top to bottom. The application in Listing 10.1 uses a VBox to lay out three TextInput controls.

LISTING 10.1

Using the VBox container

```
<?xml version="1.0" encoding="utf-8"?>
<s:Application xmlns:fx="http://ns.adobe.com/mxml/2009"
  xmlns:s="library://ns.adobe.com/flex/spark"
  xmlns:mx="library://ns.adobe.com/flex/mx">
  <mx:VBox
    horizontalCenter="0" top="20"
    borderStyle="solid" borderColor="#000000"
    horizontalAlign="center"
    paddingBottom="10" paddingLeft="10" paddingRight="10" paddingTop="10">
    <s:TextInput text="TextInput 1"/>
    <s:TextInput text="TextInput 2"/>
    <s:TextInput text="TextInput 3"/>
  </mx:VBox>
</s:Application>
```

On the Web

The code in Listing 10.1 is available in the Web site files as VBoxDemo.mxml in the chapter10 project. ■

Figure 10.2 shows the resulting application running in the Web browser.

FIGURE 10.2

An application using the VBox container

The HBox container

The HBox container behaves like the Application component when its layout is set to horizontal: It lays out nested visual components in a single row from left to right. The application in Listing 10.2 uses an HBox to lay out three TextInput controls.

LISTING 10.2

Using the HBox container

```
<?xml version="1.0" encoding="utf-8"?>
<s:Application xmlns:fx="http://ns.adobe.com/mxml/2009"
  xmlns:s="library://ns.adobe.com/flex/spark"
  xmlns:mx="library://ns.adobe.com/flex/mx">
  <mx:HBox
    horizontalCenter="0" top="20"
    borderStyle="solid" borderColor="#000000"
    horizontalAlign="center"
    paddingBottom="10" paddingLeft="10" paddingRight="10" paddingTop="10">
    <s:TextInput text="TextInput 1"/>
    <s:TextInput text="TextInput 2"/>
    <s:TextInput text="TextInput 3"/>
  </mx:HBox>
</s:Application>
```

On the Web

The code in Listing 10.2 is available in the Web site files as HBoxDemo.mxml in the chapter10 project. ■

Figure 10.3 shows the resulting application running in the Web browser.

An application using the `HBox` container

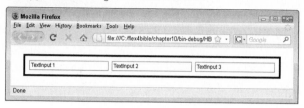

Using the Canvas container

The `Canvas` container behaves like the `Application` component when its layout is set to `absolute`. As shown in Figure 10.4, the `Canvas` container extends the `Container` class directly.

The inheritance hierarchy of the `Canvas` container

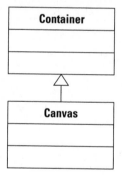

Objects that are nested within a `Canvas` determine their positions in one of these ways:

- Traditional absolute-layout properties of `x` and `y` (the number of pixels from the left and top of the `Canvas` container)
- Constraint-based positioning using anchors of `left`, `right`, `top`, `bottom`, `horizontalCenter`, and `verticalCenter`
- Advanced constraints using row- and column-based anchors

Visual components that are nested in a `Canvas` can use the following properties to set their positions relative to the `Canvas` container's top-left corner:

- `x`. The number of horizontal pixels from the `Canvas` container's left border.
- `y`. The number of vertical pixels from the `Canvas` container's top border.

The following code declares a `Label` component nested in a `Canvas`. The `Label` control's top-left corner is 10 pixels from the top and left of the `Canvas`:

```
<mx:Canvas>
   <s:Label x="10" y="10" text="Hello World!"/>
</mx:Canvas>
```

The `Canvas` container enables you to layer objects on top of each other. Paired with alpha styles that control transparency, you can create visual effects where one object appears "behind" another but shows through the "top" object.

The code in Listing 10.3 declares a `Canvas` container wrapped around three `TextInput` controls and three `VBox` containers. The `VBox` containers are arranged so that they overlap each other, and the `backgroundAlpha` setting of `.5` creates a 50 percent transparency effect.

LISTING 10.3

A Canvas container with overlapping objects

```
<s:Application xmlns:fx="http://ns.adobe.com/mxml/2009"
  xmlns:s="library://ns.adobe.com/flex/spark"
  xmlns:mx="library://ns.adobe.com/flex/mx">
  <mx:Canvas borderStyle="solid" borderColor="#000000"
    width="400" height="313"
    horizontalCenter="0" top="20">
    <s:TextInput text="TextInput 1"/>
    <s:TextInput text="TextInput 2" x="71" y="47"/>
    <s:TextInput text="TextInput 3" x="141" y="97"/>
    <mx:VBox width="100" height="100" backgroundColor="#FFFFFF"
      borderStyle="solid" borderColor="black"
      backgroundAlpha=".5" x="224" y="144"/>
    <mx:VBox width="100" height="100" backgroundColor="#666666"
      backgroundAlpha=".5" x="249" y="169"/>
    <mx:VBox width="100" height="100" backgroundColor="#000000"
      backgroundAlpha=".5" x="274" y="194"/>
  </mx:Canvas>
</s:Application>
```

On the Web

The code in Listing 10.3 is available in the Web site files as `CanvasDemo.mxml` in the `chapter10` project. ∎

Figure 10.5 shows the resulting application displayed in a browser. Notice the overlapping objects and the borders that show through.

FIGURE 10.5

A Canvas container with overlapping objects

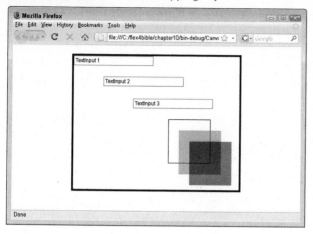

Using MX container styles

The VBox and HBox containers support styles that help to determine placement of nested objects. These styles, described in Table 10.1, control the alignment and the area around and between objects nested within the container.

TABLE 10.1

MX Box Container Styles

Style	Description	Possible Values/ Data Type	Default Value
verticalAlign	Collective vertical alignment of objects within the container	Top Middle Bottom	Top
horizontalAlign	Collective horizontal alignment of objects within the container	Left Center Right	Left
verticalGap	Number of vertical pixels between objects; applies to VBox only	Number	6
horizontalGap	Number of vertical pixels between objects; applies to HBox only	Number	6
paddingLeft	Number of pixels from left edge of container to first nested object	Number	0

continued

TABLE 10.1 *(continued)*

Style	Description	Possible Values/ Data Type	Default Value
paddingRight	Number of pixels from right edge of container to first nested object	Number	0
paddingTop	Number of pixels from top edge of container to first nested object	Number	0
paddingBottom	Number of pixels from bottom edge of container to first nested object	Number	0

The application in Listing 10.4 places nested visual components within a VBox container that sets gap, border, and padding styles using MXML style attributes.

LISTING 10.4

An application with MX Box containers and styles

```
<s:Application xmlns:fx="http://ns.adobe.com/mxml/2009"
  xmlns:s="library://ns.adobe.com/flex/spark"
  xmlns:mx="library://ns.adobe.com/flex/mx">
  <mx:VBox horizontalCenter="0" top="20"
    borderStyle="solid" borderColor="#000000"
    horizontalAlign="center"
    paddingBottom="20" paddingLeft="20" paddingRight="20" paddingTop="20"
    verticalGap="20" backgroundColor="white">
    <s:TextInput text="TextInput 1"/>
    <s:TextInput text="TextInput 2"/>
    <s:TextInput text="TextInput 3"/>
  </mx:VBox>
</s:Application>
```

On the Web

The code in Listing 10.4 is available in the Web site files as VBoxGapAndPadding.mxml **in the** chapter10 **project.** ■

The diagram in Figure 10.6 shows the placement of gap and padding styles in a VBox container.

Note

The alignment, gap, and padding styles have no effect on objects nested inside a Canvas **container, because the objects' positions are determined solely by their absolute positioning properties.** ■

Note

Developers who are familiar with CSS as implemented in Web browsers might be curious about the lack of margin styles. In HTML-based CSS, the "box model" includes padding on the inside of an object's borders, the borders themselves, and margins outside the borders that create space outside an object. Flex-based CSS omits the margin settings and implements only padding and border styles. I describe how to apply these and other styles in Chapter 11. ■

FIGURE 10.6

Using gap and padding styles

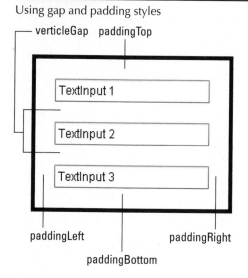

Using Spark Group Components

The Flex 4 SDK includes a new set of components derived from a superclass named GroupBase. The Group component is a direct subclass of GroupBase, and VGroup (for vertical layout) and HGroup (for horizontal layout) are derived from Group. Figure 10.7 shows a UML diagram that describes the inheritance hierarchy of the Group components.

The Spark Group components differ from the MX Box components in the following ways:

- The Group components do not support styles to implement visual displays as borders and backgrounds. These are commonly implemented with FXG-based graphics.

- The MX Box containers cannot contain instances of MXML graphics and other primitives as direct child objects; this is only possible with Spark Group components.

- Group components do not automatically generate scrollbars when their content exceeds their height or width.

- Layout settings such as alignment and gaps are implemented in Group components as properties rather than as styles.

The inheritance hierarchy of the Spark Group components

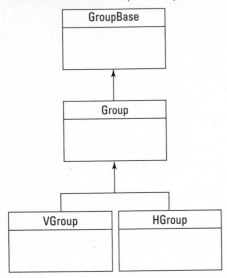

Using the Group component

The Group component implements *basic* layout (similar to the MX Canvas container's *absolute* layout). You place objects with the Group and position them using either x and y to determine the number of pixels from the container's top-left corner or use constraint properties such as top, left, bottom, and right.

The application in Listing 10.5 displays a Group component containing multiple objects. Notice that the rectangles are drawn with FXG graphics, rather than as Flex containers with backgrounds and borders. Just like the MX Canvas container, the Group component enables you to overlap objects and implement transparency.

An application with a Group component

```
<s:Application xmlns:fx="http://ns.adobe.com/mxml/2009"
  xmlns:s="library://ns.adobe.com/flex/spark"
  xmlns:mx="library://ns.adobe.com/flex/mx">
  <s:Group width="400" height="313"
    horizontalCenter="0" top="20">
    <!-- This Rect object fills the entire Group and creates the border -->
    <s:Rect width="100%" height="100%">
```

```
      <s:stroke>
        <s:SolidColorStroke color="#000000" weight="5"/>
      </s:stroke>
    </s:Rect>
    <s:TextInput text="TextInput 1" x="10" y="10"/>
    <s:TextInput text="TextInput 2" x="70" y="52"/>
    <s:TextInput text="TextInput 3" x="141" y="97"/>
    <!-- These Rect objects overlap each other with some transparency-->
    <s:Rect width="100" height="100" x="224" y="144">
      <s:fill>
        <s:SolidColor color="#999999"/>
      </s:fill>
    </s:Rect>
    <s:Rect width="100" height="100" x="249" y="169" alpha=".5">
      <s:fill>
        <s:SolidColor color="#666666"/>
      </s:fill>
    </s:Rect>
    <s:Rect width="100" height="100" x="274" y="194" alpha=".5">
      <s:fill>
        <s:SolidColor color="#000000"/>
      </s:fill>
    </s:Rect>
  </s:Group>
</s:Application>
```

On the Web

The code in Listing 10.5 is available in the Web site files as `GroupDemo.mxml` in the `chapter10` project. ∎

The completed application is shown in Figure 10.8.

Using VGroup and HGroup

The VGroup and HGroup components share all the features of Group, and add flow-based layout logic. Along with automatic vertical or horizontal alignment, these components implement the following properties that determine padding, alignment, and gaps:

- `verticalAlign`. HGroup only. Should be set to `top`, `middle`, `bottom`, `justify`, or `contentJustify`.

- `horizontalAlign`. VGroup only. Should be set to `left`, `center`, `right`, `justify`, or `contentJustify`.

- `gap`. Should be set to a number of pixels between objects. (This does the same thing as `verticalGap` and `horizontalGap` for MX Box containers, but is applied differently depending on which Spark container you're using: when used with HGroup it's applied to the horizontal gap, and when used with VGroup it's applied to the vertical gap.)

An application with a `Group` that contains MXML graphics and other Flex components

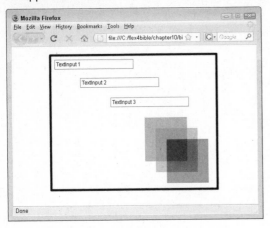

The application in Listing 10.6 declares an `HGroup` inside a `Group`. The outer `Group` implements the border with an MXML graphic; the nested `HGroup` lays out its child objects (three `TextInput` controls) from left to right.

An application with an HGroup nested inside a Group

```
<?xml version="1.0" encoding="utf-8"?>
<s:Application xmlns:fx="http://ns.adobe.com/mxml/2009"
  xmlns:s="library://ns.adobe.com/flex/spark"
  xmlns:mx="library://ns.adobe.com/flex/mx">
  <s:Group id="myGroup" width="600" height="50"
    horizontalCenter="0" top="20">
    <s:Rect width="100%" height="100%">
      <s:stroke>
        <s:SolidColorStroke color="#000000" weight="5"/>
      </s:stroke>
    </s:Rect>
    <s:HGroup
      top="10" left="10"
      height="{myGroup.height-20}" width="{myGroup.width-20}">
      <s:TextInput text="TextInput 1"/>
      <s:TextInput text="TextInput 2"/>
      <s:TextInput text="TextInput 3"/>
    </s:HGroup>
  </s:Group>
</s:Application>
```

On the Web

The code in Listing 10.6 is available in the Web site files as HGroupDemo.mxml in the chapter10 project. A similar application named VGroupDemo.mxml is included that demonstrates nesting a VGroup inside a Group for vertical layout. ■

The completed application is shown in Figure 10.9.

FIGURE 10.9

An HGroup nested within a Group, containing three TextInput controls

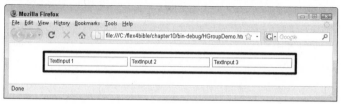

Using the Spark BorderContainer

The Spark BorderContainer component is designed to be used whenever you need a rectangular container that supports very simple styles but doesn't require a full component skin. It extends the SkinnableContainer class but typically isn't used with a custom skin. Unlike the Group components, which are designed exclusively for layout and don't display borders or background colors, the BorderContainer implements the following styles and default values:

- backgroundImage = "undefined"
- backgroundImageFillMode = "scale"
- borderAlpha = "1.0"
- borderColor = "0xB7BABC"
- borderStyle = "solid"
- borderVisible = "true"
- borderWeight = "1"
- cornerRadius = "0"
- dropShadowVisible = "false"

In addition, BorderContainer implements properties named backgroundFill (set to an instance of any class that implements the IFill interface) and borderStroke (set to an instance of any class that implements the IStroke interface). You can mix and match the border and background styles and properties as need to achieve the application's visual design.

The application in Listing 10.7 displays two instances of the BorderContainer component. The first uses style declarations for its border and background, while the second uses the more complex backgroundFill property to display a gradient fill.

LISTING 10.7

An application with two instances of the BorderContainer component

```xml
<?xml version="1.0" encoding="utf-8"?>
<s:Application xmlns:fx="http://ns.adobe.com/mxml/2009"
  xmlns:s="library://ns.adobe.com/flex/spark">
  <s:HGroup gap="40" top="20" horizontalCenter="0">
    <s:BorderContainer
      horizontalCenter="-257" top="0"
      backgroundColor="#CCCCCC"
      borderColor="#000000" borderWeight="3" width="283">
      <s:Label text="A BorderContainer with styles"
        fontSize="14" fontWeight="bold"
        horizontalCenter="0" verticalCenter="0"/>
    </s:BorderContainer>
    <s:BorderContainer width="378" borderColor="#000000" borderWeight="4">
      <s:backgroundFill>
        <s:RadialGradient>
          <s:entries>
            <s:GradientEntry color="#FFFFFF"/>
            <s:GradientEntry color="#999999"/>
          </s:entries>
        </s:RadialGradient>
      </s:backgroundFill>
      <s:Label text="A BorderContainer with a backgroundFill object"
        fontSize="14" fontWeight="bold"
        horizontalCenter="0" verticalCenter="0"/>
    </s:BorderContainer>
  </s:HGroup>
</s:Application>
```

On the Web

The code in Listing 10.7 is available in the Web site files as BorderContainerDemo.mxml **in the** chapter10 **project.** ■

Figure 10.10 shows the finished application, with the container using simple styles on the left and the version using the complex fill object on the right.

FIGURE 10.10

An application displaying two instances of BorderContainer

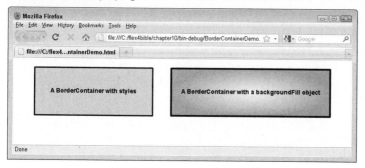

Using Panel Containers

Panel containers display a rectangular region that looks like a dialog box. Unlike the MX Box containers and the Spark Group containers, which don't have any default visual appearance, you use a Panel when you want to wrap content inside a visual presentation that sets it off from the rest of the application.

There are two versions of the Panel container: an older MX version that includes the capability to nest a ControlBar as a footer and a newer Spark version that supports declarative skins built with MXML graphics.

Cross-Reference

The process of skinning Spark components with the SparkSkin class and FXG graphics is described in Chapter 15. ■

A simple Panel is declared in MXML with a pair of <Panel> tags. The Panel container's nested components are declared between the paired tags. This code declares an MX Panel:

```
<mx:Panel title="My MX Panel">
   ... place contents here ...
</mx:Panel>
```

And this code declares a Spark Panel:

```
<s:Panel title="My Spark Panel">
   ... place contents here ...
</s:Panel>
```

Panel properties

The `Panel` component shares many properties with the `Application` container. Just as with other containers, the method you use to determine layout depends on whether you're working with MX or Spark components.

Using the layout property

Like the `Application` component, `Panel` supports the `layout` property. The MX version of `Panel` has a simple layout property that accepts values of `absolute`, `horizontal`, and `vertical` (the default). The Spark `Panel` component's `layout` property is set to an instance of a class that extends a class named `LayoutBase`. These are the same layout classes used in the Spark `Application` component, and include

- `BasicLayout` (the default)
- `VerticalLayout`
- `HorizontalLayout`
- `TileLayout`

The application in Listing 10.8 uses the Spark version of `Panel` and sets its `layout` property to an instance of `TileLayout`.

LISTING 10.8

A Spark Panel using the TileLayout class to present objects in a grid

```xml
<?xml version="1.0" encoding="utf-8"?>
<s:Application xmlns:fx="http://ns.adobe.com/mxml/2009"
  xmlns:s="library://ns.adobe.com/flex/spark"
  xmlns:mx="library://ns.adobe.com/flex/mx" >
  <s:Panel title="My Spark Panel"
    top="20" horizontalCenter="0">
    <s:layout>
      <s:TileLayout verticalGap="10" horizontalGap="20"/>
    </s:layout>
    <s:Button label="Button 1"/>
    <s:Button label="Button 2"/>
    <s:Button label="Button 3"/>
    <s:Button label="Button 4"/>
    <s:Button label="Button 5"/>
    <s:Button label="Button 6"/>
  </s:Panel>
</s:Application>
```

On the Web

The code in Listing 10.8 is available in the Web site files as `SparkPanelDemo.mxml` in the `chapter10` project. ∎

Figure 10.11 shows the result: the `Panel` component's nested child objects (six `Button` controls) are laid out in a grid with two controls per row.

FIGURE 10.11

A Spark `Panel` using the `TileLayout` class to lay out objects in a grid

Using the title and status properties

Both the MX and the Spark `Panel` containers implement a `title` property that places a label in a bold font in the left side of the `Panel` header. The MX `Panel` also implements a `status` property that places a label in a normal font aligned to the right side of the header.

Tip

While a `Panel` looks like a dialog box, it's typically presented "in-line" with the rest of the application layout, rather than as a pop-up window. When you present pop-up windows, you typically use the MX `TitleWindow` container or the `Alert` class, both of which extend the MX version of the `Panel` container and share its capabilities but are specifically designed for that use. There is also a Spark version of the `TitleWindow` container designed to be used as the superclass for custom pop-up windows in Flex 4 applications. ∎

Cross-Reference

The use of pop-up windows is described in Chapter 17. ∎

Using the MX ControlBar container

The MX ControlBar container is designed to be nested as the last component within an MX Panel or a TitleWindow. This container mimics the behavior of the HBox container, laying out its nested components horizontally, and creates a footer region below the other Panel container's nested objects with a style that matches the title bar.

Listing 10.9 shows an MX Panel with a ControlBar that lays out its child controls from left to right.

LISTING 10.9

An MX Panel with a ControlBar

```
<?xml version="1.0" encoding="utf-8"?>
<s:Application xmlns:fx="http://ns.adobe.com/mxml/2009"
  xmlns:s="library://ns.adobe.com/flex/spark"
  xmlns:mx="library://ns.adobe.com/flex/mx">
  <mx:Panel title="An MX Panel with a ControlBar"
    horizontalCenter="0" top="20"
    paddingTop="10" paddingBottom="10"
    paddingRight="10" paddingLeft="10">
    <s:VGroup>
      <s:Label text="Text 1"/>
      <s:Label text="Text 2"/>
      <s:Label text="Text 3"/>
    </s:VGroup>
    <mx:ControlBar>
      <s:Button label="Button 1"/>
      <s:Button label="Button 2"/>
      <s:Button label="Button 3"/>
    </mx:ControlBar>
  </mx:Panel>
</s:Application>
```

On the Web

The code in Listing 10.9 is available in the Web site files as ControlBarDemo.mxml in the chapter10 project. ∎

Figure 10.12 shows the resulting application. Notice that the Button controls in the ControlBar are laid out horizontally.

Tip

The MX ControlBar container always lays out its nested components horizontally. If you want to stack objects in a ControlBar vertically or place them with absolute positions, declare a VBox or Canvas container inside the ControlBar. ∎

FIGURE 10.12

An MX Panel with a ControlBar

To separate controls within a ControlBar so that they "glue" themselves to the far left and right edges, add a Spacer control between the controls with a width of 100%:

```
<mx:ControlBar>
  <s:Button label="Button 1"/>
  <mx:Spacer width="100%"/>
  <s:Button label="Button 2"/>
</mx:ControlBar>
```

Figure 10.13 shows that the component after the Spacer is pushed to the far right edge of the ControlBar.

FIGURE 10.13

An MX ControlBar with a Spacer

The invisible Spacer

Using Spark panels with control bars

The Spark Panel component implements a controlBarContent property that lays out objects horizontally as well. The application in Listing 10.10 uses this property to lay out objects at the bottom of the panel.

LISTING 10.10

A Spark Panel with control bar content

```
<?xml version="1.0" encoding="utf-8"?>
<s:Application xmlns:fx="http://ns.adobe.com/mxml/2009"
  xmlns:s="library://ns.adobe.com/flex/spark"
  xmlns:mx="library://ns.adobe.com/flex/mx" >
  <s:Panel title="A Spark Panel with a ControlBar"
    horizontalCenter="0" top="20">
    <s:layout>
      <s:VerticalLayout paddingTop="10" paddingBottom="10"
        paddingRight="10" paddingLeft="10"/>
    </s:layout>
    <s:Label text="Text 1"/>
    <s:Label text="Text 2"/>
    <s:Label text="Text 3"/>
    <s:controlBarContent>
      <s:Button label="Button 1"/>
      <s:Button label="Button 2"/>
      <s:Button label="Button 3"/>
    </s:controlBarContent>
  </s:Panel>
</s:Application>
```

On the Web

The code in Listing 10.10 is available in the Web site files as `SparkControlBarDemo.mxml` in the `chapter10` project. ∎

Using Constraint-Based Layout

Constraint-based layout enables you to place objects on the screen using anchors other than a container's top-left corner. You can implement constraint-based layout easily using Flash Builder's Design mode and Properties view or with a code-based approach. And using the new `ConstraintRow` and `ConstraintColumn` classes, you can anchor objects to regions other than the borders of the container.

Note

Constraint-based layout works only in MX containers that support absolute layout, and Spark components that use the `BasicLayout` class. When used in the MX versions of the `Application`, `Panel`, `TitleWindow`, or `Window` containers, the container's `layout` property must be set to `absolute` for constraint properties to have an effect. Because the `Canvas` container always uses `absolute` layout, constraint properties work within that container without any other changes to its property values. Constraint-based layout does not work in `VBox`, `HBox`, `ControlBar`, or other containers that don't support absolute layout. Similarly, constraint-based layout only works in Spark containers that use basic layout (that is, that have their layout property set to an instance of BasicLayout). This includes the Spark versions of Application, WindowedApplication, Window, NavigatorContent, and Group. ∎

Positioning components in Design mode

Flash Builder's Design mode has tools that can create constraint properties through a combination of selecting options in the Properties view and dragging an object with anchors in the MXML editor. Figure 10.14 shows the Constraints interface in the Flex Properties view. This interface appears whenever a component in a container with absolute layout is selected in Design view.

The Constraints interface in the Flex Properties view

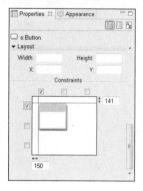

Follow these steps to create a text logo that's anchored to the application's bottom-right corner:

1. **Create a new MXML application.**

2. **If the application opens in Source mode, click the Design button.**

3. **Drag a Button control from the Components view into the application.** Place it anywhere on the screen.

4. **Set the new Button control's label property to My Button.**

5. **In the Constraints interface at the bottom of the Flex Properties view, click in the check boxes in the right anchor and the bottom anchor, as shown in Figure 10.15.**

6. **Click in the input controls in the constraint interface, and set the bottom and right anchors to 10.** You should see in the Constraints interface that the number of pixels from each anchor changes as you drag the Label control in Design view.

On the Web

The completed version of the preceding exercise is available in the Web site files as UsingConstraints Complete.mxml in the chapter10 project. ∎

FIGURE 10.15

The Constraints interface

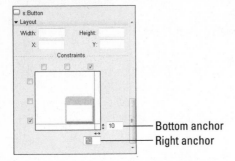

Bottom anchor
Right anchor

Using constraint properties

Each visual component supports six constraint properties. Each of the properties is datatyped as a Number and indicates the number of pixels from the named anchor:

- `left`. This property sets the number of pixels from the left edge of the container to the left edge of the nested component.

- `right`. This property sets the number of pixels from the right edge of the container to the right edge of the nested component.

- `top`. This property sets the number of pixels from the top edge of the container to the top edge of the nested component.

- `bottom`. This property sets the number of pixels from the bottom edge of the container to the bottom edge of the nested component.

- `horizontalCenter`. This property sets the number of pixels from the horizontal center of the container to the horizontal center of the nested component. A positive number offsets the component to the right of the container's horizontal center; a negative number offsets the component to the left.

- `verticalCenter`. This property sets the number of pixels from the vertical center of the container to the vertical center of the nested component. A positive number offsets the component below the container's vertical center; a negative number offsets the component above the vertical center.

The following code is generated by Design view as the user sets properties in the Constraints interface and drags the component around the screen:

```
<s:Button label="My Button" right="10" bottom="10"
    fontWeight="bold" fontSize="18"/>
```

The `right` and `bottom` properties are each set to values of 10 pixels. Each time the user resizes the application, the `Label` control changes its position relative to the application's bottom-right corner.

Sizing Containers and Controls

Four strategies are available to determine the dimensions of a container or control at runtime:

- Content. Component dimensions are determined dynamically based on the cumulative size of the component's child objects.

- Absolute. Component dimensions are determined by its width and height properties set to numeric values interpreted as pixels.

- Percentage. Component dimensions are determined by percentage of available space.

- Constraints. Component dimensions are determined by constraint-based anchor properties.

Content-based sizing

Content-based sizing means that a container or control expands to accommodate its contents. In the absence of any other sizing properties, this happens automatically. With containers, this means that the container sizes itself to accommodate and display its nested contents. With controls, this means that the control sizes itself to display its internal objects. For example, if you don't set a Button control's height or width properties, it sizes itself to display its full label and icon.

Default dimensions

Each container has a default height and width. For example, if you create a Spark Panel with this code, it has no nested components and no title property that would affect its height or width:

```
<s:Panel>
</s:Panel>
```

Other containers have different default dimensions. In the absence of nested content, the Group, VGroup, and HGroup set their height and width to 0.

Minimum and maximum dimensions

You can set properties to constrain content-based sizing. These properties set minimum and maximum dimensions to place limits on a container's capability to dynamically grow and shrink:

- minHeight. The container's minimum height in pixels.
- minWidth. The container's minimum width in pixels.
- maxHeight. The container's maximum height in pixels.
- maxWidth. The container's maximum width in pixels.

This Panel container has a minimum width and height of 200 pixels each:

```
<s:Panel minWidth="200" minHeight="200">
... nested components ...
</s:Panel>
```

The container can still expand if its contents require more space, but it can't contract to less than 200 pixels in either dimension.

Absolute sizing

Absolute sizing means that you set a component's width and height properties in absolute pixel values. This Panel container is always displayed as 200 pixels high by 200 pixels wide, regardless of its nested contents:

```
<s:Panel width="200" height="200">
</s:Panel>
```

Percentage sizing

Percentage sizing means that you set a dimension as a percentage of available space. When you set a component's size in MXML, you can declare percentage sizing with either the height and width properties or with percentHeight and percentWidth.

Percentage sizing with height and width

When you set percentage sizing with the height and width properties, you declare the values with a percentage expression, such as 50%. This Label control's width is 50 percent of the available space within its container:

```
<s:Label text="A sample text control" width="50%"/>
```

Percentage sizing with percentHeight and percentWidth

When you set percentage sizing with the percentHeight and percentWidth properties, you use numeric expressions such as 50. This Label control's width is also 50 percent of the available space within its container:

```
<s:Label text="A sample text control" percentWidth="50"/>
```

Note

You cannot set the height and width properties to new percentage values at runtime with ActionScript statements. Instead, always use percentHeight and percentWidth in ActionScript. ■

Note

The percentHeight and percentWidth properties return meaningful values only if you've previously set them through MXML declarations or ActionScript commands. Their values are not recalculated at runtime. ■

Using percentage ratios

When you declare multiple components within a container and set sizes by percentage, you can declare a total percentage of greater than 100 percent. This VBox contains three TextInput controls, each with a width property of 100 percent:

```
<s:HGroup width="450">
  <s:TextInput width="100%"/>
  <s:TextInput width="100%"/>
  <s:TextInput width="100%"/>
</s:HGroup>
```

It might seem that this means the total width of the nested component is 300 percent and would exceed the available space. Instead, the framework adds up the total percentage values and uses the ratio of the control's declared percentage value divided by the total to assign an actual percentage based on available space:

```
100% + 100% + 100% = 300% (the total)
For each component: 100% / 300% = 33.33%
```

Note

If there is a combination of percentage-based and absolute sizing, space is allotted first to the strict values. Then if the remaining space is not enough to fulfill the percentage-based items, the same ratio division is calculated and applied. ∎

Constraint-based sizing

Constraint properties also can be used to control a component's size. When a component is nested in a container with absolute layout and two constraint properties in the vertical or horizontal dimension are set, the component "stretches" at runtime to keep its edges the correct distance from the two anchors. Listing 10.11 uses a `Label` control with `right` and `left` properties that keep its edges 50 pixels from each of the Application container's horizontal edges.

LISTING 10.11

Using constraint-based sizing

```
<?xml version="1.0" encoding="utf-8"?>
<s:Application xmlns:fx="http://ns.adobe.com/mxml/2009"
  xmlns:s="library://ns.adobe.com/flex/spark"
  xmlns:mx="library://ns.adobe.com/flex/mx">
  <s:Label id="myText"
    horizontalCenter="0" top="20"
    textAlign="center"
    left="50" right="50"
    height="100%">
    <s:text>
```

continued

LISTING 10.11 *(continued)*

```
        <![CDATA[Lorem ipsum dolor sit amet, consectetur adipiscing elit.
    Curabitur rhoncus, elit in consectetur euismod, nibh enim lacinia enim,
    in hendrerit mi libero eu leo. Etiam ac nisl dapibus est egestas mollis
    at condimentum nisi. Integer commodo gravida egestas. Phasellus ac libero
    est, in iaculis velit. Curabitur molestie felis at nunc viverra id
    egestas risus facilisis. Proin at lobortis est. Curabitur non tortor
    neque, egestas feugiat sapien. Lorem ipsum dolor sit amet, consectetur
    adipiscing elit. Nam ut nunc id turpis luctus auctor et tristique dolor.
    Morbi volutpat porta tortor, non tempor nisl consequat sed. Pellentesque
    aliquam enim ac diam consectetur adipiscing. Donec odio ligula, posuere
    quis bibendum quis, sagittis nec nisi. Integer molestie interdum lacus
    non aliquet. In consectetur nisl et risus tincidunt accumsan.]]>
        </s:text>
    </s:Label>
</mx:Application>
```

On the Web

The code in Listing 10.11 is available in the Web site files as `ConstraintSizing.mxml` **in the** `chapter10` **project.** ∎

Figure 10.16 shows the resulting display. When the user resizes the application, the `Text` control expands and contracts to keep its edges the correct distance from the constraint anchors.

FIGURE 10.16

A control with constraint-based sizing

50-pixel left constraint

50-pixel right constraint

Creating a Scrolling Region

With MX containers, if a container was too small to display its nested contents, by default it displayed scrollbars that enabled the user to scroll to see the contents. This architecture was easy to use but added a lot of complexity to the container implementations.

Spark components that have child objects, such as Group and Panel, follow a different strategy. They don't generate their own scrollbars. Instead, you add an instance of a Scroller object inside the container whose content you want to scroll. The Scroller object is wrapped around a component that contains the child objects you want to scroll. This component, which can be a Group, HGroup, VGroup, or a custom component, is known as the Scroller object's *viewport*.

The application in Listing 10.12 displays a Spark Panel that wraps its content in a Scroller and a VGroup.

LISTING 10.12

An application with a scrolling panel, implemented with the Spark Scroller class

```
<?xml version="1.0" encoding="utf-8"?>
<s:Application xmlns:fx="http://ns.adobe.com/mxml/2009"
  xmlns:s="library://ns.adobe.com/flex/spark"
  xmlns:mx="library://ns.adobe.com/flex/mx">
  <s:Panel title="Spark Panel with scrolling"
    horizontalCenter="0" top="20"
    width="300" height="200">
    <s:layout>
      <s:VerticalLayout paddingTop="10" paddingBottom="10"
        paddingLeft="10" paddingRight="10"/>
    </s:layout>
    <s:Scroller width="100%" height="100%">
      <s:VGroup width="100%" height="100%">
        <s:Button label="Button 1"/>
        <s:Button label="Button 2"/>
        <s:Button label="Button 3"/>
        <s:Button label="Button 4"/>
        <s:Button label="Button 5"/>
        <s:Button label="Button 6"/>
        <s:Button label="Button 7"/>
        <s:Button label="Button 8"/>
        <s:Button label="Button 9"/>
      </s:VGroup>
    </s:Scroller>
  </s:Panel>
</s:Application>
```

On the Web

The code in Listing 10.12 is available in the Web site files as `ScrollerDemo.mxml` in the `chapter10` project. ∎

Figure 10.17 shows the completed application, with a scrolling region inside the `Panel` component's content area.

A scrolling `Panel` implemented with the `Scroller` component

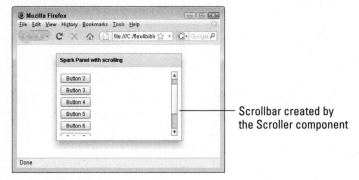

Scrollbar created by the Scroller component

Caution

The `Panel` itself can also be treated as a viewport for the `Scroller`, as in this code:

```
<s:Scroller>
  <s:Panel title="Spark Panel with scrolling">
  ... content children ...
  </s:Panel>
</s:Scroller>
```

The result of this code, however, would be to scroll the entire `Panel` (rather than just its content). ∎

Cross-Reference

You can provide custom skins to the `Scroller` component to replace its default horizontal and vertical scrollbar components. For more information on skinning of Spark components, see Chapter 15. ∎

Summary

In this chapter, I described the use of layout containers, how to size components, and how to use constraint-based layout. You learned the following:

- Layout containers are used to position other visual objects on the screen.
- The MX layout containers include VBox, HBox, and Canvas.
- The Spark layout containers include Group, HGroup, and VGroup.
- The HGroup and VGroup containers place their nested components on the screen dynamically by calculating their cumulative size.
- The Group container always uses basic layout to place objects based on x and y properties or with constraint-based properties.
- The Spark BorderContainer implements styles and properties that enable simple visual displays without having to create a custom skin.
- The Panel container creates a dialog-box presentation and supports the same layout property as the Application component.
- Constraint properties enable you to place and size objects with anchors to any of a container's borders or center positions.
- Containers can be sized based on content, absolute dimensions, percentage dimensions, or constraints.
- Spark components that have content child objects can be made scrollable by wrapping the content children inside a Group, and the Group inside a Scroller component.

Using Cascading Style Sheets

F lex applications have a default visual appearance that's determined by a combination of graphics that are embedded in the Flex SDK, known as *skins*, and various visual settings that are set through Cascading Style Sheet (CSS) declarations.

About Cascading Style Sheets

Web site developers may already be familiar with the concept of CSS, because this technology has been increasingly used to control the visual appearance of Web pages since its introduction in 1996.

The CSS recommendation is created and published by the World Wide Web Consortium (W3C), the same organization that publishes the recommendations for Hypertext Markup Language (HTML), EXtensible Markup Language (XML), and other critical Internet technologies.

Web Resource
Information about the WC3's CSS recommendation and other CSS resources is available at `www.w3.org/Style/CSS/.` ■

It's up to the vendors who actually create the Web browsers and other products to implement CSS for their own platforms. Web browsers, for example, implement various subsets of the W3C recommendation; it's only in recent years that the major browsers such as Internet Explorer and Firefox have approached compatibility in their CSS implementations.

The use of CSS to control visual appearance isn't limited to Web-based applications. Flex applications that are installed on the desktop with Adobe AIR use CSS in exactly the same manner as Flex Web applications.

IN THIS CHAPTER

Understanding style sheets

Using inline style declarations

Using style selectors

Using embedded and external style sheets

Controlling styles with ActionScript

Creating compiled style sheet files

Loading compiled style sheets at runtime

Using Flex Themes

The Flex SDK supports a concept of *themes*, which determine the overall appearance of an application. A theme is a combination of CSS declarations and graphical elements, packaged together as precompiled SWC files that can be plugged into a Flex project and its applications.

Themes are defined in Flash Builder 4 on a per-project basis. To change the theme for a Flex project, choose Project ⇨ Properties. Then, in the Properties dialog box, choose Flex Theme. As shown in the following figure, you can select from one of these prepackaged themes:

- Spark (the default)
- Wireframe
- Halo
- AeonGraphical

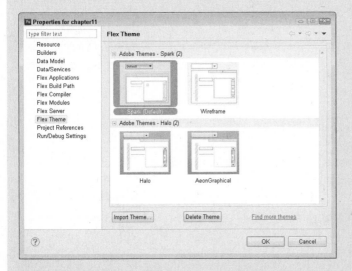

The Halo and AeonGraphical themes represent the older Flex 3 default application appearance. When you use these themes, the older MX components support all of the traditional styles, including borders, background colors, and others. When you use the new Spark-based themes (Spark and Wireframe), only the newer styles are supported.

The Flex theme architecture enables graphic designers to create and distribute prepackaged themes. The Properties dialog box displays an Import button that enables you to add themes to your Flash Builder workspace. You can download and purchase themes created by third-party graphic designers through the Adobe Web site at www.adobe.com/go/getflextheme.

The Flex framework implements significant parts of the W3C's CSS recommendation and adds features that make the technology particularly effective for implementing Flex application graphic designs.

In this chapter, I describe how to use CSS in Flex to control an application's visual appearance. I start by describing how to declare and control style sheets in a number of ways, including how to use embedded and external CSS declarations, and how to use a variety of CSS *selectors* (a way of describing how styles are applied to various parts of a Flex application). At the end of the chapter, I describe programmatic approaches to managing styles at runtime, including the use of the `styleManager` object.

On the Web

To use the sample code for this chapter, import the `chapter11.fxp` Flex project archive from the Web site files into your Flash Builder workspace. ■

What Is a Style Sheet?

A style sheet consists of rules that constitute a set of visual settings. Any particular style sheet can consist of three parts:

- **The selector.** Determines the scope of a set of rules that are declared in the style sheet. A single selector can declare multiple styles, each requiring a name and a value.

- **The style name.** Determines which style is being set.

- **The style value.** Determines the new style setting.

MXML-based declarations of styles and nonstyle properties look the same. The following application declares a `width` property and a `backgroundColor` style:

```
<?xml version="1.0" encoding="utf-8"?>
<s:Application xmlns:fx="http://ns.adobe.com/mxml/2009"
  xmlns:s="library://ns.adobe.com/flex/spark"
  xmlns:mx="library://ns.adobe.com/flex/mx"
  width="600" backgroundColor="#9B30FF">
  <s:Label
    text="This application has a purple background
    and is 600 pixels wide"/>
</s:Application>
```

To know that one is a property and the other a style, you'd have to look it up in the product documentation. You encounter differences between styles and properties when you set their values in ActionScript or actual style sheet declarations, or when you read about their use in the product documentation. Table 11.1 describes some of the differences between styles and properties.

TABLE 11.1

Differences Between Styles and Properties

Styles	Properties
Documentation is found in the Styles section for each component.	Documentation is found in the Properties section for each component.
Styles can be applied to multiple objects through embedded or external style sheets.	Properties can apply only to a single object.
When set at runtime with ActionScript, styles always use the `setStyle()` method.	Properties can be set at runtime in ActionScript with simple dot notation.
Multiple style rules can be compiled into SWF files and loaded at runtime.	Properties cannot be compiled into separate SWF files.

You can use these ways, among others, to declare styles in Flex:

- **Inline styles.** Declared as attributes in an object's MXML declaration.
- **Embedded style sheets.** Declared within an MXML file in an `<fx:Style>` tag set.
- **External style sheets.** Created as text files with a file extension of `.css`.
- **Compiled style sheets.** Created as SWF files and can be loaded at application runtime.

Regardless of how you declare a style, the name of the style and its value are always the same. For example, a style of `fontSize` is always set as a numeric value indicating the font height in terms of pixels. This style can be set in inline, embedded, external, or compiled style sheets, and its effect is always the same.

Note

Unlike the HTML implementation of CSS, Flex applications do not support any unit of measurement other than pixels. If you try to use unit-of-measurement abbreviations like `pt`, `em`, or `px`, they are either ignored or result in a compiler error, depending on the context. ■

Using Inline Style Declarations

When you declare an object in MXML, you can declare any of its styles using XML attributes. The attribute's name matches the style's name, and the style's value is declared in various ways depending on its data type.

New Feature

Flex 3 didn't support the CSS ID selector that enables you to apply a style in an embedded or external style sheet to a single object by its `id` property. As described later in this chapter, Flex 4 applications now have this capability, so you can now choose between using ID selectors and inline style declarations. ■

This `Label` control declares its `color` style to a value of red using an inline style declaration and a hexadecimal color code:

```
<s:Label text="Hello World" color="#FF0000"/>
```

Caution

Many styles have two versions of their names. For example, the `fontSize` style name uses syntax that's sometimes described as camel case, due to the use of uppercase characters in the middle of the name. This style also can be declared in an embedded or external style sheet with the hyphenated name of `font-size`. However, when setting styles in an inline declaration, you must use the camel-case version of the name, because the hyphenated version isn't recognized by the MXML parser. ■

Note

One of XML's fundamental syntax rules is that the order of attribute declaration isn't meaningful. In the MXML language, this means that you can declare property, style, and event listener attributes in any order because the order doesn't have any effect on the function or performance of the object you're declaring. ■

Declaring Style Sheets with <fx:Style>

The `<fx:Style>` element is used to either declare styles within an MXML document or to link the application to an external style sheet file.

When you type in the starting `<fx:Style>` tag in an MXML editor, Flash Builder auto-completes the tag and adds namespace declarations for all previously declared namespaces in that file. By default, this means the `<fx:Style>` element declares namespaces for Spark and MX components:

```
<fx:Style>
  @namespace mx "library://ns.adobe.com/flex/mx";
  @namespace s "library://ns.adobe.com/flex/spark";
  ...add style rules here..
</fx:Style>
```

You then add all style declarations within the `<fx:Style>` element, after the namespace declarations.

Alternatively, you can use `<fx:Style>` to reference an external style sheet file with the tag's source attribute:

```
<fx:Style source="mystyles.css"/>
```

The syntax of the style declarations is the same regardless of whether you're using an embedded or an external style sheet. Each style declaration consists of a *selector*, each of which determines the scope of a set of style declarations.

Using Style Selectors

You can declare complete style sheets either embedded within an MXML source-code file or in a separate, external CSS file. Either way, the style sheet contains one or more *selectors*. The Flex 4 implementation of CSS has the following kinds of selectors:

- **Type selectors.** Declare a set of styles that are applied to all instances of that ActionScript type.

- **Descendant selectors.** Declare a set of styles based on the containership of an object.

- **Style name selectors.** Traditionally known as *class* selectors. Declare a set of styles within an arbitrarily named collection that is then applied to multiple components through the styleName property.

- **ID selectors.** Declare a set of styles that are applied to components based on their id property.

- **The global selector.** Declares a set of styles that are applied to all components within the application.

New Feature

ID and descendant selectors are new in the Flex 4 SDK. ∎

Regardless of which selector you use, the syntax is similar: the selector, followed by a block of style declarations wrapped in braces. Each style declaration consists of a name and a value, separated by a colon (:). The style declaration should be ended with a semicolon (;) to separate it from other style declarations.

Using type selectors

A type selector consists of the name of an ActionScript class that represents a visual component, followed by a code block containing one or more style declarations. The selector consists of a namespace prefix and a component name, separated with the | character.

This type selector declares a set of styles that are applied to all Spark Label controls:

```
s|Label {
  color:#ff0000;
  font-size:14;
}
```

Because ActionScript class names are case-sensitive, you must spell type selectors exactly the same as the names of the ActionScript visual components to which the styles are being applied.

Caution

Type selectors can be declared only in the application, not in a custom component. If you try to use a type selector in a component, a compiler warning is generated and the style(s) won't be applied. ∎

Note

Property names in embedded or external style sheets can use either camel case or hyphenated syntax. Flash Builder's code completion tool always suggests camel-case names in inline style declarations (which are required) and hyphenated syntax in embedded or external styles. Because you get help with hyphenated names in the latter context, all code samples in this chapter follow that standard. ■

Understanding CSS namespaces

The Flex 4 SDK includes components from multiple namespaces. In CSS declarations, you have to be specific about which component you're applying a style to. For example, there are both MX and Spark versions of `Button`, `Panel`, and other visual components. A style declaration must be specific about which version of a component the declaration targets.

New Feature

CSS namespaces are new in the Flex 4 SDK. ■

When you create a new `<fx:Style>` tag set in an MXML document, Flash Builder automatically adds the MX and Spark namespaces declarations associated with their common prefixes:

```
<fx:Style>
  @namespace mx "library://ns.adobe.com/flex/mx";
  @namespace s "library://ns.adobe.com/flex/spark";
  ...add style declarations here...
</fx:Style>
```

Web Resource

The CSS namespace implementation in Flex 4 is based on the CSS Namespaces Module of the Namespaces in XML recommendation from the W3C, available at `www.w3.org/TR/css3-namespace`. ■

Each @namespace declaration associates a prefix with the appropriate namespace: mx for the MX namespace and s for Spark. You then compose each type selector with the appropriate prefix, the | character as a separator, and then the name of the component to which the styles should be applied:

```
<fx:Style>
  @namespace mx "library://ns.adobe.com/flex/mx";
  @namespace s "library://ns.adobe.com/flex/spark";
  s|Label
  {
    font-size:24;
  }
</fx:Style>
```

Caution

The | separator character can't have any spaces around it. If there are additional space characters between the namespace, the separator, and the type, the compiler fails with an `Unexpected character` error. ■

Tip

If an MXML document contains CSS declarations for either Spark or MX components, but not both, you can simplify the CSS declaration to use only one default namespace. Declare the namespace without a prefix, like this:

```
@namespace "library://ns.adobe.com/flex/spark";
```

You then declare each type selector without the prefix. The result looks more like Flex 3 CSS declarations:

```
Label
{
  font-size:24;
} ■
```

Using multiple type selectors

You can apply a set of styles to multiple types using a selector consisting of a comma-delimited list. This declaration applies to all instances of the Spark `Label` and `RichText` controls:

```
s|Label, s|RichText {
  color:#ff0000;
  font-size:14;
}
```

Applying type selectors to custom components

Type selectors also can be used to apply styles to instances of your own custom components. For example, if you create a custom component in an MXML file named `CustomButton.mxml`, its type is `CustomButton`. Just as with type selectors for the Flex SDK's built-components, a namespace and prefix should be declared that matches the custom component's location in the project.

This style sheet applies styles to all instances of custom component named `CustomButton`, stored in the `components` folder of the project's source-code root:

```
<fx:Style>
    @namespace comps "components.*";
    comps|CustomButton
    {
      color:blue;
    }
</fx:Style>
```

Looking at type selectors and class inheritance

When you declare a type selector in a style sheet, the selector's inheritable styles apply to all instances of that type and to all instances of any of the type's subclasses (provided the styles aren't overwritten at a lower level). For example, because the `Label` and `RichText` controls are both extended from the `TextBase` superclass, the `TextBase` selector applies its style declarations for all instances of either control:

```
s|TextBase
{
  font-size:18;
  font-style:italic;
}
```

Figure 11.1 shows the resulting application with a `Label` and a `RichText` control that use the same styles.

Tip

Type selectors that designate a superclass are inherited by subclasses even when the styles used in the selector are marked in the documentation as not implementing CSS inheritance. The documentation is describing which styles are inherited based on containership.

For example, if you apply font-based styles, which are inheritable, to a `VGroup` selector, all text controls nested in `VGroup` containers use those styles. Noninheritable styles are only applied to the `VGroup` itself and not to its nested child objects. ■

FIGURE 11.1

`Label` and `RichText` using the `TextBase` selector styles

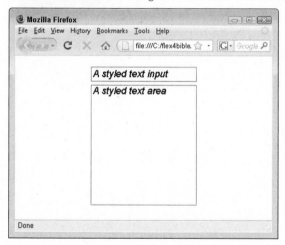

Class inheritance also is taken into account with custom components. If a custom component named `MyComponent` is extended from the `VGroup` or `HGroup` containers, it also would apply the inheritable styles declared in the `Group` selector.

Using descendant selectors

A *descendant* selector defines a set of objects by their containership. You define the selector as a set of selectors, with the containers first and the object to which the styles should be applied last, separated by space characters. This can contain multiple levels of containership. This selector applies styles to `Label` objects only when contained within a `VGroup`:

```
s|VGroup s|Label
{
  text-decoration:underline;
  font-style:italic;
}
```

The application in Listing 11.1 shows the effect of two selectors. The `Label` type selector causes all such objects to have a `font-size` of 18 pixels, while the descendant selector applies `text-decoration` and `font-style` settings only when the `Label` objects are within an `HGroup`. The objects within the `HGroup` receive styles from both selectors.

LISTING 11.1

An application using a descendant style selector

```xml
<?xml version="1.0" encoding="utf-8"?>
<s:Application xmlns:fx="http://ns.adobe.com/mxml/2009"
  xmlns:s="library://ns.adobe.com/flex/spark"
  xmlns:mx="library://ns.adobe.com/flex/mx">
  <s:layout>
    <s:VerticalLayout horizontalAlign="center" paddingTop="20" gap="15"/>
  </s:layout>
  <fx:Style>
    @namespace mx "library://ns.adobe.com/flex/mx";
    @namespace s "library://ns.adobe.com/flex/spark";
    s|Label
    {
      font-size:18;
    }
    s|HGroup s|Label
    {
      text-decoration:underline;
      font-style:italic;
    }
  </fx:Style>
  <s:VGroup>
    <s:Label text="Text objects in a VGroup"/>
    <s:Label text="Text objects in a VGroup"/>
  </s:VGroup>
```

```
    <s:HGroup>
      <s:Label text="Text objects in an HGroup"/>
      <s:Label text="Text objects in an HGroup"/>
    </s:HGroup>
  </s:Application>
```

On the Web

The code in Listing 11.1 is available in the Web site files as `DescendantSelectorDemo.mxml` in the `chapter11` project. ∎

Figure 11.2 shows the resulting application with all `Label` objects displayed with a font size of 18 pixels but only those within the `HGroup` with italics and underlining.

The result of a descendant selector

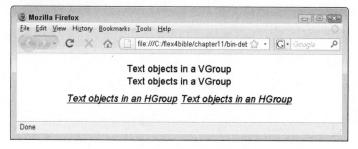

Using style name selectors

A *style name* selector, also sometimes known as a *class* selector, consists of any valid string, prepended with a period (`.`). Style names are typically created with an initial lowercase character and any mixture of uppercase and lowercase characters after that. This style name selector contains a single style declaration:

```
.redFont {
  color:#ff0000;
}
```

Note

Style name selectors are identical in purpose and declaration syntax to the HTML concept of class selectors. As with the style class in HTML, a style name defines a set of rules that can be applied to any object arbitrarily. ∎

A style name selector doesn't apply its styles to any object on its own. Instead, each object "opts in" to apply the selector's styles with the `styleName` property. This `Label` control uses the style rules in the `redFont` selector:

```
<s:Label text="Hello World" styleName="redFont"/>
```

Style name selectors can be declared in the `Application` or within any custom component. If the same style name selector is declared at two levels of the application's containership and sets conflicting values for any particular style, the declaration in the custom component takes precedence.

Note

You use the period as a prefix to the style name only in the selector definition, not in the `styleName` property. If you include the period in the `styleName` property, the settings are ignored. ■

Using ID selectors

The Flex 3 SDK (and previous versions) didn't support the ID selector. To apply a set of styles to a particular object, you typically used multiple inline style declarations or applied individual style name selectors. Flex 4 adds the ID selector syntax with a variety of optional uses.

Before applying an ID selector to an object, you must assign its `id` property to a unique value:

```
<s:TextInput id="myInput"/>
```

In the style sheet, you declare a selector by adding a `#` character as a prefix to the object's `id`. Any styles declared within the following code block are then applied to the object:

```
#myInput
{
  color:purple;
  font-size:24;
}
```

Note

ID selectors work across the entire application. If you declare another object with the same `id` in a custom component, and the ID selector is declared at the application level, the selector is applied to all objects with that `id` at any level of the application. ■

Caution

CSS ID selectors are only applied to objects when their `id` property is set explicitly. If an object is declared in ActionScript, the variable name alone isn't enough. You must also set the `id` property of the new object to match the CSS ID selector. ■

Using the global selector

The global selector has a reserved name of `global` (always declared in all lowercase). Styles declared within the `global` selector, inheritable or not, are applied to all visual components in the entire application.

Caution

There aren't many styles that you'd want to apply to the entire application. This feature's use is typically restricted to setting default font styles such as `fontFamily` and `color`. It wouldn't make sense, for example, to apply border or padding styles to every object in the application. ∎

This global declaration sets the default font family and color for the entire application:

```
global {
   font-family:Times New Roman, Times, serif;
   color:purple;
}
```

Using Embedded Style Sheets

You can embed a style sheet in an MXML application or component with the `<fx:Style>` compiler tag set. As previously described, a style sheet embedded in a custom component can include only style name selectors. Style sheets embedded in the `Application` can contain a mixture of type, style name, and global selectors.

Caution

The `<fx:Style>` tag must be declared as a direct child element of the MXML file's root element. An `<fx:Style>` tag placed within any other child element in the MXML containership results in a compiler error. ∎

New Feature

The Style tag set was declared with the `mx` prefix in Flex 3. In Flex 4, it's associated with the `fx` prefix, as in `<fx:Style>`. ∎

The code in Listing 11.2 shows an application with an embedded style sheet. The embedded style sheet's selectors and rules are applied to the entire application.

LISTING 11.2

An embedded style sheet

```
<?xml version="1.0" encoding="utf-8"?>
<s:Application xmlns:fx="http://ns.adobe.com/mxml/2009"
  xmlns:s="library://ns.adobe.com/flex/spark"
  xmlns:mx="library://ns.adobe.com/flex/mx">
  <s:layout>
    <s:VerticalLayout horizontalAlign="center" paddingTop="20"/>
  </s:layout>
  <fx:Style>
```

continued

LISTING 11.2 *(continued)*

```
  @namespace mx "library://ns.adobe.com/flex/mx";
  @namespace s "library://ns.adobe.com/flex/spark";

  global {
    font-family:Times New Roman, Times, serif;
    color:purple;
  }
  s|Label
  {
    font-size:18;
    font-style:italic;
  }
  s|Button s|Label
  {
    font-style:normal;
    font-weight:bold;
  }
  .redFont
  {
    color:#ff0000;
  }
 </fx:Style>
 <s:VGroup>
   <s:Label text="Hello World" styleName="redFont"/>
   <s:Button label="Click me"/>
 </s:VGroup>
 <s:HGroup>
   <s:Label text="Hello World"/>
   <s:Button label="Click me"/>
 </s:HGroup>
</s:Application>
```

On the Web

The code in Listing 11.2 is available in the Web site files as `EmbeddedStyles.mxml` in the `chapter11` project. ∎

Note

Notice the use of a descendant selector to control the text on the face of each `Button` control. The Spark `Button` control has a default skin that uses a `Label` object to display the value of the `label` property. The following descendant selector prevents the `Button` from displaying text that otherwise would be italicized:

```
s|Button s|Label
{
  font-style:normal;
  font-weight:bold;
} ∎
```

354

Using the Appearance View

Flash Builder 4 has a new Appearance view, shown in the following figure. The Appearance view appears automatically in Design mode, docked in a tabbed interface that's shared with the Properties view.

The Appearance view enables you to set the following styles that are added to the current application's `global` CSS selector:

- **Font.** Includes styles such as `fontFamily`, `fontSize`, `color`, `fontWeight`, `fontStyle`, `textDecoration`, `verticalAlign`, and `textAlign`.

- **Chrome.** The `chromeColor` style determines the color of borders and other graphical elements in interactive controls such as buttons, sliders, lists, and data entry controls.

- **Selection.** The `selectionColor` style determines the color of text when components are enabled and have focus.

- **Rollover.** The `rollOverColor` style determines the color of components when the mouse cursor hovers over them.

- **Focus.** The `focusColor` style determines the color of the ring around interactive components when they have focus.

- **Symbol.** The `symbolColor` style determines the color of symbols such as the checkmark in a `CheckBox` control.

- **Content Background.** The `contentBackgroundColor` and `contentBackgroundAlpha` styles determine the background color of content groups.

When you set these styles with the Appearance view, they're always declared in the `global` selector and are placed in an external CSS file that is automatically linked to the current application with an `<fx:Style>` element.

Using External Style Sheets

You can store style sheets in text files with a file extension of .css. As with embedded style sheets, an external style sheet contains a collection of style selectors, each declaring one or more style and value.

Flash Builder can create a new style sheet for you in a couple of ways:

- As a new blank `style` sheet file
- By exporting existing styles from Design view to a new external style sheet

Creating a blank style sheet

To create a new blank style sheet, choose File ➪ New ➪ CSS File from the Flash Builder menu, or right-click on a folder in the Package Explorer view and choose New ➪ CSS File. As shown in Figure 11.3, set the filename and location of the CSS file.

FIGURE 11.3

Creating a new external style sheet

Tip

You should always save external style sheets within the project's source-code root folder or in one of its subfolders. ∎

After you've created the external style sheet file, you can manually add selectors and properties. As shown in Figure 11.4, Flash Builder provides code completion support in external style sheets that helps you correctly type the property names and values. To get code completion help at any time, press Ctrl + spacebar to see available properties and values.

Code completion in an external style sheet

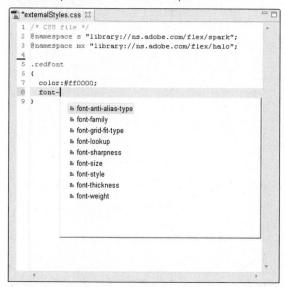

Listing 11.3 shows the contents of an external style sheet file. Notice that there is no `<fx:Style>` tag set because this is no longer an MXML file.

An external style sheet file

```
/* CSS file */
@namespace s "library://ns.adobe.com/flex/spark";
@namespace mx "library://ns.adobe.com/flex/mx";
global {
    font-family:Times New Roman, Times, serif;
    color:purple;
}
s|Label
{
```

continued

LISTING 11.3 *(continued)*

```
  font-size:18;
  font-style:italic;
}
s|Button s|Label
{
  font-style:normal;
  font-weight:bold;
}
.redFont
{
  color:#ff0000;
}
```

On the Web

The code in Listing 11.3 is available in the Web site files as `externalStyles.css` in the `chapter11` project. ■

To incorporate an external style sheet into an application, declare the `<fx:Style>` tag set with a source attribute referring to the style sheet file by its name and relative location:

```
<fx:Style source="styles.css"/>
```

Caution

When you declare `<fx:Style>` with a `source` attribute, you cannot also include nested CSS declarations. You can, however, declare more than one `<fx:Style>` tag set in an application or component. ■

Listing 11.4 shows the application now referring to an external style sheet.

LISTING 11.4

An application referring to an external style sheet

```
<?xml version="1.0" encoding="utf-8"?>
<s:Application xmlns:fx="http://ns.adobe.com/mxml/2009" xmlns:s="library://
  ns.adobe.com/flex/spark" xmlns:mx="library://ns.adobe.com/flex/mx" >
  <s:layout>
    <s:VerticalLayout horizontalAlign="center" paddingTop="20"/>
  </s:layout>
  <fx:Style source="externalStyles.css"/>
  <s:VGroup>
    <s:Label text="Hello World" styleName="redFont"/>
    <s:Button label="Click me"/>
  </s:VGroup>
```

```
<s:HGroup>
  <s:Label text="Hello World"/>
  <s:Button label="Click me"/>
</s:HGroup>
</s:Application>
```

On the Web

The code in Listing 11.4 is available in the Web site files as `ExternalStyles.mxml` **in the** `chapter11` **project.** ■

Exporting existing styles

Flash Builder enables you to export inline styles of any component instance to an external style sheet and then link the current application to that external file.

When you export styles from a component instance, you can define what kind of selector the styles should be applied to the following:

- All components (the `global` selector)
- All components with style name
- The current specific component's name
- The current specific component's name plus a style name

Follow these steps to learn how this feature works:

1. **Create a new MXML application named ExportStyles.mxml with its layout property set to VerticalLayout.**

2. **If the application opens in Source mode, switch to Design mode.**

3. **Drag a Button from the Components view into the application.**

4. **In the Flex Properties view, set the Button component's properties and styles as follows:**

   - `label`: **Click Me**
   - `color`: **#FF0000**
   - `fontWeight`: **bold**
   - `fontSize`: **14**

5. **Switch to Source view.** Your application code should look like this:

   ```
   <?xml version="1.0" encoding="utf-8"?>
   <s:Application xmlns:fx="http://ns.adobe.com/mxml/2009"
     xmlns:s="library://ns.adobe.com/flex/spark"
     xmlns:mx="library://ns.adobe.com/flex/mx">
   ```

```
<s:layout>
  <s:BasicLayout/>
</s:layout>
<s:Button label="Click Me" color="#FF0000"
  fontWeight="bold" fontSize="14"/>
</s:Application>
```

6. Switch back to Design view, and select the Button control.

7. In the Flex Properties view, click Convert to CSS, as shown in Figure 11.5.

FIGURE 11.5

Exporting styles from the Flex Properties view

Click to export to external CSS file

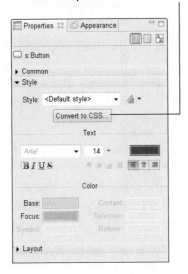

8. If prompted to save changes to the application, click Yes.

9. In the New Style Rule dialog box, shown in Figure 11.6, select New to create a new CSS style sheet.

10. **In the New CSS File dialog box, name the new style sheet newStyleSheet.** Leave the package empty to place the new style sheet in the default package and click Finish.

11. **In the New Style Rule dialog box, select Specific component and click OK.** Flash Builder should now display the new CSS file. (Note that you can also choose to move the object's properties to the global selector or to a selector that uses a style name.)

12. Save any pending changes to the file.

13. Return to the application and switch to Source view.

FIGURE 11.6

The New Style Rule dialog box

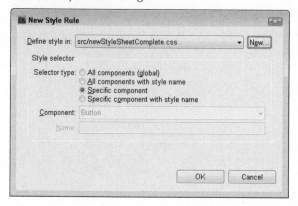

The application's source now contains an `<fx:Style>` declaration pointing to the external style sheet, and the `Button` control's inline styles have been removed:

```xml
<?xml version="1.0" encoding="utf-8"?>
<s:Application xmlns:fx="http://ns.adobe.com/mxml/2009"
  xmlns:s="library://ns.adobe.com/flex/spark"
  xmlns:mx="library://ns.adobe.com/flex/mx" >
  <s:layout>
    <s:VerticalLayout/>
  </s:layout>
  <fx:Style source="newStyleSheet.css"/>
  <s:Button label="Click Me"/>
</s:Application>
```

The external style sheet contains the styles that were part of the `Button` declaration, now applied in a type selector:

```css
/* CSS file */
@namespace s "library://ns.adobe.com/flex/spark";
@namespace mx "library://ns.adobe.com/flex/mx";
s|Button
{
  color: #FF0000;
  fontSize: 14;
  fontWeight: bold;
}
```

On the Web

The complete code from the preceding exercise is available in the Web site files as `ExportStyles Complete.mxml` and `newStyleSheetComplete.css` in the `chapter11` project. ∎

Understanding Style Data Types

When you set a style, you use syntax that's specific to the style's data type. Some styles require `String` values, others `Number` values, and still others `Array` values containing specific numbers of items.

For example, the `fontSize` style requires a numeric value. When you set this value in an MXML inline attribute, you declare it as a `String` and it's converted to a `Number` by the Flex compiler:

```
<s:Label text="Hello World" fontSize="14"/>
```

Other styles require specific `String` values. For example, the `fontWeight` style requires a `String`, but only accepts values of `bold` and `normal`:

```
<s:Label text="Hello World" fontWeight="bold"/>
```

Styles that require color values accept a number of formats. The most common color code format is hexadecimal and consists of a six-character string defining the amount of red, green, and blue in the color. The string can be prefixed by either a hash or pound character (#) or by a zero and small x (0x). If you want to store this value in a variable, you can set the hex value without quotes to an `int` (integer) or `uint` (unsigned integer) data type. This `Label` sets its font color to blue with a hexadecimal code:

```
<s:Label text="Hello World" color="0x0000FF"/>
```

Colors can also be declared using RGB (red, green, blue) percentage values. This syntax consists of the key word `rgb` followed by a comma-delimited set of percentage values representing the amount of red, green, and blue. This syntax only works in embedded or external style sheets, not in inline declarations. This style declaration means that `Label` controls have a font color of red:

```
s|Label {
  color:rgb(100%, 0%, 0%);
}
```

You also can set color values with named colors. Color names that are recognized by the Flex compiler include `aqua`, `black`, `blue`, `fuchsia`, `gray`, `green`, `lime`, `maroon`, `navy`, `olive`, `purple`, `red`, `silver`, `teal`, `white`, and `yellow`. This `Label` sets its font color to `teal` with a named color:

```
<s:Label text="Hello World" color="teal"/>
```

Style values that are typed as `Array` are declared in MXML as comma-delimited lists wrapped in brackets. The MX `Button` control's `fillColors` style requires an array of two colors that are then used to create a background gradient. As with simple color values, you can use hexadecimal or named colors:

```
<mx:Button label="Click Me" fillColors="[blue, white]"/>
```

When you declare the `Array` values in an embedded or external style sheet, you still use the comma-delimited list, but don't include the brackets. This style sheet declaration sets the `fillColors` style for all MX `Button` controls in the application with a vertical gradient of blue and white:

```
mx|Button {
  fill-colors:#0000ff,#000000;
}
```

Many of the visual effects that were achieved with complex styles in Flex 3 are now supported through the use of FXG graphics in skinnable Spark-based components. The Spark version of `Button`, for example, doesn't support the `fill-colors` style, but you can easily define a skin for the Spark `Button` that uses a gradient graphic as its background. This gives you much more flexibility; instead of being limited to two colors and a vertical gradient, you can choose from a few different kinds of gradients and include multiple color points, known as *entries*.

Using Compiled Style Sheets

Style sheets can be compiled into external SWF files and then loaded at runtime.

Note

Neither Flash Player nor the Flex framework includes a CSS parser that would enable a Flex application to parse a "raw" CSS file at runtime. The capability to load a precompiled CSS file was added to Flex in version 2.0.1. ■

Compiling style sheets

Flash Builder can create a compiled style sheet with a simple menu selection. These steps describe how to compile a style sheet:

1. Create a new external style sheet named compiledStyles.css in the current project's src folder.

2. Add a Label selector that sets the color to blue, the font-size to 18, and the font-weight to bold:

```
s|Label {
  color:blue;
  font-size:18;
  font-weight:bold;
}
```

3. Save the external style sheet file.

4. As shown in Figure 11.7, right-click the style sheet file in the Flex Navigator view and select Compile CSS to SWF.

The compiled SWF file is created in the same folder as the external style sheet and is also copied to the project's output folder.

Note

Once you have selected the Compile CSS to SWF option for any particular external style sheet, the compilation option remains selected for that file until you deselect it. Whenever Flash Builder rebuilds the project, the CSS file is recompiled as well. ■

You should see the new `compiledstyles.swf` file in the project's output folder. It's placed there, rather than in the source folder, to ensure that it's deployed with the application's other runtime assets.

Loading compiled style sheets

The compiled style sheet file is an asset that must be deployed with the application and can be dynamically loaded at runtime. Its styles can then immediately be applied to existing component instances in the application.

FIGURE 11.7

Using the Compile CSS to SWF option

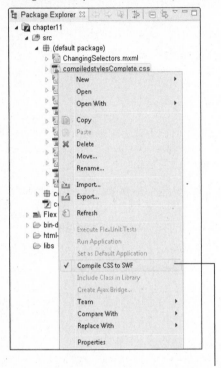

This is a toggle property; once selected,
the CSS file recompiles each time it's changed

To load the precompiled application at runtime, use the application's `styleManager` object, which implements an interface named `StyleManager2`. The `styleManager` object is a single-ton that can be referred to from any visual component in the application. It has a method named `loadStyleDeclarations()` that loads compiled style sheets and optionally updates the application's style declarations immediately.

New Feature

In Flex 3, the methods described in this section were static members of the `StyleManager` class and were called from the class itself:

```
StyleManager.loadStyleDeclarations(...style file...);
```

In Flex 4, the application now has a `styleManager` property from which you call the same methods:

```
styleManager.loadStyleDeclarations(...style file...);
```

If you're migrating an application from Flex 3 to Flex 4, just change the initial character of `StyleManager` from uppercase to lowercase and the code will work exactly as before. ∎

Follow these steps to use the `styleManager` object:

1. Create a new MXML application named `RuntimeStyles.mxml`.
2. Add a Label control with a text property of Hello World.
3. Add a Button control with a label of Load Styles.
4. Set its click event listener to execute this code:

   ```
   styleManager.loadStyleDeclarations('compiledStyles.swf');
   ```

5. Run the application.
6. **Click Load Styles.** When the application first loads, the `Label` control is displayed with its default font color, weight, and size. When you click Load Styles, the application loads the compiled style sheet and updates the `Label` control's presentation.

Listing 11.5 shows the completed application.

LISTING 11.5

An application loading a compiled style sheet at runtime

```
<?xml version="1.0" encoding="utf-8"?>
<s:Application xmlns:fx="http://ns.adobe.com/mxml/2009"
  xmlns:s="library://ns.adobe.com/flex/spark"
  xmlns:mx="library://ns.adobe.com/flex/mx">
  <s:layout>
    <s:VerticalLayout horizontalAlign="center" paddingTop="20"/>
  </s:layout>
  <fx:Script>
    <![CDATA[
      protected function button1_clickHandler(event:MouseEvent):void
      {
        styleManager.loadStyleDeclarations("compiledStylesComplete.swf");
      }
    ]]>
  </fx:Script>
  <s:Label text="Hello World"/>
  <s:Button label="Load styles" click="button1_clickHandler(event)"/>
</s:Application>
```

On the Web

The code in Listing 11.5 is available in the Web site files as `RuntimeStylesComplete.mxml` in the chapter11 project. ∎

Using the `StyleManager` class, you also can unload styles, delay style updates, and react to various events in the process of working with dynamic styles.

Controlling Styles with ActionScript

You can control styles at runtime in many ways. These tasks are available:

- Loading of compiled style sheets (described in the preceding section)
- Setting and getting styles for individual component instances
- Modifying selectors and their properties
- Changing a component instance's style name

Setting and getting style information

Every visual component in the Flex framework supports methods named `setStyle()` and `getStyle()` that enable you to set or get any particular style's values. As I described previously, you cannot use simple dot syntax to access style information (as you might with a component property). This code, for example, would produce a compiler error:

```
myText.fontSize=18;
```

The use of dot syntax to separate a component instance `id` and its members works with properties, but not with styles.

Instead, use the `setStyle()` method to reset a style's value at runtime:

```
myText.setStyle("fontSize", 18);
```

And use the `getStyle()` method to get a style's value:

```
var currentSize:Number = myLabel.getStyle("fontSize");
```

The code in Listing 11.6 shows an application with a `Label` control and two `Button` controls. Clicking Change Font Size results in modifying the `Label` control's font size at runtime. Clicking Get Font Size displays the `Label` control's current font size.

LISTING 11.6

Setting and getting style values

```
<?xml version="1.0" encoding="utf-8"?>
<s:Application xmlns:fx="http://ns.adobe.com/mxml/2009"
  xmlns:s="library://ns.adobe.com/flex/spark"
  xmlns:mx="library://ns.adobe.com/flex/mx">
  <s:layout>
    <s:VerticalLayout horizontalAlign="center" paddingTop="20"/>
  </s:layout>
```

```
<s:Label id="myText" text="Hello World" fontSize="10"/>
<s:Button label="Change Font Size"
  click="myText.setStyle('fontSize', 18)"/>
<s:Button label="Get Font Size"
  click="myText.text='Current font size: ' +
  myText.getStyle('fontSize')"/>
</s:Application>
```

On the Web

The code in Listing 11.6 is available in the Web site files as `SettingAndGettingStyles.mxml` **in the** `chapter11` **project.** ∎

As shown in Figure 11.8, the `Label` control displays its own current font size when the second button is clicked.

FIGURE 11.8

The font size changes when the ActionScript code is executed.

Caution

Styles are never bindable at runtime. This code, which tries to bind to a style's current value at runtime, succeeds upon application startup, but fails to execute when the target component's style changes at runtime:

```
<s:Label id="myText" text="{'Current font size: ' +
  myText.getStyle('fontSize')}"/>
```
∎

Modifying style selectors at runtime

You can modify style selectors at runtime with the `CSSStyleDeclaration` and `StyleManager` classes. You can use one of these approaches:

- Create an instance of CSSStyleDeclaration bound to a style name or type selector.
- Create an instance of CSSStyleDeclaration without a selector, and then use the StyleManager class's setStyleDeclaration() method to bind the styles to the selector.

Using bound CSS declarations

To bind a CSSStyleDeclaration to a style selector, pass the selector as an argument to the class's constructor method:

```
var style:CSSStyleDeclaration =
   new CSSStyleDeclaration(".redFont");
```

Then, to change the styles in the selector, use the object's setStyle() method using the same syntax as with individual component instances:

```
style.setStyle("fontSize", 18);
```

When the setStyle() method is executed, the selector and any component instances it affects are updated immediately.

Binding CSS declarations with the styleManager object

You can delay updates of styles by using unbound instances of CSSStyleDeclaration. To create an unbound style declaration, use the class's constructor method without any arguments:

```
var style:CSSStyleDeclaration = new CSSStyleDeclaration();
```

Set the style declaration's rules with the setStyle() method as described previously. Then, to bind the declaration to a style selector, call styleManager.setStyleDeclaration() with three arguments:

- The style selector name
- The CSSStyleDeclaration instance
- A Boolean value indicating whether you want to update the styles immediately

New Feature

As described previously in this section, the styleManager object is new to Flex 4. In Flex 3, you called setStyleDeclaration() as a static method of the StyleManager class. In Flex 4, this and other style management methods are now instance members of the styleManager object, a singleton that can be referred to from any object that extends UIComponent. ■

The code in Listing 11.7 declares an unbound instance of CSSStyleDeclaration, sets two styles, and then binds and updates the styles.

LISTING 11.7

Binding CSS declarations with the styleManager object

```
<?xml version="1.0" encoding="utf-8"?>
<s:Application xmlns:fx="http://ns.adobe.com/mxml/2009"
  xmlns:s="library://ns.adobe.com/flex/spark"
  xmlns:mx="library://ns.adobe.com/flex/mx">
  <s:layout>
    <s:VerticalLayout horizontalAlign="center" paddingTop="20"/>
  </s:layout>
  <fx:Script>
    <![CDATA[
      private function setFont(size:Number, weight:String):void
      {
        var style:CSSStyleDeclaration = new CSSStyleDeclaration();
        style.setStyle("fontSize", size);
        style.setStyle("fontWeight", weight);
        styleManager.setStyleDeclaration(".redFont", style, true);
      }
    ]]>
  </fx:Script>
  <fx:Style>
    @namespace mx "library://ns.adobe.com/flex/mx";
    @namespace s "library://ns.adobe.com/flex/spark";
    .redFont {
      font-size:12;
      color:red;
    }
  </fx:Style>
  <s:Label text="Hello World" styleName="redFont"/>
  <s:Button label="Change Label Font" click="setFont(36, 'bold')"/>
</s:Application>
```

On the Web

The code in Listing 11.7 is available in the Web site files as `ChangingSelectors.mxml` in the `chapter11` project. ■

Caution

The `setStyle()` method is particularly resource intensive, as it has to look up the entire inheritance tree to be correctly applied. ■

Summary

In this chapter, I described the use of Cascading Style Sheets (CSS) to effect the visual presentation of Flex applications. You learned the following:

- CSS are implemented in the Flex SDK as the primary mechanism for controlling a Flex application's visual appearance.

- You can declare styles with inline style declarations, and with embedded or external style sheets.

- Type selectors apply styles to all components that extend a certain component or set of components.

- Flex 4 adds the use of CSS namespaces to distinguish style declarations for MX or Spark components.

- Style name (also known as class) selectors define styles that are applied to components through their `styleName` property.

- The global selector applies styles to all components in the entire application.

- Styles can be manipulated programmatically with the `setStyle()` and `getStyle()` methods.

- You can compile external style sheets in SWF files that can be loaded at runtime.

Controlling Animation and Working with Drag and Drop

F lash Player was originally created as a platform for presenting animation over the Web. Future Splash Animator, the original ancestor of
the Flash authoring environment and Flash Player, was a Java-based
software product that was integrated into the browser in much the same
manner as Flash Player is today.

Millions of Flash developers worldwide create compelling content designed
for presentation in a Web application. Animation and related visual wizardry
is the most common goal, and the most common result, of documents developed in the Flash authoring environment and distributed through Flash
Player.

Animation in Flash depends largely on use of the timeline: a visual interface
that enables the developer to create animations frame by frame or through a
process known as *tweening*. Flex application developers don't have the timeline available to them. In fact, one of Macromedia's most important motiva-
tions in creating Flex was to free developers with a coding background from
having to work with the timeline at all. But a Flex application is still distributed and viewed through Flash Player. So when it's time to move objects
around the screen, a Flex developer needs code-based approaches to make it
happen.

In this chapter, I describe the use of effects to create animation in a Flex
application. I also describe how to implement drag-and-drop interfaces to
create an intuitive way to move data around an application.

On the Web

To use the sample code for this chapter, import the `chapter12.fxp` **Flex
project archive from the Web site files into your Flash Builder workspace.** ∎

IN THIS CHAPTER

Declaring effects in MXML

**Instantiating and playing
effects with ActionScript**

**Using tweening and masking
effects**

Using composite effects

**Implementing drag-and-drop
interfaces**

Using Effects

An *effect* is an ActionScript class that defines changes in a visual component's position, visibility, scaling, and other properties over a period of time. The Flex framework includes many pre-built effect classes that can be applied to visual components and played with explicit ActionScript statements or upon certain built-in effect triggers.

New Feature

The Flex 4 SDK includes a new set of effect classes that have the advantage of working on both Flex components and on primitive vector graphics defined with the new FXG syntax supported in MXML. These effect classes are members of the `spark.effects` package and can be used to animate both new Spark components and the older MX components. The older effect classes, which are members of the `mx.effects` package, are still included with the Flex 4 SDK. ■

Most pre-built effect classes in the Flex framework define changes to visual properties of control. The following new Spark effects cause changes to one or more of a visual component's properties over a period of time:

- `Animate`. Changes any arbitrary set of properties.
- `AnimateColor`. Changes a color property from a starting to an ending color.
- `AnimateFilter`. Changes properties of one of the filter classes defined in the `spark.filters` package, including `DropShadowFilter`, `GlowFilter`, `BlurFilter`, and `ShaderFilter`.
- `AnimateShaderTransition`. Performs an animation between two bitmaps using a pixel-shader program based on Flash Player's Pixel Bender technology. You can provide your own shader program or use one of those provided by this effect's subclasses, `CrossFade` and `Wipe`.
- `AnimateTransform`. Combines multiple transform animations, such as translation, scale and rotation, into a parallel effect.
- `CrossFade`. Performs a crossfade between two components or graphics. This class is extended from `AnimateShaderTransition` and is designed to be used in transitions rather than played directly.
- `Fade`. Changes the `alpha` property of a component to affect transparency.
- `Move`. Changes the component's x and y properties to modify the object's relative position within its container.
- `Move3D`. Changes the component's x, y, and z properties to modify the object's relative position within its container and its relative depth.
- `Resize`. Changes the component's `width` and `height`.
- `Rotate`. Rotates a component. You can control the angle of rotation.
- `Rotate3D`. Rotates a component in three dimensions. You can control the angle of rotation and its 3D orientation.

- `Scale`. Changes a component's relative size around its center, using `scaleX` and `scaleY` properties.

- `Scale3D`. Changes a component's relative size around its center, adding 3D functionality.

- `Wipe`. Reveals one component or graphic and hides another, performing the transformation in one of four directions (right, left, up, or down). This class is extended from `AnimateShaderTransition` and is designed to be used in transitions rather than played directly.

The following MX effects are retained from the Flex 3 SDK, and have not been rewritten in the new Spark framework. You can still use them to animate MX components but can't apply them directly to Spark components or MXML graphics:

- `Iris`. Uses a rectangular mask to reveal or hide an object. Unlike the Zoom effect, this does not change the component's dimensions.

- `WipeLeft`, `WipeRight`, `WipeUp`, and `WipeDown`. Uses a mask to reveal or hide an object in the indicated direction.

- `Zoom`. Changes the scale of a component, zooming into and out of a component's center point.

Tip

Some MX effects that haven't been rewritten can be emulated with the new Spark effects. For example, you can achieve the same result as the MX `Blur` and `Glow` effects with the Spark `AnimateFilter` effect. ■

The following MX effects are nonvisual but are played with the same sort of code as the visual effect classes:

- `Pause`. Creates a delay between multiple effects controlled in a `Sequence` (explained later in this chapter).

- `SoundEffect`. Plays an MP3 file. The MP3 file can be embedded or can be loaded at runtime.

Declaring and playing effect classes

You play effects either in a view state transition or by calling an effect object's `play()` method.

Caution

The older Flex 3 effects support an architecture known as a trigger, which plays an effect in reaction to a specific event. This code, for example, would cause an object to fade in and out in reaction to having its `visible` property set to `true` or `false`:

```
<mx:Image source="assets/flower1.jpg"
   showEffect="{myMXEffect}" hideEffect="{myMXEffect}"/>
```

If you try to use this syntax with Spark effects, the results are inconsistent. Adobe recommends that Spark effects be called directly from ActionScript code or in the context of a view state transition. ■

To get started with an effect, declare an instance of the desired effect class in either MXML or ActionScript code. This instance of the Spark Fade class will cause its target object to fade from transparent to opaque over the course of 2000 milliseconds (2 seconds):

```
<fx:Declarations>
  <s:Fade id="myFade" duration="2000"
    alphaFrom="0" alphaTo="1"/>
</fx:Declarations>
```

New Feature

As with all nonvisual objects, MXML declarations of effect objects must be wrapped in the <fx:Declarations> **element in Flex 4.** ■

Because an effect's duration is measured in milliseconds, a duration of 2000 means that the effect takes 2 seconds to play. The duration property's default value is 500 milliseconds, so the custom Fade effect plays much more slowly than the default.

To play the effect, call the effect object's play() method and pass an array containing references to all objects that should be affected:

```
myFade.play([myImage])
```

Note

Each effect class in the Flex framework has an equivalent instance class. For example, the Fade **class is matched by a** FadeInstance **class. The instance class is used internally by the framework to create new instances of the effect each time it's played. You should never declare the effect instance classes directly though.** ■

Listing 12.1 shows a complete application that declares two Fade objects. The Button components play the effects when clicked, causing the BitmapImage to fade in and out.

LISTING 12.1

Playing simple effects

```
<?xml version="1.0" encoding="utf-8"?>
<s:Application xmlns:fx="http://ns.adobe.com/mxml/2009"
  xmlns:s="library://ns.adobe.com/flex/spark">
  <fx:Declarations>
    <s:Fade id="fadeIn" alphaFrom="0" alphaTo="1"/>
    <s:Fade id="fadeOut" alphaFrom="1" alphaTo="0"/>
  </fx:Declarations>
  <s:BitmapImage id="myImage" source="@Embed('assets/flower1.jpg')"
    x="140" y="90"/>
  <s:Button x="140" y="338" label="Show Image"
    click="fadeIn.play([myImage])"/>
  <s:Button x="374" y="338" label="Hide Image"
    click="fadeOut.play([myImage])"/>
</s:Application>
```

On the Web

The code in Listing 12.1 is available in the Web site files as `PlayingEffects.mxml` in the `chapter12` project. ∎

Figure 12.1 shows the resulting application in the process of fading from visible to invisible.

Tip

You can still use the MX effects to animate Spark components by wrapping the Spark component in an MX container. For example, the `WipeLeft`, `WipeRight`, `WipeUp`, `WipeDown`, `Iris`, and certain other effects haven't been rewritten in Spark at this point. The following code wraps a Spark `Button` in a MX `Box` container, and then applies the MX `WipeRight` effect to the containing `Box`:

```
<fx:Declarations>
  <mx:WipeRight id="wipe" />
</fx:Declarations>
<mx:Box id="box" label="MX Box">
  <s:Button id="btn"
    label="Spark Button"
    click="wipe.play([box])"/>
</mx:Box> ∎
```

FIGURE 12.1

A `Fade` effect in progress

Declaring effects in ActionScript

You can explicitly construct and play an effect with ActionScript code with these steps:

1. Declare an instance of an effect class as a variable.

2. Set the effect variable's `target` property to refer to the component you want to animate.

3. Set other properties to modify the effect's behavior.

4. Call the effect class's `play()` method.

The application in Listing 12.2 creates and plays customized `Fade` effects to handle the hiding and showing of a visual component.

LISTING 12.2

Defining and playing an effect with ActionScript

```
<?xml version="1.0" encoding="utf-8"?>
<s:Application xmlns:fx="http://ns.adobe.com/mxml/2009"
  xmlns:s="library://ns.adobe.com/flex/spark"
  xmlns:mx="library://ns.adobe.com/flex/mx">
  <fx:Script>
    <![CDATA[
      import spark.effects.Fade;
      private function showImage():void
      {
        var myFade:Fade = new Fade();
        myFade.target = myImage;
        myFade.alphaFrom = 0;
        myFade.alphaTo = 1;
        myFade.play();
      }
      private function hideImage():void
      {
        var myFade:Fade = new Fade();
        myFade.target = myImage;
        myFade.alphaFrom = 1;
        myFade.alphaTo = 0;
        myFade.play();
      }
    ]]>
  </fx:Script>
  <s:BitmapImage id="myImage" source="@Embed('assets/flower1.jpg')"
    x="150" y="100"/>
  <s:Button x="150" y="375" label="Show Image" click="showImage()"/>
  <s:Button x="374" y="375" label="Hide Image" click="hideImage()"/>
</s:Application>
```

On the Web

The code in Listing 12.2 is available in the Web site files as `PlayEffectWithAS.mxml` in the `chapter12` project. ■

Tip

Effect classes also have a `targets` property that takes an array of visual components. When you call the effect class's `play()` method, the framework constructs one internal instance of the effect class for each target object and then plays them all simultaneously. ■

Using the new Spark effects

In this section I describe the most commonly used new Spark effects.

Note

I do not describe the older MX effects extensively in this book. For more information on these older effect classes, see the previous edition of this book, Flex 3 Bible (Wiley, 2008). ■

Using the Animate effect

Flex 4 has a new effect class named `Animate` that enables you to modify any number of properties, with any data types, over a period of time.

New Feature

The new `Animate` effect is designed to replace the Flex 3 `AnimateProperty` effect. In contrast to `AnimateProperty`, which only worked with numeric properties, `Animate` can be used with properties that use any data type. ■

You declare an instance of `Animate` with a `motionPaths` property consisting of an `Array` of `MotionPath` instances. Each `MotionPath` object animates a single property, and includes a `keyframes` property that in turn is an array of `Keyframe` instances. Each `Keyframe` defines a moment in `time`, set in milliseconds, and a new `value` for the named property.

The following `Animate` object has a single `MotionPath` that moves an object across the screen from left to right over the course of five seconds:

```
<s:Animate id="myAnimation">
  <s:motionPaths>
    <s:MotionPath property="x">
      <s:keyframes>
        <s:Keyframe time="0" value="0"/>
        <s:Keyframe time="5000" value="800"/>
      </s:keyframes>
    </s:MotionPath>
  </s:motionPaths>
</Animate>
```

Tip

You can simplify declarations of a `MotionPath` object by using its subclass `SimpleMotionPath`. This class takes only `property` and `value` settings and can be used when you don't need to control animation over multiple keyframes. ■

The application in Listing 12.3 causes a BitmapImage to change from so small that it's invisible to full size, and simultaneously move to a new position when the user clicks the button. Notice that the Image object's scaleX and scaleY properties are initially set to 0 to make it invisible.

LISTING 12.3

Customizing animation with the Animate effect

```xml
<?xml version="1.0" encoding="utf-8"?>
<s:Application xmlns:fx="http://ns.adobe.com/mxml/2009"
  xmlns:s="library://ns.adobe.com/flex/spark"
  xmlns:mx="library://ns.adobe.com/flex/mx">
  <fx:Declarations>
    <s:Animate id="myAnimation">
      <s:motionPaths>
        <s:MotionPath property="x">
          <s:keyframes>
            <s:Keyframe time="0" value="0"/>
            <s:Keyframe time="1000" value="{myButton.x-myImage.width-10}"/>
          </s:keyframes>
        </s:MotionPath>
        <s:MotionPath property="y">
          <s:keyframes>
            <s:Keyframe time="0" value="0"/>
            <s:Keyframe time="1000" value="{myButton.y-myImage.height-10}"/>
          </s:keyframes>
        </s:MotionPath>
        <s:MotionPath property="scaleX">
          <s:keyframes>
            <s:Keyframe time="0" value="0"/>
            <s:Keyframe time="1000" value="1"/>
          </s:keyframes>
        </s:MotionPath>
        <s:MotionPath property="scaleY">
          <s:keyframes>
            <s:Keyframe time="0" value="0"/>
            <s:Keyframe time="1000" value="1"/>
          </s:keyframes>
        </s:MotionPath>
      </s:motionPaths>
    </s:Animate>
  </fx:Declarations>
  <s:BitmapImage id="myImage" source="@Embed('assets/flower1.jpg')"
    scaleX="0" scaleY="0"/>
  <s:Button id="myButton" label="Play Animation"
    click="myAnimation.play([myImage])"
    bottom="20" right="20"/>
</s:Application>
```

On the Web

The code in Listing 12.3 is available in the Web site files as `AnimateDemo.mxml` **in the** `chapter12` **project.** ■

Figure 12.2 shows the resulting animation.

FIGURE 12.2

An `Animate` effect in progress

Resulting animation

Play Animation

Using the Fade effect

The `Fade` effect, as used in Listing 12.2, changes a component's transparency over time. It supports properties of `alphaFrom` and `alphaTo` that can be used to control the direction and level of change in the component's visibility. The default values for these properties are `0` and `1`, applied to hide or show the target component.

The `Fade` class implements a tweening effect that modifies the component's transparency level over a period of time. Whatever color or image is "behind" the target component shows through as its transparency level is changed.

Cross-Reference

The application in Listing 12.1 illustrates a good example of the `Fade` **effect.** ■

Using the Move and Move3D effects

The `Move` and `Move3D` classes implement tweening effects that do what they say: they move the component on the screen to and from specific pixel positions over a period of time. The `Move` effect supports properties of `xFrom`, `xTo`, `yFrom`, and `yTo` that define the component's position at the beginning and end of the effect. The `Move3D` class is derived from `Move` and shares its properties, and adds `zFrom` and `zTo` properties to affect the object's relative z-order. For both effects, the object's intermediate positions are then recalculated over the period of time defined by the effect's `duration` property.

Note

The `Move` effect also supports properties names `xBy` and `yBy` that enable you to move an object a certain number of horizontal and vertical pixels from its current position. The `Move3D` effect supports a `zBy` property that does the same thing for z-order. ∎

When using the `Move` effect to show and hide controls, you typically create two instances of the effect. The first, with coordinates placing the target object on screen, shows the object. The second, with coordinates set to negative values or values greater than the width of the application or other container, hides the object. Each defines specific starting and ending coordinates and is played with the `play()` method or in the context of a view state transition.

Caution

A `Move` effect's target component should always be nested in a `Group` or other container with basic layout. If the target component is nested in a container with vertical or horizontal layout and the container's dimensions change at runtime, the component's position is recalculated based on the container's layout rules. ∎

The application in Listing 12.4 defines two `Move` effects that show and hide a target component by moving it on and off the application stage. Notice that the component's positions at the start and end of the effect are either defined as specific coordinates or calculated based on the target component's dimensions.

LISTING 12.4

Using the Move effect

```
<?xml version="1.0" encoding="utf-8"?>
<s:Application xmlns:fx="http://ns.adobe.com/mxml/2009"
  xmlns:s="library://ns.adobe.com/flex/spark"
  xmlns:mx="library://ns.adobe.com/flex/mx">
  <fx:Declarations>
    <s:Move id="moveOn"
      xFrom="{0-myImage.width}" xTo="150"
      yFrom="{0-myImage.height}" yTo="100"
      duration="2000"/>
    <s:Move id="moveOff"
      xTo="{0-myImage.width}" xFrom="150"
      yTo="{0-myImage.height}" yFrom="100"
      duration="2000"/>
  </fx:Declarations>
  <s:BitmapImage id="myImage" source="@Embed('assets/flower1.jpg')"
    x="150" y="100" />
  <s:Button x="150" y="375" label="Show Image"
```

```
      click="moveOn.play([myImage])"/>
   <s:Button x="374" y="375" label="Hide Image"
      click="moveOff.play([myImage])"/>
</s:Application>
```

On the Web

The code in Listing 12.4 is available in the Web site files as `MoveDemo.mxml` **in the** `chapter12` **project.** ■

The `Move3D` effect can be used to combine vertical and horizontal movement with changes to the object's relative z-order or can be used to shrink and grow an object. The application in Listing 12.5 uses two `Move3D` instances to grow and shrink an object. It has the same visual result as the Flex 3 Zoom effect.

LISTING 12.5

Using the Move3D effect

```
<?xml version="1.0" encoding="utf-8"?>
<s:Application xmlns:fx="http://ns.adobe.com/mxml/2009"
   xmlns:s="library://ns.adobe.com/flex/spark"
   xmlns:mx="library://ns.adobe.com/flex/mx">
   <fx:Declarations>
      <s:Move3D id="bigger" zBy="-10000"/>
      <s:Move3D id="smaller" zBy="10000"/>
   </fx:Declarations>
   <s:BitmapImage id="myImage" source="@Embed('assets/flower1.jpg')"/>
   <s:Button x="150" y="375" label="Show Image"
      click="bigger.play([myImage])"/>
   <s:Button x="374" y="375" label="Hide Image"
      click="smaller.play([myImage])"/>
</s:Application>
```

On the Web

The code in Listing 12.5 is available in the Web site files as `Move3DDemo.mxml` **in the** `chapter12` **project.** ■

Using the Rotate and Rotate3D effects

The `Rotate` and `Rotate3D` effects do what they say: they rotate an object in either two or three dimensions.

The Rotate effect supports `angleFrom`, `angleTo`, and `angleBy` properties to control the direction and amount of rotation in two dimensions. It also includes a `Boolean autoCenter Transform` property that, when set to `true`, changes the rotation axis from the object's top-left corner to its center.

The application in Listing 12.6 rotates an object once in a clockwise direction.

LISTING 12.6

Using the Rotate effect

```
<?xml version="1.0" encoding="utf-8"?>
<s:Application xmlns:fx="http://ns.adobe.com/mxml/2009"
  xmlns:s="library://ns.adobe.com/flex/spark"
  xmlns:mx="library://ns.adobe.com/flex/mx">
  <fx:Declarations>
    <s:Rotate id="myRotate" angleBy="360" autoCenterTransform="true"/>
  </fx:Declarations>
  <s:BitmapImage id="myImage" source="@Embed('assets/flower1.jpg')"
    x="150" y="100" />
  <s:Button x="270" y="349" label="Rotate"
    click="myRotate.play([myImage])"/>
</s:Application>
```

On the Web

The code in Listing 12.6 is available in the Web site files as `RotateDemo.mxml` **in the** `chapter12` **project.** ■

The Rotate3D effect takes advantage of Flash Player 10's 3D capabilities and enables you to program multidimensional visual effects. It supports angleXFrom, angleXTo, angleYFrom, angleYTo, angleZFrom, and angleZTo properties to control each dimension individually. As with the Rotate effect, it supports a Boolean autoCenterTransform property that, when set to true, changes the rotation axis from the object's top-left corner to its center.

The application in Listing 12.7 rotates an object 360 degrees on all three axes over the course of two seconds.

LISTING 12.7

Using the Rotate3D effect

```
<?xml version="1.0" encoding="utf-8"?>
<s:Application xmlns:fx="http://ns.adobe.com/mxml/2009"
  xmlns:s="library://ns.adobe.com/flex/spark"
  xmlns:mx="library://ns.adobe.com/flex/mx">
  <fx:Declarations>
    <s:Rotate3D id="myRotate"
      angleXFrom="0" angleXTo="360"
      angleYFrom="0" angleYTo="360"
      angleZFrom="0" angleZTo="360"
```

```
          autoCenterTransform="true"
          duration="2000"/>
    </fx:Declarations>
    <s:BitmapImage id="myImage" source="@Embed('assets/flower1.jpg')"
      x="150" y="100" />
    <s:Button x="270" y="349" label="Rotate"
      click="myRotate.play([myImage])"/>
  </s:Application>
```

On the Web

The code in Listing 12.7 is available in the Web site files as `Rotate3DDemo.mxml` **in the** `chapter12` **project.** ■

Figure 12.3 shows the resulting visual display with the object being rotated in all three dimensions.

FIGURE 12.3

An object being rotated in three dimensions

Using composite effects

A composite effect plays two or more effects either simultaneously or consecutively. The Flex framework has two composite effects:

- **The** `Parallel` **effect.** This effect plays two or more effects at the same time.
- **The** `Sequence` **effect.** This effect plays two or more effects consecutively, with each effect starting after the previous effect has finished.

Both `Parallel` and `Sequence` effects can be declared in either MXML or ActionScript and can nest as many child effects, simple or composite, as you need to get the desired visual result.

Using Parallel effects

To create a `Parallel` effect in MXML, declare an `<mx:Parallel>` tag set and assign a unique `id`. Then, within the tag set, nest two or more effects that you want to play simultaneously:

```
<s:Parallel id="myParallelEffect">
...effect 1...
...effect 2...
...etc........
</s:Parallel>
```

The effects defined with the `<s:Parallel>` tag set don't need unique `id` properties because the entire effect is played either through association with a target component trigger or by an explicit call to the `Parallel` class's `play()` method.

The application in Listing 12.8 defines `Parallel` effects that include `Move` and `Rotate` nested effects. The visual result is an object that appears to roll on and off the application stage. Notice that the `Rotate` effect in the second `Parallel` has its `angleFrom` set to `360` and `angleTo` set to `0`. The result is a counterclockwise rotation.

LISTING 12.8

Using a Parallel effect

```xml
<?xml version="1.0" encoding="utf-8"?>
<s:Application xmlns:fx="http://ns.adobe.com/mxml/2009"
  xmlns:s="library://ns.adobe.com/flex/spark"
  xmlns:mx="library://ns.adobe.com/flex/mx" >
  <fx:Declarations>
    <s:Parallel id="moveOn" target="{imageWrapper}">
      <s:Move
        xFrom="{0-imageWrapper.width}" xTo="150"
        yFrom="100" yTo="100"/>
      <s:Rotate angleFrom="0" angleTo="360"/>
    </s:Parallel>
    <s:Parallel id="moveOff"  target="{imageWrapper}">
      <s:Move
        xTo="{0-imageWrapper.width}" xFrom="150"
        yFrom="100" yTo="100"/>
      <s:Rotate angleFrom="360" angleTo="0"/>
    </s:Parallel>
  </fx:Declarations>
  <s:Group id="imageWrapper" x="150" y="100"
    showEffect="{moveOn}" hideEffect="{moveOff}">
    <s:BitmapImage source="@Embed('assets/flower1.jpg')" />
  </s:Group>
  <s:Button x="150" y="375" label="Show Image"
    click="moveOn.play()"/>
```

```
  <s:Button x="374" y="375" label="Hide Image"
    click="moveOff.play()"/>
</s:Application>
```

On the Web

The code in Listing 12.8 is available in the Web site files as `ParallelDemo.mxml` in the `chapter12` project. ■

Tip

The `Parallel` and `Sequence` effects are part of the older MX effects system and can't operate directly on a Spark primitive object such as `BitmapImage`. The applications in Listing 12.8 and Listing 12.9 solve this by wrapping the `BitmapImage` inside a Spark `Group`, which automatically sizes itself to contain and display the image. Because `Group` is derived from `UIComponent`, it can be animated by the MX effect. ■

Note

The `Parallel`, `Sequence`, and `Pause` classes are members of the `mx.effects` package. As a convenience, the Flex 4 MXML compiler allows you to refer to them with either the MX or Spark namespace prefixes. In the codes samples in this chapter, I use the Spark namespace prefix, as in `<s:Parallel/>`, but the underlying ActionScript class is the same as if I used `<mx:Parallel/>`. ■

Using Sequence effects

The `Sequence` effect plays two or more nested effects consecutively. In this code, a `Sequence` wraps two `Move` effects. The first nested effect moves the target object horizontally, and the second moves it vertically:

```
<s:Sequence id="moveOn" target="{myImage}">
  <s:Move
    xFrom="{0-myImage.width}" xTo="150"
    yFrom="0" yTo="0"/>
  <s:Move yTo="100"/>
</s:Sequence>
```

Sometimes when using a `Sequence`, you want to create a delay between effects. The `Pause` effect is designed explicitly for this purpose: You add a `Pause` between other nested effects with a duration indicating how long the delay should be in milliseconds. This version of the `Sequence` plays the same set of `Move` effects, but it adds a one-second delay between them:

```
<s:Sequence id="moveOn" target="{myImage}">
  <s:Move
    xFrom="{0-myImage.width}" xTo="150"
    yFrom="0" yTo="0"/>
  <s:Pause duration="1000"/>
  <s:Move yTo="100"/>
</s:Sequence>
```

A Sequence effect can nest any number of child effects, enabling you to choreograph objects on the screen in sometimes elaborate ways. The application in Listing 12.9 causes an image to "bounce" across the screen with multiple Move effects nested within a Sequence. Notice that the Sequence effect handles its effectEnd event by placing the image back in its original starting position.

LISTING 12.9

An application with a Sequence effect

```
<?xml version="1.0" encoding="utf-8"?>
<s:Application xmlns:fx="http://ns.adobe.com/mxml/2009"
  xmlns:s="library://ns.adobe.com/flex/spark"
  xmlns:mx="library://ns.adobe.com/flex/mx" >
  <fx:Script>
    <![CDATA[
      [Bindable]
      private var stageWidth:Number;
      [Bindable]
      private var stageHeight:Number;
      private function bounce():void
      {
        stageHeight = stage.height;
        stageWidth = stage.width;
        trace(stageHeight + ", " + stageWidth);
        bouncingBall.play();
      }
      private function replaceBall():void
      {
        myImage.x = 0;
        myImage.y = 0;
      }
    ]]>
  </fx:Script>
  <fx:Declarations>
    <s:Sequence id="bouncingBall" target="{myImage}"
      effectEnd="replaceBall()">
      <s:Move xTo="{stageWidth/5}"   yTo="{stageHeight-myImage.height}"/>
      <s:Move xTo="{stageWidth/5*2}" yTo="{stageHeight-myImage.height*4}"/>
      <s:Move xTo="{stageWidth/5*3}" yTo="{stageHeight-myImage.height}"/>
      <s:Move xTo="{stageWidth/5*4}" yTo="{stageHeight-myImage.height*3}"/>
      <s:Move xTo="{stageWidth}"     yTo="{stageHeight-myImage.height}"/>
    </s:Sequence>
  </fx:Declarations>
  <s:BitmapImage id="myImage" source="@Embed('assets/ball.png')"/>
  <s:Button label="Bounce Ball" click="bounce()" right="10" bottom="10"/>
</s:Application>
```

On the Web

The code in Listing 12.9 is available in the Web site files as `SequenceDemo.mxml` in the `chapter12` project. ∎

Using easing classes

An easing class enables you to modify the behavior of an event that transforms a component on the screen. By default, an effect transforms an object with a linear timeline. For example, a `Move` effect changes an object's position on the screen with constant speed and motion. An easing class enables you to redefine the object's movement mathematically and modify its rate of change so that, for example, it appears to speed up as it moves closer to its endpoint.

The Flex SDK includes a set of easing objects in the `spark.effects.easing` package, each of which modifies the rate of object transformation in a different way. The `Sine` class, for example, can be used with a `Move` effect to cause the object to decelerate as it reaches its destination.

You use easing classes by creating an instance of the desired class and assigning it to the effect's `easer` property. You can either use the pre-built easing classes in the Flex SDK or you can define and use your own custom classes.

To use a pre-built easing class, declare an instance of the class in the `<fx:Declarations>` section of the MXML document. This declares an instance of the `Bounce` class:

```
<s:Bounce id="myBounce"/>
```

Then assign the easing object to the easer property of the effect class:

```
<s:Move id="myMove"
  yFrom="20" yTo="748"
  duration="2000"
  easer="{myBounce}"/>
```

The application in Listing 12.10 uses the `Bounce` easer class to cause the `BitmapImage` control to bounce as it drops onto a platform (created as an FXG graphic).

LISTING 12.10

Using an easing class

```
<?xml version="1.0" encoding="utf-8"?>
<s:Application xmlns:fx="http://ns.adobe.com/mxml/2009"
  xmlns:s="library://ns.adobe.com/flex/spark"
  xmlns:mx="library://ns.adobe.com/flex/mx">
  <fx:Script>
    <![CDATA[
      protected function button1_clickHandler(event:MouseEvent):void
      {
        myMove.yTo=platform.y-myImage.height;
```

continued

387

LISTING 12.10 *(continued)*

```
            myMove.play([myImage])
        }
    ]]>
  </fx:Script>
  <fx:Declarations>
    <s:Bounce id="myBounce"/>
    <s:Move id="myMove"
      yFrom="20" yTo="748"
      duration="2000"
      easer="{myBounce}"/>
  </fx:Declarations>
  <s:BitmapImage id="myImage" source="@Embed('assets/ball.png')"
    horizontalCenter="0" y="20"/>
  <mx:Button label="Bounce Ball"
    click="button1_clickHandler(event)"
    right="10" bottom="10"/>
  <s:Rect id="platform" width="200" height="75"
    horizontalCenter="0" bottom="0">
    <s:fill>
      <mx:SolidColor color="#666666"/>
    </s:fill>
  </s:Rect>
</s:Application>
```

On the Web

The code in Listing 12.10 is available in the Web site files as `EasingDemo.mxml` in the `chapter12` project. ∎

Using Drag-and-Drop Operations

Drag-and-drop interfaces enable users to give instructions to an application with simple mouse gestures. Pointing to an object that a person wants to manipulate is the most human of gestures, and grabbing and moving an object to change its current state is how we interact with the physical world in nearly every waking minute. The mouse turns that intuitive action into a computer instruction that graphical applications can interpret as needed.

Drag-and-drop operations can be created to visually represent various software operations:

- Selecting data
- Moving data from one location to another
- Deleting data
- Managing data relationships
- Modifying structures of information

As the designer and developer of a Flex application, you must select or create the drag-and-drop architecture that makes your interface the easiest to use.

Flex applications can implement drag-and-drop operations with two different approaches:

- The MX and Spark `List` controls and the MX `DataGrid` have built-in drag-and-drop capability.

- All visual controls can participate in drag-and-drop operations through a set of classes and events specifically designed for this purpose.

Note

Desktop applications deployed with Adobe AIR support native drag-and-drop, which enables the application user to move data, file references, and binary objects between Flex applications and other native applications with drag-and-drop gestures. ∎

Implementing drag-and-drop with List controls

All the MX and Spark `List` controls in the Flex SDK have built-in support for drag-and-drop operations. These controls include:

- `List` (both the MX and Spark versions)
- `ComboBox`
- `DataGrid`
- `TitleList`
- `HorizontalList`
- `Tree`

Each control supports a set of properties that turn on and control drag-and-drop operations:

- `dragEnabled`. This `Boolean` property, when set to `true`, enables a user to select one or more items from a `List` control and drag it or them (and underlying data) to another visual control in the application.

- `dragMoveEnabled`. This `Boolean` property, when set to `true` along with `dragEnabled`, causes items dragged from a `List` control be removed from the initiating control's data provider. This property also enables users to reorder data in a control's `dataProvider` if the control's `dropEnabled` property is set to `true`.

- `dropEnabled`. This `Boolean` property, when set to `true`, enables a `List` control to accept a drop operation. When the user completes the operation, the target object adds the operation's underlying data to its data provider. If the initiating object's `drag-MoveEnabled` property is set to `true`, the items that were dropped in the target object are removed from the initiating object's data source; otherwise, the initiating object's data provider is left in its current state.

Caution

Setting `dragMoveEnabled` to `true` without also setting `dragEnabled` to `true` has no effect on the application. You must set `dragEnabled` to `true` to initiate a `List`-based drag-and-drop operation. ■

The following code creates a `List` control and a `DataGrid` control. The `List` control can initiate a drag-and-drop operation, and the `DataGrid` can accept the dropped data:

```
<s:List dataProvider="{myData}" dragEnabled="true"/>
<mx:DataGrid dropEnabled="true">
```

Because the `DataGrid` control's `dragMoveEnabled` property isn't set to `true`, any objects dragged to the `DataGrid` are still displayed in the `List` after the operation is completed.

The application in Listing 12.11 uses `List` and `DataGrid` controls. Notice these features of the sample application:

- As the `List` row is dragged, an image of the row is generated and displayed as a visual indicator that the drag-and-drop operation is active. This image is known as the *drag proxy*.

- The drag proxy initially includes a white X in a red circle, indicating that the operation can't be completed yet. When the cursor moves over the target control with `dropEnabled` set to `true`, the white X and red circle disappear, indicating to the user that the operation can be completed.

- The `DataGrid` control's `dragMoveEnabled` property is set to true, so the data is added to the DataGrid and removed from the initiating List when the operation is completed.

LISTING 12.11

Using a List-based drag-and-drop operation

```
<?xml version="1.0" encoding="utf-8"?>
<s:Application xmlns:fx="http://ns.adobe.com/mxml/2009"
  xmlns:s="library://ns.adobe.com/flex/spark"
  xmlns:mx="library://ns.adobe.com/flex/mx"
  xmlns:views="views.*">
  <s:layout>
    <s:VerticalLayout horizontalAlign="center" paddingTop="20"/>
  </s:layout>
  <fx:Script>
    <![CDATA[
      import utilities.FormatUtilities;
    ]]>
  </fx:Script>
  <fx:Declarations>
    <s:ArrayCollection id="acBooks" source="{bookModel.book}"/>
    <fx:Model id="bookModel" source="model/books.xml"/>
  </fx:Declarations>
```

```
<fx:Style source="assets/styles.css"/>
<views:Header width="{content.width}"/>
<s:HGroup id="content">
  <s:Panel id="catalogPanel" title="Catalog">
    <s:List dataProvider="{acBooks}" labelField="title"
      height="300" width="200"
      dragEnabled="true"
      dragMoveEnabled="true"/>
  </s:Panel>
  <s:Panel title="Shopping Cart" height="{catalogPanel.height}"
    width="100%">
    <mx:DataGrid id="cart" width="100%" height="100%" dropEnabled="true">
      <mx:columns>
        <mx:DataGridColumn dataField="title" headerText="Title"
          width="300"/>
        <mx:DataGridColumn dataField="price" headerText="Price"
          labelFunction="FormatUtilities.currencyFormat"
          textAlign="right"/>
      </mx:columns>
    </mx:DataGrid>
  </s:Panel>
</s:HGroup>
</s:Application>
</s:Application>
```

On the Web

The code in Listing 12.11 is available in the Web site files as `ListDragAndDrop.mxml` in the `chapter12` project. ∎

Figure 12.4 shows the drag-and-drop operation in action.

Implementing custom drag-and-drop operations

You also can implement drag-and-drop operations manually using a set of classes and events specifically designed for the purpose. The most critical tools for this job are these ActionScript classes:

- `DragSource`. This class contains data and formatting information and serves a messaging envelope containing the data you want to move.

- `DragManager`. This class initiates and manages drag-and-drop operations containing whatever data you want the user to move in the application.

Initiating a drag-and-drop operation

The `DragSource` and `DragManager` classes are members, respectively, of the `mx.core` and `mx.managers` packages and must be imported before use:

```
import mx.core.DragSource;
import mx.managers.DragManager;
```

FIGURE 12.4

When a user drags an object into a `List` control that has `dropEnabled` set to `true`, the placement of the data in the target control's data provider is indicated by a horizontal line that appears near the mouse cursor's location.

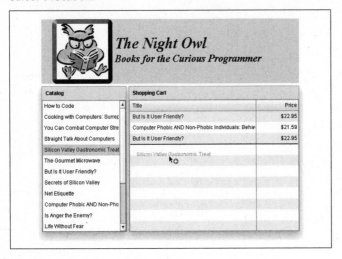

Note

Custom drag-and-drop operations can be initiated upon any mouse event; they are typically initiated upon a `mouseDown` **event (which indicates that the user has pressed the mouse button but hasn't yet released it).** ■

To initiate a custom drag-and-drop operation, follow these steps:

1. **Create an instance of the DragSource class with its no-arguments constructor method.**
2. **Populate the DragSource class with data by calling its** `addData()` **method.**
3. **Call the static method** `DragManager.doDrag()` **to start the drag-and-drop operation.**

In the following code, a `mouseDown` event on a `DataGroup` control is handled with a call to a custom method that will initiate the drag-and-drop operation:

```
<s:DataGroup id="myDataGroup"
   width="600"
   dataProvider="{acBooks}"
   itemRenderer="views.BookRenderer"
   mouseDown="initiateDrag(event)">
```

The custom `initiateDrag()` method starts by creating a `DragSource` object and filling it with data with a call to the `addData()` method. `DragSource.addData()` has two required arguments:

- A reference to the data that's being moved
- A string that identifies the format of the data

Note

When you initiate a drag-and-drop operation with a `List` control with `dragEnabled` set to `true`, the name of the `format` is always `items`. ∎

In the following method, the expression `event.target.data` returns a reference to the initiating object's underlying data.

Note

The code in the `initiateDrag()` function is wrapped in a conditional block that checks to be sure the `mouseDown` event was handled for the `DataGroup` control's item renderer, rather than for any of the visual objects inside the group. ∎

The `bookItem` format is an arbitrary string that identifies the type of data being moved. The `doDrag()` method receives three required arguments: a reference to the visual component that initiated the operation, the `DragSource` object containing the data, and a reference to the `MouseEvent` object that was passed into the current method:

```
private function initiateDrag(event:MouseEvent):void
{
  if (event.target is ItemRenderer)
  {
    var source:DragSource = new DragSource();
    var itemData:Object = event.target.data;
    source.addData(itemData,"bookItem");
    DragManager.doDrag(event.target as UIComponent, source, event,
      bookProxy, 20, 20, 1);
  }
}
```

Tip

You can call the `DragSource` class's `addData()` method multiple times to pass data in as many formats as you need. This is analogous to a clipboard operation, where data might be shared between applications in multiple formats through a copy-and-paste operation, but only formats that are common to the source and the target applications are used at any given time. ∎

Creating a proxy image

A proxy image is displayed during a drag-and-drop operation as a visual indicator of the type or content of the data being moved. When you initiate drag-and-drop with List controls, the drag proxy image is created dynamically from the current screen display. For custom drag-and-drop operations, you're responsible for providing the drag proxy image.

Note

If you don't provide a drag proxy image for a custom drag operation, a blank, partially transparent rectangle is created by the framework of the same shape and dimension as the object that initiates the operation. While this can work okay, the visual result is bland and uninformative. ∎

Drag proxy images should be embedded in the application for the best possible performance. Follow these two steps for this part of the process:

1. Embed a graphic using the `[Embed]` metadata tag, and assign it a Class variable name.

2. Instantiate a `BitMapAsset` object wrapped around a new instance of the embedded image Class.

Note

A class used as a proxy image must implement the `IFlexDisplayObject` interface. Classes that can be used for this purpose include `BitmapAsset`, `ButtonAsset`, `MovieClipAsset`, `MovieClipLoaderAsset`, `ProgrammaticSkin`, `SpriteAsset`, `SystemManager`, `TextFieldAsset`, and `UIComponent`. ■

The following code embeds an image and wraps it in a `BitMapAsset` object that's suitable for use as a proxy image:

```
[Embed(source="assets/book.png")]
private var bookImage:Class;
private var bookProxy:BitmapAsset = BitmapAsset(new bookImage());
```

You cast the instance of the proxy image class as `BitMapAsset` to fulfill the requirement that the proxy image object implements `IFlexDisplayObject` interface.

To use the proxy image in a drag-and-drop operation, pass the proxy object as the fourth argument in the call to `DragManager.doDrag()`:

```
DragManager.doDrag(event.target as UIComponent, source,
  event, bookProxy);
```

You also can control the position of the drag proxy image relative to the cursor position and the image's level of transparency. The `doDrag()` method's fifth and sixth arguments, `xOffset` and `yOffset`, determine the image's horizontal and vertical relative position, and the seventh argument, `imageAlpha`, determines the amount of transparency. This code uses the same proxy image but ensures that it's fully opaque and positioned to the top and left of the cursor:

```
DragManager.doDrag(event.target as UIComponent, source, event,
  bookProxy, 20, 20, 1);
```

Note

Positive offset values for the proxy image place the image above and to the left of the cursor, while negative values place it below and to the right. ■

Handling the dragEnter event

A target control, located where the data will be dropped, detects a drag-and-drop operation by listening for the `dragEnter` event. When the mouse cursor moves over the target object, this event generates a `DragEvent` object. The `DragEvent` class has a `dragSource` property that references the `DragSource` object that contains the operation's underlying data.

The first step in handling the `dragEnter` event is to determine whether the operation contains data in a format you can deal with in the current context. You do this by calling the `DragSource` class's `hasFormat()` method and passing in a format string you can handle. If the selected format exists in the drag source, you then accept the operation by calling `DragManager.acceptDragDrop()` and passing in a reference to the object that accepts the operation.

This code detects a particular drag format and accepts the operation:

```
private function dragEnterHandler(event:DragEvent):void
{
  if (event.dragSource.hasFormat("bookItem"))
  {
    DragManager.acceptDragDrop(event.target as UIComponent);
  }
}
```

When you call `acceptDragDrop()`, the red icon with the white X on the proxy image disappears, indicating to the user that the data is ready to be dropped.

Handling the dragDrop event

When the user drops the data over an object that has already accepted the operation (as described in the preceding section), the object dispatches a `dragDrop` event. This event also generates a `DragEvent` object. In addition to the `dragSource` property described previously, this object also has a `dragInitiator` property that references the object that initiated the operation.

The `DragSource` class has a method named `dataForFormat()`. To retrieve data that should be acted upon, call the method and pass in the format of the data you want:

```
var dragData:Object = event.dragSource.dataForFormat("bookItem");
```

After you have a reference to the dropped data, you can manipulate it in a database, move it to other data buckets in the application, or simply remove it. The following code handles the drag-and-drop operation by first getting references to data through the initiating object's underlying data object and then removing the underlying data from the `DataGroup` control's data provider:

```
private function dragDropHandler(event:DragEvent):void
{
  var dragData:Object = event.dragSource.dataForFormat("bookItem");
  var itemIndex:int = acBooks.getItemIndex(dragData);
  var bookTitle:String = dragData.title;
  acBooks.removeItemAt(itemIndex);
  Alert.show("Book deleted: " + bookTitle, "Deleted!");
}
```

The application in Listing 12.12 uses a custom drag-and-drop operation to enable a user to delete data using a trash can icon.

LISTING 12.12

A custom drag-and-drop operation

```
<?xml version="1.0" encoding="utf-8"?>
<s:Application xmlns:fx="http://ns.adobe.com/mxml/2009"
  xmlns:s="library://ns.adobe.com/flex/spark"
  xmlns:mx="library://ns.adobe.com/flex/mx"
  xmlns:views="views.*">
  <s:layout>
    <s:VerticalLayout paddingTop="20"/>
  </s:layout>
  <fx:Script>
    <![CDATA[
      import mx.controls.Alert;
      import mx.core.BitmapAsset;
      import mx.core.DragSource;
      import mx.core.UIComponent;
      import mx.events.DragEvent;
      import mx.managers.DragManager;
      import spark.components.supportClasses.ItemRenderer;
      import views.BookRenderer;
      [Embed(source="assets/book.png")]
      [Bindable]
      private var bookImage:Class;
      private var bookProxy:BitmapAsset = BitmapAsset(new bookImage());
      private function initiateDrag(event:MouseEvent):void
      {
        if (event.target is ItemRenderer)
        {
          var source:DragSource = new DragSource();
          var itemData:Object = event.target.data;
          source.addData(itemData,"bookItem");
          DragManager.doDrag(event.target as UIComponent, source, event,
            bookProxy, 20, 20, 1);
        }
      }
      private function dragEnterHandler(event:DragEvent):void
      {
        if (event.dragSource.hasFormat("bookItem"))
        {
          DragManager.acceptDragDrop(event.target as UIComponent);
        }
      }
      private function dragDropHandler(event:DragEvent):void
      {
        var dragData:Object = event.dragSource.dataForFormat("bookItem");
        var itemIndex:int = acBooks.getItemIndex(dragData);
        var bookTitle:String = dragData.title;
        acBooks.removeItemAt(itemIndex);
        Alert.show("Book deleted: " + bookTitle, "Deleted!");
      }
```

```
        ]]>
  </fx:Script>
  <fx:Declarations>
    <fx:Model id="bookModel" source="model/books.xml"/>
    <mx:ArrayCollection id="acBooks" source="{bookModel.book}"/>
  </fx:Declarations>
  <fx:Style source="assets/styles.css"/>
  <views:Header id="header"/>
  <s:HGroup>
    <s:DataGroup id="myDataGroup"
      width="600"
      dataProvider="{acBooks}"
      itemRenderer="views.BookRenderer"
      mouseDown="initiateDrag(event)">
      <s:layout>
        <s:TileLayout/>
      </s:layout>
    </s:DataGroup>
    <s:Group
      dragEnter="dragEnterHandler(event)"
      dragDrop="dragDropHandler(event)">
      <s:BitmapImage source="@Embed('assets/garbagecan.png')"/>
    </s:Group>
  </s:HGroup>
</s:Application>
```

On the Web

The code in Listing 12.12 is available in the Web site files as `CustomDragAndDrop.mxml` in the `chapter12` project. ∎

Figure 12.5 shows the resulting application, with an embedded book graphic used both as a data icon and as a drag proxy image. When the user drags a book to the trash can, the data is deleted from the application.

Custom drag-and-drop operations give you the freedom to react to user gestures in many ways. These are some other strategies you can use in your applications:

- **You can explicitly handle** `dragDrop` **events on list-based controls instead of relying on the automatic list control behaviors.** For example, you may react to the `dragDrop` event by calling a Web service and manipulating server-side data.

- **In the case where an item can be dragged from multiple sources, you can detect the originator of a drag-and-drop operation like this:**

  ```
  if (Object(event.dragInitiator).id == "bookList")
  {
    ... doWhatever() ...
  }
  ```

- **You can find out where the item is being dropped in a Halo `List`-based control using** `this.bookList.calculateDropIndex(event)` **and passing the** `DragEvent` **object.**

FIGURE 12.5

A custom drag-and-drop operation

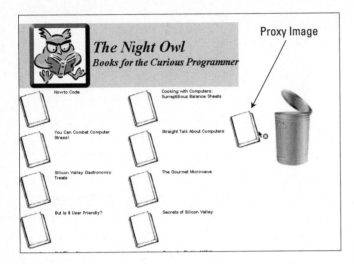

Summary

In this chapter, I described how to implement animation and drag-and-drop interfaces in Flex applications. You learned the following:

- An effect is an ActionScript class that defines changes in a visual component's position, visibility, scaling, and other properties over a period of time.

- The framework has many pre-built effect classes that control animation.

- Each effect class has a set of properties you can set to control animation.

- You can play an effect with explicit ActionScript statements or by incorporating it into a view state transition.

- Triggers, which were used extensively with Flex 3 effects, are generally not recommended for use with the new Spark effects.

- You can use drag-and-drop operations to create an intuitive interface for managing data in a Flex application.

- MX and Spark `List` controls implement drag-and-drop with the `dragEnabled` and `dropEnabled` properties.

- You can create highly customized drag-and-drop interfaces with the `DragManager` and `DragSource` classes.

Managing View States

F lex applications define view states as particular presentations of a
visual component. In each moment of the user's interactions with the
application, each visual component presents itself in a particular form
known as its *current view state*. Flex enables you to define as many different
view states as you like for the `Application` and for each of its custom
MXML components using declarative code, and then enables you to switch
easily between states by setting the `Application` or custom component's
`currentState` property.

View state management in Flex is designed primarily for application scenarios where the `Application` or component uses a significant portion of its
presentation in multiple situations and makes incremental changes to its presentation for each new situation. This sort of incremental change is different
from application navigation, where the user moves between multiple different layers, or views, that don't share content with each other.

In Flex 4, you always declare view states in MXML. In Flex 3, you could
also use ActionScript code to declare view states, but the resulting code
was verbose and difficult to maintain. Even further, the MXML view state
code has been dramatically altered since Flex 3, resulting in much cleaner
MXML declarations.

When you switch view states at runtime, you can make the change abruptly
or, using *transitions*, you can choreograph the change with ActionScript-
based *effects*. (As described in Chapter 12, effects implement Flash-based
animation to make objects appear, disappear, move, or change size and orientation using predefined animations.) A transition is a class that enables
you to easily associate effects with view state changes.

In this chapter, I describe how to create and use view states in Flex applications and how to use transitions and effects to animate the changes.

IN THIS CHAPTER

Understanding view states

**Defining view states in
Design mode**

Defining view states in MXML

**Switching view states at
runtime**

**Managing view states in
components**

**Using transitions to animate
view states**

On the Web

To use the sample code for this chapter, import the `chapter13.zip` Flex project archive from the Web site files into your Flash Builder workspace. ■

Understanding View States

View states are used to define incremental changes to an existing view. For example, a login form that initially requests a user name and password can, with the addition of a few more controls, also be used as a registration form. Any visual objects you declare are by default included in the form's initial presentation. To create different versions of the form, you declare new view states with unique names.

View states are declared with MXML code. You can either code a view state manually or, using Flash Builder's Design mode, generate the required code based on changes you make to a component at design time.

View states are identified by creating new `State` objects and setting their `name` property, which is a `String` value that you assign in MXML code. Each visual component that's displayed on the screen in a Flex application has an initial view state that's named by default `State1`. The default state is defined by all the object's current property and style settings, event handlers, and in the case of containers, nested child components in its display list, and it's represented by the main MXML in the document.

New Feature

In Flex 3, the `name` of the default state was a blank `String`. In Flex 4, the default value of the `current-State` property is the name of the first `State` object declared in the `states` property (an array). ■

Caution

Flex 4 state names cannot include periods, spaces, or other special characters. This ensures that the code used in MXML declarations to set attributes for particular states is syntactically correct. For example, this Label is only bold in a state named "boldState":

```
<s:Label text="Hello World" fontWeight.boldState="bold"/>
```

If the state name were allowed to be set as "bold.State" (with the period), the code to set the property would be:

```
<s:Label text="Hello World" fontWeight.bold.State="bold"/>
```

The parser would fail on this declaration. ■

Examples of things you can change in a view state include:

- Adding and removing nested child objects in a container
- Setting values of properties and styles
- Changing handlers for events of the component or, in the case of a container, its nested child components

Each of these actions is known as an *override:* That is, you're overriding the state on which the new state is based.

Note

You can only define view states for an application or a separate MXML component. You can't define view states for nested child components within a main application or component source code file. So to get started with view states, you first decide whether the view state will be defined at the application level or within a custom component. However, after you have made that choice, the process of declaring and controlling the view state is the same. ■

Defining View States in Design View

Flash Builder has a States view that shows up by default only when the Flex Development perspective is active and the current application or component is being edited in Design view. As shown in Figure 13.1, the States view has a toolbar that includes these buttons:

- New State
- Duplicate State
- Edit State
- Delete State

FIGURE 13.1

Flash Builder's States view

Creating a new state

You can create a new view state by clicking the New State button on the toolbar, or by right-clicking in the States view and selecting New State from the context menu. The New State dialog box, shown in Figure 13.2, asks for these properties:

401

- **Name.** A non-blank `String` value is required.

- **Duplicate of.** This asks which state the new view state is based on.

- **Blank State.** This selection results in the removal of any existing visual objects from the new state. You can easily change this in the code after the state has been created.

- **Set as start state.** This check box enables you to assign the new state as the application or component's starting state upon instantiation.

FIGURE 13.2

The New State dialog box in Design view

Caution

Unlike in Flex 3, where a new state was based on an existing state and received cascading changes at runtime, the new Duplicate of selection in the New State dialog box only defines the new state's initial settings as of the moment you create it. ■

In the following example, an application contains a data entry form that asks the user for flight departure and return dates. In the form's default state, all information is requested. In an alternative state, controls are removed from the form for a one-way itinerary.

Try these steps to add a new state to an existing application and then add an incremental view state:

1. **Open** `ViewStatesBegin.mxml` **from the chapter13 project's** `src` **folder.**

2. **Run the application in a browser.** As shown in Figure 13.3, the application displays a flight information data entry form, similar to those seen on popular travel-booking Web sites. In the application's default state, it displays form controls for arrival and departure dates, but it doesn't make any changes if the user selects the One Way radio button.

3. **Return to Flash Builder.** If the application currently is displayed in Source mode, switch to Design mode.

4. **Locate the States view in the upper-right corner of Flash Builder.** Notice that the States view displays a single state labeled `State1`.

5. **As shown in Figure 13.4, right-click anywhere in the States view and select New State.**

6. **In the New State dialog box, set the new state's name to** `oneway` **and click OK.**

FIGURE 13.3

The application's default state

FIGURE 13.4

Creating a new view state from the States view's context menu

Caution

As with ActionScript identifiers, view state names are case-sensitive. Whatever you name the state in this step is how you'll refer to it in your ActionScript code. ■

As shown in Figure 13.5, the States view now displays the new view state and indicates with a selection bar which view state is currently active.

FIGURE 13.5

The States view with the new state set as currently active

The currently selected state

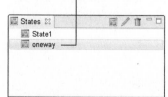

Defining a view state's overrides

To define a view state's override actions in Design view, first select the appropriate view state from the States view or the State selector. Then make changes to the Application or component with these design time actions:

- Add components to the state by dragging from the Components view.
- Remove components by selecting and deleting them.
- Change components' properties and styles through the Flex Properties view.
- Change event handlers through the Flex Properties view.

You can select the current view state either from the States view or, as shown in Figure 13.6, from the view state selection menu in the Design view editor toolbar.

FIGURE 13.6

The State selector in the Design view editor

Tip

When working with an application or component whose width or height exceeds the available dimensions of the Design view editor, you may not see scrollbars appear. Remember that you can use the Zoom and Pan tools to move around the design surface. ∎

Follow these steps to make incremental changes to the application:

1. Reopen `ViewStatesBegin.mxml` in Flash Builder's Design mode.

2. Using either the States view or the State selector, set the current view state to oneway.

3. Select the `SimpleText` control with the text value of Return, and press Delete to remove the control from the view state.

4. Select the `DateField` control in the same area of the application, and delete it as well.

5. To test the view states in Design view, set the current state to `State1`. You should see that the two controls you deleted are displayed in their original locations.

6. Switch back again to the oneway state. You should see that the two controls are removed from the current display.

Listing 13.1 shows the application after adding and defining the oneway state.

LISTING 13.1

The view states application

```xml
<?xml version="1.0" encoding="utf-8"?>
<s:Application xmlns:fx="http://ns.adobe.com/mxml/2009"
  xmlns:s="library://ns.adobe.com/flex/spark"
  xmlns:mx="library://ns.adobe.com/flex/mx">
  <s:states>
    <s:State name="State1"/>
    <s:State name="oneway"/>
  </s:states>
  <fx:Style>
    @namespace mx "library://ns.adobe.com/flex/mx";
    @namespace s "library://ns.adobe.com/flex/spark";

    s|Label { font-weight:bold }
  </fx:Style>
  <mx:Image x="23" y="10" source="assets/airplane.png"/>
  <s:Label text="Flight Search" fontSize="14"
    fontWeight="bold" x="104" y="33"/>
  <s:Panel title="Select travel dates"
    width="421" height="200" id="panel1" x="23" y="78">
    <s:Label x="10" y="10" text="From (city or airport):"/>
    <s:Label x="214" y="10" text="To (city or airport):"/>
    <mx:DateField x="61" y="77" id="returnDate"/>
    <s:TextInput x="10" y="36" id="departInput"/>
    <s:Label x="10" y="79" text="Depart:"/>
    <s:TextInput x="214" y="36" id="returnInput"/>
    <s:Label x="214" y="79" text="Return:" id="label1" includeIn="State1"/>
    <mx:DateField x="270" y="77" id="departDate" includeIn="State1"/>
    <s:Group bottom="0" width="100%">
      <s:layout>
        <s:HorizontalLayout paddingLeft="10" paddingRight="10"
          paddingBottom="10"/>
      </s:layout>
```

continued

```
        <s:RadioButton label="Round Trip" selected="true"/>
        <s:RadioButton label="One Way"/>
        <mx:Spacer width="100%"/>
        <s:Button label="Search"/>
      </s:Group>
    </s:Panel>
</s:Application>
```

On the Web

The code in Listing 13.1 is available in the Web site files as `ViewStatesComplete.mxml` in the `chapter13` project. ■

Switching View States at Runtime

All visual components support the `currentState` property to enable switching from one view state to another at runtime. The value of `currentState` is a simple `String`, so this code switches the current `Application` or component's state to `oneway`:

```
this.currentState = "oneway";
```

To return to the default state, set `currentState` to its name:

```
this.currentState = "State1";
```

Try the following steps with the airfare search application described in the preceding section:

1. Reopen `ViewStatesBegin.mxml` in Flash Builder, and switch to Source view.

2. Locate these `RadioButton` control declarations:
   ```
   <mx:RadioButton label="Round Trip" selected="true"/>
   <mx:RadioButton label="One Way"/>
   ```

3. Add a `click` event handler to the `RadioButton` control labeled One Way that changes the `currentState` to `oneway`:
   ```
   <s:RadioButton label="One Way" click="currentState='oneway'"/>
   ```

4. Add a `click` event handler to the `RadioButton` control labeled Round Trip that changes the `currentState` to `State1` (the default state):
   ```
   <s:RadioButton label="Round Trip" selected="true"
     click="currentState='State1'"/>
   ```

5. **Run the application, and click the `RadioButton` controls to switch between view states.** You should see that the two controls appear and disappear as you click the `RadioButton` controls to switch view states.

You can also control view states with bindings. Instead of explicit ActionScript statements, set the Application or component's `currentState` property using a binding expression that gets its current value from a visual control or other data source.

In the following code, two `RadioButton` controls are grouped together with a `RadioButtonGroup`. Each `RadioButton` has its `value` set to an explicit state name or a blank string (the Base state):

```
<fx:Declarations>
  <s:RadioButtonGroup id="typeGroup"/>
</fx:Declarations>
<s:RadioButton groupName="typeGroup"
  label="Round Trip" value="State1" selected="true"/>
<s:RadioButton groupName="typeGroup"
  label="One Way" value="oneway"/>
```

In the `<s:Application>` start tag, the `currentState` is set with a binding expression that executes each time the user clicks one of the `RadioButton` controls:

```
<s:Application xmlns
  xmlns:fx="http://ns.adobe.com/mxml/2009"
  xmlns:s="library://ns.adobe.com/flex/spark"
  xmlns:mx="library://ns.adobe.com/flex/mx">
  currentState="{typeGroup.selectedValue}">
```

The application is functionally identical to the version using explicit ActionScript statements, but updates its current state based on the binding expression's evaluated result.

Declaring View States in MXML

A view state is represented by the `<s:State>` tag set and is always assigned a name:

```
<s:State name="myNewState">
... state declaration ...
</s:State>
```

To declare one or more view states in a main application or custom component file, wrap the `<s:State>` declaration tags within `<s:states>` tags:

```
<?xml version="1.0" encoding="utf-8"?>
<s:Application xmlns:fx="http://ns.adobe.com/mxml/2009"
  xmlns:s="library://ns.adobe.com/flex/spark"
  xmlns:mx="library://ns.adobe.com/flex/mx">
  <s:states>
    <s:State name="State1"/>
    <s:State name="oneway"/>
  </s:states>
  ... declare visual objects ...
</s:Application>
```

The `<s:states>` element must always be declared as a child element of the `Application` or component root; you cannot nest state declarations within other child MXML tag sets unless they are in an `<fx:Component>` tag set (used with custom item renderers, which are described in Chapter 19).

Tip

Technically speaking, it doesn't matter whether the `<s:states>` tag set is at the top, bottom, or middle of the MXML code, as long as it's a direct child of the MXML file's root element and doesn't separate visual components from each other. ■

Once a state has been declared, you can then indicate which controls are a part of the state with the `includeIn` or `excludeFrom` attributes. You can also modify properties, styles, and event handlers by adding new MXML attributes to the affected component declarations.

Adding and removing components

By default a component declared in MXML is a part of all the application or parent components states. You determine which components are included in a state by setting the component's `includeIn` or `excludeFrom` attributes.

New Feature

In Flex 3, you added and removed visual objects with the `AddChild` and `RemoveChild` elements, declared within an `<mx:State>` tag. In Flex 4, each component is essentially responsible for its own placement and behavior. ■

For example, this Button control would only appear in a state named `state2`:

```
<s:Button label="Search" includeIn="state2"/>
```

And this Button would appear in all states *except* for `state3`:

```
<s:Button label="Search" excludeFrom="state3"/>
```

Caution

You can use either `includeIn` or `excludeFrom` in any particular component, but you can't use both. The following code would result in a compiler error:

```
<s:Button label="Search" includeIn="state2"
   excludeFrom="state3"/> ■
```

You can set either of these attributes to a comma-delimited list of state names. For example, this Button would appear in `state2` and `state3`, but no others:

```
<s:Button label="Search" includeIn="state2,state3"/>
```

The state of a control when it appears and disappears during a state change isn't affected. For example, a `TextInput` control might be shown in `state1` and not in `state2`. But although not currently visible, its current state (such as the value the user has typed) isn't disturbed. This is because the state management framework controls visibility by adding and removing the object from its container's display list, and not by creating or destroying it in memory. Once a control has been instantiated as part of a change to a named state, it stays in memory unless you explicitly remove it by setting it to `null` or you reset it by calling its constructor.

Overriding properties, styles, and event handlers

You override properties, styles, and event handlers in a view state by adding an attribute to a component's MXML declaration consisting of the property, style, or event name, followed by a period and the name of the state in which the change should be applied. For example, the following `Label` object would have a `fontSize` of 12 pixels in its default state, but would be 18 pixels in a state named `state2`:

```
<s:Label text="Hello World"
  fontSize="12" fontSize.state2="18"/>
```

You follow exactly the same pattern for properties and event handlers. This `Button` would call one event handler function in the default state, and a different one in `state2`:

```
<s:Button label="click me"
  click="default_clickHandler(event)"
  click.state2="state2_clickHandler(event)"/>
```

Caution

Because state names are declared as `String` values rather than as ActionScript identifiers or variable names, the compiler isn't able to track inconsistencies between your declared state names and the states you try to use in your MXML attributes. Any mismatches between state names will result in application runtime errors. ■

The application in Listing 13.2 presents a login data entry form wrapped in a `Panel` container.

LISTING 13.2

An application prior to adding view states

```
<?xml version="1.0" encoding="utf-8"?>
<s:Application xmlns:fx="http://ns.adobe.com/mxml/2009"
  xmlns:s="library://ns.adobe.com/flex/spark"
  xmlns:mx="library://ns.adobe.com/flex/mx">
<s:layout>
  <s:VerticalLayout horizontalAlign="center" paddingTop="20"/>
</s:layout>
<s:Panel title="Log In Form" id="panel1" width="307" height="139">
  <mx:Form id="form1">
    <mx:FormItem label="User Name:">
      <s:TextInput id="userNameInput"/>
    </mx:FormItem>
    <mx:FormItem label="Password:">
```

continued

LISTING 13.2 *(continued)*

```
            <s:TextInput id="passwordInput"/>
        </mx:FormItem>
      </mx:Form>
      <s:controlBarContent>
        <s:Button label="Log In"/>
        <mx:Spacer width="100%"/>
        <mx:LinkButton label="Register as new user" id="stateButton"/>
      </s:controlBarContent>
    </s:Panel>
</s:Application>
```

On the Web

The code in Listing 13.2 is available in the Web site files as `UsingOverridesBegin.mxml` **in the** `chapter13` **project.** ∎

As shown in Figure 13.7, the application's `Form` contains two `TextInput` controls wrapped in `FormItem` containers.

FIGURE 13.7

A data entry form before adding view states

In a new `register` state, the following changes will be made to the form:

- The `Panel` component's title and its `Button` and `LinkButton` label will change to reflect the current state.
- The `LinkButton` control's `click` event handler will switch back to the default state.
- The `Form` will display an extra `TextInput` control wrapped in a `FormItem`.

Figure 13.8 shows the application running in the new register state.

Listing 13.3 shows the completed application with all view state declarations and changes to the `currentState` property.

FIGURE 13.8

The application with the new view state active

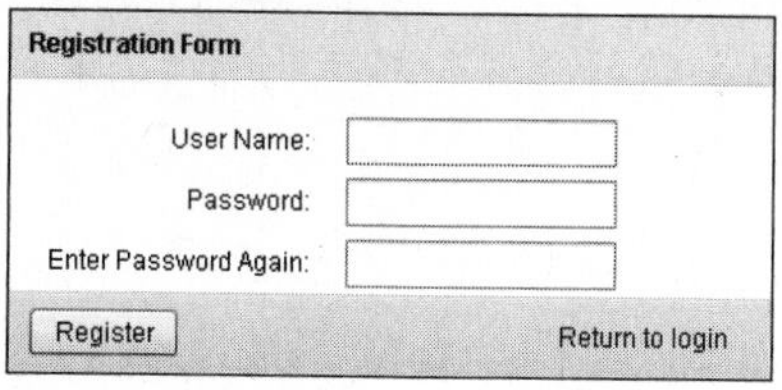

LISTING 13.3

Another application with complete view state declarations

```xml
<?xml version="1.0" encoding="utf-8"?>
<s:Application xmlns:fx="http://ns.adobe.com/mxml/2009"
  xmlns:s="library://ns.adobe.com/flex/spark"
  xmlns:mx="library://ns.adobe.com/flex/mx">
  <s:states>
    <s:State name="default"/>
    <s:State name="register"/>
  </s:states>
  <s:layout>
    <s:VerticalLayout horizontalAlign="center" paddingTop="20"/>
  </s:layout>
  <s:Panel title="Log In Form" id="panel1" width="307"
    height="139" height.register="167"
    title.register="Registration Form"
    width.register="363">
    <mx:Form id="form1">
      <mx:FormItem label="User Name:">
        <s:TextInput id="userNameInput"/>
      </mx:FormItem>
      <mx:FormItem label="Password:">
        <s:TextInput id="passwordInput"/>
      </mx:FormItem>
      <mx:FormItem includeIn="register" label="Enter Password Again:">
        <s:TextInput/>
      </mx:FormItem>
    </mx:Form>
    <s:controlBarContent>
      <s:Button label="Log In" label.register="Register"/>
      <mx:Spacer width="100%"/>
      <mx:LinkButton label="Register as new user" id="stateButton"
```

continued

411

LISTING 13.3 *(continued)*

```
        click="currentState='register'"
        click.register="currentState='default'"
        label.register="Return to login"/>
    </s:controlBarContent>
  </s:Panel>
</s:Application>
```

On the Web

The code in Listing 13.3 is available in the Web site files as `UsingOverridesComplete.mxml` in the `chapter13` project. ■

Managing View States in Components

You can declare a view state inside a custom component. The rules are the same as for a main application file: You can only apply the view state to the entire component, not to its nested child objects.

You can then control that component's `currentState` either internally or from the component instance parent object. Remember that code within a custom component uses `this` to refer to the current instance of the component. The following code switches the `currentState` of the component instance to a new state:

```
        this.currentState = 'myNewState';
```

Listing 13.4 defines a custom `Label` component that has a view state named `rollOverState`. When the component's `rollOver` event is dispatched, it changes to the new state; when the `rollOut` event occurs, it returns to its base state. The view state contains `<mx:SetStyle>` tags that override the component's `color` and `textDecoration` styles.

LISTING 13.4

A custom component with a view state

```
<?xml version="1.0" encoding="utf-8"?>
<s:Group xmlns:fx="http://ns.adobe.com/mxml/2009"
  xmlns:s="library://ns.adobe.com/flex/spark"
  currentState='default'
  rollOver="currentState='rollover'"
  rollOut="currentState='default'">
  <s:states>
    <s:State name="default"/>
    <s:State name="rollover"/>
  </s:states>
```

```
<fx:Script>
  <![CDATA[
    [Bindable]
    public var text:String="Default Text";
  ]]>
</fx:Script>
<s:Label text="{text}"
  color.rollover="#0000FF"
  textDecoration.rollover="underline"/>
</s:Group>
</s:Group>
```

On the Web

The code in Listing 13.4 is available in the Web site files as `components/RollOverText.mxml` in the chapter13 **project.** ■

Using the custom component is a simple matter of declaring an instance and setting any standard Label properties or styles. The application in Listing 13.5 uses MXML to declare an instance of the component.

LISTING 13.5

Using a custom component with view states

```
<?xml version="1.0" encoding="utf-8"?>
<s:Application xmlns:fx="http://ns.adobe.com/mxml/2009"
  xmlns:s="library://ns.adobe.com/flex/spark"
  xmlns:mx="library://ns.adobe.com/flex/mx"
  xmlns:components="components.*">
  <components:RollOverText
    text="Hello World"
    fontSize="18"
    horizontalCenter="0" top="20"/>
</s:Application>
```

On the Web

The code in Listing 13.5 is available in the Web site files as `TestRollover.mxml` in the chapter13 **project.** ■

Tip

In the application in Listing 13.5, the custom component instance's `fontSize` style affects the component's contained `SimpleText` control because `fontSize` is an inheritable style. ■

Using Transitions

Transitions are a way of associating animations, implemented as Flex effects, with runtime changes from one view state to another. By default, when you switch to a view state that changes the visibility, size, or position of objects on the screen, the change is visually abrupt. A transition enables you to slow down and choreograph the change so that it's easier and more fun to watch.

As with view states, you typically declare transitions using MXML code. Each visual component has a `transitions` property. The `transitions` property is an `Array` containing one or more instances of the Transition class. To declare transitions in MXML, you create an `<s:transitions>` tag set as a direct child of the main application or component file's root element, often right after the `<s:states>` declaration. Then nest as many `<s:Transition>` tag sets within `<s:transitions>` as you need:

```
<s:Application...>
  <s:states>
    ...declare <s:State> elements here...
  </s:states>
  <s:transitions>
    ...declare <s:Transition> elements here...
  </s:transitions>
  ... declare visual objects here ...
</s:Application>
```

Note

In the Flex 4 SDK, the `State` and `Transition` classes are still members of the MX package `mx.states`, so they're sometimes declared with an `mx` prefix. However, the Flex 4 SDK declares these classes in both the MX and Spark namespace manifests, so you can use either namespace prefix. ■

Declaring a transition

Each transition is declared as an `<s:Transition>` tag with these properties:

- `fromState`. The name of the starting state.
- `toState`. The name of the ending state.

Each of these properties can be set to either an explicit state name or a wildcard (*), the default for both properties, to indicate that the transition applies to all state changes.

You then indicate which animation you want to play by nesting the appropriate effect class within the `<s:Transition>` tag set. The effect should have its `target` or `targets` property set to indicate which objects should be animated.

This transition is applied by moving from a state named `state1` to a state named `state2`. It has the effect of applying a `Fade` effect to an object that's being added in the state:

```
<s:transitions>
  <s:Transition fromState="state1" toState="state2">
    <s:Fade target="{addedObject}"/>
  </s:Transition>
</s:transitions>
```

Using Parallel and Sequence effects in transitions

You also can use Parallel or Sequence effects to introduce more complex animation.

Using the Parallel effect in a transition

The Parallel effect combines multiple effects that execute simultaneously. The following transition causes a Move effect and a Zoom effect to play simultaneously, creating the visual effect of an object "exploding" from the top-left corner of the application into its final position:

```
<s:Transition fromState="*" toState="detail">
  <s:Parallel target="{detailImage}">
    <s:Move xFrom="0" yFrom="0" xTo="300" yTo="50"/>
    <s:Zoom zoomHeightFrom="0" zoomWidthFrom="0"
      zoomHeightTo="1" zoomWidthTo="1"/>
  </s:Parallel>
</s:Transition>
```

Using the Sequence effect in a transition

As described earlier in this chapter, the Sequence effect enables you to play multiple effects consecutively. The following code declares a Transition with a Sequence that executes a horizontal Move effect first, and follows it with a vertical Move:

```
<s:Transition fromState="*" toState="detail">
  <s:Sequence target="{detailImage}">
    <s:Move xFrom="0" yFrom="0" xTo="300" yTo="0"/>
    <s:Move xFrom="300" yFrom="0" xTo="300" yTo="300"/>
  </s:Sequence>
</s:Transition>
```

The effects framework includes the following special classes that are designed to control when an object is added or removed from a presentation or when other actions are taken relative to when particular visual effects are executed in a transition:

- AddAction. Defines when an object is added to the presentation.
- CallAction. Calls a function of the defined target object.
- RemoveAction. Defines when an object is removed from the presentation.
- SetAction. Sets the value of a named property of an object.

Take the following example transition that's designed to execute when an object is removed from the current container as a result of a change in view state:

```
<s:Transition fromState="detail" toState="default">
  <s:Fade target="{detailImage}"/>
</s:Transition>
```

By default, the object with an id of detailImage would be removed from the presentation before any effects are played, so the Fade effect would never be played. You can solve this by nesting the desired effect in a Sequence and explicitly indicating when the object should be removed from the container's display list (after the Fade is executed):

```
<s:Transition fromState="detail" toState="default">
  <s:Sequence target="{detailImage}">
    <s:Fade/>
    <s:RemoveAction/>
  </s:Sequence>
</s:Transition>
```

The application in Listing 13.6 uses Transition declarations to animate the change in an object's position and transparency. The function that's executed when the user clicks down on the mouse button first sets the target object's location in the second state based on the values of the click event's MouseEvent.stageX and MouseEvent.stageY properties. As a result, the graphic explodes onto the stage from the top-left corner of the application and moves to the coordinates of the mouseDown event.

LISTING 13.6

An application with transition

```
<?xml version="1.0" encoding="utf-8"?>
<s:Application xmlns:fx="http://ns.adobe.com/mxml/2009"
  xmlns:s="library://ns.adobe.com/flex/spark"
  xmlns:mx="library://ns.adobe.com/flex/mx"
  currentState="state1"
  mouseDown="mouseDownHandler(event)"
  mouseUp="mouseUpHandler(event)">
  <s:states>
    <s:State name="state1"/>
    <s:State name="state2"/>
  </s:states>
  <s:transitions>
    <s:Transition id="myTransition" fromState="*" toState="*">
      <s:Parallel target="{myGraphic}">
        <s:Move />
        <s:Fade />
```

```
        </s:Parallel>
      </s:Transition>
    </s:transitions>
    <fx:Script>
      <![CDATA[
        import mx.events.EffectEvent;
        [Bindable]
        private var targetX:Number;
        [Bindable]
        private var targetY:Number;
        protected function mouseDownHandler(event:MouseEvent):void
        {
          targetX = event.stageX - (myGraphic.width / 2);
          targetY = event.stageY - (myGraphic.height / 2);
          currentState = "state2";
        }
        protected function mouseUpHandler(event:MouseEvent):void
        {
          currentState='state1';
        }
      ]]>
    </fx:Script>
    <s:Ellipse id="myGraphic" width="200" height="200"
      x.state1="-200" y.state1="-200"
      x.state2="{targetX}" y.state2="{targetY}"
      alpha.state1="0" alpha.state2="1">
      <s:fill>
        <s:RadialGradient>
          <s:entries>
            <s:GradientEntry color="red"/>
            <s:GradientEntry color="blue"/>
          </s:entries>
        </s:RadialGradient>
      </s:fill>
    </s:Ellipse>
    <s:Label text="Click anywhere for state 2" fontSize="14"
      horizontalCenter="0" verticalCenter="0"/>
  </s:Application>
```

On the Web

The code in Listing 13.6 is available in the Web site files as `TransitionDemo.mxml` **in the** `chapter13` **project.** ∎

Figure 13.9 shows the resulting application with transitions and effects.

FIGURE 13.9

The transition and effect cause the graphic to explode onto the screen.

Click anywhere for State 2

Summary

In this chapter, I described how to use view states to manage different looks in a Flex application. You learned the following:

- A view state is defined as a particular presentation of a visual component.

- View states are typically declared in MXML code.

- Flash Builder's Design mode can help you generate view state code that uses MXML declarations.

- You control which state is active at runtime by changing the value of the main application or component file's currentState property.

- You can declare view states within a custom component.

- Transitions enable you to associate effects (programmatic animations) with changes from one view state to another.

- You declare transitions with MXML code.

- Each transition can be declared with a toState and a fromState property.

- You can associate Parallel or Sequence effects with a transition for more complex visual effects.

Declaring Graphics with MXML and FXG

O ne of the Flex 4 SDK most important features is the capability to redefine the appearance of visual controls with *programmatic skins*.

The concept of skinning, or programming a component's visual appearance, isn't new to Flex. In past versions, you could create your own skin as an ActionScript class. By overriding certain methods that are called at runtime from the Flex framework and using the Flash drawing application programming interface (API) to declare vector graphics, you could essentially create an entire visual presentation without ever using graphical applications like Adobe Photoshop and Illustrator.

This strategy, however, was slow and cumbersome. And, because the graphical applications I've mentioned couldn't interpret the ActionScript code and preview its results, you just had to use your imagination (and a lot of graph paper) to figure out how to code the image you wanted to create.

Adobe Systems introduced the FXG language to help solve this programming challenge. FXG, which stands for Flash XML Graphics, is an XML-based graphics interchange file format that describes low-level vector graphics, with specific attention paid to how Flash Player renders graphics.

In Flex 4, you can declare FXG graphics either as part of an MXML file or by incorporating FXG files exported from Creative Suite products as embedded graphics. You can then mix these FXG graphics with other visual components in a skinning class that determines a component's appearance at runtime.

In this chapter, I first describe the structure of FXG and how it's incorporated into the new version of MXML. Then, in Chapter 15, I show you how to create your own skin classes and associate them with your applications and custom components.

IN THIS CHAPTER

Understanding FXG

Declaring vector graphics in MXML

Using ActionScript primitive graphics

Adding visual effects to MXML graphics

Creating FXG files in Illustrator and Photoshop

Working with FXG files in Flex applications

On the Web

To use the sample code for this chapter, import the `chapter14.fxp` **Flex project archive file from the Web site files into your Flash Builder workspace.** ■

Declaring Vector Graphics in MXML

As previously described, FXG is an XML-based declarative format that enables you to either declare vector graphics within an MXML file or exchange graphical declarations between software applications that support the format using FXG files.

There are two versions of the FXG specification: versions 1 and 2. Starting with Creative Suite 4, Adobe's graphical authoring tools (Illustrator, Photoshop, and Fireworks) were able to import and export FXG files. In Creative Suite 4 (CS4), these software products work with FXG version 1, while the CS5 versions of these applications and the Flex 4 SDK support both versions 1 and 2.

Note

The FXG 2 specification includes updates, name changes, and a few extra properties in various elements and attributes. Adobe decided to make version 2 a full revision rather than a 1.x maintenance release because the CS4 products already support FXG 1.0. A full version-number update ensures that each version of the Creative Suite product can easily tell whether it's working with a version it understands. ■

Web Resource

The specification for FXG 1.0 is available on Adobe's open-source Web site at `http://opensource.adobe.com/wiki/display/flexsdk/FXG+1.0+Specification`**. The FXG 2.0 specification is available at** `http://opensource.adobe.com/wiki/display/flexsdk/FXG+2.0+Specification`**. The CS5 products such as Illustrator and Fireworks are able to export the new format, and the Flex 4 SDK is able to use the exported files.** ■

You can define a vector graphic either in text files with a file extension of `.fxg` (referred to in this chapter as *FXG files*), or as MXML-based declarations of ActionScript objects that are based on a set of classes. In either case, the graphics are rendered by Flash Player at runtime and are dependent on Flash Player's graphical rendering capabilities.

Drawing lines and shapes

The FXG specification defines elements named `<Graphic>`, `<Ellipse>`, `<Line>`, `<Path>`, and `<Rect>`. In an FXG file, you "draw" a shape by declaring an element of the appropriate name and setting its attributes.

To accomplish the same thing in MXML, the Flex 4 SDK includes a package named `spark.primitives`. This package contains the following ActionScript classes that you can use to declare vector graphics:

- `Ellipse`. Draws an elliptical shape. If its height and width are identical, it draws a circle.

- `Line`. Draws a straight line from one set of coordinates to another.

- `Path`. Draws a shape based on a set of drawing commands, creating multiple shape segments.

- `Rect`. Draws a rectangular shape. If its height and width are identical, it draws a square.

The `spark.primitives` package also includes the following classes that are used to group graphics together and embed graphical files in conventional formats such as PNG, GIF, and JPG:

- `BitmapImage`. A class that embeds bitmap data defined in a graphical file. The file can be in any one of the conventional bitmap file formats: PNG, JPG, or GIF.

- `Graphic`. A nonvisual class that can be used to group multiple FXG graphics together. When you place multiple FXG graphics within an instance of the `Graphic` class, they overlap each other using a layout architecture similar to a `Group` with a layout of `BasicLayout`.

Drawing lines

The `Line` class draws a line on the screen. As with all such primitives, it must be placed within a Spark application or component. Its `width` and `height` properties determine its horizontal and vertical length, while the `stroke` property determines its color and style.

The `stroke` property must be set to an instance of a class that implements the `IStroke` interface. Examples of such classes in the Flex 4 SDK include `GradientStroke` and `SolidColorStroke`.

Caution

The `Line` class's `stroke` property defaults to `null`. If you don't set the stroke to an instance of a class that implements the `IStroke` interface, the line is invisible. ■

The following code draws a simple horizontal line. The stroke property is set to an instance of `SolidColorStroke` with a color of black (`#000000`) and a weight of 2 pixels:

```
<s:Line width="700">
  <s:stroke>
    <s:SolidColorStroke color="#000000" weight="2"/>
  </s:stroke>
</s:Line>
```

Using gradient strokes

As with the `fill` property used with shapes that are drawn with the `Rect`, `Ellipse`, and `Path` classes (described in the following sections), the `stroke` property can be set to a gradient of two or more colors with the `GradientStroke` class or with one of its subclasses, `LinearGradientStroke` and `RadialGradientStroke`.

The gradient stroke classes support a property named `entries` that's set to an array of two or more instances of the `GradientEntry` class. The following code draws a horizontal line that's 10 pixels wide and has five entries:

```
<s:Line width="700">
  <s:stroke>
    <s:LinearGradientStroke weight="10">
      <s:entries>
        <s:GradientEntry color="#000000"/>
        <s:GradientEntry color="#ffffff"/>
        <s:GradientEntry color="#000000"/>
        <s:GradientEntry color="#ffffff"/>
        <s:GradientEntry color="#000000"/>
      </s:entries>
    </s:LinearGradientStroke>
  </s:stroke>
</s:Line>
```

Figure 14.1 shows the resulting line, with alternating black and white colors.

FIGURE 14.1

A horizontal line with a gradient stroke

Drawing rectangular and elliptical shapes

The two most commonly used primitive vector graphic classes are `Rect` and `Ellipse`. Respectively, they render rectangular and elliptical shapes on the screen. Both support `fill` and `stroke` properties, which enable you to define the outer border and inner fill of the shape you're drawing.

Each shape's `fill` property can be set to an instance of a class that implements the `IFill` interface. Examples of such classes in the Flex 4 SDK include:

- `BitmapFill`
- `LinearGradient`
- `RadialGradient`
- `SolidColor`

And, as described in the previous section on the `Line` class, each shape's `stroke` property is set to an instance of a class that implements the `IStroke` interface.

Note

All shape classes support the x, y, top, bottom, left, right, horizontalCenter, and verticalCenter properties to control a shape's position within its container, and the height and width properties to control its dimensions. As with all Flex visual components, the height and width can be set either to a numeric value representing a certain number of pixels or to a percentage value. ■

The following MXML code defines a rectangle with dimensions of 400 pixels width by 300 pixels height. The rectangle's outer border is a solid black line with a weight of 2 pixels, and the fill is a solid light gray:

```
<s:Rect width="400" height="300"
  horizontalCenter="0" verticalCenter="0" >
  <s:fill>
    <s:SolidColor color="#EEEEEE"/>
  </s:fill>
  <s:stroke>
    <s:SolidColorStroke color="#000000" weight="2"/>
  </s:stroke>
</s:Rect>
```

Figure 14.2 shows the resulting shape, a simple rectangle with a light gray fill and a black stroke.

FIGURE 14.2

This simple shape is defined as an instance of the Rect class.

Drawing arbitrary shapes with the Path class

The Path class enables you to declare any shape based on a set of commands that replicate the features of the Flash drawing API. Its data property is a string that executes cursor placement and drawing operations. The data string alternates commands and sets of numeric values. Each command is notated with a single alphabetical character, as follows:

- **C.** Draw a cubic Bezier curve. The first two values are the first set of control coordinates, the second two values are the second set of control coordinates, and the last two values are the drawing destination.
- **H.** Draw a horizontal line from the current cursor coordinate to a new X coordinate.
- **L.** Draw a line from the current cursor position to a set of coordinates. For example, the command L 100 100 causes a line to be drawn from the current cursor position to X and Y coordinates of 100 and 100.
- **M.** Move the cursor to a set of coordinates. For example, the command M 50 100 causes the cursor to be placed at an X coordinate of 50 and a Y coordinate of 100.
- **Q.** Draw a quadratic Bezier curve. The first two values are the control coordinates, and the last two are the drawing destination.
- **V.** Draw a vertical line from the current cursor coordinate to a new Y coordinate.
- **Z.** Close the path.

The following simple `Path` object draws a horizontal line starting at X and Y positions of 100, and then draws a horizontal line to an X position of 500. The color and weight of the path are determined by its `stroke` property:

```
<s:Path data="M 100 100 H 500 Z">
  <s:stroke>
    <s:SolidColorStroke color="black" weight="5"/>
  </s:stroke>
</s:Path>
```

Note

If you change any command to a lowercase character, it's evaluated as a coordinate relative to the current cursor position instead of an absolute coordinate within the vector graphic's container. For example, a `data` property of `M 100 100 h 500 Z` creates a horizontal line that's 500 pixels wide, starting at an X position of 100, whereas if you use the uppercase `H`, the line is 400 pixels wide (drawn from 100 to 500 pixels). ∎

Caution

Errors in the `data` property's commands don't cause compilation or runtime errors; instead, the shape probably won't be drawn. ∎

More complex `Path` objects can be drawn with more commands, and multiple shapes and lines can be drawn in the same `Path` object by moving the cursor and initiating new draw commands. The following object draws a curved arrow using a series of lines and cubic Bezier curves:

```
<s:Path data="M 20 0
  C 50 0 50 35 20 35
  L 15 35 L 15 45
  L 0  32 L 15 19
  L 15 29 L 20 29
  C 44 29 44 6 20 6">
```

```
  <s:stroke>
    <s:SolidColorStroke color="0x888888"/>
  </s:stroke>
  <s:fill>
    <s:LinearGradient rotation="90">
      <s:GradientEntry color="0x000000" alpha="0.8"/>
      <s:GradientEntry color="0xFFFFFF" alpha="0.8"/>
    </s:LinearGradient>
  </s:fill>
</s:Path>
```

Figure 14.3 shows the resulting vector graphic: a curved arrow with a linear gradient.

FIGURE 14.3

A curved arrow drawn with the `Path` class

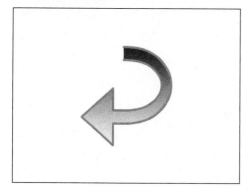

Note

White space, such as extra space, tab, or line feed characters, is ignored in the `data` property's value. In the preceding code, I've added space characters and line feeds to make the `data` property more readable. This doesn't affect the application's performance or functionality. ∎

Adding visual effects

The primitive vector graphic classes support many properties that enable you to modify their appearance. Examples include gradient fills and strokes, drop shadows and other filters, and scaling, or resizing, of vector graphics. In this section I describe some of the most commonly used effects from which you can choose.

Using gradient fills

The `fill` property that's supported by the `Rect`, `Ellipse`, and `Path` classes can be set to a solid color with the `SolidColor` class or to a gradient with either `RadialGradient` or `LinearGradient`. Each does exactly what its name implies:

- LinearGradient. Defines a change in colors in a linear using calculation from one coordinate to another. By default the gradient is calculated from left to right, but it can be adjusted by changing the gradient class's direction property; for example, to change the gradient to go from top to bottom, change the LinearGradient object's direction to 90.

- RadialGradient. Defines a change in colors starting from the certain point in an object (by default its center) and radiating outward to its borders. You can set the focalPoint Ratio and rotation properties to change the point from which the gradient radiates.

The application in Listing 14.1 defines two Ellipse shapes. The first uses a radial gradient, and the seconds uses a linear gradient. Each is modified by the focalPointRatio and rotation properties to create a particular visual appearance.

LISTING 14.1

Two shapes with gradient fills

```
<?xml version="1.0" encoding="utf-8"?>
<s:Application xmlns:fx="http://ns.adobe.com/mxml/2009"
  xmlns:s="library://ns.adobe.com/flex/spark"
  xmlns:mx="library://ns.adobe.com/flex/mx">
  <fx:Style>
    @namespace s "library://ns.adobe.com/flex/spark";
    s|Label { font-size:14; font-weight:bold; }
  </fx:Style>
  <s:layout>
    <s:VerticalLayout gap="20" horizontalAlign="center" paddingTop="20"/>
  </s:layout>
  <s:Label text="Radial Gradient"/>
  <s:Ellipse width="200" height="100"
    horizontalCenter="0" verticalCenter="0" >
    <s:fill>
      <s:RadialGradient focalPointRatio="-.1" rotation="45">
        <s:entries>
          <s:GradientEntry color="#FFFFFF"/>
          <s:GradientEntry color="#000000"/>
        </s:entries>
      </s:RadialGradient>
    </s:fill>
    <s:stroke>
      <s:SolidColorStroke color="#000000" weight="2"/>
    </s:stroke>
  </s:Ellipse>
  <s:Label text="Linear Gradient"/>
  <s:Ellipse width="200" height="100"
    horizontalCenter="0" verticalCenter="0">
```

```
    <s:fill>
      <s:LinearGradient rotation="45">
        <s:entries>
          <s:GradientEntry color="#FFFFFF"/>
          <s:GradientEntry color="#000000"/>
        </s:entries>
      </s:LinearGradient>
    </s:fill>
    <s:stroke>
      <s:SolidColorStroke color="#000000" weight="2"/>
    </s:stroke>
  </s:Ellipse>
</s:Application>
```

On the Web

The code in Listing 14.1 is available in the Web site files in the `chapter14` **project as** `GradientDemos.mxml`. ■

Figure 14.4 shows visual result: two `Ellipse` objects with different types of gradient fills.

FIGURE 14.4

These ellipse objects use, respectively, a linear and a radial gradient fill.

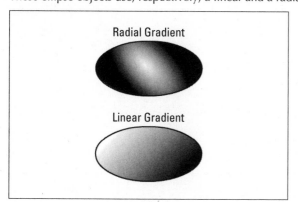

The `fill` property contains an array of `GradientEntry` objects. Each can be assigned a `ratio` value from 0 to 1 that determines where in the graphical element the color change occurs. The following `Path` object uses a `RadialGradient` with many instances of the `GradientEntry` class. They alternate colors and determine where the colors change in the graphical element with their ratio values:

```
<s:Path data="M 0 40 L 40 0 L 105 0 L 144 40 L 144 51
               L 105 90 L 40 90 L 0 51 L 0 40 Z ">
  <s:fill>
    <s:RadialGradient>
      <s:GradientEntry color="#333333" ratio="0" alpha="1"/>
      <s:GradientEntry color="#CCCCCC" ratio="0.09" alpha="1"/>
      <s:GradientEntry color="#333333" ratio="0.37" alpha="1"/>
      <s:GradientEntry color="#CCCCCC" ratio="0.89" alpha="1"/>
      <s:GradientEntry color="#333333" ratio="0.99" alpha="1"/>
    </s:RadialGradient>
  </s:fill>
</s:Path>
```

Figure 14.5 shows the result: a symmetrical polygon with a series of concentric radial gradients.

FIGURE 14.5

A symmetrical polygon with a radial gradient fill defined with primitive vector graphic classes declared in MXML

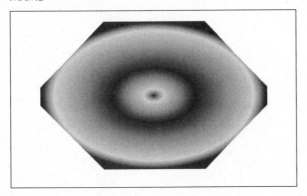

Reusing graphic elements with <fx:Library> and <fx:Definition>

The Flex 4 SDK adds a new MXML element named <fx:Library> that you use to define graphic elements that can then be reused anywhere in the same MXML document. Within the <fx:Library> element, you define one or more <fx:Definition> element. Each <fx:Definition> describes a graphic element.

Caution

The <fx:Library> tag must be placed as the first child element within the MXML document's root element. If you place any other tags before it, a compiler error is generated. ■

The application in Listing 14.2 defines a single vector graphic as a *library definition*. Its name is set as CurvedArrow. In the body of the application, there are three instances of the graphic. Each sets its scaleX and scaleY properties to a different value. The resulting application displays three instances of the arrow. Even though they're different sizes, they all show clean curves and smooth gradient fills.

LISTING 14.2

A library definition shape used multiple times

```
<?xml version="1.0" encoding="utf-8"?>
<s:Application xmlns:fx="http://ns.adobe.com/mxml/2009"
  xmlns:s="library://ns.adobe.com/flex/spark">
  <fx:Library>
    <fx:Definition name="CurvedArrow">
      <s:Path data="M 20 0
        C 50 0 50 35 20 35
        L 15 35 L 15 45
        L 0 32 L 15 19
        L 15 29 L 20 29
        C 44 29 44 6 20 6">
        <s:stroke>
          <s:SolidColorStroke color="0x888888"/>
        </s:stroke>
        <s:fill>
          <s:LinearGradient rotation="90">
            <s:GradientEntry color="0x000000" alpha="0.8"/>
            <s:GradientEntry color="0xFFFFFF" alpha="0.8"/>
          </s:LinearGradient>
        </s:fill>
      </s:Path>
    </fx:Definition>
  </fx:Library>
  <s:HGroup horizontalCenter="0" top="20">
    <fx:CurvedArrow scaleX="1" scaleY="1"/>
    <fx:CurvedArrow scaleX="2" scaleY="2"/>
    <fx:CurvedArrow scaleX="4" scaleY="4"/>
  </s:HGroup>
</s:Application>
```

On the Web

The code in Listing 14.2 is available in the Web site files in the `chapter14` project as `ScalingGraphics.mxml`. ∎

New Feature

The `<fx:Library>` MXML tag is new in Flex 4. You use it to define reusable graphic elements. Each reusable graphical element is defined in an `<fx:Definition>` class with a `name` property. The definition becomes an ActionScript class at compilation time. You can then declare instances of the reusable graphic element by referring to its name as an MXML tag with the `fx` prefix. For example, in Listing 14.2, the `<fx:Library>` tag is a direct child of `<s:Application>`. It contains this definition:

```
<fx:Definition name="CurvedArrow">
  <s:Path.../>
</fx:Definition>
```

The resulting CurvedArrow **graphical element can then be used anywhere in the visual content of the document in which the** <fx:Library> **tag is declared.** ∎

Scaling graphic elements

An MXML graphic is rendered as a vector graphic; this means that its rendering is calculated mathematically rather than as a set of pixels (as is the case with bitmap graphics). As a result, you can increase or decrease the size of the graphic (a process known as *scaling*) without disturbing the graphic's resolution. When you do the same thing with a bitmap graphic, it's often *pixilated*, showing jagged edges. With vector graphics, the rendering stays clean and attractive.

In Listing 14.2, the graphic that's defined in the <fx:Library> section is rendered three times, each time with a different value for the object's scaleY and scaleY properties:

```
<fx:CurvedArrow scaleX="1" scaleY="1"/>
<fx:CurvedArrow scaleX="2" scaleY="2"/>
<fx:CurvedArrow scaleX="4" scaleY="4"/>
```

Figure 14.6 shows the result, with the three versions of the arrow graphic displayed side by side. Notice that the graphic's curves are smooth regardless of the scale. This is a benefit of vector graphics: because their presentation is calculated mathematically, they can adjust to whatever scale your application needs.

FIGURE 14.6

A graphic element displayed in three scales

Applying filters

Each of the primitive vector graphic classes supports the `filters` property, an array of objects derived from one of the classes in the `spark.filters` package. The following filter classes are included in the Flex 4 SDK:

- `BevelFilter`
- `BlurFilter`
- `ColorMatrixFilter`
- `ConvolutionFilter`
- `DisplacementMapFilter`
- `DropShadowFilter`
- `GlowFilter`
- `GradientBevelFilter`
- `GradientFilter`
- `GradientGlowFilter`
- `ShaderFilter`

Each filter class supports a set of properties that modify its effect on the graphical element. For example, the following `Path` object adds two filters, a drop shadow, and a blur:

```
<s:Path data="M 20 0
  C 50 0 50 35 20 35
  L 15 35 L 15 45
  L 0  32 L 15 19
  L 15 29 L 20 29
  C 44 29 44 6 20 6">
  <s:stroke>
    <s:SolidColorStroke color="0x888888"/>
  </s:stroke>
  <s:fill>
    <s:LinearGradient rotation="90">
      <s:GradientEntry color="0x000000" alpha="0.8"/>
      <s:GradientEntry color="0xFFFFFF" alpha="0.8"/>
    </s:LinearGradient>
  </s:fill>
  <s:filters>
    <s:DropShadowFilter distance="20" color="#333333"/>
    <s:BlurFilter/>
  </s:filters>
</s:Path>
```

Figure 14.7 shows two versions of the resulting graphical element side by side. The first is the graphical element without the filters; the second shows the changes implemented by the filters.

FIGURE 14.7

A graphical element before and after adding filters

Using FXG Files

An FXG file is a text file written in the FXG format. You can create FXG files with Adobe's graphical editing products and use the files as embedded graphics in Flex 4 applications. In this section I first describe how to create and export graphics in Photoshop, Illustrator, and Fireworks. I then show how to use the resulting files as ActionScript classes in your Flex applications.

Creating FXG graphics with Creative Suite software

Starting with Creative Suite 4, Adobe added features to Photoshop, Illustrator, and Fireworks that enable you to create and export graphics in FXG format. The resulting files can be used in your Flex applications as embedded graphics.

Creating FXG graphics with Photoshop

Adobe Photoshop is primarily used to create and manipulate bitmap graphics, so it might seem at first like FXG wouldn't be useful to Photoshop developers. However, wrapping bitmap files in FXG gives you a very easy and convenient way of exporting a graphic in a format that can be used as an ActionScript class in your Flex applications.

Follow these steps to export a Photoshop file as FXG:

1. Open the file in Photoshop.

2. Choose File ⇨ Save As.

3. Set the Format to FXG (*.fxg).

4. Select the folder in which you want to create the file.

5. Set the filename using the .fxg file extension and click Save.

A sample FXG file built in Photoshop might look like this:

```
<?xml version="1.0" encoding="utf-8" ?>
<Graphic version="1.0" viewHeight="300" viewWidth="400"
  d:locked="false" xmlns="http://ns.adobe.com/fxg/2008"
  xmlns:d="http://ns.adobe.com/fxg/2008/dt">
  <BitmapGraphic
  source="@Embed('PhotoshopGraphic.assets/images/Background.png')"
  repeat="false" d:locked="true" d:userLabel="Background"/>
  <BitmapGraphic width="400" height="300"
  source="@Embed('PhotoshopGraphic.assets/images/Shape 1.png')"
  repeat="false" d:userLabel="Shape_1"/>
  <BitmapGraphic width="400" height="300"
  source="@Embed('PhotoshopGraphic.assets/images/Shape 2.png')"
  repeat="false" d:userLabel="Shape_2"/>
  <BitmapGraphic width="400" height="300"
  source="@Embed('PhotoshopGraphic.assets/images/Shape 3.png')"
  repeat="false" d:userLabel="Shape_3"/>
</Graphic>
```

The root element is always <Graphic>, and each bitmap graphic in the file is referenced by an instance of the <BitmapGraphic> element. The binary graphic files themselves are created in PNG format and saved in an assets/images subfolder in the same folder as the FXG file.

To use this file in your Flex application, create the FXG file and its associated assets folder anywhere in your Flex project's source-code root folder.

Creating FXG graphics with Illustrator

Adobe Illustrator is primarily designed to enable the creation of vector-based graphic art. While designers can work with bitmap formats in Illustrator to some extent, they typically move to Adobe Photoshop when building graphics that are primarily bitmap-based.

Starting with Illustrator CS4, users can save their vector graphic files in FXG format. In Illustrator CS4, the resulting files are in FXG 1.0, while in Illustrator CS5, the format is updated to FXG 2.0. Regardless of the version, you can use the resulting FXG files in Flex 4 applications in a number of ways.

Figure 14.8 shows a vector graphic in Illustrator CS4. The graphic was created with a variety of Illustrator tools, including a simple rectangular shape.

To create an FXG file in Illustrator that describes this shape and can be used in Flex 4, follow these steps:

1. **Create or open a file in Illustrator.**
2. **Choose File ⇨ Save As.**
3. **In the Save As dialog box, set the Save as type option to FXG (*.fxg) and assign a file name with an extension of .fxg.**
4. **Click Save.**
5. **In the FXG Options dialog box, shown in Figure 14.9, set any desired options.**
6. **Click OK to save the file.**

FIGURE 14.8

A vector graphic created in Illustrator CS4

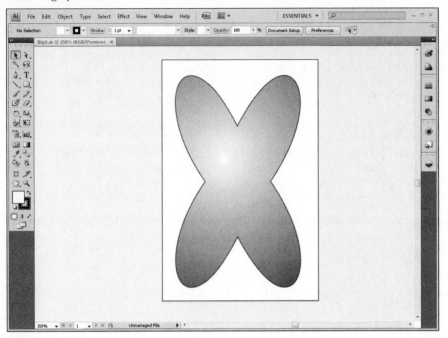

FIGURE 14.9

The FXG Options dialog box for FXG exporting

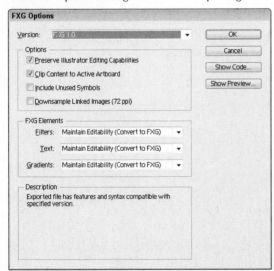

Listing 14.3 shows the contents of the resulting FXG file. The XML markup in the file describes the vector graphic in mathematical terms and includes metadata that's used by Illustrator to parse and enable later modification of the file.

LISTING 14.3

An FXG file created by Illustrator CS4 that describes a shape with a gradient fill

```
<?xml version="1.0" encoding="utf-8" ?>
<Graphic version="1.0" viewHeight="367" viewWidth="247.5"
  ai:appVersion="14.0.0.367" d:id="1" xmlns="http://ns.adobe.com/fxg/2008"
  xmlns:ai="http://ns.adobe.com/ai/2008"
  xmlns:d="http://ns.adobe.com/fxg/2008/dt">
  <Library/>
  <Group x="21.5342" y="23.8696" d:id="2" d:type="layer"
    d:userLabel="Layer 1">
    <Group d:id="3">
      <Group ai:knockout="0">
        <Path ai:knockout="0" data="M151.206 161.63C246.726 294.045 180.796
  401.39 99.4658 245.871 18.1367 401.39 -47.7939 294.045 47.7256 161.63
  -47.7939 29.2144 18.1367 -78.1294 99.4658 77.3901 180.796 -78.1294
  246.726 29.2144 151.206 161.63Z" >
          <fill>
            <RadialGradient x="77.084" y="125.323" scaleX="582.81"
              scaleY="582.81">
              <GradientEntry color="#ffffff" ratio="0"/>
              <GradientEntry color="#231f20" ratio="1"/>
            </RadialGradient>
          </fill>
        </Path>
        <Path winding="nonZero" ai:knockout="0" data="M151.206
  161.63C246.726 294.045 180.796 401.39 99.4658 245.871 18.1367 401.39
  -47.7939 294.045 47.7256 161.63 -47.7939 29.2144 18.1367 -78.1294 99.4658
  77.3901 180.796 -78.1294 246.726 29.2144 151.206 161.63Z" >
          <stroke>
            <SolidColorStroke color="#231f20" caps="none" weight="1"
              joints="miter" miterLimit="4"/>
          </stroke>
        </Path>
      </Group>
    </Group>
  </Group>
  <Private>
    <ai:PrivateElement d:ref="#1">
      <ai:SaveOptions>
        <ai:Dictionary>
          <ai:DictEntry name="includeXMP" value="0" valueType="Boolean"/>
          <ai:DictEntry name="writeImages" value="1" valueType="Boolean"/>
```

continued

LISTING 14.3   *(continued)*

```
            <ai:DictEntry name="aiEditCap" value="1" valueType="Boolean"/>
            <ai:DictEntry name="versionKey" value="1" valueType="Integer"/>
            <ai:DictEntry name="includeSymbol" value="0" valueType="Boolean"/>
            <ai:DictEntry name="preserveTextPolicy" value="3"
              valueType="Integer"/>
            <ai:DictEntry name="preserveFilterPolicy" value="3"
              valueType="Integer"/>
            <ai:DictEntry name="preserveGradientPolicy" value="3"
              valueType="Integer"/>
            <ai:DictEntry name="rasterizeResolution" value="72"
              valueType="Integer"/>
            <ai:DictEntry name="downsampleLinkedImages" value="0"
              valueType="Boolean"/>
            <ai:DictEntry name="clipToActiveArtboard" value="1"
              valueType="Boolean"/>
          </ai:Dictionary>
        </ai:SaveOptions>
        <ai:DocData base="BigX.assets/images"/>
        <ai:Artboards originOffsetH="58.5" originOffsetV="595.5"
          rulerCanvasDiffH="306" rulerCanvasDiffV="-396" zoom="1.5">
          <ai:Artboard active="1" bottom="228.5" index="0" left="58.5"
            right="306" top="595.5"/>
          <ai:ArtboardsParam all="0" range="" type="0"/>
        </ai:Artboards>
    </ai:PrivateElement>
    <ai:PrivateElement d:ref="#2">
      <ai:LayerOptions colorType="ThreeColor">
        <ai:ThreeColor blue="257" green="128.502" red="79.31"/>
      </ai:LayerOptions>
    </ai:PrivateElement>
    <ai:PrivateElement ai:hashcode="0327efec167b7fabf49517bf0010d041"
      d:ref="#3">
      <ai:Ellipse evenOdd="1" height="324" knockout="0" width="199"
        x="-0.034" y="-0.37">
        <ai:Stroke colorType="ThreeColor" miterLimit="4" weight="1">
          <ai:ThreeColor blue="0.125" green="0.122" red="0.137"/>
        </ai:Stroke>
        <ai:Fill colorType="Gradient">
          <ai:Gradient gradientType="radial" length="292.978"
            originX="77.466" originY="125.63">
            <ai:GradientStops>
              <ai:GradientStop colorType="ThreeColor" rampPoint="0">
                <ai:ThreeColor blue="1" green="1" red="1"/>
              </ai:GradientStop>
              <ai:GradientStop colorType="ThreeColor" rampPoint="100">
                <ai:ThreeColor blue="0.125" green="0.122" red="0.137"/>
              </ai:GradientStop>
            </ai:GradientStops>
```

```
        </ai:Gradient>
      </ai:Fill>
      <ai:ArtStyle>
        <ai:LiveEffects>
          <ai:LiveEffect index="0" isPre="1" major="1" minor="0"
            name="Adobe Punk and Bloat">
            <ai:Dictionary>
              <ai:DictEntry name="d_factor" value="48" valueType="Real"/>
            </ai:Dictionary>
          </ai:LiveEffect>
        </ai:LiveEffects>
      </ai:ArtStyle>
    </ai:Ellipse>
  </ai:PrivateElement>
  </Private>
</Graphic>
```

Tip

Illustrator sometimes generates bitmap files that render various visual effects and are used in addition to the XML-based description of a graphic's primary vector art. All of the Creative Suite products create a special folder, known as the `assets` folder, that's associated with the FXG file and is used to store such dependent files. For example, an FXG file named `BigX.fxg` has an associated assets folder named `BigX.assets`. As with FXG files created in Photoshop, these bitmap files are referred to in the FXG file with the `<BitMapGraphic>` tag. This folder must be copied along with the FXG file into your Flex project in order for the graphical element to be rendered correctly. ■

Creating FXG graphics with Fireworks

Adobe Fireworks CS4 is a hybrid graphics editing product that deals well with both bitmap and vector graphics. When you create a graphic from scratch with Fireworks, and primarily use its vector graphic tools, the resulting artwork can be exported as a pure FXG file that can then be used in a Flex 4 application.

Figure 14.10 shows a vector graphic created in Fireworks CS4. This is the same graphic element that was originally created in Illustrator; I show it here to make the point that you can create similar vector art in both products.

To save the vector graphic in FXG format, follow these steps:

1. **Choose Commands ⇨ Export to FXG from the Fireworks menu.**

2. **In the Select Folder dialog box, select the folder in which you want to save the FXG file.**

3. **Enter the filename of the FXG file you want to create and click OK.**

FIGURE 14.10

A vector graphic in Fireworks CS4

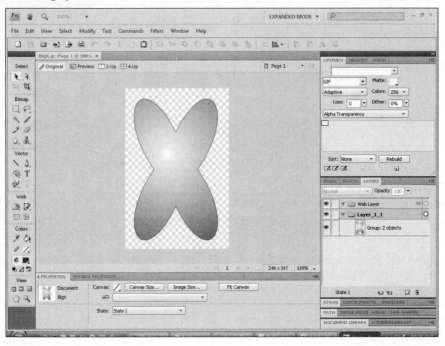

Listing 14.4 shows the contents of the resulting FXG file created by Fireworks CS4.

LISTING 14.4

An FXG file created by Fireworks CS4 that describes a shape with a gradient fill

```
<?xml version="1.0" encoding="UTF-8"?>
<Graphic version="1.0" xmlns="http://ns.adobe.com/fxg/2008"
  xmlns:fw="http://ns.adobe.com/fxg/2008/fireworks"
  viewHeight= "367" viewWidth= "248">
  <Library>
  </Library>
  <Group id="Page_1" fw:type="page">
    <Group id="State_1" fw:type="state">
      <Group id="Layer_1_1" fw:type="layer">
        <Group id="undefined">
```

```
        <Path winding="evenOdd" data="M 173 186 C 269 318 203 425 121 270
C 40 425 -26 318 69 186 C -26 53 40 -54 121 101 C 203 -54 269 53 173 186
Z " blendMode="normal" alpha="1">
          <fill>
            <RadialGradient x = "99" y = "150" scaleX = "584"
              scaleY = "584" rotation = "0">
              <GradientEntry color="#ffffff" ratio="0" alpha="1"/>
              <GradientEntry color="#ffffff" ratio="0.01" alpha="1"/>
              <GradientEntry color="#231f20" ratio="0.99" alpha="1"/>
              <GradientEntry color="#231f20" ratio="1" alpha="1"/>
            </RadialGradient>
          </fill>
        </Path>
        <Path winding="nonZero" data="M 173 186 C 269 318 203 425 121 270
C 40 425 -26 318 69 186 C -26 53 40 -54 121 101 C 203 -54 269 53 173 186
Z "
          blendMode="normal" alpha="1">
          <stroke>
            <SolidColorStroke color="#231f20" weight="1"/>
          </stroke>
        </Path>
      </Group>
    </Group>
   </Group>
  </Group>
</Graphic>
```

Note

Notice that the FXG markup generated by Fireworks is considerably more concise than the version created by Illustrator. In general, you can create more reusable FXG markup code in Fireworks. If you have existing artwork that was created as a native Illustrator file (with a file extension of .ai), you can open that file in Fireworks and then export it as FXG to create the most concise possible FXG file. ■

Using FXG files in Flex applications

Once you've created your FXG files with Photoshop, Illustrator, or Fireworks, you can embed them in a Flex application in a couple of ways:

- Use the `<s:BitmapGraphic>` tag to embed an FXG graphic with the `@Embed()` compiler directive.

- Treat FXG files as ActionScript classes and instantiate them with both MXML and ActionScript code.

Note

Unlike the FXG ActionScript classes that I described earlier in this chapter, graphics that are drawn with FXG files cannot be modified at runtime by changes to its properties. If you need your FXG graphic to be modifiable at runtime, consider copying and pasting the FXG code from the file into an MXML document. ■

Embedding FXG graphics with <s:BitmapImage>

The `<s:BitmapImage>` tag is used in Flex 4 MXML files to embed graphical elements as bit-maps. To use this strategy, set the tag's source attribute to the name and location of the FXG file, wrapped in the `@Embed()` compiler directive:

```
<s:BitmapImage source="@Embed('fxgGraphics/FWGraphic.fxg')"/>
```

Caution

When you embed an FXG graphic in this fashion, the vector graphic is transcoded at compile time into a bit-map graphic. As a result, if you then try to scale the graphic, you might see pixilation and other artifacts normally associated with bitmap graphics. ■

Using FXG files as ActionScript classes

You can also use FXG files as ActionScript classes, instantiating and placing them in your applications using either MXML or ActionScript code.

To add an FXG file as a graphical element with MXML, first declare a custom namespace in the MXML document that associates an XML prefix with the folder (package) in which the FXG file is stored:

```
<s:Application xmlns:fx="http://ns.adobe.com/mxml/2009"
   xmlns:s="library://ns.adobe.com/flex/spark"
   xmlns:mx="library://ns.adobe.com/flex/mx"
   xmlns:fxgGraphics="fxgGraphics.*">
</s:Application>
```

Then place the graphic element in the application or within a Spark component by referring to the file name (without the `.fxg` extension) as an MXML tag name:

```
<fxgGraphics:MyFXGGraphic/>
```

Tip

The resulting ActionScript class is extended from the `SpriteVisualElement` class and can use any of that class's properties, methods, and events. For example, to enable a click behavior you can listen for the graphic element's `click` event and respond by executing your own ActionScript code. You can even make the cursor change to a hand shape when it hovers over the graphic by setting the graphic element's `buttonMode` property to `true`:

```
<fxgGraphics:MyFXGGraphic
   click="fwgraphic1_clickHandler(event)"
   buttonMode="true"/> ■
```

If you prefer, you can use ActionScript code to declare, instantiate, and place an instance of an FXG graphic in your application. The application in Listing 14.5 creates and places an FXG graphic on the screen upon application startup. It then sets various properties and event handler to use the graphic as a lightweight button.

LISTING 14.5

An application using an FXG file as an ActionScript class

```
<?xml version="1.0" encoding="utf-8"?>
<s:Application xmlns:fx="http://ns.adobe.com/mxml/2009"
  xmlns:s="library://ns.adobe.com/flex/spark"
  xmlns:mx="library://ns.adobe.com/flex/mx"
  creationComplete="application1_creationCompleteHandler(event)">
  <fx:Script>
    <![CDATA[
      import fxgGraphics.FWGraphic;
      import mx.controls.Alert;
      import mx.events.FlexEvent;

      private var graphic:FWGraphic = new FWGraphic();
      protected function application1_creationCompleteHandler(
        event:FlexEvent):void
      {
        this.contentGroup.addElement(graphic);
        graphic.buttonMode = true;
        graphic.addEventListener(MouseEvent.CLICK, graphic_clickHandler);
        graphic.scaleX=.5;
        graphic.scaleY=.5;
        graphic.horizontalCenter=0;
        graphic.verticalCenter=0;
      }
      protected function graphic_clickHandler(event:MouseEvent):void
      {
        Alert.show("You clicked the graphic", "Alert");
      }
    ]]>
  </fx:Script>
</s:Application>
```

On the Web

The code in Listing 14.5 is available in the Web site files in the `chapter14` project as `FireworksFXGDemo.mxml`. ∎

Summary

In this chapter, I described tools that help you debug a Flex application. You learned the following:

- FXG is an XML-based markup language that is used to describe vector graphic elements and embed bitmap graphics.

- The Flex 4 SDK includes ActionScript classes in the `spark.primitives` package that reproduce the effect of their equivalent FXG elements and mimic their syntax when declared with MXML.

- You can use the primitive vector graphic classes to declare vector graphics in MXML or instantiate and add them to your Flex application at runtime with ActionScript.

- Adobe Photoshop, Illustrator, and Fireworks can import and export FXG files.

- FXG files can be embedded in Flex applications as bitmap graphics.

- FXG files can be treated as ActionScript classes in Flex applications.

Skinning Spark Components

As I described in Chapter 14, one of the Flex 4 SDK's most important new features is the capability to redefine the appearance of visual controls with *programmatic skins*.

In past versions of the Flex SDK, you could create your own skin as an ActionScript class. By overriding certain methods that are called at runtime from the Flex framework and using the Flash drawing application programming interface (API) to declare vector graphics, you could define an entire visual presentation without ever using graphical applications like Adobe Photoshop and Illustrator.

This strategy, however, was slow and cumbersome. And, because the graphical applications I've mentioned couldn't interpret the ActionScript code and show you a preview of its results, you had to use your imagination (and a lot of graph paper) to figure out how to code the image you wanted to create.

In Flex 4, skins are now defined as MXML components that are extended from new classes named `Skin` and `SparkSkin`. You can bind the skin component to an application or custom component at compile time or runtime with its `skinClass` style. The skin class can be constructed with a combination of vector graphics, bitmap graphics, and Flex components to achieve whatever design ideas your application requires.

IN THIS CHAPTER

Declaring skins as MXML components

Using skin states and skin parts

Binding custom skins to Spark components

Making copies of existing custom skins

Customizing component appearance with graphic elements

In this chapter, I describe how to define custom skins using the new MXML architecture, and then how to attach them to your applications and custom components.

On the Web

To use the sample code for this chapter, import the `chapter15.fxp` **Flex project archive file from the Web site files into your Flash Builder workspace.** ■

Creating and Using Spark Custom Skins

A custom skin component for a Flex 4 application or any of its Spark components is based on the new `Skin` and `SparkSkin` classes. You can start either by creating a new copy of a component's default skin class (a step made very easy by Flash Builder 4) or you can create a new fresh component that extends the `Skin` class. While it's possible to create such components in either MXML or ActionScript, most developers find that the MXML approach is much easier and the resulting code far more readable.

Skinning a Spark application

You can create a new custom skin using the new architecture for any component that includes the new `SkinnableComponent` class in its inheritance hierarchy. `SkinnableComponent` extends `UIComponent`, which means that Spark components can be added as display children of any Spark or MX containers.

In this section, I describe how to create a new custom skin for the Spark `Application` component, but most of the techniques also apply to all other Spark components.

Creating a custom skin

To create a new custom skin, start by creating a new custom MXML component. As with all MXML components and ActionScript classes, I recommend that you place your custom skins in a specially named package under your Flex project's source-code root folder.

If you're using the Flex project that's available for download from the Web, you'll see that it already has a package named `skins` under the source-code root folder. If you're working on your own Flex project, you'll need to create this new package:

1. **Open the Flex project in Flash Builder.**
2. **Right-click the default package in the Package Explorer view and choose New ⇨ Package.**
3. **As shown in Figure 15.1, name the new package** skins.
4. **Click Finish.**

FIGURE 15.1

Creating a new package in the Package Explorer

Next create a new skin component:

1. **In the Package Explorer, right-click the new `skins` package and choose New ➪ MXML Component.**

2. **In the New MXML Component dialog box, shown in Figure 15.2, type CustomAppSkin in the Filename field.**

3. **Accept the Layout default value of None.**

4. **Click the Browse button next to Based on.**

5. **Select spark.skins.SparkSkin and click OK.**

6. **Delete the default values in the Width and Height settings.**

7. **Click Finish to create the new skin component.**

The code for the new skin component looks like this:

```
<?xml version="1.0" encoding="utf-8"?>
<s:SparkSkin xmlns:fx="http://ns.adobe.com/mxml/2009"
  xmlns:s="library://ns.adobe.com/flex/spark"
  xmlns:mx="library://ns.adobe.com/flex/mx">
  <fx:Declarations>
    <!-- Place non-visual elements
       (e.g., services, value objects) here -->
  </fx:Declarations>
</s:SparkSkin>
```

FIGURE 15.2

Creating a new Spark skin component

The new skin component's code looks like that of any other custom component and can contain instances of any Flex component. Its difference lies in its superclass. Because its root element is <s:SparkSkin>, its purpose is to implement the component's visual design.

Associating the skin with the host component

After creating the new skin component, you should associate it with the Spark component it's designed to modify. You create the association with the [HostComponent] metadata tag. This tag takes as its only attribute a string that describes the fully qualified package and name of the component:

```
[HostComponent("spark.components.Button")]
```

As with the [Event] metadata tag, [HostComponent] is placed inside the <fx:Metadata> element. Follow these steps to add the component association to the new custom skin:

1. **Add a blank line under the** <s:SparkSkin> **starting tag.**

2. Add the following code to the component:

```
<fx:Metadata>
  [HostComponent("spark.components.Application")]
<fx:Metadata>
```

In your skin component, you'll be able to refer to the host component's properties using ActionScript code and binding expressions. You refer to the host object with an id of host Component, and to its properties using dot notation. For example, in a custom skin for the Application component, you could output the application's current height and width to the screen with the following Label and binding expression:

```
<s:Label text="{hostComponent.width},{hostComponent.height}"/>
```

Declaring required skin states

In the next step, you declare view states to match the host component's required skin states. You don't have to refer to these view states in the component's visual design. For example, the Spark Application component has two required states. If you want the application to look the same in all view states, you just set the skin's objects, properties, and styles without any state notation. But you must declare the states or a runtime error is generated when the skin is bound to the application at runtime.

First look at the host component's documentation to find out which states are required:

1. Open the Flex help system.

2. Search for spark.components.Application.

3. After opening the help screen for the Application component, click Skin States.

4. If necessary, click Show Inherited Skin States to see the states inherited from the Application component's superclasses.

As shown in Figure 15.3, the Application component requires the following skin states:

- disabled

- normal

FIGURE 15.3

The Spark application component's required skin states

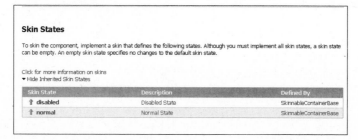

5. **Return to the new skin component file in Flash Builder.**

6. **Add the following code after the default `<fx:Declarations>` element:**

```
<s:states>
  <s:State name="normal" />
  <s:State name="disabled" />
</s:states>
```

In the skin code, you'll be able to designate inclusion or exclusion of particular objects depending on which state the application is in with the `includeIn` and `excludeFrom` properties. For example, the following `Group` is only included in the `normal` state:

```
<s:Group id="normalGroup" minWidth="0" minHeight="0"
  includeIn="normal" >
  ... visual controls and graphics ...
</s:Group>
```

You're also able to control individual properties and styles with dot notation. The following style overrides the skin's default `chromeColor` setting only when the application's state is `disabled`:

```
chromeColor.disabled="#EEEEEE"
```

Adding required skin parts

Spark components typically implement one or more required skin parts. These are typically used for specific functionality in the component. For example, the `Application` component requires a skin part named `contentGroup` that must implement the `Group` component or one of its subclasses. This is the actual container used to lay out the visual children declared with MXML in the `Application`. Or in button skins, the `labelDisplay` skin part is a `TextBase` object that will display the label of any button that uses that skin. If you don't declare the required skin parts in your custom skin, the application fails at runtime when it tries to use the skin part; in the case of `contentGroup`, it fails when it tries to add visual controls declared with MXML to the group upon application startup.

As with skin states, you can look at the documentation to find out which skin parts are required by the host component.

Follow these steps to declare the Application component's required `contentGroup` skin part:

1. **In `CustomAppSkin.mxml`, place the cursor above the closing `</s:Application>` tag.**

2. **Add the following code:**

```
<s:Group id="contentGroup"/>
```

At this point, the custom skin should look like this:

```
<?xml version="1.0" encoding="utf-8"?>
<s:SparkSkin xmlns:fx="http://ns.adobe.com/mxml/2009"
  xmlns:s="library://ns.adobe.com/flex/spark"
  xmlns:mx="library://ns.adobe.com/flex/mx">
  <fx:Metadata>
```

```
    [HostComponent("spark.components.Application")]
  </fx:Metadata>
  <fx:Declarations>
    <!-- Place non-visual elements
      (e.g., services, value objects) here -->
  </fx:Declarations>
  <s:states>
    <s:State name="normal" />
    <s:State name="disabled" />
  </s:states>
  <s:Group id="contentGroup"/>
</s:SparkSkin>
```

The custom skin doesn't implement a visual design yet, but it has everything you need to make it compatible with the Spark `Application` component.

Adding vector graphics to the skin

The next step is to add visual objects to the skin. Because the custom skin uses the default basic layout, objects can be overlaid on top of each other, and you can use constraint-based layout properties such as top, left, bottom, and right to position objects relative to the skin's borders.

Visual objects that are added to the layout in the host component should appear in the application's background. To make this happen, just declare any FXG graphics in the skin component's code above the declaration of the `contentGroup` object.

Follow these steps to add a background color and a frame with a drop shadow to the application's appearance:

1. In `CustomAppSkin.mxml`, place the cursor above the Group with an `id` of `contentGroup` and make a new blank line.

2. Declare a rectangle that covers the entire application canvas and has a solid light gray color of #CCCCCC:

   ```
   <s:Rect width="100%" height="100%">
     <s:fill>
       <s:SolidColor color="#cccccc"/>
     </s:fill>
   </s:Rect>
   ```

3. Add another rectangle after the first, but still before the `contentGroup` object. This rectangle is constrained to 20 pixels from all application borders, uses rounded corners, and has a drop-shadow filter:

   ```
   <s:Rect left="20" right="20" top="20" bottom="20"
     radiusX="15" radiusY="15">
     <s:fill>
       <s:SolidColor color="#eeeeee"/>
     </s:fill>
     <s:filters>
       <s:DropShadowFilter/>
     </s:filters>
   </s:Rect>
   ```

The custom skin now creates a framed appearance. Next you'll add settings to ensure that visual objects that are added to the application from the host component are placed within the visual area created by the frame. You do this by adding constraint properties to the `contentGroup` object in the custom skin.

4. **Add** `left`, `right`, `top`, **and** `bottom` **properties to the** `contentGroup` **object, setting all values to 30.** This causes any visual objects added to the Application to be placed within the rounded rectangle with extra padding of 10 pixels on all borders:

```
<s:Group id="contentGroup"
  left="30" right="30" top="30" bottom="30"/>
```

Note

The visual frame created by the rectangle graphic is constrained to 20 pixels from the application's borders. If you set the `contentGroup` object's constraints to 30 pixels, it results in a 10-pixel padding between the frame borders and the first visual objects in the layout. ■

The custom skin is now complete. Listing 15.1 shows the completed code.

LISTING 15.1

A completed custom skin for the Spark Application component

```
<?xml version="1.0" encoding="utf-8"?>
<s:SparkSkin xmlns:fx="http://ns.adobe.com/mxml/2009"
  xmlns:s="library://ns.adobe.com/flex/spark"
  xmlns:mx="library://ns.adobe.com/flex/mx">
  <fx:Declarations>
    <!-- Place non-visual elements (e.g., services, value objects) here -->
  </fx:Declarations>
  <fx:Metadata>
    [HostComponent("spark.components.Application")]
  </fx:Metadata>
  <s:states>
    <s:State name="normal" />
    <s:State name="disabled" />
  </s:states>
  <s:Rect width="100%" height="100%">
    <s:fill>
      <s:SolidColor color="#cccccc"/>
    </s:fill>
  </s:Rect>
  <s:Rect left="20" right="20" top="20" bottom="20"
    radiusX="15" radiusY="15">
    <s:fill>
      <s:SolidColor color="#eeeeee"/>
    </s:fill>
```

```
      <s:filters>
        <s:DropShadowFilter/>
      </s:filters>
    </s:Rect>
    <s:Group id="contentGroup"
      left="30" right="30" top="30" bottom="30"/>
  </s:SparkSkin>
```

On the Web

The code in Listing 15.1 is available in the Web site files in the `chapter15` project as `CustomAppSkinComplete.mxml`. ∎

Binding a custom skin to a Spark component

You bind a custom skin to a Spark component using the component's `skinClass` style. This style is declared in the `SkinnableComponent` class and is therefore available to all of its subclasses.

Note

The `skinClass` style's type is set to `Class`, but the class must extend `UIComponent`. Skins designed for use with Spark components should extend `SparkSkin`. ∎

As with all styles, you can set the `skinClass` style in many ways:

- As an inline declaration for a particular component instance.
- In a style sheet to affect all instances of a particular component.
- At runtime using the `setStyle()` method.

Assigning a skin for a single component

You assign a skin to a single component instance at compile time by setting `skinClass` with an inline style declaration. When assigning a skin to the `Application` component, this strategy makes the most sense, since by definition there is only one instance of that component.

The value of the `skinClass` style should be set to the fully qualified package and name of the custom skin component. To use the custom skin that was created in the previous section, set the `<s:Application>` tag's skinClass attribute to `skins.CustomAppSkin`.

The application in Listing 15.2 uses the custom skin class that's shown in Listing 15.1.

LISTING 15.2

An application using a custom skin

```xml
<?xml version="1.0" encoding="utf-8"?>
<s:Application xmlns:fx="http://ns.adobe.com/mxml/2009"
  xmlns:s="library://ns.adobe.com/flex/spark"
  xmlns:mx="library://ns.adobe.com/flex/mx"
  skinClass="skins.CustomAppSkinComplete">
  <s:Label text="My Skinned Application" top="20" horizontalCenter="0"
    fontSize="36"/>
</s:Application>
```

On the Web

The code in Listing 15.2 is available in the Web site files in the `chapter15` **project as**
`AppWithCustomSkin.mxml.` ∎

Figure 15.4 shows the resulting application with the custom skin applied.

FIGURE 15.4

An application with a custom skin

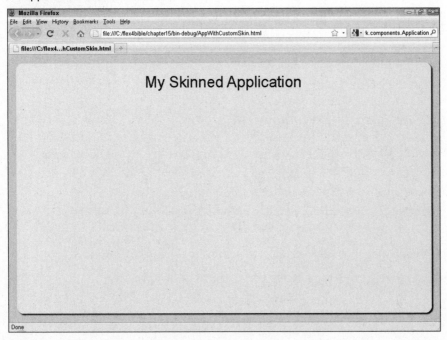

Setting a custom skin with a style sheet declaration

You can also apply custom skins with style sheet declarations. While this strategy is most useful when applying a skin to a group of components (such as all objects that are instances of a particular Spark component), it can be used with any Spark component, including `Application`.

As with all styles, the declaration starts with a CSS selector that defines which components will have the style applied. You can use type selectors, style name selectors (also known as class selectors), contextual selectors, or any other syntax that's supported in the Flex 4 SDK.

The value of the `skinClass` style is set using the `ClassReference()` compiler directive. You pass the fully qualified package and name of the custom skin component. The following code assigns a skin named `MyCustomButtonSkin` to all instances of the Spark `Button` component:

```
s|Button: ClassReference("skins.MyCustomButtonSkin");
```

The application in Listing 15.3 uses a style sheet declaration to assign the custom application skin to the application.

LISTING 15.3

An application using a custom skin assigned in a style sheet

```
<?xml version="1.0" encoding="utf-8"?>
<s:Application xmlns:fx="http://ns.adobe.com/mxml/2009"
  xmlns:s="library://ns.adobe.com/flex/spark"
  xmlns:mx="library://ns.adobe.com/flex/mx">
  <fx:Style>
    @namespace s "library://ns.adobe.com/flex/spark";
    @namespace mx "library://ns.adobe.com/flex/mx ";
    s|Application
    {
      skinClass:ClassReference("skins.CustomAppSkinComplete");
    }
  </fx:Style>
  <s:Label text="My Skinned Application" top="20" horizontalCenter="0"
    fontSize="36"/>
</s:Application>
```

On the Web

The code in Listing 15.3 is available in the Web site files in the `chapter15` project as `AppWithSkinStyleSheet.mxml`. ■

Loading custom skins at runtime

You can also load a custom skin at runtime using the `setStyle()` method or any of the techniques available with the `StyleManager` class. For example, the following code adds the custom skin to the application:

```
this.setStyle("skinClass", skins.CustomAppSkinComplete);
```

You can also get a reference to the class being currently used as a skin using the `getStyle()` method:

```
var currentSkin:Class = this.getStyle("skinClass") as Class;
```

The application in Listing 15.4 switches between the application's default skin and a custom skin each time you click the button. Notice that the appearance of the application changes, and the relative positions of the `Label` and `Button` also change because the custom skin uses different constraint properties to lay out the application's visual objects.

LISTING 15.4

An application loading custom and default skins at runtime

```
<?xml version="1.0" encoding="utf-8"?>
<s:Application xmlns:fx="http://ns.adobe.com/mxml/2009"
  xmlns:s="library://ns.adobe.com/flex/spark">
  <fx:Script>
    <![CDATA[
      import skins.CustomAppSkinComplete;
      protected var oldSkin:Class;
      protected function clickHandler(event:MouseEvent):void
      {
        if (oldSkin == null)
        {
          oldSkin = this.getStyle("skinClass") as Class;
          this.setStyle("skinClass", CustomAppSkinComplete);
          skinButton.label = "Load Original Skin";
        }
        else
        {
          this.setStyle("skinClass", oldSkin);
          oldSkin = null;
          skinButton.label = "Load Custom Skin";
        }
      }
    ]]>
  </fx:Script>
  <s:Label text="My Skinned Application" top="20" horizontalCenter="0"
    fontSize="36"/>
  <s:Button id="skinButton" label="Load Custom Skin"
```

```
    click="clickHandler(event)"
    top="100" horizontalCenter="0"/>
</s:Application>
```

On the Web

The code in Listing 15.4 is available in the Web site files in the `chapter15` **project as**
`AppLoadStyleAtRuntime.mxml.` ∎

Skinning Other Spark Components

You can create custom skins for all Spark components, including your own custom components. In this section I describe the specific code you need to skin the Spark `Button` and `List` components.

Creating a new skin

In Flash Builder 4, you can get started with custom skinning by creating a copy of a component's default skin class. This tool is available only from Flash Builder's design mode.

Follow these steps to create a copy of the Spark `Button` component's default skin:

1. **Open** `AppWithButtons.mxml` **in Flash Builder.** Notice that the application uses a completed version of the custom application skin created in a previous section of this chapter and declares a number of `Button` objects laid out vertically and centered:

   ```
   <?xml version="1.0" encoding="utf-8"?>
   <s:Application xmlns:fx="http://ns.adobe.com/mxml/2009"
     xmlns:s="library://ns.adobe.com/flex/spark"
     skinClass="skins.CustomAppSkinComplete">
     <s:layout>
       <s:VerticalLayout paddingTop="20" horizontalAlign="center"/>
     </s:layout>
     <s:Button label="Button 1"/>
     <s:Button label="Button 2"/>
     <s:Button label="Button 3"/>
     <s:Button label="Button 4"/>
   </s:Application>
   ```

2. **View the application in Design mode.**

3. **Right-click the first button and select Create Skin, as shown in Figure 15.5.**

   Flash Builder displays a dialog box, shown in Figure 15.6, with options for creating a new MXML component based on the `Button` object's default skin. In the case of the `Button` component, the new MXML component is extended from `spark.skins.SparkSkin` and copied from `spark.skins.spark.ButtonSkin`.

FIGURE 15.5

Creating a custom skin from Design mode

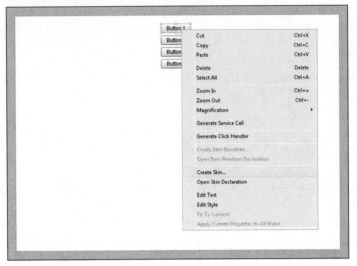

FIGURE 15.6

Creating a copy of a component skin

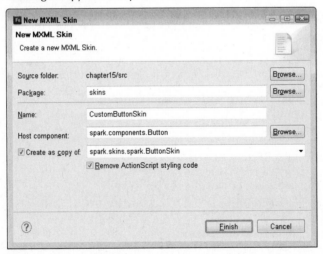

4. Set Package to skins.

5. Set Name to CustomButtonSkin.

6. Check the option to Remove ActionScript styling code.

7. **Click Finish.** The new custom skin should be created and opened in Design mode.

8. **Click the Source button to look at the new skin component's code.**

Listing 15.5 shows the new component's code.

LISTING 15.5

A new custom skin copied from the Button component's default skin

```
<?xml version="1.0" encoding="utf-8"?>
<!--
ADOBE SYSTEMS INCORPORATED
Copyright 2008 Adobe Systems Incorporated
All Rights Reserved.
NOTICE: Adobe permits you to use, modify, and distribute this file
in accordance with the terms of the license agreement accompanying it.
-->
<!--- The default skin class for the Spark Button component.
@langversion 3.0
@playerversion Flash 10
@playerversion AIR 1.5
@productversion Flex 4
-->
<s:SparkSkin xmlns:fx="http://ns.adobe.com/mxml/2009" xmlns:s="library://
  ns.adobe.com/flex/spark"
 xmlns:fb="http://ns.adobe.com/flashbuilder/2009" minWidth="21"
  minHeight="21" alpha.disabled="0.5">
 <!-- host component -->
 <fx:Metadata>
   <![CDATA[
   /**
   * @copy spark.skins.spark.ApplicationSkin#hostComponent
   */
   [HostComponent("spark.components.Button")]
   ]]>
 </fx:Metadata>
 <!-- states -->
 <s:states>
   <s:State name="up" />
   <s:State name="over" />
   <s:State name="down" />
   <s:State name="disabled" />
 </s:states>
 <!-- layer 1: shadow -->
 <!--- @private -->
 <s:Rect id="shadow" left="-1" right="-1" top="-1" bottom="-1" radiusX="2">
   <s:fill>
     <s:LinearGradient rotation="90">
```

continued

LISTING 15.5   (continued)

```
          <s:GradientEntry color="0x000000"
            color.down="0xFFFFFF"
            alpha="0.01"
            alpha.down="0" />
          <s:GradientEntry color="0x000000"
            color.down="0xFFFFFF"
            alpha="0.07"
            alpha.down="0.5" />
        </s:LinearGradient>
      </s:fill>
  </s:Rect>
  <!-- layer 2: fill -->
  <!--- @private -->
  <s:Rect id="fill" left="1" right="1" top="1" bottom="1" radiusX="2">
    <s:fill>
      <s:LinearGradient rotation="90">
        <s:GradientEntry color="0xFFFFFF"
          color.over="0xBBBDBD"
          color.down="0xAAAAAA"
          alpha="0.85" />
        <s:GradientEntry color="0xD8D8D8"
          color.over="0x9FA0A1"
          color.down="0x929496"
          alpha="0.85" />
      </s:LinearGradient>
    </s:fill>
  </s:Rect>
  <!-- layer 3: fill lowlight -->
  <!--- @private -->
  <s:Rect id="lowlight" left="1" right="1" top="1" bottom="1" radiusX="2">
    <s:fill>
      <s:LinearGradient rotation="270">
        <s:GradientEntry color="0x000000" ratio="0.0" alpha="0.0627" />
        <s:GradientEntry color="0x000000" ratio="0.48" alpha="0.0099" />
        <s:GradientEntry color="0x000000" ratio="0.48001" alpha="0" />
      </s:LinearGradient>
    </s:fill>
  </s:Rect>
  <!-- layer 4: fill highlight -->
  <!--- @private -->
  <s:Rect id="highlight" left="1" right="1" top="1" bottom="1" radiusX="2">
    <s:fill>
      <s:LinearGradient rotation="90">
        <s:GradientEntry color="0xFFFFFF"
          ratio="0.0"
          alpha="0.33"
          alpha.over="0.22"
          alpha.down="0.12"/>
        <s:GradientEntry color="0xFFFFFF"
          ratio="0.48"
```

```
          alpha="0.33"
          alpha.over="0.22"
          alpha.down="0.12" />
        <s:GradientEntry color="0xFFFFFF"
          ratio="0.48001"
          alpha="0" />
      </s:LinearGradient>
    </s:fill>
  </s:Rect>
  <!-- layer 5: highlight stroke (all states except down) -->
  <!--- @private -->
  <s:Rect id="highlightStroke" left="1" right="1" top="1" bottom="1"
   radiusX="2" excludeFrom="down">
    <s:stroke>
      <s:LinearGradientStroke rotation="90" weight="1">
        <s:GradientEntry color="0xFFFFFF" alpha.over="0.22" />
        <s:GradientEntry color="0xD8D8D8" alpha.over="0.22" />
      </s:LinearGradientStroke>
    </s:stroke>
  </s:Rect>
  <!-- layer 6: highlight stroke (down state only) -->
  <!--- @private -->
  <s:Rect id="hldownstroke1" left="1" right="1" top="1" bottom="1"
   radiusX="2" includeIn="down">
    <s:stroke>
      <s:LinearGradientStroke rotation="90" weight="1">
        <s:GradientEntry color="0x000000" alpha="0.25" ratio="0.0" />
        <s:GradientEntry color="0x000000" alpha="0.25" ratio="0.001" />
        <s:GradientEntry color="0x000000" alpha="0.07" ratio="0.0011" />
        <s:GradientEntry color="0x000000" alpha="0.07" ratio="0.965" />
        <s:GradientEntry color="0x000000" alpha="0.00" ratio="0.9651" />
      </s:LinearGradientStroke>
    </s:stroke>
  </s:Rect>
  <!--- @private -->
  <s:Rect id="hldownstroke2" left="2" right="2" top="2" bottom="2"
   radiusX="2" includeIn="down">
    <s:stroke>
      <s:LinearGradientStroke rotation="90" weight="1">
        <s:GradientEntry color="0x000000" alpha="0.09" ratio="0.0" />
        <s:GradientEntry color="0x000000" alpha="0.00" ratio="0.0001" />
      </s:LinearGradientStroke>
    </s:stroke>
  </s:Rect>
  <!-- layer 7: border - put on top of the fill so it doesn't disappear when
    scale is less than 1 -->
  <!--- @private -->
  <s:Rect id="border" left="0" right="0" top="0" bottom="0" width="69"
   height="20" radiusX="2">
```

continued

459

LISTING 15.5   *(continued)*

```
    <s:stroke>
      <s:LinearGradientStroke rotation="90" weight="1">
        <s:GradientEntry color="0x000000"
          alpha="0.5625"
          alpha.down="0.6375" />
        <s:GradientEntry color="0x000000"
          alpha="0.75"
          alpha.down="0.85" />
      </s:LinearGradientStroke>
    </s:stroke>
  </s:Rect>
  <!-- layer 8: text -->
  <!--- @copy spark.components.supportClasses.ButtonBase#labelDisplay -->
  <s:Label id="labelDisplay"
    textAlign="center"
    verticalAlign="middle"
    maxDisplayedLines="1"
    horizontalCenter="0" verticalCenter="1"
    left="10" right="10" top="2" bottom="2">
  </s:Label>
</s:SparkSkin>
```

On the Web

The code in Listing 15.5 is available in the Web site files in the `chapter15` project as `CustomButtonSkinComplete.mxml`. ■

Note

Notice in the generated code that Flash Builder adds a new XML namespace to the custom skin component's root element:

```
xmlns:fb="http://ns.adobe.com/flashbuilder/2009"
```

The custom `fb` prefix is used to mark certain MXML tags as having been generated for a particular purpose. If you had elected to include ActionScript styling code in the generated skin component, the `fb` prefix would have been used to mark an `<fx:Script>` tag as having a `purpose` attribute with a value of styling:

```
<fx:Script fb:purpose="styling">
   ... scripting code ...
</fx:Script>
```

These special properties are placed in the code only for purposes of documentation and don't affect the application's performance or functionality. ■

The component that you started with now has its `skinClass` style set to the new component:

```
<s:Button label="Button 1" skinClass="skins.CustomButtonSkin"/>
```

Assigning custom skins with CSS

As described in a previous section of this chapter, the `skinClass` attribute is an inline style declaration that styles only the current `Button` instance. If you want to style all instances of the `Button` class throughout the application, first remove the `skinClass` attribute from the MXML code you used to create the custom skin, and then declare `skinClass` in a style sheet that affects the entire application by following these steps:

1. Open `AppWithButtons.mxml` in Source mode.
2. Remove the `skinClass` attribute from the first `Button` object.
3. Add the following code above the first `<s:Button>` declaration:

```
<fx:Style>
  @namespace s "library://ns.adobe.com/flex/spark";
  s|Button {
    skinClass: ClassReference("skins.CustomButtonSkin");
  }
</fx:Style>
```

The application in Listing 15.6 uses a completed version of the custom button skin for all instances of the `Button` component throughout the application.

LISTING 15.6

An application using a custom skin for all instances of Button

```
<?xml version="1.0" encoding="utf-8"?>
<s:Application xmlns:fx="http://ns.adobe.com/mxml/2009"
  xmlns:s="library://ns.adobe.com/flex/spark"
  skinClass="skins.CustomAppSkinComplete">
  <s:layout>
    <s:VerticalLayout paddingTop="20" horizontalAlign="center"/>
  </s:layout>
  <fx:Style>
    @namespace s "library://ns.adobe.com/flex/spark";
    s|Button {
      skinClass: ClassReference("skins.CustomButtonSkinComplete");
    }
  </fx:Style>
  <s:Button label="Button 1"/>
  <s:Button label="Button 2"/>
  <s:Button label="Button 3"/>
  <s:Button label="Button 4"/>
</s:Application>
```

On the Web

The code in Listing 15.6 is available in the Web site files in the `chapter15` project as
`AppWithButtonsComplete.mxml`. ∎

Customizing the skin

Next you can make some changes to the existing skin. In the following example, I add `color`,
`fontSize`, `fontWeight`, and `textDecoration` attributes to the `Label` at the bottom of the
custom skin to affect how all of the button labels are displayed.

To customize the skin, follow these steps:

1. Open `CustomButtonSkin.mxml` in Source mode.

2. Locate the `Label` component toward the bottom of the file with an `id` of
   `displayLabel`.

3. Set the `Label` component's color to purple and its `fontSize` to 18:

   `color="purple" fontSize="18"`

4. Locate the `<s:states>` element.

5. Add a `stateGroups` attribute of `overOrDown` to both the over state and the down
   state:

   ```
   <s:states>
     <s:State name="up" />
     <s:State name="over" stateGroups="overOrDown"/>
     <s:State name="down" stateGroups="overOrDown"/>
     <s:State name="disabled" />
   </s:states>
   ```

6. Return to the `Label` at the bottom of the custom skin and add the following attributes to cause the label to be bold and underlined in the over and down states:

   `fontWeight.overOrDown="bold" textDecoration.overOrDown="underline"`

7. Save the custom skin file and run the `AppWithButtons` application.

New Feature

The `stateGroups` attribute is new in the Flex 4 SDK. It enables you to group states together when particular
changes will be made to properties, styles, or event handlers based on two or more states. You don't need to
pre-declare a state group; instead, just declare the `stateGroups` attribute in whichever states you want to
group together, and then refer to the group using dot syntax just as you do with individual states. ∎

As shown in Figure 15.7, the skinned application now displays the `Button` objects using the new
custom skin.

You can now follow the same workflow to skin any Spark component using FXG and bitmap
graphics and applying your own distinct designs to your Flex 4 applications.

The custom skin in Listing 15.7 uses elliptical shapes instead of rectangles, but otherwise is nearly identical to the code in the original skin.

FIGURE 15.7

An application using buttons with custom skins

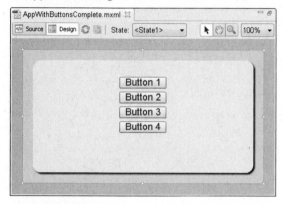

LISTING 15.7

A custom button skin with elliptical shapes

```
<?xml version="1.0" encoding="utf-8"?>
<s:SparkSkin xmlns:fx="http://ns.adobe.com/mxml/2009"
  xmlns:s="library://ns.adobe.com/flex/spark"
  minWidth="21" minHeight="21" alpha.disabled="0.5">
  <fx:Metadata>
    [HostComponent("spark.components.Button")]
  </fx:Metadata>
  <fx:Script>
    <![CDATA[
      static private const exclusions:Array = ["labelDisplay"];
      override public function get colorizeExclusions():Array {
        return exclusions;}
      override protected function initializationComplete():void
      {
        useChromeColor = true;
        super.initializationComplete();
      }
    ]]>
  </fx:Script>
```

continued

LISTING 15.7   (continued)

```
<!-- states -->
<s:states>
  <s:State name="up" />
  <s:State name="over" stateGroups="overOrDown"/>
  <s:State name="down" stateGroups="overOrDown"/>
  <s:State name="disabled" />
</s:states>
<!-- layer 1: shadow -->
<s:Ellipse id="shadow" left="-1" right="-1" top="-1" bottom="-1" >
  <s:fill>
    <s:LinearGradient rotation="90">
      <s:GradientEntry color="0x000000"
        color.down="0xFFFFFF"
        alpha="0.01"
        alpha.down="0" />
      <s:GradientEntry color="0x000000"
        color.down="0xFFFFFF"
        alpha="0.07"
        alpha.down="0.5" />
    </s:LinearGradient>
  </s:fill>
</s:Ellipse>
<!-- layer 2: fill -->
<s:Ellipse id="fill" left="1" right="1" top="1" bottom="1" >
  <s:fill>
    <s:LinearGradient rotation="90">
      <s:GradientEntry color="0xFFFFFF"
        color.over="0xBBBDBD"
        color.down="0xAAAAAA"
        alpha="0.85" />
      <s:GradientEntry color="0xD8D8D8"
        color.over="0x9FA0A1"
        color.down="0x929496"
        alpha="0.85" />
    </s:LinearGradient>
  </s:fill>
</s:Ellipse>
<!-- layer 3: fill lowlight -->
<s:Ellipse id="lowlight" left="1" right="1" bottom="1" height="9" >
  <s:fill>
    <s:LinearGradient rotation="90">
      <s:GradientEntry color="0x000000" alpha="0.0099" />
      <s:GradientEntry color="0x000000" alpha="0.0627" />
    </s:LinearGradient>
  </s:fill>
</s:Ellipse>
<!-- layer 4: fill highlight -->
<s:Ellipse id="highlight" left="1" right="1" top="1" height="9" >
```

```
    <s:fill>
      <s:SolidColor color="0xFFFFFF"
        alpha="0.33"
        alpha.over="0.22"
        alpha.down="0.12" />
    </s:fill>
</s:Ellipse>
<!-- layer 5: highlight stroke (all states except down) -->
<s:Ellipse id="highlightStroke" left="1" right="1" top="1" bottom="1"
  excludeFrom="down">
  <s:stroke>
    <s:LinearGradientStroke rotation="90" weight="1">
      <s:GradientEntry color="0xFFFFFF" alpha.over="0.22" />
      <s:GradientEntry color="0xD8D8D8" alpha.over="0.22" />
    </s:LinearGradientStroke>
  </s:stroke>
</s:Ellipse>
<!-- layer 6: highlight stroke (down state only) -->
<s:Ellipse left="1" top="1" bottom="1" width="1" includeIn="down">
  <s:fill>
    <s:SolidColor color="0x000000" alpha="0.07" />
  </s:fill>
</s:Ellipse>
<s:Ellipse right="1" top="1" bottom="1" width="1" includeIn="down">
  <s:fill>
    <s:SolidColor color="0x000000" alpha="0.07" />
  </s:fill>
</s:Ellipse>
<s:Ellipse left="2" top="1" right="2" height="1" includeIn="down">
  <s:fill>
    <s:SolidColor color="0x000000" alpha="0.25" />
  </s:fill>
</s:Ellipse>
<s:Ellipse left="1" top="2" right="1" height="1" includeIn="down">
  <s:fill>
    <s:SolidColor color="0x000000" alpha="0.09" />
  </s:fill>
</s:Ellipse>

<!-- layer 7: border - put on top of the fill so it doesn't disappear when
  scale is less than 1 -->
<s:Ellipse id="border" left="0" right="0" top="0" bottom="0" width="69"
  height="20" >
  <s:stroke>
    <s:LinearGradientStroke rotation="90" weight="1">
      <s:GradientEntry color="0x000000"
        alpha="0.5625"
        alpha.down="0.6375" />
```

continued

LISTING 15.7 *(continued)*

```xml
          <s:GradientEntry color="0x000000"
            alpha="0.75"
            alpha.down="0.85" />
        </s:LinearGradientStroke>
      </s:stroke>
    </s:Ellipse>

    <!-- layer 8: text -->
    <!---
    @copy spark.components.supportClasses.ButtonBase#labelDisplay
    -->
    <s:Label id="labelDisplay"
      textAlign="center"
      verticalAlign="middle"
      maxDisplayedLines="1"
      horizontalCenter="0" verticalCenter="1"
      left="10" right="10" top="10" bottom="10"
      color="purple" fontSize="14"
      fontWeight.overOrDown="bold"
      textDecoration.overOrDown="underline">
    </s:Label>

  </s:SparkSkin>
```

On the Web

The code in Listing 15.7 is available in the Web site files in the `skins` **package of the** `chapter15` **project as**
`EllipticalButtonSkin.mxml`. ∎

To use this customized skin, change the style declaration in `AppWithButtons.mxml` to:

```xml
<fx:Style>
  @namespace s "library://ns.adobe.com/flex/spark";
  s|Button {
    skinClass: ClassReference("skins.EllipticalButtonSkin");
  }
</fx:Style>
```

When you run the application, it now appears as shown in Figure 15.8.

FIGURE 15.8

An application with custom skins for its Button components

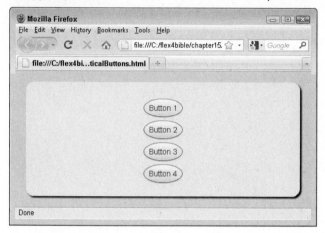

Summary

In this chapter, I described how to use the Flex 4 SDK's new skinning architecture to create and use custom skins for Spark components. You learned the following:

- You declare custom skins in Flex 4 as MXML components.

- Custom skins for Spark components are subclassed from the new SparkSkin class.

- A custom skin can combine vector and bitmap graphics to implement any desired visual design.

- The [HostComponent] metadata tag associates a custom skin with its host component.

- Custom skins must declare the host component's required skin states.

- Custom skins can declare objects with the id of a skin part declared by the host component.

- You use the skinClass style to load a skin into a component.

- The skinClass style can be set with inline attributes, embedded or external style sheets, or loaded at runtime by using the setStyle() method or the StyleManager class.

Managing Application Navigation

I n any application that supports more than a single task on a single screen, you need to provide the user with a way of navigating from one area of the application to another. The areas of the application that can be presented only one screen at a time are commonly known as *views*.

In Flex applications, you handle navigation by switching between the application's views, or by modifying the current state of a view. Unlike classic Web applications, which define views as complete HTML pages that are requested and loaded by the browser one at a time, a Flex application's views are pre-defined and downloaded as part of the entire application. Unless you're using an advanced architecture such as runtime modules, switching from one view to another doesn't require new requests to a Web server, as it would in a Web site.

In this chapter, I describe how to manage navigation in a Flex application by managing stacks of views.

Note

I use the term *view* throughout this chapter to describe a rectangular visual presentation that presents and/or collects information from the user. The term is taken from the application development architecture known as model-view-controller, a way of breaking up an application into small parts with specific functions. ∎

Web Resource

These sites have extensive technical information about the role of views in model-view-controller style development:

```
http://ootips.org/mvc-pattern.html
http://c2.com/cgi/wiki?
  ModelViewControllerAsAnAggregateDesignPattern
http://st-www.cs.uiuc.edu/users/smarch/st-docs/mvc.html ∎
```

IN THIS CHAPTER

Understanding classic Web navigation

Understanding Flex navigation

Using the `ViewStack` **container**

Navigating with ActionScript

Using navigator bar containers

Using menu controls

Using other navigator containers

On the Web

To use the sample code for this chapter, import the `chapter16.zip` Flex project archive from the Web site files into your Flash Builder workspace. ■

Understanding Classic Web Navigation

Navigation in a Web site or an application built completely as a set of HTML pages is based on the capabilities of the Web browser. When a user clicks hyperlinks or submits information through HTML data entry forms, the Web browser handles navigation by sending HTTP (Hypertext Transfer Protocol) requests to a Web server for each new page.

Classic Web applications, which dynamically generate their screens one page at a time, deliver each application view as a separate page upon request. The application's views don't exist in the browser until they're requested and delivered. And when the browser navigates to any new page, the current page is completely unloaded from memory.

Note

This discussion of classic Web application architecture does not take into account AJAX-style development, which enables you to load more than one screen into browser memory at a time. Some, but not all, of the advantages of Flex development also can be realized with AJAX (Asynchronous JavaScript and XML). ■

Classic Web application architecture has certain advantages, such as infinite scalability (measured by the number of views that are possible in an application without negatively affecting performance). But its limitations include the following:

- **Classic Web applications can't store data persistently in client-side memory.** As each page is unloaded from the browser, the data in its memory is lost.

  - **Some Web architectures solve data persistence by passing data from page to page as the user navigates through the application.** ASP.NET, for example, has an architecture known as the `ViewState` that passes data as part of each form post. This works with small amounts of data, but larger data packets can cause client-side performance issues because passing so much data to and from the server can create an impression of sluggishness.

  - **Other Web architectures solve the state issue by storing session data on the server and synchronizing client access to the data with cookies (variables generated by the server and returned by the client on each new page request).** While server-side session management relieves the client of the need to manage data persistently, it can create user scalability issues. Each time a new user visits the application, additional server memory is required. In addition, cookies can be disabled by the user, rendering this solution ineffective.

- **The browser has to rebuild the view each time it's visited.** Because browsers have no inherent client-side state management, the graphical presentation of a page must be recalculated and rendered anew on each visit to the page. The browser offers caching of image and other assets to speed up this process, but graphical presentation in a Web page is necessarily limited.

- **HTML and JavaScript aren't interpreted identically by every Web browser.** In fact, one of the most costly and time-consuming aspects of classic Web application development is testing, because you must test your application on each combination of operating system, browser, and version that you want to support. Some Web application vendors handle this issue by limiting the platforms on which an application is supported. For example, Intuit's QuickBooks Online, while a powerful and reliable Web application, is supported only on Microsoft Internet Explorer on Windows and Safari on Mac — no Firefox users allowed!

Understanding Flex Navigation

Navigation in Flex applications is handled at two levels with navigator containers and view states. The difference between these strategies can be described as one of the amount of visual change during a move from one presentation to another:

- **Navigator containers.** Use these when you want to replace a rectangular region of a Flex application (a view) with a completely different visual presentation.

- **View states.** Use these when you want to modify an existing view, by adding or removing visual components or by changing components' properties, styles, or event listeners.

In some cases, either a navigator container or a view state can get the job done, but for the most part the choice is clear: Use a navigator container to move from one view to another, and use a view state to change an existing view.

Cross-Reference
Detailed information about view states is available in Chapter 13. ∎

Using Navigator Containers

You create a stack of views using one of the navigator containers provided in the Flex framework. The `ViewStack` class is the simplest of these navigator containers. You declare the `ViewStack` container as a parent container that nests a collection of view components and displays only one of its nested views at any given time.

The `ViewStack` container doesn't have any user interface controls that enable the user to select a current view, so it's typically controlled either with ActionScript code or with navigator bar components that use the `ViewStack` as a data provider and dynamically generate interactive components to control navigation.

Declaring a ViewStack in MXML

To create a `ViewStack` in MXML, declare an `<mx:ViewStack>` tag set. Then declare each nested container within the `<mx:ViewStack>` tag set. You can nest either pre-built containers from the Flex framework or your own custom components. The containers you nest within the `ViewStack` can be either layout or navigator containers.

New Feature

The `ViewStack`, `TabNavigator`, **and** `Accordion` **navigator containers were originally designed so they could only contain instances of the original MX container classes such as** `VBox`, `HBox`, **and** `Panel`. **This rule is enforced via the nested object's inheritance hierarchy: Each of the components nested directly within a** `ViewStack` **must include** `mx.core.Container` **as one of its superclasses. If you nest most Spark components directly in a** `ViewStack`, **a type coercion error is generated at runtime when the framework tries to cast the object as** `Container`.

To solve this, nest the Spark component inside a new component named `NavigatorContent`. **This container implements a new interface named** `INavigatorContent`, **making it compatible with the MX navigator containers. To use Spark containers in a** `ViewStack` **(or in its related navigator containers,** `TabNavigator` **and** `Accordion`), **nest them in an instance of** `NavigatorContent`. ■

Each container nested within a navigator container, whether implemented as a `ViewStack`, `TabNavigator`, or `Accordion`, should have a `label` property. The `label` is an arbitrary `String` that's used in many circumstances to describe the container's purpose to the user. You don't always need the `label` property, but if you bind the stack to a navigator container that generates interactive components such as `Buttons`, or if you use the `TabNavigator` or `Accordion` containers, the value of each nested container's `label` is displayed on the interactive component that navigates to that child container.

This code creates a `ViewStack` with five views or layers:

```
<mx:ViewStack id="views">
  <mx:HBox/>
  <mx:VBox/>
  <mx:Canvas/>
  <s:NavigatorContent>
    <s:Panel/>
  <s:/NavigatorContent>
  <views:MyCustomComponent/>
</mx:ViewStack>
```

The first three views are instances of MX containers, the fourth is a Spark `Panel` wrapped in `NavigatorContent`, and the last is an instance of a custom component that's extended from a compatible container component.

Using custom components in a navigator container

The views nested within a navigator container can be defined as custom components in MXML. As described previously, a custom component that's nested in a navigator container must extend either the Spark `NavigatorContent` component or one of the MX container classes. These include `HBox`, `VBox`, `Canvas`, `Panel`, `Form`, and others.

The custom component in Listing 16.1 displays a `Label` control and a `DataGrid` wrapped in a `NavigatorContent` container.

LISTING 16.1

A custom component suitable for use in a navigator container

```xml
<?xml version="1.0" encoding="utf-8"?>
<s:NavigatorContent xmlns:fx="http://ns.adobe.com/mxml/2009"
  xmlns:s="library://ns.adobe.com/flex/spark"
  xmlns:mx="library://ns.adobe.com/flex/mx"
  width="400" height="300">
  <s:layout>
    <s:VerticalLayout horizontalAlign="center"/>
  </s:layout>
  <s:Label text="Author List" styleName="logo"/>
  <mx:DataGrid>
    <mx:columns>
      <mx:DataGridColumn dataField="title" headerText="First Name"/>
      <mx:DataGridColumn dataField="price" headerText="Last Name"/>
    </mx:columns>
  </mx:DataGrid>
</s:NavigatorContent>
```

On the Web

The code in Listing 16.1 is available in the Web site files as `views/Authors.mxml` in the `chapter16` project. View components named `Books.mxml` and `ShoppingCart.mxml` are also used in these examples. ■

Creating a ViewStack in Design mode

You can use Flash Builder's Design mode to visually create a `ViewStack` and its nested views. As described previously, each of the nested views must be a container, as an instance of either a Flex framework container class or a custom component that includes the `Container` class in its inheritance hierarchy.

Note

Flash Builder's Design mode refers to the layers of a `ViewStack` as panes, and the documentation sometimes refers to them as panels. These terms refer to the nested view containers within the `ViewStack`. ■

On the Web

The steps in this section assume that you've downloaded the files from the Web site and imported the `chapter16` project. ■

Follow these steps to create a `ViewStack` in Design mode:

1. **Open `BookStore.mxml` from the `chapter16` project.** Notice that the application already has an instance of a custom `Header` component and a few layout settings:

```xml
<?xml version="1.0" encoding="utf-8"?>
<s:Application xmlns:fx="http://ns.adobe.com/mxml/2009"
  xmlns:s="library://ns.adobe.com/flex/spark"
  xmlns:mx="library://ns.adobe.com/flex/mx"
  xmlns:views="views.*">
  <s:layout>
    <s:VerticalLayout horizontalAlign="left"
      paddingTop="20" paddingLeft="20"/>
  </s:layout>
  <fx:Style source="assets/styles.css"/>
  <views:Header/>
</s:Application>
```

2. **Run the application.** As shown in Figure 16.1, you should see that the `Header` component displays an image, some text, and a background image.

3. **Return to Flash Builder, and switch to Design mode.**

The starting application with a custom `Header` component

4. **Look in the Components view's Navigators section, and drag a** ViewStack **into the application below the header.** As shown in Figure 16.2, the ViewStack is represented visually by a rectangular outlined area and a toolbar with + and – buttons to add and remove views, and < and > buttons to navigate from one view to the next.

A starting ViewStack

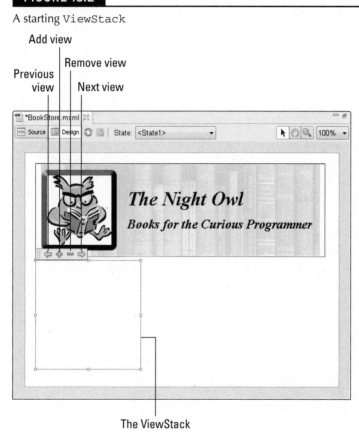

The ViewStack

5. **Click the + button to add a new view to the** ViewStack. As shown in Figure 16.3, the Insert Pane dialog box prompts you to select a component to instantiate as a layer of the ViewStack. The list of available components includes all containers from the Flex framework and all the application's custom components that are eligible for use in the context of a navigator container.

6. **Set the** Label **of the new pane as Catalog.**

7. Select Books from the list of available containers.

8. Click OK to add the new pane to the ViewStack.

9. Repeat Steps 5 through 8, and add an instance of the Authors container with a label of Authors.

The Insert Pane dialog box

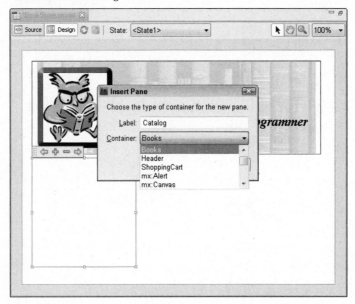

10. Repeat Steps 5 through 8 again, and add an instance of the ShoppingCart container with a label of Shopping Cart.

11. Click the left arrow button three times to return to the first layer of the ViewStack. It should be blank.

12. Click the – button to remove the first layer, leaving only the three you added.

13. **Run the application.** When the application appears, it should display the Books container, because it was the first layer declared within the ViewStack.

Note

The application displays only one layer at this point, because you haven't added any interactive components to control navigation. ∎

14. Return to Flash Builder, and switch to Source mode.

The generated ViewStack code looks like this:

```
<mx:ViewStack id="viewstack1" width="200" height="200">
  <views:Books label="Catalog" width="100%" height="100%">
  </views:Books>
  <views:Authors label="Authors" width="100%" height="100%">
  </views:Authors>
  <views:ShoppingCart label="Shopping Cart" width="100%"
    height="100%">
  </views:ShoppingCart>
</mx:ViewStack>
```

The Design mode tool for generating `ViewStack` code makes a great start but has these issues:

- **The `ViewStack` is always generated with an initial `height` and `width` of 200 pixels each.** You can change the `ViewStack` dimensions in Design mode by dragging the `ViewStack` handles, or in the Properties view. And of course, you can always change or remove the dimensions completely in Source mode.

- **Design mode has no mechanism for visually reordering a `ViewStack` container's layers.** If you want to change the order of the views, you must do so in Source mode by changing the order of the child containers.

- **All containers' MXML declarations are generated with tag sets, such as:**

  ```
  <views:Books label="Catalog" width="100%" height="100%">
  </views:Books>
  ```

  Particularly when using custom components, the MXML code would be more efficient with empty tag syntax:

  ```
  <views:Books label="Catalog" width="100%" height="100%"/>
  ```

  This is purely a matter of code aesthetics though, and it doesn't have any negative effect on application functionality or performance.

After generating a `ViewStack` in Design mode, revise the generated code as needed in Source mode.

Working with navigator containers in ActionScript

When a navigator container is initially constructed and displayed, it displays the currently active view (by default, the first view declared in the stack). You can change the active view at runtime with ActionScript commands that reference one of these `ViewStack` properties:

- `selectedIndex:int`. The numeric index position of the active container within the stack.
- `selectedChild:Container`. The object reference of the active container within the stack.

Using selectedIndex

The `selectedIndex` property returns the index position of the currently active container, as determined by the order of the `ViewStack` container's display list. When declaring a `ViewStack` in MXML, the display list order and the order of MXML declaration are the same.

As with all index operations in ActionScript, indexing starts at 0. So the first container with the view stack is at position 0, the second at position 1, and so on.

To change the currently selected view by index, set the stack's `selectedIndex` property to the numeric index of the container you want to activate. This code makes the `viewstack1` container's second layer visible and active:

```
<s:Button label="Authors" click="viewstack1.selectedIndex=1"/>
```

Because indexing always begins at 0, this `Button` would enable the user to navigate to the first layer of a stack:

```
<s:Button label="First Layer" click="viewstack1.selectedIndex=0"/>
```

Using numChildren

The `numChildren` property returns the total number of layers in the stack as an `int` value. Taking into account the 0-based indexing offset, clicking this `Button` would result in navigating to the last layer of a stack:

```
<s:Button label="Last Layer"
  click="viewstack1.selectedIndex=viewstack1.numChildren-1"/>
```

Navigating forward and backward through view stack layers

You can navigate forward and backward through layers of a view stack by incrementing or decrementing the stack's `selectedIndex` property. This `Button` would enable the user to move to the previous layer of a stack:

```
<s:Button label="Authors" click="viewstack1.selectedIndex--"/>
```

Note

The `selectedIndex` property of a `ViewStack` can't be set to less than 0. If the `Button` control in the preceding code is clicked when the `ViewStack` container's `selectedIndex` is already set to 0, the command is ignored and there is no runtime error. ∎

You also can navigate forward through a stack, but if you set the `selectedIndex` to a value greater than the stack's highest available index, an "array out of bounds" error results. You can prevent this by wrapping the code to navigate forward in a conditional clause that checks to be sure that the last container in the stack isn't already active:

```
private function navForward():void
{
  if (viewstack1.selectedIndex != viewstack1.numChildren-1)
  {
    viewstack1.selectedIndex++;
  }
}
```

Alternatively, you can set the `Button` control's `enabled` property to `false` when `selectedIndex` indicates that a forward or backward navigation either wouldn't work or would result in a runtime error. Binding expressions that evaluate `selectedIndex` and return a `Boolean` value to the `enabled` property can handle this task dynamically.

The following Button control that navigates forward is enabled only when the ViewStack container's selectedIndex isn't already set to the highest index:

```
<s:Button label="Next &gt;&gt;"
  click="viewstack1.selectedIndex++"
  enabled="{viewstack1.selectedIndex != viewstack1.numChildren-1}"/>
```

Managing binding issues

In the preceding code example, the binding expression used in the enabled property might be executed upon application startup before the ViewStack container's numChidren property can be correctly evaluated. If this happens, you might see that the Button controls are incorrectly enabled and disabled upon application startup.

To fix this sort of timing issue, call the ViewStack container's executeBindings() method with a recursive argument of true to reevaluate all its dependent binding expressions. If you call this method upon the ViewStack container's creationComplete event, it evaluates any bound property values such as numChildren again and the Button control's enabled states will be correctly calculated:

```
<mx:ViewStack id="viewstack1" width="400" height="200"
    creationComplete="executeBindings(true)">
  <views:Books label="Catalog" width="100%" height="100%"/>
  <views:Authors label="Authors" width="100%" height="100%"/>
  <views:ShoppingCart label="Shopping Cart" width="100%"
    height="100%"/>
</mx:ViewStack>
```

The application in Listing 16.2 implements forward and backward navigation with a ViewStack and Button controls. Each Button control has its enabled property set through a binding expression, and the ViewStack re-executes its bindings upon its creationComplete event.

LISTING 16.2

An application using forward and backward navigation

```
<?xml version="1.0" encoding="utf-8"?>
<s:Application xmlns:fx="http://ns.adobe.com/mxml/2009"
  xmlns:s="library://ns.adobe.com/flex/spark"
  xmlns:mx="library://ns.adobe.com/flex/mx"
  xmlns:views="views.*">
  <s:layout>
    <s:VerticalLayout horizontalAlign="left"
      paddingTop="20" paddingLeft="20"/>
  </s:layout>
  <fx:Style source="assets/styles.css"/>
  <views:Header/>
  <s:HGroup>
```

continued

LISTING 16.2 (continued)

```
  <s:Button label="&lt;&lt; Previous"
    click="viewstack1.selectedIndex--"
    enabled="{viewstack1.selectedIndex != 0}"/>
  <s:Button label="Next &gt;&gt;"
    click="viewstack1.selectedIndex++"
    enabled="{viewstack1.selectedIndex !=
    viewstack1.numChildren-1}"/>
</s:HGroup>
<mx:ViewStack id="viewstack1" width="400" height="200"
  creationComplete="executeBindings(true)">
  <views:Books label="Catalog" width="100%" height="100%"/>
  <views:Authors label="Authors" width="100%" height="100%"/>
  <views:ShoppingCart label="Shopping Cart" width="100%" height="100%"/>
</mx:ViewStack>
</s:Application>
```

On the Web

The code in Listing 16.2 is available in the Web site files as `BookStoreIndexNavigation.mxml` in the `chapter16` project. ∎

Figure 16.4 shows the resulting application, with Previous and Next buttons to handle backward and forward navigation.

Using selectedChild

The `ViewStack` container's `selectedChild` property accesses the stack's currently visible view by its object reference. To use this property, each of the stack's nested containers should be assigned a unique `id`:

```
<mx:ViewStack id="viewstack1">
  <views:Books id="booksView"/>
  <views:Authors id="authorsView"/>
  <views:ShoppingCart id="cartView"/>
</mx:ViewStack>
```

To select an active view by the container's unique `id`, set the `ViewStack` container's `selectedChild`:

```
<s:Button label="Shoppping Cart"
  click="viewstack1.selectedChild=cartView"/>
```

Note

Notice that there are no quotes around the `cartView` container's `id` when it's assigned in this way. You're accessing the `id` as a variable or component instance `id`, not a `String` value. ∎

FIGURE 16.4

An application with forward and backward navigation

Note

When navigating with `selectedChild` set to a container's unique `id`, because your navigation will be hard-coded, you typically don't need to assign a `label` property to each container. The `label` property becomes useful when dynamically generating user interface controls for navigation. ∎

The application in Listing 16.3 implements navigation using `Button` controls for each of the nested containers in a `ViewStack`. Each `Button` control explicitly navigates to its container by the container's unique `id`.

LISTING 16.3

An application using explicit navigation by unique id

```
<?xml version="1.0" encoding="utf-8"?>
<s:Application xmlns:fx="http://ns.adobe.com/mxml/2009"
  xmlns:s="library://ns.adobe.com/flex/spark"
  xmlns:mx="library://ns.adobe.com/flex/mx"
  xmlns:views="views.*">
  <s:layout>
```

continued

LISTING 16.3   *(continued)*

```
   <s:VerticalLayout horizontalAlign="left"
      paddingTop="20" paddingLeft="20"/>
   </s:layout>
   <fx:Style source="assets/styles.css"/>
   <views:Header/>
   <s:HGroup>
     <s:Button label="Catalog"
       click="viewstack1.selectedChild=booksView"/>
     <s:Button label="Authors"
       click="viewstack1.selectedChild=authorsView"/>
     <s:Button label="Shopping Cart"
       click="viewstack1.selectedChild=cartView"/>
   </s:HGroup>
   <mx:ViewStack id="viewstack1" width="400" height="200">
     <views:Books id="booksView" width="100%" height="100%"/>
     <views:Authors id="authorsView" width="100%" height="100%"/>
     <views:ShoppingCart id="cartView" width="100%" height="100%"/>
   </mx:ViewStack>
 </s:Application>
```

On the Web

The code in Listing 16.3 is available in the Web site files as `BookStoreReferenceNavigation.mxml` **in the** `chapter16` **project.** ∎

Figure 16.5 shows the resulting application, with explicit `Button` controls to handle navigation to each nested container.

Managing creation policy

The `ViewStack`, `TabNavigator`, and `Accordion` containers support a property named `creationPolicy` that manages the manner in which their nested view containers are instantiated at runtime. These are possible values of `creationPolicy`:

- `auto` (the default)
- `all`
- `none`
- `queued`

When `creationPolicy` is set to the default of `auto`, only the initially active view is completely instantiated at first. The other view containers also are instantiated, but their child controls are left `null`. Any attempt to address these objects in ActionScript code while they're not yet instantiated results in a null error.

FIGURE 16.5

An application with explicit navigation by unique `id`

This behavior is known as *deferred instantiation* and is a strategy for optimizing client-side performance in Flash Player. In a navigator container that contains dozens of views or more, if the application has to instantiate all the content before the user can interact with anything, significant delays can occur. To prevent this issue, the default behavior makes content visible as early as possible.

You see the effect of deferred instantiation when you try to initialize some property of a nested component before the user decides to visit that content at runtime and get a runtime error. You can solve this by setting the navigator container's `creationPolicy` property to `all`, meaning that all the views are instantiated during the navigator container's instantiation. This strategy can work fine in a small- to medium-size application that doesn't have a large number of nested views, or if you need to interact with child objects of nested views prior to the user viewing them.

Alternatively, you can set `creationPolicy` to `none`, meaning that you don't want the nested components ever to be instantiated automatically, and then take complete control over the process by explicitly calling the nested container's `createComponentsFromDescriptors()` method when you see fit.

Note

The `Container` class implements such methods as `addChild()`, `addChildAt()`, and `removeChild()` that enable you to explicitly control the contents and order of a container's nested child objects at runtime. You can use these methods to control not just which objects have been instantiated, but which are currently nested children of a navigator container. ■

Tip

The `creationPolicy` property is also implemented in layout containers. Layout containers instantiate all their child objects at the same time by default. If you prefer to take control over the instantiation process, set the layout container's `creationPolicy` property to `none`, and then instantiate the child objects as necessary using with the container's `createComponentsFromDescriptors()` method. ∎

Finally, the effect of setting `creationPolicy` to `queued` means that you want to instantiate all objects automatically, but instead of creating all objects simultaneously (as with the setting of `all`), each nested view component's content is instantiated only after the prior component's instantiation has been completed.

Managing navigator container dimensions

By default, navigator containers size to the first visible child container. Any subsequent navigation results in bumping the child container up to the top left if it is smaller than the instantiated size, or the implementation of scrollbars if the container is larger.

You can set the height and width of a navigator container using absolute pixel dimensions, percentage dimensions, or dynamic sizing. You can use two common strategies for handling navigator container sizing:

- **Set the navigator container's dimensions to specific pixel or percentage dimensions, and then set the nested container sizes to 100 percent height and width.** Each of the nested view containers then resizes to fill the available space in the navigator container.

- **Set the nested containers to specific pixel dimensions, and set the navigator container's resizeToContent property to true.** The navigator container then resizes to accommodate each newly active view as the user navigates through the application.

Caution

Setting `resizeToContent` to `true` forces the navigator container to remeasure and redraw itself as the user navigates through the application. This can cause interesting and unintended visual effects, particularly when the navigator container has a visible border or background. ∎

Using Navigator Bar Containers

If you want a user to be able to navigate to any container within a `ViewStack`, you can use one of the navigator bar containers that are included with the Flex framework. The framework uses four navigator bar containers:

- `ButtonBar`. Generates one `Button` control for each nested container. There are both MX and Spark versions of `ButtonBar`. The Spark version implements toggle buttons, making the `ToggleButtonBar` component unnecessary.

- `LinkBar`. Generates one MX `LinkButton` control for each nested container.

- `TabBar`. Generates one `Tab` for each nested container.

- `ToggleButtonBar`. Generates one MX `Button` control for each nested container and shows the current selection through the `Button` control's `toggle` behavior.

Note

You won't find a `Tab` component or ActionScript class in the Flex documentation, but it's used internally as a style selector to manage a `TabBar`'s visual presentation. Because each `Tab` is an instance of this internal class, you can change certain styles such as the amount of padding within each `Tab`:

```
<fx:Style>
 @namespace mx "library://ns.adobe.com/flex/mx";
 mx|Tab {
     padding-left:10;
     padding-bottom:0;
     padding-top:0;
     padding-right:10;
}
</fx:Style> ■
```

Using a data collection as a dataProvider

Each of the navigator bar containers has a `dataProvider` property that you can set either to a collection of data or to a `ViewStack` by referencing its `id`. The MX navigator bar containers can accept an `Array` or `ArrayCollection`, while the Spark `ButtonBar` can accept an `ArrayList` or `ArrayCollection`, but not an `Array`.

When using a data collection as the navigator bar's `dataProvider`, the navigator bar generates one interactive component for each of the `dataProvider` object's data items.

The application in Listing 16.4 generates a Spark `ButtonBar` using a `dataProvider` set from an `ArrayList` of complex objects. Because the Array contains three data items, the user sees three `Button` objects.

LISTING 16.4

A LinkBar with items generated from an ArrayCollection

```
<?xml version="1.0" encoding="utf-8"?>
<s:Application xmlns:fx="http://ns.adobe.com/mxml/2009"
  xmlns:s="library://ns.adobe.com/flex/spark"
  xmlns:mx="library://ns.adobe.com/flex/mx">
  <fx:Script>
    <![CDATA[
      import spark.events.IndexChangeEvent;
      protected function buttonbar_changeHandler(
        event:IndexChangeEvent):void
```

continued

LISTING 16.4 *(continued)*

```
        {
            var buttonURL:String = buttonData.getItemAt(event.newIndex).url;
            var request:URLRequest = new URLRequest(buttonURL);
            navigateToURL(request);
        }
    ]]>
  </fx:Script>
  <fx:Declarations>
    <s:ArrayList id="buttonData">
      <fx:Object>
        <fx:label>Adobe</fx:label>
        <fx:url>http://www.adobe.com</fx:url>
      </fx:Object>
      <fx:Object>
        <fx:label>Google</fx:label>
        <fx:url>http://www.google.com</fx:url>
      </fx:Object>
      <fx:Object>
        <fx:label>Microsoft</fx:label>
        <fx:url>http://www.microsoft.com</fx:url>
      </fx:Object>
    </s:ArrayList>
  </fx:Declarations>
  <s:ButtonBar change="buttonbar_changeHandler(event)"
    dataProvider="{buttonData}"
    horizontalCenter="0" top="20"/>
</s:Application>
```

On the Web

The code in Listing 16.4 is available in the Web site files as `NavBarWithArrayData.mxml` in the `chapter16` project. ■

Note

In the preceding code, the `<fx:Object>` tags are declared separately and then bound to the `ButtonBar` object's `dataProvider`. ■

Note

The `label` and `url` property names are arbitrary and not predefined in the `Object` class, but the `fx` prefix is required because they're declared within the `<fx:Object>` tag set. The value of the `label` property is used in the labels of the navigator bar container's generated controls because the container's `labelField` property defaults to `label`. You can use any other named object property for this purpose by setting the `labelField` to the property you want to use. ■

Handling navigator bar events

When a navigator bar's `dataProvider` is set as a data collection, it doesn't automatically do anything when the user clicks one of its controls. Instead, you handle the navigator bar's `itemClick` event for MX controls, and the change event for the Spark `ButtonBar`, by executing some ActionScript code.

The `itemClick` event generates an event object typed as `mx.events.ItemClickEvent`. This object has an `item` property that references the underlying data of the interactive component that was clicked. Within an event handler function, the expression `event.item` returns the underlying data, and from that point you can reference the selected object's data properties.

The change event generates an event object typed as `spark.events.IndexChangeEvent`. The object has properties named `newIndex` and `oldIndex` that tell you which object has been selected by the user (based on its index position in the data collection) and which object was selected before the event.

The application in Listing 16.4 handles the `change` event of a Spark `ButtonBar` control and responds by navigating to the selected URL.

Using a ViewStack as a dataProvider

When you pass a `ViewStack` to a navigator bar as its `dataProvider`, the navigator bar generates one interactive control for each of the `ViewStack` container's nested views. Each nested container's `label` property is passed to each generated `Button`, `LinkButton`, or `Tab` for display. It also automatically causes its bound `ViewStack` to navigate to the related view when a control in the bar is clicked.

You set a `ViewStack` as a `dataProvider` with a binding expression:

```
<s:ButtonBar dataProvider="{viewstack1}"/>
```

The application in Listing 16.5 uses a `ToggleButtonBar` that generates one toggle button for each nested container of a `ViewStack`.

LISTING 16.5

An application using a navigator bar container

```
<?xml version="1.0" encoding="utf-8"?>
<s:Application xmlns:fx="http://ns.adobe.com/mxml/2009"
  xmlns:s="library://ns.adobe.com/flex/spark"
  xmlns:mx="library://ns.adobe.com/flex/mx"
  xmlns:views="views.*">
  <s:layout>
    <s:VerticalLayout horizontalAlign="left"
      paddingTop="20" paddingLeft="20"/>
```

continued

LISTING 16.5 *(continued)*

```
    </s:layout>
     <fx:Style source="assets/styles.css"/>
     <views:Header/>
     <s:ButtonBar dataProvider="{viewstack1}"/>
     <mx:ViewStack id="viewstack1" width="400" height="200">
       <views:Books label="Catalog" width="100%" height="100%"/>
       <views:Authors label="Authors" width="100%" height="100%"/>
       <views:ShoppingCart label="Shopping Cart" width="100%" height="100%"/>
     </mx:ViewStack>
   </s:Application>
```

On the Web

The code in Listing 16.5 is available in the Web site files as `BookStoreNavBar.mxml` **in the** `chapter16` **project.** ■

Figure 16.6 shows the resulting application, with generated toggle button controls to handle navigation to each nested container.

Note

The Spark `ButtonBar` **component's primary advantage over the MX navigation toolbars is that it supports custom skins using the new Spark skinning architecture. It also differs from the MX** `ButtonBar` **in that it toggles buttons automatically as navigation occurs, staying in sync with its bound ViewStack. In this behavior it's closest in functionality to the MX** `ToggleButtonBar`. ■

Managing navigator bar presentation

Each of the MX navigator bar containers has a `direction` property that can be used to lay out the container vertically. For example, this `LinkBar` stacks its generated `LinkButton` controls vertically:

```
<mx:LinkBar dataProvider="{viewstack1}" direction="vertical"/>
```

The application in Listing 16.6 uses a vertical `LinkBar` wrapped in an `HBox` container. Binding expressions are used to match the component's width and height properties as needed.

LISTING 16.6

An application using a vertical navigator bar container

```
<?xml version="1.0" encoding="utf-8"?>
<s:Application xmlns:fx="http://ns.adobe.com/mxml/2009"
  xmlns:s="library://ns.adobe.com/flex/spark"
```

```
  xmlns:mx="library://ns.adobe.com/flex/mx"
  xmlns:views="views.*">
  <s:layout>
    <s:VerticalLayout horizontalAlign="left"
      paddingTop="20" paddingLeft="20"/>
  </s:layout>
  <fx:Style source="assets/styles.css"/>
  <views:Header id="header"/>
  <s:HGroup width="{header.width}">
    <mx:LinkBar dataProvider="{viewstack1}"
      direction="vertical"
      backgroundColor="white" backgroundAlpha=".8"
      height="{viewstack1.height}"/>
    <mx:ViewStack id="viewstack1" width="100%" height="200">
      <views:Books label="Catalog" width="100%" height="100%"/>
      <views:Authors label="Authors" width="100%" height="100%"/>
      <views:ShoppingCart label="Shopping Cart" width="100%" height="100%"/>
    </mx:ViewStack>
  </s:HGroup>
</s:Application>
```

FIGURE 16.6

An application using a navigator bar container

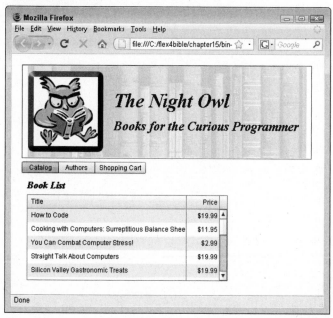

On the Web

The code in Listing 16.6 is available in the Web site files as `BookStoreVerticalNav.mxml` **in the** `chapter16` **project.** ■

Figure 16.7 shows the resulting application, with a vertical `LinkBar` displaying stacked `LinkButton` controls.

An application using a vertical navigator bar container

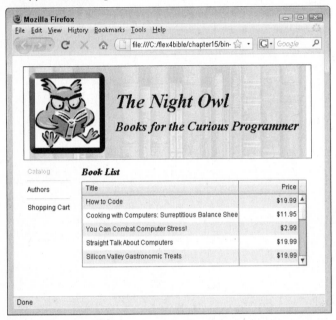

The Spark `ButtonBar` component's `direction` property takes values of `ltr` and `rtl`, which controls the order of button creation (left-to-right or right-to-left). Its `layout` property is like the same property as implemented in the Spark `Application`, `Panel` and `List` components: it accepts an instance of one of the layout classes such as `VerticalLayout`, `HorizontalLayout`, or `TileLayout`.

The application in Listing 16.7 displays a Spark `ButtonBar` with its buttons stacked vertically.

An application using a vertical Spark ButtonBar component

```
<?xml version="1.0" encoding="utf-8"?>
<s:Application xmlns:fx="http://ns.adobe.com/mxml/2009"
```

```
xmlns:s="library://ns.adobe.com/flex/spark"
xmlns:mx="library://ns.adobe.com/flex/mx"
xmlns:views="views.*">
<s:layout>
  <s:VerticalLayout horizontalAlign="left"
    paddingTop="20" paddingLeft="20"/>
</s:layout>
<fx:Style source="assets/styles.css"/>
<views:Header id="header"/>
<s:HGroup width="{header.width}">
  <s:ButtonBar dataProvider="{viewstack1}"
    height="{viewstack1.height}">
    <s:layout>
      <s:VerticalLayout/>
    </s:layout>
  </s:ButtonBar>
  <mx:ViewStack id="viewstack1" width="100%" height="200">
    <views:Books label="Catalog" width="100%" height="100%"/>
    <views:Authors label="Authors" width="100%" height="100%"/>
    <views:ShoppingCart label="Shopping Cart" width="100%" height="100%"/>
  </mx:ViewStack>
</s:HGroup>
</s:Application>
```

On the Web

The code in Listing 16.7 is available in the Web site files as `BookStoreVerticalButtonBar.mxml` **in the** `chapter16` **project.** ■

Note

The Spark `ButtonBar` **is a skinnable component. Its default skin declares each button object as an instance of** `spark.components.ButtonBarButton`, **which extends the Spark** `ToggleButton` **component. You can change the appearance of the** `ButtonBar` **component and its child button objects by creating custom skins both for the navigator container and for its children.** ■

Using Menu Controls

Flex provides three menu controls that you can use to create styles of navigation interfaces. They include the MX `Menu`, `MenuBar`, and `PopupMenuButton` controls. Of these three controls, the `Menu` and `MenuBar` define their menus with a hierarchical data structure, represented as XML, and notify you of user selections with both an `itemClick` and `change` event.

The `PopupMenuButton` control differs from the other menu controls, in that it displays only a single-level menu and notifies you of a user selection with its `change` event. In this section I describe the details of using the `Menu` and `MenuBar` controls. The `PopupMenuButton` control is described in Chapter 17.

You can use the `Menu` and `MenuBar` controls, combined with event listeners and ActionScript event handler functions, to create a customized navigation interface.

Menu data providers

The data that determines the structure of a `Menu` or `MenuBar` is typically represented hierarchically and can be one of these types:

- A `String` containing valid XML text
- An `XMLNode`
- An `XMLList`
- Any object that implements `ICollectionView`
- An `Array`

Any other object passed as a menu data provider is automatically wrapped in an `Array` with the object as its first and only item.

The most common sort of data used to determine menu structure is an `XMLList`. You can declare an `XMLList` in the application with MXML code and nested XML markup:

```
<fx:Declarations>
  <mx:XMLList id="menuData">
    <menuitem label="Lists">
      <menuitem label="Catalog" view="catalogView"/>
      <menuitem label="Authors" view="authorsView"/>
    </menuitem>
    <menuitem label="Shopping">
      <menuitem label="Shopping Cart" view="cartView"/>
    </menuitem>
  </mx:XMLList>
</fx:Declarations>
```

Tip

As with all nonvisual objects, instances of `XML` and `XMLList` must be declared inside an `<fx:Declarations>` element in Flex 4 applications. ■

You can select any element and attribute names you like in the XML structure, but you should follow these recommendations when using a menu control with a `ViewStack`:

- **Each menu item should have a consistently named attribute to serve as the visible label for each menu node.** In the preceding example, this attribute is named `label`. Notice that all menu items at all levels of the hierarchy have this attribute.

- **Menu items that cause navigation should have an attribute whose value matches the unique `id` of a nested container in a `ViewStack`.** This can help you simplify the ActionScript code you write to handle the menu control's events.

To use the data in a menu control, pass the XMLList structure to the control as its dataProvider property in a binding expression. Also set the menu control's labelField to an E4X (ECMAScript for XML) expression that references the label attribute in each menu node:

```
<mx:MenuBar id="myMenuBar" dataProvider="{menuData}"
   labelField="@label"/>
```

Cross-Reference

Detailed information about retrieving XML and parsing it with E4X is available in Chapters 23 and 24. ■

Caution

If you forget to set the menu control's labelField to a consistently named attribute or property of the underlying data, the labels of the menu items sometimes present raw XML because the control doesn't have any instructions for parsing the data. ■

Handling menu events

When the user selects an item from either the Menu or MenuBar control, it dispatches an item Click event that generates an event object typed as mx.events.MenuEvent. This event object has an item property that references the underlying data that drove the creation of the selected menu item. Within an event handler function, the expression event.item references the data, and the E4X expression can be used to access the selected XML node's attributes. For example, the expression event.item.@view references the XML node's view attribute.

You can listen for the itemClick event with MXML or ActionScript. This MenuBar has an attribute-based itemClick event listener that passes the event object to a custom event handler function named menu_ClickHandler():

```
<mx:MenuBar id="myMenuBar" dataProvider="{menuData}"
   labelField="@label" itemClick="menu_ClickHandler(event)"/>
```

To listen for the same event with an ActionScript statement, use the addEventListener() method to listen for the event named by the constant MenuEvent.ITEM_CLICK:

```
navMenu.addEventListener(MenuEvent.ITEM_CLICK, menu_ClickHandler);
```

The custom event handler can then access the selected XML node's attributes and use them to execute navigation. This event handler function retrieves the node's view attribute with an array-style expression to change the active view container of the ViewStack:

```
import mx.events.MenuEvent;
private function menu_ClickHandler(event:MenuEvent):void
{
  viewstack1.selectedChild = this[event.item.@view];
}
```

Using the Menu control

The Menu control presents a set of cascading menus in response to a user event. Because this control is always presented in response to an event, and not as a static part of the application's visual interface, it can be instantiated only with ActionScript, not with MXML.

To create a Menu, instantiate it with the Menu class's static `createMenu()` method and pass two arguments:

- The Menu object's parent container
- The Menu object's data provider

Then present the Menu with its `show()` method, passing optional `xShow` and `yShow` coordinates as arguments. This event handler function responds to a mouse event by creating a Menu with a data provider named menuData and the application as the parent window, and then displays it at the mouse event's `stageX` and `stageY` coordinates.

The application in Listing 16.8 uses a Menu populated with an XMLList as its `dataProvider`.

LISTING 16.8

Using the Menu control

```
<?xml version="1.0" encoding="utf-8"?>
<s:Application xmlns:fx="http://ns.adobe.com/mxml/2009"
  xmlns:s="library://ns.adobe.com/flex/spark"
  xmlns:mx="library://ns.adobe.com/flex/mx">
  <s:layout>
    <s:VerticalLayout horizontalAlign="left"
      paddingTop="20" paddingLeft="20"/>
  </s:layout>
  <fx:Script>
    <![CDATA[
      import mx.events.MenuEvent;
      import mx.controls.Alert;
      import mx.controls.Menu;
      private function showMenu(event:MouseEvent):void
      {
        var navMenu:Menu = Menu.createMenu(this, menuData);
        navMenu.labelField="@label";
        navMenu.addEventListener(MenuEvent.ITEM_CLICK, menuClickHandler);
        navMenu.show(event.stageX,event.stageY);
      }
      private function menuClickHandler(event:MenuEvent):void
      {
        Alert.show("You selected " + event.item.@label, "Menu Selection");
      }
    ]]>
  </fx:Script>
```

```
<fx:Declarations>
  <fx:XMLList id="menuData">
    <menuitem label="Lists">
      <menuitem label="Catalog" view="catalogView"/>
      <menuitem label="Authors" view="authorsView"/>
    </menuitem>
    <menuitem label="Shopping">
      <menuitem label="Shopping Cart" view="cartView"/>
    </menuitem>
  </fx:XMLList>
</fx:Declarations>
<s:Button label="Click for Menu" click="showMenu(event)"/>
</s:Application>
```

On the Web

The code in Listing 16.8 is available in the Web site files as `MenuDemo.mxml` **in the** `chapter16` **project.** ∎

Figure 16.8 shows the resulting application. The Menu pops up when the mouse button is released while over the Label control.

FIGURE 16.8

Using the Menu control

Using the MenuBar control

The MenuBar control presents a horizontal list of menu items with cascading pull-down sub-menus. It uses the same sort of data and generates the same events as the Menu control. Unlike the Menu, it's designed to be placed in a static position in the application and serve as a navigation or functional menu, so it's typically declared in MXML:

```
<mx:MenuBar id="myMenuBar" dataProvider="{menuData}"
  labelField="@label" itemClick="menuClickHandler(event)"/>
```

The application in Listing 16.9 uses a MenuBar for navigation in the sample bookstore application. The MenuBar is placed in the Application component's controlBarContent section, causing it to "dock" at the top of the application's interface.

LISTING 16.9

Using the MenuBar control

```
<?xml version="1.0" encoding="utf-8"?>
<s:Application xmlns:fx="http://ns.adobe.com/mxml/2009"
  xmlns:s="library://ns.adobe.com/flex/spark"
  xmlns:mx="library://ns.adobe.com/flex/mx"
  xmlns:views="views.*">
  <s:layout>
    <s:VerticalLayout horizontalAlign="left"
      paddingTop="20" paddingLeft="20"/>
  </s:layout>
  <fx:Style source="assets/styles.css"/>
  <fx:Script>
    <![CDATA[
      import mx.events.MenuEvent;
      private function menuClickHandler(event:MenuEvent):void
      {
        viewstack1.selectedChild = this[event.item.@view];
      }
    ]]>
  </fx:Script>
  <fx:Declarations>
    <fx:XMLList id="menuData">
      <menuitem label="Lists">
        <menuitem label="Catalog" view="catalogView"/>
        <menuitem label="Authors" view="authorsView"/>
      </menuitem>
      <menuitem label="Shopping">
        <menuitem label="Shopping Cart" view="cartView"/>
      </menuitem>
    </fx:XMLList>
  </fx:Declarations>
  <s:controlBarContent>
    <mx:MenuBar id="myMenuBar"
      dataProvider="{menuData}"
      labelField="@label" itemClick="menuClickHandler(event)"/>
  </s:controlBarContent>
  <views:Header/>
  <mx:ViewStack id="viewstack1" width="400" height="200">
    <views:Books id="catalogView" label="Catalog"
      width="100%" height="100%"/>
    <views:Authors id="authorsView" label="Authors"
      width="100%" height="100%"/>
```

```
      <views:ShoppingCart id="cartView" label="Shopping Cart"
        width="100%" height="100%"/>
    </mx:ViewStack>
  </s:Application>
```

On the Web

The code in Listing 16.9 is available in the Web site files as `BookStoreMenuBar.mxml` in the `chapter16` project. ∎

Figure 16.9 shows the resulting application, with the `MenuBar` placed in the application's control bar area.

FIGURE 16.9

Using the MenuBar control

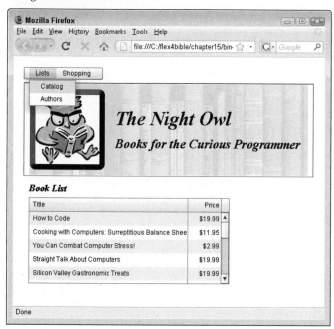

Using Other Navigator Containers

The `TabNavigator` and `Accordion` navigator containers provide the same form of navigation functionality as the `ViewStack` in that they nest a stack of containers and display only one of the containers at a time. Unlike the `ViewStack`, though, the `TabNavigator` and `Accordion` have their own user interface to enable the user to navigate between views.

The TabNavigator container

The MX TabNavigator container provides a set of tabs, similar in appearance to a TabBar, but more visually integrated with the rest of the container. Unlike the ViewStack, which is invisible by default, the TabNavigator has a default border.

The MXML syntax of the TabNavigator is identical to that of the ViewStack: You wrap its nested containers within the appropriate MXML tag set. As with the ViewStack, you can wrap only those components within a TabNavigator that include the Container class in their inheritance hierarchy:

```
<mx:TabNavigator id="views">
  <mx:HBox/>
  <mx:VBox/>
  <mx:Canvas/>
  <s:NavigatorContent/>
  <views:MyCustomComponent/>
</mx:TabNavigator >
```

Caution

Just like the MX ViewStack container, the MX TabNavigator container's direct child objects must be instances of MX containers such as HBox, VBox, and Canvas, or be an instance of the Spark NavigatorContent component. If you want to host a Spark container in a TabNavigator, wrap it inside a NavigatorContent. ∎

For example, in the bookstore application that's been used previously in this chapter, to use a TabNavigator instead of a ViewStack, you'd follow these steps:

1. Change the MXML tag set wrapping the custom components from <mx:ViewStack> to <mx:TabNavigator>.

2. Delete any navigator bar control or custom navigator controls that you might have been using to provide a navigation interface.

Listing 16.10 shows the application using a TabNavigator instead of a ViewStack.

```
LISTING 16.10
```

An application using a TabNavigator

```xml
<?xml version="1.0" encoding="utf-8"?>
<s:Application xmlns:fx="http://ns.adobe.com/mxml/2009"
  xmlns:s="library://ns.adobe.com/flex/spark"
  xmlns:mx="library://ns.adobe.com/flex/mx"
  xmlns:views="views.*">
  <s:layout>
    <s:VerticalLayout horizontalAlign="left"
      paddingTop="20" paddingLeft="20"/>
  </s:layout>
```

```
<fx:Style source="assets/styles.css"/>
<views:Header/>
<mx:TabNavigator id="viewstack1" width="400" height="300">
  <views:Books label="Catalog" width="100%" height="100%"/>
  <views:Authors label="Authors" width="100%" height="100%"/>
  <views:ShoppingCart label="Shopping Cart" width="100%" height="100%"/>
</mx:TabNavigator>
</s:Application>
```

On the Web

The code in Listing 16.10 is available in the Web site files as `BookStoreTabNav.mxml` **in the** `chapter16` **project.** ∎

Figure 16.10 shows the resulting application, with a `TabNavigator` providing the navigation interface. Notice that the tabs are visually integrated with the container that wraps the application content.

FIGURE 16.10

An application using a `TabNavigator`

The Accordion container

The `Accordion` navigator container provides navigation through a set of *headers* that slide vertically to expose or hide nested views as needed. The `openDuration` property determines how long it takes to change from one panel to the next. You set this value in milliseconds; for example, setting `openDuration` to 500 means it takes one-half second to move from one panel to the next.

New Feature

In Flex 3, the `openDuration` property was set by default to 500. In the Flex 4 SDK, it's set to 0 by default, so you see an abrupt switch between panels instead of a sliding animation. ∎

Web Resource

The `Accordion` container slides only vertically, not horizontally. Doug McCune has created and shared a horizontal `Accordion` that you can download from `http://dougmccune.com/blog/2007/01/27/horizontal-accordion-component-for-flex.` ∎

Caution

Just like the MX `ViewStack` container, the MX `Accordion` container's direct child objects must be instances of MX containers such as `HBox`, `VBox`, and `Canvas` or the Spark `NavigatorContent` component. ∎

The MXML syntax of the `Accordion` is identical to that of the `ViewStack`: You wrap its nested containers within the appropriate MXML tag set. As with the `ViewStack` and `TabNavigator`, you can wrap only those components within an `Accordion` that include the `Container` class in their inheritance hierarchy:

```
<mx:Accordion id="views" openDuration="500">
  <mx:HBox/>
  <mx:VBox/>
  <mx:Canvas/>
  <s:NavigatorContent/>
  <views:MyCustomComponent/>
</mx:Accordion >
```

For example, in the bookstore application that's been used previously as an example in this chapter, to use an `Accordion` instead of a `ViewStack`, you'd follow these steps:

1. Change the MXML tag set wrapping the custom components from `<mx:ViewStack>` to `<mx:Accordion>`.

2. Delete any navigator bar control or custom navigator controls that you might have been using to provide a navigation interface.

Listing 16.11 shows the application using an `Accordion` instead of a `ViewStack`.

LISTING 16.11

An application using an Accordion

```xml
<?xml version="1.0" encoding="utf-8"?>
<s:Application xmlns:fx="http://ns.adobe.com/mxml/2009"
  xmlns:s="library://ns.adobe.com/flex/spark"
  xmlns:mx="library://ns.adobe.com/flex/mx"
  xmlns:views="views.*">
  <s:layout>
    <s:VerticalLayout horizontalAlign="left"
      paddingTop="20" paddingLeft="20"/>
  </s:layout>
  <fx:Style source="assets/styles.css"/>
  <views:Header/>
  <mx:Accordion id="viewstack1" width="400" height="300"
    openDuration="500">
    <views:Books label="Catalog" width="100%" height="100%"/>
    <views:Authors label="Authors" width="100%" height="100%"/>
    <views:ShoppingCart label="Shopping Cart" width="100%" height="100%"/>
  </mx:Accordion>
</s:Application>
```

On the Web

The code in Listing 16.11 is available in the Web site files as `BookStoreAccordion.mxml` in the `chapter16` project. ∎

Figure 16.11 shows the resulting application, with an `Accordion` providing the navigation interface. Notice that the tabs are visually integrated with the container that wraps the application content.

TabNavigator and Accordion keyboard shortcuts

The `TabNavigator` and `Accordion` containers support the following set of keyboard shortcuts that enable the user to navigate with key presses instead of mouse gestures:

- **Down Arrow** and **Right Arrow.** Selects the next tab or header, wrapping from last to first, but doesn't change the active view. Pressing Enter or the spacebar then triggers navigation.

- **End.** Navigates to last view.

- **Home.** Navigates to first view.

- **Page Down.** Navigates to the next view, wrapping from last to first.

- **Page Up.** Navigates to the previous view, wrapping from first to last.

- **Up Arrow** and **Left Arrow.** Selects the previous tab or header, wrapping from first to last, but doesn't change the active view. Pressing Enter or the spacebar then triggers navigation.

FIGURE 16.11

An application using an Accordion

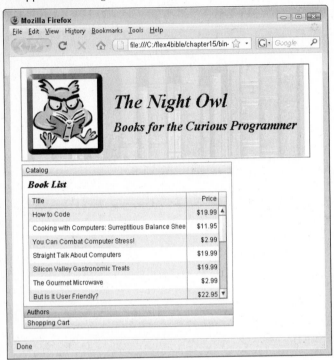

Summary

In this chapter, I described techniques for creating navigation interfaces in Flex applications. You learned the following:

- Classic Web applications handle navigation by requesting and loading individual Web pages into the browser one at a time.

- Flex applications contain all their views in the compiled application.

- The ViewStack container nests multiple view containers and displays only one at a time.

- You can manage navigation with ActionScript commands or with a navigator bar container.

- The navigator bar containers automate navigation when bound to a ViewStack.

- The menu controls can be used with event listeners and ActionScript to create a navigation interface.

- The TabNavigator and Accordion containers combine ViewStack functionality with their own navigation interfaces.

Working with Pop-up Windows

In applications that are built for windows-style operating systems, such as Microsoft Windows, Mac OS X, and the various windowing interfaces on Linux and other operating systems, pop-up windows are commonly used to get the user's attention, provide information, and collect data. Not all Flex applications have or require pop-up windows, but they're a common interface that users of these operating systems easily recognize and know how to use.

Flex applications are able to present pop-up windows in a variety of forms. Whether you want to display a simple information message or create a more customized user experience, you have these options:

- **The `Alert` class.** This class creates a simple pop-up dialog box displaying simple `String` values. You can also use the `Alert` class to enable the user to confirm or cancel an operation before it's executed, and it can include a custom graphical icon.

- **The `PopUpMenuButton` control.** This control displays a two-part `Button` control that displays a single-level pop-up menu when clicked.

- **The `PopUpButton` control.** This control combines a `Button` with any other visual component that you want to display when clicked.

- **Custom pop-up windows.** These windows can be created with the `TitleWindow` container and presented and managed with the `PopUpManager` class.

In this chapter, I describe each option and provide examples of how you can use these classes and controls.

On the Web

To use the sample code for this chapter, import the `chapter17.zip` **Flex project archive from the Web site files into your Flash Builder workspace.** ■

IN THIS CHAPTER

Understanding pop-up windows

Using the `Alert` **class**

Using the `PopUpMenuButton` **control**

Using the `PopUpButton` **control**

Creating and displaying custom pop-up windows

Using the Alert Class

The `mx.controls.Alert` class can present dialog boxes as pop-up windows that either present simple informational messages or enable the user to accept or decline an operation. In addition, the pop-up windows generated by the `Alert` class can include a custom graphical icon in their presentation.

The `Alert` class displays a pop-up dialog box in response to a call to the class's static `show()` method. The syntax of the method is:

```
show(text:String = "", title:String = "",
  flags:uint = 0x4, parent:Sprite = null,
  closeHandler:Function = null,
  iconClass:Class = null, defaultButtonFlag:uint = 0x4):Alert
```

Note

All the `show()` method's arguments are marked as optional, but you almost always pass in the first text argument (the string you want to display in the body of the pop-up window). ∎

Note

Before calling the `Alert` class's methods, it must be imported. You can import the `Alert` class with this explicit import statement:

```
import mx.controls.Alert;
```

You also can import the class with a wildcard statement that includes all classes in the `mx.controls` package:

```
import mx.controls.*;
```
∎

Presenting pop-up windows with Alert.show()

The most common use of the `Alert` class is to present a simple dialog box with up to two text messages. To present this sort of dialog box, call the class's `show()` method and pass in two `String` arguments:

```
Alert.show("This is a simple informational message", "Alert Title");
```

The first `String` argument passed into `Alert.show()` appears in the body of the dialog box, and the second `String` appears as the dialog box title.

Figure 17.1 shows a simple `Alert` pop-up dialog box with the two text messages.

Controlling Alert window modality

A pop-up window that's *modal* blocks the user from interacting with the rest of the application as long as the dialog box appears on the screen. In Flex, some pop-up windows are modal and others aren't.

When you present a pop-up window with the `Alert` class, it's modal by default, so the user has to click a button or otherwise close the window before continuing his work with the rest of the application.

FIGURE 17.1

A simple `Alert` pop-up dialog box

Modal pop-up windows in Flex have a special feature that lets the user know the application isn't currently available as long as the pop-up window is visible. When the pop-up window appears on the screen, the rest of the application is blurred so that its appearance clearly indicates to the user that he can't use it until he takes some action. The visual result, where the dialog box is presented in clear resolution and the remainder of the application is blurry, is a visual indicator that the user must take some action to continue.

You can make the `Alert` class present a non-modal window by passing the `Alert.NONMODAL` constant into the `show()` method as a *flag*. The `Alert` class has other constants designed for use as flags that are used to determine which buttons are displayed in the pop-up window.

Flags are passed into the `show()` method as the third argument. This code creates a non-modal pop-up window:

```
Alert.show("This is a non-modal Alert window",
    "Non-modal Alert", Alert.NONMODAL);
```

Figure 17.2 shows three instances of the resulting non-modal pop-up window. This is possible because the user can click multiple times on the background application without closing the `Alert` window. Notice that the application in the background isn't blurry and can accept user focus.

Tip

You also can present a non-modal pop-up window with a custom container based on `TitleWindow` and managed with `PopUpManager`. ■

FIGURE 17.2

A non-modal Alert dialog box

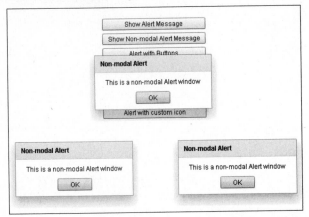

Managing Alert window buttons

You can present a pop-up window created by the Alert class with buttons labeled Yes, No, OK, and Cancel. You determine which buttons will be presented with the show() method's flags argument. To include more than one flag, separate them with the bitwise OR operator (|) and wrap the entire expression in parentheses.

This call to Alert.show() presents a dialog box with Yes and No buttons, shown in Figure 17.3:

```
Alert.show("This is an Alert dialog box with custom buttons",
    "Alert with Buttons", (Alert.YES | Alert.NO));
```

Non-modal dialog boxes with multiple buttons

If you want to present an Alert dialog box with multiple buttons and make it non-modal, include the Alert.NONMODAL constant in the flags argument:

```
Alert.show(
    "This is a non-modal Alert dialog box with custom buttons",
    "Non-modal Alert with Buttons",
    (Alert.YES | Alert.NO | Alert.NONMODAL));
```

Setting button labels

The labels of the various buttons are determined by these static properties of the Alert class:

- yesLabel. The label on the Yes button.
- noLabel. The label on the No button.
- okLabel. The label on the OK button.
- cancelLabel. The label on the Cancel button.

FIGURE 17.3

An Alert pop-up dialog box with multiple buttons

These properties should be set prior to calling the `Alert.show()` method. In addition, because buttons in the `Alert` dialog box don't automatically resize themselves based on their labels, you may need to explicitly set the `Alert.buttonWidth` property to specific width in terms of pixels:

```
private function alertWithButtonLabels():void
{
  Alert.yesLabel = "Fer sure!!!";
  Alert.noLabel = "NO WAY!!";
  Alert.buttonWidth = 100;
  Alert.show("This is an Alert dialog box with custom button labels",
    "Alert with Button Labels", (Alert.YES | Alert.NO));
}
```

Figure 17.4 shows an Alert dialog box with custom button labels.

FIGURE 17.4

An Alert dialog box with custom button labels

Setting a default button

When an `Alert` pop-up window has multiple buttons, the first button is the default. If the user presses Enter or Return without any other window interactions, it's the equivalent of clicking that button. To change the default button, pass the selected button's flag constant in the `show()`

method's seventh argument. Because you have to pass in all other arguments, just pass `null` in the arguments you aren't using:

```
Alert.show("This Alert dialog box's default button is Cancel",
  "Alert with default Button",
  (Alert.OK | Alert.CANCEL),
  null, null, null,
  Alert.CANCEL);
```

The user can click other buttons or press Tab to move focus from one button to another, but if he presses Enter or Return immediately upon the pop-up dialog box's appearance, the `close` event handler indicates that the default button was clicked.

Handling Alert window events

When you add multiple buttons to an `Alert` dialog box, you usually want to react in some way to whichever button the user clicks. When the user clicks any button to close the dialog box, an event object typed as `mx.events.CloseEvent` is generated. To find out which button was clicked, create a custom event handler function that accepts this event object as its only argument and returns `void`. Within the event handler function, the event object's `detail` property references the flag constant representing that button.

```
private function alertCloseHandler(event:CloseEvent):void
{
  if (event.detail == Alert.OK)
  {
    Alert.show("You clicked " + Alert.okLabel,
      "Close Event Handler");
  }
  else
  {
    Alert.show("You clicked " + Alert.cancelLabel,
      "Close Event Handler");
  }
}
```

Tip

You may want to use the `close` event handler function even if your pop-up window only has a single button. For example, you can use it to store a reminder that the user has been warned about a particular condition so you don't have to show the pop-up window again. ■

You designate the event handler function by passing the function name as the `show()` method's fifth argument:

```
Alert.show("An Alert dialog box with close event handler",
  "Alert Event Handler", (Alert.OK | Alert.CANCEL),
  null, alertCloseHandler);
```

When the user clicks any of the pop-up dialog box's buttons, the `close` event is handled by the custom event handler and you have an opportunity to execute ActionScript code.

In the resulting application, shown in Figure 17.5, the user is informed as to which button was clicked.

The response to handling the `Alert` class `close` event

Using a custom graphical icon

You can display a graphical icon in the body of the `Alert` pop-up window with the `iconClass` argument. Graphical icons must be embedded in the application, so you first declare the graphic with the `[Embed]` metadata tag and assign it a `Class` variable name:

```
[Embed(source="assets/questionicon.png")]
private var questionIcon:Class;
```

In the call to `Alert.show()`, pass the `Class` variable representing the graphic as the sixth argument:

```
Alert.show("An Alert dialog box with custom icon",
    "Alert Event Handler", 0, null, null,
    questionIcon);
```

Figure 17.6 shows the `Alert` dialog box with the custom icon.

An Alert dialog box with a custom icon graphic

Tip

Graphics designed for use as icons in the `Alert` pop-up window should be small and their backgrounds either should be transparent (a reason to use GIF, PNG, or SWF files) or should match the `contentBackground Color` style of the window. ∎

Note

The graphic used in this example was created in Adobe Fireworks, but you can use any graphics application you're familiar with to create the required assets. ∎

The application in Listing 17.1 contains demo code for all the preceding uses of the `Alert. show()` method.

LISTING 17.1

Using the Alert.show() method

```
<?xml version="1.0" encoding="utf-8"?>
<s:Application xmlns:fx="http://ns.adobe.com/mxml/2009"
  xmlns:s="library://ns.adobe.com/flex/spark"
  xmlns:mx="library://ns.adobe.com/flex/mx">
  <s:layout>
    <s:VerticalLayout horizontalAlign="center" paddingTop="20"/>
  </s:layout>
  <fx:Script>
    <![CDATA[
      import mx.controls.Alert;
      import mx.events.CloseEvent;

      [Embed(source="assets/questionicon.png")]
      private var questionIcon:Class;

      private function simpleAlert():void
      {
        Alert.show("This is a simple informational message", "Alert Title");
      }
      private function nonModalAlert():void
      {
        Alert.show("This is a non-modal Alert window",
          "Non-modal Alert", Alert.NONMODAL);
      }
      private function alertWithButtons():void
      {
        Alert.show("This is an Alert dialog with multiple buttons",
          "Alert with Buttons",
          (Alert.YES | Alert.NO));
      }
      private function alertWithButtonLabels():void
      {
        Alert.yesLabel = "Fer sure!!!";
```

```
         Alert.noLabel = "NO WAY!!";
         Alert.buttonWidth = 100;
         Alert.show("This is an Alert dialog with custom button labels",
            "Alert with Button Labels",
            (Alert.YES | Alert.NO));
      }
      private function alertWithDefaultButton():void
      {
         Alert.show("This Alert dialog's default button is Cancel",
            "Alert with default Button", (Alert.OK | Alert.CANCEL),
            null, null, null, Alert.CANCEL);
      }
      private function alertWithCloseHandler():void
      {
         Alert.show("An Alert dialog with close event handler",
            "Alert Event Handler", (Alert.OK | Alert.CANCEL),
            null, alertCloseHandler);
      }
      private function alertCloseHandler(event:CloseEvent):void
      {
         if (event.detail == Alert.OK)
         {
            Alert.show("You clicked " + Alert.okLabel,
               "Close Event Handler");
         }
         else
         {
            Alert.show("You clicked " + Alert.cancelLabel,
               "Close Event Handler");
         }
      }
      private function alertWithCustomIcon():void
      {
         Alert.show("An Alert dialog with custom icon",
            "Alert Event Handler", 0, null, null,
            questionIcon);
      }
   ]]>
</fx:Script>
<s:Button label="Show Alert Message"
  click="simpleAlert()"
  width="{widestButton.width}"/>
<s:Button label="Show Non-modal Alert Message"
  click="nonModalAlert()" id="widestButton"/>
<s:Button label="Alert with Buttons"
  click="alertWithButtons()"
  width="{widestButton.width}"/>
<s:Button label="Alert with event handler"
  click="alertWithCloseHandler()"
  width="{widestButton.width}"/>
```

continued

LISTING 17.1   *(continued)*

```
    <s:Button label="Alert with Button Labels"
      click="alertWithButtonLabels()"
      width="{widestButton.width}"/>
    <s:Button label="Alert with Default Button"
      click="alertWithDefaultButton()"
      width="{widestButton.width}"/>
    <s:Button label="Alert with custom icon"
      click="alertWithCustomIcon()"
      width="{widestButton.width}"/>
  </s:Application>
```

On the Web

The code in Listing 17.1 is available in the Web site files as `AlertDemos.mxml` in the `chapter17` project. The graphic file used in the custom icon example is available as `questionicon.png` in the project's `src/assets` folder. ■

Using CSS selectors with the Alert class

You can change the `Alert` pop-up window's appearance with these CSS (Cascading Style Sheets) selectors:

- **The `mx|Alert` type selector.** This selector affects the body of the pop-up window. Most styles that you might use with the Panel container also work on the Alert dialog box.

- **The `.windowStyles` style name selector.** This selector affects the text in the title area of the pop-up window. You can change the name of this class selector with the `Alert` class's `titleStyleName` style, but it should always be set on a global basis for the entire application. Setting this value with `setStyle()` for only one call to `Alert.show()` can result in incorrect sizing.

These styles can be set in the `Alert` type selector to change the overall appearance of the window:

- `contentBackgroundColor`. This style changes the background of the window's content area.

- **Font styles.** `color`, `fontSize`, `fontFamily`, and so on affect the text in the window's content area.

Caution

In the Flex 3 SDK, the `Alert` class supported window styles, including `cornerRadius` and `rounded BottomCorners`, that affected the outer edges of the window, and border styles such as `borderStyle` and `borderColor` that affected the outer border of the window. These no longer work in Flex 4 when using the default Spark theme. This theme only supports a limited number of styles, including `chromeColor`, `color`, `contentBackgroundColor`, `focusColor`, `symbolColor`, `selectionColor`, and `rollOverColor`. ■

Font styles also can be set in the `.windowStyles` selector to change the appearance of text in the `Alert` pop-up window's header region.

Caution

The windowStyles **selector is also used by the MX** Panel **and** TitleWindow **containers. Any changes to the selector are applied to all instances of these containers as well as pop-up windows created by the** Alert **class. Spark** Panel **and** TitleWindow **components are not affected in this way.** ■

The application in Listing 17.2 contains an embedded style sheet that changes styles for both the pop-up window's body and title area. The window has a typewriter font in the content area and a sans serif font in the title.

LISTING 17.2

Changing the Alert window's appearance with styles

```
<?xml version="1.0" encoding="utf-8"?>
<s:Application xmlns:fx="http://ns.adobe.com/mxml/2009"
  xmlns:s="library://ns.adobe.com/flex/spark"
  xmlns:mx="library://ns.adobe.com/flex/mx">
  <fx:Style>
    @namespace mx "library://ns.adobe.com/flex/mx";
    @namespace s "library://ns.adobe.com/flex/spark";

    mx|Alert {
      content-background-color:#CCCCCC;
      chrome-color:#999999;
      font-family:Courier, "_typewriter";
    }
    .windowStyles {
      font-family:Arial, "_sans";
      font-size:14;
      font-style:italic;
      color:#FFFFFF;
    }
  </fx:Style>
  <fx:Script>
    <![CDATA[
      import mx.controls.Alert;

      private function simpleAlert():void
      {
        Alert.show("This is an Alert dialog box with styles applied",
          "Alert Title");
      }
    ]]>
  </fx:Script>
  <s:Button label="Alert with Style"
    click="simpleAlert()"
    horizontalCenter="0" top="20"/>
</s:Application>
```

On the Web

The code in Listing 17.2 is available in the Web site files as `AlertWithStyles.mxml` **in the** `chapter17` **project.** ■

As shown in Figure 17.7, the `Alert` pop-up window uses the `mx|Alert` and `.windowStyles` selectors to determine its visual presentation.

FIGURE 17.7

An `Alert` pop-up window, customized with CSS

Using the PopUpMenuButton Control

The `PopUpMenuButton` control combines the functionality of a `Button` with a menu. It's presented as a two-part visual component, including a simple `Button` and an icon representing a down arrow. When the user clicks the control, it presents a menu populated with items from its data provider.

Caution

Unlike the `Menu` **and** `MenuBar` **controls, the** `PopUpMenuButton` **doesn't support cascading menus. It's similar in some ways to the** `ComboBox` **control, in that it presents a single list of available items. But whereas the** `ComboBox` **presents only a single control and behavior, the Button control in the** `PopUpMenuButton` **supports all standard Button events.** ■

Creating a data provider

The data provider for a `PopUpMenuButton` can be an `XMLList`, `XMLListCollection`, `Array`, or `ArrayCollection`. If you use an `XMLList`, ensure that each of its XML nodes contains only simple values in the form of attributes or child nodes with text. Because cascading menus aren't possible, you can't use a deeply nested XML structure.

This `XMLList` is designed as a compatible data source for the `PopUpMenuButton` control:

```
<fx:Declarations>
  <fx:XMLList id="xSizes">
    <node label="Small" value="S"/>
    <node label="Medium" value="M"/>
    <node label="Large" value="L"/>
  </fx:XMLList>
</fx:Declarations>
```

The data provider also could be expressed as this `ArrayCollection`:

```
<fx:Declarations>
  <fx:ArrayCollection id="acSizes">
    <fx:Object>
      <fx:label>Small</fx:label>
      <fx:value>Small</fx:value>
    </fx:Object>
    <fx:Object>
      <fx:label>Medium</fx:label>
      <fx:value>M</fx:value>
    </fx:Object>
    <fx:Object>
      <fx:label>Large</fx:label>
      <fx:value>L</fx:value>
    </fx:Object>
  </fx:ArrayCollection>
</fx:Declarations>
```

Whether you use an XML- or Array-based data set, the `PopUpMenuButton` displays a single-level menu when the user clicks the control's arrow icon, as shown in Figure 17.8.

FIGURE 17.8

A `PopUpMenuButton` control

Click the arrow icon to open the menu

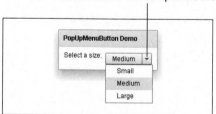

Handling events

As with the `Menu` and `MenuBar` controls, the `PopUpMenuButton` dispatches an `itemClick` event when the user selects an item from the pop-up menu. The same event is dispatched when the user clicks the `Button` portion of the control (the part of the control that displays its label).

The itemClick event generates an event object typed as mx.events.MenuEvent, which has an item property that refers to the selected data item.

In the context of an event handler method, the expression event.item refers to the data item, and you can use E4X notation to refer to data node attributes or simple dot notation to refer to named properties of selected objects in an ArrayCollection.

The application in Listing 17.3 uses a PopUpMenuButton control with data populated from an XMLList. When the user clicks the Button portion of the control or selects an item from its menu, the itemClick event is dispatched and the messages are displayed that indicate which item has been selected.

LISTING 17.3

Using the PopUpMenuButton control

```xml
<?xml version="1.0" encoding="utf-8"?>
<s:Application xmlns:fx="http://ns.adobe.com/mxml/2009"
  xmlns:s="library://ns.adobe.com/flex/spark"
  xmlns:mx="library://ns.adobe.com/flex/mx">
  <s:layout>
    <s:VerticalLayout horizontalAlign="center"
      paddingTop="20" gap="20"/>
  </s:layout>
  <fx:Script>
    <![CDATA[
      import mx.events.MenuEvent;

      private function itemClickHandler(event:MenuEvent):void
      {
        resultLabel.text = "Menu label: " + event.item.@label;
        resultValue.text = "Menu value: " + event.item.@value;
      }
    ]]>
  </fx:Script>
  <fx:Declarations>
    <fx:XMLList id="xSizes">
      <node label="Small" value="S"/>
      <node label="Medium" value="M"/>
      <node label="Large" value="L"/>
    </fx:XMLList>
  </fx:Declarations>
  <s:Panel title="PopUpMenuButton Demo"
    horizontalCenter="0" top="20">
    <s:layout>
      <s:HorizontalLayout
        paddingTop="10" paddingLeft="10"
        paddingRight="10" paddingBottom="10"/>
    </s:layout>
```

```
    <s:Label text="Select a size:"/>
    <mx:PopUpMenuButton id="p2"
      dataProvider="{xSizes}"
      labelField="@label"
      itemClick="itemClickHandler(event);"/>
  </s:Panel>
  <mx:Spacer height="50"/>
  <s:Label id="resultLabel"/>
  <s:Label id="resultValue"/>
</s:Application>
```

On the Web

The code in Listing 17.3 is available in the Web site files as `PopUpMenuButtonDemo.mxml` in the `chapter17` project. ∎

As shown in Figure 17.9, when the user clicks the `Button` portion of the control or selects an item from the pop-up menu, the `itemClick` event is handled.

FIGURE 17.9

Handling the `PopUpMenuButton` control's `itemClick` event

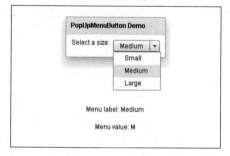

Using the PopUpButton control

The `PopUpButton` control enables you to create a `Button` made up of two sub-buttons, a main display button and a pop-up button, that when clicked present any other visual control as a pop-up window. The only requirement for the component you use as the pop-up window is that it must include the `UIComponent` class in its inheritance hierarchy. You can use any pre-built container or control or any custom component as a pop-up window.

The `PopUpButton` control is commonly declared in MXML code somewhere in an Application or custom component:

```
<mx:PopUpButton id="myPopup" label="My Popup Button"/>
```

You then define the control's pop-up window and the window's events and data with ActionScript code.

Declaring the pop-up window

The pop-up window displayed by a `PopUpButton` is created at runtime and is typically instantiated in ActionScript code. You first create an instance of the component you want to use, but don't add it to the current `Application` or component's display list. The component is then bound to the `PopUpButton` with the `popUp` property.

This code declares an instance of a `DateChooser` control outside any functions. Then, in a function that's called upon application startup, the component is bound to the `PopUpButton` control's `popUp` property:

```
[Bindable]
private var myDateChooser:DateChooser = new DateChooser();
private function initPopUpButton():void {
  myDateChooser.selectedDate = new Date();
  myPopUpButton.popUp = myDateChooser;
}
```

Handling events and managing pop-up behavior

The rules for handling a `PopUpButton` control's events depend on which component you use as the pop-up window. For example, if you use a pre-built control such as the `DateChooser`, you depend on that control's data and events to manage behavior at runtime.

In the current example, when the user selects a date from the `DateChooser` control, it dispatches a change event with an event object typed as `mx.events.CalendarLayoutChangeEvent`. Because the `DateChooser` control has been instantiated with ActionScript code, any event listeners must be created with the `addEventListener()` method:

```
myDateChooser.addEventListener(CalendarLayoutChangeEvent.CHANGE,
  dateChangeHandler);
```

You can then call the `PopUpButton` control's `close()` method to close the pop-up window:

```
private function dateChangeHandler(
  event:CalendarLayoutChangeEvent):void {
    myPopup.close();
}
```

Tip

Even when objects aren't currently displayed on the screen, they still exist in application memory, which enables you to access any of their properties. In this example, you can use the `selectedDate` property of the `DateChooser` even after it's no longer displayed. ∎

The application in Listing 17.4 uses a `PopUpButton` to display a DateChooser control as a pop-up window.

LISTING 17.4

Using a PopUpButton control

```xml
<?xml version="1.0" encoding="utf-8"?>
<s:Application xmlns:fx="http://ns.adobe.com/mxml/2009"
  xmlns:s="library://ns.adobe.com/flex/spark"
  xmlns:mx="library://ns.adobe.com/flex/mx"
  creationComplete="initPopupButton()">
  <s:layout>
    <s:VerticalLayout
      horizontalAlign="center"
      paddingTop="20" gap="20"/>
  </s:layout>
  <fx:Script>
    <![CDATA[
      import mx.controls.DateChooser;
      import mx.events.CalendarLayoutChangeEvent;

      [Bindable]
      private var myDateChooser:DateChooser = new DateChooser();

      private function initPopupButton():void
      {
        myDateChooser.selectedDate = new Date();
        myDateChooser.addEventListener(CalendarLayoutChangeEvent.CHANGE,
          dateChangeHandler);
        myPopupButton.popUp = myDateChooser;
        myPopupButton.executeBindings(true);
      }
      private function
        dateChangeHandler(event:CalendarLayoutChangeEvent):void
      {
        resultText.text = "You selected " +
          df.format(myDateChooser.selectedDate);
        myPopupButton.close();
      }
    ]]>
  </fx:Script>
  <fx:Declarations>
    <mx:DateFormatter id="df" formatString="M/D/YYYY"/>
  </fx:Declarations>
  <s:Panel title="Using the PopUpButton Control">
    <s:layout>
```

continued

LISTING 17.4 *(continued)*

```
        <s:HorizontalLayout
          paddingTop="10" paddingBottom="10"
          paddingRight="10" paddingLeft="10"/>
      </s:layout>
      <s:Label text="Select a date:"/>
      <mx:PopUpButton id="myPopupButton"
        label="{df.format(myDateChooser.selectedDate)}"
        width="135"/>
    </s:Panel>
    <mx:Spacer height="160"/>
    <s:Label id="resultText"/>
  </s:Application>
```

On the Web

The code in Listing 17.4 is available in the Web site files as `PopUpButtonDemo.mxml` in the `chapter17` project. ■

Note

The `PopUpButton` component has a Boolean `openAlways` property that can be used to display a component's pop-up object when the user clicks the main button. The pop-up object is always displayed when you click the pop-up button or press the spacebar, regardless of the setting of the `openAlways` property. ■

Figure 17.10 shows the resulting application displaying the `DateChooser` control in response to a user clicking the `PopUpButton`.

FIGURE 17.10

Using the `PopUpButton` control

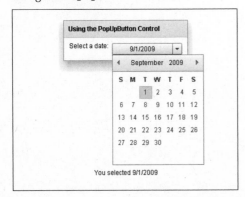

Working with Custom Pop-up Windows

You can create custom pop-up windows in a Flex application for many purposes:

- Presenting detailed information to the user that's too complex to easily fit into an `Alert` dialog box

- Collecting configuration and preference information before executing an operation

- Providing a pop-up window that can be reused as a custom component

- Collecting data through a data entry form wrapped in a pop-up window

Tip

A custom pop-up window component must be extended from a class that implements the `IFlexDisplay Object` interface. This interface is implemented by the `UIComponent` class, which in turn is in the inheritance hierarchy of all MX containers and controls. This essentially means that any component can be used as a custom pop-up window. If you want to create a custom pop-up window based on a Spark component, though, you should base your custom pop-up window on the Spark `TitleWindow` component. ■

Defining a custom pop-up window

Custom pop-up windows can be defined as custom MXML components. If you want to create a window that looks like a dialog box, you can use either the `Panel` or `TitleWindow` container. While either component has the appearance of a dialog box, the Spark `Panel` component can't be dragged around the screen by the user. If you want full dialog box functionality, create your custom pop-up window components as subclasses of the `TitleWindow` component.

Creating the component

The steps for creating an MXML component that will be used as a pop-up window are the same as for any other MXML component:

1. **Create a new MXML component based on spark.components.TitleWindow.**

2. **Save the new component in your project as a file with the .mxml file extension.**

The following code defines an MXML component designed to collect login information, and it might be saved as a file named `LoginWindow.mxml`:

```
<?xml version="1.0" encoding="utf-8"?>
<s:TitleWindow xmlns:fx="http://ns.adobe.com/mxml/2009"
  xmlns:s="library://ns.adobe.com/flex/spark"
  xmlns:mx="library://ns.adobe.com/flex/mx"
  title="Please Log In">
  <mx:Form>
    <mx:FormItem label="User Name:">
      <s:TextInput id="userInput"/>
    </mx:FormItem>
    <mx:FormItem label="Password:">
```

```
                <s:TextInput displayAsPassword="true" id="passwordInput"/>
            </mx:FormItem>
            <mx:FormItem direction="horizontal">
              <s:Button label="Log In"/>
              <s:Button label="Cancel"/>
            </mx:FormItem>
          </mx:Form>
        </s:TitleWindow>
```

Sharing data with events

The custom component that will be used as a pop-up window should share information with the rest of the application using custom events. The LoginWindow component described in the preceding code sample would share events for logging in and for canceling the operation. In order to share the login information, you need to create a custom event class to contain the login data.

Listing 17.5 is a custom event class with public properties for the user name and password values that will be collected by the custom component.

LISTING 17.5

A custom event class designed for use with a custom Login component

```
package events
{
  import flash.events.Event;
  public class LoginEvent extends Event
  {
    public var username:String;
    public var password:String;
    public function LoginEvent(type:String,
      bubbles:Boolean=false, cancelable:Boolean=false)
    {
      super(type, bubbles, cancelable);
    }
    override public function clone():Event
    {
      var ev:LoginEvent = new LoginEvent(this.type);
      ev.username = this.username;
      ev.password = this.password;
      return ev;
    }
  }
}
```

On the Web

The code in Listing 17.5 is available in the Web site files as LoginEvent.as in the chapter17 project's src/events folder. ■

522

When the user clicks the custom component's Log In button, the component shares data with the application by constructing and dispatching a custom event object:

```
var event:LoginEvent = new LoginEvent("login");
event.username = userInput.text;
event.password = passwordInput.text;
dispatchEvent(event);
```

And if the user clicks `Cancel`, the custom component dispatches a `cancel` event, with the event object typed as the standard `Event` class:

```
dispatchEvent(new Event("cancel"));
```

Listing 17.6 shows a completed custom component designed for use as a pop-up window that can share data with the application using custom events. Nothing in the preceding code indicates that this component will be used as a pop-up window; it could just as easily be declared with an MXML tag set in the application to appear inline in the application.

LISTING 17.6

A custom component ready for use as a pop-up window

```
<?xml version="1.0" encoding="utf-8"?>
<s:TitleWindow xmlns:fx="http://ns.adobe.com/mxml/2009"
  xmlns:s="library://ns.adobe.com/flex/spark"
  xmlns:mx="library://ns.adobe.com/flex/mx"
  title="Please Log In">
  <fx:Metadata>
    [Event(name="login", type="events.LoginEvent")]
  </fx:Metadata>
  <fx:Script>
    <![CDATA[
      import events.LoginEvent;
      private function login():void
      {
        var event:LoginEvent = new LoginEvent("login");
        event.username = userInput.text;
        event.password = passwordInput.text;
        dispatchEvent(event);
      }
      public function setInitialFocus():void
      {
        userInput.setFocus();
      }
    ]]>
  </fx:Script>
  <mx:Form>
    <mx:FormItem label="User Name:">
```

continued

LISTING 17.6   *(continued)*

```
        <s:TextInput id="userInput"/>
      </mx:FormItem>
      <mx:FormItem label="Password:">
        <s:TextInput displayAsPassword="true" id="passwordInput"/>
      </mx:FormItem>
    </mx:Form>
    <s:controlBarContent>
      <s:Button label="Log In" click="login()"/>
    </s:controlBarContent>
  </s:TitleWindow>
```

On the Web

The code in Listing 17.6 is available in the Web site files as `LoginTitleWindow.mxml` in the `chapter17` project's `src/popups` folder. ∎

Managing custom pop-up windows with the PopUpManager class

The `PopUpManager` is a singleton class with static methods that you use to manage custom pop-up windows at runtime. It has two methods that you can use to present a pop-up window:

- `addPopUp()`. Adds a new top-level window using a component that's already been instantiated and is ready to use.

- `createPopUp()`. Creates a new instance of a component, presents the component as a pop-up window, and returns a reference.

Of these two methods, the `addPopUp()` method is more useful, because it enables you to construct and preconfigure a visual object prior to presenting it as a pop-up window.

The `PopUpManager` also has these methods that you use to manipulate the position and order of pop-up windows:

- `bringToFront()`. Gives top-level presentation and focus to a particular window.

- `centerPopUp()`. Positions a pop-up window in the horizontal and vertical center of its parent window.

Finally, `PopUpManager` has a `removePopUp()` method to remove top-level windows from the display when they're no longer needed, though they will still exist in application memory.

Adding a pop-up window to the display

To add a new pop-up window to the application at runtime using the `addPopUp()` method, first declare an instance of the custom component you want to present. This declaration will likely be outside of any functions so the pop-up window reference persists between function calls:

```
private var popup:LoginWindow;
```

Within a function that you call to display the pop-up window, instantiate the component and create any required event listeners with accompanying event handler functions. The `LoginWindow` component in this example dispatches events named `login` and `cancel`, so it requires two `addEventListener()` calls:

```
popup = new LoginWindow();
popup.addEventListener("login", loginHandler);
popup.addEventListener("cancel", cancelHandler);
```

To present the window on-screen, call `PopUpManager.addPopUp()` with these arguments:

- `childList:String`. The display child list in which you're adding the pop-up window. Possible values include `PopUpManagerChildList.APPLICATION`, `PopUpManagerChildList.POPUP`, and `PopUpManagerChildList.PARENT` (the default).

- `modal:Boolean`. This argument determines whether the custom pop-up window is modal. If not passed in, it defaults to `false`.

- `parent:DisplayObject`. The parent window over which the pop-up window is displayed.

- `window:IFlexDisplayObject`. The component reference you just instantiated.

After adding the pop-up window to the application interface, you can center the window over its parent window with a call to `PopUpManager.centerPopUp()`. If necessary, you can ensure that the new window has top-level focus with a call to `PopUpManager.bringToFront()`.

This makes a call to `PopUpManager.addPopup()` to present the `LoginWindow` custom component as a modal pop-up window and then centers it on the parent component:

```
PopUpManager.addPopUp(popup, this, true);
PopUpManager.centerPopUp(popup);
```

Caution

If you don't explicitly center the pop-up window with `PopUpManager.centerPopUp()`, the window appears in the top-left corner of the parent window. ■

Figure 17.11 shows the resulting pop-up window. Notice the application's blurry appearance in the background, indicating that the user must dismiss the window before interacting with the rest of the application.

Removing a pop-up window

To remove a pop-up window, use the `PopUpManager` class's static `removePopUp()` method. The method takes a single argument that references the pop-up window instance:

```
PopUpManager.removePopUp(popup);
```

FIGURE 17.11

The `LoginWindow` component as a pop-up window can now be dragged by the user, and the rest of the application is disabled due to the modality of the pop-up.

You also can call the method from within the component to cause it to remove itself from the interface:

```
PopUpManager.removePopUp(this);
```

The application in Listing 17.7 uses the `LoginWindow` component as a pop-up window. In each of its custom event handler functions, it explicitly closes the pop-up window with a call to `PopUpManager.removePopUp()`.

LISTING 17.7

An application using a custom pop-up window

```
<?xml version="1.0" encoding="utf-8"?>
<s:Application xmlns:fx="http://ns.adobe.com/mxml/2009"
  xmlns:s="library://ns.adobe.com/flex/spark"
  xmlns:mx="library://ns.adobe.com/flex/mx">
  <fx:Script>
    <![CDATA[
      import events.LoginEvent;
      import mx.controls.Alert;
      import mx.managers.PopUpManager;
      import popups.LoginTitleWindow;

      private var popup:LoginTitleWindow;

      private function showLoginWindow():void
      {
        popup = new LoginTitleWindow();
        popup.addEventListener(Event.CLOSE, closeHandler);
        popup.addEventListener("login", loginHandler);
```

```
      popup.addEventListener("cancel", closeHandler);
      PopUpManager.addPopUp(popup, this, true)
      PopUpManager.centerPopUp(popup);
      popup.setInitialFocus();
    }
    private function loginHandler(event:LoginEvent):void
    {
      Alert.show("You logged in as " + event.username +
        " with a password of " + event.password, "Login Successful");
      PopUpManager.removePopUp(popup);
    }
    private function closeHandler(event:Event):void
    {
      Alert.show("You cancelled the login operation", "Login Cancelled");
      PopUpManager.removePopUp(popup);
    }
  ]]>
</fx:Script>
<s:Button label="Log In" click="showLoginWindow()"
  horizontalCenter="0" top="20"/>
</s:Application>
```

On the Web

The code in Listing 17.7 is available in the Web site files as UseCustomPopUp.mxml **in the** chapter17 **project.** ∎

The TitleWindow container is a subclass of Panel, so it shares all of that container's features: It contains a title bar, a caption, a border, and a content area, and like the Panel, it can host a controlBarContent area with wizard-like buttons at the bottom.

The TitleWindow displays a close button in its upper-right corner, creating a common visual interface for pop-up windows.

The close button doesn't actually close the pop-up window. Instead, it dispatches a close event with an event object typed as mx.events.CloseEvent. Upon instantiating the custom component (and prior to adding it as a pop-up window), create a listener for the close event:

```
    popup.addEventListener(CloseEvent.CLOSE, closeHandler);
```

Then, in the event handler function, call PopUpManager.removePopUp() to remove the pop-up window from the application interface:

```
    private function closeHandler(event:CloseEvent):void
    {
      Alert.show("You canceled the login operation", "Login Canceled");
      PopUpManager.removePopUp(popup);
    }
```

If you don't want to display the close button in the custom pop-up window, just create a custom skin for your pop-up and modify it as needed. To do this, follow these steps:

1. **Open the custom pop-up window file in Flash Builder's Design mode.**

2. **Right-click anywhere on the design area and select Create Skin.**

3. **As shown in Figure 17.12, enter the package and name of the new skin you want to create. As with all custom components, you should place the skin component in a subfolder of the project's source-code root.**

FIGURE 17.12

Creating a new custom skin based on the `TitleWindow` component's default skin

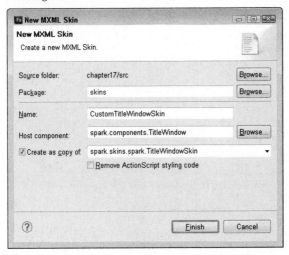

4. **Set Host component to spark.components.TitleWindow.**

5. **Select Create a copy of and use the default value spark.skins.spark. TitleWindowSkin (this is the default skin for the Spark TitleWindow component).**

6. **Click Finish to create the new custom skin.**

7. **When the new custom skin file appears in Flash Builder's Design mode, click the close icon in the skin's upper-right corner as shown in Figure 17.13.**

8. **Press Delete to remove the button from the skin.** Alternatively, you can use Source mode and comment out the `<s:Button>` tag.

9. **Save your changes.**

10. Open the custom pop-up window file in Source mode and look at the <s:TitleWindow> starting tag. It now includes the skinClass attribute that assigns your new custom skin:

```
<s:TitleWindow xmlns:fx="http://ns.adobe.com/mxml/2009"
  xmlns:s="library://ns.adobe.com/flex/spark"
  xmlns:mx="library://ns.adobe.com/flex/mx"
  title="Please Log In"
  skinClass="skins.CustomTitleWindowSkin">
```

FIGURE 17.13

The close button is a part of the Spark TitleWindow component's skin and can be deleted.

The TitleWindow skin's default close button

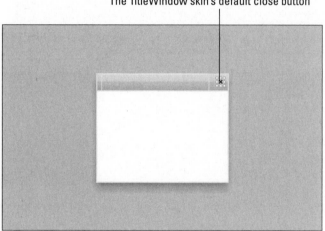

Note

The TitleWindow **component's close icon is defined as an optional skin part, so when you delete it from the skin it doesn't result in any compilation errors.** ∎

If you want to use the custom skin with all dialog boxes in your application, you can set the skinClass style in an embedded or external style sheet. For example, this CSS code assigns the new skin for all components that are based on the Spark TitleWindow component:

```
<fx:Style>
  @namespace s "library://ns.adobe.com/flex/spark";
  s|TitleWindow {
    skinClass: ClassReference("skins.CustomTitleWindowSkin");
  }
</fx:Style>
```

Summary

In this chapter, I described how to create pop-up windows as part of a Flex application interface. You learned the following:

- Pop-up windows are typically used to present and collect information in a windowing style application.

- You use the `Alert` class to present simple informational messages and to enable a user to confirm or decline an operation.

- The `PopUpMenuButton` control combines a `Button` and single-level `Menu` that's similar in presentation to a `ComboBox`.

- You use the `PopUpButton` control to present any visual container or control as a pop-up window.

- Custom pop-up windows are defined in the same way as any custom component.

- The Spark `TitleWindow` is designed to be used as a custom pop-up window and enables dragging of the resulting window by the user.

- You can remove the close button from the `TitleWindow` interface by creating a custom skin.

- You use the `PopUpManager` class's static methods to add and remove custom pop-up windows at runtime.

Part III

Working with Data

IN THIS PART

Chapter 18
Modeling and Managing Data

Chapter 19
Using List Controls

Chapter 20
Using Advanced List Controls

Chapter 21
Using the Flex Charting Controls

Chapter 22
Working with Data Entry Forms

Chapter 23
Working with HTTPService
and XML

Chapter 24
Managing XML with E4X

Modeling and Managing Data

F lex applications are *stateful*; that is, they have the capability to remember data persistently for the duration of the user's session in a way that classic Web applications usually don't. One of the most common tasks you must accomplish as an application developer is to create a framework for storing data that the application can use at runtime.

The content of an application's data can come from many sources: XML files, databases or other server-side resources, or remote functions wrapped by and exposed as SOAP-style or Representational State Transfer (REST)-style Web services. Regardless of how the data comes to an application, though, a Flex application stores the data in exactly the same way: as a data model.

In this chapter, I describe common techniques for modeling data in Flex applications. I start with creating single-object data models: ActionScript classes designed to hold one instance of a data entity at a time. (A data instance might represent a row in a database table or a single element in an XML file.) You can represent such data instances with the `<fx:Model>` tag, a generic data object, or, more commonly, you create your own custom ActionScript classes, known variously by the design pattern names *Value Object* and *Transfer Object*.

In the second part of the chapter, I describe the use of data collections: ordered collections of data instances managed by the `ArrayList` and `ArrayCollection` classes. I describe how and where to declare these classes and then describe how to use the powerful `ArrayCollection` class to filter, sort, bookmark, and traverse data in client application memory.

On the Web

To use the sample code for this chapter, import the `chapter18.fxp` Flex project archive from the Web site files into your Flex Builder workspace. ■

IN THIS CHAPTER

Using the `<fx:Model>` **tag to model data items**

Embedding data with `<fx:Model>`

Creating value object classes in ActionScript

Storing data sets in client memory with the `ArrayList` **and** `ArrayCollection` **classes**

Filtering and sorting data with the `ArrayCollection` **class**

Traversing, searching, and bookmarking data objects with the `IViewCursor` **interface**

Creating a Data Model

A data model is a way of representing data (information) in a client application. It's a truism of database applications that you can't do much without knowing your data structure. Take an application that represents the personal information of your contact list. Whether you store this data in an e-mail client or a complex server-side database application such as SQL Server or MySQL, the software that manages the data has to know its structure.

In classic relational databases, data is stored in tables. Each table has columns that represent the bits of data that are created for each row in the table. A database table representing contact information might have any number of columns. Each column has a name and a data type. For example, a contacts table might have the data structure shown in Table 18.1.

TABLE 18.1

A Simple Database Table Structure

Column Name	Primary Key	Data Type	Length	Null OK
contactId	X	Integer		
firstName		String	50	
lastName		String	50	
dob		Date		x
address		String	50	x
city		String	20	x
zipCode		String	10	x
telephone		String	15	x

When data is returned to a Flex application in this structure, you need a way to store it. The goal is to create an object that can serve as a container for this data and can share this data structure to the best of the Flex framework's capability.

Figure 18.1 shows a UML diagram describing the structure of an object that would be able to hold this data.

You can create a data model to store the data in two ways: by using the <fx:Model> tag to declare a generic untyped data object and by creating a custom ActionScript class. Of these approaches, the custom ActionScript version is significantly more powerful and flexible. The <fx:Model> approach is fast and easy to code, and it might be used during early prototyping of an application, but an application that's built for durability and easy long-term maintenance generally requires custom ActionScript classes to represent data in Flex application memory.

FIGURE 18.1

A UML diagram describing a class with data structure

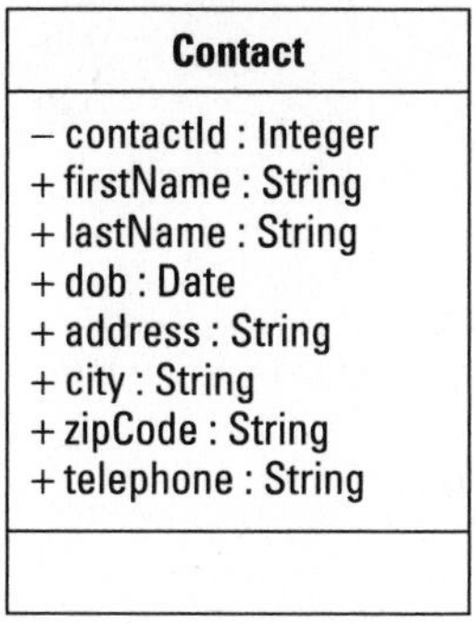

Contact
− contactId : Integer
+ firstName : String
+ lastName : String
+ dob : Date
+ address : String
+ city : String
+ zipCode : String
+ telephone : String

Using the <fx:Model> element

The <fx:Model> element compiles XML markup into a generic ActionScript Object.

New Feature

The <fx:Model> element was used with the mx prefix in previous versions of the Flex SDK. As with all nonvisual elements, it must be declared within an <fx:Declarations> **element in a Flex 4 application.** ■

You could implement the data structure described in the UML diagram in Figure 18.1 as a data object with this code:

```
<fx:Declarations>
  <fx:Model id="myContact">
   <data>
    <contactId>1</contactId>
    <firstName>Joe</firstName>
    <lastName>Adams</lastName>
    <address>123 Main Street</address>
    <city>Anywhere</city>
    <state>WA</state>
    <zipCode>12345</zipCode>
    <dob>11/28/1959</dob>
    <telephone>555-123-4567</telephone>
   </data>
  </fx:Model>
</fx:Declarations>
```

You also can fill Model properties dynamically from user interface components using binding expressions:

```
<fx:Declarations>
  <fx:Model id="myContact">
```

```
            <data>
              <contactId>0</contactId>
              <firstName>{firstNameInput.text}</firstName>
              <lastName>{lastNameInput.text}</lastName>
              <dob>{myDataField.selectedDate}</dob>
              ... additional elements and bindings...
            </data>
          </fx:Model>
       </fx:Declarations>
```

At runtime, as the user interacts with form controls, the controls' values are passed to the Model object through the binding expressions.

Caution

The use of binding expressions to dynamically fill Model properties has an obvious benefit of creating and filling a data object declaratively, but this technique also has a drawback that might not be immediately apparent. When you fill a Model property from a binding expression, its initial value is null. If you don't explicitly set initial values with ActionScript statements, you can end up sending the data object to remote server functions such as Web services where null values can cause runtime errors. If you encounter this problem, an easy solution is to initialize the object's properties upon application startup in an initialization function:

```
myModel.firstName="";
myModel.lastName="";
```

On the other hand, setting default values is a built-in benefit of custom ActionScript classes used as value objects, described later in this chapter. ■

The application in Listing 18.1 declares a single data object using the <fx:Model> tag and then displays its values in Label controls with binding expressions.

LISTING 18.1

Declaring a data object with <fx:Model>

```
<?xml version="1.0" encoding="utf-8"?>
<s:Application xmlns:fx="http://ns.adobe.com/mxml/2009"
  xmlns:s="library://ns.adobe.com/flex/spark"
  xmlns:mx="library://ns.adobe.com/flex/mx">
  <fx:Declarations>
    <fx:Model id="contact">
      <data>
        <contactId>1</contactId>
        <firstName>Joe</firstName>
        <lastName>Adams</lastName>
        <address>123 Main Street</address>
        <city>Anywhere</city>
        <state>WA</state>
        <zipCode>12345</zipCode>
        <dob>11/28/1959</dob>
        <telephone>555-123-4567</telephone>
```

```
      </data>
    </fx:Model>
  </fx:Declarations>
  <s:VGroup top="20" horizontalCenter="0">
    <s:Label text="{contact.firstName} {contact.lastName}"/>
    <s:Label text="{contact.address}"/>
    <s:Label text="{contact.city}, {contact.state} {contact.zipCode}"/>
    <s:Label text="{contact.dob}"/>
    <s:Label text="{contact.telephone}"/>
  </s:VGroup>
</s:Application>
```

On the Web

The code in Listing 18.1 is available in the Web site files as `ModelDemo.mxml` in the `chapter18` project. ∎

Benefits of <fx:Model>

The advantage of the `<fx:Model>` tag is its simplicity. It's very easy to declare a bit of hard-coded data with these benefits:

- **The object and all its properties are automatically bindable.** You don't have to include the `[Bindable]` metadata tag, and you can refer to any of the object's properties with binding expressions, as in:

  ```
  <s:Label text="{contact.firstName} {contact.lastName}"/>
  ```

- **The `<fx:Model>` tag uses simple XML syntax to declare its property names.**

After a data object has been declared with the `<fx:Model>` tag, you refer to its data using dot syntax. The object's id, assigned in the `<fx:Model>` start tag, actually refers to the model's root element if there is a sole root element. In the preceding example, this element is named `<data>`, but its name isn't important; you refer to the root by the model object's `id` and then to its named properties as child objects of the model:

```
contact.firstName
```

Drawbacks of <fx:Model>

These drawbacks of the `<fx:Model>` tag prevent its being truly useful to model objects in production applications:

- **The properties are always String values; the `<fx:Model>` architecture doesn't give you any way to set specific data types.**

- **You can declare only a single instance of an object.** Unlike strongly typed ActionScript classes, which are designed to be instantiated as many times as necessary, if you want another data object you have to declare it explicitly.

- **Because `<fx:Model>` is a compiler tag that doesn't represent an ActionScript class, it has no methods or properties.**

Importing data with <fx:Model>

The <fx:Model> tag does have one very useful capability: It can be used to compile data into an application. This technique is useful only when two circumstances are true:

- **It is a relatively small amount of data.** Large amounts of embedded data result in an increase in the size of the compiled application. For applications that are deployed over the Web, embedding data results in a slower download and longer delay before the application starts for the first time. On the positive side, the data is instantly available to the application without having to be downloaded at runtime.

- **The data is completely static.** If any of the data under consideration might change during the lifetime of the application, you should load the data at runtime using the HTTPService component or another runtime loading mechanism.

To embed data with the <fx:Model> tag, first save it as an XML file. The names of the XML file's data elements can be anything you like; the only requirements are that the XML file be well formed and have a single root element. The following XML structure is suitable for use with the <fx:Model> tag:

```
<?xml version="1.0" encoding="UTF-8"?>
<data>
  <book>
    <title_id>BU1032</title_id>
    <title>How to Program Good</title>
    <pub_id>1528</pub_id>
    <au_id>409-56-7008</au_id>
    <price>19.99</price>
    <notes>A guide to creating great software.</notes>
    <pubdate>2005-01-15</pubdate>
  </book>
  ... additional <book> elements ...
</data>
```

Assuming the preceding XML markup is saved in a text file named books.xml in the project source root's data subfolder, the code to import and embed the data looks like this:

```
<fx:Model id="bookData" source="data/books.xml"/>
```

As with hard-coded data, the Model element's id points to the XML structure's root element. From there, the data typing of each element depends on the number of elements with a particular name. If the preceding structure contains two or more <book> elements, the expression book-Data.book returns an Array. If the XML structure's root element contains only a single child <book> element, the expression bookData.book instead returns an ActionScript Object.

Tip

To ensure that you always have an `Array` to work with, you can use the `ArrayUtil.toArray()` method wrapped around an expression that might return an `Object` due to the number of elements in the XML data structure. At application startup, declare a separate `Array` variable and fill it as shown here:

```
import mx.utils.ArrayUtil;
[Bindable]
private var bookArray:Array;
private function initApp():void
{
  bookArray = ArrayUtil.toArray(bookData.book);
} ▪
```

Using Value Objects

A *value object*, also known variously as a *transfer object*, a *data transfer object*, and a *bean*, is a class designed to hold data for a single instance of a data entity. The design pattern is named Transfer Object in the world of Java Enterprise Edition (JEE) application server development, where it's implemented as a Java class.

Web Resource

The Transfer Object design pattern is described in the J2EE design pattern catalog at `http://java.sun.com/blueprints/corej2eepatterns/Patterns/TransferObject.html`. In the most recent version on the Sun Web site, the graphics still refer to the design pattern as Value Object, its old name. Don't be confused; it's really the same pattern! ▪

Value object classes have these advantages over the `<fx:Model>` tag:

- Class properties can be strongly datatyped. Each property is declared with standard variable declaration syntax and typically has a data type declared after the colon:

  ```
  public var myDateProperty:Date;
  ```

- Class properties can have default values. As when declaring a variable inside or outside a function, you can declare default values by appending the value after an = assignment operator. This code declares a `Date` property with the default set to the current date:

  ```
  public var myDateProperty:Date = new Date();
  ```

- You can use implicit setter and getter accessor methods. Accessor methods enable complex logic and authentication when setting or getting data and creating read-only properties (properties that can be read from the application but can only be set internally within the value object class).

- When you integrate a Flex client application with an application server that supports data transfer with AMF (Action Message Format), such as ColdFusion, BlazeDS, LiveCycle Data Services, PHP, and others, client-side value object classes defined in ActionScript can be mapped to equivalent classes on the server (written in the server's native language, such as Java, ColdFusion Markup Language, PHP, or C#). This enables you to pass data between the application tiers with minimal code in both tiers.

Using the New ActionScript Class wizard

You can use Flex Builder's ActionScript Class wizard to create a simple ActionScript class. Follow these steps to create a new value object class to represent Book data:

1. **Open the `chapter18` project if it isn't already open.** Notice that the project contains a `valueObjects` package.

2. **Right-click on the `valueObjects` package and select New ⇨ ActionScript Class.**

3. **Set the class name as Contact, as shown in Figure 18.2.**

4. **Click Finish to create the new ActionScript class.**

The New ActionScript Class wizard

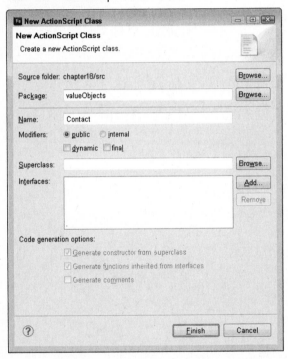

The completed ActionScript class is created in the file `Contact.as` in the `valueObjects` folder and should appear in the Source view editor as follows:

```
package valueObjects
{
  public class Contact
  {
```

```
    public function Contact()
    {
    }
  }
}
```

The class is ready to fill in with properties and other functionality.

Value object class syntax

Value objects are implemented in Flex as simple ActionScript classes, and their syntax is determined by basic ActionScript syntax requirements. In this section, I describe each part of a value object class, its purpose, and some best practice recommendations.

Declaring a package

A *package* is a collection of related classes. As in many other languages, including both Java and ColdFusion, packages are tied to the folder structure of an application's source code.

In ActionScript 3.0, each public ActionScript class must be wrapped inside a package declaration that's implemented as a code block. The package declaration tells the compiler where the class is stored based on its package within the project's source root folder or other locations in the project's build path.

As shown in Figure 18.3, the Contact value object class is stored in the `valueObjects` subfolder of the project's source root.

FIGURE 18.3

The project structure, including the `valueObjects` subfolder

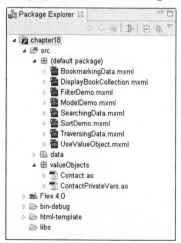

The package declaration looks like this:

```
package valueObjects
{
...public class declaration here...
}
```

Caution

When you generate a new class file with the New ActionScript Class wizard, the package declaration is created for you. However, if you move the class source code later, you're responsible for manually updating the package declaration in the class source code. ■

Declaring the public class

The class declaration for a public class is placed inside the package code block. Value object classes are always declared as `public`, so they can be used by the rest of the application. Also, value object classes typically don't explicitly extend any other class, as they usually don't have to inherit existing functionality.

The name of an ActionScript public class must match the name of the source-code file in which it's defined. The name is case-sensitive, and by convention always has an initial uppercase character.

The public class declaration looks like this:

```
package valueObjects
{
  public class Contact
  {
    ...class members declared here...
  }
}
```

As noted in the preceding example, members of the class, including properties, functions, and constants, are declared inside the class declaration's code block.

Tip

You can declare private classes in an ActionScript class source-code file. These classes are available for use only by the public class in whose source-code file the private class is declared. The private class doesn't actually have a `private` access modifier declaration, and it's declared outside the package declaration:

```
package valueObjects
{
  public class Book
  {
    public var page1:Page = new Page();
    public function Book()
    {
    }
```

```
    }
}
class Page
{
  public var pageNumber:int;
  public var text:String;
} ∎
```

Declaring ActionScript class properties

ActionScript class properties are declared as variables, using this syntax:

```
[access modifier] var [property name]:[data type];
```

The access modifiers at the beginning of a property declaration should be one of these keywords:

- `internal`. Properties that can be set and read by the current class and by any classes in the same package.

- `private`. Properties that can only be set and read by instances of the class in which they're declared.

- `protected`. Properties that can be set and read by the current class and by any of its subclasses.

- `public`. Properties that can be set and read by the rest of the application.

Note

The default access modifier is `internal`; if you leave the access modifier off a property declaration, the property is available only to the current class and any other classes in the same package. You'll also see a compiler warning indicating that you should include an explicit access modifier. ∎

The name of a property is subject to naming rules for all ActionScript identifiers: It can include alphabetical, numeric, and underscore characters, and it must start with an alphabetical character or an underscore. The following naming conventions are considered to be best practices by most developers:

- The initial character in a property name is lowercase.

- Private properties have an initial underscore (_) character.

Neither of these conventions is a technical requirement, but by following them you create code that makes sense to other developers.

To add public properties representing the data structure in Table 18.1, follow these steps:

1. Open the `Contact.as` file you created in the previous exercise.

2. Place the cursor inside the class declaration's code block, but before the constructor method.

3. Declare each of the required properties with appropriate data types, as follows:

```
public var contactId:int=0;
public var firstName:String;
public var lastName:String;
public var dob:Date;
public var address:String;
public var city:String;
public var zipCode:String;
public var telephone:String;
```

4. Save the file to disk.

Making properties bindable

Value objects benefit from having their properties marked as bindable, so that as the property values change at runtime, they can broadcast those changes to any objects with binding expressions.

You can make individual properties bindable by adding the [Bindable] metadata tag before each property declaration. This code makes the firstName and lastName properties bindable, but doesn't do the same for the contactId property:

```
public var contactId:int=0;
[Bindable]
public var firstName:String;
[Bindable]
public var lastName:String;
```

Alternatively, you can add a single [Bindable] tag before the class declaration to make all its properties bindable:

```
package valueObjects
{
  [Bindable]
  public class Contact
  {
    public var contactId:int=0;
    public var firstName:String;
    public var lastName:String;
    ... remaining property declarations ...
  }
}
```

Follow these steps to make all the value object class's properties bindable:

1. Open Contact.as.

2. Create an empty line just before the class declaration, and add a [Bindable] metadata tag.

3. Save the changes to disk.

Listing 18.2 shows the completed value object `Contact` class.

LISTING 18.2

A completed value object class

```
package valueObjects
{
  [Bindable]
  public class Contact
  {
    public var contactId:int=0;
    public var firstName:String;
    public var lastName:String;
    public var dob:Date;
    public var address:String;
    public var city:String;
    public var zipCode:String;
    public var telephone:String;
    public function Contact()
    {
    }
  }
}
```

On the Web

A completed class that's similar to Listing 18.2 is available in the Web site files as `ContactComplete.as` in the `chapter18` project. ∎

Using private properties and accessor methods

If you prefer, you can use private properties and set and get accessor methods. This is a preferred syntax for some developers, because it follows the object-oriented practice of encapsulation and hiding data members from public usage.

To declare a private property in an ActionScript class, replace the public access modifier with the keyword `private`. If you like, you also can follow the practice of using an underscore (_) prefix as the property name's initial character:

```
private var _firstName:String;
```

To make the property accessible to the rest of the application, you then create set and get accessor methods. In ActionScript 3, these methods use explicit `set` and `get` keywords to indicate that the functions should be accessed by the class consumer as though they were properties.

A set accessor method receives a single argument and returns void. The body of the method sets the corresponding private variable's value from the argument:

```
public function set contactId(v:int):void
{
    this._contactId = v;
}
```

A get accessor method receives no arguments and returns the value of its corresponding private property:

```
public function get contactId():int
{
    return _contactId;
}
```

Note

Unlike in Java, where setter and getter accessor methods are enforced by application frameworks that explicitly call value object methods such as `getFirstName()`, in ActionScript, methods whose names are preceded by the `get` and `set` keywords are implicitly recognized as properties by the compiler. As a result, you can't name a private property with the same identifier as a getter or setter accessor method. This is one reason the convention of prefixing private property names with the underscore character is commonly followed: It guarantees that the identifier for the private property and for its corresponding accessor methods are different from each other. ■

Note

If you create a `get` accessor method for a private property, but not a `set` method, the property is considered "read-only" to the rest of the application. ■

Generating getter and setter functions in Flash Builder 4

Flash Builder 4 includes a new feature that enables you to quickly convert a public property to a private property with a public getter and setter method. To do this, follow these steps:

1. Open `Contact.as` from the `valueObjects` folder.
2. Place the cursor anywhere in the name of the first property, `contactID`.
3. Select Source ⇨ Generate Getter/Setter from the Flash Builder menu.
4. Click OK in the Generate Getter/Setter dialog box, shown in Figure 18.4.

You should see the following changes in your code:

- The `public` property should now be `private`, and it should have an underscore character as a prefix:

  ```
  private var _contactId:int=0;
  ```
- There should be two new functions with the `set` and `get` keywords, both named for the original property:

```
public function get contactId():int
{
  return _contactId;
}
public function set contactId(v:int):void
{
  _contactId = v;
}
```

Generating getter and setter methods

Listing 18.3 shows part of the ActionScript class using private properties and accessor methods, instead of public properties.

Using private properties and getter/setter accessor methods

```
package valueObjects
{
  [Bindable]
  public class ContactPrivateVars
  {
    private var _contactId:int=0;
    private var _firstName:String;
    private var _lastName:String;
```

continued

LISTING 18.3 *(continued)*

```
    ... more property declarations...

    public function get lastName():String
    {
      return _lastName;
    }
    public function set lastName(v:String):void
    {
      _lastName = v;
    }
    public function get firstName():String
    {
      return _firstName;
    }
    public function set firstName(v:String):void
    {
      _firstName = v;
    }
    public function get contactId():int
    {
      return _contactId;
    }
    public function set contactId(v:int):void
    {
      _contactId = v;
    }
    ...more getter and setter functions...
  }
}
```

On the Web

The code in Listing 18.3 is available in the Web site files as `ContactPrivateVars.as` in the `chapter18`
project. ■

Tip

Just as with public properties, you can make individual accessor method properties bindable by adding the
`[Bindable]` metadata tag before the method declaration:

```
[Bindable]
public function set firstName(newValue:String):void
{
  this._firstName = newValue;
}
 public function get firstName():String
{
  return this._firstName;
} ■
```

Note

Accessor methods provide an opportunity to perform other tasks in addition to just getting and setting the properties. For example, if you want to use local shared objects, a set accessor method provides an opportunity to save the new value to disk. Or, if a property is only available to users with a particular level of security, you can check permissions before changing or returning the property. ■

Instantiating value object classes

You can create instances of value object classes using either MXML or ActionScript.

Instantiating with MXML

To create an instance of a value object class in MXML, follow these steps:

1. **Declare a custom namespace prefix associated with the package containing the ActionScript class.** The custom namespace prefix should be placed in the MXML file's root element (for example, in the <s:Application> start tag):

   ```
   <s:Application xmlns:fx="http://ns.adobe.com/mxml/2009"
     xmlns:s="library://ns.adobe.com/flex/spark"
     xmlns:mx="library://ns.adobe.com/flex/mx"
     xmlns:valueObjects="valueObjects.*">
   </s:Application>
   ```

2. **Within an** <fx:Declarations> **element, declare an MXML tag using the custom namespace prefix, followed by the component name (without the .mxml extension).** As with instances of pre-built components in the Flex framework, assign an id attribute to serve the object's unique identifier:

   ```
   <fx:Declarations>
     <valueObjects:Contact id="contact"/>
   </fx:Declarations>
   ```

Setting object properties in MXML

You can set a value object's properties as either attributes or child elements. When assigning properties as XML attributes, you can include binding expressions to set values from visual components or other data sources. For example, this instance of the Contact object gets its property values from TextInput and other data entry controls:

```
<fx:Declarations>
  <valueObjects:Contact id="myContact"
    firstName="{firstNameInput.text}"
    lastName="{lastNameInput.text}"
    dob="{dobSelector.selectedDate}"/>
</fx:Declarations>
```

Alternatively, you can declare value object properties using child element syntax:

```
<fx:Declarations>
  <valueObjects:Contact id="myContact">
    <valueObjects:firstName>
```

```
                        {firstNameInput.text}
                    </valueObjects:firstName>
                    <valueObjects:lastName>
                        {lastNameInput.text}
                    </valueObjects:lastName>
                    <valueObjects:dob>
                        {firstNameInput.text}
                    </valueObjects:dob>
                </valueObjects:ContactComplete>
            </fx:Declarations>
```

Note

The choice of using attributes or child elements in this case is purely one of coding style; both approaches result in passing values from visual controls to a value object's properties as the user interacts with the controls. Notice, however, that when using child element syntax, you must include the value object class's namespace prefix on each tag, while with attribute-style syntax, the prefix isn't required (and in fact can't be used). As a result, attribute-style syntax is much more concise and, unsurprisingly, more popular. ∎

The application in Listing 18.4 declares an instance of the Contact value object class and populates its public properties with binding expressions that refer to the properties of interactive controls.

LISTING 18.4

Using a value object in MXML

```
<?xml version="1.0" encoding="utf-8"?>
<s:Application xmlns:fx="http://ns.adobe.com/mxml/2009"
  xmlns:s="library://ns.adobe.com/flex/spark"
  xmlns:mx="library://ns.adobe.com/flex/mx"
  xmlns:valueObjects="valueObjects.*">
  <fx:Declarations>
    <valueObjects:ContactComplete id="contact"
      firstName="{firstNameInput.text}"
      lastName="{lastNameInput.text}"
      dob="{dobSelector.selectedDate}"/>
    <mx:DateFormatter id="formatter" formatString="MMMM D, YYYY"/>
  </fx:Declarations>
  <s:VGroup top="20" horizontalCenter="0">
    <s:TextInput id="firstNameInput"/>
    <s:TextInput id="lastNameInput"/>
    <mx:DateField id="dobSelector"/>
    <s:Label text="First Name: {contact.firstName}"/>
    <s:Label text="Last Name: {contact.lastName}"/>
    <s:Label text="Date of Birth: {formatter.format(contact.dob)}"/>
  </s:VGroup>
</s:Application>
```

On the Web

The code in Listing 18.4 is available in the Web site files as `UseValueObject.mxml` in the `chapter18` project. ∎

Instantiating value objects with ActionScript

Because a value object is an ActionScript class, you can create an instance of the class with this simple variable declaration. If you want to be able to use binding expressions to get data out of the class at runtime, be sure to include the `[Bindable]` metadata tag before the variable declaration:

```
private var myContact:Contact = new Contact();
```

You then set object properties with dot syntax:

```
myContact.firstName = firstNameInput.text
myContact.lastName = lastNameInput.text
myContact.dob = dobSelector.selectedDate;
```

Using customized constructor methods

After the value object is populated with data, you can send it to a server through a `RemoteObject` or `WebService` request, or store it persistently in client application memory for later use.

If you're planning to instantiate a value object class with ActionScript code, you might want to customize the class's constructor method to allow values to be set upon object construction. As with all ActionScript classes, the constructor method for a value object class follows these rules:

- **The name of the constructor method is the same as the class name and is case-sensitive.**

- **You can have only a single constructor method.** ActionScript 3.0 doesn't support method overloading (the capability to create two or more methods that share a name but differ by the number or data types of their arguments).

- **A constructor method never returns a value and doesn't require a return data type declaration.**

In this example, the constructor method has been customized to accept arguments containing initialization data:

```
public function ContactCustomConstructor(
   contactId:int, firstName:String, lastName:String, dob:Date,
   address:String, city:String, zipCode:String, telephone:String)
{
   this.contactId = contactId;
   this.firstName = firstName;
   this.lastName = lastName;
   this.dob = dob;
   this.address = address;
   this.zipCode = zipCode;
   this.telephone = telephone;
}
```

551

Note

In the preceding code, the names of arguments and the names of their corresponding public properties are identical. In the body of the constructor method, the prefix `this` is used to resolve ambiguity between the public property (referred to explicitly) and the argument of the same name. Without the prefix, the argument name takes precedence. ∎

Using default argument values

In ActionScript 3.0, if you declare an argument in the constructor without a default value, the argument must be passed during object instantiation. This can cause a problem with objects that you also want to instantiate with MXML code, because this sort of instantiation always executes the class's constructor method but isn't capable of passing arguments:

```
<fx:Declarations>
  <valueObjects:ContactCustomConstructor id="myContact"/>
</fx:Declaration>
```

Using the preceding constructor method signature, this MXML declaration would cause a compiler error and prevent you from successfully building or running the application.

You can solve this problem by adding default values to each of the constructor method's arguments, as in the following example:

```
public function ContactCustomConstructor(
  contactId:int=0, firstName:String=null, lastName:String=null,
  dob:Date=null, address:String=null, city:String=null,
  zipCode:String=null, telephone:String=null)
{
  if (contactId != 0)
    this.contactId = contactId;
  if (firstName != null)
    this.firstName = firstName;
  ... remaining property settings ...
}
```

If the class with this version of the constructor method is declared in MXML, the arguments are passed with their default values. Conditional code in the constructor method can then determine whether to pass the values to their corresponding public properties.

Using Data Collections

A data collection is an ordered list of data objects stored in client application memory. Flex provides ActionScript classes named `ArrayCollection` and `ArrayList` that are designed for this purpose. More than a simple `Array`, the `ArrayList`, and `ArrayCollection` classes have these advantages:

- Unlike an `Array`, `ArrayList` and `ArrayCollection` reliably execute binding expressions that refer to their stored data.

- The `ArrayCollection` class implements a set of interfaces that provide client-side data filtering, sorting, bookmarking, and traversal.

- An `ArrayCollection` can be serialized for transport over the Web in requests to Web services, remoting services, and messaging services.

New Feature

The `ArrayList` class is new to the Flex 4 SDK. It's a lighter-weight class than `ArrayCollection`, as it's designed simply to contain data at runtime and not to perform extensive data management tasks. Also, when you get data from a server using RPC components such as `HTTPService` and `WebService`, the data is frequently returned automatically as an `ArrayCollection`. ■

Cross-Reference

In addition to the `ArrayCollection` class, the Flex SDK also includes a class named `XMLListCollection` that serves many of the same purposes but is designed to manage hierarchical data represented in XML format. The `XMLListCollection` class is described in detail in Chapter 24. ■

Declaring an ArrayCollection

As with most ActionScript classes, data collection variables can be declared with either MXML or ActionScript. To declare an `ArrayCollection` in MXML, use the `<s:ArrayCollection>` tag and assign its `id` property:

```
<fx:Declarations>
  <s:ArrayCollection id="myData"/>
</fx:Declarations>
```

Note

When you declare a data collection variable with MXML, the variable is immediately instantiated and made bindable. ■

Alternatively, you can use this ActionScript code to declare and instantiate the `ArrayCollection` variable. If you want to bind to the collection's data, use the `[Bindable]` metadata tag before the variable declaration:

```
import mx.collections.ArrayCollection;
[Bindable]
private var myData:ArrayCollection;
```

Note

The `ArrayCollection` class must be imported and explicitly instantiated when used in ActionScript code. When you use the `<s:ArrayCollection>` tag, you don't need to import the class, and it's automatically instantiated. ■

Setting a data collection object's source property

The `ArrayCollection` and `ArrayList` classes have a `source` property that refers to a raw `Array` containing its data. You can set a data collection object's `source` in a number of ways:

- By passing the `Array` into the data collection class's constructor method:

  ```
  myData = new ArrayList(myArray);
  ```

- With an ActionScript statement after the `ArrayCollection` has been instantiated:

  ```
  myData.source = ["red", "green", "blue"];
  ```

- In an MXML declaration, nested in `<s:source>` tags:

  ```
  <fx:Declarations>
    <s:ArrayCollection id="acColors">
      <s:source>
        <fx:String>Red</fx:String>
        <fx:String>Green</fx:String>
        <fx:String>Blue</fx:String>
      </s:source>
    </s:ArrayCollection>
  <fx:Declarations>
  ```

Tip

In the preceding MXML declaration, the `ArrayCollection` object's source property is already known by the compiler to be an `Array`. This is why you can then immediately declare individual data elements in a list. A longhand version of this code might look like this:

```
<fx:Declarations>
  <s:ArrayCollection id="acColors">
    <s:source>
      <fx:Array>
        <fx:String>Red</fx:String>
        <fx:String>Green</fx:String>
        <fx:String>Blue</fx:String>
      </fx:Array>
    </s:source>
  </s:ArrayCollection>
</fx:Declarations> ■
```

If you're working with data that's been embedded into the application with the `<fx:Model>` tag, the model's repeating elements are exposed to the ActionScript environment as an `Array`. This code would wrap the `Array` in an `ArrayCollection` using a binding expression:

```
<fx:Declarations>
  <fx:Model id="bookData" source="data/books.xml"/>
  <s:ArrayList id="bookData" source="{bookData.book}">
</fx:Declarations>
```

Accessing data at runtime

Both the `ArrayList` and `ArrayCollection` classes implement the `IList` interface. The following `IList` methods and properties enable you to dynamically get, add, and remove data at runtime:

- `addItem(item:Object)`. Appends a data item to the end of the collection.

- `addItemAt(item:Object, index:int)`. Adds a data item in the collection at the declared index position. Existing data items are shifted downward to make room for the new data item.

- `getItemAt(index:int, prefetch:int=0)`. Returns a data item at the declared index position. The optional prefetch argument is used when an `ArrayCollection` contains *managed data* to indicate how many rows of data should be fetched from the server.

- `length:int`. Returns the number of items in the `ArrayCollection`.

- `removeAll()`. Clears all items from the collection.

- `removeItemAt(index:int)`. Removes a data item from the `ArrayCollection` object.

- `setItemAt(item:Object, index:int)`. Replaces a data item in the declared index position.

Note

The term managed data refers to data that's managed by and accessed through Adobe LiveCycle Data Services' Data Management Service. ∎

The application in Listing 18.5 shows the use of an `ArrayCollection` to handle data that's embedded from an XML file. When the user clicks the application's Remove Item button, the `ArrayCollection` object's `removeItemAt()` method is called to remove the selected data item.

LISTING 18.5

Using an ArrayCollection

```
<?xml version="1.0" encoding="utf-8"?>
<s:Application xmlns:fx="http://ns.adobe.com/mxml/2009"
  xmlns:s="library://ns.adobe.com/flex/spark"
  xmlns:mx="library://ns.adobe.com/flex/mx">
  <s:layout>
    <s:VerticalLayout horizontalAlign="center" paddingTop="20"/>
  </s:layout>
  <fx:Declarations>
    <fx:Model id="bookData" source="data/books.xml"/>
    <s:ArrayCollection id="acBooks" source="{bookData.book}"/>
  </fx:Declarations>
  <fx:Script>
    <![CDATA[
      private function removeDataItem():void
      {
```

continued

LISTING 18.5   *(continued)*

```
        if (booksGrid.selectedIndex != -1)
        {
          acBooks.removeItemAt(booksGrid.selectedIndex);
        }
      }
    ]]>
  </fx:Script>
  <mx:DataGrid id="booksGrid" dataProvider="{acBooks}"/>
  <s:Button label="Remove Data" click="removeDataItem()"/>
</s:Application>
```

On the Web

The code in Listing 18.5 is available in the Web site files as `DisplayBookCollection.mxml` in the `chapter18` project. ■

Managing data at runtime

The `ArrayCollection` class implements a number of interfaces to enable you to dynamically manage data in client application memory at runtime. These interfaces include:

- `ICollectionView`. Has methods for filtering and sorting data at runtime.
- `IList`. Has the methods described previously for adding, removing, and accessing data at runtime.

In addition, the `ArrayCollection` class's `createCursor()` method returns an `IViewCursor` object that enables you to bookmark and traverse data in memory, much like you might do with a server-side database that supports cursor operations. In this section, I describe the use of the `ICollectionView` and `IViewCursor` interfaces that support dynamic data management in the client application.

You can filter data that's managed by the `ArrayCollection` class without having to make additional calls to remote servers. This is a major benefit of Flex applications, compared to the model typically used in a classic Web application. In classic Web applications, each time the user requests a filtered view of data, the application makes a call to a dynamic server page (whether built in ColdFusion, ASP.NET, PHP, or some other Web server technology). The dynamic server page executes a database query to get a filtered data set, and the application server returns a response formatted in HTML.

Flex applications are *stateful*; they have their own data management tools that can execute most data management operations without having to communicate with the server. As a result, these applications can support many more concurrent users, as each user contributes the processing power of her own local computer system to the task at hand.

Filtering data

The `ArrayCollection` class executes filtering through its `filterFunction` property. This property is designed to reference an ActionScript function that you create and customize. A function designed for filtering always has this signature:

```
private function functionName(item:Object):Boolean
```

The item argument can be either a generic ActionScript `Object` variable or a strongly typed value object. When you execute a filter, the `ArrayCollection` class loops through its source data and executes the filter function once for each data item. If the filtering function returns `true`, the current data item is included in the resulting filtered view; if it returns `false`, the data item is hidden and won't be visible to the user unless and until the filter is removed.

The following filtering function examines a property of a data item and compares it to a value provided by the user through a visual component. If the data item property and the user-provided value match, the function returns `true`, indicating that the data item should be included in the filtered view:

```
private function filterOnAuthor(item:Object):Boolean
{
  if (item.au_id == authorList.selectedItem.au_id)
  {
    return true;
  }
  else
  {
    return false;
  }
}
```

The preceding code also could be written more concisely, using the comparison of the two values as a `Boolean` expression:

```
private function filterOnAuthor(item:Object):Boolean
{
  return (item.au_id == authorList.selectedItem.au_id);
}
```

Because this function will be called by the `ArrayCollection` once for each of its data items, you should keep the filtering function brief.

To use the filter function, first assign the function to the `ArrayCollection` class's `filterFunction` property by its name. Then call the `ArrayCollection` object's `refresh()` method to cause the filtering to happen:

```
acBooks.filterFunction=filterOnAuthor;
acBooks.refresh();
```

If the application's current state is such that you want to remove the filter, set `filterFunction` to a value of `null` and then again call the `refresh()` method. In the following code, a conditional statement evaluates whether the user has selected the first item in a `ComboBox` control. This item represents a value of "all records," so the `filterFunction` is set to `null` if the condition is true. Otherwise, the `filterFunction` is set to the custom ActionScript function designed to execute the filter. The call to `refresh()` is then executed at the end of the conditional block:

```
private function executeFilter():void
{
  if (authorList.selectedIndex == 0)
  {
    acBooks.filterFunction = null;
  }
  else
  {
    acBooks.filterFunction=filterOnAuthor;
  }
  acBooks.refresh();
}
```

The application in Listing 18.6 implements a filter using two data sets. The first data set, representing authors, is displayed in a `DropDownList` control. As the application starts up, an additional data item is added at the beginning of this data set representing a choice of All Authors.

At runtime, each time the user selects an author (or All Authors), the `executeFilter()` method is called. As a result, the `filterFunction` is set and the call to `refresh()` causes the filter to be applied.

LISTING 18.6

Implementing a filtering function

```
<?xml version="1.0" encoding="utf-8"?>
<s:Application xmlns:fx="http://ns.adobe.com/mxml/2009"
  xmlns:s="library://ns.adobe.com/flex/spark"
  xmlns:mx="library://ns.adobe.com/flex/mx"
  creationComplete="app_creationCompleteHandler()">
  <s:layout>
    <s:VerticalLayout horizontalAlign="center" paddingTop="20"/>
  </s:layout>
  <fx:Declarations>
    <fx:Model id="authorModel" source="data/authors.xml"/>
    <fx:Model id="bookModel" source="data/books.xml"/>
    <s:ArrayCollection id="acAuthors" source="{authorModel.author}"/>
    <s:ArrayCollection id="acBooks" source="{bookModel.book}"/>
  </fx:Declarations>
  <fx:Script>
```

```
    <![CDATA[
      private function app_creationCompleteHandler():void
      {
        acAuthors.addItemAt("All Authors", 0);
        authorList.selectedIndex = 0;
      }
      private function getAuthorName(item:Object):String
      {
        if (item is String)
        {
          return item as String;
        }
        else
        {
          return item.au_fname + " " + item.au_lname;
        }
      }
      private function filterOnAuthor(item:Object):Boolean
      {
        return (item.au_id == authorList.selectedItem.au_id);
      }
      private function executeFilter():void
      {
        if (authorList.selectedIndex == 0)
        {
          acBooks.filterFunction = null;
        }
        else
        {
          acBooks.filterFunction=filterOnAuthor;
        }
        acBooks.refresh();
      }
    ]]>
  </fx:Script>
  <mx:DataGrid id="bookGrid" dataProvider="{acBooks}" width="350">
    <mx:columns>
      <mx:DataGridColumn dataField="title" headerText="Title"/>
      <mx:DataGridColumn dataField="price" headerText="Price"/>
    </mx:columns>
  </mx:DataGrid>
  <s:DropDownList id="authorList"
    width="200"
    dataProvider="{acAuthors}"
    labelFunction="getAuthorName"
    change="executeFilter()"/>
</s:Application>
```

On the Web

The code in Listing 18.6 is available in the Web site files as `FilterDemo.mxml` in the `chapter18` project. ■

Cross-Reference

The application in Listing 18.6 includes the use of the Spark `DropDownList` and the MX `DataGrid` controls. These features of the Flex SDK are described in Chapter 19. ■

Sorting data

The `ArrayCollection` sorts data through use of its `sort` property. The sort property references an instance of the `mx.collections.Sort` class. This class in turn has a `fields` property that references an `Array` containing instances of `mx.collections.SortField`.

The `SortField` class supports these `Boolean` properties that determine which named property of an `ArrayCollection` object's data items to sort on and how to execute the sort operation:

- `caseInsensitive` defaults to `false`, meaning that sort operations are case-sensitive by default.
- `descending` defaults to `false`, meaning that sort operations are ascending by default.
- `numeric` defaults to `false`, meaning that sort operations are text-based by default.

You can instantiate a `SortField` object and set all of its `Boolean` properties in the constructor method call, using this syntax:

```
var mySortField:SortField = new SortField(
    'propName', caseInsensitive, descending, numeric);
```

All the constructor method arguments are optional, so the following code creates a `SortField` object that sorts on a `lastName` field and uses the default settings of case-sensitive, ascending, and text:

```
var mySortField:SortField = new SortField('lastName');
```

To sort on multiple named properties, add the `SortField` objects to the array in the order of sort precedence — the first `SortField` object is the primary sort, and so on:

```
var mySort:Sort = new Sort();
mySort.fields = new Array();
mySort.fields.push(new SortField('price', false, false, true));
mySort.fields.push(new SortField('title'));
```

After creating the `Sort` object and populating its `fields` property with the `Array` of `SortField` objects, the last step is to assign the `ArrayCollection` object's sort property and call its `refresh()` method:

```
acBooks.sort = mySort;
acBooks.refresh();
```

Note

The implementation of sorting functionality as a collection of objects enables you to save a customized Sort object and reuse it elsewhere in your application. ■

The application in Listing 18.7 executes a sort operation using the ArrayCollection's sort property and two SortField objects.

LISTING 18.7

Executing a sort operation

```
<?xml version="1.0" encoding="utf-8"?>
<s:Application xmlns:fx="http://ns.adobe.com/mxml/2009"
  xmlns:s="library://ns.adobe.com/flex/spark"
  xmlns:mx="library://ns.adobe.com/flex/mx">
  <s:layout>
    <s:VerticalLayout horizontalAlign="center" paddingTop="20"/>
  </s:layout>
  <fx:Declarations>
    <fx:Model id="bookModel" source="data/books.xml"/>
    <s:ArrayCollection id="acBooks" source="{bookModel.book}"/>
  </fx:Declarations>
  <fx:Script>
    <![CDATA[
      import mx.collections.SortField;
      import mx.collections.Sort;
      private function executeSort():void
      {
        var mySort:Sort = new Sort();
        mySort.fields = new Array();
        mySort.fields.push(new SortField('price', false, false, true));
        mySort.fields.push(new SortField('title'));
        acBooks.sort = mySort;
        acBooks.refresh();
      }
    ]]>
  </fx:Script>
  <mx:DataGrid id="bookGrid" dataProvider="{acBooks}" width="350">
    <mx:columns>
      <mx:DataGridColumn dataField="title" headerText="Title"/>
      <mx:DataGridColumn dataField="price" headerText="Price"/>
    </mx:columns>
  </mx:DataGrid>
  <s:Button label="Sort Data" click="executeSort()"/>
</s:Application>
```

On the Web

The code in Listing 18.7 is available in the Web site files as `SortDemo.mxml` in the `chapter18` project. ■

Tip

The `Sort` class has a property named `compareFunction` that can be assigned to a custom ActionScript function. This is useful if you need to execute a sort operation that's based on comparisons other than simple numeric or text values. The signature of the function you assign is as follows:

```
function [name](item1:Object, item2:Object,
    fields:Array = null):int
```

The function should return one of these values: −1 if the first item should appear above the second in the sorted view, 1 if the second item should appear first, and 0 if the two items are equivalent for purposes of sorting. ■

Using data cursors

The `ArrayCollection` class has a function named `createCursor()` that returns an object implementing the `IViewCursor` interface. The `IViewCursor` object has properties and methods supporting these client-side data management tasks:

- Traversing the data forward and backward
- Searching the data for particular values
- Accessing a particular object in the collection at the cursor's location
- Bookmarking data so you can easily return to bookmarked items

In order to use an `ArrayCollection` cursor object, declare a variable typed as the `IViewCursor` interface. It's typically best to declare this variable as a persistent property outside of any functions, so you can then refer to the object from anywhere else in the code:

```
import mx.collections.IViewCursor;
private var cursor:IViewCursor;
private function initApp():void
{
    cursor = acBooks.createCursor();
}
```

After the cursor has been created, you can then use its features to manage code in the client application.

Traversing data

The properties and methods the `IViewCursor` interface supports that enable you to move through data one item at a time and determine the current cursor position are as follows:

- `afterLast:Boolean`. Returns `true` if the current cursor position is after the last data item.
- `beforeFirst:Boolean`. Returns `true` if the current cursor position is before the first data item.
- `current:Object`. Returns a reference to the data item at the current cursor position.

- `moveNext():Boolean`. Moves the cursor to the next data item in the collection. This method returns `false` if the cursor can't move forward (because it's already at the end of the collection).

- `movePrevious():Boolean`. Moves the cursor to the previous data item in the collection. This method returns `false` if the cursor can't move backward (because it's already at the start of the collection).

Note

When you first create a cursor from a collection, the cursor's initial position is the collection's first item (unless the collection is empty). ■

The application in Listing 18.8 uses a cursor to loop through a collection and collect values from each of its data items.

LISTING 18.8

Using a cursor to traverse and collect data from a collection

```
<?xml version="1.0" encoding="utf-8"?>
<s:Application xmlns:fx="http://ns.adobe.com/mxml/2009"
  xmlns:s="library://ns.adobe.com/flex/spark"
  xmlns:mx="library://ns.adobe.com/flex/mx">
  <s:layout>
    <s:VerticalLayout horizontalAlign="center" paddingTop="20"/>
  </s:layout>
  <fx:Declarations>
    <fx:Model id="bookModel" source="data/books.xml"/>
    <s:ArrayCollection id="acBooks" source="{bookModel.book}"/>
    <mx:CurrencyFormatter id="formatter" precision="2"/>
  </fx:Declarations>
  <fx:Script>
    <![CDATA[
      import mx.collections.IViewCursor;
      import mx.controls.Alert;
      private var cursor:IViewCursor;
      private function collectData():void
      {
        cursor = acBooks.createCursor();
        var total:Number = 0;
        while (!cursor.afterLast)
        {
          total += Number(cursor.current.price);
          cursor.moveNext();
        }
        Alert.show("The average price of a book is " +
          formatter.format(total / acBooks.length),
          "Average Price");
```

continued

LISTING 18.8   (continued)

```
      }
    ]]>
  </fx:Script>
  <mx:DataGrid id="bookGrid" dataProvider="{acBooks}" width="350">
    <mx:columns>
      <mx:DataGridColumn dataField="title" headerText="Title"/>
      <mx:DataGridColumn dataField="price" headerText="Price"/>
    </mx:columns>
  </mx:DataGrid>
  <s:Button label="Get Average Price" click="collectData()"/>
</s:Application>
```

On the Web

The code in Listing 18.8 is available in the Web site files as TraversingData.mxml **in the** chapter18 **project.** ■

Finding data with a cursor

The IViewCursor interface supports these methods to search an ArrayCollection for a data item:

- findAny(item:Object):Boolean. Locates an item with specific values anywhere in the ArrayCollection.

- findFirst(item:Object):Boolean. Locates the first item with specific values.

- findLast(item:Object):Boolean. Locates the last item with specific values.

Before executing any of these methods to locate data, the ArrayCollection must first be sorted on at least one of the properties on which you're searching. Then, to locate a data item, create an object with matching named properties set to the data that you want to search. For example, if you want to search on a title property of the objects in your collection, create a new Object with that named property set to the value you want to locate:

```
var searchObject:Object = {title:bookGrid.selectedItem.title};
var found:Boolean = cursor.findAny(searchObject);
```

If the search operation is successful, the function returns true. You can then get a reference to the data item that was located by referring to the cursor object's current property:

```
var foundObject:Object = cursor.current;
```

In the application in Listing 18.9, the application uses two ArrayCollection objects. The first is a catalog of data. When the user selects an item and clicks to add the object to the second ArrayCollection, a shopping cart — an IViewCursor — object is used to determine whether the object is already in the cart. If the object isn't found, it's added to the cart collection; if it is found, the object's quantity property is incremented by 1.

LISTING 18.9

Locating data with a cursor

```
<?xml version="1.0" encoding="utf-8"?>
<s:Application xmlns:fx="http://ns.adobe.com/mxml/2009"
  xmlns:s="library://ns.adobe.com/flex/spark"
  xmlns:mx="library://ns.adobe.com/flex/mx"
  creationComplete="app_creationCompleteHandler()">
  <fx:Declarations>
    <fx:Model id="bookModel" source="data/books.xml"/>
    <s:ArrayCollection id="acBooks" source="{bookModel.book}"/>
    <s:ArrayCollection id="acCart"/>
    <mx:CurrencyFormatter id="formatter" precision="2"/>
  </fx:Declarations>
  <fx:Script>
    <![CDATA[
      import mx.collections.IViewCursor;
      import mx.collections.Sort;
      import mx.collections.SortField;
      private var cursor:IViewCursor;
      private function app_creationCompleteHandler():void
      {
        var mySort:Sort = new Sort();
        mySort.fields = [new SortField('title')];
        acCart.sort = mySort;
        acCart.refresh();
      }
      private function addToCart():void
      {
        var searchObject:Object = {title:bookGrid.selectedItem.title};
        cursor = acCart.createCursor();
        if (cursor.findAny(searchObject))
        {
          cursor.current.quantity ++;
        }
        else
        {
          bookGrid.selectedItem.quantity=1;
          acCart.addItem(bookGrid.selectedItem);
        }
      }
      private function removeFromCart():void
      {
        acCart.removeItemAt(cartGrid.selectedIndex);
      }
    ]]>
  </fx:Script>
  <s:HGroup horizontalCenter="0" top="20">
```

continued

LISTING 18.9   *(continued)*

```
    <s:Panel title="Catalog">
      <s:layout>
        <s:VerticalLayout paddingBottom="10" paddingTop="10"
          paddingRight="10"  paddingLeft="10"/>
      </s:layout>
      <mx:DataGrid id="bookGrid" dataProvider="{acBooks}" width="350">
        <mx:columns>
          <mx:DataGridColumn dataField="title" headerText="Title"/>
          <mx:DataGridColumn dataField="price" headerText="Price"/>
        </mx:columns>
      </mx:DataGrid>
      <s:controlBarContent>
        <s:Button label="Add to Cart" click="addToCart()"
          enabled="{bookGrid.selectedIndex!=-1}"/>
      </s:controlBarContent>
    </s:Panel>
    <s:Panel title="Shopping Cart">
      <s:layout>
        <s:VerticalLayout paddingBottom="10" paddingTop="10"
          paddingRight="10"  paddingLeft="10"/>
      </s:layout>
      <mx:DataGrid id="cartGrid" dataProvider="{acCart}"
        width="350" sortableColumns="false">
        <mx:columns>
          <mx:DataGridColumn dataField="title" headerText="Title"/>
          <mx:DataGridColumn dataField="quantity" headerText="Quantity"/>
        </mx:columns>
      </mx:DataGrid>
      <s:controlBarContent>
        <s:Button label="Remove from Cart"
          click="removeFromCart()"
          enabled="{cartGrid.selectedIndex!=-1}"/>
      </s:controlBarContent>
    </s:Panel>
  </s:HGroup>
</s:Application>
```

On the Web

The code in Listing 18.9 is available in the Web site files as `SearchingData.mxml` in the `chapter18` project. ∎

Bookmarking data

The properties and methods the IViewCursor interface defines that enable you to bookmark data items and then easily find them again are as follows:

- bookmark:CursorBookmark. A property that refers to the cursor's current bookmark.
- seek(bookmark:CursorBookmark, offset:int = 0, prefetch:int = 0):void. A method that can be used to locate a bookmark and reposition the cursor to that location, or to an offset relative to the bookmark location.

To create a bookmark, first position a cursor object on the data item you want to mark. Then create a variable typed as the CursorBookmark class that references the cursor's bookmark property:

```
import mx.collections.CursorBookmark;
private var myBookmark:CursorBookmark;
private function bookMarkIt():void
{
  myBookMark = cursor.bookmark;
}
```

To return the cursor to the bookmarked position, call the cursor's seek() method and pass the CursorBookmark object:

```
cursor.seek(myBookmark);
```

The application in Listing 18.10 uses a CursorBookmark object to "remember" which data item was most recently added to the shopping cart. When the user clicks the application's Add Another button, the cursor's seek() method is called to return to that data item and increment its quantity property.

LISTING 18.10

Using a cursor bookmark

```
<?xml version="1.0" encoding="utf-8"?>
<s:Application xmlns:fx="http://ns.adobe.com/mxml/2009"
  xmlns:s="library://ns.adobe.com/flex/spark"
  xmlns:mx="library://ns.adobe.com/flex/mx"
  creationComplete="app_creationCompleteHandler()">
  <fx:Declarations>
    <fx:Model id="bookModel" source="data/books.xml"/>
    <s:ArrayCollection id="acBooks" source="{bookModel.book}"/>
    <s:ArrayCollection id="acCart"/>
    <mx:CurrencyFormatter id="formatter" precision="2"/>
  </fx:Declarations>
  <fx:Script>
    <![CDATA[
```

continued

LISTING 18.10   *(continued)*

```
    import mx.collections.CursorBookmark;
    import mx.collections.IViewCursor;
    import mx.collections.Sort;
    import mx.collections.SortField;
    private var cursor:IViewCursor;
    [Bindable]
    private var myBookmark:CursorBookmark;
    private function app_creationCompleteHandler():void
    {
      var mySort:Sort = new Sort();
      mySort.fields = [new SortField('title')];
      acCart.sort = mySort;
      acCart.refresh();
    }
    private function addToCart():void
    {
      cursor = acCart.createCursor();
      var searchObject:Object = {title:bookGrid.selectedItem.title};
      if (cursor.findAny(searchObject))
      {
        cursor.current.quantity ++;
      }
      else
      {
        bookGrid.selectedItem.quantity=1;
        acCart.addItem(bookGrid.selectedItem);
        cursor.findAny(searchObject);
      }
      myBookmark = cursor.bookmark;
    }
    private function addAnother():void
    {
      cursor.seek(myBookmark);
      cursor.current.quantity++;
      cartGrid.selectedItem=cursor.current;
    }
    private function removeFromCart():void
    {
      acCart.removeItemAt(cartGrid.selectedIndex);
    }
  ]]>
</fx:Script>
<s:HGroup horizontalCenter="0" top="20">
  <s:Panel title="Catalog">
    <s:layout>
      <s:VerticalLayout paddingBottom="10" paddingTop="10"
        paddingRight="10"  paddingLeft="10"/>
    </s:layout>
```

```
      <mx:DataGrid id="bookGrid" dataProvider="{acBooks}" width="350">
        <mx:columns>
          <mx:DataGridColumn dataField="title" headerText="Title"/>
          <mx:DataGridColumn dataField="price" headerText="Price"/>
        </mx:columns>
      </mx:DataGrid>
      <s:controlBarContent>
        <s:Button label="Add to Cart" click="addToCart()"
          enabled="{bookGrid.selectedIndex!=-1}"/>
      </s:controlBarContent>
    </s:Panel>
    <s:Panel title="Shopping Cart">
      <s:layout>
        <s:VerticalLayout paddingBottom="10" paddingTop="10"
          paddingRight="10"  paddingLeft="10"/>
      </s:layout>
      <mx:DataGrid id="cartGrid" dataProvider="{acCart}"
        width="350" sortableColumns="false">
        <mx:columns>
          <mx:DataGridColumn dataField="title" headerText="Title"/>
          <mx:DataGridColumn dataField="quantity" headerText="Quantity"/>
        </mx:columns>
      </mx:DataGrid>
      <s:controlBarContent>
        <s:Button label="Remove from Cart" click="removeFromCart()"
          enabled="{cartGrid.selectedIndex!=-1}"/>
        <s:Button label="Add Another" click="addAnother()"
          enabled="{myBookmark != null}"/>
      </s:controlBarContent>
    </s:Panel>
  </s:HGroup>
</s:Application>
```

On the Web

The code in Listing 18.10 is available in the Web site files as `BookmarkingData.mxml` in the `chapter18` project. ■

Summary

In this chapter, I described how to model and manage data in a Flex application using value object classes, the `ArrayCollection` class, and the `IViewCursor` interface. You learned the following:

- You can model individual data items with the `<fx:Model>` tag or with custom ActionScript classes that implement the Value Object design pattern.

- Objects modeled with `<fx:Model>` can't declare default values or apply specific data types to their properties.

- Custom ActionScript classes that implement the Value Object design pattern can best model the structure of a server-side database table.

- You can use the `<fx:Model>` tag to embed data in an application.

- You should only embed data that's small in scope and won't change.

- The `ArrayCollection` and `ArrayList` classes are designed to manage data in a Flex client application.

- Both `ArrayCollection` and `ArrayList` are wrapper classes around an `Array` and do a better job than the `Array` of reliably executing bindings when its data changes.

- You can use the `ArrayCollection` class to sort and filter data in a client application without having to make additional requests to an application server.

- The `IViewCursor` interface gives you the ability to traverse, search, and bookmark data stored in an `ArrayCollection`.

Using List Controls

Most Flex applications are designed for the purpose of presenting and managing data in some form. As a result, one of the most popular families of visual controls in the Flex framework includes those known as *list controls*.

A list control is defined as a component that has a `dataProvider` property that enables you to populate the control with dynamic data. The data provided to a list control can be in the form of either hierarchical or relational data, and the type of data you want to present frequently determines which control you use. In addition to being able to display relational or hierarchical data, list controls have a common set of properties, methods, and events that enable the user to select one or more items with mouse and keyboard gestures.

The Flex 4 SDK includes both the older MX list controls such as `DataGrid`, `AdvancedDataGrid`, and `OlapDataGrid` and newer controls based on the new Spark component architecture:

- **The `List` component.** This component behaves by default like an HTML `<select>` control and displays data items to the user in a list box. After you learn how to use the `List` control, you have most of the information you need to use other such controls. You can populate controls with data, listen for events indicating that the user has selected or started to drag data, set common styles, and so on. It supports the Spark layout architecture, so you can display a horizontal or tile layout instead of the default vertical list.

- **The `DropDownList` and `ComboBox` components.** These components also behave like an HTML `<select>` control but use a drop-down list instead of a static list.

- **The `ButtonBar` component.** This component has the same appearance and behavior as an MX `ToggleButtonBar`, presenting a set of `ToggleButton` controls horizontally, but is controlled programmatically just like other Spark list controls.

IN THIS CHAPTER

Understanding list controls

Providing data to list controls

Using dynamic data providers

Controlling list item labels

Using list control events and properties

Handling user data selections

Using custom item renderers

On the Web

To use the sample code for this chapter, import the `chapter19.fxp` project from the Web site files into any folder on your disk. ∎

In this chapter, I describe in general terms how to use all list controls. I include information on how to populate these controls with data, how to control data presentation with custom generation of item labels and renderers, and how to handle events indicating that the user wants to select and manipulate data.

Cross-Reference

The unique capabilities of other list controls, including the MX `DataGrid`, `TileList`, and `HorizontalList`, and the new Spark components, are described in Chapter 20. ∎

Table 19.1 describes the components that have the capability to display dynamic data and support user interaction using the list control model. In the Architecture column I show which component architecture the most recent version of the component implements.

TABLE 19.1

The List Controls

Control	Architecture	Description
Advanced DataGrid	MX	This component implements all the features of the MX `DataGrid` control but adds the capability to group and aggregate data and can sort on multiple columns. This component is part of the Flex Data Visualization components and is available only with a Flash Builder Premiere license.
ButtonBar	Spark	This new component presents Spark `ToggleButton` objects horizontally. The appearance and behavior are similar to the MX `ToggleButtonBar`, but the application programming interface (API) follows the list model, implementing the `change` event and `selected Item` and `selectedIndex` properties.
ComboBox	Spark	This component presents a drop-down list of simple string values. The presentation of this component is similar to an HTML `<select>` control that has its `size` property set to 1, but enables the user to enter an arbitrary string instead of selecting an item from the list.
DataGrid	MX	This component presents a grid with multiple rows and columns. It is used to present data received from a server-side database or other data source that uses the spreadsheet-like rows-and-columns structure of relational database tables.
DropDownList	Spark	Extended from the Spark `List` control, this control shows a drop-down list from which the user can select a value. Its `layout` property enables you to lay the list out with vertical, horizontal, or tile layout.

Control	Architecture	Description
Horizontal List	MX	This component presents a horizontal list of data items, typically rendered with a custom item renderer. (For the Spark architecture, use a `List` with `layout` set to `HorizontalLayout`.)
List	Spark	This component presents a list box of data items. By default, the presentation of this component is similar to an HTML `<select>` control that has its size property set to a value greater than 1. Its `layout` property enables you to lay out the list's items with a Spark layout object such as `HorizontalLayout` or `TileLayout`.
OlapDataGrid	MX	This component expands on the `AdvancedDataGrid` and supports presentation of results from an Online Analytical Processing (OLAP) query.
TileList	MX	This component presents a grid of data items, typically rendered with a custom item renderer. (For the Spark architecture, use a `List` with `layout` set to `TileLayout`.)
Tree	MX	This component presents hierarchical data, commonly supplied by the contents of an XML file.

In addition to the components listed in Table 19.1, the Flex SDK includes a set of MX-based list controls designed for use in Adobe AIR applications. These controls provide the user with the ability to inspect and manipulate files and directories in the local file system and cannot be used in Flex applications that are deployed over the Web. They include the `FileSystemList`, `FileSystemComboBox`, `FileSystemDataGrid`, and `FileSystemTree` components.

Most of the information in this chapter and in Chapter 20 about list and `DataGrid` controls applies equally to these AIR-based controls, but these controls add functionality that enables them to populate their data from the directory and file contents of the local file system. They also implement additional properties and methods that are designed to support their unique purpose.

Note

Other MX components extend a class named `ComboBase` and therefore must be considered members of the family of list controls as well. The `ColorPicker` control is designed to enable selection of a color value from a grid of "Web-safe" colors, and the `DateField` control presents a pop-up calendar control. The components aren't often thought of as list controls, but they support the same set of properties, methods, and events as their cousins. In the Flex 4 SDK, there are no Spark equivalents to these components. ■

Each list control has its own unique visual presentation and behavior. As the developer, you select the control most suited to your application's requirements.

Figure 19.1 shows examples of the `List`, `DataGrid`, and `DropDownList` controls, each using the same set of data as its data provider.

On the Web

The application displayed in Figure 19.1 is available in the Web site files as `ListControls.mxml` in the `chapter19` project. ■

FIGURE 19.1

Commonly used list controls

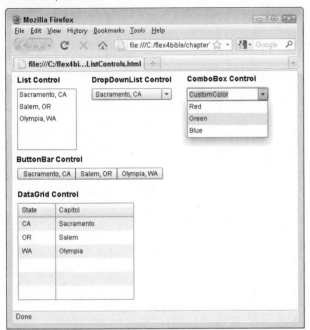

Using Data Providers

The data you provide to a list control must be in the form of an ActionScript object, but for most purposes you typically provide a set of data that's been wrapped in one of the data collection classes: either the `ArrayList` or `ArrayCollection` classes for data that's in rows and columns or the `XMLListCollection` class for hierarchical data.

The Spark and MX list controls have the same basic rules for their data providers: the data must be provided as an ordered data collection. But the Spark controls (`List`, `DropDownList`, and `ComboBox`) specify that the data object must implement the `IList` interface, whereas the MX controls accept any ActionScript `Object`. In practical terms, this means that the MX `DataGrid` and other related controls can accept a raw `Array` as their `dataProvider`, while the new Spark controls require an `ArrayList`, `ArrayCollection`, or other class that implements the interface.

The `List`, `DropDownList`, and `ComboBox` controls are distinguished from the `DataGrid` and its related controls in that they present only a single column of data. They can present data from a collection of complex objects, but by default they present only one value in each list item. In contrast, the `DataGrid` control is designed to present data in multiple columns.

Using hard-coded data providers

You can embed data in a Flex application for use by either a specific instance of a list control or as a separate data object that's then linked to a control through a binding expression. Hard-coding means that you declare actual data in the code, rather than retrieving it from an external data source at runtime.

Caution

As described in Chapter 18, when you embed data in a Flex application, the compiled application file expands accordingly. You should embed data only when it's a small amount of content and won't change during the lifetime of the application. ■

Nesting hard-coded data in a data provider

When using a list control, you can nest hard-coded data in the declaration of a list control's `data-Provider` by declaring the property with child-element syntax rather than attribute syntax. The following code presents a `List` control populated with a hard-coded data provider containing an `ArrayList` of simple `String` values:

```
<s:List id="sizeList">
  <s:dataProvider>
    <s:ArrayList>
      <fx:String>Small</fx:String>
      <fx:String>Medium</fx:String>
      <fx:String>Large</fx:String>
    </s:ArrayList>
  </s:dataProvider>
</s:List>
```

You also can declare the `dataProvider` with hard-coded collections of complex objects by nesting multiple `<fx:Object>` declarations within the `<s:dataProvider>` tag set:

```
<s:List id="stateList" labelField="stateName">
  <s:dataProvider>
    <s:ArrayList>
      <fx:Object>
        <fx:stateName>California</fx:stateName>
        <fx:capitol>Sacramento</fx:capitol>
      </fx:Object>
      <fx:Object>
        <fx:stateName>Oregon</fx:stateName>
        <fx:capitol>Salem</fx:capitol>
      </fx:Object>
      <fx:Object>
        <fx:stateName>Washington</fx:stateName>
        <fx:capitol>Olympia</fx:capitol>
      </fx:Object>
    <s:ArrayList>
  </s:dataProvider>
</s:List>
```

Note

With MX controls, you can leave out the `<s:ArrayList>` element and nest the data elements directly with the `<mx:dataProvider>`. This isn't possible with Spark list controls, because the MXML compiler doesn't know which implementing class of the `IList` interface to use. ■

Modifying data with the ArrayList API

Because data is passed to the `dataProvider` as an `ArrayList` or `ArrayCollection` object, the class's API can be used to access and manipulate the data. Even though the original data is hard-coded, the following ActionScript statement code would add a new item to the `List` object's `dataProvider` when it contains simple `String` values:

```
sizeList.dataProvider.addItem('Extra Large');
```

And this code would add a new item when it contains complex objects:

```
stateList.dataProvider.addItem({state:'New York','Albany'});
```

The application in Listing 19.1 uses a `List` object with a hard-coded data provider and then enables the user to add data to the object with the `addItem()` method.

LISTING 19.1

A List control with hard-coded data

```xml
<?xml version="1.0" encoding="utf-8"?>
<s:Application xmlns:fx="http://ns.adobe.com/mxml/2009"
  xmlns:s="library://ns.adobe.com/flex/spark"
  xmlns:mx="library://ns.adobe.com/flex/mx">
  <s:layout>
    <s:VerticalLayout horizontalAlign="center" paddingTop="20"/>
  </s:layout>
  <s:List id="sizeList">
    <s:dataProvider>
      <s:ArrayList>
        <fx:String>Small</fx:String>
        <fx:String>Medium</fx:String>
        <fx:String>Large</fx:String>
      </s:ArrayList>
    </s:dataProvider>
  </s:List>
  <s:HGroup>
    <s:Label text="New Item:"/>
    <s:TextInput id="itemInput"/>
    <s:Button label="Add Item"
      click="sizeList.dataProvider.addItem(itemInput.text)"/>
  </s:HGroup>
</s:Application>
```

On the Web

The code in Listing 19.1 is available in the Web site files as `ListWithHardCodedData.mxml` in the `chapter19` project. ∎

Declaring separate data objects with MXML tags

You also can provide hard-coded data to a Spark list control from an `<s:ArrayList>` element declared within an `<fx:Declarations>` element or in ActionScript code. The application in Listing 19.2 declares an `ArrayList` and then provides the data to the `List` object through a binding expression.

LISTING 19.2

A List control with data provided through a binding expression

```
<?xml version="1.0" encoding="utf-8"?>
<s:Application xmlns:fx="http://ns.adobe.com/mxml/2009"
  xmlns:s="library://ns.adobe.com/flex/spark"
  xmlns:mx="library://ns.adobe.com/flex/mx">
  <s:layout>
    <s:VerticalLayout horizontalAlign="center" paddingTop="20"/>
  </s:layout>
  <fx:Declarations>
    <s:ArrayList id="myData">
      <fx:String>Small</fx:String>
      <fx:String>Medium</fx:String>
      <fx:String>Large</fx:String>
    </s:ArrayList>
  </fx:Declarations>
  <s:List id="sizeList" dataProvider="{myData}"/>
  <s:HGroup>
    <s:Label text="New Item:"/>
    <s:TextInput id="itemInput"/>
    <s:Button label="Add Item"
      click="sizeList.dataProvider.addItem(itemInput.text)"/>
  </s:HGroup>
</s:Application>
```

On the Web

The code in Listing 19.2 is available in the Web site files as `ListWithBoundData.mxml` in the `chapter19` project. ∎

Using dynamic data providers

Data retrieved from an external source, such as the results of a remote server call through the Remote Procedure Call (RPC) components, or data retrieved from a local database (for an AIR desktop application) is typically stored in a data collection object. As described in Chapter 18, the data collection is typically declared in ActionScript code with the `[Bindable]` metadata tag or in MXML code.

In ActionScript code, the declaration looks like this:

```
import mx.collections.ArrayList;
[Bindable]
private var myData:ArrayList = new ArrayList();
```

And in MXML, it looks like this:

```
<s:ArrayList id="myData"/>
```

Note

Data objects that are declared in MXML are immediately instantiated and always bindable. ■

Regardless of how the data collection is declared, by making it bindable, you make it possible to pass the data to a List control with a simple binding expression:

```
<s:List id="sizeList" dataProvider="{myData}"/>
```

Using RPC components

You can choose to retrieve data dynamically from many sources, including the Flex SDK components that are grouped together as the RPC classes. These classes are distinguished from each other by the data format they use to communicate with a remote server:

- HTTPService. This class sends simple HTTP requests to URLs that return data formatted as simple text or XML. For example, a call to an RSS feed from a blog or content-based Web site would be executed using the HTTPService class.

- RemoteObject. This class sends and receives messages formatted in Action Message Format (AMF). This binary format is defined by Adobe and implemented in many of its server products, including LiveCycle Data Services, BlazeDS, and ColdFusion.

- WebService. This class retrieves data from a server with calls formatted in the industry-standard SOAP format.

These components and their methodologies are described starting in Chapter 23. All, however, are capable of returning data sets in the form of ArrayList or ArrayCollection objects that are suitable for use as List control data providers.

Note

The AMF data format was published by Adobe Systems in 2007 to support development of independent application server products that are compatible with Flex- and Flash-based applications. ■

Retrieving local data in AIR applications

If you're building an AIR-based desktop application, you can retrieve data from local XML files using the File and FileStream classes or from the local SQLite embedded database with classes such as SQLConnection and SQLStatement. These classes aren't designed to return data in the ArrayList format directly; you typically need to manually wrap data into your data collection objects with explicit ActionScript code.

Controlling List Item Labels

If a List control's data provider contains simple values (such as String, Number, or Date), these values are displayed on each item by default. If the data provider contains complex objects (either instances of the ActionScript Object class or of your own custom value object classes), you can determine the text labels that are displayed in a List control's items using one of these strategies:

- The labelField property enables you to point to a specific named property of each object whose values should be displayed.
- The labelFunction property enables you to customize each item's label with your own ActionScript code.

Using the labelField property

Most List controls support the labelField property. This property enables you to indicate which of the named properties of data items in the control's data provider is displayed at runtime.

The default value of labelField is label. As a result, if the data provider's objects have a property named label, that property's value is displayed. In the following code, the ArrayList contains data objects with a label property. The List control displays the label property's value on each of its items:

```
<fx:Declarations>
  <s:ArrayList id="stateData">
    <fx:Object>
      <fx:label>CA</fx:label>
      <fx:capitol>Sacramento</fx:capitol>
    </fx:Object>
    <fx:Object>
      <fx:label>OR</fx:label>
      <fx:capitol>Salem</fx:capitol>
    </fx:Object>
  </s:ArrayList>
</fx:Declarations>
<s:List id="stateList" dataProvider="{stateData}"/>
```

More commonly, the complex objects in the data collection have property names that are determined by the structure of a database table, XML file, value object, or other existing data source. If you forget to set the labelField property on a List control that displays complex data objects, the control displays labels consisting of a set of [] characters wrapped around the word object and the object's data type. If the data item is cast as an ActionScript Object, the result looks like this:

```
[object Object]
```

As shown in Figure 19.2, the results aren't particularly useful, even when working with a value object class.

FIGURE 19.2

A List control displaying a complex data object with no labelField setting

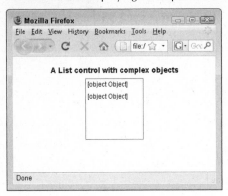

To fix this behavior, you explicitly set the List control's labelField to the name of the property you want to display:

```
<fx:Declarations>
  <s:ArrayList id="stateData">
    <fx:Object>
      <fx:state>CA</fx:state>
      <fx:capitol>Sacramento</fx:capitol>
    </fx:Object>
    <fx:Object>
      <fx:state>OR</fx:state>
      <fx:capitol>Salem</fx:capitol>
    </fx:Object>
  </s:ArrayList>
</fx:Declarations>
<s:List id="stateList" dataProvider="{stateData}"
  labelField="state"/>
```

Figure 19.3 shows the same List control, this time displaying the value of the property named in the control's labelField property.

The application in Listing 19.3 uses the List control's labelField property to determine which property value of each data object is displayed at runtime.

LISTING 19.3

Using the labelField property

```
<?xml version="1.0" encoding="utf-8"?>
<s:Application xmlns:fx="http://ns.adobe.com/mxml/2009"
  xmlns:s="library://ns.adobe.com/flex/spark"
```

```
  xmlns:mx="library://ns.adobe.com/flex/mx"
  xmlns:vo="vo.*">
  <s:layout>
    <s:VerticalLayout horizontalAlign="center" paddingTop="20"/>
  </s:layout>
  <fx:Declarations>
    <s:ArrayList id="stateData">
      <vo:StateVO>
        <vo:state>CA</vo:state>
        <vo:capitol>Sacramento</vo:capitol>
      </vo:StateVO>
      <vo:StateVO>
        <vo:state>OR</vo:state>
        <vo:capitol>Salem</vo:capitol>
      </vo:StateVO>
      <vo:StateVO>
        <vo:state>WA</vo:state>
        <vo:capitol>Olympia</vo:capitol>
      </vo:StateVO>
    </s:ArrayList>
  </fx:Declarations>
  <s:Label text="A List control with value objects and labelField"
    fontSize="14" fontWeight="bold" width="215"
    verticalAlign="middle" textAlign="center"/>
  <s:List id="stateList" width="200"
    dataProvider="{stateData}" labelField="capitol"/>
</s:Application>
```

FIGURE 19.3

A List control displaying a complex data object with the labelField set to one of the properties of the data provider's complex data objects

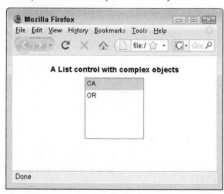

On the Web

The code in Listing 19.3 is available in the Web site files as `UsingLabelField.mxml` **in the** `chapter19` **project.** ∎

Using the labelFunction property

Most `List` controls implement the `labelFunction` property to enable you to customize the label that appears on each of the control's items at runtime. You can control both how the data will be displayed and enable each label to show multiple properties from your data objects. The `labelFunction` property points to the name of a function that follows a specific signature:

```
[access modifier] function [functionName](item:Object):String
```

The access modifier for a custom label function can be anything you like, although when you're calling the function from within the same application or component in which it's defined, the access modifier is typically set to private because it's most often used only from within. The name of the function's only argument (`item` in the example syntax) can be anything you like, but it should be typed as either an `Object` or a custom class implementing the Value Object design pattern, depending on what type of data is stored in your `List` control's `dataProvider` collection. And the function always returns a `String`, because its purpose is to generate a label for each of the `List` control's visual items.

At runtime, the `List` control calls the named function each time it needs to render an item visually. It passes the current data object to the custom function as its `item` argument and then displays the returned `String` value. The following is an example of a function that's compatible with the `labelFunction` architecture:

```
private function getStateLabel(item:StateVO):String
{
  return item.capitol + ", " + item.state;
}
```

The application in Listing 19.4 displays a `List` control where each visual item's label is generated by the custom `getStateLabel()` function.

LISTING 19.4

Using the labelFunction property

```
<?xml version="1.0" encoding="utf-8"?>
<s:Application xmlns:fx="http://ns.adobe.com/mxml/2009"
  xmlns:s="library://ns.adobe.com/flex/spark"
  xmlns:mx="library://ns.adobe.com/flex/mx"
  xmlns:vo="vo.*">
  <s:layout>
    <s:VerticalLayout horizontalAlign="center" paddingTop="20"/>
  </s:layout>
  <fx:Declarations>
```

```
<s:ArrayList id="stateData">
  <vo:StateVO>
    <vo:state>CA</vo:state>
    <vo:capitol>Sacramento</vo:capitol>
  </vo:StateVO>
  <vo:StateVO>
    <vo:state>OR</vo:state>
    <vo:capitol>Salem</vo:capitol>
  </vo:StateVO>
  <vo:StateVO>
    <vo:state>WA</vo:state>
    <vo:capitol>Olympia</vo:capitol>
  </vo:StateVO>
</s:ArrayList>
</fx:Declarations>
<fx:Script>
  <![CDATA[
    import vo.StateVO;
    private function getStateLabel(item:StateVO):String
    {
      return item.capitol + ", " + item.state;
    }
  ]]>
</fx:Script>
<s:Label text="A List control with value objects and labelFunction"
  fontSize="14" fontWeight="bold" width="215"
  textAlign="center"/>
<s:List id="stateList" width="200"
  dataProvider="{stateData}" labelFunction="getStateLabel"/>
</s:Application>
```

On the Web

The code in Listing 19.4 is available in the Web site files as `UsingLabelFunction.mxml` in the `chapter19` project. ■

The resulting application is shown in Figure 19.4. Notice that each of the `List` control's labels is generated using both of the data object's named properties, concatenated with literal strings to separate the values.

Note

The `DataGrid` component doesn't implement the `labelField` or `labelFunction` properties directly. Instead, these properties are implemented in the `DataGridColumn` component so you can easily customize the presentation of individual columns. A label function written for a `DataGridColumn` must accept an additional argument: a reference to the `DataGridColumn` that is calling the label function. ■

FIGURE 19.4

A List control displaying `String` values calculated in a `labelFunction`

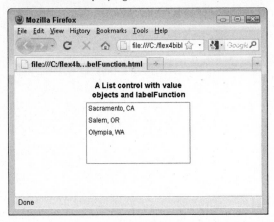

List Control Events and Properties

All `List` controls support these events to notify you of user actions and other important updates to a control:

- **change**. Notifies you that the user has selected an item using either a mouse or keyboard gesture.

- **changing**. Notifies you that the user has attempted to select an item using either a mouse or a keyboard gesture. This event is cancelable, thus preventing the selection from occurring.

`List` controls also support these properties that can be used to detect which data the user currently has selected:

- **allowMultipleSelections:Boolean**. When set to `true`, this enables the user to select more than one item at a time by holding down Ctrl while clicking items.

- **doubleClickEnabled:Boolean**. When this property is set to `true`, the `List` control detects double-clicks on its items and dispatches a `doubleClick` event.

- **selectedIndex:int**. This is the numeric index of the currently selected item.

- **selectedIndices:Array**. This is an array of indices of the currently selected items, when the `List` control's `allowMultipleSelection` property is set to `true`.

- **selectedItem:Object**. This is the data object underlying the `List` control's currently selected row or cell.

- **selectedItems:Array**. This is an array of currently selected objects, when the `List` control's `allowMultipleSelection` property is set to `true`.

In addition, each `List` control supports unique events and properties designed for that control's specific purpose and capabilities.

Caution

The `ComboBox` and `DropDownList` **controls do not support the** `allowMultipleSelection,selected Indices,` **or** `selectedItems` **properties.** ■

Handling User Data Selections

When a user selects items in a `List` control, she's indicating that she wants to use the selected item's underlying data. When this occurs, the `List` control dispatches a `change` event. After this event occurs, you can use the control's `selectedItem` and `selectedIndex` properties to detect which item has been selected.

Using the change event

The `change` event is implemented in all Spark and MX `List` controls. In Spark controls, it dispatches an event object typed as `spark.events.IndexChangeEvent`, which has a `newIndex` property that indicates by index which data item was selected by the user.

You can detect which data item was selected by the user by referring to the event object's `new Index` property and passing it to the `getItemAt()` method of the `ArrayList` data provider:

```
changeMessage = "You clicked on " +
    event.target.dataProvider.getItemAt(event.newIndex);
```

Caution

This technique notifies you that the user changed their selection, an item, but it doesn't always indicate that the expression `event.target.dataProvider.getItemAt(event.newIndex)` returns a valid value. In most `List` controls, the user can hold down Ctrl (Cmd on the Mac) and click to deselect an item, in which case you get a `change` event that can't be distinguished from the event that occurs when selecting an item. When nothing is selected, the `getItemAt()` expression causes a runtime error. The value of `newIndex` is -1, and when you pass that value to the `ArrayList` class's `getItemAt()` method, it results in a `RangeError` with the message "Index '-1' specified is out of bounds". ■

Using the selectedItem property

You can also use the `List` control's `selectedItem` property, which always returns a reference to the data object that drove the creation of the currently selected list item. If the user has deselected all items in a `List` control, `selectedItem` returns `null`:

```
if (event.target.selectedItem == null)
{
  changeMessage = "None selected";
}
else
{
  changeMessage = "You selected " + event.target.selectedItem;
}
```

The application in Listing 19.5 uses a `List` control and a change event listener. Each time the change event is dispatched by the `List` control, an event handler function inspects the control's `selectedItem` and displays a message indicating which item (if any) is currently selected.

LISTING 19.5

Using the change event and selectedItem property

```
<?xml version="1.0" encoding="utf-8"?>
<s:Application xmlns:fx="http://ns.adobe.com/mxml/2009"
  xmlns:s="library://ns.adobe.com/flex/spark"
  xmlns:mx="library://ns.adobe.com/flex/mx">
  <s:layout>
    <s:VerticalLayout horizontalAlign="center" paddingTop="20"/>
  </s:layout>
  <fx:Script>
    <![CDATA[
      [Bindable]
      private var changeMessage:String="None selected";
      private function changeHandler(event:Event):void
      {
        if (event.target.selectedItem == null)
          changeMessage = "None selected";
        else
          changeMessage = "You selected " + event.target.selectedItem;
      }
    ]]>
  </fx:Script>
  <fx:Declarations>
    <s:ArrayList id="myData">
      <fx:String>Small</fx:String>
      <fx:String>Medium</fx:String>
      <fx:String>Large</fx:String>
    </s:ArrayList>
  </fx:Declarations>
  <s:List id="sizeList" width="200" dataProvider="{myData}"
    change="changeHandler(event)"/>
  <s:Label text="{changeMessage}" fontSize="12"/>
</s:Application>
```

On the Web

The code in Listing 19.5 is available in the Web site files as `ChangeEventDemo.mxml` **in the** `chapter19` **project.** ∎

When testing this application, try holding down Ctrl (Windows) or Cmd (Mac) and clicking an item that's already selected. You should see the message "None selected" displayed, because the control's `selectedItem` property now returns `null`.

Using the selectedIndex property

All `List` controls implement the `selectedIndex` property, which returns the index position of the control's currently selected item. Because all indexing in ActionScript starts at 0, if the first item is selected the `selectedIndex` property returns 1, the second returns 2, and so on. When you use a `List` or `ComboBox` control in a data entry form, you can place a data item as the first item in a list that indicates that the user is selecting all options:

```
<s:DropDownList id="categoryList" change="changeHandler(event)">
  <s:dataProvider>
    <s:ArrayList>
      <fx:String>All Categories</fx:String>
      <fx:String>Comedy</fx:String>
      <fx:String>Drama</fx:String>
      <fx:String>Action</fx:String>
      <fx:String>Horror</fx:String>
    </s:ArrayList>
  </s:dataProvider>
</s:DropDownList>
```

The following code detects whether the user has selected the first item, indicating she wants all categories or a specific category:

```
private function changeHandler(event:Event):void
{
  if (categoryList.selectedIndex == 0)
  {
    Alert.show("You selected all categories", "Everything!");
  }
  else
  {
    Alert.show("You selected " + categoryList.selectedItem,
      "One Thing!");
  }
}
```

If no items are currently selected in a `List` control, the `selectedIndex` property returns a value of -1. This is particularly useful when you want to detect a state where the user hasn't yet selected a value from a `List` or `DataGrid` control:

```
private function changeHandler(event:Event):void
{
  if (categoryList.selectedIndex == -1)
  {
    Alert.show("You haven't selected anything!", "Nothin!");
  }
  else
  {
    Alert.show("You selected " + categoryList.selectedItem,
      "One Thing!");
  }
}
```

Note

When using a MX `ComboBox` with its `editable` property set to the default value of `false`, its `selected Index` property never returns -1, because some item is always selected. When you set editable to `true` and the user types a value into the `TextInput` portion of the control at runtime, `selectedIndex` returns -1 to indicate the user has provided a custom value. ■

Selecting complex data objects

When a `List` control's data provider is a collection of complex objects instead of simple values, you can refer to selected data objects' named properties using either dot syntax or array-style syntax. Dot syntax is more common, because, especially when working with classes that implement the Value Object design pattern, they enable Flex Builder and the compiler to validate property names and provide code completion.

For example, when a user selects an item that represents a complex data object from a `List` control, you should first cast the control's `selectedItem` property as the appropriate ActionScript class. You can then refer to the object's named properties and gain the benefit of Flex Builder's and the compiler's syntax checking and code completion tools:

```
var selectedState:StateVO = stateList.selectedItem as StateVO;
var selectedCapitol = selectedState.capitol;
```

If you prefer, you can use array-style syntax to refer to a data object's named properties:

```
var selectedCapitol = stateList.selectedItem["capitol"];
```

This syntax enables you to use variables containing the names of the properties. The following code would have the same functional result as the other preceding examples:

```
var fieldName:String = "capitol";
var selectedCapitol = stateList.selectedItem[fieldName];
```

Particularly when using data model classes that implement the Value Object design pattern, you may want to declare a bindable instance of the class to store the most recently selected data item. This `StateVO` value object class contains two properties, both of which are bindable due to the use of the `[Bindable]` metadata tag before the class declaration:

```
package vo
{
  [Bindable]
  public class StateVO
  {
    public var state:String;
    public var capitol:String;
    public function StateVO()
    {
    }
  }
}
```

The application in Listing 19.6 uses a ComboBox with a data provider containing multiple instances of a value object class. Upon application startup, and then again when the user selects an item from the control, a reference to the currently selected data item is saved to the selected-State variable.

Notice that this variable is marked as bindable, and its internal [Bindable] tag also marks its properties as bindable. Both levels of "bindability" are required in order for the Label controls to successfully display the selected object's properties whenever the user selects new data.

LISTING 19.6

Selecting complex data objects

```xml
<?xml version="1.0" encoding="utf-8"?>
<s:Application xmlns:fx="http://ns.adobe.com/mxml/2009"
  xmlns:s="library://ns.adobe.com/flex/spark"
  xmlns:mx="library://ns.adobe.com/flex/mx"
  xmlns:vo="vo.*">
  <s:layout>
    <s:VerticalLayout horizontalAlign="center" paddingTop="20"/>
  </s:layout>
  <fx:Script>
    <![CDATA[
      import vo.StateVO;
      [Bindable]
      private var selectedState:StateVO;
      private function setSelectedState():void
      {
        selectedState=stateList.selectedItem as StateVO;
      }
    ]]>
  </fx:Script>
  <fx:Declarations>
    <s:ArrayList id="stateData">
      <vo:StateVO>
        <vo:state>CA</vo:state>
        <vo:capitol>Sacramento</vo:capitol>
      </vo:StateVO>
      <vo:StateVO>
        <vo:state>OR</vo:state>
        <vo:capitol>Salem</vo:capitol>
      </vo:StateVO>
      <vo:StateVO>
        <vo:state>WA</vo:state>
        <vo:capitol>Olympia</vo:capitol>
      </vo:StateVO>
    </s:ArrayList>
  </fx:Declarations>
```

continued

LISTING 19.6 *(continued)*

```
   <s:DropDownList id="stateList"
      width="200"
      dataProvider="{stateData}"
      labelField="capitol"
      change="setSelectedState()"/>
   <s:Label text="Selected State Information:"/>
   <s:Label text="State: {selectedState.state}"/>
   <s:Label text="Capitol: {selectedState.capitol}"/>
</s:Application>
```

On the Web

The code in Listing 19.6 is available in the Web site files as `SelectingComplexObjects.mxml` in the `chapter19` project. ■

Using Custom Item Renderers

By default, `List` controls display simple strings in their visual items. As described previously, you can customize the string that's displayed with the control's `labelField` and `labelFunc-tion` properties, but if you want to create a more complex display, you need to use a custom item renderer.

MX `List` controls enable you to declare both item renderers and item editors. The differences between renderers and editors can be described as follows:

- Item renderers primarily display information, while item editors enable the user to modify the data that's stored in the `List` control's data provider.

- Item renderers display in every item of the `List` control regardless of the user's interactions with the control. Item editors are displayed only when the user clicks to start editing the item.

- Item renderers also can be marked as editors. In this case, they're still displayed on every item of List control like a normal item renderer. But, like an item editor, they enable the user to modify the data in the `List` control's data provider.

The Spark List controls support only item renderers, and not item editors, but you can write your own logic to create renderers with an editable interface.

Note

The use of custom item renderers is described in this chapter, because they can be used with all `List` controls. Custom item editors are described in Chapter 20 in the section about the `DataGrid` control. ■

You declare a `List` control's custom item renderer as a visual component that you want the control to instantiate each time it needs to render an item visually. Each of the `List` controls has a default item renderer class that it assigns to its `itemRenderer` property. The default `item Renderer` class for MX List controls is `mx.controls.listClasses.ListItemRenderer`, while the default `itemRenderer` class for Spark list controls is `spark.skins.spark. DefaultItemRenderer`. Both default `itemRenderer` classes are designed to display a simple `String` value to the user.

When you declare a custom renderer, you override this default selection and have the freedom to create much more complex presentations.

You can declare custom item renderers in these ways:

- **Drop-in renderers.** These are visual components that you assign to an MX `List` control without any changes to the renderer component's default property or style settings. These are only available with MX list controls.

- **Inline renderers.** These are components you define and nest within an MXML declaration of the `List` control.

- **Component renderers.** These are separate visual components that you define as MXML components or ActionScript classes and assign to the `List` control's `itemRenderer` property in an MXML declaration. You also can assign a component renderer at runtime with ActionScript code by using the `mx.core.ClassFactory` class.

Using drop-in item renderers

A drop-in renderer is a visual component that you assign to a MX `List` control's `itemRenderer` or `itemEditor` properties using its complete package and class name. A limited number of components implement the `IDropInListItemRenderer` interface, making them eligible for this use. They include:

- `Button`
- `CheckBox`
- `DateField`
- `Image`
- `Label`
- `NumericStepper`
- `Text`
- `TextArea`
- `TextInput`

Caution
Spark list controls don't support drop-in item renderers. ∎

At runtime, for each item the `List` control renders, it creates an instance of the visual component you name as the renderer and passes data to the default property for that component. For example, if you use an Image component as your custom renderer, the data is passed to the control's source property. The Label, Text, TextArea, and TextInput controls have a default property of text, and each of the other controls has its own unique property.

If a List control's data provider contains String values, each containing the location of a graphic image you want to display instead of a label, you assign the itemRenderer using the fully qualified name of the component's equivalent ActionScript class:

```
<mx:List id="answerList" dataProvider="{answerData}"
    itemRenderer="mx.controls.Image"/>
```

Caution

When assigning a drop-in or a component item renderer, you must include the entire package and class name in the itemRenderer or itemEditor declaration. Including an import statement for the class you're using as the renderer does not eliminate this requirement. ■

The application in Listing 19.7 uses an ArrayList of String values, each containing the name of an image file in the project's source root. The List control's variableRowHeight property is set to true, enabling each row of the control to adjust to the image it displays.

LISTING 19.7

Using a drop-in item renderer

```
<?xml version="1.0" encoding="utf-8"?>
<s:Application xmlns:fx="http://ns.adobe.com/mxml/2009"
  xmlns:s="library://ns.adobe.com/flex/spark"
  xmlns:mx="library://ns.adobe.com/flex/mx">
  <fx:Declarations>
    <s:ArrayList id="answerData">
      <fx:String>assets/yesImage.png</fx:String>
      <fx:String>assets/noImage.png</fx:String>
      <fx:String>assets/maybeImage.png</fx:String>
    </s:ArrayList>
  </fx:Declarations>
  <mx:List id="answerList" dataProvider="{answerData}"
    itemRenderer="mx.controls.Image"
    rowCount="{answerData.length}"
    variableRowHeight="true"
    horizontalCenter="0" top="20"
    width="80" height="140"/>
</s:Application>
```

On the Web

The code in Listing 19.7 is available in the Web site files as DropinRenderer.mxml in the chapter19 project. ■

Figure 19.5 shows the resulting application. Its MX List control displays the images based on the values in the control's data provider.

FIGURE 19.5

An MX List control with a drop-in item renderer

Note

Drop-in item renderers work effectively with both MX single-column controls such as the List and ComboBox and with DataGridColumn components in the context of a DataGrid. Drop-in item editors can't be used very effectively in single-column controls, because with the drop-in architecture you don't have the ability to control positioning, set object properties, or override default behaviors. ∎

Tip

You can use the labelFunction and labelField properties to affect the string that is passed to the drop-in renderers. For example, this function designed for use with labelFunction adds a URL path to an image reference:

```
private function doIt(item:Object):String
{
  return "http://www.myUrl.com/" + item as String;
} ∎
```

Using inline renderers and editors

An inline renderer is an MXML component that you nest with the declaration of the List control. You first nest an itemRenderer or itemEditor child element with the List control's MXML tags, and then within that control, you nest a set of <fx:Component> tags. Within the <fx:Component> tags, you can nest the control or container from which you want to extend the custom component.

With MX list controls, the item renderer can be extended from any MX control or container. For example, the following code declares a custom component that's extended from the VBox container:

```
<mx:List id="myList" dataProvider="{myData}">
  <mx:itemRenderer>
    <fx:Component>
      <mx:VBox>
      ... nested components ...
      </mx:VBox>
    </fx:Component>
  </mx:itemRenderer>
</mx:List>
```

With Spark list controls, the item renderer should be extended from a new Spark component named ItemRenderer:

```
<s:List id="myList" dataProvider="{myData}">
  <s:itemRenderer>
    <fx:Component>
      <s:ItemRenderer>
      ... nested components ...
      </s:ItemRenderer>
    </fx:Component>
  </s:itemRenderer>
</s:List>
```

Note

In object-oriented terms, an inline item renderer is a local anonymous class. Such classes have the benefit of being declared within the context of their use, in this case within the List control for which it's designed. The drawback of using an anonymous class is that it can't be reused in a different context. ■

Note

The <fx:Component> declaration is a compiler tag and doesn't represent a specific ActionScript class. Its purpose is to create a new component scope within an MXML file. Variables declared within the <fx:Component> tag set are local to the custom component and, unless declared public, aren't accessible to the containing application or component. Also, within the scope of the <fx:Component> tag set, the expression this refers to the current instance of the custom component and not to the application or containing component. ■

MX visual components and the Spark ItemRenderer class implement a bindable data property designed for use in the custom item renderer architecture. At runtime, the List control creates an instance of the renderer component for each of its data items and passes the data provider's current data item to the component instance's data property.

Within the component code, you can refer to the current data item in a binding expression to use its information. In the application in Listing 19.8, the List control displays the same image as before, but this time the image file's location is determined in the custom item renderer by including a literal string in the Image control declaration. The item renderer is based on the Spark ItemRenderer container and includes both the image and a Label control that displays the raw data.

LISTING 19.8

Using an inline renderer

```
<?xml version="1.0" encoding="utf-8"?>
<s:Application xmlns:fx="http://ns.adobe.com/mxml/2009"
  xmlns:s="library://ns.adobe.com/flex/spark"
  xmlns:mx="library://ns.adobe.com/flex/mx">
  <fx:Declarations>
    <s:ArrayList id="answerData">
      <fx:String>yesImage.png</fx:String>
      <fx:String>noImage.png</fx:String>
      <fx:String>maybeImage.png</fx:String>
    </s:ArrayList>
  </fx:Declarations>
  <s:List id="myList" dataProvider="{answerData}" width="300"
    horizontalCenter="0" top="20">
    <s:itemRenderer>
      <fx:Component>
        <s:ItemRenderer width="100%">
          <s:layout>
            <s:VerticalLayout gap="10" horizontalAlign="center"
              paddingTop="10" paddingBottom="10"
              paddingLeft="10" paddingRight="10"/>
          </s:layout>
          <mx:Image source="assets/{data}"/>
          <s:Label text="The value of the data property is {data}"
            width="100%"/>
        </s:ItemRenderer>
      </fx:Component>
    </s:itemRenderer>
  </s:List>
</s:Application>
```

On the Web

The code in Listing 19.8 is available in the Web site files as `InlineRenderer.mxml` **in the** `chapter19` **project.** ■

Using an inline or component renderer also makes working with data providers containing complex objects easier. The `List` control's `data` property is data typed as an ActionScript `Object` and is compatible with any sort of data object that might be passed from the `List` control's data provider. For example, if the data object has an `imageSource` property, the custom item renderer can use that property in a binding expression to pass values to its nested visual controls:

```
<mx:Image source="imageLocation/{data.imageSource}"/>
```

In the application in Listing 19.9, the `List` control's data provider contains objects with `value` and `imageSource` properties. The `Image` component used as the custom item renderer receives its source from the data object's `imageSource` property through a binding expression. The `Label` control at the bottom of the application displays the `value` property of the `List` control's currently selected data object through a binding expression of `myList.selectedItem.value`.

LISTING 19.9

Using complex data objects in a custom item renderer

```xml
<?xml version="1.0" encoding="utf-8"?>
<s:Application xmlns:fx="http://ns.adobe.com/mxml/2009"
  xmlns:s="library://ns.adobe.com/flex/spark"
  xmlns:mx="library://ns.adobe.com/flex/mx">
  <s:layout>
    <s:VerticalLayout horizontalAlign="center" paddingTop="20"/>
  </s:layout>
  <fx:Declarations>
    <s:ArrayList id="answerData">
      <fx:Object>
        <fx:value>Yes</fx:value>
        <fx:imageSource>yesImage.png</fx:imageSource>
      </fx:Object>
      <fx:Object>
        <fx:value>No</fx:value>
        <fx:imageSource>noImage.png</fx:imageSource>
      </fx:Object>
      <fx:Object>
        <fx:value>Maybe</fx:value>
        <fx:imageSource>maybeImage.png</fx:imageSource>
      </fx:Object>
    </s:ArrayList>
  </fx:Declarations>
  <s:List id="myList" dataProvider="{answerData}" width="300" height="260">
    <s:itemRenderer>
      <fx:Component>
        <s:ItemRenderer width="100%">
          <s:layout>
            <s:VerticalLayout gap="10" horizontalAlign="center"
              paddingTop="10" paddingBottom="10"
              paddingLeft="10" paddingRight="10"/>
          </s:layout>
          <mx:Image source="assets/{data.imageSource}"/>
          <s:Label text="Image Source: {data.imageSource}"/>
        </s:ItemRenderer>
      </fx:Component>
    </s:itemRenderer>
  </s:List>
  <s:Label text="{myList.selectedItem.value}"
    fontSize="14"/>
</s:Application>
```

On the Web

The code in Listing 19.9 is available in the Web site files as `InlineRendererComplexObjects.mxml` in the `chapter19` project. ■

The resulting application is shown in Figure 19.6.

Note

You cannot create an empty `<fx:Component>` tag set; it must have a single nested child element indicating which visual component you're extending. The content of an inline component can include ActionScript code, `<fx:Binding>`, `<fx:Model>`, and `<s:State>` tags, and pretty much anything else you might declare in a custom component in a separate MXML file. ■

An application with a Spark List control using a complex item renderer

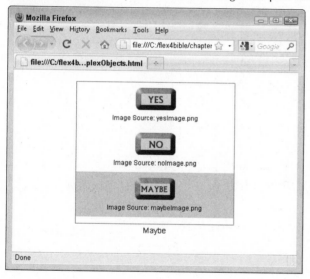

Using component item renderers

A component item renderer is a separate class that can be created as either an MXML component or an ActionScript class that extends an existing visual component from the Flex framework. As with all visual components, the custom component has the same `data` property as was described in the previous section on inline components. At runtime, the `List` control creates an instance of the named component for each item it needs to render and passes the data provider's current data object to the component instance's `data` property.

Note

This chapter describes how to create custom components with MXML. For details of creating components in ActionScript, see the product documentation. ∎

You create item renderers as MXML components in the same manner as any other component. If you're using Flex Builder, you can use the New MXML Component wizard to create an MXML component source-code file.

If you are using your custom renderer with an MX List object, its root element is the visual component that you want your custom component to extend. If it is a Spark item renderer, its root element is the new `ItemRenderer` class. The objects nested within the component's root element can use the `data` object and its named properties (determined by the `List` control's data provider) to display information dynamically.

Tip

You should create custom components in packages with descriptive names reflecting the use of the components they contain. For example, in the sample application described in this section, the custom components are stored in a `renderers` package. Although it works technically to create custom components directly in the default package, this practice can create file management and application maintenance issues. ∎

The custom component in Listing 19.10 extends the `ItemRenderer` container and contains an `Image` component. It uses its `data` property to set the nested object's properties through binding expressions.

LISTING 19.10

A custom item renderer component built with MXML

```
<?xml version="1.0" encoding="utf-8"?>
<s:ItemRenderer xmlns:fx="http://ns.adobe.com/mxml/2009"
  xmlns:s="library://ns.adobe.com/flex/spark"
  xmlns:mx="library://ns.adobe.com/flex/mx"
  width="100%">
  <s:layout>
    <s:VerticalLayout gap="10" horizontalAlign="center"
      paddingTop="10" paddingBottom="10"
      paddingLeft="10" paddingRight="10"/>
  </s:layout>
  <mx:Image source="assets/{data.imageSource}"/>
  <s:Label text="Image source: {data.imageSource}"/>
</s:ItemRenderer >
```

On the Web

The code in Listing 19.10 is available in the Web site files as `renderers/ImageRenderer.mxml` **in the** `chapter19` **project.** ∎

You use the custom renderer component with the same syntax as a drop-in renderer, supplying the fully qualified name and path of the component in the List control's itemRenderer or item Editor property:

```
<s:List id="myList" dataProvider="{answerData}"
    itemRenderer="renderers.ImageRenderer"/>
```

Note

When you provide the name of the custom renderer class to the List control, it is not a binding expression, and the class name isn't wrapped in braces ({}). You're providing the class definition in a similar way to how event handler functions are passed to addEventListener(). Instances of classes are wrapped in binding expressions; class definitions are passed solely by name without binding syntax. ■

The application in Listing 19.11 uses the custom component renderer to display all of each data object's values.

LISTING 19.11

Using a custom component renderer

```
<?xml version="1.0" encoding="utf-8"?>
<s:Application xmlns:fx="http://ns.adobe.com/mxml/2009"
  xmlns:s="library://ns.adobe.com/flex/spark"
  xmlns:mx="library://ns.adobe.com/flex/mx">
  <s:layout>
    <s:VerticalLayout horizontalAlign="center" paddingTop="20"/>
  </s:layout>
  <fx:Declarations>
    <s:ArrayList id="answerData">
      <fx:Object>
        <fx:value>Yes</fx:value>
        <fx:imageSource>yesImage.png</fx:imageSource>
      </fx:Object>
      <fx:Object>
        <fx:value>No</fx:value>
        <fx:imageSource>noImage.png</fx:imageSource>
      </fx:Object>
      <fx:Object>
        <fx:value>Maybe</fx:value>
        <fx:imageSource>maybeImage.png</fx:imageSource>
      </fx:Object>
    </s:ArrayList>
  </fx:Declarations>
  <s:List id="myList" dataProvider="{answerData}"
    itemRenderer="renderers.ImageRenderer"/>
  <s:Label text="{myList.selectedItem.value}"
    fontSize="14"/>
</s:Application>
```

On the Web

The code in Listing 19.11 is available in the Web site files as `UsingComponentRenderers.mxml` in the chapter19 project. ∎

Customizing Spark item renderers with view states

In addition, the Spark `ItemRenderer` class can react to view states that are controlled by the consuming List control. These view states are named `normal`, `hovered`, and `selected`. To use the view states in the custom item renderer, declare them in the component's `<s:States>` section:

```
<s:states>
  <s:State name="normal"/>
  <s:State name="hovered"/>
  <s:State name="selected"/>
</s:states>
```

You can now use these view states in your MXML declarations, including or excluding components or changing their properties or styles using dot syntax. For example, this rectangle changes appearance depending on the view state passed into the item renderer by the consuming list control:

```
<s:Rect includeIn="hovered, selected"
    height="100%" width="100%">
    <s:stroke>
    <s:SolidColorStroke
        color.hovered="#666666"
        color.selected="#000000"
        weight="1"/>
    </s:stroke>
    <s:fill>
      <s:SolidColor
        color.hovered="#EEEEEE"
        color.selected="#999999"/>
    </s:fill>
  </s:Rect>
```

The custom component in Listing 19.12 changes the appearance of each list item depending on which view state is set by the consuming list control.

LISTING 19.12

Using a custom item renderer with view states

```
<?xml version="1.0" encoding="utf-8"?>
<s:ItemRenderer xmlns:fx="http://ns.adobe.com/mxml/2009"
  xmlns:s="library://ns.adobe.com/flex/spark"
  xmlns:mx="library://ns.adobe.com/flex/mx">
```

```
<s:states>
  <s:State name="normal"/>
  <s:State name="hovered"/>
  <s:State name="selected"/>
</s:states>
<s:Rect includeIn="hovered, selected"
  height="100%" width="100%">
  <s:stroke>
    <s:SolidColorStroke
      color.hovered="#666666"
      color.selected="#000000"
      weight="1"/>
  </s:stroke>
  <s:fill>
    <s:SolidColor
      color.hovered="#EEEEEE"
      color.selected="#999999"/>
  </s:fill>
</s:Rect>
<s:VGroup
  paddingTop="5" paddingBottom="5"
  paddingLeft="5" paddingRight="5">
  <s:Label
    horizontalCenter="0"
    fontWeight.selected="bold"
    text="State: {data.state}"/>
  <s:Label
    horizontalCenter="0"
    fontWeight.selected="bold"
    text="Capitol: {data.capitol}"/>
</s:VGroup>
</s:ItemRenderer>
```

On the Web

The code in Listing 19.12 is available in the Web site files as `RendererWithViewStates.mxml` in the `chapter19` project's `renderers` folder. An application that uses the component is available as `UsingRenderersWithViewStates.mxml`. ∎

The resulting application is shown in Figure 19.7.

Cross-Reference

You can also create custom skins for Spark item renderers class that implement complex visual displays. I describe how to create custom skins for Spark components in Chapter 15. ∎

FIGURE 19.7

An application with a Spark List control using an item renderer with view states

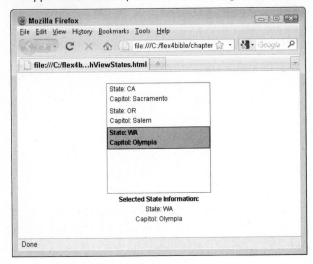

Summary

In this chapter, I described how to use the basic functions of List controls. You learned the following:

- A List control presents data to the user and enables him make data selections with mouse or keyboard gestures.

- All list controls implement a common set of properties and events to determine their presentation and behavior.

- The list controls include the Spark List, DropDownList, ComboBox and ButtonBar, and the MX List, ComboBox, DataGrid, TileList, HorizontalList, Tree, AdvancedDataGrid, and OLAPDataGrid controls.

- MX list controls designed exclusively for use with AIR applications populate their data with information from the local client file system.

- You handle user selections with the change event and the selectedItem and selectedIndex properties.

- You can customize the labels presented in list control items with the labelField and labelFunction properties.

- Custom item renderers can be used with all list controls to create a more complex visual presentation.

- Custom item renderers can be declared using the drop-in, inline, or component architectures.

- Item renderers for Spark list controls only support inline and component architectures but can be used with view states and custom skins.

Using Advanced List Controls

A ll list controls are not created equal. The two simplest list controls — the Spark and MX `List` controls — display a single column of values and support the common functionality of custom labels, item renderers, and so on. But other, more advanced list controls, such as the `ComboBox` and `DropDownList`, are really compound controls that add features such as enabling users to enter their own arbitrary values.

More complex list controls — such as the Spark `ButtonBar` and the MX `DataGrid`, `Tree`, `TileList`, and `HorizontalList` — have their own unique capabilities. And as I described briefly in Chapter 19, the Adobe AIR-based list controls have the capability to populate data from the local file system.

In Chapter 19, I described functionality that's common to all list controls, from the most fundamental to the most advanced. In this chapter, I describe the unique capabilities of specific data-driven controls, starting with the `DropDownList` and `ComboBox` and working up to the `TileList`, `HorizontalList`, and `DataGrid`.

On the Web

To use the sample code for this chapter, import the `chapter20.fxp` project from the Web site files into any folder on your disk. ∎

Using ComboBox and DropDownList Controls

The `ComboBox` and `DropDownList` controls are most like the basic `List` control in that they each display items in a single column by default. The Spark versions of these controls support the `layout` property that enables display of a list's items horizontally or as a set of tiled cells.

IN THIS CHAPTER

Using the Spark
`DropDownList` **and**
`ButtonBar` **components**

Using `ComboBox` **controls**

Creating a bindable
`DropDownList` **component**

Using the `DataGrid` **control**

Selecting and customizing
`DataGrid` **columns**

Presenting custom labels in
a `DataGrid` **column**

Using custom item editors in
a `DataGrid` **column**

Using the `TileList` **and**
`HorizontalList` **controls**

Using the
`AdvancedDataGrid`
control

Using the prompt property

Both the MX ComboBox and the Spark DropDownList implement the prompt property. This property's value is a String that's displayed to users if they haven't yet selected a value from the control's data list. The application in Listing 20.1 displays a DropDownList with a prompt.

LISTING 20.1

An application with a DropDownList control

```xml
<?xml version="1.0" encoding="utf-8"?>
<s:Application xmlns:fx="http://ns.adobe.com/mxml/2009"
  xmlns:s="library://ns.adobe.com/flex/spark"
  xmlns:mx="library://ns.adobe.com/flex/mx"
  xmlns:vo="vo.*">
  <s:layout>
    <s:VerticalLayout horizontalAlign="center" paddingTop="20"/>
  </s:layout>
  <fx:Declarations>
    <s:ArrayList id="stateData">
      <vo:StateVO>
        <vo:state>CA</vo:state>
        <vo:capitol>Sacramento</vo:capitol>
      </vo:StateVO>
      <vo:StateVO>
        <vo:state>OR</vo:state>
        <vo:capitol>Salem</vo:capitol>
      </vo:StateVO>
      <vo:StateVO>
        <vo:state>WA</vo:state>
        <vo:capitol>Olympia</vo:capitol>
      </vo:StateVO>
    </s:ArrayList>
  </fx:Declarations>
  <s:VGroup width="300" gap="20">
    <s:Label text="DropDownList Control" styleName="label"
      fontSize="14" fontWeight="bold"/>
    <s:DropDownList
      id="dropdownState"
      prompt="Select a State"
      dataProvider="{stateData}"
      labelField="state" width="124"/>
    <s:Label text="selectedIndex: {dropdownState.selectedIndex}"/>
    <s:Label text="selectedItem: {dropdownState.selectedItem.capitol},
      {dropdownState.selectedItem.state}"/>
  </s:VGroup>
</s:Application>
```

On the Web

The code in Listing 20.1 is available in the Web site files as `DropDownDemo.mxml` in the `chapter20` project. ■

Figure 20.1 shows the resulting application.

FIGURE 20.1

A `DropDownList` control with a `prompt`

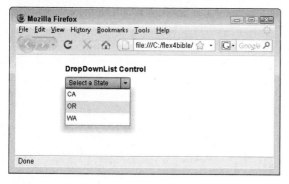

Note

There's a subtle difference in behavior between the MX `ComboBox` and the Spark `DropDownList`. When a `ComboBox` doesn't have its `prompt` property assigned, it automatically selects the first item in its `dataProvider` and sets `selectedIndex` to 0. The `DropDownList` doesn't automatically select its first data item; instead its `selectedIndex` is always set to −1 (nothing selected) by default, `selectedItem` defaults to `null`, and it displays an empty string in the prompt area. ■

Using the ComboBox control

The MX and Spark `ComboBox` controls appear at first glance to be simple drop-down list controls. Their name, however, indicates that there's more to their capabilities. This component is actually a compound control that includes both a `List` and a `TextInput`.

The MX `ComboBox` control's nested `TextInput` isn't visible by default; instead, it appears only when the control's `editable` property is set to `true`. Used in this way, the user has an option of either selecting an item from the control's `List` or typing an arbitrary `String` value into the control.

The Spark version of `ComboBox` always displays its `TextInput` control; if you don't want to allow the user to enter arbitrary values, use the Spark `DropDownList` instead.

The following code declares a Spark `ComboBox` with `prompt` set to a string that prompts the user accordingly:

```
<s:ComboBox id="sizeCB"
  dataProvider="{sizeData}"
  prompt="Select an item"/>
```

Tip

You can use the MX ComboBox **control's** prompt **property even if it isn't editable. When you set** prompt **to a value other than** null**, the** ComboBox **object's** selectedIndex **returns –1 and its** selectedItem **returns** null**. Once the user selects an item,** selectedItem **and** selectedIndex **reflect the currently selected item and its position in the** ArrayCollection **being used as the control's** dataProvider**. ■**

Figure 20.2 shows the resulting control displaying an initial prompt in the TextInput that appears as a result of the editable property being set to true.

FIGURE 20.2

A ComboBox with a prompt

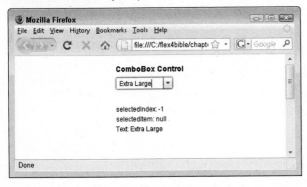

As with the List control, when the user selects an item from a ComboBox control's list, the selectedItem and selectedIndex properties point respectively to the selected data object and its ordinal position within the control's data provider. When the user types a value into the TextInput portion of the control, however, the control's properties are set as follows:

- selectedItem returns null for MX controls, and the value the user typed in for Spark controls.
- selectedIndex returns –1 for the MX control and –3 for the Spark control.
- prompt returns the user-entered value (MX version only).
- text returns the user-entered value (MX version only).

Tip

While the MX ComboBox **control's** prompt **and** text **properties return the same value, only the** text **property is bindable. If you try to use** prompt **in a binding expression, you get a compiler warning indicating that the binding won't update at runtime if the property changes. ■**

The application in Listing 20.2 uses a Spark ComboBox with its dataProvider set to an ArrayList containing simple String values. The Label controls use binding expressions to display the control's current text, selectedIndex, and selectedItem properties.

LISTING 20.2

Using an editable ComboBox

```
<?xml version="1.0" encoding="utf-8"?>
<s:Application xmlns:fx="http://ns.adobe.com/mxml/2009"
  xmlns:s="library://ns.adobe.com/flex/spark"
  xmlns:mx="library://ns.adobe.com/flex/mx"
  xmlns:vo="vo.*" width="495" height="421">
  <s:layout>
    <s:VerticalLayout horizontalAlign="center" paddingTop="20"/>
  </s:layout>
  <fx:Declarations>
    <s:ArrayList id="sizeData">
      <fx:String>Small</fx:String>
      <fx:String>Medium</fx:String>
      <fx:String>Large</fx:String>
    </s:ArrayList>
  </fx:Declarations>
  <s:VGroup>
    <s:Label text="ComboBox Control" styleName="label"
      fontSize="14" fontWeight="bold"/>
    <s:ComboBox id="cbSize"
      dataProvider="{sizeData}"/>
    <mx:Spacer height="20"/>
    <s:Label text="selectedIndex: {cbSize.selectedIndex}"/>
    <s:Label text="selectedItem: {cbSize.selectedItem}"/>
  </s:VGroup>
</s:Application>
```

On the Web

The code in Listing 20.2 is available in the Web site files as `ComboBoxDemo.mxml` in the `chapter20` project. ■

Selecting complex data objects with ActionScript

The `ComboBox` and `DropDownList` controls have a particular weakness in that you can't easily set their initial values when working with a data provider containing complex objects. In HTML code, it's common to set a `<select>` control's currently selected item by looping through the `<option>` tags and matching a property of the data set to values of the options. For example, ColdFusion supports the `<cfselect>` command that dynamically generates an HTML `<select>` control based on the contents of a query object. It determines which row is selected by matching the `selected` attribute's value with the values from the field designated in the `value` attribute:

```
<cfselect name="sizeList" size="1" query="qData"
  value="valueField" display="labelField"
  selected="selectedValue">
</select>
```

607

Each Web application server language that generates HTML code dynamically has its own unique way of accomplishing this task, but the goal is always to generate an HTML `<select>` tag with `<option>` tags for each data item and select one of the control's rows when the control is first presented.

The `ComboBox` and `DropDownList` controls don't provide this capability directly. Assume that the data provider for a `DropDownList` contains complex objects with named properties, as in this example:

```
<fx:Declarations>
  <s:ArrayList id="stateData">
    <vo:StateVO>
      <vo:state>CA</vo:state>
      <vo:capitol>Sacramento</vo:capitol>
    </vo:StateVO>
    ... more value objects ...
  </s:ArrayList>
</fx:Declarations>
```

If you want a `DropDownList` or `ComboBox` to indicate that one of its data items is selected based on a value that you pass in, you have to write a bit of additional code. The code in Listing 20.3 defines a subclass of `DropDownList` that adds two public properties and one public method:

- `selectField:String`. The name of a property of the `dataProvider` collection's data objects you can name as a data point to compare to a value.

- `selectFieldValue:*`. A value you pass in to compare to the named field.

- `updateSelection()`. A public method you can call at any time to update the control's selection based on the two previously named properties. This method is called automatically upon the component's `creationComplete` event, but can also be called explicitly from anywhere in the application.

LISTING 20.3

A custom DropDownList that implements selection of complex objects

```
package components
{
  import mx.events.FlexEvent;
  import spark.components.DropDownList;

  public class SelectableDropDown extends DropDownList
  {
    public var selectField:String = "";
    public var selectFieldValue:* = null;

    public function SelectableDropDown()
    {
      super();
      this.addEventListener(FlexEvent.CREATION_COMPLETE,
```

```
      creationCompleteHandler);
  }
  private function creationCompleteHandler(event:FlexEvent):void
  {
    updateSelection();
  }
  public function updateSelection():void
  {
    if (selectField != "" && selectFieldValue != null &&
      dataProvider != null)
    {
      var dataObj:Object;
      for (var i:Number=0; i<dataProvider.length; i++)
      {
        dataObj = dataProvider.getItemAt(i);
        if (dataObj[selectField] == selectFieldValue)
        {
          selectedIndex = i;
          break;
        }
      }
    }
  }
}
```

On the Web

The code in Listing 20.3 is available in the Web site files as `SelectableDropDown.as` in the `chapter20` project's `components` package. ∎

If the custom control's `selectField` property is left to its default of an empty string, it behaves just like its superclass. If you pass in a named property and a value to compare, it updates itself automatically upon creation completion or whenever you call its public `updateSelection()` method.

Listing 20.4 shows an application that uses the custom component.

LISTING 20.4

Using a custom DropDownList component

```
<?xml version="1.0" encoding="utf-8"?>
<s:Application xmlns:fx="http://ns.adobe.com/mxml/2009"
  xmlns:s="library://ns.adobe.com/flex/spark"
  xmlns:mx="library://ns.adobe.com/flex/mx"
  xmlns:vo="vo.*" xmlns:components="components.*">
```

continued

LISTING 20.4 *(continued)*

```
  <s:layout>
    <s:VerticalLayout horizontalAlign="center" paddingTop="20"/>
  </s:layout>
  <fx:Declarations>
    <s:ArrayList id="stateData">
      <vo:StateVO>
        <vo:state>CA</vo:state>
        <vo:capitol>Sacramento</vo:capitol>
      </vo:StateVO>
      <vo:StateVO>
        <vo:state>OR</vo:state>
        <vo:capitol>Salem</vo:capitol>
      </vo:StateVO>
      <vo:StateVO>
        <vo:state>WA</vo:state>
        <vo:capitol>Olympia</vo:capitol>
      </vo:StateVO>
    </s:ArrayList>
  </fx:Declarations>
  <s:VGroup width="300">
    <s:Label text="Selectable DropDownList Control" styleName="label"
      fontSize="14" fontWeight="bold"/>
    <components:SelectableDropDown
      id="dropdownState"
      prompt="Select a State"
      dataProvider="{stateData}"
      labelField="state" width="124"
      selectField="state"
      selectFieldValue="WA"/>
    <mx:Spacer height="20"/>
    <s:Label text="selectedIndex: {dropdownState.selectedIndex}"/>
    <s:Label text="selectedItem: {dropdownState.selectedItem.capitol},
      {dropdownState.selectedItem.state}"/>
  </s:VGroup>
</s:Application>
```

On the Web

The code in Listing 20.4 is available in the Web site files as `SelectableDropDownDemo.mxml` in the `chapter20` project. The application also uses `StateVO.as` in the project source root's `vo` package and `SelectableDropDown.as` in the `components` package. ∎

Using the Spark ButtonBar control

The Flex 4 SDK implements a new control named `ButtonBar`, which I initially described in
Chapter 16. Its purpose is to display a set of buttons based on a `dataProvider` object that
implements the `IList` interface (usually a `ViewStack`, an `ArrayList`, or an `Array`
`Collection`). Its API is similar to that of the `List` control in that it supports the change event
that informs you the user has selected a new data item, and the `selectedItem` and `selected`
`Index` properties that enable you to get or set the currently selected item.

Just like the Spark `List` control described in Chapter 19, the `ButtonBar` enables you to set its
label with the `labelField` and `labelFunction` properties. The application in Listing 20.5
generates a `ButtonBar` with three buttons. Each button's label is generated by the `getState-`
`Label` method as a result of the `ButtonBar` component's `labelFunction` property.

LISTING 20.5

An application using a ButtonBar component

```
<?xml version="1.0" encoding="utf-8"?>
<s:Application xmlns:fx="http://ns.adobe.com/mxml/2009"
  xmlns:s="library://ns.adobe.com/flex/spark"
  xmlns:mx="library://ns.adobe.com/flex/mx"
  xmlns:vo="vo.*">
  <s:layout>
    <s:VerticalLayout horizontalAlign="center" paddingTop="20"/>
  </s:layout>
  <fx:Script>
    <![CDATA[
      import spark.events.IndexChangeEvent;
      import vo.StateVO;
      protected function getStateLabel(item:StateVO):String
      {
        return item.capitol + ", " + item.state;
      }
      protected function buttons_changeHandler(event:IndexChangeEvent):void
      {
        var stateObj:StateVO = event.target.selectedItem as StateVO;
        out.text="You selected " + stateObj.capitol + ", " +
          stateObj.state;
      }
    ]]>
  </fx:Script>
  <fx:Declarations>
    <s:ArrayList id="stateData">
      <vo:StateVO>
        <vo:state>CA</vo:state>
        <vo:capitol>Sacramento</vo:capitol>
      </vo:StateVO>
```

continued

LISTING 20.5 *(continued)*

```
      <vo:StateVO>
        <vo:state>OR</vo:state>
        <vo:capitol>Salem</vo:capitol>
      </vo:StateVO>
      <vo:StateVO>
        <vo:state>WA</vo:state>
        <vo:capitol>Olympia</vo:capitol>
      </vo:StateVO>
    </s:ArrayList>
  </fx:Declarations>
  <s:Label text="ButtonBar Control" fontSize="14" fontWeight="bold"/>
  <s:ButtonBar id="buttons"
    dataProvider="{stateData}"
    labelFunction="getStateLabel"
    change="buttons_changeHandler(event)"/>
  <s:Label id="out"/>
</s:Application>
```

On the Web

The code in Listing 20.5 is available in the Web site files as `ButtonBarDemo.mxml` in the `chapter20` project. ∎

Figure 20.3 shows the resulting application, displaying the `ButtonBar` control and its currently selected values.

FIGURE 20.3

A Spark `ButtonBar` control

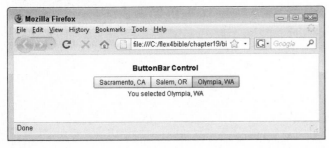

Tip

The `ButtonBar` control supports keyboard shortcuts that enable the user to navigate and select buttons. When the user presses the left or right arrow keys, a selection indicator shows that the previous or next button is selected, and when she presses the spacebar, the `ButtonBar` selects the highlighted button and dispatches a `change` event just as though the button has been pressed.

By default, the arrow keys move the selection indicator forward and backward, but you can set the ButtonBar control's arrowKeysWrapFocus property to true to cause the selection indicator to wrap from the last to the first button when pressing the right arrow key, or from first to last when pressing the left arrow key. ■

Cross-Reference

The ButtonBar control can also be used in combination with a ViewStack to implement a simple application navigation interface. I describe in Chapter 16 how to bind the ViewStack to the ButtonBar control's dataProvider property to automatically generate buttons for each of its nested views. ■

Using the DataGrid Control

The DataGrid control is one of the most popular controls in the Flex SDK. It displays relational data in the form of rows and columns, and enables the user to easily scroll through and select data. In addition, the DataGrid can be made editable, enabling the user to edit multiple rows of data in batches instead of having to navigate to a data entry form interface for each row he wants to modify.

Note

The Flex 4 SDK does not include Spark versions of the DataGrid component and its advanced extensions, AdvanceDataGrid and OlapDataGrid. Adobe intends to create Spark versions in a later revision of the SDK, but for now you should use the MX versions. ■

In terms of inheritance hierarchy, the DataGrid is directly extended from ListBase; as a result, it shares most of the events and properties of the List component. Figure 20.4 shows the inheritance tree of the DataGrid. The FileSystemDataGrid (used in AIR applications) and the PrintDataGrid (optimized for printing) are extended from DataGrid and inherit all its behaviors.

FIGURE 20.4

The MX DataGrid inheritance hierarchy

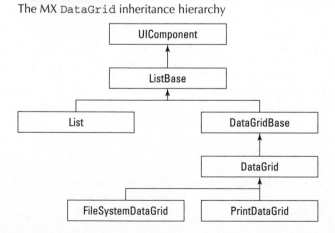

The `DataGrid` control has these built-in features:

- It displays multiple columns, each dedicated to displaying one named property of its data provider's data items.
- It displays column headers, which you can customize with simple strings or complex displays.
- The data display is sortable by the user when she clicks a column heading. This actually results in sorting the `DataGrid` object's underlying data collection.
- The user can change the order of the columns by clicking and dragging the columns.
- The user can resize columns by clicking and dragging the borders between the columns.
- Data is displayed in rows with alternating row colors.
- Scrolling through large amounts of data is supported through an architecture known as deferred instantiation.
- When integrated with Adobe's LiveCycle Data Services or a similar application server that supports the Data Management Service architecture, you can easily enable paging through large amounts of server-side data without overwhelming Flash Player memory.
- You can lock rows and columns to prevent scrolling. ,

Tip
When you provide data to a `DataGrid` control, it should always be in the form of an `ArrayCollection` or `ArrayList` containing complex objects. The objects should have named properties that in turn contain either simple values that can be directly displaying in the `DataGrid` controls columns and or that can be used by item renderer components to create customized displays. Because the purpose of a `DataGrid` is to display more than a single column, it doesn't make sense to provide it with an `ArrayCollection` containing simple string values. ■

Customizing the DataGrid display

The `DataGrid` control provides many features that enable you to customize how it's displayed:

- The `height` and `width` can be set in absolute pixels or percentage of available space.
- The `rowCount` property can determine the control's height based on the number of rows you display.
- The `alternatingItemColors` style is set to an `Array` of colors. When set with two colors, the items' backgrounds alternate between them. If you set this style to an `Array` with more than two colors, the items loop through the colors and display them in order of declaration.
- The `columns` property determines which columns are displayed to the user.

In this section, I describe some of the techniques that are most commonly used in customizing the `DataGrid` control.

The default columns display

By default, the `DataGrid` control generates columns for its data provider based on the property names of the first object in the data set.

Note

Ideally, all the data objects in a data collection have the same number of properties and identical names. When you enable the `DataGrid` to generate its columns automatically, it does so based only on the properties in the first item of the `dataProvider`. ■

In the following XML structure, each data object has eight properties, named (in order of declaration) `contactid`, `firstname`, `lastname`, `streetaddress`, `city`, `state`, `email`, and `phone`:

```
<?xml version="1.0"?>
<contacts>
  <row>
    <contactid>1</contactid>
    <firstname>Brad</firstname>
    <lastname>Lang</lastname>
    <streetaddress>3004 Buckhannan Avenue</streetaddress>
    <city>Syracuse</city>
    <state>NY</state>
    <email>Brad.C.Lang@trashymail.com</email>
    <phone>315-449-9420</phone>
  </row>
  <row>
    <contactid>2</contactid>
    <firstname>Kevin</firstname>
    <lastname>Mount</lastname>
    <streetaddress>341 Private Lane</streetaddress>
    <city>Montgomery</city>
    <state>GA</state>
    <email>Kevin.J.Mount@trashymail.com</email>
    <phone>229-329-4001</phone>
  </row>
    ... additional <row> elements ...
</contacts>
```

Web Resource

The contact information used in this section of the book and elsewhere is fake. If you need fake data with which to test and benchmark your application, try the Web site at `www.fakenamegenerator.com`. You can order large amounts of fake data in a variety of data formats. This service only charges you if you need the data in a hurry. ■

As with the `List` and `ComboBox` controls, you pass data into the `DataGrid` with the `dataProvider` property. The application in Listing 20.6 uses code that embeds data from the XML file with the `<fx:Model>` tag and wraps it in an `ArrayList`. The data is then passed to the `DataGrid` with a binding expression.

LISTING 20.6

Default DataGrid column generation

```xml
<?xml version="1.0" encoding="utf-8"?>
<s:Application xmlns:fx="http://ns.adobe.com/mxml/2009"
  xmlns:s="library://ns.adobe.com/flex/spark"
  xmlns:mx="library://ns.adobe.com/flex/mx">
  <fx:Declarations>
    <fx:Model id="contactData" source="data/contacts.xml"/>
    <s:ArrayList id="contactAC" source="{contactData.row}"/>
  </fx:Declarations>
  <mx:DataGrid id="contactGrid" dataProvider="{contactAC}"
    horizontalCenter="0" top="20"/>
</s:Application>
```

On the Web

The code in Listing 20.6 is available in the Web site files as `DataGridDefaultColumns.mxml` in the `chapter20` project. ∎

At runtime, the `DataGrid` examines the first data object in its `dataProvider` and then generates one column for each of the data object's named properties. The columns are arranged in alphabetical order, rather than the order in which the properties are declared in the XML file. (The data objects are cast as instances of the ActionScript `Object` class, which doesn't maintain its properties in any specific order.)

Figure 20.5 shows the resulting display, with the `DataGrid` showing all eight available columns of data.

FIGURE 20.5

A `DataGrid` with default column display

Controlling the column display

You determine the number and order of columns displayed by the `DataGrid` with its `columns` property. The `columns` property is an `Array` of `DataGridColumn` instances, typically declared like this:

```
<mx:DataGrid id="contactGrid" dataProvider="{contactAC}">
  <mx:columns>
    <mx:DataGridColumn ... property settings.../>
    <mx:DataGridColumn ... property settings.../>
  </mx:columns>
</mx:DataGrid>
```

The `DataGridColumn` control determines how each individual column is displayed. Its key properties include:

- `dataField:String`. This is the name of the property you want the column to display. This value is case-sensitive and must exactly match the property names of the data provider's items.

- `headerText:String`. This is the string value you want to display in the column header.

- `width:Number`. This is the width of the column in absolute pixels. (You cannot set a column's width based on a percentage of available space in the `DataGrid` without doing some calculations at runtime.)

This `DataGridColumn` declaration creates a column that displays each data object's `firstname` property, displays the header text of "First Name," and has an explicit width of 100 pixels:

```
<mx:DataGridColumn dataField="firstname"
  headerText="First Name" width="100"/>
```

Columns are displayed in the order of their declaration: The first `DataGridColumn` is leftmost in the `DataGrid` display, the second is to its right, and so on. The application in Listing 20.7 declares a `DataGrid` with three columns displaying the data provider's `firstname`, `lastname`, and `email` properties.

LISTING 20.7

A DataGrid with explicit column settings

```
<?xml version="1.0" encoding="utf-8"?>
<s:Application xmlns:fx="http://ns.adobe.com/mxml/2009"
  xmlns:s="library://ns.adobe.com/flex/spark"
  xmlns:mx="library://ns.adobe.com/flex/mx">
  <fx:Declarations>
    <fx:Model id="contactData" source="data/contacts.xml"/>
    <s:ArrayList id="contactAC" source="{contactData.row}"/>
  </fx:Declarations>
 <mx:DataGrid id="contactGrid" dataProvider="{contactAC}"
```

continued

617

LISTING 20.7 *(continued)*

```
      horizontalCenter="0" top="20">
      <mx:columns>
        <mx:DataGridColumn
          dataField="firstname" headerText="First Name"
          width="100"/>
        <mx:DataGridColumn
          dataField="lastname" headerText="Last Name"
          width="100"/>
        <mx:DataGridColumn
          dataField="email" headerText="Email Address"
          width="250"/>
      </mx:columns>
    </mx:DataGrid>
  </s:Application>
```

On the Web

The code in Listing 20.7 is available in the Web site files as `DataGridExplicitColumns.mxml` in the `chapter20` project. ■

Figure 20.6 shows the resulting application, with three columns of data displayed in the order of their declaration in the `DataGrid` control's `columns` property.

FIGURE 20.6

A `DataGrid` with explicit columns

Note

Even though only certain columns are displayed to the user, the `DataGrid` control's `selectedItem` property still refers to the complete data object represented by the currently selected row. In many data-oriented applications, you don't display the values of each row's unique identifiers (primary keys in database parlance) to the user. That information, however, is always available. In the application in Listing 20.7, for example, the expression `contactGrid.selectedItem.contactid` would refer to the unique identifier for the currently selected data item. ■

Tip

If you specify a column's property by setting `dataField`, this will be the property that the column sorts on when you click the header. If you don't specify `dataField` (which is possible if you use a renderer or `labelFunction` to render a column's cells), this row isn't automatically sortable. ∎

Displaying custom labels in DataGrid column cells

In Chapter 18, I described how to use the `labelFunction` property with the `List`, `DropDownList`, and `ComboBox` controls. The `labelFunction` property also is implemented in the `DataGridColumn` component, but the function you create to format that column's labels has a slightly different signature.

As a reminder, the signature for a custom function compatible with the `List` and `ComboBox` controls looks like this:

```
private function getFormattedLabel(item:Object):String
```

When the function is assigned to a `DataGridColumn`, the function signature changes to:

```
private function getFormattedLabel(item:Object,
    column:DataGridColumn):String
```

The difference is the addition of the function's second argument, which is a reference to the `DataGridColumn` object that calls the function at runtime.

In the data set used in this chapter, each data item has a phone property formatted with hyphens:

```
315-555-9420
```

If, instead, you want to format the phone number with parentheses around the area code, you might declare an instance of the `PhoneFormatter` class:

```
<mx:PhoneFormatter id="formatter"/>
```

Then create the custom formatting function:

```
private function getPhoneLabel(item:Object,
    column:DataGridColumn):String
{
}
```

The `PhoneFormatter` requires a value that can be parsed as a number, so within the formatting function, you first strip the hyphen characters from the data item's value. You can do this a couple of ways; the following code uses a regular expression and replaces all instances of the hyphen character with a blank string:

```
var pattern:RegExp = /-/g;
var phoneValue:String = item.phone.replace(pattern, "");
```

Finally, return the formatted value by passing the resulting expression to the `PhoneFormatter` object's `format()` method:

```
return formatter.format(phoneValue);
```

Listing 20.8 shows the complete application with a `DataGridColumn` that displays each contact's phone number with the format (315) 555-9420.

LISTING 20.8

Using a custom formatting function in a DataGridColumn

```
<?xml version="1.0" encoding="utf-8"?>
<s:Application xmlns:fx="http://ns.adobe.com/mxml/2009"
  xmlns:s="library://ns.adobe.com/flex/spark"
  xmlns:mx="library://ns.adobe.com/flex/mx">
  <fx:Script>
    <![CDATA[
      import mx.controls.dataGridClasses.DataGridColumn;
      private function getPhoneLabel(
        item:Object, column:DataGridColumn):String
      {
        var pattern:RegExp = /-/g;
        var phoneValue:String = item.phone.replace(pattern, "");
        return formatter.format(phoneValue);
      }
    ]]>
  </fx:Script>
  <fx:Declarations>
    <fx:Model id="contactData" source="data/contacts.xml"/>
    <s:ArrayList id="contactAC" source="{contactData.row}"/>
    <mx:PhoneFormatter id="formatter"/>
  </fx:Declarations>
  <mx:DataGrid id="contactGrid" dataProvider="{contactAC}"
    horizontalCenter="0" top="20">
    <mx:columns>
      <mx:DataGridColumn dataField="firstname" headerText="First Name"
        width="100"/>
      <mx:DataGridColumn dataField="lastname" headerText="Last Name"
        width="100"/>
      <mx:DataGridColumn dataField="email" headerText="Email Address"
        width="250"/>
      <mx:DataGridColumn dataField="phone" headerText="Phone Number"
        width="150" labelFunction="getPhoneLabel"/>
    </mx:columns>
  </mx:DataGrid>
</s:Application>
```

On the Web

The code in Listing 20.8 is available in the Web site files as `DataGridFormatLabels.mxml` **in the** `chapter20` **project.** ■

Figure 20.7 shows the resulting application with formatted phone numbers in the last column of the `DataGrid` control.

FIGURE 20.7

A `DataGridColumn` with custom label formatting

Using a dynamic data field

As I described previously, the custom formatting function for a `DataGridColumn` requires an argument that references the `DataGridColumn` that is calling the function. The purpose of this argument is to enable you to determine the data field of the current data item dynamically.

For example, if the data provider's data items have phone values in two different properties and you want to format them both with the same logic, you can identify the property you want to format with the array-style expression `item[column.dataField]`. The `dataField` property of the `DataGridColumn` returns the name of the property currently being processed, so you need only one custom function to format as many data properties as needed:

```
private function getPhoneLabel(item:Object,
        column:DataGridColumn):String
{
  var dataValue:String = item[column.dataField];
  var pattern:RegExp = /-/g;
  var phoneValue:String = dataValue.replace(pattern, "");
  return formatter.format(phoneValue);
}
```

Debugging a custom formatting function

It can be instructive to add a `trace()` statement to the body of a custom formatting function. As you scroll up and down in a `DataGrid`, the trace statement in the custom function is executed each time the data grid column has to be formatted:

```
private function getPhoneLabel(item:Object,
  column:DataGridColumn):String
{
  var dataValue:String = item[column.dataField];
  var pattern:RegExp = /-/g;
  var phoneValue:String = item.phone.replace(pattern, "");
  trace("original value: " + dataValue + ", " +
    "formatted value: " +   formatter.format(phoneValue));
  return formatter.format(phoneValue);
}
```

Figure 20.8 shows the resulting output in Flash Builder's Console view when the application is run in debug mode. The Console view displays the trace statements continuously as you scroll up and down in the `DataGrid`.

FIGURE 20.8

Debugging a custom formatting function

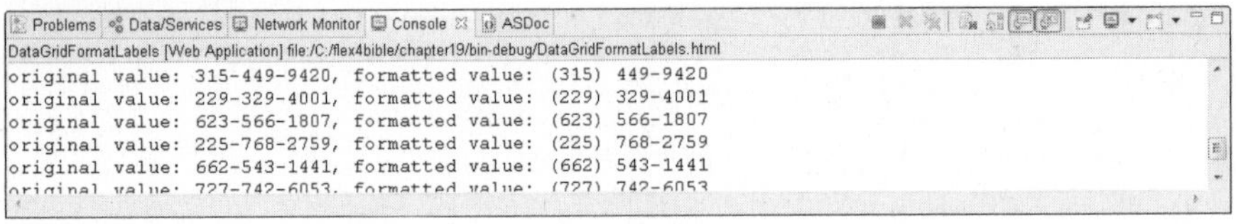

Tip

One of the advantages of the `DataGrid` control is that it reuses its visual objects as you scroll. Just like the Spark `DataGroup` component, `DataGrid` populates existing visual controls with new data and creates the appearance of a smooth scrolling experience.

As a result, you can populate the `DataGrid` and other list controls with significant amounts of data without causing Flash Player to bog down or overload its memory usage. When you run the application described previously with trace statements, try scrolling up and down. You'll notice that the function is called frequently as you scroll, and the existing visual objects are updated with new data. ■

Advanced Item Renderers and Editors

As described in Chapter 18, all list controls support the custom item renderer and editor architectures. In an MX `DataGrid` control, an item renderer or editor is used in a specific column, so the `itemRenderer` and `itemEditor` properties are implemented in the `DataGridColumn` component.

Just as with the `List` control, item renderer and editor components for the `DataGridColumn` can be declared in three ways:

- **Drop-in renderers.** These are visual components that you assign to a list control without any changes to the renderer component's default property or style settings.

- **Inline renderers.** These are components you define and nest within an MXML declaration of the list control.

- **Component renderers.** These are separate visual components that you define as MXML components or ActionScript classes and assign to the list control's `itemRenderer` property in an MXML declaration. You also can assign a component renderer at runtime with ActionScript code by using the `mx.core.ClassFactory` class (described next).

Cross-Reference
For more information on the three types of item renderer declarations, see Chapter 19. ■

At runtime, the `DataGridColumn` creates an instance of the component and passes its data provider's current data item as the renderer object's `data` property. Within the custom component, whether declared inline or as a separate component, you use the data object's properties with either ActionScript statements or binding expressions to populate visual objects and create your custom presentation.

Using the dataChange event

In the following example, a `DataGrid` component displays contact information from the `contacts.xml` file. In the first column of the `DataGrid`, the contact's first and last names are displayed as a single concatenated string. This task can be easily handled with a custom label formatting function:

```
private function getNameLabel(item:Object,
    column:DataGridColumn):String
{
    return item.firstname + " " + item.lastname;
}
```

In the second column, the `DataGrid` will display the contact's full address, formatted as a single `Text` control using HTML markup for bold and other formatting. To handle this requirement, you can use the `dataChange` event to update a custom component's display at runtime. This event is dispatched within the custom component whenever the value of its data property is updated. You can respond to the event by explicitly updating the custom component's nested objects as needed.

The custom component in Listing 20.9 is extended from the MX `Text` component. When the component's `dataChange` event is dispatched, it responds by updating its own `htmlText` property with the data object's new property values.

LISTING 20.9

A custom component updating its display with the dataChange event

```xml
<?xml version="1.0" encoding="utf-8"?>
<mx:Text xmlns:fx="http://ns.adobe.com/mxml/2009"
  xmlns:mx="library://ns.adobe.com/flex/mx"
  dataChange="updateHTML()">
  <fx:Script>
    <![CDATA[
      private function updateHTML():void
      {
        htmlText = data.city + ", " + data.state + "\n" +
          "<b>Phone:</b> " + data.phone + "\n" +
          "<b>Email:</b> " + data.email + "\n";
      }
    ]]>
  </fx:Script>
</mx:Text>
```

On the Web

The code in Listing 20.9 is available in the Web site files as `AddressRenderer.mxml` in the `chapter20` project's `renderers` package. ∎

The application in Listing 20.10 uses the custom component as an item renderer to display complete formatted address information in the `DataGrid` control's second column. Notice that the `DataGrid` control's `selectable` property is set to `false`. This makes it easier for the user to select the custom component's text value for copying. Also, its `variableRowHeight` property is set to `true` to enable the `DataGrid` columns to adjust their height as needed.

LISTING 20.10

An application using a component item renderer

```xml
<?xml version="1.0" encoding="utf-8"?>
<s:Application xmlns:fx="http://ns.adobe.com/mxml/2009"
  xmlns:s="library://ns.adobe.com/flex/spark"
  xmlns:mx="library://ns.adobe.com/flex/mx">
  <s:layout>
    <s:VerticalLayout horizontalAlign="center" paddingTop="20"/>
  </s:layout>
  <fx:Script>
    <![CDATA[
      import mx.controls.dataGridClasses.DataGridColumn;
      private function getNameLabel(
        item:Object, column:DataGridColumn):String
      {
        return item.firstname + " " + item.lastname;
```

```
        }
    ]]>
  </fx:Script>
  <fx:Declarations>
    <fx:Model id="contactData" source="data/contacts.xml"/>
    <s:ArrayList id="contactAC" source="{contactData.row}"/>
  </fx:Declarations>
  <mx:DataGrid id="contactGrid" dataProvider="{contactAC}"
    selectable="false" variableRowHeight="true" rowCount="5">
    <mx:columns>
      <mx:DataGridColumn dataField="firstname" headerText="Full Name"
        width="150" labelFunction="getNameLabel"
        fontWeight="bold" fontSize="14"/>
      <mx:DataGridColumn headerText="Address Info"  width="350"
        itemRenderer="renderers.AddressRenderer"/>
    </mx:columns>
  </mx:DataGrid>
</s:Application>
```

On the Web

The code in Listing 20.10 is available in the Web site files as `DataGridCustomRenderer.mxml` in the `chapter20` project. ∎

Figure 20.9 shows the resulting application, with each contact's full name in the left column and complete formatted address information in the right column. The user can select the text in the right column and then right-click (or Ctrl+click on the Mac) to copy the text with the pop-up context menu.

FIGURE 20.9

A custom item renderer using the `dataChange` event

Using Spark item renderers

The Flex 4 SDK includes components named `MXDataGridItemRenderer` and `MXAdvancedDataGridItemRenderer`. These Spark-based components are designed to be used as the root elements for custom item renderers used by the MX `DataGrid` and `AdvancedDataGrid` controls. They enable you to use vector graphics and advanced text rendering, even though the containing component is an MX-based control.

You can create a new item renderer for a `DataGrid` by following these steps:

1. In the Package Explorer view, right-click on the package in which you want to create a new renderer component.

2. Choose New ⇨ MXML Item Renderer.

3. Select the template Item Renderer for MX DataGrid.

4. Click Finish to create the new item renderer component.

Listing 20.11 shows a completed Spark item renderer for a `DataGridColumn` that incorporates a radial gradient background defined with an FXG graphic and Spark-based `Label` controls to display the text.

LISTING 20.11

An application using a Spark item renderer

```xml
<?xml version="1.0" encoding="utf-8"?>
<s:MXDataGridItemRenderer xmlns:fx="http://ns.adobe.com/mxml/2009"
  xmlns:s="library://ns.adobe.com/flex/spark"
  focusEnabled="true">
  <s:Rect width="100%" height="100%">
    <s:fill>
      <s:RadialGradient>
        <s:entries>
          <s:GradientEntry color="#CCCCCC"/>
          <s:GradientEntry color="#EEEEEE"/>
        </s:entries>
      </s:RadialGradient>
    </s:fill>
  </s:Rect>
  <s:VGroup top="5" bottom="5" right="10" left="10">
    <s:Label text="{data.streetaddress}"/>
    <s:Label text="{data.city}, {data.state}"/>
    <s:Label fontWeight="bold" text="{data.phone}"/>
  </s:VGroup>
</s:MXDataGridItemRenderer>
```

On the Web

The code in Listing 20.11 is available in the Web site files as `SparkAddressRenderer.mxml` in the renderers package of the `chapter20` project. ■

Figure 20.10 shows the resulting application.

A DataGrid with a Spark-based item renderer with FXG graphics

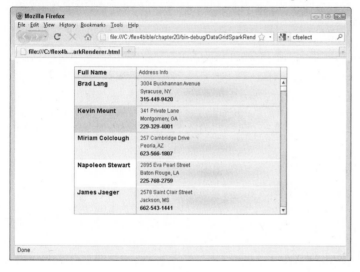

Using item editors

Like an item renderer, an item editor is a custom component that you display instead of the default label in a `DataGridColumn` cell. An item editor, however, is always an interactive control that enables the user to make changes to the data it represents. As with item renderers, you can declare an item editor using a drop-in, inline, and component syntax.

Before you can use an item editor, the `DataGrid` must have its `editable` property set to `true`. When you do this, the `DataGrid` automatically displays an item editor in any cell the user clicks. The default item editor is the `TextInput` control, so when the user clicks into an editable cell, he's presented with a `TextInput` that enables him to change the data. When he clicks or tabs out of the cell, the new data is saved to the `DataGrid` component's data provider in application memory.

When you set the `DataGrid` component's `editable` property to `true`, all its columns are automatically editable. Each `DataGridComponent` has an `editable` property as well; you stop editing of any particular column by setting its `editable` property to `false`.

In the following code, the DataGrid is editable, but editing is prevented in the firstname and lastname columns. As a result, only the data in the phone column can be changed by the user:

```
<mx:DataGrid id="contactGrid" dataProvider="{contactAC}"
  editable="true" selectable="false">
  <mx:columns>
    <mx:DataGridColumn dataField="firstname" headerText="First Name"
        width="100" editable="false"/>
    <mx:DataGridColumn dataField="lastname" headerText="Last Name"
        width="100" editable="false"/>
    <mx:DataGridColumn dataField="phone" headerText="Phone"
        width="100"/>
  </mx:columns>
</mx:DataGrid>
```

When the user clicks a cell in the phone column, a TextInput control is displayed to allow editing.

Caution

If you apply a labelFunction to a column that's also editable and uses the default item editor, the user will be editing the value returned from the labelFunction and not the column's original data. ∎

Using drop-in item editors

To use a component as a drop-in item editor for an MX DataGrid control, it must implement the IDropInListItemRenderer interface, and it must be interactive, enabling the user to make changes to data. Only a small number of components in the Flex SDK qualify on both counts; they include:

- Button
- CheckBox
- DateField
- NumericStepper
- TextArea
- TextInput

To declare a drop-in editor in a DataGridColumn, you assign the component to the DataGridColumn component's itemEditor (if you want to see the component appear only when the user clicks a cell to edit it), or to its itemRenderer (if you want to see it appear on all rows). In either case, you assign the component by its fully qualified class name, including the package prefix:

```
<mx:DataGridColumn dataField="selected"
  itemEditor="mx.controls.CheckBox"
  ... remainder of declaration ...
/>
```

I describe the details of each strategy in the following sections.

Using the itemEditor and editorDataField properties

When you declare an `itemEditor` for a `DataGridColumn`, you also have to set the `DataGridColumn` control's `editorDataField` property to indicate which field of the item editor component contains the value entered by the user. At runtime, the changed value is transferred back to the current data object's property (the property that's named as the `DataGridColumn` component's `dataField`).

For example, if you use a `CheckBox` control as an item editor, the `editorDataField` property should be set to `selected`. For a `TextInput` control, `editorDataField` should be set to `text` (the default), for a `NumericStepper`, it should be `value`, and so on.

When you set the `itemEditor` property to a named component, that component is instantiated only when the user clicks into the cell. For example, the following code indicates that a `CheckBox` control should appear only when the user clicks:

```
<mx:DataGridColumn dataField="selected"
   itemEditor="mx.controls.CheckBox"
   editorDataField="selected"
   headerText="" width="50"/>
```

Unless the user has clicked a cell that's editable, the column's actual value is displayed as a label. When the user clicks in a cell, it displays the `CheckBox` control.

Using the rendererIsEditor property

If you want the item editor component to be displayed in every row of the `DataGrid`, follow these steps:

1. **Assign the editor component** `DataGridColumn` **component's** `itemRenderer` **property instead of** `itemEditor`.

2. **Set the** `DataGridColumn` **component's** `rendererIsEditor` **property to** `true`.

The following code causes the `CheckBox` control to appear in every row, regardless of whether the user has clicked into the cell:

```
<mx:DataGridColumn dataField="selected"
   itemRenderer="mx.controls.CheckBox"
   rendererIsEditor="true"
   editorDataField="selected"
   headerText="" width="50"/>
```

The application in Listing 20.12 uses an `itemRenderer` in its first `DataGrid` that's set with `rendererIsEditor` to `true`. The renderer is a drop-in component based on `mx.controls.CheckBox`. At application startup, the `initApp()` method loops through the `ArrayList` being used as the `DataGrid` component's data provider and adds a `selected` property to each object. That property is then both displayed and edited through the `CheckBox` that appears on every row.

When the user clicks Show Selected, the application loops through the first data provider and locates all data items with selected set to `true` and adds them to a second `ArrayList` that's displayed in a separate `DataGrid`.

Note

Notice in Listing 20.12 that the `DataGrid` control's `selectable` property is set to `false`. This turns off the default selection and highlighting functionality of the `DataGrid` to enable the user to more easily click the `CheckBox` controls in the left column. ∎

LISTING 20.12

Setting a renderer as an editor

```
<?xml version="1.0" encoding="utf-8"?>
<s:Application xmlns:fx="http://ns.adobe.com/mxml/2009"
  xmlns:s="library://ns.adobe.com/flex/spark"
  xmlns:mx="library://ns.adobe.com/flex/mx"
  creationComplete="app_creationCompleteHandler(event)">
  <s:layout>
    <s:VerticalLayout horizontalAlign="center" paddingTop="20"/>
  </s:layout>
  <fx:Script>
    <![CDATA[
      import mx.events.FlexEvent;
      import mx.collections.ArrayList;
      [Bindable]
      protected var selectedData:ArrayList = new ArrayList();
      protected function app_creationCompleteHandler(event:FlexEvent):void
      {
        //Add a selected property to each data object on startup
        for (var i:int=0;i < collection.length; i++)
        {
          var contact:Object = collection.getItemAt(i);
          contact.selected=false;
        }
      }
      protected function button1_clickHandler(event:MouseEvent):void
      {
        selectedData = new ArrayList();
        for (var i:Number=0; i<collection.length; i++)
        {
          if (collection.getItemAt(i).selected)
          {
            selectedData.addItem(collection.getItemAt(i));
          }
        }
      }
    ]]>
  </fx:Script>
  <fx:Declarations>
    <fx:Model id="contactData" source="data/contacts.xml"/>
    <s:ArrayList id="collection" source="{contactData.row}"/>
  </fx:Declarations>
```

```
<s:HGroup>
  <s:Panel title="Available Data">
    <mx:DataGrid id="contactGrid" dataProvider="{collection}"
      editable="true" selectable="false">
      <mx:columns>
        <mx:DataGridColumn dataField="selected"
          itemRenderer="mx.controls.CheckBox"
          rendererIsEditor="true" editorDataField="selected"
          width="20" headerText=""/>
        <mx:DataGridColumn dataField="firstname" headerText="First Name"
          width="100" editable="false"/>
        <mx:DataGridColumn dataField="lastname" headerText="Last Name"
          width="100" editable="false"/>
      </mx:columns>
    </mx:DataGrid>
  </s:Panel>
  <s:Panel title="Selected Data">
    <mx:DataGrid id="selectedGrid" dataProvider="{selectedData}">
      <mx:columns>
        <mx:DataGridColumn dataField="firstname" headerText="First Name"/>
        <mx:DataGridColumn dataField="lastname" headerText="Last Name"/>
      </mx:columns>
    </mx:DataGrid>
  </s:Panel>
</s:HGroup>
<s:Button label="Show Selected" click="button1_clickHandler(event)"/>
</s:Application>
```

On the Web

The code in Listing 20.12 is available in the Web site files as `DataGridDropinEditor.mxml` in the `chapter20` project. ■

Figure 20.11 shows the resulting `DataGrid` with a `CheckBox` on every row. When the user clicks one of the `CheckBox` components, its `selected` value is saved to the appropriate data object's `selected` property.

Tip

When you allow the user to edit data through an editable `DataGrid`, changes are made to the data collection that's stored in client memory. If you want to save the data to a persistent data store on the server (or on the client, in the case of an Adobe AIR-based desktop application), you need to write code to transfer the changed data. If the persistent data store is on the server, you can accomplish this with the Remote Procedure Call (RPC) components (`HTTPService`, `WebService`, or `RemoteObject`) or with the Data Management Service (if using LiveCycle Data Services). With a desktop-based application, you could use the local SQLite database that's embedded in Adobe AIR. ■

FIGURE 20.11

A renderer displaying every row with rendererIsEditor set to true

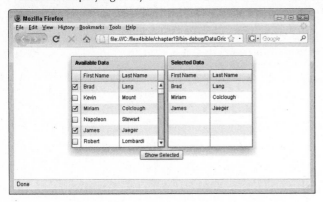

Using inline and component editors

As with custom renderers, you can declare custom item editor components with either inline syntax or as separate components. The benefits of using this syntax instead of drop-in components are that you're free to use any combination of visual controls and containers, and you can override the components' default property and style settings.

For example, imagine that you wanted to use the DateField control as an item editor, but you modify its default behavior in some way. You might set its editable property to true to enable the user to enter a date directly (without having to pick it from the pop-up calendar control) or restrict its available dates:

```
<mx:DataGridColumn dataField="dob" editorDataField="selectedDate">
  <mx:itemEditor>
    <fx:Component>
      <mx:DateField maxYear="2000" editable="true"/>
    </fx:Component>
  </mx:itemEditor>
</mx:DataGridColumn>
```

Because the DateField component is declared with the itemEditor property, it's displayed only when the user clicks the cell containing the date value.

Cross-Reference

The use of the <fx:Component> tag to define a separate component is described in Chapter 19's section about creating item renderers. ■

The application in Listing 20.13 shows the use of a DateField as an inline item editor. Upon application startup, the data is retrieved dynamically using an HTTPService component (described in Chapter 21). When the data is returned, the data objects in the ArrayCollection are transformed into instances of the ContactVO class. This is critical for this example, because the ContactVO class has a dob property typed as a Date, which makes it compatible with the DateField control that is then used as the property's editor in the DataGrid.

LISTING 20.13

Using an inline item editor

```
<?xml version="1.0" encoding="utf-8"?>
<s:Application xmlns:fx="http://ns.adobe.com/mxml/2009"
  xmlns:s="library://ns.adobe.com/flex/spark"
  xmlns:mx="library://ns.adobe.com/flex/mx"
  creationComplete="contactService.send()">
  <s:layout>
    <s:VerticalLayout horizontalAlign="center" paddingTop="20"/>
  </s:layout>
  <fx:Script>
    <![CDATA[
      import mx.collections.ArrayCollection;
      import mx.controls.dataGridClasses.DataGridColumn;
      import mx.rpc.events.ResultEvent;

      import vo.ContactVO;
      [Bindable]
      private var collection:ArrayCollection;
      private function resultHandler(event:ResultEvent):void
      {
        collection = event.result.contacts.row;
        for (var i:int=0; i<collection.length; i++)
        {
          var newContact:ContactVO =
            new ContactVO(collection.getItemAt(i));
          collection.setItemAt(newContact, i);
        }
      }
      private function getDateLabel(
        item:ContactVO, column:DataGridColumn):String
      {
        return dateFormatter.format(item.dob);
      }
    ]]>
  </fx:Script>
  <fx:Declarations>
    <mx:DateFormatter id="dateFormatter" formatString="MM/DD/YYYY"/>
    <s:HTTPService id="contactService"
      url="data/contactsWithDates.xml"
      result="resultHandler(event)"/>
  </fx:Declarations>
 <mx:DataGrid id="contactGrid" dataProvider="{collection}" rowCount="5"
```

continued

LISTING 20.13 *(continued)*

```
    editable="true">
    <mx:columns>
      <mx:DataGridColumn dataField="firstname" headerText="First Name"
        width="100"/>
      <mx:DataGridColumn dataField="lastname" headerText="Last Name"
        width="100"/>
      <mx:DataGridColumn dataField="dob" editorDataField="selectedDate"
        headerText="Date of Birth"
        labelFunction="getDateLabel">
        <mx:itemEditor>
          <fx:Component>
            <mx:DateField maxYear="2000" editable="true"/>
          </fx:Component>
        </mx:itemEditor>
      </mx:DataGridColumn>
    </mx:columns>
  </mx:DataGrid>
</s:Application>
```

On the Web

The code in Listing 20.13 is available in the Web site files as `DataGridInlineEditor.mxml` **in the** `chapter20` **project.** ∎

Figure 20.12 shows the resulting pop-up calendar control that's part of the `DateField`. When the user clicks the cell displaying the date, he sees the `DateField`; when he clicks the `DateField` control's button, the calendar control pops up. Because the `DateField` control's `editable` property is `true`, the user also can click into the `TextInput` portion of the `DateField` and type a value directly.

FIGURE 20.12

An `itemEditor` declared within inline syntax to enable custom properties and behaviors to be declared

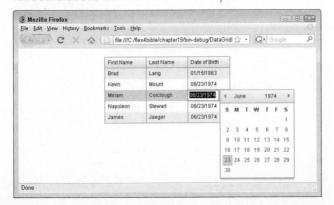

Using List Controls with Horizontal and Tile Layout

The MX `HorizontalList` and `TileList` controls share nearly all the behaviors and capabilities of the `DataGrid` and `List` controls:

- Data provided to a `HorizontalList` or `TileList` is typically displayed using a custom item renderer, declared either inline or as a separate component.

- The `change` event notifies you that the user has selected a data item.

- The `selectedItem` property returns a reference to the selected data item.

- The `allowMultipleSelection` property enables users to select multiple data items by clicking while holding down Ctrl (or ⌘ on the Mac) and Shift.

- As the user scrolls, existing visual objects are reused and their data is populated with the new data. As with the `DataGrid` control, this creates a smooth scrolling experience while enabling these controls to display large amounts of data without overusing Flash Player memory.

Cross-Reference

The new Spark `List` control's `layout` property enables you to lay out the control's data items horizontally or in tile format. If you prefer to use the new Spark skinning architecture, see the instructions for the Spark List control in Chapter 18. ■

The difference between the `HorizontalList` and `TileList` controls has to do with their layout. As implied by their component names, the `HorizontalList` lays out cells in a single row, whereas the `TileList` lays out cells in a similar fashion to the Tile container, as a grid of objects in rows and columns.

The `TileList` and `HorizontalList` controls are almost always used with custom item renderers that determine the presentation of each of the list's cells. As with the other list controls, you declare the item renderer component with drop-in, inline, or component syntax.

The application in Listing 20.14 uses an MX `TileList` control and an inline renderer to display the contents of an XML file that refers to image files in the project's `assets` folder. The renderer component uses properties of each XML `<slide>` element to present an `Image` and a `Label` wrapped in a `VBox` container.

The `TileList` is wrapped inside a `Panel` container. When the user clicks in one of the `TileList` control's cells, the detail region is updated through the use of binding expressions.

LISTING 20.14

An MX TileList control presenting dynamic data

```xml
<?xml version="1.0" encoding="utf-8"?>
<s:Application xmlns:fx="http://ns.adobe.com/mxml/2009"
  xmlns:s="library://ns.adobe.com/flex/spark"
  xmlns:mx="library://ns.adobe.com/flex/mx">
  <s:layout>
    <s:VerticalLayout horizontalAlign="center" paddingTop="20"/>
  </s:layout>
  <fx:Declarations>
    <fx:Model id="slideModel" source="data/slideshow.xml"/>
    <s:ArrayCollection id="slideAC" source="{slideModel.slide}"/>
  </fx:Declarations>
  <s:Panel title="My Photos" height="430" width="525">
    <s:layout>
      <s:VerticalLayout
        paddingLeft="10" paddingRight="10"
        paddingTop="10" paddingBottom="10"/>
    </s:layout>
    <mx:TileList
      id="slideList" dataProvider="{slideAC}"
      width="100%" height="100%"
      rowHeight="125" columnWidth="120">
      <mx:itemRenderer>
        <fx:Component>
          <mx:VBox horizontalScrollPolicy="off" verticalScrollPolicy="off"
            verticalAlign="middle" horizontalAlign="center">
            <mx:Image source="assets/thumbs/{data.source}"/>
            <mx:Label text="{data.caption}"/>
          </mx:VBox>
        </fx:Component>
      </mx:itemRenderer>
    </mx:TileList>
  </s:Panel>
  <s:Panel title="Selected Photo" width="372" height="320">
    <s:layout>
      <s:VerticalLayout
        paddingLeft="10" paddingRight="10"
        paddingTop="10" paddingBottom="10"
        horizontalAlign="center"/>
    </s:layout>
    <mx:Image source="assets/{slideList.selectedItem.source}"/>
    <s:Label text="{slideList.selectedItem.caption}"
      fontSize="14" fontWeight="bold"/>
  </s:Panel>
</s:Application>
```

On the Web

The code in Listing 20.14 is available in the Web site files as `MXTileList.mxml` in the `chapter20` project. ■

Figure 20.13 shows the resulting application, with graphic images and their captions laid out in a gridlike format.

An MX `TileList` control displaying an inline item renderer

The `HorizontalList` control uses the same architecture, enabling the user to scroll sideways through content. In the application in Listing 20.15, the change event handler saves the current `selectedItem` to a bindable `Object`. When the item is selected, the `VBox` container at the bottom of the application becomes visible due to its use of a binding expression in its enabled property.

LISTING 20.15

Using the MX HorizontalList control

```xml
<?xml version="1.0" encoding="utf-8"?>
<s:Application xmlns:fx="http://ns.adobe.com/mxml/2009"
  xmlns:s="library://ns.adobe.com/flex/spark"
  xmlns:mx="library://ns.adobe.com/flex/mx">
  <fx:Script>
    <![CDATA[
      import mx.events.ListEvent;

      protected function slideList_changeHandler(event:ListEvent):void
      {
        currentImage=event.target.selectedItem;
        detailPanel.visible=true;
      }
    ]]>
  </fx:Script>
  <s:layout>
    <s:VerticalLayout horizontalAlign="center" paddingTop="20"/>
  </s:layout>
  <fx:Declarations>
    <fx:Model id="slideModel" source="data/slideshow.xml"/>
    <s:ArrayCollection id="slideAC" source="{slideModel.slide}"/>
    <fx:Object id="currentImage"/>
  </fx:Declarations>
  <s:Panel title="My Photos" width="80%">
    <s:layout>
      <s:VerticalLayout
        paddingLeft="10" paddingRight="10"
        paddingTop="10" paddingBottom="10"/>
    </s:layout>
    <mx:HorizontalList
      id="slideList" dataProvider="{slideAC}"
      width="100%" height="125" rowHeight="125" columnWidth="120"
      change="slideList_changeHandler(event)">
      <mx:itemRenderer>
        <fx:Component>
          <mx:VBox horizontalScrollPolicy="off" verticalScrollPolicy="off"
            verticalAlign="middle" horizontalAlign="center">
            <mx:Image source="assets/thumbs/{data.source}"/>
            <mx:Label text="{data.caption}"/>
          </mx:VBox>
        </fx:Component>
      </mx:itemRenderer>
    </mx:HorizontalList>
  </s:Panel>
  <mx:Spacer height="50"/>
  <s:Panel id="detailPanel" title="Selected Photo"
    width="372" height="320" visible="false">
    <s:layout>
      <s:VerticalLayout
```

```
        paddingLeft="10" paddingRight="10"
        paddingTop="10" paddingBottom="10"
        horizontalAlign="center"/>
  </s:layout>
  <mx:Image source="assets/{currentImage.source}"/>
  <s:Label text="{currentImage.caption}"
    fontSize="14" fontWeight="bold"/>
  </s:Panel>
</s:Application>
```

On the Web

The code in Listing 20.15 is available in the Web site files as `HorizontalListDemo.mxml` **in the** `chapter20` **project.** ∎

Figure 20.14 shows the resulting application, after an item has been selected from the `HorizontalList` control.

FIGURE 20.14

A `HorizontalList` control with selected information displayed in a detail region

The Spark version of the `List` control supports a layout property that can be set to an instance of `HorizontalLayout` or `TileLayout`. You use `ItemRenderer` as the base class of its custom item renderers, as shown in the application in Listing 20.16.

LISTING 20.16

An application with a Spark List using the TileLayout class

```xml
<?xml version="1.0" encoding="utf-8"?>
<s:Application xmlns:fx="http://ns.adobe.com/mxml/2009"
  xmlns:s="library://ns.adobe.com/flex/spark"
  xmlns:mx="library://ns.adobe.com/flex/mx">
  <s:layout>
    <s:VerticalLayout horizontalAlign="center" paddingTop="20"/>
  </s:layout>
  <fx:Declarations>
    <fx:Model id="slideModel" source="data/slideshow.xml"/>
    <s:ArrayCollection id="slideAC" source="{slideModel.slide}"/>
  </fx:Declarations>
  <s:Panel title="My Photos" height="430" width="550">
    <s:layout>
      <s:VerticalLayout
        paddingLeft="10" paddingRight="10"
        paddingTop="10" paddingBottom="10"/>
    </s:layout>
    <s:List id="slideList" dataProvider="{slideAC}"
      width="100%" height="100%" >
      <s:layout>
        <s:TileLayout rowHeight="125" columnWidth="120"/>
      </s:layout>
      <s:itemRenderer>
        <fx:Component>
          <s:ItemRenderer>
            <s:layout>
              <s:VerticalLayout horizontalAlign="center"/>
            </s:layout>
            <mx:Image source="assets/thumbs/{data.source}"/>
            <s:Label text="{data.caption}"/>
          </s:ItemRenderer>
        </fx:Component>
      </s:itemRenderer>
    </s:List>
  </s:Panel>
  <s:Panel title="Selected Photo" width="372" height="320">
    <s:layout>
      <s:VerticalLayout
        paddingLeft="10" paddingRight="10"
        paddingTop="10" paddingBottom="10"
        horizontalAlign="center"/>
    </s:layout>
    <mx:Image source="assets/{slideList.selectedItem.source}"/>
    <s:Label text="{slideList.selectedItem.caption}"
      fontSize="14" fontWeight="bold"/>
  </s:Panel>
</s:Application>
```

On the Web

The code in Listing 20.16 is available in the Web site files as `SparkTileList.mxml` in the `chapter20` project. ■

Web Resource

The photos used in these examples are from the Web site www.pdphoto.org, dedicated to providing free public domain photos. Most of their photos are completely free. ■

Using the AdvancedDataGrid Control

The `AdvancedDataGrid` control is an extended version of the `DataGrid` control that adds these features:

- Sorting by multiple columns
- Row- and column-based styling
- Displaying hierarchical data with an embedded `Tree` component
- Dynamic grouping of "flat" data into a hierarchical display
- Grouping of multiple columns under a single heading
- Multicolumn item renderers

Note

The `AdvancedDataGrid` control is available only as part of the Data Visualization components license. This package also includes the Flex charting controls. The license is sold on a per-developer basis, so there aren't any ongoing royalties for using these controls. Unlike in the Flex 2 product line, the charting and other Data Visualization components aren't sold as stand-alone products; they're available only as part a Flash Builder Premium license. ■

Hierarchical data display

As with the `DataGrid`, the `AdvancedDataGrid` control's data provider is typically in the form of an `ArrayCollection`. To use the hierarchical data display feature, the objects in the data set should include at least one "grouping" property that can be used to collect and group data items based on their identical values in that property.

You can display data that is already in hierarchical form, such as the data created in this ActionScript code:

```
var employeeAC:ArrayCollection = new ArrayCollection();
employeeAC.source =
  [{department:"Shipping",
    children: [
      {firstname:"Kevin", lastname:"Mount"},
      {firstname:"Robert", lastname:"Lombardi"}]},
   {department:"Marketing",
```

```
      children: [
        {firstname:"Brad", lastname:"Lang"},
        {firstname:"James", lastname:"Jaeger"}]}
  ];
```

Notice that the data is structured as an `Array` containing multiple `Object` instances, written in ActionScript shorthand notation. Each `Object` contains a `department` property designed as the grouping field and an `Array` named `children` that contains additional data objects.

You pass this type of data to the `AdvancedDataGrid` by first wrapping it in an instance of the `HierarchicalData` class. This class has a `childrenField` property that defines which field of each object is expected to contain child objects. Its default value is `children`, so the data described in the ActionScript code has the expected structure and field names already.

Note

The `AdvancedDataGrid` component handles XML-based data intuitively. Child XML nodes are rendered as nodes of the component's nested `Tree` control. ∎

The `columns` property of the `AdvancedDataGrid` control should contain instances of the `AdvancedDataGridColumn` component. Its `dataField` and `headerText` properties behave just like the `DataGridColumn`, and its style enables you to specify the color and font on a per-column basis.

The application in Listing 20.17 uses a hierarchical data set and an `AdvancedDataGrid` to display grouped data.

LISTING 20.17

The AdvancedDataGrid control with hierarchical data

```xml
<?xml version="1.0" encoding="utf-8"?>
<s:Application xmlns:fx="http://ns.adobe.com/mxml/2009"
  xmlns:s="library://ns.adobe.com/flex/spark"
  xmlns:mx="library://ns.adobe.com/flex/mx"
  creationComplete="initData()">
  <s:layout>
    <s:VerticalLayout horizontalAlign="center" paddingTop="20"/>
  </s:layout>
  <fx:Script>
    <![CDATA[
      import mx.collections.ArrayCollection;
      [Bindable]
      private var employeeAC:ArrayCollection = new ArrayCollection();

      private function initData():void
      {
        employeeAC.source = [
          {department:"Shipping",
```

```
                children: [{firstname:"Kevin", lastname:"Mount"},
                    {firstname:"Robert", lastname:"Lombardi"}]},
            {department:"Marketing",
                children: [{firstname:"Brad", lastname:"Lang"},
                    {firstname:"James", lastname:"Jaeger"}]}
            ];
        }
    ]]>
  </fx:Script>
  <mx:AdvancedDataGrid id="employeeGrid">
    <mx:dataProvider>
      <mx:HierarchicalData source="{employeeAC}"/>
    </mx:dataProvider>
    <mx:columns>
      <mx:AdvancedDataGridColumn dataField="department"
        headerText="Department" fontWeight="bold"/>
      <mx:AdvancedDataGridColumn dataField="firstname"
        headerText="First Name"/>
      <mx:AdvancedDataGridColumn dataField="lastname"
        headerText="Last Name"/>
    </mx:columns>
  </mx:AdvancedDataGrid>
</s:Application>
```

On the Web

The code in Listing 20.17 is available in the Web site files as `AdvDataGridDemo.mxml` **in the** `chapter20` **project.** ■

The resulting application is shown in Figure 20.15. The user can click the grouped values in the leftmost column to expand the tree nodes and see the child rows.

The `AdvancedDataGrid` component

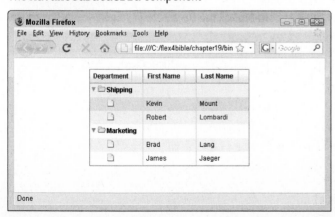

Grouping flat data

Flat data is typically defined as a conventional `ArrayCollection` containing rows and columns, such as you might import into a Flex application with a call to a database query. You can group this type of data structure in an `AdvancedDataGrid` control by wrapping it in a `GroupingCollection2` object. This object contains one or more nested `GroupingField` objects that define which columns or properties you want to group on.

In MXML, you prepare the data like this:

```
<mx:GroupingCollection2 id="gc" source="{dataCollection}">
  <mx:grouping>
    <mx:Grouping>
      <mx:GroupingField name="department"/>
    </mx:Grouping>
  </mx:grouping>
</mx:GroupingCollection2>
```

New Feature

The `GroupingCollection2` **class replaces** `GroupingCollection`**, which was used in Flex 3 for the same purpose and is now deprecated. The new class provides better performance but shares the same API as the old version.** ■

The `GroupingCollection2` is then passed to the `AdvancedDataGrid` component's `dataProvider`. To make the `GroupingCollection2` update its view, you must call its `refresh()` method. In the following code, the `refresh()` method is called when the grid component's `initialize` event is dispatched:

```
<mx:AdvancedDataGrid id="myAdvancedGrid"
  dataProvider="{gc}"
  initialize="gc.refresh()">
  ... column declarations ...
</mx:AdvancedDataGrid>
```

The application in Listing 20.18 uses a flat data set from an XML file and groups it with the `GroupingCollection2` object.

LISTING 20.18

Grouping flat data with the GroupingCollection2 and AdvancedDataGrid

```
<?xml version="1.0" encoding="utf-8"?>
<s:Application xmlns:fx="http://ns.adobe.com/mxml/2009"
  xmlns:s="library://ns.adobe.com/flex/spark"
  xmlns:mx="library://ns.adobe.com/flex/mx">
  <s:layout>
    <s:VerticalLayout horizontalAlign="center" paddingTop="20"/>
  </s:layout>
  <fx:Declarations>
```

```
      <fx:Model id="empModel" source="data/employees.xml"/>
      <s:ArrayCollection id="employeeAC" source="{empModel.row}"/>
   </fx:Declarations>
   <mx:AdvancedDataGrid id="employeeGrid" initialize="gc.refresh()">
      <mx:dataProvider>
         <mx:GroupingCollection2 id="gc" source="{employeeAC}">
            <mx:grouping>
               <mx:Grouping>
                  <mx:GroupingField name="department"/>
               </mx:Grouping>
            </mx:grouping>
         </mx:GroupingCollection2>
      </mx:dataProvider>
      <mx:columns>
         <mx:AdvancedDataGridColumn dataField="department"
            headerText="Department" fontWeight="bold"/>
         <mx:AdvancedDataGridColumn dataField="firstname"
            headerText="First Name"/>
         <mx:AdvancedDataGridColumn dataField="lastname"
            headerText="Last Name"/>
      </mx:columns>
   </mx:AdvancedDataGrid>
</s:Application>
```

On the Web

The code in Listing 20.18 is available in the Web site files as `AdvDataGridFlatData.mxml` **in the** `chapter20` **project.** ∎

Figure 20.16 shows the resulting application with two of the groups expanded to display their child data items.

FIGURE 20.16

An `AdvancedDataGrid` with grouped data from a flat data provider

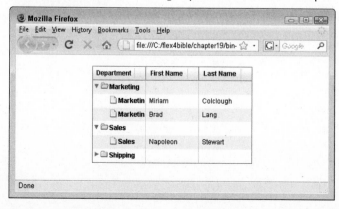

Summary

In this chapter, I described how to use advanced techniques with list controls. You learned the following:

- The Spark `DropDownList` control is similar to the MX `ComboBox`, but implements the new Spark skinning architecture.
- The Spark ButtonBar control displays a set of buttons laid out horizontally, based on a `dataProvider` that implements the `IList` interface.
- The `ComboBox` control's `editable` property produces a `TextInput` control into which the user can type an arbitrary String value, instead of selecting an item from the list.
- You can create your own custom `DropDownList` control that selects a complex object from its `dataProvider` based on properties you pass in at runtime.
- A default `DataGrid` displays columns for each named property of the first data item in its data provider.
- You determine selection and order of column display in a `DataGrid` with the `columns` property, which in turn contains a set of `DataGridColumn` objects declared in the order in which you want the columns displayed.
- The `DataGridColumn` component implements the `labelFunction`, `itemRenderer`, and `itemEditor` for customization of its appearance.
- The `dataChange` event can be used for customizing item renderer appearance at runtime with ActionScript code.
- Item editors can be declared to appear only on the current row with the `itemEditor` property or on every row with the `itemRenderer` and `rendererIsEditor` properties.
- The `DataGridColumn` component's `editorDataField` property should be set to the name of the item editor's property that contains data updated by the user.
- The `TileList` and `HorizontalList` controls display data in grid- or row-style layouts and use custom item renderers to determine the visual appearance of their cells.
- The `AdvancedDataGrid` component is available with the Data Visualization components (part of Flash Builder Premium).
- The `AdvancedDataGrid` component can present hierarchical and flat data in groups, along with summaries and other advanced data display features.

Using the Flex Charting Controls

IN THIS CHAPTER

Understanding the Flex Charting controls

Understanding chart types

Declaring charts in MXML

Setting chart properties and styles

Using pie and financial charts

Using bar and column charts

Using line and area charts

The Flex charting controls enable to you to represent numeric and statistical data visually in a graphical, interactive format. When presented in its raw form, numeric data can be difficult for users to interpret and grasp. When presented visually, in the form of pie charts, bar charts, and other graphical patterns, the data can be understood much more easily.

Consider the following visual presentations. The application in Figure 21.1 uses the following raw data, stored in an XML file:

```xml
<?xml version="1.0"?>
<data>
  <row>
    <fruit>Apples</fruit>
    <sales>34</sales>
  </row>
  <row>
    <fruit>Oranges</fruit>
    <sales>23</sales>
  </row>
  <row>
    <fruit>Pears</fruit>
    <sales>45</sales>
  </row>
</data>
```

Figure 21.1 shows the data display in a `DataGrid` and a `BarChart` control. The `DataGrid` shows the data in its raw form, while the chart makes the data more understandable to the user.

The data is clearly presented either way, but the graphical chart enables the user to understand its meaning on a more intuitive level. Applications that make extensive use of charting controls are sometimes known as *dashboard* applications because, like a car's dashboard, they give the user a sense of the data with a quick glance.

The Flex Charting controls are included in the Flex Data Visualization components package and are part of the per-developer license for Flash Builder 3 Premium. In Flex 2, the charting components were available under separate license; beginning with Flex 3, they're delivered only with the premium version of the development environment. After you purchase a Flash Builder Premium license, you can include the charting controls in as many applications as you like without any ongoing royalties.

FIGURE 21.1

A data set displayed in a `DataGrid` and a `BarChart`

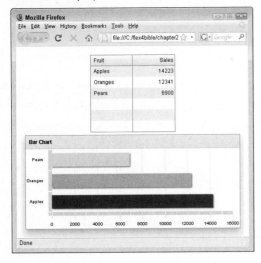

Caution

You can test the charting components and other Data Visualization components (such as the `AdvancedDataGrid` control) in your Flex applications without a license, but they're displayed with a watermark in the background that prevents their use in a production application. ■

On the Web

To use the sample code for this chapter, import the `chapter20.fxp` project from the Web site files into any folder on your disk. ■

Understanding Flex's Types of Charts

The Flex Charting controls include nine distinct types of charts, each implemented as a particular Flex component. Each chart type requires data that's passed in with a component known as the *series class*.

Note

In the Flex 4 SDK, the existing MX versions of the charting controls have not been replaced by newer Spark versions. ∎

The structure of a data series designed for use by a charting control is frequently determined by the structural requirements of chart type. A pie chart requires a simple set of data where each data item only requires one value. Data points for the candlestick chart require four values, representing each item's open, close, high, and low values. Check the documentation for each chart type to understand what kind of data structure it requires.

Tip

Data series is another name for data set. A data series for a chart can be represented as an `Array`, `ArrayList`, or `ArrayCollection`; if you'll be making changes to the data at runtime, `ArrayList` or `ArrayCollection` is the usual choice. ∎

Note

Pie charts can accept any object as a `dataProvider` that implements the `IList` or `ICollectionView` interfaces. In the examples in this chapter, I use an `ArrayCollection` to provide data for the charts, but you can also use the simpler `ArrayList` class if you prefer. ∎

Table 21.1 describes the different types of charts in the Flex Charting controls. For each chart type, its Flex control name and matching series class are noted, along with a description of the chart type's characteristics.

TABLE 21.1

Flex Chart Types

Chart Type	Charting Component	Series Class	Characteristics
Area	AreaChart	AreaSeries	Similar to a line chart, but fills the area beneath the line with a fill pattern. Often used to represent a timeline with associated data.
Bar	BarChart	BarSeries	Presents data as a set of horizontal bars representing data levels across an x axis. Nearly identical in usage to the column chart, which presents data as vertical bars.
Bubble	BubbleChart	BubbleSeries	Represents data structures with three values for each data point: the x axis, the y axis, and the size of the symbol. Each data point is represented by a filled circle that covers some portion of the chart.

continued

TABLE 21.1			_(continued)_
Chart Type	**Charting Component**	**Series Class**	**Characteristics**
Candlestick	`CandleStick-Chart`	`CandleStick-Series`	Represents financial data with each data point representing high, low, opening, and closing values. All four values are required. To represent data points without the opening value, see the HighLowOpenClose chart type.
Column	`ColumnChart`	`ColumnSeries`	Presents data as a set of vertical bars representing data levels across a y axis. Nearly identical in usage to the bar chart, which presents data as horizontal bars.
HighLow-OpenClose	`HLOCChart`	`HLOCseries`	Represents financial data with each data point representing high, low, opening, and closing values. The opening value is optional.
Line	`LineChart`	`LineSeries`	Represents data as a set of points connected with straight lines. Similar to an area chart in usage, but doesn't fill the area beneath the lines. Particularly useful for representing and comparing multiple related data series.
Pie	`PieChart`	`PieSeries`	A circular chart where each data point requires only one value. The aggregate of all data points should add up to 100 (or 100%), because the purpose of a pie chart is to show the relative size of each "slice" of the pie. This component can also display a doughnut chart, with a hollow area in the center.
Plot	`PlotChart`	`PlotSeries`	A chart where each data item has three data points: x position, y position, and radius to determine the visible area covered by the data point. By default, data points for the first series are represented by a diamond graphic, the second by a circle, and the third by a square.

Declaring Chart Controls

You declare a chart control in the same manner as any other Flex visual control. You place it on the screen within a container — use the container's horizontal, vertical, or basic layout to position the chart — and use either absolute pixel or percentage-based sizing to set its `height` and `width`.

Tip

Unlike images, charting controls do not have a concept of aspect ratio. If you set one dimension of a chart to a particular size, it doesn't have any effect on the other dimension: The chart's `height` and `width` properties are set independently. ∎

As with all visual controls, charting controls can be declared in either MXML or ActionScript code. For example, a simple pie chart declared in MXML looks like this:

```
<mx:PieChart dataProvider="{salesData}"
  height="100%" width="100%">
  <mx:series>
    <mx:PieSeries field="sales" labelField="fruit"
      labelPosition="inside" explodeRadius=".05"/>
  </mx:series>
</mx:PieChart>
```

Figure 21.2 shows the resulting chart, displaying each data point as a wedge of the pie. The explodeRadius property, which has a range of possible values from 0 to 1, determines how much separation is displayed between each wedge of the pie.

The same chart could be created with this ActionScript code:

```
import mx.charts.series.PieSeries;
import mx.charts.PieChart;
private function createChart():void
{
  var series:PieSeries = new PieSeries();
  series.field="sales";
  series.labelField="fruit";
  series.explodeRadius=.01;
  series.setStyle("labelPosition", "inside");
  var chart:PieChart = new PieChart();
  chart.visible=true;
  chart.dataProvider=salesData;
  chart.percentWidth=100;
  chart.percentHeight=100;
  chart.series=[series];
  contentGroup.addElement(chart)
}
```

FIGURE 21.2

A simple pie chart

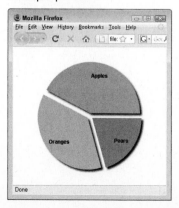

As with many visual controls, the ActionScript code required to create and display the chart is significantly more verbose than the equivalent MXML, but you should choose the coding style you prefer. There is no difference in function or performance between the two approaches.

Setting Chart Properties and Styles

Each chart type has its own individual requirements and unique behaviors that respond to its particular properties and styles. In this section, I describe the behaviors of each family of charts and how they respond to particular settings.

Using pie charts

As I described previously, a pie chart is declared with the `PieChart` component, and its data is provided with the `PieSeries` class. Pie charts have these characteristics:

- A pie chart requires only a single data series. Unlike other, more complex charts, the pie chart is designed to show one set of data and illustrate the percentage of the total of the series' data points.
- Each data point is presented as a wedge of the pie.
- The fill colors of the pie wedges are set to default values that you can override.
- The pie wedges are presented with no default gap; you create gaps by applying various `explode` properties.
- Each wedge has a default drop-shadow filter that you can remove or override.

Setting wedge labels

The wedge label is a string value that's displayed on or near each pie wedge. You control the label's position with the `DataSeries` class's `labelPosition` style, which has these possible values:

- `none` (**default**). No label is displayed.
- `callout`. The label is displayed outside the pie with a line connecting it to its pie wedge.
- `inside`. The label is displayed inside its pie wedge.
- `insideWithCallout`. The label is displayed inside its pie wedge if it fits or outside with a callout connector if it doesn't.
- `outside`. The label is displayed outside the pie wedge, with added callout connectors where necessary.

You determine the value of the label with the `DataSeries` class's `labelField` or `labelFunction` property. The `labelField` behaves just like the same named property in list controls; you're naming a data property containing the value you want to display. This declaration would cause the raw value of each data item's sales property to be displayed inside the matching pie wedge:

```
labelField="sales" labelPosition="inside"
```

For more complex label presentations, you can use the `labelFunction` property to point to a function that's called at runtime to render each pie wedge. A custom label function for the `PieSeries` class requires four arguments:

- `field:String`. The name of the field being rendered.
- `index:Number`. The ordinal position of the current data item in the chart's data provider.
- `item:Object`. The data item represented by the current pie wedge.
- `percentValue:Number`. The percent of the total value represented by the current pie wedge.

This custom label function uses a `NumberFormatter` object to format both the sales value and the `percentValue` argument:

```
private function getWedgeLabel(item:Object, field:String,
  index:Number, percentValue:Number):String
{
  return item.fruit + ": $" + nf.format(item.sales) +
  " (" + nf.format(percentValue) + "%)";
}
```

As with the `labelFunction` property of the list controls, you set the property's value to the callback function's name:

```
<mx:PieSeries field="sales" labelFunction="getWedgeLabel"/>
```

The application in Listing 21.1 declares a custom label function suitable for use as a custom label function for the `PieSeries` class.

LISTING 21.1

A pie chart with a custom label function

```
<s:Application xmlns:fx="http://ns.adobe.com/mxml/2009"
  xmlns:s="library://ns.adobe.com/flex/spark"
  xmlns:mx="library://ns.adobe.com/flex/mx">
  <fx:Declarations>
    <fx:Model id="pieModel" source="data/PieData.xml"/>
    <s:ArrayCollection id="pieData" source="{pieModel.row}"/>
    <mx:NumberFormatter id="nf" precision="1" rounding="nearest"/>
  </fx:Declarations>
  <fx:Style>
    @namespace s "library://ns.adobe.com/flex/spark";
    @namespace mx "library://ns.adobe.com/flex/mx";
    mx|PieChart
    {
      font-size:12;
    font-weight:bold;
    {
```

continued

LISTING 21.1   *(continued)*

```
      }
    </fx:Style>
    <fx:Script>
      <![CDATA[
        private function getWedgeLabel(
          item:Object, field:String, index:Number, percentValue:Number):String
        {
          return item.fruit + ": $" + nf.format(item.sales) +
            " (" + nf.format(percentValue) + "%)";
        }
      ]]>
    </fx:Script>
    <mx:PieChart dataProvider="{pieData}"
      height="90%" width="90%"
      horizontalCenter="0" verticalCenter="0">
      <mx:series>
        <mx:PieSeries field="sales" labelFunction="getWedgeLabel"
          labelPosition="callout" explodeRadius=".01"/>
      </mx:series>
    </mx:PieChart>
  </s:Application>
```

On the Web

The code in Listing 21.1 is available in the Web site files as `PieChartCustomLabel.mxml` **in the** `chapter20` **project.** ∎

Figure 21.3 shows the resulting application with customized labels presented as callouts connected to their respective pie wedges.

Exploding the pie

The pie chart has two methods for *exploding*, or *separating*, the wedges. The `exploderRadius` property, when set to a value greater than 0 (with a maximum of 1), pushes all wedges outward from the chart's center.

The following pie chart sets its `explodeRadius` property with a binding expression that references a slider's current value. As the user manipulates the slider, the pie wedges move farther apart:

```
    <s:VGroup>
      <s:Label text="Explode Radius: {explodeSlider.value}"
        fontSize="14" fontWeight="bold"/>
      <mx:HSlider id="explodeSlider" minimum="0" maximum="1"
        snapInterval=".01" liveDragging="true" value=".3"/>
    </s:VGroup>
    <mx:PieChart dataProvider="{pieData}"
      height="100%" width="100%">
```

```
<mx:series>
  <mx:PieSeries field="sales" labelFunction="getWedgeLabel"
    labelPosition="callout"
    explodeRadius="{explodeSlider.value}"/>
</mx:series>
</mx:PieChart>
```

A pie chart with customized labels

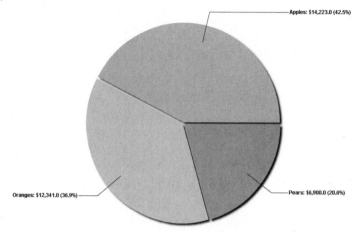

Figure 21.4 shows the visual result: The pie wedges shrink and move apart as the value of `explodeRadius` increases.

Exploding the pie

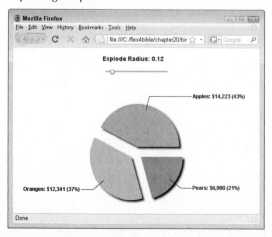

Caution

Setting `explodeRadius` to the maximum value of 1 causes the pie wedges to disappear. ∎

Exploding one pie wedge

```
<s:Application xmlns:fx="http://ns.adobe.com/mxml/2009"
  xmlns:s="library://ns.adobe.com/flex/spark"
  xmlns:mx="library://ns.adobe.com/flex/mx">
  <s:layout>
    <s:VerticalLayout
      gap="40" horizontalAlign="center"
      paddingTop="20" paddingRight="20" paddingLeft="20"/>
  </s:layout>
  <fx:Declarations>
    <fx:Model id="pieModel" source="data/PieData.xml"/>
    <s:ArrayCollection id="pieData" source="{pieModel.row}"/>
    <mx:NumberFormatter id="nf" precision="1" rounding="nearest"/>
  </fx:Declarations>
  <fx:Style>
    @namespace s "library://ns.adobe.com/flex/spark";
    @namespace mx "library://ns.adobe.com/flex/mx";
    mx|PieChart
    {
      font-size:12;
      font-weight:bold;
    }
  </fx:Style>
  <fx:Script>
    <![CDATA[
      private function getWedgeLabel(
        item:Object, field:String, index:Number, percentValue:Number):String
      {
        return item.fruit + ": $" + nf.format(item.sales) +
          " (" + nf.format(percentValue) + "%)";
      }
    ]]>
  </fx:Script>
  <s:VGroup horizontalAlign="center">
    <s:Label text="Explode Radius: {explodeSlider.value}"
      fontSize="14" fontWeight="bold"/>
    <s:HSlider  id="explodeSlider" minimum="0" maximum="1"
      snapInterval=".01" liveDragging="true" value=".3" width="200"/>
  </s:VGroup>
  <mx:PieChart dataProvider="{pieData}"
    height="100%" width="100%">
    <mx:series>
```

```
    <mx:PieSeries field="sales" labelFunction="getWedgeLabel"
       labelPosition="callout"
       perWedgeExplodeRadius="{[0,0,explodeSlider.value]}"/>
    </mx:series>
  </mx:PieChart>
</s:Application>
```

On the Web

The code in Listing 21.2 is available in the Web site files as `PieExplode.mxml` **in the** `chapter20` **project.** ■

Figure 21.5 shows the result: One pie wedge is exploded from the rest of the chart.

FIGURE 21.5

Exploding one pie wedge

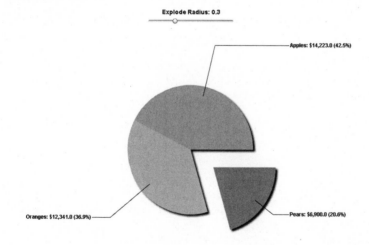

Creating a doughnut chart

A doughnut chart is essentially a pie chart with a hole in the middle. You turn a pie into a doughnut by setting the `PieChart` control's `centerRadius` property to a value greater than 0. The value is measured as the distance from the center of the chart to the inner edge of the wedges, equaling a percentage of the pie's total radius.

The application in Listing 21.3 generates a doughnut chart with a center radius that's 30 percent of the total pie radius.

LISTING 21.3

Displaying a doughnut chart

```xml
<?xml version="1.0" encoding="utf-8"?>
<s:Application xmlns:fx="http://ns.adobe.com/mxml/2009"
  xmlns:s="library://ns.adobe.com/flex/spark"
  xmlns:mx="library://ns.adobe.com/flex/mx">
  <fx:Declarations>
    <fx:Model id="pieModel" source="data/PieData.xml"/>
    <s:ArrayCollection id="pieData" source="{pieModel.row}"/>
  </fx:Declarations>
  <mx:PieChart dataProvider="{pieData}"
    height="100%" width="100%" innerRadius=".3"
    fontSize="14" fontWeight="bold">
    <mx:series>
      <mx:PieSeries field="sales" labelField="fruit"
        labelPosition="inside"/>
    </mx:series>
  </mx:PieChart>
</s:Application>
```

On the Web

The code in Listing 21.3 is available in the Web site files as `DoughnutDemo.mxml` **in the** `chapter20` **project.** ∎

Figure 21.6 shows the result: a chart with a hole in the center.

FIGURE 21.6

A doughnut chart

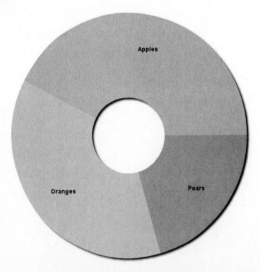

Using multiple data series

A pie chart declared with multiple data series displays its data as a set of concentric circles. When creating this type of chart, the `PieChart` doesn't need a `dataProvider`; instead, you assign a unique `dataProvider` to each `PieSeries`. When the chart is rendered, the first data series is displayed in the center of the pie, the second surrounds the first, and so on:

```
<mx:PieChart>
  <mx:series>
    <mx:PieSeries dataProvider="{pieData}" field="sales"
      labelPosition="none"/>
    <mx:PieSeries dataProvider="{pieData2}" field="sales"
      labelPosition="callout"/>
  </mx:series>
</mx:PieChart>
```

Notice that the first series (the inner circle) has its `labelPosition` style set to none, while the second (the outer circle) is set to `callout`. This results in a single label for each item, displayed outside the chart.

The application in Listing 21.4 declares a pie chart as a doughnut with two data series.

LISTING 21.4

A pie chart with two data series

```
<?xml version="1.0" encoding="utf-8"?>
<s:Application xmlns:fx="http://ns.adobe.com/mxml/2009"
  xmlns:s="library://ns.adobe.com/flex/spark"
  xmlns:mx="library://ns.adobe.com/flex/mx">
  <fx:Declarations>
    <fx:Model id="pieModel" source="data/PieData.xml"/>
    <fx:Model id="pieModel2" source="data/PieData2.xml"/>
    <s:ArrayCollection id="pieData" source="{pieModel.row}"/>
    <s:ArrayCollection id="pieData2" source="{pieModel2.row}"/>
  </fx:Declarations>
  <fx:Style>
    @namespace s "library://ns.adobe.com/flex/spark";
    @namespace mx "library://ns.adobe.com/flex/mx";

    mx|PieSeries {
      fills:#333333,#999999,#FFFFFF;
    }
  </fx:Style>  <mx:PieChart height="100%" width="100%"
    fontSize="14" fontWeight="bold"
    left="20" right="20" top="20" bottom="20">
    <mx:series>
      <mx:PieSeries field="sales" labelField="fruit"
        dataProvider="{pieData}" labelPosition="callout"/>
```

continued

659

LISTING 21.4 *(continued)*

```
    <mx:PieSeries field="sales" labelField="fruit"
        dataProvider="{pieData2}" labelPosition="callout"/>
    </mx:series>
  </mx:PieChart>
</s:Application>
```

On the Web

The code in Listing 21.4 is available in the Web site files as `PieMultipleSeries.mxml` **in the** `chapter20`
project. ▪

Figure 21.7 shows the result: a pie chart with multiple data series displayed as concentric circles.

FIGURE 21.7

A pie chart with multiple data series

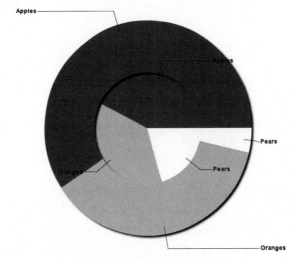

Controlling fill colors and backgrounds

You can override the fill colors of each wedge of a pie chart with the `fills` property of the
`PieSeries` class. This property is an `Array` containing objects that implement the `IFill` interface. You can use these classes for this purpose:

- `BitMapFill`. Fills an object with a bitmap graphic.
- `LinearGradient`. Fills an object with a linear gradient, defined as an `Array` of
  `GradientEntry` objects.

- RadialGradient. Fills an object with a radial gradient, defined as an `Array` of `GradientEntry` objects.

- SolidColor. Fills an object with a single solid color, defined by a hexadecimal color code or a named color that's recognized by the Flex compiler.

To select solid fill colors for a pie chart, declare the `PieSeries` object's `fills` property as an `<mx:fills>` tag set, and nest one `<mx:SolidColor>` declaration for each data element. The following code sets three fill colors of red, green, and blue:

```
<mx:PieChart dataProvider="{pieData}">
  <mx:series>
    <mx:PieSeries field="sales" labelField="fruit"
      labelPosition="inside">
      <mx:fills>
        <mx:SolidColor color="#FF0000"/>
        <mx:SolidColor color="#00FF00 "/>
        <mx:SolidColor color="#0000FF "/>
      </mx:fills>
    </mx:PieSeries>
  </mx:series>
</mx:PieChart>
```

For a pie chart with more than one data series, you set each series individually, because each instance of the `PieSeries` has its own `fills` property.

The application in Listing 21.5 selects colors of black, gray, and white for its three wedges. Figure 21.8 shows the finished pie chart.

LISTING 21.5

A pie chart with custom fill colors

```
<?xml version="1.0" encoding="utf-8"?>
<s:Application xmlns:fx="http://ns.adobe.com/mxml/2009"
  xmlns:s="library://ns.adobe.com/flex/spark"
  xmlns:mx="library://ns.adobe.com/flex/mx">
  <fx:Declarations>
    <fx:Model id="pieModel" source="data/PieData.xml"/>
    <s:ArrayCollection id="pieData" source="{pieModel.row}"/>
  </fx:Declarations>
  <s:Group top="50" bottom="50" left="20" right="20">
    <mx:PieChart height="100%" width="100%">
      <mx:series>
        <mx:PieSeries field="sales" labelField="fruit"
          dataProvider="{pieData}" labelPosition="callout"
          fontSize="14" fontWeight="bold"
          height="100%" width="100%">
```

continued

LISTING 21.5 *(continued)*

```
        <mx:fills>
           <mx:SolidColor color="#000000"/>
           <mx:SolidColor color="#999999"/>
           <mx:SolidColor color="#FFFFFF"/>
        </mx:fills>
      </mx:PieSeries>
    </mx:series>
   </mx:PieChart>
  </s:Group>
</s:Application>
```

On the Web

The code in Listing 21.5 is available in the Web site files as `PieSetFillColors.mxml` **in the** `chapter20`
project. ∎

Figure 21.8 shows the resulting pie chart with specific fill colors.

FIGURE 21.8

A pie chart with black, gray, and white fill colors

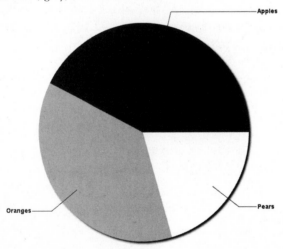

Using financial charts

The Flex framework contains two types of charts for use with financial data:

- **The candlestick chart.** This chart represents financial data as a series of candlesticks, each representing high, low, opening, and closing points for a data series.

- **The HighLowOpenClose (HLOC).** This chart is similar but doesn't require opening values for its data series.

The data structure for these two charts is similar. Each data point should have values that can be assigned to these properties of the `CandlestickSeries` or `HLOCSeries` objects:

- `closeField`. Represents the data item's closing value; required for both charts.

- `highField`. Represents the data item's high value; required for both charts.

- `lowField`. Represents the data item's low value; required for both charts.

- `openField`. Represents the data item's opening value; optional for the HLOC chart, and required for the candlestick chart.

The two charts differ in how they represent these values. As shown in Figure 21.9, the HLOC chart displays a vertical stroke for each data item showing the high and low values and two short strokes protruding from the main display. The stroke pointing to the left is the open value, and the stroke pointing to the right is the close value.

FIGURE 21.9

The icon for a HLOC chart

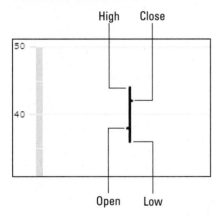

As shown in Figure 21.10, the candlestick chart displays a box indicating the high and low values as vertical lines, and the open and close values as a box. If the close value is higher than the open value, the box is filled; if the open value is higher, the box is empty.

FIGURE 21.10

Icons for the candlestick chart

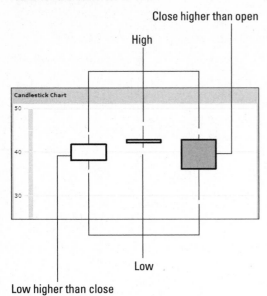

The application in Listing 21.6 shows a data set displayed in its raw form in a `DataGrid` and then rendered visually in an HLOC and a candlestick chart.

LISTING 21.6

Data rendered in an HLOC and a candlestick chart

```xml
<?xml version="1.0" encoding="utf-8"?>
<s:Application xmlns:fx="http://ns.adobe.com/mxml/2009"
  xmlns:s="library://ns.adobe.com/flex/spark"
  xmlns:mx="library://ns.adobe.com/flex/mx">
  <s:layout>
    <s:VerticalLayout horizontalAlign="center"
      paddingTop="20" paddingBottom="20"
      paddingRight="20" paddingLeft="20" gap="20"/>
  </s:layout>
  <fx:Declarations>
    <fx:Model id="financialModel" source="data/FinancialData.xml"/>
    <s:ArrayCollection id="financialData" source="{financialModel.row}"/>
  </fx:Declarations>
  <mx:DataGrid dataProvider="{financialData}" rowCount="3"/>
  <s:HGroup width="100%" height="100%">
    <s:Panel title="HLOC Chart" height="100%" width="100%">
      <mx:HLOCChart dataProvider="{financialData}"
```

```
            height="100%" width="100%">
            <mx:horizontalAxis>
              <mx:LinearAxis minimum="-1" maximum="3" interval="1"/>
            </mx:horizontalAxis>
            <mx:series>
              <mx:HLOCSeries dataProvider="{financialData}"
                highField="high" lowField="low"
                openField="open" closeField="close">
                <mx:stroke>
                  <mx:SolidColorStroke color="black" weight="3"/>
                </mx:stroke>
                <mx:openTickStroke>
                  <mx:SolidColorStroke color="black" weight="3"/>
                </mx:openTickStroke>
                <mx:closeTickStroke>
                  <mx:SolidColorStroke color="black" weight="3"/>
                </mx:closeTickStroke>
              </mx:HLOCSeries>
            </mx:series>
          </mx:HLOCChart>
        </s:Panel>
        <s:Panel title="Candlestick Chart" height="100%" width="100%">
          <mx:CandlestickChart dataProvider="{financialData}"
            height="100%" width="100%">
            <mx:horizontalAxis>
              <mx:LinearAxis minimum="0" maximum="4" interval="1"/>
            </mx:horizontalAxis>
            <mx:series>
              <mx:CandlestickSeries dataProvider="{financialData}"
                highField="high" lowField="low"
                openField="open" closeField="close"
                xField="quarter">
                <mx:boxStroke>
                  <mx:SolidColorStroke color="black" weight="3"/>
                </mx:boxStroke>
              </mx:CandlestickSeries>
            </mx:series>
          </mx:CandlestickChart>
        </s:Panel>
      </s:HGroup>
    </s:Application>
```

On the Web

The code in Listing 21.6 is available in the Web site files as `FinancialCharts.mxml` **in the** `chapter20`
project. ■

Figure 21.11 shows the resulting application, with the raw data displayed in the `DataGrid` and
the two charts side by side.

FIGURE 21.11

The HLOC and candlestick charts, side by side

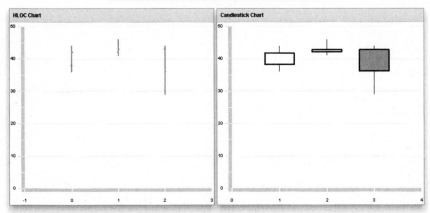

Using bar, column, line, and area charts

The bar, column, line, and area charts are all designed to render and compare values graphically along an x and a y axis. The data structure for all four of these charts is identical. Each requires one or more data series, each consisting of an `Array` or `ArrayCollection` of name/value pairs. As with the pie chart, the value should be numeric (a *chartable value*), but whereas the pie chart illustrates each value's percentage of the whole, these charts display values next to each for the purpose of comparison or trend analysis.

The data for a bar, column, line, or area chart series can be represented in ActionScript or MXML, or retrieved dynamically from an application server at runtime. A compatible data series, rendered in MXML, might look like this:

```xml
<?xml version="1.0"?>
<data>
  <row>
    <fruit>Apples</fruit>
    <sales>14223</sales>
  </row>
  <row>
    <fruit>Oranges</fruit>
    <sales>12341</sales>
  </row>
  <row>
    <fruit>Pears</fruit>
```

```
        <sales>6900</sales>
      </row>
    </data>
```

Using bar and column charts

The bar and column charts are identical in their fundamental structure and purpose: They're used to compare values or show changes in values over time. As shown in Figure 21.12, these two charts are distinguished by the dimension in which they represent numeric values: The bar chart displays horizontal bars pushing out from the chart's left-inner border, while the column chart displays vertical columns rising from the chart's bottom-inner border.

FIGURE 21.12

A bar chart and a column chart representing the same data

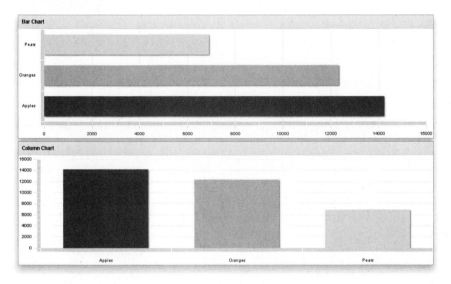

You declare a bar or column chart with much the same syntax as a pie chart, but you must include a declaration of one axis of the chart. For a bar chart, which uses the x axis to render its numeric values, you provide an explicit <mx:verticalAxis> declaration. Within the axis declaration, you declare an instance of one of these axis components:

- CategoryAxis. Treats alphanumeric values as category names along the axis.
- DateTimeAxis. Lays out date/time values along the axis.
- LinearAxis. Treats numeric data points as a set of linear values along the axis.
- LogAxis. Maps numerical values logarithmically along the axis.

Tip

The DateTimeAxis **plots values evenly across an access using a data set containing instances of the ActionScript** Date **class. It also can work with a set of string labels when you provide a custom parsing function to transform the strings into dates it can handle.** ▪

The following BarChart uses a set of categories (the names of fruit in the data set) as its vertical axis:

```
<mx:BarChart dataProvider="{salesData}">
  <mx:verticalAxis>
    <mx:CategoryAxis dataProvider="{salesData}"
      categoryField="fruit"/>
  </mx:verticalAxis>
  <mx:series>
    <mx:BarSeries xField="sales" yField="fruit"/>
  </mx:series>
</mx:BarChart>
```

The result, as shown in the bar chart in Figure 21.12, is to display the categorical data from the fruit field, named in the CategoryField property.

Tip

The CategoryAxis **component has its own** dataProvider **property and does not inherit this value from the** BarChart **or** ColumnChart **in which it's nested. Even when they share the same data, the data provider must be declared twice.** ▪

Similarly, the ColumnChart control needs a horizontalAxis declaration to indicate what values are displayed beneath the chart:

```
<mx:ColumnChart dataProvider="{salesData}">
  <mx:horizontalAxis>
    <mx:CategoryAxis dataProvider="{salesData}"
      categoryField="fruit"/>
  </mx:horizontalAxis>
  <mx:series>
    <mx:ColumnSeries xField="fruit" yField="sales"/>
  </mx:series>
</mx:ColumnChart>
```

Both the ColumnChart and BarChart controls implement these properties to determine which values are used on each axis of the chart:

- xField. The name of the property containing values for the x axis.
- yField. The name of the property containing values for the y axis.

The application in Listing 21.7 displays a bar chart and a column chart side by side, using the same data set.

LISTING 21.7

A bar and a column chart

```xml
<?xml version="1.0" encoding="utf-8"?>
<s:Application xmlns:fx="http://ns.adobe.com/mxml/2009"
  xmlns:s="library://ns.adobe.com/flex/spark"
  xmlns:mx="library://ns.adobe.com/flex/mx">
  <s:layout>
    <s:VerticalLayout paddingTop="20" paddingBottom="20"
      paddingRight="20" paddingLeft="20"/>
  </s:layout>
  <fx:Style>
    @namespace s "library://ns.adobe.com/flex/spark";
    @namespace mx "library://ns.adobe.com/flex/mx";
    mx|BarSeries, mx|ColumnSeries {
      fills:#333333,#999999,#CCCCCC;
    }
  </fx:Style>
  <fx:Declarations>
    <fx:Model id="salesModel" source="data/salesData.xml"/>
    <s:ArrayCollection id="salesData" source="{salesModel.row}"/>
  </fx:Declarations>
  <s:Panel title="Bar Chart" height="100%" width="100%">
    <mx:BarChart dataProvider="{salesData}"
      height="100%" width="100%">
      <mx:verticalAxis>
        <mx:CategoryAxis dataProvider="{salesData}" categoryField="fruit"/>
      </mx:verticalAxis>
      <mx:series>
        <mx:BarSeries xField="sales" yField="fruit"/>
      </mx:series>
    </mx:BarChart>
  </s:Panel>
  <s:Panel title="Column Chart" height="100%" width="100%">
    <mx:ColumnChart dataProvider="{salesData}"
      height="100%" width="100%">
      <mx:horizontalAxis>
        <mx:CategoryAxis dataProvider="{salesData}" categoryField="fruit"/>
      </mx:horizontalAxis>
      <mx:series>
        <mx:ColumnSeries xField="fruit" yField="sales"/>
      </mx:series>
    </mx:ColumnChart>
  </s:Panel>
</s:Application>
```

On the Web

The code in Listing 21.7 is available in the Web site files as `BarAndColumnDemo.mxml` in the `chapter20` project. ∎

Using line and area charts

The line and area charts are nearly identical to each other in structure, with their primary visual difference lying in how they represent a trend visually. As shown in Figure 21.13, the area chart fills the area beneath the trend line with a fill color or bitmap, and the line chart leaves the area below the line blank.

FIGURE 21.13

Line and area charts representing the same data

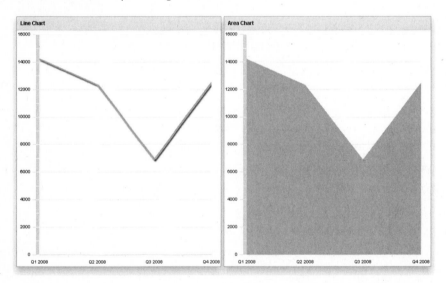

As with the `ColumnChart` control, the `LineChart` and `AreaChart` require a `horizontalAxis` that determines which values are displayed below the chart, along the x axis:

```
<mx:LineChart dataProvider="{trendData}">
  <mx:horizontalAxis>
    <mx:CategoryAxis dataProvider="{trendData}"
      categoryField="quarter"/>
  </mx:horizontalAxis>
  <mx:series>
    <mx:LineSeries xField="quarter" yField="sales"/>
  </mx:series>
</mx:LineChart>
```

The application in Listing 21.8 displays a line chart and an area chart using the same data.

Line and area charts

```xml
<?xml version="1.0" encoding="utf-8"?>
<s:Application xmlns:fx="http://ns.adobe.com/mxml/2009"
  xmlns:s="library://ns.adobe.com/flex/spark"
  xmlns:mx="library://ns.adobe.com/flex/mx">
  <s:layout>
    <s:HorizontalLayout verticalAlign="middle"
      paddingTop="20" paddingBottom="20"
      paddingRight="20" paddingLeft="20"/>
  </s:layout>
  <fx:Declarations>
    <fx:Model id="trendModel" source="data/trendData.xml"/>
    <s:ArrayCollection id="trendData" source="{trendModel.row}"/>
  </fx:Declarations>
  <s:Panel title="Line Chart" height="100%" width="100%">
    <mx:LineChart dataProvider="{trendData}"
      height="100%" width="100%">
      <mx:horizontalAxis>
        <mx:CategoryAxis dataProvider="{trendData}"
          categoryField="quarter"/>
      </mx:horizontalAxis>
      <mx:series>
        <mx:LineSeries xField="quarter" yField="sales"/>
      </mx:series>
    </mx:LineChart>
  </s:Panel>
  <s:Panel title="Area Chart" height="100%" width="100%">
    <mx:AreaChart dataProvider="{trendData}"
      height="100%" width="100%">
      <mx:horizontalAxis>
        <mx:CategoryAxis dataProvider="{trendData}"
          categoryField="quarter"/>
      </mx:horizontalAxis>
      <mx:series>
        <mx:AreaSeries xField="quarter" yField="sales"/>
      </mx:series>
    </mx:AreaChart>
  </s:Panel>
</s:Application>
```

On the Web

The application in Listing 21.8 is available in the Web site files as `LineAndAreaDemo.mxml` in the `chapter20` project. ■

Both the LineSeries and AreaSeries components can adjust the shape of their lines based on their form property. As displayed in Figure 21.13, the form property has these possible values:

- curve. Draws curves between data points.
- horizontal. Draws vertical lines from the x coordinate of the current point to the x coordinate of the next point.
- reverseStep. Draws vertical and then horizontal lines to connect data points.
- segment (the default). Draws straight lines to connect data points.
- step. Draws horizontal and then vertical lines to connect data points.
- vertical. Draws vertical lines from the y coordinate of the current point to the y coordinate of the next point.

Figure 21.14 shows the six different forms of line charts.

FIGURE 21.14

The different forms of line charts

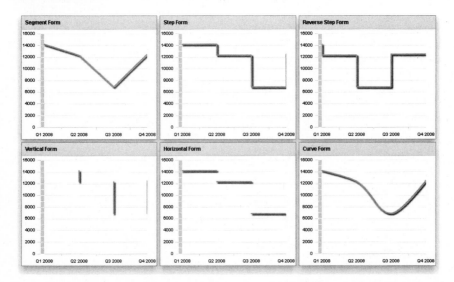

On the Web

The application shown in Figure 21.14 is available in the Web site files as LineFormDemo.mxml in the chapter20 project. ■

Summary

In this chapter, I described how to use the Flex Charting controls to display data graphically in a Flex application. You learned the following:

- The Flex Charting controls are part of the Data Visualization components and are included with a license for Flash Builder 4 Premium.
- There are nine types of charts.
- You can determine the visual presentation of a chart by setting its data, properties, and styles.
- Pie charts also can be displayed as doughnut charts with hollow centers.
- HLOC and candlestick charts are designed to show financial information.
- The bar, column, line, and area charts are designed to show comparative or trend data.

Working with Data Entry Forms

W hen you start to integrate data into a Flex application, you have to solve the problem of how to get data into the Flex runtime environment. As you have seen in earlier chapters, you can embed data into the application using hard-coded MXML or ActionScript, or by integrating data into the application with the `<fx:Model>` tag. These strategies, however, only work for data that's both small and static.

For existing data that's retrieved from a server-based resource, such as a database or an EXtensible Markup Language (XML) file, you can use Remote Procedure Call (RPC) components such as `HTTPService`, `WebService`, and `RemoteObject`.

Cross-Reference

For more information about `HTTPService`, `WebService`, **and** `RemoteObject` **RPC components, see Chapters 23, 25, 26, 28, and 29.** ∎

And then there's data that comes from the user. Unless an application is used exclusively with static data or content retrieved from a server at runtime, a data-centric application must collect data from the user. In this chapter, I describe using the following tools for building data entry form components:

- The `Form`, `FormHeading`, and `FormItem` components for laying out a data entry form

- `Validator` components to validate a user's data entry

- Custom value object and event classes to share data with the rest of the application

This chapter also includes tutorials that enable you to integrate many of the techniques described in preceding chapters, including using containers and controls (Chapters 8 and 10), creating custom MXML components (Chapter

IN THIS CHAPTER

Using the `Form` **container**

Creating a `Form` **component**

Laying out `Form` **controls with the** `FormItem` **container**

Validating data entry

Sharing data with value objects and custom events

5), modeling data with custom ActionScript classes (Chapter 17), and creating and dispatching custom event objects (Chapter 7).

On the Web

To use the sample code for this chapter, import the `chapter22.fxp` **project from the Web site files into any folder on your disk. ▪**

Using the Form Container

The `Form` component is a MX-based layout container that's responsible for laying out `Form` controls and labels in an intuitive, consistent manner.

Tip

Unlike the HTML `<form>` **element, which collects data and posts it to a server-based resource with an HTTP request, the Flex** `Form` **container does not handle application navigation or packaging of data collected from the user. Instead, you (the developer) are responsible for declaring data collection objects and sharing them with the application. The** `Form` **container is never directly responsible for application navigation in Flex; this is handled with the** `ViewStack` **and related navigator containers. ▪**

Note

In the Flex 4 SDK, the `Form` **container and its related components,** `FormHeading` **and** `FormItem`**, have not been rewritten in the new Spark component architecture. Use the MX versions of these components. ▪**

As with all containers in the Flex framework, the `Form` can be declared inline in an application or component or used as the superclass for a custom component. The `Form` container's background and border style settings are fully transparent by default, but you can modify these styles just as you can with the `Box` containers. This `Form`, for example, has a light gray background and a solid border:

```
<mx:Form backgroundColor="#EEEEEE" borderStyle="solid" >
  ... nested components ...
</mx:Form>
```

You can nest any visual components within a `Form`, and they lay out in a single column stacked vertically, just like with the `VGroup` container. But the following components have special behaviors when nested within a `Form` container:

- `FormHeading`. This label-style control automatically left-aligns itself in the controls column.

- `FormItem`. Use this special container to nest the `Form`'s controls. Controls are stacked in a single column placed on the right side of the `Form`.

Every `Form` has two columns. Each nested `FormItem` container has a `label` property. All labels in the `FormItem` containers within a single `Form` are right-aligned with each other by default and stacked in a single column placed on the left side of the form.

The application in Listing 22.1 declares a Form container with two columns, one on the left for labels and the other on the right for controls. The FormItem containers are nested within the Form and are declared in the order of their vertical presentation. The FormHeading control displays its label value left-aligned above the column containing the controls.

LISTING 22.1

A simple Form container

```
<?xml version="1.0" encoding="utf-8"?>
<s:Application xmlns:fx="http://ns.adobe.com/mxml/2009"
  xmlns:s="library://ns.adobe.com/flex/spark"
  xmlns:mx="library://ns.adobe.com/flex/mx">
  <mx:Form backgroundColor="#EEEEEE" borderStyle="solid"
    verticalCenter="0" horizontalCenter="0">
    <mx:FormHeading label="My Custom Form" fontSize="14"/>
    <mx:FormItem label="First Name:">
      <s:TextInput id="firstNameInput"/>
    </mx:FormItem>
    <mx:FormItem label="Last Name:">
      <s:TextInput id="lastNameInput"/>
    </mx:FormItem>
  </mx:Form>
</s:Application>
```

On the Web

The code in Listing 22.1 is available in the Web site files as SimpleForm.mxml in the chapter22 project. ■

Figure 22.1 shows the resulting form, with two TextInput controls and a Button control displayed in a single column.

FIGURE 22.1

A simple data entry form

Using the FormHeading control

The FormHeading control is optional; it displays a label that's aligned with the controls that are wrapped in FormItem containers. These default style settings make it display in a larger font than a default Label control:

- fontSize. Sets the label to a default of 12 pixels.

- fontWeight. Sets the label to a default of bold (compared to normal for other text controls).

You can use as many FormHeading objects as you like. For example, in a multi-part form, you might add a FormHeading at the top of each section, as shown in Listing 22.2.

LISTING 22.2

A form with multiple headings

```
<?xml version="1.0" encoding="utf-8"?>
<s:Application xmlns:fx="http://ns.adobe.com/mxml/2009"
  xmlns:s="library://ns.adobe.com/flex/spark"
  xmlns:mx="library://ns.adobe.com/flex/mx">
  <mx:Form>
    <mx:FormHeading label="Your Personal Information"/>
    <mx:FormItem label="First Name:">
      <s:TextInput id="firstNameInput"/>
    </mx:FormItem>
    <mx:FormItem label="Last Name:">
      <s:TextInput id="lastNameInput"/>
    </mx:FormItem>
    <mx:FormHeading label="Your Address"/>
    <mx:FormItem label="Address:">
      <s:TextInput id="address1Input"/>
      <s:TextInput id="address2Input"/>
    </mx:FormItem>
    <mx:FormItem label="City/State/Zip:" direction="horizontal">
      <s:TextInput id="cityInput"/>
      <s:TextInput id="stateInput" width="30"/>
      <s:TextInput id="zipInput" width="60"/>
    </mx:FormItem>
    <mx:FormItem>
      <mx:Button label="Save Information"/>
    </mx:FormItem>
  </mx:Form>
</s:Application>
```

On the Web

The code in Listing 22.2 is available in the Web site files as MultipleFormHeadings.mxml in the chapter22 project. ∎

Figure 22.2 shows the resulting application, with FormHeading controls above each section of the data entry form.

FIGURE 22.2

Using multiple FormHeading controls

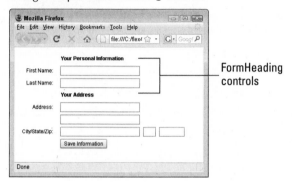

FormHeading controls

Some developers prefer not to use the FormHeading, instead wrapping the Form container in a Panel. The Panel container's title is then used to display a heading, and the FormHeading isn't necessary. The application in Listing 22.3 uses a Spark Panel with a button in its control bar area.

LISTING 22.3

A Form inside a Panel

```
<?xml version="1.0" encoding="utf-8"?>
<s:Application xmlns:fx="http://ns.adobe.com/mxml/2009"
  xmlns:s="library://ns.adobe.com/flex/spark"
  xmlns:mx="library://ns.adobe.com/flex/mx">
  <s:Panel title="My Custom Form"
    horizontalCenter="0" top="20">
    <mx:Form>
      <mx:FormItem label="First Name:">
        <s:TextInput id="firstNameInput"/>
      </mx:FormItem>
      <mx:FormItem label="Last Name:">
        <s:TextInput id="lastNameInput"/>
      </mx:FormItem>
    </mx:Form>
    <s:controlBarContent>
      <s:Button label="Click Me"/>
    </s:controlBarContent>
  </s:Panel>
</s:Application>
```

On the Web

The code in Listing 22.3 is available in the Web site files as `FormInPanel.mxml` in the `chapter22` project. ■

Figure 22.3 shows the resulting application. The `Form` is wrapped inside a `Panel`, and the `Button` is displayed in the Panel container's control bar area.

A `Form` wrapped inside a `Panel`

Using the FormItem container

The `FormItem` container is nested within a `Form` container and in turn contains one or more data entry controls. The container's `label` property is used to set a string value that is displayed in the `Form` container's left column.

Controlling label alignment

By default, the labels in a `Form` container are right-aligned. If you want to change their alignment to left or center, follow these steps:

1. **Create a style selector for the `FormItem` container.**
2. **Within the selector, assign the `labelStyleName` style to an arbitrary style name.**
3. **Declare the style name selector with `text-align` set to the new alignment value.**

The following `<fx:Style>` tag set handles each of these tasks:

```
<fx:Style>
  @namespace s "library://ns.adobe.com/flex/spark";
  @namespace mx "library://ns.adobe.com/flex/mx";
  .leftAlignedLabels {
    text-align: left;
  }
  mx|FormItem {
```

```
        labelStyleName:leftAlignedLabels;
    }
</fx:Style>
```

Figure 22.4 shows the visual result. The labels within the `Form` container's left column are now left-aligned.

FIGURE 22.4

A form with left-aligned labels and horizontal layout

Left-aligned columns

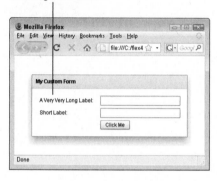

Controlling FormItem layout

Controls within the `FormItem` container are stacked vertically by default. You can change the layout rules for any particular `FormItem` container by setting its `direction` property to `horizontal`. The following code causes the three `TextInput` controls to lay out side by side, instead of being stacked on top of each other:

```
<mx:FormItem label="City/State/Zip:" direction="horizontal">
  <s:TextInput id="cityInput"/>
  <s:TextInput id="stateInput"/>
  <s:TextInput id="zipInput"/>
</mx:FormItem>
```

Caution

If a `FormItem` **container with its** `direction` **set to** `horizontal` **has its width restricted to a point where there isn't room for all its nested controls, it "wraps" the controls to the next line. The solution is to widen the** `FormItem` **container.** ■

Setting a default button

In most Web browsers, when the cursor is in an HTML form's text field and the user presses Enter or Return, the first "submit" button behaves as though the user has clicked it. This is known as *default button* behavior and is automatic in those browsers that support it.

The Flex Form container does not have an automatic default button, but you can create the behavior by setting the Form container's defaultButton property. This property is designed to refer to a Button object somewhere in the current application or component; you set it with a binding expression that refers to the target Button object by its id.

Setting a default button in Flex causes these behaviors:

- When any control in the Form container has focus, the default button shows a colored glow, indicating that pressing Enter or Return is the same as clicking the button.
- When the user presses Enter or Return, the Button object's click event is dispatched.

The application in Listing 22.4 has a simple Form container with its defaultButton property set to a Button control with an id of saveButton. The user can click the button or press Enter or Return with the cursor in a TextInput control; either way, the Button object's click event is dispatched.

LISTING 22.4

A Form with a default button

```
<?xml version="1.0" encoding="utf-8"?>
<s:Application xmlns:fx="http://ns.adobe.com/mxml/2009"
  xmlns:s="library://ns.adobe.com/flex/spark"
  xmlns:mx="library://ns.adobe.com/flex/mx">
  <fx:Script>
    <![CDATA[
      import mx.controls.Alert;
      private function saveButton_clickHandler(event:MouseEvent):void
      {
        Alert.show("You clicked the button", "Click Handler");
      }
    ]]>
  </fx:Script>
  <fx:Style>
    @namespace s "library://ns.adobe.com/flex/spark";
    @namespace mx "library://ns.adobe.com/flex/mx";
    mx|Form {
      background-color:#EEEEEE;
      border-style:solid;
      border-color:#000000;
    }
  </fx:Style>
  <mx:Form defaultButton="{saveButton}"
    horizontalCenter="0" verticalCenter="0">
    <mx:FormHeading label="Your Personal Information"/>
    <mx:FormItem label="First Name:">
      <s:TextInput id="firstNameInput"/>
    </mx:FormItem>
    <mx:FormItem label="Last Name:">
```

```
        <s:TextInput id="lastNameInput"/>
      </mx:FormItem>
      <mx:FormItem>
        <s:Button id="saveButton"
          label="Save Information"
          click="saveButton_clickHandler(event)"/>
      </mx:FormItem>
    </mx:Form>
  </s:Application>
```

On the Web

The code in Listing 22.4 is available in the Web site files as `FormDefaultButton.mxml` in the `chapter22` project. ∎

Tip

The default button does not have to be nested inside the `Form` container. The `defaultButton` property references the button object by its `id`, so as long as the button control is "in scope" the default button behavior works as expected. This is particularly useful if you want to nest a `Button` object in the control bar area of a `Panel` (outside the `Form` container). ∎

Using Custom Form Components

Data entry forms can be designed as fully encapsulated components that handle all the normal tasks of data entry:

- Presentation of a data entry interface
- Collection and validation of data entered by the user
- Sharing of data with the rest of the application with custom value object and event classes

In this section, I describe the steps to create and use a custom `Form` component.

Creating a custom Form component

You can create a custom `Form` component as an MXML component with `<mx:Form/>` as its root element. Flash Builder does a particularly nice job of helping you lay out `Form` components in Design view. Try these steps to create a simple `Form` component:

1. **Open the `chapter22` project from the Web site files.** Notice that the project's source root folder has a package named `forms`.
2. **Right-click (Ctrl+click on the Mac) the `forms` package.**
3. **Select New ⇨ MXML Component from the context menu.**

4. **In the New MXML Component wizard, set these properties (shown in Figure 22.5):**

   - Filename: **LoginForm.mxml**
   - Based on: **mx.containers.Form**
   - Width: **[blank value]**
   - Height: **[blank value]**

Creating a Form component with the New MXML Component wizard

5. **Click Finish to create the new component.** The new component should appear in Flash Builder.

6. **If the component opens in Design mode, click Source to switch to Source mode.**

The beginning code for the Form component looks like this:

```
<?xml version="1.0" encoding="utf-8"?>
<mx:Form xmlns:fx="http://ns.adobe.com/mxml/2009"
  xmlns:s="library://ns.adobe.com/flex/spark"
  xmlns:mx="library://ns.adobe.com/flex/mx">
  <fx:Declarations>
    <!-- Place non-visual elements
      (e.g., services, value objects) here -->
  </fx:Declarations>
</mx:Form>
```

Switch to Design mode to see the beginning Form component presentation. It shows up as a small rectangle; if you created it without a default width and height, it appears with the Form container's minimum dimensions.

Adding controls to a Form component

When you are building a `Form` component, Flash Builder's Design mode lets you easily drag and drop the objects you want to use from the Components view. Each time you add a control to a `Form` container, Design view automatically wraps the control in a new `FormItem` container. You can then set the `FormItem` container's `label` property, drag its handles to resize it, set other properties and styles in the Flex Properties view, and otherwise customize the control's appearance and behavior.

Follow these steps to add data entry form controls to the `LoginForm` component that was described in the preceding section:

1. Open the `LoginForm.mxml` file in Design mode.

2. Locate the `TextInput` control in the Text section of the Components view.

3. **Drag the control into the editor region, and drop it inside the `Form` area.** As shown in Figure 22.6, you should see that the `TextInput` control is wrapped in a `FormItem` container automatically, with a default `label` property of `Label`.

FIGURE 22.6

A `TextInput` control wrapped in a `FormItem` container in Design mode

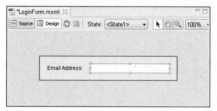

4. **Double-click the `FormItem` container's label region.** When the label turns into an input control, type the label **Email Address:**.

5. Click the new `TextInput` control in Design view.

6. In the Properties view, change the `TextInput` control's `id` to `emailInput`.

7. Drag another `TextInput` control from the Components view into the form.

Caution

To ensure that a new `FormItem` container is wrapped around the new control, make sure the blue insertion line that's displayed during the drag-and-drop operation is as wide as the existing `FormItem` container (shown in Figure 22.7). If it's the size of the `TextInput` control when you release the mouse button, the new `TextInput` control will be dropped into the existing `FormItem` container. ∎

8. **Double-click the label of the new `FormItem` container and change it to `Password:`.**

9. Change the new `TextInput` control's `id` to `passwordInput`.

FIGURE 22.7

The insertion indicator is the width of the existing `FormItem`, meaning that you'll create a new `FormItem` when you drop the component.

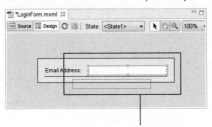

The blue insertion indicator

10. Drag a `Button` control into the `Form` and place it below the existing `FormItem` container, in its own container.

11. Double-click the new `Button` control and change its label to Log In.

12. Double-click the label of the new `FormItem` container and delete the default value. The component should now appear as it does in Figure 22.8.

FIGURE 22.8

The `Form` component in its current state

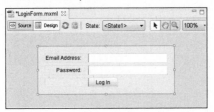

13. Switch to Source mode.

The `Form` component's source code should now look like this:

```
<?xml version="1.0" encoding="utf-8"?>
<mx:Form xmlns:fx="http://ns.adobe.com/mxml/2009"
        xmlns:s="library://ns.adobe.com/flex/spark"
        xmlns:mx="library://ns.adobe.com/flex/mx">
  <mx:FormItem label="Email Address:">
    <s:TextInput id="emailInput"/>
  </mx:FormItem>
  <mx:FormItem label="Password:">
    <s:TextInput id="passwordInput"/>
  </mx:FormItem>
```

```
<mx:FormItem>
  <s:Button label="Log In"/>
</mx:FormItem>
</mx:Form>
```

You'll continue to build your custom form component later in this chapter.

Caution

When creating a `Form` component in Design mode, it's easy to accidentally change the `id` property of the `FormItem` container instead of its nested component. The purpose of the `id` is to enable you to easily collect data from the `Form` controls when the user clicks the button or otherwise indicates that data entry is complete. You care about the data in the controls, not any data that might be associated with the `FormItem` containers. ■

Validating Data Entry

When a user enters data into any database application, you typically want to ensure that it matches specific criteria before sending it to the server or saving it into a persistent data store. Flex provides a set of ActionScript classes in the `mx.validators` package that are designed for this purpose. Each of the following classes validates a particular data type:

- `CreditCardValidator`. Checks that a `String` has the correct length and prefix and passes the Luhn mod10 algorithm for the specified card type.

Web Resource

For more information on the Luhn mod10 algorithm, visit this entry at Wikipedia: http://en.wikipedia.org/wiki/Luhn_algorithm. ■

- `CurrencyValidator`. Checks that a `String` matches a valid currency pattern; can be customized for particular locales and other specific rules.

- `DateValidator`. Checks that a `Date`, `String`, or `Object` variable contains a valid date value; can be customized for particular date ranges.

- `EmailValidator`. Checks that a `String` follows the common pattern of an e-mail address.

- `NumberValidator`. Checks that a value is a `Number` or a `String` that can be parsed as a number; can be customized for particular numeric ranges and other rules.

- `PhoneNumberValidator`. Checks that a value matches a valid phone number pattern; can be customized for particular locales and other specific rules.

- `RegExpValidator`. Checks that a `String` matches a regular expression.

- `SocialSecurityValidator`. Checks that a `String` matches a valid Social Security number pattern.

- `StringValidator`. Checks for `String` values that match your specific criteria, including minimum and maximum length.

- `ZipCodeValidator`. Checks that a `String` matches a valid ZIP code pattern.

All validator classes are extended from `mx.validators.Validator`, so they're all used the same basic way.

Creating a validator object

You can create validator objects with either MXML or ActionScript. Each validator object is assigned to a single control and implements these required properties that determine its behavior at runtime:

- `property`. The name of the source object's property that contains the value to be validated.
- `source`. A reference to the data entry control being validated.

For example, assume your data entry form includes this `TextInput` control, which you want to validate as an e-mail address:

```
<s:TextInput id="emailInput"/>
```

The validator object declaration for this control would minimally include the source, referencing the `TextInput` control's `id` in a binding expression, and the property, referencing the input control's `text` property as a string:

```
<fx:Declarations>
  <mx:EmailValidator id="myValidator"
    source="{emailInput}" property="text"/>
</fx:Declarations>
```

New Feature

In Flex 4 applications, validator controls declared with MXML tags must be placed inside an `<fx:Declarations/>` element. ∎

The equivalent functionality in ActionScript looks like this:

```
import mx.validators.EmailValidator;
var myValidator:EmailValidator;
private function initApp():void
{
  myValidator = new EmailValidator;
  myValidator.source = emailInput;
  myValidator.property = "text";
}
```

Controlling validation with trigger events

By default, validation occurs either when the user completes a change to a control's value or when he simply clicks or tabs into the control to give it focus and then clicks or tabs again to remove focus. This automatic validation is controlled by two properties that are shared by all validator classes:

- `trigger`. A reference that points to an object that will trigger validation.
- `triggerEvent`. A String containing the name of the event that will trigger validation.

Validation happens automatically when a control loses focus because the validator object's trigger property defaults to the value of its source property (the control being validated) and `trigger Event` defaults to the `valueCommitted` event. Normally, this event occurs when a change is made or the control simply loses focus.

You can change when validation occurs by changing these properties' values. For example, in an application where you want all controls to be validated when the user clicks a button, you would follow these steps:

1. Add a unique `id` to the `Button` control you want to use as the trigger.
2. Set each validator object's `trigger` property to the `Button` control's `id` in a binding expression.
3. Set each validator object's `triggerEvent` property to the event name `click`.

Follow these steps to add automatic validation to the `LoginForm` component you created in previous sections of this chapter:

1. Open `LoginForm.mxml` in Source view.
2. Locate the `Button` control with a label of `Log In`, and add an `id` of `loginButton`.
3. After the `<mx:Form>` start tag, declare an `<fx:Declarations>` tag set.
4. Within the `<fx:Declarations>` tag set, declare an `EmailValidator` object with MXML code. Set its `id` to `emailValidator`, `source` to the `emailInput` control, `property` to `text`, `trigger` to `loginButton`, and `triggerEvent` to `click`:

   ```
   <fx:Declarations>
     <mx:EmailValidator id="emailValidator"
       source="{emailInput}" property="text"
       trigger="{loginButton}" triggerEvent="click"/>
   </fx:Declarations>
   ```

5. Add a `StringValidator` object inside the `<fx:Declarations>` element with an `id` of `passwordValidator`. Set its `source` to `passwordInput` and all other properties exactly like the first validator object:

   ```
   <mx:StringValidator id="passwordValidator"
     source="{passwordInput}" property="text"
     trigger="{loginButton}" triggerEvent="click"/>
   ```

The `Form` component in Listing 22.5 uses identical `trigger` and `triggerEvent` properties to automatically trigger two different validator objects when a `Button` control is clicked.

LISTING 22.5

A Form component using automatic validation

```xml
<?xml version="1.0" encoding="utf-8"?>
<mx:Form xmlns:fx="http://ns.adobe.com/mxml/2009"
  xmlns:s="library://ns.adobe.com/flex/spark"
  xmlns:mx="library://ns.adobe.com/flex/mx">
  <fx:Declarations>
    <mx:EmailValidator id="emailValidator"
      source="{emailInput}" property="text"
      trigger="{loginButton}" triggerEvent="click"/>
    <mx:StringValidator id="passwordValidator"
      source="{passwordInput}" property="text"
      trigger="{loginButton}" triggerEvent="click"/>
  </fx:Declarations>
  <mx:FormItem label="Email Address:">
    <s:TextInput id="emailInput"/>
  </mx:FormItem>
  <mx:FormItem label="Password:">
    <s:TextInput id="passwordInput"/>
  </mx:FormItem>
  <mx:FormItem>
    <s:Button id="loginButton" label="Log In"/>
  </mx:FormItem>
</mx:Form>
```

On the Web

The code in Listing 22.5 is available in the Web site files as `LoginFormAutoValidation.mxml` in the forms folder of the `chapter22` project. ∎

To see the effect of this form, follow these steps to create a new application and incorporate the Form component:

1. Create a new MXML application named `ValidationDemo.mxml`.

2. Add an instance of the new `LoginForm` component. Set its id property to `login-Form`.

Note

As you type, Flash Builder should add the required custom `forms` namespace prefix for the `forms` folder to the `<s:Application>` tag. ∎

3. Set the `LoginForm` object's `horizontalCenter` property to 0 and `top` to 20. The application code should appear as follows:

```xml
<?xml version="1.0" encoding="utf-8"?>
<s:Application xmlns:fx="http://ns.adobe.com/mxml/2009"
```

```
xmlns:s="library://ns.adobe.com/flex/spark"
xmlns:mx="library://ns.adobe.com/flex/mx"
xmlns:forms="forms.*">
   <forms:LoginForm id="loginForm" horizontalCenter="0" top="20"/>
</s:Application>
```

4. **Run the application in a browser.**

5. **Click the** `LoginForm`**'s Log In button to trigger validation.**

At runtime, as the user clicks the button to trigger validation, each of the validator objects examines the named property of its `source` data entry control. If validation rules pass, the user sees no feedback. If a validation rule is broken, the source control displays a red border to the user. When the user moves the cursor over the control, she sees a pop-up window displaying the error message, as shown in Figure 22.9.

FIGURE 22.9

A form displaying a validation error message

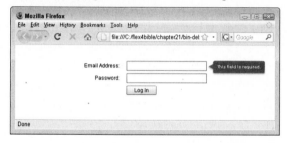

Controlling validation with ActionScript

Trigger-based validation lets users know that they have entered invalid values but doesn't give you (the developer) an opportunity to handle the situation and decide whether to continue with form processing or cancel processing and display an error. In the previous examples, if you were to execute a function on the button's `click` event, that function would execute regardless of whether the validation passed.

For most `Form` components, triggering validation with ActionScript code enables you to find out immediately whether all your validations have passed and to take appropriate action.

Disabling validation trigger events

When you use programmatic validation, you typically disable the automatic validation that results from using the `trigger` and `triggerEvent` properties. You accomplish this by removing the validator object's `trigger` property and setting `triggerEvent` to a blank String:

```
<mx:EmailValidator id="emailValidator"
   source="{emailInput}" property="text"
   triggerEvent=""/>
```

Because no event can be dispatched that would have a blank string for its event name, this results in disabling any event-based validation. This is necessary as deleting both properties would cause default validation to occur upon the `valueCommitted` event of the source object.

Triggering individual validator objects with ActionScript

To programmatically trigger validation on a single validator object, call the object's `validate()` method. This method returns an instance of the `ValidationResultEvent` event class:

```
var validObj:ValidationResultEvent =
    emailValidator.validate();
```

As with all event classes, `ValidationResultEvent` has a `type` property. You determine whether validation has succeeded by comparing the event object's `type` to the event name constants `VALID` and `INVALID`. For example, this conditional ActionScript block would execute only if validation is passed:

```
if (validObj.type == ValidationResultEvent.VALID)
{
    ... process data ...
}
```

The version of the custom `Form` component in Listing 22.6 triggers validation programmatically on two separate validator objects and then evaluates both resulting event objects to determine whether the `Form`'s data is valid.

LISTING 22.6

A Form component with programmatic validation of one validator object at a time

```xml
<?xml version="1.0" encoding="utf-8"?>
<mx:Form xmlns:fx="http://ns.adobe.com/mxml/2009"
  xmlns:s="library://ns.adobe.com/flex/spark"
  xmlns:mx="library://ns.adobe.com/flex/mx">
  <fx:Script>
    <![CDATA[
      import mx.controls.Alert;
      import mx.events.ValidationResultEvent;
      private function isValid():Boolean
      {
        var emailObj:ValidationResultEvent = emailValidator.validate();
        var pwordObj:ValidationResultEvent = passwordValidator.validate();
        return (emailObj.type == ValidationResultEvent.VALID &&
          pwordObj.type == ValidationResultEvent.VALID);
      }
      protected function loginButton_clickHandler(event:MouseEvent):void
      {
        if (isValid())
          Alert.show("Data is valid", "Validation Logic");
        else
```

```
        Alert.show("There are form errors", "Validation Logic");
      }
    ]]>
  </fx:Script>
  <fx:Declarations>
    <mx:EmailValidator id="emailValidator"
      source="{emailInput}" property="text"
      triggerEvent=""/>
    <mx:StringValidator id="passwordValidator"
      source="{passwordInput}" property="text"
      triggerEvent=""/>
  </fx:Declarations>
  <mx:FormItem label="Email Address:">
    <s:TextInput id="emailInput"/>
  </mx:FormItem>
  <mx:FormItem label="Password:">
    <s:TextInput id="passwordInput"/>
  </mx:FormItem>
  <mx:FormItem>
    <s:Button id="loginButton" label="Log In"
      click="loginButton_clickHandler(event)"/>
  </mx:FormItem>
</mx:Form>
```

On the Web

The code in Listing 22.6 is available in the Web site files as `LoginFormSingleValidation.mxml` in the forms folder of the `chapter22` project. ∎

Triggering multiple validator objects with ActionScript

As a data entry form becomes more complex, with additional controls and validators, calling the `validate()` method on each validator object can be cumbersome. An alternative approach is to use the `Validator` class's static `validateAll()` method to trigger multiple validator objects simultaneously.

To use this approach, call `validateAll()` and pass in an `Array` of validator objects:

```
var arInvalid:Array = Validator.validateAll(
  [emailValidator, passwordValidator]);
```

The `validateAll()` method returns an `Array` containing `ValidationResultEvent` objects only for those validator objects that fail validation. If the `Array` has no items, this means that all validators passed their validation rules. The following code evaluates the returned `Array`:

```
if (arInvalid.length == 0)
{
  Alert.show("Data is valid", "Validation Logic");
  return true;
}
```

Try these steps to add programmatic validation of multiple validator objects to the LoginForm component described in previous sections:

1. Open LoginForm.mxml in Source view.

2. For both of the existing validator objects, remove their trigger property and set their triggerEvent to a blank string:

```
<mx:EmailValidator id="emailValidator"
   source="{emailInput}" property="text" triggerEvent=""/>
<mx:StringValidator id="passwordValidator"
   source="{passwordInput}" property="text" triggerEvent=""/>
```

3. Add an <fx:Script> tag set just below the </fx:Declarations> end tag.

4. Create a new private function named isValid() that accepts no arguments and returns void.

5. Within the function body, use the Validator.validateAll() method to trigger both the emailValidator and the passwordValidator objects:

```
var arInvalid:Array = Validator.validateAll(
   [emailValidator, passwordValidator]);
```

As you type the code, Flash Builder might automatically add an import statement for the Validator class. If this doesn't happen, add this import statement above the isValid() function:

```
import mx.validators.Validator;
```

6. Add the following code after the call to validateAll() to evaluate whether validation rules were passed:

```
if (arInvalid.length == 0)
{
   Alert.show("Data is valid", "Validation Logic");
   return true;
}
else
{
   Alert.show("There are form errors", "Validation Logic");
   return false;
}
```

7. Locate the Button control with the Log In label, and add a click event handler that calls the isValid() method:

```
<s:Button id="loginButton" label="Log In"
   click="isValid()"/>
```

8. Save the Form component file, and open ValidatorDemo.mxml, the application that was created in a preceding exercise.

9. Run the application, and try clicking the form's button to trigger validation.

As shown in Figure 22.10, you should see that validation is triggered and a pop-up window produced by the Alert class is displayed. After you click OK to clear the pop-up window, a validation error message is displayed when you move the cursor over any control with a red border.

Tip

The `target` of the `ValidationResultEvent` objects in the `Array` refers back to the validator object that failed. You can then refer to the validator object's `source` property to get a reference to the control that was validated, or the `message` property to access the validation error message as a `String`. ∎

Results of validation with ActionScript

Controlling validation rules and error messages

Each validator class has a set of validation rules and equivalent error messages that are displayed when the rules are broken. One of these rules, named `required`, is implemented on the `Validator` superclass and, therefore, is used for all validator objects.

The `required` rule is a `Boolean` value that defaults to `true`. As a result, when you apply a validator object to a `Form` control, you're automatically indicating that the control's value can't be left blank. When this rule is broken, the value of the validator object's `requiredFieldError` property is displayed in the pop-up error message. The default error message for the `required-FieldError` (in the American English locale) is "This field is required." You can customize the error message by setting the appropriate property:

```
<mx:EmailValidator id="emailValidator"
  source="{emailInput}" property="text" triggerEvent=""
  requiredFieldError="Email address can't be left blank"/>
<mx:StringValidator id="passwordValidator"
  source="{passwordInput}" property="text" triggerEvent=""
  requiredFieldError="Password can't be left blank"/>
```

Each of the two validator objects now has its own distinct error message. As shown in Figure 22.11, the user gets better, more specific feedback when she makes a data entry error.

Table 22.1 describes some commonly used validation rules and equivalent error message properties. This is not an exhaustive list; see the product documentation for a complete list of validation rules and their equivalent error message property names.

FIGURE 22.11

A customized validation error message

TABLE 22.1

Examples of Validation Rules and Error Messages

Rule Name	Values	Error Name	Implemented By
required	Boolean	requiredFieldError	All validator classes
minLength	Numeric	tooShortError	StringValidator
maxLength	Numeric	tooLongError	StringValidator
domain	real | int	integerError	NumberValidator
minValue	Numeric	lowerThanMinError	NumberValidator, CurrencyValidator
maxValue	Numeric	exceedsMaxError	NumberValidator, CurrencyValidator
[automatic validation for NumberValidator, CurrencyValidator, and DateValidator]	N/A	invalidCharError	NumberValidator, CurrencyValidator
[Automatic validation for EmailValidator]	N/A	invalidCharError, invalidDomainError, invalidIPDomainError, invalidPeriods InDomainError, missingAtSignError, missingPeriod InDomainError, missingUsernameError, tooManyAtSignsError	EmailValidator
[Automatic validation for DateValidator]	n/a	wrongDayError, wrongLengthError, wrongMonthError, wrongYearError	DateValidator

696

Follow these steps to add custom error messages to the `LoginForm` component:

1. **Open `LoginForm.mxml` in Source mode.**

2. **Set the `emailValidator` object's `requiredFieldError` property to Email address can't be left blank.**

3. **Set the `passwordValidator` object's `requiredFieldError` property to Password can't be left blank.**

    The code for the validator objects should now look like this:

    ```
    <mx:EmailValidator id="emailValidator"
      source="{emailInput}" property="text" triggerEvent=""
      requiredFieldError="Email address can't be left blank"/>
    <mx:StringValidator id="passwordValidator"
      source="{passwordInput}" property="text" triggerEvent=""
      requiredFieldError="Password can't be left blank"/>
    ```

4. **Save the `Form` component file, and open `ValidatorDemo.mxml`, the application that was created in a preceding exercise.**

5. **Run the application, and try clicking the form button to trigger validation.** You should see the custom error messages displayed for each of the `Form` controls.

Sharing Data with the Application

When you use data entry form components, you share data with the application with custom events. Each data entry form requires two custom ActionScript classes:

- A value object class that models the `Form`'s data
- A custom event class that is dispatched from the `Form` component

Cross-Reference

Detailed information about using custom event classes is available in Chapter 7. Detailed information on modeling data with the Value Object design pattern is available in Chapter 16. ■

Modeling Form data with a value object

To share data from a `Form` component, you first create an instance of a value object class and populate the object with data from the `Form`'s controls. You can accomplish this with either MXML or ActionScript code.

Listing 22.7 shows a custom ActionScript value object class with public properties for each of the `Form` component's controls.

LISTING 22.7

A custom ActionScript class that implements the Value Object design pattern

```
package vo
{
  [Bindable]
  public class LoginVO
  {
    public var email:String;
    public var password:String;

    public function LoginVO()
    {
    }
  }
}
```

On the Web

The code in Listing 22.7 is available in the Web site files as `LoginVO.as` in the vo package of the `chapter22` project. ∎

Populating value object data with MXML

To declare and populate the value object with data in MXML, declare the object and set each of its properties to one of the Form control's values with binding expressions:

```
<vo:LoginVO id="formDataObj"
    email="{emailInput.text}"
    password="{passwordInput.text}"/>
```

At runtime, each of the value object's properties is populated when its matching data entry control executes the binding expression.

Caution

When working with value object properties that have complex data types such as a Date, the MXML approach has a liability: If the user never interacts with the data entry control, the value in the declaration is never set. To handle this, you can set each property with a default value within the value object class:

```
public var myDateProperty:Date = new Date();
```

If you don't do this, in some cases the value object's property ends up set as null (depending on how the user interacts with the form). ∎

Populating value object data with ActionScript

You also can create and populate a value object with ActionScript code. This approach is sometimes preferred because you can examine values and take action based on various conditions. The code to create and populate the value object in ActionScript might look like this:

```
var loginObj:LoginVO = new LoginVO();
loginObj.email = emailInput.text;
loginObj.password = passwordInput.text;
```

Because data is being passed to the value object in ActionScript statements, you have the opportunity to further validate or modify data before sharing it with the rest of the application.

Dispatching a custom event

As described in Chapter 7, you create custom event classes to "wrap" and share particular types of data with the rest of the application. Because data from the `Form` controls is contained within a value object, you typically create a custom event class with one public property data typed as the custom value object class.

The custom event class in Listing 22.8 has a single `login` property data typed as the `LoginVO` class. Notice that this event class sets its `bubbles` property by passing a value of `true` as the second argument in the `super()` constructor method call. It also overrides the `clone()` method, allowing you to re-dispatch the event object from within an event handler function if necessary.

LISTING 22.8

A bubbling custom event object with a value object public property

```
package events
{
  import flash.events.Event;
  import vo.LoginVO;
  public class LoginEvent extends Event
  {
    public var login:LoginVO;
    public function LoginEvent(type:String, login:LoginVO)
    {
      super(type, true);
      this.login = login;
    }
    override public function clone():Event
    {
      return new LoginEvent(type, login);
    }
  }
}
```

On the Web

The code in Listing 22.8 is available in the Web site files as `LoginEvent.as` in the events package of the `chapter22` project. ∎

To use this custom event and share data with the rest of the application, follow these steps in the Form component:

1. Declare an `<fx:Metadata>` tag set.

2. Declare an `[Event]` metadata tag for a custom event that uses the custom event class.

3. To share data with the rest of the application, add code that:

   a. Creates the value object and populates it with data

   b. Creates the custom event object and populates its public property with the value object

   c. Dispatches the custom event object

Follow these steps to complete the custom Form component:

1. Open the `LoginForm.mxml` file in Source mode.

2. After the `<mx:Form>` start tag, add an `<fx:Metadata>` tag set.

3. Within the `<fx:Metadata>` tag set, declare a custom event with a name of `login` and a type of `events.LoginEvent`:

   ```
   <fx:Metadata>
     [Event(name="login", type="events.LoginEvent")]
   </fx:Metadata>
   ```

4. In the `<fx:Script>` section, create a new `protected` function with no arguments named `clickHandler()` that void:

   ```
   protected function clickHandler():void
   {
   }
   ```

5. Within the new function, add a conditional evaluation that executes the `isValid()` function:

   ```
   if (isValid())
   {
   }
   ```

6. Within the conditional block, add the following code to create and populate the value object with data:

   ```
   if (isValid())
   {
     var loginObj:LoginVO = new LoginVO();
     loginObj.email = emailInput.text;
     loginObj.password = passwordInput.text;
   }
   ```

7. Add code to create the custom event object, set its `login` property to the value object, and dispatch the event:

```
var e:LoginEvent = new LoginEvent("login", loginObj);
dispatchEvent(e);
```

8. In the `isValid()` function, comment out or delete the code that displays an Alert pop-up window.

9. Locate the button control, and change its `click` event listener to call the `clickHandler()` method and pass the event object:

```
<s:Button id="loginButton" label="Log In"
  click="clickHandler(event)"/>
```

10. Save the `LoginForm` component.

Listing 22.9 shows the completed `Form` component with validation and data sharing through a custom event and a value object.

LISTING 22.9

A completed Form component with validation and data sharing

```
<?xml version="1.0" encoding="utf-8"?>
<mx:Form xmlns:fx="http://ns.adobe.com/mxml/2009"
  xmlns:s="library://ns.adobe.com/flex/spark"
  xmlns:mx="library://ns.adobe.com/flex/mx">
  <fx:Metadata>
    [Event(name="login", type="events.LoginEvent")]
  </fx:Metadata>
  <fx:Declarations>
    <mx:EmailValidator id="emailValidator"
      source="{emailInput}" property="text" triggerEvent=""
      requiredFieldError="Email address can't be left blank"/>
    <mx:StringValidator id="passwordValidator"
      source="{passwordInput}" property="text" triggerEvent=""
      requiredFieldError="Password can't be left blank"/>
  </fx:Declarations>
  <fx:Script>
    <![CDATA[
      import events.LoginEvent;
      import mx.validators.Validator;
      import vo.LoginVO;
      private function isValid():Boolean
      {
        var arInvalid:Array = Validator.validateAll(
          [emailValidator, passwordValidator]);
        if (arInvalid.length == 0)
          return true;
        else
```

continued

LISTING 22.9   (continued)

```
        return false;
    }
    private function clickHandler():void
    {
      if (isValid())
      {
        var loginObj:LoginVO = new LoginVO();
        loginObj.email = emailInput.text;
        loginObj.password = passwordInput.text;
        var e:LoginEvent = new LoginEvent("login", loginObj);
        dispatchEvent(e);
      }
    }
  ]]>
</fx:Script>
<mx:FormItem label="Email Address:">
  <s:TextInput id="emailInput"/>
</mx:FormItem>
<mx:FormItem label="Password:">
  <s:TextInput id="passwordInput"/>
</mx:FormItem>
<mx:FormItem>
  <s:Button id="loginButton" label="Log In"
    click="clickHandler()"/>
</mx:FormItem>
</mx:Form>
```

On the Web

The code in Listing 22.9 is available in the Web site files as `LoginFormComplete.mxml` in the `src/forms` folder of the `chapter22` project. ■

The final step in the process is to handle the custom event from the application. Follow these steps to integrate the Form component into a new MXML application:

1. Create a new MXML application named `FormComponentDemo.mxml` and delete its default `<fx:Declarations>` element.

2. Set the application's `layout` property to an instance of `<s:VerticalLayout>` with its `horizontalAlign` property set to `center`.

3. Add an instance of the `LoginForm` control.

The code so far should look like this:

```xml
<?xml version="1.0" encoding="utf-8"?>
<s:Application xmlns:fx="http://ns.adobe.com/mxml/2009"
  xmlns:s="library://ns.adobe.com/flex/spark"
  xmlns:mx="library://ns.adobe.com/flex/mx"
  xmlns:forms="forms.*">
  <s:layout>
    <s:VerticalLayout horizontalAlign="center"/>
  </s:layout>
  <forms:LoginForm id="loginForm"/>
</s:Application>
```

4. Add an `<fx:Script>` tag set to the application.

5. Within the script section, add a bindable private variable named myLogin, typed as the LoginVO class.

As you code, Flash Builder should add the required import statement:

```
import vo.LoginVO;
[Bindable]
private var myLogin:LoginVO;
```

6. Add a private function named loginHandler() that receives an event argument typed as LoginEvent and returns void.

7. Within the private function, save the event object's login property to the bindable myLogin variable:

```
private function loginHandler(event:LoginEvent):void
{
  myLogin = event.login;
}
```

8. Add a login event listener to the LoginForm component instance that calls loginHandler() and passes the event object:

```xml
<forms:LoginForm id="loginForm" login="loginHandler(event)"/>
```

9. Add a Label control to the bottom of the application that displays the myLogin object's email property:

```xml
<s:Label text="Email address: {myLogin.email}"/>
```

10. Add another Label control to the bottom of the application that displays the myLogin object's password property:

```xml
<s:Label text="Password: {myLogin.password}"/>
```

11. Run the application, and test the form by entering valid data and clicking Log In. You should see that the value object is passed from the Form component to the application and its data is displayed in the Label controls as a result of their binding expressions.

Listing 22.10 shows the completed application with a completed version of the custom form component.

LISTING 22.10

An application using a custom Form component

```
<?xml version="1.0" encoding="utf-8"?>
<s:Application xmlns:fx="http://ns.adobe.com/mxml/2009"
  xmlns:s="library://ns.adobe.com/flex/spark"
  xmlns:mx="library://ns.adobe.com/flex/mx"
  xmlns:forms="forms.*">
  <s:layout>
    <s:VerticalLayout horizontalAlign="center"/>
  </s:layout>
  <fx:Script>
    <![CDATA[
      import events.LoginEvent;
      import vo.LoginVO;
      [Bindable]
      private var myLogin:LoginVO;
      private function loginHandler(event:LoginEvent):void
      {
        myLogin = event.login;
      }
    ]]>
  </fx:Script>
  <forms:LoginFormComplete id="loginForm" login="loginHandler(event)"/>
  <s:Label text="Email address: {myLogin.email}"/>
  <s:Label text="Password: {myLogin.password}"/>
</s:Application>
```

On the Web

The code in Listing 22.10 is available in the Web site files as `FormComponentDemoComplete.mxml` in the `src` folder of the `chapter22` project. ∎

Figure 22.12 shows the resulting application displaying data it receives from the form component as a result of handling its custom event.

Tip

You can manually trigger the validation interface by setting any visual component's `errorString` property to a nonblank `String`. When `errorString` is set to a nonblank `String`, the visual component displays the same red border and displays the property's value in the same pop-up error display window when the mouse hovers over the component, as when validation errors are passed to a control by a validator class. You can also explicitly remove the validation interface from a visual component by setting its `errorString` to a blank `String` or null. ∎

FIGURE 22.12

An application displaying data received in a form component's custom event

Data from form component

Summary

In this chapter, I described how to build and use data entry form components in Flex applications. You learned the following:

- The `Form` container lays out labels in one column and controls in another column.
- The `FormHeading` control is optional and displays a label aligned inside the `Form` container's controls column.
- The `FormItem` container is nested within the `Form` container.
- The `label` properties of all `FormItem` containers within the `Form` are right-aligned by default, but they can also be adjusted to center or left alignment.
- The `FormItem` container can nest multiple controls that are stacked vertically by default.
- Flash Builder's Design view enables you to quickly create `Form` components by adding `FormItem` containers to controls as they're dragged from the Components view.
- Data validation is handled with validator objects.
- You can trigger validation with trigger events or explicit ActionScript code.
- `Form` components share data with the rest of the application with custom value object and event classes.

Working with HTTPService and XML

IN THIS CHAPTER

Understanding RPC and REST Web services

Understanding HTTP communications

Generating HTTP data connection code with Flash Builder 4

Using the HTTPService **control**

Retrieving data at runtime

Parsing XML formatted data

Passing parameters to an application server

Generating HTTPService **code with Flash Builder**

Working with Flash Player security

A pplications built with the Flex framework are commonly both dynamic and data-centric: They use, present, and enable users to modify data that's imported at runtime from a server-based data store (or, in the case of desktop applications running on Adobe AIR, a local database).

Flash Player and Adobe AIR don't have the capability to communicate directly with server-based data storage applications such as database and Lightweight Directory Access Protocol (LDAP) servers. Instead, they're designed to communicate with *middleware* application servers using a variety of protocols.

The Flex framework includes three Remote Procedure Call (RPC) components that enable you to integrate your Flex applications with common application server products. Of these, the HTTPService component has the most flexibility in terms of the format of messages that are exchanged between the client and server at runtime. Unlike the other RPC components, you can use the HTTPService component with any application server, because it exchanges data in the form of simple HTTP (Hypertext Markup Language) parameters and XML (EXtensible Markup Language) of any flavor.

Flash Builder 4 adds a new set of code generation features described as the *data-centric development* tools. These new tools enable you to quickly build data-centric applications that trade data at runtime with multiple application servers using any of the RPC architectures.

In this chapter, I first describe how to define a Flash Builder 4 *data connection* — a set of ActionScript classes that enable requests and retrieval of data from an application server. Then I describe how to do it all manually — how to create and use an HTTPService component, how to parse the results, and how to view those results using a Flex visual control. I also describe how to send data from a Flex application to a dynamic application server using HTTP requests that are similar to those that are sent from a Web browser using a hyperlink or a data entry form.

On the Web

To use the sample code for this chapter, import the `chapter23.fxp` **Flex project archive file from the Web site files into your Flash Builder workspace.** ∎

Using RPC and REST Architectures

RPC and REST are acronyms that represent architectural styles. Unlike SOAP and AMF (Action Message Format), which are implemented by the other RPC components, RPC and REST are more like design patterns: They describe ways in which successful Web-based applications have been designed in the past.

Understanding the Representational State Transfer architecture

REST stands for Representational State Transfer, and it represents a software architecture or design pattern that can be implemented with numerous client-based and server-based platforms for the Web. A "RESTful" architecture enables a local client system to retrieve resources stored in a remote system without necessarily requiring a remote dynamic application server.

According to Roy Fielding, who coined the term, REST is intended to "evoke an image of how a well-designed Web application behaves: a network of Web pages (a virtual state-machine), where the user progresses through an application by selecting links (state transitions), resulting in the next page (representing the next state of the application) being transferred to the user and rendered for their use." In short, a Web site that returns either Web pages or structured data in the form of XML pages based on requests to consistently formatted requests is RESTful.

REST architecture is marked by these characteristics and benefits:

- **Data is "pulled" from the server to the client.** When implemented with HTTP, the request is sent from a Web browser and the response comes from a Web server.

- **Requests are stateless and do not depend on data stored persistently in the server.** When you add statefulness to HTTP request/response systems with cookies or other token architectures, the application becomes less RESTful.

- **Caching is implemented to improve performance**. In the context of a Flex application, the use of static XML files that can be cached by the underlying Web browser improves performance when the data is requested multiple times.

- **A uniform interface is used to simplify programming.** In the context of Flex, this is implemented through the use of standard HTTP requests.

- **Named resources are identified and retrieved by their URLs**. When you add query string parameters in a POST request, the system becomes more like RPC and less like REST.

- **Server-side code written according to the principles of REST is guaranteed to be compatible with any client-side application development platform that supports industry-standard HTTP and XML.**

You can use the `HTTPService` component in a REST-style application because, like the Web browser, it can communicate with its requests formatted as simple URL.

Web Resource

Detailed descriptions of the REST architecture are available at these Web sites: `www.xfront.com/REST-Web-Services.html` **and** `http://en.wikipedia.org/wiki/Representational_State_Transfer.` ■

Understanding the Remote Procedure Call architecture

RPC represents a software architecture that enables a computer program in one operating environment to cause functions (also known as *methods*, *operations*, or *subroutines*) to be executed in separate, remote operating environments. As described previously, Flex applications can participate in RPC relationships with remote application servers using multiple architectures and techniques.

RPC-style architectures are typically implemented in Flex with a dynamic Web server that can respond to complex HTTP requests. All three RPC components communicate with the server over the HTTP protocol; they differ, however, in the format of the messages that are exchanged between client and server:

- **The `HTTPService` component.** This component makes standard HTTP requests to any Web server environment, including calls to both static and dynamic Web pages, and uses either plain text or any well-formed XML language as its message format.

- **The `RemoteObject` component.** This component, described in Chapters 26 and 27, communicates with application servers using the binary AMF.

- **The `WebService` component.** This component, described in Chapter 25, makes requests to, and handles responses from, application servers that support the industry-standard SOAP message format.

The `RemoteObject` and `WebService` components are limited in the servers with which they can communicate:

- `RemoteObject`. Requests work only with servers that implement AMF, including ColdFusion, LiveCycle Data Services, and BlazeDS among Adobe products, and numerous third-party and open-source products that are designed to be installed on top of ASP.NET, PHP, and Java Enterprise Edition (also known as J2EE) application servers.

- `WebService`. Requests work only with servers that use the SOAP protocol, including ColdFusion, ASP.NET, and J2EE servers that include a SOAP Web service library such as Apache's AXIS.

In contrast, you can use the `HTTPService` component to create an RPC-style application that uses any application server, because using well-formed XML as a message format can be accomplished nearly universally.

You can use all three RPC components to implement an RPC-style software architecture where functions are called from the server to retrieve and modify data. Whereas the `WebService` and

`RemoteObject` components are always used to implement RPC, because they always call functions (called *operations* in Web services and *methods* in remote objects), you can use the `HTTPService` component to implement RPC, REST, or a hybrid of the two.

Creating Data-Centric Applications with Flash Builder 4

Flash Builder 4 adds a new set of features grouped together as the data centric development tools. These tools include the capability to generate code for these application tasks:

- Connecting to services hosted by remote application servers

- Converting returned data to strongly typed value object classes

- Binding returned data to visual controls such as `List` and `DataGrid`

- Presenting data entry forms with returned data already filled into the form's controls

These features are available for use with the following servers and remote applications:

- Adobe ColdFusion

- LiveCycle Data Services

- BlazeDS

- PHP

- SOAP-based Web service providers

- RESTful data providers returning data as well-formed XML

In this section I describe how to use these new tools to generate code for retrieving and handling well-formed XML-formatted data from any application server or from the local disk when using Adobe AIR.

Creating and managing data connections

You can define a remote HTTP service in any Flex project. (When working with certain specific application servers such as ColdFusion, you must first associate the Flex project with that server.) You'll need the following information before you get started:

- The URL or relative address of the XML file or server page that provides the data

- Any named parameters that are required if you're making a call to a dynamic remote server page

Creating the service

In this example, I use a static XML file that's stored in a subdirectory of the deployed application directory as the source data for the service:

1. **Create a new MXML application named** `UseDataConnection.mxml` **and view it in Source mode.**

2. **Set its layout property to an instance of** `<s:VerticalLayout>` **with** `horizontalAlign` **set to** `center` **and** `paddingTop` **set to** 20.

   ```
   <s:layout>
     <s:VerticalLayout horizontalAlign="center" paddingTop="20"/>
   </s:layout>
   ```

3. **Select Data ⇨ Connect to HTTP from the Flash Builder menu.**

4. **In the Connect to Data/Service dialog box, shown in Figure 23.1, click in the Operation Name column of the Operations grid and enter** getContacts.

5. **Click in the URL column and type** data/contacts.xml.

6. **In the Service Details section, set Service Name to** `ContactService`. Notice that the Service package defaults to `services.contactservice`, and the Custom DataType Package defaults to `valueObjects`.

7. **Click Finish to complete the code generation operation.**

FIGURE 23.1

Configuring an HTTP connection and its operations

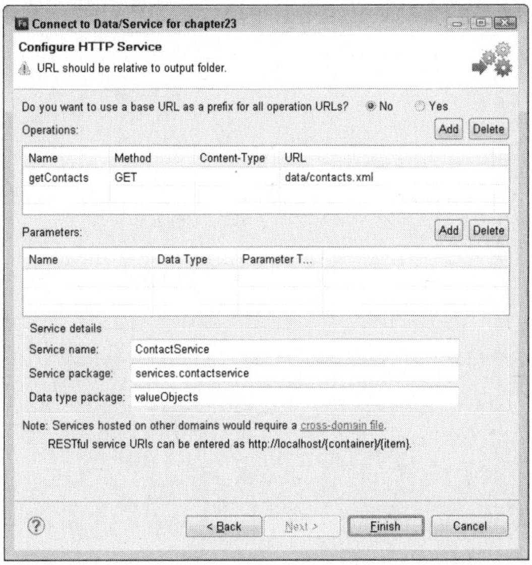

The resulting generated code is created in the Service package, which defaults to `services.`[`service name`]. A new ActionScript class is generated there; for example, the preceding steps create a new class named `ContactService`. This class is derived from a superclass, in this case named `_Super_ContactService`.

Tip

You can customize the subclass, which you'll call directly in your application, adding custom properties and methods as needed. If you change the properties of the data connection in Flash Builder, the super class will be regenerated, but the subclass is left intact with any changes you might have made. ■

Modifying the connection's properties

Data connections are managed in Flash Builder's new Data/Services view. From this view, you can select a service and modify its properties, configure the return data types of any of the service class's operations, and start the process of binding an operation's data to a visual control.

Follow these steps to modify a service's properties:

1. **Right-click the service name in the Data/Services view.**

2. **Select Properties from the context menu.** When the Properties dialog box appears, you can add, delete, or modify any of the data connection's operations.

3. **After making any changes to the data connection's properties, click Finish to regenerate the data connection's superclass.**

Reviewing the generated code

The connection is represented in the Flash Builder interface in the Data/Services view, which in turn points to the set of classes previously described. Follow these steps to explore the generated code:

1. **Open the generated package in the Package Explorer view.** If you followed the previous instructions to create the data connection, the package is named `services.contactservice`.

2. **Open** `ContactService.as`.

The code for this class is very simple; it extends another class named `_Super_ContactService`:

```
/**
 * This is a generated sub-class of _ContactService.as
 * and is intended for behavior customization.  This class
 * is only generated when there is no file already present
 * at its target location.  Thus custom behavior that you
 * add here will survive regeneration of the super-class.
 **/
package services.contactservice
{
  public class ContactService extends _Super_ContactService
  {
  }
}
```

Note

The class you open might not be as clean as the preceding example. I've added indentation and eliminated some of the white space in the generated code to make it more readable. But the comments tell you what you need to know: This class can be customized and won't be overwritten if you generate the data connection again. ■

Listing 23.1 shows the generated superclass code (cleaned up for readability).

LISTING 23.1

A generated superclass that defines how to connect to a server and retrieve XML-formatted data

```
package services.contactservice
{
  import mx.rpc.AsyncToken;
  import fr.core.model_internal;
  import mx.rpc.AbstractOperation;
  import valueObjects.Contact
  import fr.services.wrapper.HTTPServiceWrapper;
  import mx.rpc.http.HTTPMultiService;
  import mx.rpc.http.Operation;
  import com.adobe.serializers.xml.XMLSerializationFilter;
  [ExcludeClass]
  internal class _Super_ContactService extends HTTPServiceWrapper
  {
    private static var serializer0:XMLSerializationFilter =
      new XMLSerializationFilter();
    public function _Super_ContactService()
    {
      _serviceControl = new HTTPMultiService("");
      var operations:Array = new Array();
      var operation:Operation;
      var argsArray:Array;
      operation = new Operation(null, "getContacts");
      operation.url = "data/contacts.xml";
      operation.method = "GET";
      operation.serializationFilter = serializer0;
      operation.properties = new Object();
      operation.properties["xPath"] = "/::row";
      operation.resultElementType = Contact;
      operations.push(operation);
      _serviceControl.operationList = operations;
      model_internal::initialize();
    }
    public function getContacts() : AsyncToken
    {
      var _internal_operation:AbstractOperation =
        _serviceControl.getOperation("getContacts");
      var _internal_token:AsyncToken = _internal_operation.send() ;

      return _internal_token;
    }
  }
}
```

After reading the remainder of this chapter, you might want to return to this page and review the generated code. You'll see that it mimics what you can do manually with the `HTTPService` component: request and parse data in XML format.

Note

The generated code uses a class named `HTTPMultiService` to send requests to the server. In later sections of this chapter, I describe how to use `HTTPService` to manage a single server location; `HTTPMultiService` enables you to manage multiple related server locations but shares most of the `HTTPService` component's features. ■

Defining a return data type

When data is returned from an `HTTPService` request, it's defined by default as an ActionScript `Object`. As I described in Chapter 18, Flex applications can realize enormous benefits from using strongly typed value object classes instead of generic instances of `Object`. Flash Builder 4 can parse your returned XML data and automatically generate the required value object class. When the data is then returned from the server, it appears in the application as the class you've selected.

Generating the code

To dynamically generate value object code, you'll need to provide a sample of the XML data that will be received from the server. If you're working with an application server, you'll be able to provide the page location's URL (Uniform Resource Locator) and Flash Builder will retrieve and parse the returned XML. In some cases, Flash Builder automatically uses a sample of the data, but to be sure you have it available as you're using the wizard, first open the XML file in Flash Builder or another text editor and copy its contents to the system clipboard.

1. Open `contacts.xml` from the Flex project's `src/data` folder.

2. Select all the file's contents and copy it to the clipboard.

3. Go to the Data/Services view.

4. Right-click (or Ctrl+click on a Mac) the `getContacts()` operation and select Configure Return Type, as shown in Figure 23.2.

   In the first screen of the Configure Operation Return Type wizard, shown in Figure 23.3, you can select either auto-detection of the XML data structure or select an existing ActionScript class to use as a value object.

5. Accept the default option to auto-detect the return type from sample data and click Next.

6. In the next screen, select Enter sample XML/JSON response.

7. If the data isn't already displayed in the text area below the radio buttons, paste the XML data from the system clipboard, as shown in Figure 23.4. Then click Next.

8. In the next screen, open the Select root selector drop-down list and choose row as the XML node that represents a single instance data item (see Figure 23.5).

FIGURE 23.2

Configuring the return type from the Data/Services view

FIGURE 23.3

Choosing auto-detection of the XML data structure

FIGURE 23.4

Passing the data as pasted XML data

FIGURE 23.5

Configuring the return type's properties

9. **Enter** Contact **as the name of the return type.** Note that you must do this in the correct order, to override the wizard's automatic setting of the return type name to match the selected XML node.

10. **Leave the Is Array? option selected.**

11. **In the grid of data properties, change the Type Name of** contactid **to** int.

12. **Click Finish to complete the operation and generate the value object.**

The getContacts() operation now shows a return type of Contact[]; the [] characters indicate that the returned data will be in the form of an Array.

Reviewing the generated code

You'll find three new ActionScript classes in the Flex project's valueObjects folder:

- Contact.as. The value object class you'll use in your application. As with the generated ContactService class, this is a subclass that can be customized and won't be overwritten if you regenerate the return data type at a later time.

- _ContactEntityMetadata. A class that manages object bindings, collections that contain the class, and other runtime tasks.

- _Super_Contact.as. The superclass that defines the names and data types of the value object class's properties.

The Contact.as file contains the subclass declaration, initialization code, and comments describing the class structure. The comments indicating which code should not be modified are particularly important:

```
/**
 * This is a generated sub-class of _Contact.as and is intended for
 * behavior customization.  This class is only generated when there
 * is no file already present at its target location.  Thus custom
 * behavior that you add here will survive regeneration of the
 * super-class.
 *
 * NOTE: Do not manually modify the RemoteClass mapping unless
 * your server representation of this class has changed and you've
 * updated your ActionScriptGeneration,RemoteClass annotation on the
 * corresponding entity
 **/
package valueObjects
{
  import com.adobe.fiber.core.model_internal;

  public class Contact extends _Super_Contact
  {
    /**
     * DO NOT MODIFY THIS STATIC INITIALIZER - IT IS NECESSARY
     * FOR PROPERLY SETTING UP THE REMOTE CLASS ALIAS FOR THIS CLASS
     * Calling this static function will initialize RemoteClass
```

```
    * aliases for this value object as well as all of the value
    * objects corresponding to entities associated to this value
    * object's entity.
    */
  public static function _initRemoteClassAlias() : void
  {
    _Super_Contact.model_internal::initRemoteClassAliasSingle(
      valueObjects.Contact);
    _Super_Contact.model_internal::
      initRemoteClassAliasAllRelated();
  }

  model_internal static function
   initRemoteClassAliasSingleChild() : void
  {
    _Super_Contact.model_internal::initRemoteClassAliasSingle(
      valueObjects.Contact);
  }
  {
    _Super_Contact.model_internal::initRemoteClassAliasSingle(
      valueObjects.Contact);
  }
  /**
   * END OF DO NOT MODIFY SECTION
   **/

 }
}
```

The superclass defines the class's private properties and implements matching getter/setter accessor methods for each:

```
[ExcludeClass]
public class _Super_Contact extends flash.events.EventDispatcher
   implements com.adobe.fiber.valueobjects.IValueObject {
   model_internal static function initRemoteClassAliasSingle(
     cz:Class) : void
   {
   }
   model_internal static function initRemoteClassAliasAllRelated()
     : void
   {
   }
   model_internal var _dminternal_model : _ContactEntityMetadata;
  /**
  * properties
  */
  private var _internal_contactid : int;
  private var _internal_firstname : String;
  private var _internal_lastname : String;
  ... more private properties ...
  [Bindable(event="propertyChange")]
```

```
public function get contactid() : int
{
  return _internal_contactid;
}
[Bindable(event="propertyChange")]
public function get firstname() : String
{
  return _internal_firstname;
}
... more setters and getters ...
```

If you're interested, you can open these generated classes on your system and explore them in depth; or you can move on to the next step, binding the returned data to a visual control.

Binding returned data to visual controls

After defining an HTTP connection and its operations and configuring an operation's return type, the next step is to display the returned data in a visual control.

1. **Open the UseDataConnection application in Design mode.**

2. **Go to the Data Controls section of the Components view, and drag a** `DataGrid` **into the application.** As shown in Figure 23.6, the `DataGrid` initially shows three columns.

FIGURE 23.6

A `DataGrid` created in Design mode

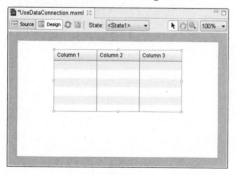

3. **Right-click (or Ctrl+click on a Mac) the DataGrid and select Bind To Data.**

Tip

You can also start the binding operation by selecting Data ➪ Bind to Data from the Flash Builder menu or by dragging the operation from the Data/Services view onto the `DataGrid`. ■

4. **In the Bind To Data dialog box, shown in Figure 23.7, select the Service and Operation that you want to bind to.**

FIGURE 23.7

Binding data to a visual control

5. **Click OK.** You should see that the DataGrid displays all the data properties returned from the operation.

6. **With the DataGrid still selected, go to the Properties view and click Configure Columns.**

7. **In the Configure Columns dialog box, remove columns that you don't want to display and then click OK to save your changes.** Figure 23.8 shows the dialog box after configuring the DataGrid to display just four columns.

FIGURE 23.8

Configuring DataGrid columns

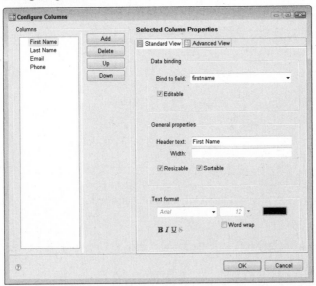

8. **Save and run the application.** As shown in Figure 23.9, you should see that the application automatically retrieves and displays the data upon startup.

Data returned using code generated by Flash Builder

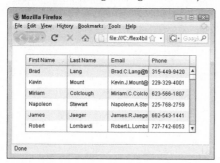

Listing 23.2 shows the completed application code. Notice that the use of the generated service and value object classes makes the application code itself very simple.

A completed application using generated HTTP data connection code

```xml
<?xml version="1.0" encoding="utf-8"?>
<s:Application xmlns:fx="http://ns.adobe.com/mxml/2009"
  xmlns:s="library://ns.adobe.com/flex/spark"
  xmlns:mx="library://ns.adobe.com/flex/mx"
  xmlns:contactservice="services.contactservice.*">
  <fx:Script>
    <![CDATA[
      import mx.events.FlexEvent;
      import mx.controls.Alert;
      protected function dataGrid_creationCompleteHandler(
        event:FlexEvent):void
      {
        getContactsResult.token = contactService.getContacts();
      }
    ]]>
  </fx:Script>
  <s:layout>
    <s:VerticalLayout horizontalAlign="center" paddingTop="20"/>
  </s:layout>
```

continued

LISTING 23.2   *(continued)*

```
<fx:Declarations>
  <s:CallResponder id="getContactsResult"/>
  <contactservice:ContactService id="contactService"
    fault="Alert.show(event.fault.faultString)" showBusyCursor="true"/>
</fx:Declarations>
<mx:DataGrid id="dataGrid"
  creationComplete="dataGrid_creationCompleteHandler(event)"
  dataProvider="{getContactsResult.lastResult}" editable="true">
  <mx:columns>
    <mx:DataGridColumn headerText="First Name" dataField="firstname"/>
    <mx:DataGridColumn headerText="Last Name" dataField="lastname"/>
    <mx:DataGridColumn headerText="Email" dataField="email"/>
    <mx:DataGridColumn headerText="Phone" dataField="phone"/>
  </mx:columns>
</mx:DataGrid>
</s:Application>
```

Declaring and Configuring HTTPService Objects

While the new code generation tools are fast and easy to use and generate code that's adequate for most simple Flex applications, it's also important to understand how the generated code works. In the next sections of this chapter I describe the `HTTPService` and `CallResponder` components and detail how to use them in a data-centric Flex application.

You can declare and configure an `HTTPService` object in either MXML or ActionScript code. For applications that communicate only with a single network resource, the MXML approach might be simpler and easier to implement. In more complex applications that use multiple network resources, ActionScript classes and methods that dynamically generate `HTTPService` objects as needed can be easier to manage.

Creating an HTTPService object

The MXML syntax to create an `HTTPService` object looks like this:

```
<fx:Declarations>
  <s:HTTPService id="myService" url="data/contacts.xml"/>
</fx:Declarations>
```

As with all Flex components, the object's `id` property is used to identify it uniquely in the context of the current application or component. The `url` property (discussed in detail in the next section) can be set with either a literal `String`, as in this example, or with a binding expression if you want to be able to switch to a different network resource at `runtime`.

New Feature

As with all nonvisual components, an HTTPService object declared in MXML must be wrapped in an <fx:Declarations> element in Flex 4. ■

Note

The HTTPService and other RPC classes are declared in the both the MX and the Spark MXML manifests, so you can use either the mx: or the s: prefix. Flash Builder auto-completes these declarations with the s: prefix by default. ■

The equivalent ActionScript code looks like this:

```
import mx.rpc.http.HTTPService;
private var myService:HTTPService =
new HTTPService("data/contacts.xml");
```

Alternatively, you can declare the object first and then set its url in a separate statement:

```
private var myService:HTTPService = new HTTPService();
myService.url = "data/contacts.xml";
```

The Flex framework's class library has two HTTPService classes. The first, which is imported in the preceding example, is a member of the mx.rpc.http package and is used in ActionScript code. The other version of the HTTPService class is a subclass of the first and is a member of the mx.rpc.http.mxml package. This is the version you use when you instantiate the object with the <s:HTTPService> tag.

The versions are nearly identical with only one difference. The MXML version implements an initialized() method that's designed to be called after the object's instantiation. When you declare the HTTPService object in MXML, this method is called automatically; you only need to call it yourself if you instantiate this version of the class in ActionScript code.

New Feature

In Flex 3, the showBusyCursor property, which causes an animated cursor to be displayed for the duration of an HTTPService request/response cycle, and the concurrency property, which determines how multiple concurrent requests to the same network resource are handled, were declared in the MXML version of HTTPService. In Flex 4, these have been moved to the superclass, mx.rpc.http.HTTPService, and are therefore available regardless of how you declare or instantiate the RPC object. ■

Tip

ActionScript-based declarations of HTTPService should be placed outside of any function declarations, so that the object is accessible from all functions in the current application or component. ■

Essential HTTPService properties

Whether you use the MXML or ActionScript approach, the HTTPService component implements these properties that determine where the request is made and what HTTP methods are used:

- concurrency:String. A rule that determines how to handle multiple concurrent calls to the same network resource.
- method:String. The HTTP method to be used.
- resultFormat:String. The format in which the data should be returned.
- showBusyCursor:Boolean. When true, causes an animated cursor to appear for the duration of the request/response cycle.
- url:String. The Web address to which the request is sent.

The details of these properties are described in the following sections.

Setting the url property

The url property is set to the network address to which the HTTP service should be sent. For a Flex application designed for Web deployment, this can be either a relative or absolute address. For example, if the Flex application is retrieving a static XML file that's on the same server and within the same directory structure, the url could be set as follows:

```
myHTTPService.url = "data/contacts.xml";
```

For Web-based applications, the expression data/contacts.xml means that the XML file is in a data subfolder on the same server from which the Flex application downloads at runtime.

For desktop applications deployed with Adobe AIR, or for Web applications that need to retrieve data from a domain other than one from which the application is downloaded, you can set the url as an absolute address. This statement sets url to an absolute location on the Web:

```
myHTTPService.url = "http://www.myserver.com/data/contacts.xml";
```

And this sets the location to a file in the application's installed files directory in an Adobe AIR application:

```
var f:File = File.applicationDirectory.resolvePath(
  "data/contacts.xml");
myHTTPService.url = f.nativePath;
```

Caution

If you need to retrieve content at runtime from a different domain on the Web, you may need to deal with Flash Player's cross-domain security constraint. See the information on using the cross-domain permissions file later in this chapter and how to use the Proxy Service that's included with LiveCycle Data Services and BlazeDS in Chapter 26. ■

The network resource to which you send an HTTPService request can be either a static text file or a dynamic application server page that generates a response upon demand. As long as the response is in a form that the HTTPService component is able to parse (usually a well-formed XML file), the response will be read and understood when it's received from the server.

Setting the method property

The HTTPService component's method property supports the following values:

- GET (the default)
- POST
- PUT (only with AIR or a proxy service)
- DELETE (only with AIR or a proxy service)
- OPTIONS (only with a proxy service)
- HEAD (only with a proxy service)
- TRACE (only with a proxy service)

In RPC-style applications, the HTTPService component is mostly used with the GET and POST methods, while REST-style approaches sometimes use PUT and DELETE requests.

Caution

Flash Player 10 only supports HTTP requests with methods of GET and POST. Desktop applications deployed with AIR also can use the PUT and DELETE request methods. To use PUT and DELETE requests in a Web application, or any other request methods, you must send requests through a server-side proxy such as the Proxy Service provided by LiveCycle Data Services and BlazeDS (described in Chapter 24). ■

For example, Flex developers who use Ruby on Rails as their application server sometimes follow a RESTful pattern where the HTTPService method determines what kind of data manipulation is being requested by the client application. Each of the following methods is treated as a "verb" that indicates what should be done with the data passed in the request:

- **DELETE request.** Results in deleting existing data in the server tier.
- **GET request.** Retrieves a representation of data without making any changes to the version in the server's persistent data store.
- **POST request.** Results in creating a new data item in the server tier.
- **PUT request.** Results in modifying existing data in the server tier.

Web Resource

For more information on using a RESTful approach with Ruby on Rails, visit the Ruby documentation at http://api.rubyonrails.org/classes/ActionController/Resources.html. An article by Derek Wischusen on integrating HTTPService and Ruby on Rails is available at www.adobe.com/devnet/flex/articles/flex2_rails_print.html. ■

Tip

The resthttpservice library, available at http://code.google.com/p/resthttpservice, is a free open-source Flex component that's fully REST-aware and can serve as a replacement for the HTTPService class. A tutorial about it is available online at:

```
http://blogs.4point.com/taylor.bastien/2009/04/
    flex-and-rest-is-it-time-to-scrub-out-soap.html. ■
```

Setting the resultFormat property

The `resultFormat` property determines how data is exposed in the Flex application when it's received from the server. The possible values are listed here:

- `array`. The top-level object is returned as the first item in an ActionScript `Array`.

- `e4x`. Well-formed XML is returned as an ActionScript `XML` object that can be parsed and modified with EcmaScript for XML (E4X) syntax.

- `flashvars`. Data formatted as name/value pairs is parsed into an ActionScript `Object` with named properties. For example, the following `String` value is a well-formed `flashvars` value:

  `firstName=Joe&lastName=Smith`

- `object` **(the default)**. Well-formed XML is returned as a tree of ActionScript objects. When a single element exists in a particular level of the XML hierarchy with a particular name, it's returned as an instance of the `ObjectProxy` class; when multiple elements of the same name are returned, they're wrapped in an `ArrayCollection`.

- `text`. The response is returned as a simple `String` value.

- `xml`. Well-formed XML is returned as an ActionScript `XMLNode` object that can be parsed with Document Object Model (DOM) code.

  The resulting ActionScript `Object` would have two properties named `firstName` and `lastName`.

Cross-Reference
The use of E4X to parse well-formed XML is described in Chapter 24. ■

Setting the concurrency property

The concurrency property is implemented only with the MXML version of the `HTTPService` component and determines how the responses from multiple concurrent requests will be handled. The property's possible values are listed here:

- `last`. Issuing another request before the last one was completed results in canceling the first request.

- `multiple` **(the default)**. Multiple responses are handled as they're received from the server, and it's up to you (the developer) to create a code pattern that enables you to identify the responses for each request. The `AsyncToken` class, an instance of which is returned from the `send()` method, can be helpful in this circumstance.

- `single`. You can have only a single request active at any given time. Issuing another request before the last one was completed results in a runtime error.

The following code results in canceling any pending `HTTPService` requests when a new request is sent:

```
<s:HTTPService id="myService"
url="data/contacts.xml"
concurrency="last"/>
```

Sending and Receiving Data

You send an HTTP request with the HTTPRequest object's send() method. For example, if you want to retrieve data upon application startup, you can call the send() method in the application's creationComplete event handler:

```
<s:Application xmlns:fx="http://ns.adobe.com/mxml/2009"
  xmlns:s="library://ns.adobe.com/flex/spark"
  xmlns:mx="library://ns.adobe.com/flex/mx"
  creationComplete=»myService.send()»>
  <fx:Declarations>
    <s:HTTPService id="myService" url="data/contacts.xml"/>
  </fx:Declarations>
</s:Application>
```

Alternatively, you can send the request upon a user event, such as the click event handler of a Button component:

```
<s:Button label="Make request" click="service.send()"/>
```

Note

The send() method accepts an optional parameters argument typed as an Object that enables you to send parameters to dynamic application server pages. I describe this technique later in this chapter. ■

Understanding asynchronous communications

All the Flex framework's RPC components send and receive data asynchronously. This means that when you send a request, Flash Player's ActionScript Virtual Machine (AVM) doesn't pause in its code execution and wait for data to be returned. This architecture is similar to how a Web browser's XMLHttpRequest object handles JavaScript requests for data: Requests are sent, and the responses are handled through event listeners.

For ColdFusion developers, Flex's HTTPService and ColdFusion's <cfhttp> tags behave differently. ColdFusion handles responses to its <cfhttp> command synchronously, meaning that it waits for data to be returned before going to the next line of code. Two major differences between the runtime environments account for this.

First, ColdFusion pages are transient and stay in server memory only until they've generated and returned HTML to the requesting Web browser. Asynchronous operations require a runtime environment that stays in memory and can listen for a response. Also, ColdFusion is multithreaded and can afford to allocate a thread to wait for a response. Flash Player is single-threaded; if it had to wait for a response, the application would have to suspend all other operations such as animations and user interactions until the data came back.

Handling HTTPService responses

You can handle the response from a server with two approaches:

- With a binding expression that references returned data
- With event listeners that execute ActionScript code when data is returned

Of these approaches, the binding expression is simpler and easier to code, but it gives much less flexibility and power in terms of how you handle the returned data. In contrast, the event listener architecture gives you the opportunity to debug, inspect, manipulate, and save returned data persistently.

Using a binding expression

The `HTTPService` component's `lastResult` property is a reference variable that gives you access to the data that's returned from the server. When the service object's `resultFormat` property is set to the default value of `object` and you retrieve well-formed XML, the expression `myService.lastResult` refers to an instance of the `ObjectProxy` class that represents the XML document.

The following code represents the contents of an XML file named `contacts.xml`:

```
<?xml version="1.0"?>
<contacts>
  <row>
    <contactid>1</contactid>
    <firstname>Brad</firstname>
    <lastname>Lang</lastname>
    <streetaddress>3004 Buckhannan Avenue</streetaddress>
    <city>Syracuse</city>
    <state>NY</state>
    <email>Brad.C.Lang@trashymail.com</email>
    <phone>315-449-9420</phone>
  </row>
  ... additional <row> elements ...
</contacts>
```

When an XML file is structured with multiple repeating elements of the same name, as is the case with the `<row>` element in this XML structure, the `HTTPService` components generates an `ArrayCollection` that "wraps" the data. To display the data from a `DataGrid` or other data visualization component, use a binding expression that starts with the `HTTPService` object's `id` and `lastResult` property and then "walks" down the XML hierarchy to the repeating element name.

The following `DataGrid` component uses the content of the repeating `<row>` elements as its data provider:

```
<mx:DataGrid dataProvider="{contactService.lastResult.data.row}"/>
```

Try these steps in the `chapter23` project:

1. **Open `contacts.xml` file from the project's `src/data` folder.** Notice that the XML file has a root element named `<contacts>` and repeating elements named `<row>`. Each `<row>` element has a consistent internal structure consisting of named properties for contactId, firstname, lastname, and so on.

2. Create a new MXML application named `HTTPServiceWithBindings.mxml` and view it in Source mode.

3. Set its layout property to an instance of `<s:VerticalLayout>` with `horizontalAlign` set to `center`.

   ```
   <s:layout>
     <s:VerticalLayout horizontalAlign="center"/>
   </s:layout>
   ```

4. Add an `<fx:Declarations>` element after the closing `</s:layout>` tag.

5. Add an `<s:HTTPService>` tag set between the `<fx:Declarations>` tags. Set its id to `contactService` and its `url` property to `data/contacts.xml`:

   ```
   <s:HTTPService id="contactService"
     url="data/contacts.xml"/>
   ```

6. Add an `<s:Button>` component below the `<s:HTTPService>` tag. Set its label to **Get Data** and its `click` event listener to call the `HTTPService` object's `send()` method:

   ```
   <s:Button label="Get Data" click="contactService.send()"/>
   ```

7. Add a `DataGrid` component below the `<mx:Button>` tag. Set its `dataProvider` to display the `HTTPService` component's returned data using a binding expression that references the XML file's repeating `<row>` elements:

   ```
   <mx:DataGrid
     dataProvider="{contactService.lastResult.contacts.row}"/>
   ```

8. Run the application, and click the Get Data button to send the request. You should see the XML file's data displayed in the `DataGrid`, as shown in Figure 23.10.

The completed application is shown in Listing 23.3

LISTING 23.3

Using a binding expression to display retrieved data

```xml
<?xml version="1.0" encoding="utf-8"?>
<s:Application xmlns:fx="http://ns.adobe.com/mxml/2009"
  xmlns:s="library://ns.adobe.com/flex/spark"
  xmlns:mx="library://ns.adobe.com/flex/mx">
  <s:layout>
    <s:VerticalLayout horizontalAlign="center" paddingTop="20"/>
  </s:layout>
  <fx:Declarations>
    <s:HTTPService id="contactService" url="data/contacts.xml"/>
  </fx:Declarations>
  <s:Button label="Get Data" click="contactService.send()"/>
  <mx:DataGrid
    dataProvider="{contactService.lastResult.contacts.row}"/>
</s:Application>
```

FIGURE 23.10

Data retrieved from the XML file and displayed in the DataGrid

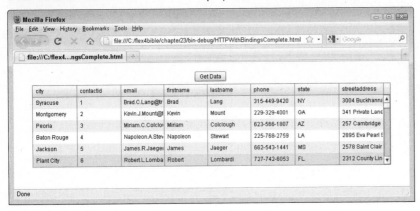

On the Web

The code in Listing 23.3 is available in the Web site files as `HTTPWithBindingsComplete.mxml` in the `src` folder of the `chapter23` project. ■

Tip

When you retrieve content from the local hard disk instead of a Web server, a file access runtime error might occur. To fix this issue, you can place the application in a local security sandbox and block network access. You do this in the project properties by adding the following compiler argument to the Flex project's compiler arguments:

```
-use-network=false  ■
```

Figure 23.11 shows the Flex Compiler section of the project properties screen with the additional `-use-network` compiler argument.

Handling the result event

When data is returned from the remote server, the `HTTPService` object dispatches a `result` event, whose event object is typed as `mx.rpc.events.ResultEvent`. This `ResultEvent` class has a `result` property that refers to the returned data.

FIGURE 23.11

Placing an application in the local sandbox to guarantee access to local files

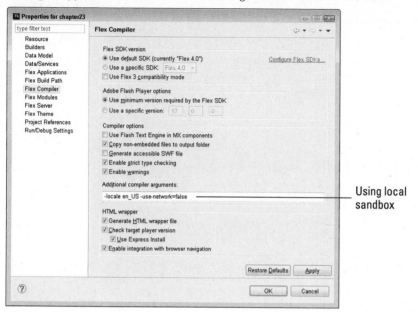

Note

The `ResultEvent` class also has a `headers` property that in theory should return the HTTP response headers from the Web server. In practice, this object frequently returns `null`. ∎

To handle and save data using the `result` event, follow these steps:

1. **Declare a bindable variable outside of any function that acts as a persistent reference to the returned data.** If you're expecting a set of repeating data elements, cast the variable as an `ArrayCollection`:

```
import mx.collections.ArrayCollection;
[Bindable]
private var myData:ArrayCollection
```

2. **Create an event handler function that will be called when the event is dispatched.** The function should receive a single event argument typed as `ResultEvent` and return `void`:

```
private function resultHandler(event:ResultEvent):void
{
}
```

Tip

You can use Flash Builder 4's new event handler generation capabilities to create the handler function automatically. When you auto-complete the `result` event in the `HTTPService` MXML declaration, Flash Builder prompts you to generate the result handler. It then creates the event handler function with the method signature described in the preceding step. ■

3. **Within the event handler function, use the event.result expression to refer to the data that's returned from the server.** Walk down the XML hierarchy to get to the repeating data elements, and return that expression to the bindable `ArrayCollection` variable:

```
myData = event.result.contacts.row;
```

You can listen for the `result` event with either an MXML attribute-based event listener or a call to the ActionScript `addEventListener()` method. The attribute-based event listener looks like this:

```
<s:HTTPService id="contactService"
  url="http://localhost/contacts.xml"
  result="resultHandler(event)"/>
```

When using `addEventListener()` to create an event listener, you can designate the event name with the `String` value `result` or with the `ResultEvent` class's `RESULT` constant:

```
var myService:HTTPService = new HTTPService();
myService.url = "data/contacts.xml";
myService.addEventListener(ResultEvent.RESULT, resultHandler);
```

The application in Listing 23.4 retrieves a data set at runtime using an `HTTPService` object's `result` event. Data is saved to a persistent `ArrayCollection` variable that's been marked as `[Bindable]` and then displayed in a `DataGrid` using a binding expression.

LISTING 23.4

An application using the HTTPService component and a result event

```
<?xml version="1.0" encoding="utf-8"?>
<s:Application xmlns:fx="http://ns.adobe.com/mxml/2009"
  xmlns:s="library://ns.adobe.com/flex/spark"
  xmlns:mx="library://ns.adobe.com/flex/mx">
  <s:layout>
    <s:VerticalLayout horizontalAlign="center" paddingTop="20"/>
  </s:layout>
  <fx:Script>
    <![CDATA[
      import mx.rpc.events.ResultEvent;
      import mx.collections.ArrayCollection;
      [Bindable]
      private var myData:ArrayCollection
```

```
  protected function contactService_resultHandler(
    event:ResultEvent):void
  {
    myData = event.result.contacts.row;
  }
  ]]>
</fx:Script>
<fx:Declarations>
  <s:HTTPService id="contactService" url="data/contacts.xml"
    result="contactService_resultHandler(event)"/>
</fx:Declarations>
<s:Button label="Get Data" click="contactService.send()"/>
<mx:DataGrid dataProvider="{myData}"/>
</s:Application>
```

On the Web

The code in Listing 23.4 is available in the Web site files as `HTTPResultEvent.mxml` in the `src` folder of the `chapter23` project. ■

Tip

It may seem at first glance that the use of the `result` event simply takes more code than a binding expression. Many advantages to this approach, however, make the extra code worthwhile. By processing the returned data in an event handler function, you have the opportunity to debug or modify data when it's returned to the server, and the persistent variable enables you to refer to the data at any later point.

It's also possible for a single service to return different data structures depending on which parameters are sent in the request. In this case, binding directly to the results isn't possible, because you have to extract data from the result with expressions that can differ depending on the circumstance. ■

Handling the fault event

When an `HTTPService` request results in an error, the `HTTPRequest` object dispatches a `fault` event, whose event object is typed as `mx.rpc.events.FaultEvent`. This event object has a `fault` property typed as `mx.rpc.Fault`, which has these properties:

- `faultCode:String`. A code that indicates the nature of the fault and whether it occurred in the client or server environment.

- `faultDetail:String`. An additional message that sometimes contains useful information.

- `faultString:String`. The error message.

- `message:String`. A string consisting of all the previous values concatenated together with | characters used as separators.

When you debug a `fault` event, you can easily see the structure of the event object. Figure 23.12 shows the Variables view during a debugging session showing the structure of the `FaultEvent` and `Fault` objects.

FIGURE 23.12

The Variables view displaying fault information during a debugging session

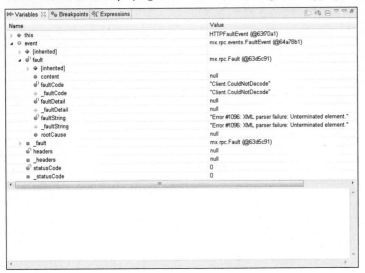

To handle a `fault` event, create an event handler function that receives an event argument typed as `FaultEvent`. Within the body of the function, you can deal with the fault however you like. This suppresses the ugly error message that appears in response to unhandled faults in the debug player. The following code collects fault information from the event object and displays it to the user with an `Alert` pop-up window:

```
private function faultHandler(event:FaultEvent):void
{
    Alert.show(event.fault.faultString, event.fault.faultCode);
}
```

Figure 23.13 shows the resulting application with the `Alert` dialog box showing the user the `faultString` and `faultCode` values.

As with the `result` event, you can listen for the `fault` event with either an MXML attribute-based event listener or the `addEventListener()` method. The MXML attribute version looks like this:

```
<s:HTTPService id="contactService"
  url="data/contactsMalformed.xml"
  result="resultHandler(event)"
  fault="faultHandler(event)"/>
```

When using `addEventListener()` to create an event listener, you can designate the event name with the `String` value `fault` or with the `FaultEvent` class's `FAULT` constant:

```
var myService:HTTPService = new HTTPService();
myService.url = "data/contacts.xml";
myService.addEventListener(ResultEvent.RESULT, resultHandler);
myService.addEventListener(FaultEvent.FAULT, faultHandler);
```

FIGURE 23.13

Displaying fault information to the user

The application in Listing 23.5 shows the use of the `fault` event with an MXML-based event listener.

LISTING 23.5

Using the fault event

```
<?xml version="1.0" encoding="utf-8"?>
<s:Application xmlns:fx="http://ns.adobe.com/mxml/2009"
  xmlns:s="library://ns.adobe.com/flex/spark"
  xmlns:mx="library://ns.adobe.com/flex/mx">
  <s:layout>
    <s:VerticalLayout horizontalAlign="center" paddingTop="20"/>
  </s:layout>
  <fx:Script>
    <![CDATA[
      import mx.collections.ArrayCollection;
      import mx.controls.Alert;
      import mx.rpc.events.FaultEvent;
      import mx.rpc.events.ResultEvent;
      [Bindable]
      private var myData:ArrayCollection
      private function resultHandler(event:ResultEvent):void
```

continued

LISTING 23.5 *(continued)*

```
    {
      myData = event.result.contacts.xml;
    }
    private function faultHandler(event:FaultEvent):void
    {
      Alert.show(event.fault.faultString, event.fault.faultCode);
    }
  ]]>
 </fx:Script>
 <fx:Declarations>
   <s:HTTPService id="contactService" url="data/contactsMalformed.xml"
     result="resultHandler(event)"
     fault="faultHandler(event)"/>
 </fx:Declarations>
 <s:Button label="Get Data" click="contactService.send()"/>
 <mx:DataGrid dataProvider="{contactService.lastResult.contacts.row}"/>
</s:Application>
```

On the Web

The code in Listing 23.5 is available in the Web site files as `HTTPFaultEvent.mxml` in the `src` folder of the `chapter23` project. ∎

Tip

All RPC components, including `HTTPService`, implement a `requestTimeout` property that sets a timeout value in terms of seconds. For example, if you set `requestTimeout` to a value of 10 and the server doesn't respond within ten seconds, a `fault` event is dispatched. ∎

Note

The `result` and `fault` events work exactly the same for all RPC components and use the same set of event classes, `ResultEvent` and `FaultEvent`. The only significant difference lies in the structure of the data returned in a `result` event. For example, `HTTPService`, when used to retrieve XML, returns data as a set of objects or as an E4X-compatible `XML` object, depending on the value of its `resultFormat` property. In contrast, `WebService` and `RemoteObject` return data based on data types declared in metadata returned from the server. In all cases, though, you access the returned data by referencing the `ResultEvent` object's `result` property. ∎

Working with CallResponder and AsyncToken

The `CallResponder` class is designed to enable you to assign multiple result and event handlers for different application scenarios. Instead of binding a single set of event handlers to the RPC component, you assign the handlers to a particular `CallResponder` object:

```
<s:HTTPService id="contactService" url="data/contacts.xml"/>
<s:CallResponder id="getDataResponder"
  result="getData_resultHandler(event)"
  fault="faultHandler(event)"/>
```

New Feature

The `CallResponder` **class is new to the Flex 4 SDK and is also included in the most recent version of the Flex 3 SDK.** ∎

At runtime, you select the responder you want to use by passing the `AsyncToken` that's returned from the service call to the `token` property of the responder object:

```
getDataResponder.token = contactService.send();
```

When the RPC request's data is returned, the responder object dispatches its `result` event and calls your custom event handler function. Similarly, any exception causes the responder to dispatch its `fault` event.

Note

As shown in the first section of this chapter on data-centric code generation, the `CallResponder` **and** `AsyncToken` **can also be used to set up a data binding relationship with a visual control. After associating the** `CallResponder` **with the call by assigning its token to the value returned from the service call, you can then refer to the** `CallResponder` **object's** `lastResult` **property in a binding expression:**

```
<mx:DataGrid id="dataGrid"
  dataProvider="{getDataResponder.lastResult}"/> ∎
```

Using the AsyncToken Class

The `AsyncToken` class is a dynamic object that enables you to add arbitrary named properties to the object at runtime and associate a remote server call with a responder object. Every request to a remote operation through an RPC component returns an instance of `AsyncToken` that stays in application memory for the duration of the remote request. After making the request, you can add as many bits of information as you need to track the purpose of the request or other important details:

```
var token:AsyncToken = contactService.send();
token.myProp1 = "Any property value";
```

When data is returned in the `result` or `fault` event handlers, you can retrieve the arbitrary properties from the event object's `token` property:

```
protected function resultHandler(event:ResultEvent):void
{
  var savedProp = event.token.myProp1;
}
```

Using `AsyncToken`, you can "remember" information about the asynchronous call between the time it's made and the time its data is returned or a fault is thrown.

The application in Listing 23.6 uses a `CallResponder` object to declare a pair of result and event handlers. After the `HTTPService` object's `send()` method is called, the application then binds the responder to the call by adding the responder to the returned `AsyncToken`. The result event handler is successfully called when the data is returned, and the data is captured and displayed.

LISTING 23.6

An application using a CallResponder

```xml
<?xml version="1.0" encoding="utf-8"?>
<s:Application xmlns:fx="http://ns.adobe.com/mxml/2009"
  xmlns:s="library://ns.adobe.com/flex/spark"
  xmlns:mx="library://ns.adobe.com/flex/mx">
  <s:layout>
    <s:VerticalLayout horizontalAlign="center" paddingTop="20"/>
  </s:layout>
  <fx:Script>
    <![CDATA[
      import mx.collections.ArrayCollection;
      import mx.controls.Alert;
      import mx.rpc.AsyncToken;
      import mx.rpc.events.FaultEvent;
      import mx.rpc.events.ResultEvent;
      [Bindable]
      private var myData:ArrayCollection
      protected function button1_clickHandler(event:MouseEvent):void
      {
        getDataResponder.token = contactService.send();
      }
      protected function getData_resultHandler(event:ResultEvent):void
      {
        myData = event.result.contacts.row;
      }
      protected function faultHandler(event:FaultEvent):void
      {
        Alert.show(event.fault.faultString, event.fault.faultCode);
      }
    ]]>
  </fx:Script>
  <fx:Declarations>
    <s:HTTPService id="contactService" url="data/contacts.xml"/>
    <s:CallResponder id="getDataResponder"
      result="getData_resultHandler(event)"
      fault="faultHandler(event)"/>
  </fx:Declarations>
  <s:Button label="Get Data" click="button1_clickHandler(event)"/>
  <mx:DataGrid dataProvider="{myData}"/>
</s:Application>
```

On the Web

The code in Listing 23.6 is available in the Web site files as `CallResponderDemo.mxml` in the `src` folder of the `chapter23` project. ■

Working with ItemResponder and AsyncToken

Developers who prefer to work entirely with ActionScript to manage their service calls sometimes use a pattern that includes the Flex framework's `ItemResponder` and `AsyncToken` classes.

Note

The `ItemResponder` and `AsyncToken` classes work nearly exactly the same with all RPC components. ■

The `ItemResponder` class can be used instead of the `CallResponder`, attribute-based event listeners, or the `addEventListener()` method to handle and dispatch event objects to ActionScript event handler functions. To use `ItemResponder`, you first create custom event handler functions to handle an RPC request's `result` and `fault` events. Each event handler function receives an `AsyncToken` argument in addition to the expected event object. For example, the `result` handler function signature looks like this:

```
private function resultHandler(event:ResultEvent,
  token:AsyncToken):void
{
  ... handle returned data ...
}
```

The `fault` event handler function looks like this:

```
private function faultHandler(event:FaultEvent,
  token:AsyncToken):void
{
  ... handle fault ...
}
```

Before you make the RPC request, you create an instance of the `ItemResponder` class and pass references to the `result` and `fault` event handler functions as constructor method arguments:

```
var responder:ItemResponder =
  new ItemResponder(resultHandler,faultHandler);
```

Note

As with `addEventListener()`, you're passing the functions as objects, and not calling them directly, so you only pass the function names and not their complete calling syntax. ■

The next steps are as follows:

1. Make the RPC request and return an instance of `AsyncToken`.

2. Add the `ItemResponder` object to the `AsyncToken` object's array of responders with its `addResponder()` method.

```
var token:AsyncToken = contactService.send();
token.addResponder(responder);
```

When the asynchronous request is completed, the `AsyncToken` object calls the appropriate event handler function, depending on whether a `result` or `fault` event is dispatched by the RPC component. The event handler function receives both its event object and a reference to the `AsyncToken` object that called it.

The application in Listing 23.7 uses `ItemResponder` and `AsyncToken` objects to manage an asynchronous request and its result and fault events.

LISTING 23.7

Using ItemResponder and AsyncToken

```
<?xml version="1.0" encoding="utf-8"?>
<s:Application xmlns:fx="http://ns.adobe.com/mxml/2009"
  xmlns:s="library://ns.adobe.com/flex/spark"
  xmlns:mx="library://ns.adobe.com/flex/mx">
  <s:layout>
    <s:VerticalLayout horizontalAlign="center" paddingTop="20"/>
  </s:layout>
  <fx:Script>
    <![CDATA[
      import mx.collections.ArrayCollection;
      import mx.collections.ItemResponder;
      import mx.controls.Alert;
      import mx.rpc.AsyncToken;
      import mx.rpc.events.FaultEvent;
      import mx.rpc.events.ResultEvent;
      import mx.rpc.http.HTTPService;
      [Bindable]
      private var myData:ArrayCollection
      private var contactService:HTTPService = new HTTPService();
      private function getData():void
      {
        contactService.url="data/contacts.xml";
        var responder:ItemResponder =
          new ItemResponder(resultHandler,faultHandler);
        var token:AsyncToken = contactService.send();
        token.addResponder(responder);
      }
      private function resultHandler(event:ResultEvent,
        token:AsyncToken):void
      {
```

```
        myData = event.result.contacts.row;
      }
      private function faultHandler(event:FaultEvent, token:AsyncToken):void
      {
        Alert.show(event.fault.faultString, event.fault.faultCode);
      }
    ]]>
  </fx:Script>
  <s:Button label="Get Data" click="getData()"/>
  <mx:DataGrid dataProvider="{myData}"/>
</s:Application>
```

On the Web

The code in Listing 23.7 is available in the Web site files as `ItemResponderDemo.mxml` in the `src` folder of the `chapter23` project. ∎

Tip

It's a common practice to create individual custom classes to manage each unique RPC request. Each custom class uses a common naming convention for both the function that creates and executes an RPC request, such as `execute()`, and its event handler methods, such as `resultHandler()` and `faultHandler()`. Known as the Command design pattern, this approach enables you to manage complex applications with dozens or thousands of unique server requests and is at the heart of the Cairngorm microarchitecture that's used by developers of large Flex applications. ∎

Web Resource

Steven Webster provides an excellent description of the Command design pattern (in the context of the Cairngorm microarchitecture) in his six-part series on Cairngorm at `www.adobe.com/devnet/flex/articles/cairngorm_pt1.html`. ∎

Working with Value Objects

XML-formatted data retrieved with the `HTTPService` component is always exposed as an `ArrayCollection` of `ObjectProxy` instances. If you prefer to work with strongly typed value object classes, you can create a simple set of code that transforms the `Object` instances into your value objects. This process has two steps:

1. **Create a value object class with the appropriate properties and set the value object class's constructor method to accept an optional argument typed as the ActionScript** `Object` **class.** Within the constructor method, if the `Object` argument was passed in, transfer its property values to the equivalent properties in the current instance of the value object class:

```
public function Contact(data:Object = null)
{
  if (data != null)
  {
    this.contactid = Number(data.contactid);
    this.firstname = data.firstname;
    this.lastname = data.lastname;
    ... set additional properties ...
  }
}
```

2. At runtime, in the `result` event handler, loop through the `ArrayCollection` and create one new instance of the value object for each data item, and then replace the original object with the `ArrayCollection` class's `setItemAt()` method:

```
private function resultHandler(event:ResultEvent):void
{
  var obj:Contact;
  myData = event.result.contacts.row;
  for (var i:int=0; i<myData.length; i++)
  {
    obj = new Contact(myData.getItemAt(i));
    myData.setItemAt(obj, i);
  }
}
```

Note

Notice that the value object class's constructor method explicitly typecasts properties as necessary. This is a major benefit of creating the extra code to transfer data from generic instances of the Object class to strongly typed value objects: Data is correctly cast and easier to use in other code throughout the application. ∎

The application in Listing 23.8 retrieves data from the server and then loops through the `ArrayCollection` to replace each generic `Object` with an equivalent value object. When the user selects a row from the `DataGrid`, a bindable instance of the value object named `current-Contact` is filled in with the selected data and its details are displayed in the `Panel`.

LISTING 23.8

Using value objects with data from an HTTPService request

```
<?xml version="1.0" encoding="utf-8"?>
<s:Application xmlns:fx="http://ns.adobe.com/mxml/2009"
  xmlns:s="library://ns.adobe.com/flex/spark"
  xmlns:mx="library://ns.adobe.com/flex/mx"
  creationComplete="contactService.send()">
  <s:layout>
    <s:VerticalLayout horizontalAlign="center" paddingTop="20"/>
  </s:layout>
  <fx:Script>
    <![CDATA[
```

```
    import mx.collections.ArrayCollection;
    import mx.events.ListEvent;
    import mx.rpc.events.ResultEvent;

    import vo.Contact;
    [Bindable]
    private var myData:ArrayCollection
    [Bindable]
    private var currentContact:Contact;
    private function contactService_resultHandler(event:ResultEvent):void
    {
      var obj:Contact;
      myData = event.result.contacts.row;
      for (var i:int=0; i<myData.length; i++)
      {
        obj = new Contact(myData.getItemAt(i));
        myData.setItemAt(obj, i);
      }
    }
    protected function datagrid1_changeHandler(event:ListEvent):void
    {
      currentContact = event.target.selectedItem as Contact;
    }
  ]]>
</fx:Script>
<fx:Declarations>
  <s:HTTPService id="contactService" url="data/contacts.xml"
    result="contactService_resultHandler(event)"/>
</fx:Declarations>
<mx:DataGrid dataProvider="{myData}"
  change="datagrid1_changeHandler(event)">
  <mx:columns>
    <mx:DataGridColumn dataField="firstname" headerText="First Name"/>
    <mx:DataGridColumn dataField="lastname" headerText="Last Name"/>
  </mx:columns>
</mx:DataGrid>
<s:Panel title="Current Contact" width="300">
  <mx:Form>
    <mx:FormItem label="First Name:">
      <s:Label text="{currentContact.firstname}"/>
    </mx:FormItem>
    <mx:FormItem label="Last Name:">
      <s:Label text="{currentContact.lastname}"/>
    </mx:FormItem>
    <mx:FormItem label="City:">
      <s:Label text="{currentContact.city}"/>
    </mx:FormItem>
  </mx:Form>
</s:Panel>
</s:Application>
```

On the Web

The code in Listing 23.8 is available in the Web site files as `HTTPValueObjects.mxml` in the `src` folder of the `chapter23` project. The `Contact` value object class is defined in `Contact.as` in the `src/vo` subfolder. ∎

Passing Parameters to Server Pages

When you use the `HTTPService` component to make calls to dynamic pages that are managed by an application server, you frequently need to pass parameters. The syntax for passing parameters is the same regardless of whether you use the `HTTPService` component with `GET` or `POST` requests.

You can pass parameters in an `HTTPService` request two ways:

- Named parameters that are packaged in an ActionScript `Object`
- Bound parameters that are set up in the `HTTPService` object declaration

Using named parameters

To pass parameters by name, first create an instance of an ActionScript `Object`. The `Object` class is dynamic, meaning that you can add arbitrary named properties at runtime. Set each parameter as a named property of the properties object, and then pass the properties object as the only argument in the object's `send()` method.

The ActionScript code to accomplish these tasks might look like this:

```
private function sendData():void
{
  var params:Object = new Object();
  params.firstname="Joe";
  params.lastname="Smith";
  contactService.send(params);
}
```

You also can use shorthand ActionScript code to create an object and pass it in a single statement:

```
private function sendData():void
{
  contactService.send({firstname:"Joe", lastname:"Smith"});
}
```

If the `HTTPService` object's method property is set to `GET`, the parameters are appended to the request URL. The first part of the resulting HTTP request would look like this:

```
GET /?firstname=Joe&lastname=Smith HTTP/1.1
```

In contrast, if the HTTPService object's method property is set to POST, the parameters are appended to the end of the HTTP request. The following is a literal POST request header sent from a Flex application hosted by Microsoft Internet Explorer 6:

```
POST / HTTP/1.1
Accept: */*
Accept-Language: en-US
Referer: file://C:\flex4bible\workspace\chapter23\
   bin-debug\HTTPSendParams.swf
x-flash-version: 9,0,115,0
Content-Type: application/x-www-form-urlencoded
Content-Length: 28
Accept-Encoding: gzip, deflate
User-Agent: Mozilla/4.0 (compatible; MSIE 6.0; Windows NT 5.1; SV1;
   .NET CLR 1.1.4322; .NET CLR 2.0.50727; .NET CLR 3.0.04506.648; .
   NET CLR 3.5.21022)
Host: localhost
Connection: Keep-Alive
Cache-Control: no-cache
firstname=Joe&lastname=Smith
```

Using bound parameters

You can set up bound parameters in an HTTPService declaration so that named properties are sent with a consistent source. For example, assume that you've declared a bindable instance of a value object that stores current values:

```
[Bindable]
private var myContact:Contact;
```

If you know that the parameters you send with HTTPService always get their values from this object, you can declare the relationship using binding expressions:

```
<s:HTTPService id="contactService" url="myAppPage.php"
  result="resultHandler(event)">
  <s:request>
    <firstname>{myContact.firstname}</firstname>
    <lastname>{myContact.lastname}</lastname>
  </s:request>
</s:HTTPService>
```

When you call the HTTPService object's send() method with no arguments, the named parameters in the <s:request> tag set are sent with exactly the same HTTP request syntax as with the named parameters syntax described previously.

Cross-Reference
To fully demonstrate the use of HTTPRequest parameters, you need an application server that can receive and respond to parameterized requests. ■

Handling Cross-Domain Policy Issues

When Flash Player is asked to make a request to a domain other than the one from which the current Flash document was downloaded, it needs to have permission from the target domain. This issue frequently comes up when you're using data from a third-party data provider, but it also can be relevant when you have two or more domains in a single organization.

Figure 23.14 describes the circumstance in which cross-domain permission is required. If a Flex application downloaded from one domain makes an HTTP request to a different domain, Flash Player automatically seeks cross-domain permission via a request for a cross-domain policy file from the remote domain.

The goal of the cross-domain security constraint is to prevent malicious code from "taking over" the user's Flash Player and making repeated requests to arbitrary Web-based resources.

FIGURE 23.14

Cross-domain permission is required in this circumstance.

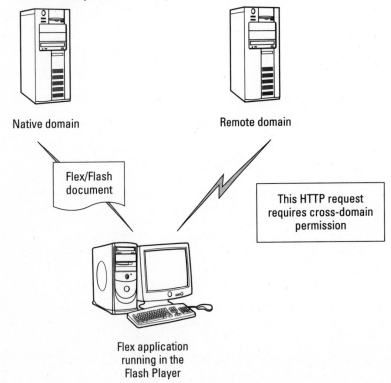

Native domain

Remote domain

Flex/Flash
document

This HTTP request
requires cross-domain
permission

Flex application
running in the
Flash Player

Tip

Cross-domain permission is required for all HTTP requests to remote domains, including attempts to retrieve content with the `HTTPService` **component, make remote procedure calls with the** `WebService` **and** `RemoteObject` **components, and download image or Flash documents with the** `Image` **or** `SWFLoader` **components. The same restriction is applied to Flash documents that use the** `URLLoader` **or** `XMLSocket` **classes to connect to remote domains.** ∎

The cross-domain policy file is an XML file that is always named `crossdomain.xml` and placed in the Web root of the remote domain. At runtime, when Flash Player determines that cross-domain permission is required to execute a task, it tries to download this file from the remote domain's root folder. If it finds the file, it parses it and looks for permissions that have been granted to the domain from which the Flash document or Flex application was originally down-loaded.

The cross-domain policy file looks like this:

```
<?xml version="1.0"?>
<!DOCTYPE cross-domain-policy SYSTEM
   "http://www.adobe.com/xml/dtds/cross-domain-policy.dtd">
<cross-domain-policy>
  <allow-access-from domain="www.domain1.com" />
  <allow-access-from domain="domain2.com" />
  <allow-access-from domain="*.domain3.com" />
</cross-domain-policy>
```

Each `<allow-access-from>` element gives permission to Flash documents downloaded from the domain named in the domain attribute to make HTTP requests to the server on which the cross-domain file is stored.

Starting with Flash Player 7, the cross-domain policy rules enforce rules on a per-domain basis without regard for partial combinations of host names and domain names. So, for example, if a Flex application is downloaded from a URL starting with `mydomain.com` and the cross-domain policy file has a declaration that allows access from `www.mydomain.com`, Flash Player does not consider permission to have been granted. The domain names must match exactly, and there is no Domain Name Service (DNS) lookup for IP addresses.

Wildcard characters are supported, however. The following declaration would grant HTTP request permission to documents downloaded from `mydomain.com`, `www.mydomain.com`, and any other URL that ends with `mydomain.com`:

```
<allow-access-from domain="*.mydomain.com" />
```

Web Resource

Complete information on creating a cross-domain security file, including how to handle requests to secure pages from a Flash document that was loaded from a nonsecure Web page, is available on the Web at `www.adobe.com/go/tn_14213`. ∎

Summary

In this chapter, I described how to use the `HTTPService` component to send and receive data over the Web. You learned the following:

- Flash Builder 4 helps you build data-centric applications quickly and easily with new code generation features.

- The Flex SDK contains three RPC components: the `RemoteObject`, `WebService`, and `HTTPService` classes.

- Only the `HTTPService` component is completely portable among application servers, because it can use any XML or plain text format for its messages.

- You can declare an `HTTPService` object in either MXML or ActionScript.

- You handle data returned from an `HTTPService` request with either binding expressions or event handlers.

- The new `CallResponder` class enables you to separate the definitions of `result` and `fault` event handlers from the `HTTPService` component declaration.

- XML-formatted data is parsed automatically and delivered as either a tree of ActionScript objects and data collections or an E4X-compatible `XML` object.

- Parameters can be passed with either an `Object` that serves as a collection of name/value pairs or with bindings declared in MXML.

- Cross-domain constraint issues can be solved by placing a cross-domain policy file in the Web root of the remote domain.

Managing XML with E4X

XML (EXtensible Markup Language) has become a lingua franca for data exchange on the Web. When the XML standard was originally defined in 1998, its purpose was to define a common set of syntax rules that could be applied to multiple applications. XML isn't a language in itself, so much as it's a set of rules that define how markup languages designed for data representation should behave.

There have been a few attempts over the years to extend the XML recommendation and go beyond the original version 1.0, but each attempt has foundered. It's generally agreed that the rules of XML as they currently stand do what the standard should do, and each proposed addition has run into some sort of opposition.

The developer tools for working with XML, however, have continued to evolve. From the earliest XML processing APIs such as the Document Object Model (DOM) and the Simple API for XML (SAX), to more recent innovations such as JDOM for Java developers and the XML processing classes in the .NET framework, organizations that are responsible for creating programming languages and development platforms continue to improve the lot of developers who work with XML. The goal is always to make it as easy to parse and modify XML-formatted data as possible.

EcmaScript for XML (E4X) is one such toolkit. E4X was defined by Ecma International in the ECMA-357 standard and is implemented as a part of ActionScript 3. Any application running in Flash Player 9 or later has access to the E4X API and can use its simple syntax to parse, extract data from, and modify XML and XMLList objects stored in application memory.

In this chapter, I describe how to use E4X and ActionScript-based XML classes to parse and modify XML-formatted data in Flex applications.

IN THIS CHAPTER

Understanding E4X

Creating an XML object

Using XMLList objects

Using the XMLListCollection class

Parsing XML with E4X

Modifying XML with E4X

Working with XML namespaces

Tip

E4X also is implemented in other derivations of EcmaScript, including SpiderMonkey (the JavaScript engine that's embedded in the Gecko browser kernel), Rhino (Mozilla's Java-based JavaScript engine), and Adobe Acrobat's implementation of JavaScript. ■

On the Web

To use the sample code for this chapter, import the `chapter24.fxp` project from the Web site files into any folder on your disk. ■

Using XML Classes

Flash documents and Flex applications written with ActionScript 2 had access to an XML class that enabled the developer to extract data from an XML file or data packet. This object used DOM programming to extract information.

DOM-style programming has certain advantages: The coding style is implemented in many languages, so if you know how to code with DOM in one language, you can easily adapt your skills to another.

However, DOM programming tends to be verbose and require lots of extensive looping (loops within loops within loops) to get to the data you want.

Consider this XML content:

```
<?xml version="1.0"?>
<invoices>
  <invoice>
    <customer>Smith, Maria</customer>
    <items>
      <lineitem price="21.41" quantity="4">Widget</lineitem>
      <lineitem price="2.11" quantity="14">Mouse</lineitem>
      <lineitem price="8.88" quantity="3">Wrench</lineitem>
    </items>
  </invoice>
</invoices>
```

Using the old-style `XMLDocument` and `XMLNode` objects, you would first "walk" the XML tree to get a reference to the collection of elements you want to evaluate. Then, to locate a `<lineitem>` element with a particular text node (the item description), you'd loop through the elements and use conditional statements to evaluate each data item:

```
var arItems:Array=
  xmlDocument.firstChild.firstChild.childNodes[1].childNodes;
var arResult:Array = new Array();
for (var i:int=0; i<xInvoices.length; i++)
{
  var currentNode:XMLNode = arItems[i] as XMLNode;
```

```
    if (currentNode.attributes.price == '21.41')
    {
      arResult.push(currentNode)
    }
  }
}
```

With E4X you would first assign the XML file's root element to a new-style XML object. You can then extract the element representing the "Widget" with the simple expression:

```
var xResult:XMLList = xInvoices..lineitem.(@price=21.41);
```

This example makes clear that E4X offers a much more concise and readable syntax for finding and extracting data from an XML data structure.

Tip

The old XML class functionality was refactored into classes named XMLNode and XMLDocument in ActionScript 3. These are considered "legacy" classes that enable you to use DOM-style programming if you prefer. However, after developers understand and master the use of E4X to accomplish XML processing tasks, they usually don't go back. ■

In ActionScript 3, Flex developers can use the following XML classes to manage XML-formatted data at runtime:

- XML. A new version of the XML class that supports E4X expressions to parse and modify data at runtime. The XML class has only one root node.

- XMLList. A class representing an ordered set of XML objects. The XMLList class is similar to an Array in that it contains objects in fixed order. Also, like an Array, it doesn't have a complete API to manage, modify, and reliably execute bindings when its data changes at runtime.

- XMLListCollection. A "wrapper" class that manages an ArrayList. Just as the ArrayCollection provides sorting, filtering, and other advanced features for managing an Array, the XMLListCollection implements a powerful API that manages an XMLList and reliably executes bindings when its data changes at runtime.

The first step in using these classes is to create a new-style XML object.

Creating an XML object

The XML class represents a single XML node and can be created in a number of ways:

- With a hard-coded XML structure in an ActionScript statement
- With the MXML <mx:XML> tag
- By parsing an XML-formatted String value
- By retrieving XML-formatted data with the HTTPService component with its resultFormat property set to e4x

Declaring a hard-coded XML structure in ActionScript

You can declare an XML object and set its data in a single statement by using a value in the assignment statement structured as XML:

```
var sales:XML =
  <sales>
    <item type="apples" price="4.53" quantity="6"/>
    <item type="oranges" price="3.35" quantity="10"/>
    <item type="pears" price="5.16" quantity="3"/>
  </sales>;
```

Note

Notice that the XML structure isn't wrapped in quotes. When using an XML object, the data type is XML, not a String value, so quotation marks aren't required; in fact, using quotation marks would cause a syntax error. ■

Tip

You can use binding expressions within attribute and element values to populate data into an XML structure at the moment of its creation. ■

The sales object in this example points to the XML structure's root element. The E4X expression that refers to the object's `<item>` elements is:

```
sales.item
```

Parsing an XML-formatted string value

If you have an XML-formatted string value that you've read from a server-based data source (for example, as a string stored in a database table column), you can transform the string into an XML object by passing the string value in a call to the XML class's constructor method.

For example, this code creates a well-formed XML data packet as a String variable (remember, because it's a String and not XML yet, you do need to use quotation marks):

```
var stringData:String = '<sales>' +
  '<item type="apples" price="4.53" quantity="6"/>' +
  '<item type="oranges" price="3.35" quantity="10"/>' +
  '<item type="pears" price="5.16" quantity="3"/>' +
  '</sales>';
```

To transform the `stringData` variable into an XML object that can be managed with E4X, declare the XML object with a call to its constructor method and pass the String as the only argument:

```
var xmlData:XML = new XML(stringData);
```

As with the first example, the XML object points to the XML document's root element, so the E4X expression `xmlData.item` refers to the set of `<item>` elements that are direct children of the root.

Declaring an XML object in MXML

The `<fx:XML>` tag declares an `XML` object using nested XML markup. The tag's `format` property is set either to `xml` to create a legacy `XMLNode` object or to `e4x` (the default) to create an `XML` object that can be managed with E4X expressions. The following code declares the `XML` object with this MXML syntax:

```
<fx:XML format="e4x" id="xmlData">
  <sales>
    <item type="apples" price="4.53" quantity="6"/>
    <item type="oranges" price="3.35" quantity="10"/>
    <item type="pears" price="5.16" quantity="3"/>
  </sales>
</fx:XML>
```

As with the version declared in ActionScript, the `XML` object's `id` is a reference to the root element (not an XML document), so the expression `xmlData.item` refers to the set of `<item>` elements that are direct children of the root.

Importing XML with HTTPService

The `HTTPService` component's `resultFormat` property can be set to `e4x`, causing the retrieved data to be represented as an `XML` object. The `HTTPService` object, for example, retrieves an external XML-formatted file:

```
<s:HTTPService id="salesService"
  url="data/sales.xml"
  resultFormat="e4x"
  result="resultHandler(event)"/>
```

In the `result` event handler function, you capture the returned data by casting `event.result` as an `XML` object:

```
private var xmlData:XML;
private function resultHandler(event:ResultEvent):void
{
  xmlData = event.result as XML;
}
```

Again, the `xmlData` object refers to the root element of the retrieved XML document, not to the document itself.

Controlling parsing with XML properties

An `XML` object refers to a single XML element node, whether it's the XML document's root element or one of its children.

The XML class supports the following static properties that determine how it parses and exposes data to E4X expressions:

- `ignoreComments`. When `true`, this expression strips comments out of an XML string during the parsing process.

- `ignoreProcessingInstructions`. When `true`, this expression strips processing instructions out of an XML string during the parsing process.

- `ignoreWhitespace`. When `true`, this expression removes beginning and ending white space characters from text nodes during the parsing process.

To use any of these static properties, set their value before creating an `XML` object. For example, the following XML packet contains extra white space before and after the data.

```
<data>
  <firstname>Joe      </firstname>
</data>
```

By default, the extra white space is removed during parsing, because the `ignoreWhitespace` property is set to `true` by default. To preserve white space around text nodes, set `ignore-Whitespace` to `false` before creating the `XML` object:

```
XML.ignoreWhitespace = false;
var xmlData=<data>
  <firstname>Joe      </firstname>
</data>;
```

Now the E4X expression `xmlData.firstname` returns the value of the text node, and the extra spaces are preserved.

Using the XMLList class

The `XMLList` class is an ordered set of `XML` or `XMLList` objects. While it is a collection of potentially disparate XML data, most commonly the objects in an `XMLList` share a common structure. Like an ActionScript `Array`, it maintains the objects in the order of initial declaration or parsing, or in the most recent order based on changes you've made to the data through calls to object methods (or, in this case, E4X expressions).

You can create an `XMLList` object with an explicit MXML declaration that nests multiple `XML` nodes:

```
<fx:XMLList id="xList">
  <item type="apples" price="4.53" quantity="6"/>
  <item type="oranges" price="3.35" quantity="10"/>
  <item type="pears" price="5.16" quantity="3"/>
</fx:XMLList>
```

Or, if you already have an `XML` object in memory, you can use an E4X expression that refers to a set of elements. For example, if an `XML` object named `xmlData` contains two or more `<item>` child elements, the expression `xmlData.item` returns an `XMLList` object:

```
var xmlData:XML =
  <sales>
```

```
          <item type="apples" price="4.53" quantity="6"/>
          <item type="oranges" price="3.35" quantity="10"/>
          <item type="pears" price="5.16" quantity="3"/>
      </sales>;
  var salesList:XMLList = xmlData.item;
```

This expression xmlData.item uses the dot (.) operator to navigate to the XML object's named child element. If only one element with the name (in this case, item) exists, the expression returns an XML object. When more than one element of the same name is found, the expression returns an XMLList.

Tip

When an XMLList contains only a single XML object, you can call any methods or properties of the XML class as though they were members of the XMLList. When the XMLList contains more than a single XML object, you can only call methods and properties implemented by the XMLList class. ■

Using the XMLListCollection class

The XMLListCollection class is a wrapper for the XMLList, in the same way the ArrayCollection wraps an Array. Like ArrayCollection, it extends the ListCollectionView superclass. As a result, it provides a rich API for storing, sorting, filtering, and modifying its contained data.

The XMLListCollection class's source property is typed as an XMLList (again like the ArrayCollection and Array), so you can instantiate and initialize an XMLListCollection object and associate it with an XMLList in a number of ways:

- Assign the XMLList to the source property after first instantiating the XMLListCollection:

  ```
  [Bindable]
  private var xCollection:XMLListCollection =
    new XMLListCollection();
  xCollection.source = xmlList;
  ```

- Pass the XMLList to the XMLListCollection constructor method:

  ```
  [Bindable]
  private var xCollection:XMLListCollection =
    new XMLListCollection(xmlList);
  ```

- Declare the XMLListCollection in MXML, and assign the source with an attribute and a binding expression:

  ```
  <s:XMLListCollection id="xCollection" source="{xmlList}"/>
  ```

Note

As with all MXML declarations, the MXML version of the object is automatically instantiated and made bindable. The ActionScript versions must be explicitly marked as bindable if you want to use binding expressions to update other components when the data changes at runtime. ■

In addition to the `ListCollectionView` API that enables you to add, update, and manipulate data at runtime, the `XMLListCollection` supports a small set of methods that are specifically designed to access hierarchical data. For example, the `attribute()` function enables you to search the `XMLList` for all nested XML child objects that share a named attribute. `XMLListCollection` also implements a `copy()` method that returns a "deep" copy of its `XMLList`.

Note

E4X expressions can be called only from an XML or `XMLList` object, not from an `XMLListCollection`. The `XMLListCollection` is typically used to represent the final result of an E4X expression and pass it to visual controls or other application components through bindings. ■

Using E4X Expressions

EcmaScript for XML (E4X) is an expression language that enables you to extract and manipulate data stored in XML objects with simple expressions. By using E4X, you can eliminate the significantly more verbose ActionScript code that would otherwise be required.

Web Resource

The specification for E4X is available at this URL:

```
www.ecma-international.org/publications/
    standards/Ecma-357.htm.  ■
```

The examples in this section use the `invoices.xml` shown in Listing 24.1. This file uses a multi-level hierarchical data structure to represent simple invoice information.

LISTING 24.1

A file named invoices.xml representing a set of business invoices

```
<?xml version="1.0"?>
<invoices>
  <invoice>
    <customer>
      <firstname>Maria</firstname>
      <lastname>Smith</lastname>
    </customer>
    <items>
      <lineitem price="21.41" quantity="4">Widget</lineitem>
      <lineitem price="2.11" quantity="14">Mouse</lineitem>
      <lineitem price="8.88" quantity="3">Wrench</lineitem>
    </items>
  </invoice>
  <invoice>
    <customer>
      <firstname>John</firstname>
```

```
      <lastname>Jones</lastname>
    </customer>
    <items>
      <lineitem price="7.41" quantity="84">Mouse</lineitem>
      <lineitem price="0.91" quantity="184">Mousepad</lineitem>
    </items>
  </invoice>
</invoices>
```

On the Web

The code in Listing 24.1 is available in the Web site files as `invoices.xml` in the `src/data` folder of the `chapter24` project. ∎

Note

The structure of the sample XML file in Listing 24.1 intentionally mixes values represented in attributes and text nodes. A well-structured XML file would be more consistent; this one is designed to represent a varied set of parsing challenges. ∎

Figure 24.1 shows a sample application using E4X.

An application designed to demonstrate parsing of XML with E4X

Extracting data from XML objects

You can extract data from an XML object using an E4X expression that mixes various operators and data comparisons. In this section, I describe each operator and expression and provide code samples.

Tip

E4X expressions are an aspect of the ActionScript language and are 100 percent accurate only when used in their compiled form. Some programmers have tried to create a runtime E4X parser. For example, Michael Labriola's E4XParser component is described at this URL:

```
www.adobe.com/devnet/flex/articles/e4x.html
```

Runtime E4X parsers are designed to be used in applications where the structure and element/attribute names of an XML data packet aren't known at compile time. Use these with care and lots of testing, however; runtime E4X parsers might not handle all possible E4X expressions and occasionally return different results than when the same expression is evaluated in a compiled Flex application. ■

Using dot notation

As I described previously, an ActionScript XML object that's been created from XML notation refers to the structure's root element, not to the XML document itself. If an HTTPService component imports the XML document in Listing 24.1 and passes the ResultEvent object to an event handler function, the expression event.result refers to the <invoices> element. You typically save the returned data to a variable typed as XML and then use E4X expressions to extract data as needed:

```
[Bindable]
private var xInvoices:XML;
private function resultHandler(event:ResultEvent):void
{
   xInvoices = event.result as XML;
}
```

Starting at the root element, you then "walk" down the XML hierarchy one level at a time using simple dot notation and element names. So, for example, this code extracts all elements named <invoice> that are child elements of the root:

```
xReturn = xInvoices.invoice;
```

The returned XMLList looks like this:

```
<invoice>
  <customer>
    <firstname>Maria</firstname>
    <lastname>Smith</lastname>
  </customer>
  <items>
    ... all <lineitem> elements ...
  </items>
</invoice>
<invoice>
```

```
<customer>
  <firstname>John</firstname>
  <lastname>Jones</lastname>
</customer>
<items>
  ... all <lineitem> elements ...
</items>
</invoice>
```

Using array notation

When two or more elements have the same name at the same level of the XML hierarchy, you can refer to individual items as `Array` elements. As with all ActionScript array and index notation, indexing starts at 0. This statement extracts the second element named `invoice`:

```
xReturn = xInvoices.invoice[1];
```

The resulting XML object looks like this:

```
<invoice>
  <customer>
    <firstname>John</firstname>
    <lastname>Jones</lastname>
  </customer>
  <items>
    <lineitem price="7.41" quantity="84">Mouse</lineitem>
    <lineitem price="0.91" quantity="184">Mousepad</lineitem>
  </items>
</invoice>
```

After you've found an element using array notation, you can continue down the XML hierarchy with extended dot notation. This code extracts the customer element that's a child of the first invoice element:

```
xReturn = xInvoices.invoice[0].customer
```

The resulting XML object looks like this:

```
<customer>
  <firstname>Maria</firstname>
  <lastname>Smith</lastname>
</customer>
```

Tip

An E4X expression can return either an `XML` or `XMLList` object, depending on whether the expression returns a single node or more than one node. This can cause typecasting issues, because you can't use implicit coercion to automatically cast `XML` as `XMLList`, or vice versa.

The solution: Both classes are directly extended from the ActionScript `Object` class, so if you're using a single variable that will accept either type of result, cast it as `Object`:

```
var xReturn:Object;
```

The consequence of this approach is that as you code, you won't get as much assistance from Flash Builder and the compiler (in terms of code completion and compile-time syntax checking), but as long as you code correctly, everything works fine at runtime. ■

Using the descendant accessor operator

A single dot (.) causes the expression to look at direct child elements of the current XML object. You also can do a deep search of the XML hierarchy for elements by their names with the double-dot (..) descendant accessor operator. This enables you to search for all elements of the same name, regardless of their position or how many parent elements there are between the current element and the one you're looking for.

This code extracts all <customer> elements regardless of their position in the content:

```
xReturn = xInvoices..customer;
```

The resulting XMLList object looks like this:

```
<customer>
  <firstname>Maria</firstname>
  <lastname>Smith</lastname>
</customer>
<customer>
  <firstname>John</firstname>
  <lastname>Jones</lastname>
</customer>
```

Tip

When an E4X expression doesn't find any results, it doesn't return null or undefined as you might expect. Instead, it returns an empty XMLList object. You can check whether you got results by calling the object's length() method and inspecting the result:

```
if (xReturn.length() == 0)
{
    errorMessage = "No XML nodes were found";
}
```

The length() method is implemented in both the XML and XMLList classes, so you can safely call it without knowing in advance which type of object you're working with. ■

Filtering XML data with predicate expressions

A predicate expression enables you to filter data in an XML object, accomplishing tasks similar to the WHERE clause in an SQL statement. The predicate expression itself is an ActionScript comparison expression wrapped in parentheses. You append the predicate to the part of the E4X expression that indicates what data you want to return, separated with a dot operator.

This ActionScript extracts all <customer> elements that have a <lastname> child element matching the String value Jones:

```
xReturn = xInvoices..customer.(lastname=='Jones')
```

The resulting XML node looks like this:

```
<customer>
  <firstname>John</firstname>
  <lastname>Jones</lastname>
</customer>
```

Caution

Notice that the predicate expression uses the ActionScript == equality operator, not the single equals (=) assignment operator. If you use the assignment operator in this expression, it changes all `<lastname>` elements' text nodes to `Jones` and returns them as an `XMLList`. ∎

You also can filter on values stored as text nodes in elements. For example, the XML structure sets `<lineitem>` descriptions as text nodes:

```
<items>
  <lineitem price="21.41" quantity="4">Widget</lineitem>
  <lineitem price="2.11" quantity="14">Mouse</lineitem>
  <lineitem price="8.88" quantity="3">Wrench</lineitem>
</items>
```

You can refer to an element's `toString()` method in a predicate expression to return the node value instead of the XML node itself and then compare the text node's value to any other value. This code extracts all `<lineitem>` elements whose text nodes equal the `String` value `Mouse`:

```
xReturn = xInvoices..lineitem.(toString()=='Mouse');
```

The result is an `XMLList` that looks like this:

```
<lineitem price="2.11" quantity="14">Mouse</lineitem>
<lineitem price="7.41" quantity="84">Mouse</lineitem>
```

You also can compare values to an element's attributes. You refer to attributes using the @ character as a prefix to the attribute's name. This command extracts all `<lineitem>` elements where the price is less than 8:

```
xReturn = xInvoices..lineitem.(@price < 8);
```

The result is an `XMLList` that looks like this:

```
<lineitem price="2.11" quantity="14">Mouse</lineitem>
<lineitem price="7.41" quantity="84">Mouse</lineitem>
<lineitem price="0.91" quantity="184">Mousepad</lineitem>
```

When you compare values in an E4X expression, typecasting of literal numeric expressions depends on whether you wrap the expression in quotation marks. This version of the expression would execute a `String`-based filter, because the literal value is wrapped in quotation marks:

```
xReturn = xInvoices..lineitem.(@price < '8');
```

The resulting XMLList includes all <lineitem> elements where the first character of the price attribute comes before the character "8" in terms of alphanumeric sorting:

```
<lineitem price="21.41" quantity="4">Widget</lineitem>
<lineitem price="2.11" quantity="14">Mouse</lineitem>
<lineitem price="7.41" quantity="84">Mouse</lineitem>
<lineitem price="0.91" quantity="184">Mousepad</lineitem>
```

This pattern follows the JavaScript standard of typecasting literal values based on how they're expressed. A numeric literal with quotation marks is actually a String, while the same value without the quotation marks is a Number.

The application in Listing 24.2 tests each of the expressions described in this section and returns the result to a TextArea control. It uses an ActionScript helper class that contains all the expressions being tested.

LISTING 24.2

A demo application for testing E4X expressions

```
<?xml version="1.0" encoding="utf-8"?>
<s:Application xmlns:fx="http://ns.adobe.com/mxml/2009"
  xmlns:s="library://ns.adobe.com/flex/spark"
  xmlns:mx="library://ns.adobe.com/flex/mx"
  creationComplete="app_creationCompleteHandler()">
<s:layout>
  <s:HorizontalLayout/>
</s:layout>
<fx:Script>
  <![CDATA[
    import helpers.E4XParsingHelper;
    import mx.rpc.events.ResultEvent;
    import mx.collections.ArrayCollection;

    [Bindable]
    private var acExpressions:ArrayCollection;
    [Bindable]
    private var xInvoices:XML;
    private function app_creationCompleteHandler():void
    {
      invoiceService.send();
      acExpressions = new ArrayCollection(
        E4XParsingHelper.getExpressionsArray());
      XML.prettyIndent=2;
    }
    private function resultHandler(event:ResultEvent):void
    {
```

```
          xInvoices = event.result as XML;
        }
        private function evaluate():void
        {
          var xReturn:Object = E4XParsingHelper.evalE4X(xInvoices,
            expList.selectedIndex);
          if (xReturn.length() == 0)
          {
            resultString.text = "No XML nodes were found";
          }
          else
          {
            resultString.text = xReturn.toXMLString();
          }
        }
      }
    ]]>
  </fx:Script>
  <fx:Declarations>
    <s:HTTPService id="invoiceService"
      url="data/invoices.xml" resultFormat="e4x"
      result="resultHandler(event)"/>
  </fx:Declarations>
  <mx:VDividedBox width="50%" height="100%">
    <s:Panel title="XML being searched:" width="100%" height="100%">
      <s:TextArea width="100%" height="100%" editable="false"
        text="{xInvoices.toXMLString()}"/>
    </s:Panel>
    <s:Panel id="expListPanel" title="Select an E4X expression:"
      width="100%" height="100%" >
      <s:List id="expList" dataProvider="{acExpressions}"
        width="100%" change="evaluate()"/>
    </s:Panel>
  </mx:VDividedBox>
  <s:Panel title="Result as an XML String" height="100%" width="100%">
    <s:TextArea width="100%" height="100%" id="resultString"/>
  </s:Panel>
</s:Application>
```

On the Web

The code in Listing 24.2 is available in the Web site files as `E4XParsing.xml` in the default package in the `src` **folder of the** `chapter24` **project.** ■

The helper E4XParsingHelper class in Listing 24.3 contains all the test expressions in two forms: The Array of Strings is used by the demo application to display the expressions being evaluated, while the static evalE4X() method executes precompiled E4X expressions as requested by the user.

LISTING 24.3

The E4XParsingHelper class, containing all expressions being tested in the demo application

```
package helpers
{
  public class E4XParsingHelper
  {
    public var arExpressions:Array;
    public static function getExpressionsArray():Array
    {
      var arExpressions:Array = new Array();
      arExpressions.push("xInvoices.invoice");
      arExpressions.push("xInvoices.invoice[1]");
      arExpressions.push("xInvoices.invoice[0].customer");
      arExpressions.push("xInvoices..customer");
      arExpressions.push("xInvoices..customer.(lastname=='Jones')");
      arExpressions.push("xInvoices..lineitem.(toString()=='Mouse')");
      arExpressions.push("xInvoices..lineitem.(@price < 8)");
      arExpressions.push("xInvoices..lineitem.(@price < '8')");
      return arExpressions;
    }
    public static function evalE4X(xInvoices:XML, expIndex:int):Object
    {
      switch (expIndex)
      {
        case 0: return xInvoices.invoice;
        case 1: return xInvoices.invoice[1];
        case 2: return xInvoices.invoice[0].customer;
        case 3: return xInvoices..customer;
        case 4: return xInvoices..customer.(lastname=='Jones');
        case 5: return xInvoices..lineitem.(toString()=='Mouse');
        case 6: return xInvoices..lineitem.(@price < 8);
        case 7: return xInvoices..lineitem.(@price < '8');
        default: return new XMLList();
      }
    }
  }
}
```

On the Web

The code in Listing 24.3 is available in the Web site files as `E4XParsingHelper.as` in the `helpers` package of the `chapter24` project. ■

Tip

You can add new test expressions to the helper class by adding a new item to the `Array` in the `get ExpressionsArray()` method and adding an equivalent case statement in the `evalE4X()` method. ■

Modifying data in XML objects

You can use E4X expressions to add, remove, and modify elements in an XML object. For example, if an XML object starts with a simple root element, it's a simple matter to add both elements and attributes and to change the values of existing attributes and text nodes.

Changing existing values

You can change existing values in an XML object by using an E4X expression to identify one or more XML nodes and then assign a new value to them. For example, the XML structure that was used as a starting point in the preceding section has a root element with child `<invoice>` elements. Each `invoice` has `customer.firstname` and `customer.lastname` nodes.

The following code changes the `firstname` of the first invoice's customer to a new value of "Harry":

```
xInvoices.invoice[0].customer.firstname='Harry';
```

After modification, the `<customer>` element for the first `<invoice>` looks like this:

```
<customer>
  <firstname>Harry</firstname>
  <lastname>Smith</lastname>
</customer>
```

You also can modify existing attribute values by referring to the attribute name with the @ character as a prefix. This code changes the price attribute of the first `<lineitem>` in the first `<invoice>`:

```
xInvoices.invoice[0].items.lineitem[0].@price=12.50;
```

The `<lineitem>` element looks like this after the code has been executed:

```
<lineitem price="12.5" quantity="4">Widget</lineitem>
```

Notice that the `String` representation of the value is truncated to remove the trailing zero. That's because with no quotation marks around the numeric value on the right side of the assignment operator, it's first evaluated as a `Number` and then saved as a `String` in the XML. You can force formatting of numeric values by wrapping quotation marks around the literal expression:

```
xInvoices.invoice[0].items.lineitem[0].@price='12.50';
```

The modified `<lineitem>` element now retains the formatting, as shown here:

```
<lineitem price="12.50" quantity="4">Widget</lineitem>
```

Adding elements and attributes

The same E4X syntax that modifies existing elements and attributes can be used to add new nodes. Simply put, if a node to which you refer in an assignment doesn't already exist, the assignment creates it.

This command adds a new `<city>` element to the first `<customer>` element and sets its value:

```
xInvoices.invoice[0].customer.city='Seattle';
```

After the code has been executed, the resulting <customer> element looks like this:

```
<customer>
  <firstname>Maria</firstname>
  <lastname>Smith</lastname>
  <city>Seattle</city>
</customer>
```

The same approach works with attributes. This command adds an inStock attribute to the first <lineitem> in the first invoice:

```
xInvoices.invoice[0].items.lineitem[0].@inStock=true
```

After the code is executed, the modified <lineitem> element looks like this:

```
<lineitem price="21.41" quantity="4" inStock="true">Widget</lineitem>
```

Caution

You can make an assignment to only one XML object at a time. If the E4X expression on the left side of an assignment identifies more than one XML element, a runtime error occurs. ∎

Deleting elements and attributes

The delete operator is used to remove data from an XML object at runtime. You start with the delete operator at the beginning of the statement and follow it with an E4X expression that identified the node you want to remove.

This command removes the second invoice in the XML object:

```
delete xInvoices.invoice[1];
```

In some cases, you can remove whole sets of elements. This command empties the items element of the first invoice:

```
delete xInvoices.invoice[0].items.lineitem;
```

After the code is executed, the first <invoice> looks like this:

```
<invoice>
  <customer>
    <firstname>Maria</firstname>
    <lastname>Smith</lastname>
  </customer>
  <items/>
</invoice>
```

You can also remove attributes with the delete operator. This code removes the quantity attribute from the first <lineitem> in the first <invoice>.

```
delete xInvoices.invoice[0].items.lineitem[0].@quantity;
```

After the code is executed, the modified `<lineitem>` element looks like this:

```
<lineitem price="21.41">Widget</lineitem>
```

Tip

All E4X expressions that modify XML **objects return a reference to the modified XML. For example, this statement both modifies an** XML **object and returns a reference to the modified data:**

```
var xNew:XML = xInvoices.invoice[0].customer.city='Seattle'; ∎
```

The application in Listing 24.4 uses a helper class, `E4XChangingHelper`, to demonstrate each of the expressions described in this section.

LISTING 24.4

An application that demonstrates modifying data with E4X

```
<?xml version="1.0" encoding="utf-8"?>
<s:Application xmlns:fx="http://ns.adobe.com/mxml/2009"
  xmlns:s="library://ns.adobe.com/flex/spark"
  xmlns:mx="library://ns.adobe.com/flex/mx"
  creationComplete="initApp()">
  <s:layout>
    <s:HorizontalLayout/>
  </s:layout>
  <fx:Script>
    <![CDATA[
      import helpers.E4XChangingHelper;
      import mx.rpc.events.ResultEvent;
      import mx.collections.ArrayCollection;
      [Bindable]
      private var acExpressions:ArrayCollection;
      [Bindable]
      private var xInvoices:XML;
      private function initApp():void
      {
        invoiceService.send();
        acExpressions = new ArrayCollection(
          E4XChangingHelper.getExpressionsArray());
        XML.prettyIndent=2;
      }
      private function resultHandler(event:ResultEvent):void
      {
        xInvoices = event.result as XML;
      }
      private function evaluate():void
      {
        var tempXML:XML = new XML(xInvoices.toXMLString());
       E4XChangingHelper.evalE4X(tempXML, expList.selectedIndex);
```

continued

LISTING 24.4 *(continued)*

```
            resultString.text = tempXML.toXMLString();
        }
    ]]>
  </fx:Script>
  <fx:Declarations>
    <mx:HTTPService id="invoiceService"
      url="data/invoices.xml" resultFormat="e4x"
      result="resultHandler(event)"/>
  </fx:Declarations>
  <mx:VDividedBox width="50%" height="100%">
    <s:Panel title="XML being searched:" width="100%" height="100%">
      <s:TextArea width="100%" height="100%" editable="false"
        text="{xInvoices.toXMLString()}"/>
    </s:Panel>
    <s:Panel id="expListPanel" title="Select an E4X expression:"
      width="100%" height="100%" >
      <mx:List id="expList" dataProvider="{acExpressions}"
        width="100%" rowCount="{acExpressions.length}"
        change="evaluate()"/>
    </s:Panel>
  </mx:VDividedBox>
  <s:Panel title="Result as an XML String" height="100%" width="50%">
    <s:TextArea width="100%" height="100%" id="resultString"/>
  </s:Panel>
</s:Application>
```

On the Web

The code in Listing 24.4 is available in the Web site files as `E4XChanging.mxml` in the default package in the `src` folder of the `chapter24` project. ∎

The ActionScript helper class in Listing 24.5 contains all the expressions that the application is designed to evaluate.

LISTING 24.5

A helper class containing expressions for modifying XML data

```
package helpers
{
  public class E4XChangingHelper
  {
    public var arExpressions:Array;

    public static function getExpressionsArray():Array
    {
      var arExpressions:Array = new Array();
```

```
      arExpressions.push(
        "xInvoices.invoice[0].customer.firstname='Harry'");
      arExpressions.push(
        "xInvoices.invoice[0].items.lineitem[0].@price=12.50");
      arExpressions.push(
        "xInvoices.invoice[0].items.lineitem[0].@price='12.50'");
      arExpressions.push(
        "xInvoices.invoice[0].customer.city='Seattle'");
      arExpressions.push(
        "xInvoices.invoice[0].items.lineitem[0].@inStock=true");
      arExpressions.push(
        "delete xInvoices.invoice[1]");
      arExpressions.push(
        "delete xInvoices.invoice[0].items.lineitem");
      arExpressions.push(
        "delete xInvoices.invoice[0].items.lineitem[0].@quantity");
      return arExpressions;
    }
    public static function evalE4X(xInvoices:XML, expIndex:int):void
    {
      switch (expIndex)
      {
        case 0:
          xInvoices.invoice[0].customer.firstname='Harry';
          break;
        case 1:
          xInvoices.invoice[0].items.lineitem[0].@price=12.50;
          break;
        case 2:
          xInvoices.invoice[0].items.lineitem[0].@price='12.50';
          break;
        case 3:
          xInvoices.invoice[0].customer.city='Seattle';
          break;
        case 4:
          xInvoices.invoice[0].items.lineitem[0].@inStock=true;
          break;
        case 5:
          delete xInvoices.invoice[1];
          break;
        case 6:
          delete xInvoices.invoice[0].items.lineitem;
          break;
        case 7:
          delete xInvoices.invoice[0].items.lineitem[0].@quantity;
          break;
      }
    }
  }
}
```

On the Web

The code in Listing 24.5 is available in the Web site files as `E4XPChangingHelper.as` in the `helpers` package of the `chapter24` project. ∎

Tip

You can add new test expressions to the helper class by adding a new item to the `Array` in the `getExpressionsArray()` method and adding an equivalent case statement in the `evalE4X()` method. ∎

Working with Namespaces

XML namespaces constitute a simple way to distinguish and group element and attribute names as members of groups, essentially allowing for the use of different "flavors" of XML in a single document. For example, MXML uses a default namespace to identify the FX elements of the MXML language to the Flex compiler (`http://ns.adobe.com/mxml/2009`), other namespaces for MX and Spark components, and enables you to create your own custom namespaces to identify directories as packages containing classes and components, such as in the declaration `xmlns:forms="forms.*"`.

E4X enables you to incorporate namespace notation into expressions that identify elements for extraction or modification. There are two basic steps to using namespaces in E4X:

1. Create a `namespace` object that represents a namespace in the XML content you're parsing or modifying.

2. Refer to the `namespace` object as a prefix for the elements or attributes you want to locate.

The following XML packet uses three namespaces to distinguish elements that share a name:

```
private var xTravel:XML =
<travel
  xmlns:train="http://www.bardotech.com/train"
  xmlns:plane="http://www.bardotech.com/airplane"
  xmlns:car="http://www.bardotech.com/automobile">
  <journey>
    <train:traveltime>8 hours</train:traveltime>
    <plane:traveltime>1 hour</plane:traveltime>
    <car:traveltime>3 days</car:traveltime>
  </journey>
</travel>
```

To extract a `<traveltime>` element and distinguish it from the other elements of the same name, first declare namespace objects that are mapped to the namespaces in the XML data. You can do this two ways.

If you want to identify namespaces by their URI, use the ActionScript's `namespace` keyword to create a namespace object by the URI:

```
private namespace train = "http://www.bardotech.com/train";
private namespace plane = «http://www.bardotech.com/airplane»;
private namespace car = "http://www.bardotech.com/automobile";
```

Alternatively, if you want to identify namespaces by their prefixes as assigned in the XML structure, create variables typed as the `Namespace` class. Assign each namespace by calling the `XML` object's `namespace()` method and passing the selected namespace prefix:

```
private var train:Namespace = xTravel.namespace("train");
private var plane:Namespace = xTravel.namespace("plane");
private var car:Namespace = xTravel.namespace("car");
```

Note

The `Namespace` class is a top-level Flash Player class, meaning that it isn't a member of any particular package and can be used without requiring an `import` statement. ■

Tip

Notice that the names of the ActionScript `namespace` objects match the namespace prefixes in the XML content. This isn't technically necessary; as long as the namespace Uniform Resource Identifier (URI) or prefix match, XML elements will be identified correctly. But consistency between data and code notation certainly doesn't hurt. ■

After the `namespace` objects have been declared, you can use them as element and attribute prefixes in E4X expressions. The namespace object's name is separated from the element or attribute name with the `::` operator to qualify the node as being a member of the selected namespace.

The following code extracts the `<traveltime>` element that's qualified with the `plane` namespace:

```
traveltime = xTravel.journey.plane::traveltime;
```

The application in Listing 24.6 declares an XML structure and then enables the user to indicate which of the three `<traveltime>` values she wants to see.

LISTING 24.6

Using XML namespaces in E4X

```
<?xml version="1.0" encoding="utf-8"?>
<s:Application xmlns:fx="http://ns.adobe.com/mxml/2009"
  xmlns:s="library://ns.adobe.com/flex/spark"
  xmlns:mx="library://ns.adobe.com/flex/mx">
```

continued

LISTING 24.6 *(continued)*

```
<s:layout>
  <s:VerticalLayout horizontalAlign="center" paddingTop="20"/>
</s:layout>
<fx:Style>
  @namespace s "library://ns.adobe.com/flex/spark";
  @namespace mx "library://ns.adobe.com/flex/mx";

  s|RadioButton {
    font-size:12;
    font-weight:bold;
  }
</fx:Style>
<fx:Declarations>
  <s:RadioButtonGroup id="vehicleGroup" itemClick="getTravelTime()"/>
</fx:Declarations>
<fx:Script>
  <![CDATA[
    [Bindable]
    private var travelTime:String="Choose a vehicle";
    private var xTravel:XML =
      <travel
        xmlns:train="http://www.bardotech.com/train"
        xmlns:plane="http://www.bardotech.com/airplane"
        xmlns:car="http://www.bardotech.com/automobile">
        <journey>
          <train:traveltime>8 hours</train:traveltime>
          <plane:traveltime>1 hour</plane:traveltime>
          <car:traveltime>3 days</car:traveltime>
        </journey>
      </travel>
    private namespace train = "http://www.bardotech.com/train";
    private namespace plane = "http://www.bardotech.com/airplane";
    private namespace car = "http://www.bardotech.com/automobile";
    private function getTravelTime():void
    {
      var vehicle:String = vehicleGroup.selectedValue as String;
      switch (vehicle)
      {
        case "plane":
          travelTime = xTravel.journey.plane::traveltime;
          break;
        case "train":
          travelTime = xTravel.journey.train::traveltime;
          break;
        case "car":
          travelTime = xTravel.journey.car::traveltime;
      }
    }
```

```
    ]]>
  </fx:Script>
  <s:Panel title="Select a vehicle" width="135">
    <s:layout>
      <s:VerticalLayout paddingBottom="5" paddingLeft="5"
        paddingRight="5" paddingTop="5"/>
    </s:layout>
    <s:RadioButton label="Plane" value="plane"
      groupName="vehicleGroup"/>
    <s:RadioButton label="Train" value="train"
      groupName="vehicleGroup"/>
    <s:RadioButton label="Automobile" value="car"
      groupName="vehicleGroup"/>
    <s:controlBarContent>
      <s:Label text="{travelTime}"/>
    </s:controlBarContent>
  </s:Panel>
</s:Application>
```

On the Web

The code in Listing 24.6 is available in the Web site files as `E4XWithNamespaces.mxml` **in the default package in the** `src` **folder of the** `chapter24` **project.** ■

Figure 24.2 shows the resulting application, displaying the results of an E4X expression with namespaces to the user.

An application using E4X with namespaces

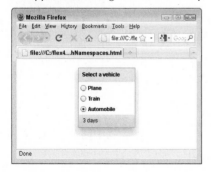

Summary

In this chapter, I described how to use E4X to parse and modify data stored in XML objects in Flex application memory at runtime. You learned the following:

- E4X stands for EcmaScript for XML.

- E4X is a standard of Ecma International that is implemented in ActionScript 3 and in certain other languages and platforms.

- E4X enables you to parse, extract, and modify XML-based data at runtime with simple, concise expressions.

- E4X is a part of the compiled ActionScript language and is not designed for runtime evaluation of arbitrary expressions.

- Array-style syntax is combined with various operators to "walk" the XML hierarchy.

- The `delete` operator removes elements and attributes at runtime.

- XML with namespaces can be accurately parsed using namespace objects and the namespace qualification operator (`::`).

Part IV

Integrating Flex Applications with Application Servers

IN THIS PART

Chapter 25
Working with SOAP-Based
Web Services

Chapter 26
Integrating Flex Applications
with BlazeDS and Java

Chapter 27
Using the Message Service
with BlazeDS

Chapter 28
Integrating Flex Applications
with ColdFusion

Chapter 29
Integrating Flex Applications
with PHP

Working with SOAP-Based Web Services

In Chapter 23, I described the use of the Flex `HTTPService` component to make requests and handle responses from Web resources formatted as arbitrary XML data structures. The strength of REST (Representational State Transfer) and generic XML is that you can create and use Web services that employ any arbitrary data structure. The potential weakness of this strategy is that each application must have specific knowledge of the particular XML structure being used.

SOAP-based Web services take a different approach: They employ industry-standard XML languages to format both messages and metadata. The SOAP language itself is used to format requests and responses between a client and a server, while WSDL (Web Services Description Language) is used to declare to Web service consumers the structure and capabilities of Web service operations.

Note

The term SOAP started as an acronym for Simple Object Access Protocol. Starting with version 1.2, it became simply SOAP. ∎

The strength of SOAP-based Web services lies in their industry-level standardization and their capability to accept strongly typed parameters and return values in a way that RESTful operations typically can't. Their weakness lies in the verbose nature of the messages that are exchanged between the client and the server. Because SOAP-based Web services send and receive data in XML, the message packets are significantly larger than the same data encoded in AMF (Action Message Format; the binary format used by the `RemoteObject` class).

IN THIS CHAPTER

Understanding SOAP

Understanding WSDL

Using the `WebService` component

Handling `WebService` component events

Calling Web service operations and displaying data with Flash Builder data connections

SOAP servers and clients are designed to be interoperable, so that you can easily call functions (known in SOAP as *operations*) from objects on remote servers without knowing what platform is hosting the service or what programming language was used to develop it, because many support SOAP. And, as data is passed between client and server, its data types are maintained as long as both tiers of the application use compatible types.

Web Resource

The SOAP and WSDL recommendations are managed by the World Wide Web Consortium (W3C), which also manages the recommendations for XML, HTML, and HTTP. The most recent recommendations are available at `www.w3.org/TR/soap` **and** `www.w3.org/TR/wsdl`.

For a history of SOAP, check out Dave Winer's "Dave's History of SOAP" at `www.xmlrpc.com/stories/storyReader$555` **and Don Box's "A Brief History of SOAP" at** `http://webservices.xml.com/pub/a/ws/2001/04/04/soap.html`. ■

On the Web

To use the sample code for this chapter, import the `chapter25.fxp` **project from the Web site files into any folder on your disk. The sample Web service files are built in the CFML (ColdFusion Markup Language) programming language for use with Adobe ColdFusion and should work with either ColdFusion 8 or 9. You can download the free developer edition of ColdFusion from** `www.adobe.com/products/coldfusion`. ■

Understanding SOAP

SOAP is an XML language that's used to format messages sent between clients and servers in RPC (Remote Procedure Call)–style applications. Its purpose is to allow client applications to call functions of remote objects that are defined and hosted in a server-based environment.

When a remote operation is called from a SOAP client application, the request message is encoded in the SOAP language as an XML package with a root element named `<Envelope>`. The following SOAP packet was generated by a Flex application calling a remote operation named `helloWorld`:

```
<SOAP-ENV:Envelope
 xmlns:SOAP-ENV="http://schemas.xmlsoap.org/soap/envelope/"
 xmlns:xsd="http://www.w3.org/2001/XMLSchema"
 xmlns:xsi="http://www.w3.org/2001/XMLSchema-instance">
  <SOAP-ENV:Body
   SOAP-ENV:encodingStyle=
     "http://schemas.xmlsoap.org/soap/encoding/">
   <intf:helloWorld xmlns:intf="http://flex4bible"/>
  </SOAP-ENV:Body>
</SOAP-ENV:Envelope>
```

When the response comes back from the server, it's encoded in the same XML language. The following SOAP response was generated by a Web service written in CFML and hosted by Adobe ColdFusion:

```
<?xml version="1.0" encoding="utf-8"?>
<soapenv:Envelope
  xmlns:soapenv="http://schemas.xmlsoap.org/soap/envelope/"
  xmlns:xsd="http://www.w3.org/2001/XMLSchema"
  xmlns:xsi="http://www.w3.org/2001/XMLSchema-instance">
 <soapenv:Body>
  <ns1:helloWorldResponse
   soapenv:encodingStyle="http://schemas.xmlsoap.org/soap/encoding/"
   xmlns:ns1="http://flex4bible">
   <helloWorldReturn
     xsi:type="xsd:string">Hello World</helloWorldReturn>
  </ns1:helloWorldResponse>
 </soapenv:Body>
</soapenv:Envelope>
```

If you compare the outgoing and incoming SOAP data packets, you'll see that they use the same XML namespace, http://schemas.xmlsoap.org/soap/envelope/, to define the elements and attributes of the SOAP language. They differ in certain minor details, such as the capitalization of namespace prefixes (Flex uses SOAP-ENV, while ColdFusion uses soap-env), but they agree on the important elements of Web-based communications.

The magic of SOAP, however, is that you don't need to know these details. SOAP-based client and server software is responsible for creating an abstraction layer that enables the developer to make calls to remote operations using code that's only minimally different from that used to call local methods.

A SOAP-based Web service can be built with many different programming languages and hosted on many operating systems. To host a service, you need an application server that knows how to read and write SOAP message packets. Similarly, the client application uses an implementation of SOAP that handles the serialization and deserialization of the SOAP message packets as data is sent and received.

Some SOAP-based software packages implement both server and client functionality. For example, Apache's Axis (http://ws.apache.org/axis/) is a popular Java-based implementation of SOAP that implements client and server functionality and can be used freely with any Java-based application. Other implementations, such as the Flex SDK's WebService component, include only a SOAP client.

This chapter describes how to use the WebService component to make calls to SOAP-based Web services. While the examples in this chapter are written against a Web service built and hosted in Adobe ColdFusion, Flex applications are interoperable with many SOAP server implementations. For example:

- Microsoft ASP.NET implements SOAP as a feature named XML Web Services.

- Apache Axis includes implementations of SOAP for client-side and server-side Java-based applications on most operating systems.

- Adobe ColdFusion (used in this chapter) implements SOAP as an option for calling ColdFusion Component (CFC) functions and uses the <cfinvoke> command to call functions from most SOAP servers. The most recent versions, ColdFusion 8 and 9, run on Windows, Mac OS X, Linux, Solaris, and AIX.

- Many open-source and built-in implementations of SOAP also are available for various scripting languages, including PHP, Python, and Ruby.

Note

Whenever possible, most developers prefer to use the `RemoteObject` component to integrate Flex applications with ColdFusion, Java-based applications like LiveCycle Data Services and BlazeDS, and other non-Adobe products, such as OpenAMF, AMFPHP, and WebOrb, that support the Remoting Service architecture and binary AMF. This is primarily due to the performance advantage you get with AMF.

SOAP, while supporting strongly defined data types, is formatted as XML and generates much larger data packets than AMF-enabled architectures. Web service integration tends to be used for integration with third-party data vendors who support the SOAP standard or with application servers with particularly strong SOAP support, such as ASP.NET. ∎

Understanding WSDL

Web Services Description Language (WSDL) is an XML language that's used to declare to Web service consumers the structure and capabilities of Web service operations. In order to consume a Web service, a Flex application must be able to read and parse a WSDL file at runtime that tells the `WebService` component everything it needs to know in order to successfully call the service's operations.

WSDL is a somewhat complex language, but many SOAP server implementations, including Apache Axis, ASP.NET's XML Web Services, and ColdFusion, can dynamically generate a WSDL file for a native class exposed as a Web service in response to an HTTP request from a client application. For all these application servers, you generate a WSDL file by sending an HTTP request from a client application to the service URL and appending a query string variable named `wsdl`.

Take as an example a ColdFusion Component (CFC) named `SoapService.cfc` that's designed to be called as a Web service. If the CFC is stored in a subfolder of the Web root named `services`, and ColdFusion is installed on your local server and connected to a Web server running on the default port 80, the CFC's URL would be:

```
http://localhost/services/SoapService.cfc
```

To generate the WSDL file, append a query string parameter named `wsdl`:

```
http://localhost/services/SoapService.cfc?wsdl
```

ColdFusion responds by generating the WSDL content and returning it to the requesting application. Similar patterns are used by other common SOAP server applications. This is an example of a WSDL URI for Apache Axis:

```
http://localhost/myJEEApp/services/MyWebService?wsdl
```

And this is an example for ASP.NET:

```
http://localhost/myDotNetApp/MyWebService.asmx?wsdl
```

Note

The address of the WSDL document on the Web is referred to in Flash Builder and the Flex documentation as the WSDL URI (Uniform Resource Identifier). ■

Web Resource

The WSDL language is managed by the W3C. The current recommendation is available at `www.w3.org/TR/` `wsdl.` ■

WSDL is standardized across vendors and application servers and usually looks pretty much the same regardless of its generating server software. The following sample WSDL page was generated by ColdFusion for a CFC with a single `helloWorld()` operation:

```
<?xml version="1.0" encoding="UTF-8"?>
<wsdl:definitions targetNamespace="http://flex4bible"
  xmlns:apachesoap="http://xml.apache.org/xml-soap"
  xmlns:impl="http://flex4bible" xmlns:intf="http://flex4bible"
  xmlns:soapenc="http://schemas.xmlsoap.org/soap/encoding/"
  xmlns:tns1="http://rpc.xml.coldfusion"
  xmlns:wsdl="http://schemas.xmlsoap.org/wsdl/"
  xmlns:wsdlsoap="http://schemas.xmlsoap.org/wsdl/soap/"
  xmlns:xsd="http://www.w3.org/2001/XMLSchema">
<!--WSDL created by ColdFusion version 8,0,0,176276-->
 <wsdl:types>
  <schema targetNamespace="http://rpc.xml.coldfusion"
    xmlns="http://www.w3.org/2001/XMLSchema">
   <import namespace="http://schemas.xmlsoap.org/soap/encoding/"/>
   <complexType name=»CFCInvocationException»>
    <sequence/>
   </complexType>
  </schema>
 </wsdl:types>
<wsdl:message name=»CFCInvocationException»>
   <wsdl:part name=»fault» type=»tns1:CFCInvocationException»/>
 </wsdl:message>
 <wsdl:message name=»helloWorldResponse»>
   <wsdl:part name=»helloWorldReturn» type=»xsd:string»/>
 </wsdl:message>
 <wsdl:message name=»helloWorldRequest»>
 </wsdl:message>
 <wsdl:portType name=»SoapService»>
    <wsdl:operation name=»helloWorld»>
       <wsdl:input message=»impl:helloWorldRequest»
         name=»helloWorldRequest»/>
       <wsdl:output message=»impl:helloWorldResponse»
         name=»helloWorldResponse»/>
```

```
                <wsdl:fault message=»impl:CFCInvocationException»
                   name=»CFCInvocationException»/>
                </wsdl:operation>
        </wsdl:portType>
        <wsdl:binding name=»SoapService.cfcSoapBinding»
           type=»impl:SoapService»>
           <wsdlsoap:binding style=»rpc»
              transport=»http://schemas.xmlsoap.org/soap/http»/>
              <wsdl:operation name=»helloWorld»>
                <wsdlsoap:operation soapAction=»»/>
                <wsdl:input name=»helloWorldRequest»>
                  <wsdlsoap:body
                     encodingStyle=»http://schemas.xmlsoap.org/soap/encoding/»
                     namespace=»http://flex4bible» use=»encoded»/>
                </wsdl:input>
                <wsdl:output name=»helloWorldResponse»>
                   <wsdlsoap:body
                     encodingStyle=»http://schemas.xmlsoap.org/soap/encoding/»
                     namespace=»http://flex4bible» use=»encoded»/>
                </wsdl:output>
                <wsdl:fault name=»CFCInvocationException»>
                   <wsdlsoap:fault
                     encodingStyle=»http://schemas.xmlsoap.org/soap/encoding/»
                     name=»CFCInvocationException»
                     namespace=»http://flex4bible» use=»encoded»/>
                </wsdl:fault>
             </wsdl:operation>
          </wsdl:binding>
          <wsdl:service name=»SoapServiceService»>
        <wsdl:documentation xmlns:wsdl=»http://schemas.xmlsoap.org/wsdl/»>
           A ColdFusion web service built as a CFC
        </wsdl:documentation>
        <wsdl:port binding=»impl:SoapService.cfcSoapBinding»
           name=»SoapService.cfc»>
          <wsdlsoap:address
             location=»http://localhost:8500/flex4bible/SoapService.cfc»/>
          </wsdl:port>
        </wsdl:service>
      </wsdl:definitions>
```

The details of the WSDL language are beyond the scope of this book, but one thing is clear from this example: WSDL isn't designed to be human readable (at least without serious study). Its purpose is to inform a software-based Web service consumer (in this case, a Flex client application) about a service's metadata. It includes detailed information about an operation's name, what parameters and data types the operation expects, what type of data is returned in the operation's response, and where the request to call the operation should be sent at runtime.

Web Resource

You can find many tutorials on WSDL on the Web. For one that's concise, check out `http://msdn2.`
`microsoft.com/en-us/library/ms996486.aspx.` ■

Using the WebService Component

In this section, I describe how to use the `WebService` component to make calls to Web service functions and handle the resulting data. The sample applications call Web services written in CFML and hosted on ColdFusion 8, so if you want to run the sample applications on your own system, you'll first need to download and install ColdFusion 8 from Adobe Systems.

Installing ColdFusion

ColdFusion is available for download from `www.adobe.com/products/coldfusion/` and can be installed and run in "developer" mode on your local system without any license fees. Versions are available for Windows, Mac OS X, and other operating systems.

Tip

The Web service examples in this chapter don't have any database dependencies, so they should run success-fully on any of ColdFusion's supported operating systems. The code should run successfully in either ColdFusion 8 or ColdFusion 9. ∎

After installing ColdFusion, follow these steps to set up the sample Web service included with the Flex project:

1. **Create a folder under the ColdFusion server's Web root named** `flex4bible`. The default Web root folder in this environment is `C:\ColdFusion9\wwwroot` on Windows and `/Applications/ColdFusion9/wwwroot` on Mac OS X.

2. **Locate the files and directories in the ColdFusionFiles folder within the** `chapter25` **project.**

3. **Copy and paste the files into the new** `flex4bible` **folder under the ColdFusion Web root.**

You should have these files and directories:

- `Application.cfc`. A file that controls the ColdFusion application's configuration.
- `data`. A folder containing an XML file that represents the data used in the Web service.
- `SoapService.cfc`. The Web service file.
- `TestPage.cfm`. A ColdFusion page you can call from a browser to make sure the code works before using it as a Web service.

Note

The Flex application examples for this chapter assume that ColdFusion has been installed with the "develop-ment" Web server, which runs with port 8500. A request to the CFC in this environment would be sent to `http://localhost:8500/flex4bible/SoapService.cfc?wsdl`. If you have the Web service com-ponent installed in another folder or if ColdFusion is running on another port, you'll need to modify the exam-ple applications as necessary to point to the correct port and location. ∎

Creating a WebService object

As with the `HTTPService` component that was described in Chapter 23, the `WebService` component can be instantiated with either MXML or ActionScript code. The component's `wsdl` property is a `String` value that contains the URL from which the service's WSDL can be retrieved at runtime.

To create a `WebService` object in MXML, declare it with a unique `id` and set its `wsdl` property as in this example:

```
<s:WebService id="myService"
   wsdl="http://localhost:8500/flex4bible/SoapService.cfc?wsdl"/>
```

New Feature

In Flex 4 applications, the `<s:WebService>` tag must be placed within the `<fxDeclarations>` element. ■

Tip

As with the `HTTPService` component, if a Web-based Flex application and a Web service it calls are hosted in the same domain, you can use a relative URL in the `wsdl` property. In this example, you could shorten the `wsdl` property to `/flex4bible/SoapService.cfc?wsdl`. ■

To declare a `WebService` object in ActionScript, you can create the object and then set its `wsdl` property in a separate statement:

```
var myService:WebService = new WebService();
myService.wsdl =
   "http://localhost:8500/flex4bible/SoapService.cfc?wsdl"
```

Alternatively, you can pass the `wsdl` location into the `WebService` constructor method:

```
var myService:WebService = new WebService(
   "http://localhost:8500/flex4bible/SoapService.cfc?wsdl");
```

Loading the WSDL content

When you use MXML to declare a `WebService` object, it requests and downloads the WSDL content from the `wsdl` location upon object construction (usually as the application starts up). When using ActionScript code to declare the `WebService` object, you have to explicitly load the WSDL content by calling the object's `loadWSDL()` method. If the `wsdl` property is already set, you can call `loadWSDL()` without any arguments:

```
var myService:WebService = new WebService(
   "http://localhost:8500/flex4bible/SoapService.cfc?wsdl");
myService.loadWSDL();
```

Another approach is to pass the `wsdl` location into `loadWSDL()` and handle both tasks at the same time:

```
var myService:WebService = new WebService();
myService.loadWSDL(
  "http://localhost:8500/flex4bible/SoapService.cfc?wsdl");
```

Invoking an operation

To invoke an operation, you call it as if the operation is a method of the `WebService` object, as follows:

```
myService.helloWorld();
```

Handling the load event

Whether you use ActionScript or MXML to declare a `WebService` object, it dispatches an event named `load` when the WSDL content has been successfully retrieved and parsed. The `WebService` object can make calls to Web service operations only after this task is complete, so it's common to make initial calls to Web service operations upon the `load` event being dispatched. In MXML, the code to make an initial call when the `WebService` component is ready looks like this:

```
<s:WebService id="myService"
  wsdl="http://localhost:8500/flex4bible/SoapService.cfc?wsdl"
  load="myService.helloWorld()"/>
```

You also can use `addEventListener()` to handle the `load` event and make an initial call to the Web service operation:

```
import mx.rpc.soap.LoadEvent;
private function initApp():void
{
  myService.addEventListener(LoadEvent.LOAD, callService);
}
private function callService(event:LoadEvent):void
{
 myService.helloWorld();
}
```

Note

The `LoadEvent` class implements a `document` property typed as `XMLDocument` that represents the WSDL document that was loaded from the server. This is a legacy XML object that you can parse with Document Object Model (DOM)–style programming. In highly dynamic applications, the `document` property enables you to parse and present options to users for calling Web service operations without having to hard code the operation names in your Flex application. ■

Tip

You also can make initial calls to Web service operations from the `Application` component's life cycle events, such as `initialize` or `creationComplete`. If these events are dispatched before the `WebService` component has successfully read its WSDL content, your pending calls are placed in a queue. When the `load` event is dispatched, queued calls are sent to the Web service provider automatically. ■

Handling Web service results

As with the `HTTPService` component, Web service requests and responses are handled asynchronously. This means that when you send a request, Flash Player's ActionScript Virtual Machine (AVM) doesn't pause in its code execution and wait for data to be returned. Instead, you call the Web service operation and then use either binding expressions or event listeners to handle and process the returned data.

Using binding expressions

A binding expression can be used to pass data returned from a call to a Web service operation to a visual control or other component that's capable of acting as a binding destination. A binding expression for a Web service operation consists of three parts, separated with dots:

- The `WebService` object's unique `id` or variable name
- The name of the Web service operation
- The `lastResult` property

Using the example in the previous section, where the `WebService` object has an `id` of `myService` and the Web service operation is named `helloWorld()`, the binding expression to pass returned data to a Flex component would be:

```
myService.helloWorld.lastResult
```

Caution

The operation name is used to create a temporary instance of the `Operation` class that, in turn, implements the `lastResult` property. There are a number of versions of this class, including versions for SOAP and Remoting, and within each of these categories are separate versions for use with `WebService` objects declared in ActionScript and in MXML. ■

The application in Listing 25.1 uses binding expressions to handle and display both a simple String returned from the Web service's `helloWorld()` operation and an `ArrayCollection` returned from the service's `getAllContacts()` operation.

LISTING 25.1

Handling Web service results with binding expressions

```xml
<?xml version="1.0" encoding="utf-8"?>
<s:Application xmlns:fx="http://ns.adobe.com/mxml/2009"
  xmlns:s="library://ns.adobe.com/flex/spark"
  xmlns:mx="library://ns.adobe.com/flex/mx">
  <fx:Declarations>
    <s:WebService id="myService"
      wsdl="http://localhost:8500/flex4bible/SoapService.cfc?wsdl"/>
  </fx:Declarations>
  <s:layout>
```

```
    <s:VerticalLayout horizontalAlign="center" paddingTop="20"/>
  </s:layout>
  <s:Button label="Get String" click="myService.helloWorld()"/>
  <s:Label text="{myService.helloWorld.lastResult}" fontSize="12"/>
  <s:Button label="Get Data" click="myService.getAllContacts()"/>
  <mx:DataGrid dataProvider="{myService.getAllContacts.lastResult}">
    <mx:columns>
      <mx:DataGridColumn dataField="firstname" headerText="First Name"/>
      <mx:DataGridColumn dataField="lastname" headerText="Last Name"/>
    </mx:columns>
  </mx:DataGrid>
</s:Application>
```

On the Web

The code in Listing 25.1 is available in the Web site files as `WebServiceWithBindings.mxml` **in the** `src`
folder of the `chapter25` **project.** ∎

Figure 25.1 shows the resulting application, displaying a simple string and a complex data set
returned from the Web service.

FIGURE 25.1

Displaying Web service results

Using the result event

As with the `HTTPService` component, you can handle results of a call to a Web service operation
with the `WebService` component's result event. This event dispatches an event object typed as
`mx.rpc.events.ResultEvent`, the same event object that's used by `HTTPService` and
`RemoteObject`. The event object's `result` property references the returned data.

To handle and save data using the `result` event, follow these steps:

1. **Declare a bindable variable outside of any functions that acts as a persistent reference to the returned data.** Cast the variable's type depending on what you expect to be returned by the Web service operation. For example, if the data type declared in the WSDL document is `soapenc:Array` or is a custom type derived from that type (such as ColdFusion's `impl:ArrayOf_xsd_anyType`), the `WebService` component casts the returned data as an `ArrayCollection`:

   ```
   import mx.collections.ArrayCollection;
   [Bindable]
   private var myData:ArrayCollection
   ```

2. **Create an event handler function that will be called when the event is dispatched.** The function should receive a single event argument typed as `ResultEvent` and return `void`:

   ```
   private function resultHandler(event:ResultEvent):void
   {
   }
   ```

3. **Within the event handler function, use the `event.result` expression to refer to the data that's returned from the server.** Unlike with the `HTTPService` component, where you have to walk down the XML hierarchy to get to the returned data, the expression `event.result` returns a strongly typed `ArrayCollection` and can be passed directly to the persistent variable:

   ```
   myData = event.result as ArrayCollection;
   ```

Note

When passing the value of `event.result` directly to a variable, you have to explicitly declare the type of the returned data using the ActionScript `as` operator. `ResultEvent.result` is typed in the API as an `Object`; explicit casting tells both the compiler and Flash Builder's code syntax checker that the data is expected to arrive already formatted as an `ArrayCollection`. ■

You can listen for the result event with either an MXML attribute-based event listener or a call to the ActionScript `addEventListener()` method. The attribute-based event listener looks like this:

```
<s:WebService id="myService"
  wsdl="http://localhost:8500/flex4bible/SoapService.cfc?wsdl"
  result="resultHandler(event)"/>
```

When using `addEventListener()` to create an event listener, you can designate the event name with the String value result or with the `ResultEvent` class's `RESULT` constant:

```
var myService:WebService = new WebService();
myService.loadWSDL(
  "http://localhost:8500/flex4bible/SoapService.cfc?wsdl");
myService.addEventListener(ResultEvent.RESULT, resultHandler);
myService.callMethod();
```

Listing 25.2 uses a `result` event handler function to capture and save data that's been returned from a Web service operation.

LISTING 25.2

Using a WebService component with a result event handler function

```xml
<?xml version="1.0" encoding="utf-8"?>
<s:Application xmlns:fx="http://ns.adobe.com/mxml/2009"
  xmlns:s="library://ns.adobe.com/flex/spark"
  xmlns:mx="library://ns.adobe.com/flex/mx">
  <fx:Declarations>
    <s:WebService id="myService"
      wsdl="http://localhost:8500/flex4bible/SoapService.cfc?wsdl"
      result="resultHandler(event)"/        >
  </fx:Declarations>
  <fx:Script>
    <![CDATA[
      import mx.collections.ArrayCollection;
      import mx.rpc.events.ResultEvent;
      [Bindable]
      private var contactData:ArrayCollection;
      private function resultHandler(event:ResultEvent):void
      {
        contactData = event.result as ArrayCollection;
      }
    ]]>
  </fx:Script>
  <s:layout>
    <s:VerticalLayout horizontalAlign="center" paddingTop="20"/>
  </s:layout>
  <s:Button label="Get Data" click="myService.getAllContacts()"/>
  <mx:DataGrid dataProvider="{contactData}">
    <mx:columns>
      <mx:DataGridColumn dataField="firstname" headerText="First Name"/>
      <mx:DataGridColumn dataField="lastname" headerText="Last Name"/>
    </mx:columns>
  </mx:DataGrid>
</s:Application>
```

On the Web

The code in Listing 25.2 is available in the Web site files as `WebServiceResultEvent.mxml` in the `src` folder of the `chapter25` project. ∎

Handling fault events

When a call to a Web service operation fails, the WebService object dispatches a fault event. Just like the HTTPService and RemoteObject components, the event object is typed as mx.rpc.events.FaultEvent. This event object has a fault property typed as mx.rpc. Fault, which has these properties:

- faultCode:String. A code that indicates the nature of the fault and whether it occurred in the client or server environment.

- faultDetail:String. An additional message that sometimes contains useful information.

- faultString:String. The error message.

- message:String. A string consisting of all of the previous values concatenated together with | characters used as separators.

To handle a fault event, create an event handler function that receives an event argument typed as FaultEvent. Within the body of the function, you can deal with the fault however you like. This code collects fault information from the event object and displays it to the user with an Alert pop-up window:

```
private function faultHandler(event:FaultEvent):void
{
   Alert.show(event.fault.faultString, event.fault.faultCode);
}
```

The application in Listing 25.3 generates a fault by calling a nonexistent operation from the Web service.

LISTING 25.3

Using the fault event

```
<?xml version="1.0" encoding="utf-8"?>
<s:Application xmlns:fx="http://ns.adobe.com/mxml/2009"
  xmlns:s="library://ns.adobe.com/flex/spark"
  xmlns:mx="library://ns.adobe.com/flex/mx">
  <fx:Declarations>
    <s:WebService id="myService"
      wsdl="http://localhost:8500/flex4bible/SoapService.cfc?wsdl"
      result="resultHandler(event)"
      fault="faultHandler(event)"/>
  </fx:Declarations>
  <fx:Script>
    <![CDATA[
      import mx.collections.ArrayCollection;
      import mx.controls.Alert;
      import mx.rpc.events.FaultEvent;
```

```
      import mx.rpc.events.ResultEvent;
      [Bindable]
      private var contactData:ArrayCollection;
      private function resultHandler(event:ResultEvent):void
      {
      contactData = event.result as ArrayCollection;
      }
      private function faultHandler(event:FaultEvent):void
      {
      Alert.show(event.fault.faultString, event.fault.faultCode);
      }
    ]]>
  </fx:Script>
  <s:layout>
    <s:VerticalLayout horizontalAlign="center" paddingTop="20"/>
  </s:layout>
  <s:Button label="Get Data" click="myService.noSuchMethod()"/>
  <mx:DataGrid dataProvider="{myService.getAllContacts.lastResult}">
    <mx:columns>
      <mx:DataGridColumn dataField="firstname" headerText="First Name"/>
      <mx:DataGridColumn dataField="lastname" headerText="Last Name"/>
    </mx:columns>
  </mx:DataGrid>
</s:Application>
```

On the Web

The code in Listing 25.3 is available in the Web site files as `WebServiceFaultEvent.mxml` **in the** `src` **folder of the** `chapter25` **project.** ∎

As shown in Figure 25.2, the application responds by displaying the fault information in a pop-up window produced by the `Alert` class.

Handling events of multiple operations

When a Flex application needs to handle result and fault events from more than one operation of a single Web service, you need to distinguish which event handler method will be used for the results of each operation call. You can handle this requirement with either ActionScript or MXML code.

To set up an event listener for a single method in ActionScript, call `addEventListener()` as a method of an `Operation` object either before or after making a call to the Web service operation. The following code calls a Web service's `getAllContacts()` operation and then dispatches its `result` event to an event handler function named `resultHandler()`:

```
    myService.getAllContacts();
    myService.getAllContacts.addEventListener(
      ResultEvent.RESULT, resultHandler);
```

Because `addEventListener()` is called as a method of the operation, not the `WebService` object itself, the event listener is active only for that particular operation.

To set up a similar architecture with MXML, declare the `WebService` component as a paired `<s:WebService>` tag set. Within the tags, nest multiple `<s:operation>` tags, each representing an operation you want to call. The `<s:operation>` tag is an instruction to the compiler rather than an instance of an ActionScript class. Its purpose is to configure a single operation with its own unique event handlers.

FIGURE 25.2

Responding to a `fault` event

The following MXML code declares an instance of the `WebService` component with distinct `result` event listeners for each of two operations. Because the two operations return different types of data, it's important that they each have their own event handler functions:

```
<s:WebService id="myService"
  wsdl="http://localhost:8500/flex4bible/SoapService.cfc?wsdl"
  fault="faultHandler(event)">
  <s:operation name="getAllContacts"
    result="contactsResultHandler(event)"/>
  <s:operation name="helloWorld"
    result="helloWorldHandler(event)"/>
</s:WebService>
```

The application in Listing 25.4 declares MXML-based `result` event handlers for each of two Web service operations. The `fault` event handler is declared in the `<mx:WebService>` tag and is used by both of the service's operations.

LISTING 25.4

Handling events with multiple Web service operations

```
<?xml version="1.0" encoding="utf-8"?>
<s:Application xmlns:fx="http://ns.adobe.com/mxml/2009"
  xmlns:s="library://ns.adobe.com/flex/spark"
  xmlns:mx="library://ns.adobe.com/flex/mx">
  <fx:Declarations>
    <s:WebService id="myService"
      wsdl="http://localhost:8500/flex4bible/SoapService.cfc?wsdl"
      fault="faultHandler(event)">
      <s:operation name="getAllContacts"
        result="contactsResultHandler(event)"/>
      <s:operation name="helloWorld"
        result="helloResultHandler(event)"/>
    </s:WebService>
  </fx:Declarations>
  <fx:Script>
    <![CDATA[
      import mx.collections.ArrayCollection;
      import mx.controls.Alert;
      import mx.rpc.events.FaultEvent;
      import mx.rpc.events.ResultEvent;
      [Bindable]
      private var contactData:ArrayCollection;
      [Bindable]
      private var helloData:String;
      private function contactsResultHandler(event:ResultEvent):void
      {
        contactData = event.result as ArrayCollection;
      }
      private function helloResultHandler(event:ResultEvent):void
      {
        helloData = event.result as String;
      }
      private function faultHandler(event:FaultEvent):void
      {
        Alert.show(event.fault.faultString, event.fault.faultCode);
      }
    ]]>
  </fx:Script>
  <s:layout>
    <s:VerticalLayout horizontalAlign="center" paddingTop="20"/>
  </s:layout>
  <s:Button label="Get String" click="myService.helloWorld()"/>
  <s:Label text="{helloData}" fontSize="12"/>
  <s:Button label="Get Data" click="myService.getAllContacts()"/>
  <mx:DataGrid dataProvider="{contactData}">
```

continued

793

LISTING 25.4   *(continued)*

```
    <mx:columns>
      <mx:DataGridColumn dataField="firstname" headerText="First Name"/>
      <mx:DataGridColumn dataField="lastname" headerText="Last Name"/>
    </mx:columns>
  </mx:DataGrid>
</s:Application>
```

On the Web

The code in Listing 25.4 is available in the Web site files as `WebServiceMultipleOperations.mxml` in the `src` folder of the `chapter25` project. ∎

Using the CallResponder class

One alternative approach to handling result and fault events in a more granular way is to use the new `CallResponder` class.

New Feature

The `CallResponder` class is new to the Flex 4 SDK. ∎

As with all other RPC classes, you can declare a `CallResponder` object using either MXML or ActionScript. If you declare it in MXML, you must place it inside the `<fx:Declarations>` section of an MXML document. You can then move the `result` and `fault` event handlers to the `CallResponder`:

```
<fx:Declarations>
  <s:WebService id="myService"
    wsdl=http://localhost:8500/flex4bible/SoapService.cfc?wsdl" />
  <s:CallResponder id="myResponder"
    result="contactsResultHandler(event)"
    fault="faultHandler(event)"/>
</fx:Declarations>
```

When you call a Web service operation, an instance of the `AsyncToken` class is returned. You bind the operation call to the `CallResponder` object by assigning the returned `AsyncToken` object to the responder's `token` property:

```
myResponder.token = myService.getContacts();
```

Now when you make the call to the Web service operation, the responder's `result` handler is executed if data is returned successfully, and the responder's fault handler is executed upon any exception.

The advantage of the new `CallResponder` class is that you can both realize the benefits of using MXML to declare objects and gain more flexibility in your code as you bind operation calls to specific event handlers at runtime.

Tip

The `CallResponder` class also supports the `lastResult` property. You can bind a visual control to the data returned from an operation by using a binding expression that refers to the responder object:

```
<mx:DataGrid dataProvider="{myResponder.lastResult}"/> ■
```

Processing Web service operations with ActionScript

Everything you do with the `WebService`, `CallResponder`, and other components can be done with pure ActionScript code. It's a question of style: some developers prefer to minimize the use of MXML when dealing with these non-visual classes.

There are many ways to design the code; the version in Listing 25.5 uses a `WebService` and a `CallResponder` object. Upon application startup, the service's `loadWsdl()` method is called to retrieve the service description. Then upon the load event, the operation is called. Finally, the result is handled with yet another event handler.

LISTING 25.5

Calling a Web service operation with pure ActionScript

```
<?xml version="1.0" encoding="utf-8"?>
<s:Application xmlns:fx="http://ns.adobe.com/mxml/2009"
  xmlns:s="library://ns.adobe.com/flex/spark"
  xmlns:mx="library://ns.adobe.com/flex/mx"
  creationComplete="app_creationCompleteHandler(event)">
  <fx:Script>
    <![CDATA[
      // ActionScript file
      import mx.collections.ArrayCollection;
      import mx.controls.Alert
      import mx.events.FlexEvent;
      import mx.rpc.CallResponder;
      import mx.rpc.Fault;
      import mx.rpc.events.FaultEvent;
      import mx.rpc.events.ResultEvent;
      import mx.rpc.soap.LoadEvent;
      import mx.rpc.soap.WebService;

      private const wsdl:String =
        "http://localhost:8500/flex4bible/SoapService.cfc?wsdl";
      [Bindable]
      private var contactData:ArrayCollection;
      private var service:WebService = new WebService();
      private var responder:CallResponder = new CallResponder();

      protected function app_creationCompleteHandler(event:FlexEvent):void
```

continued

LISTING 25.5 *(continued)*

```
      {
        responder.addEventListener(ResultEvent.RESULT, resultHandler);
        responder.addEventListener(FaultEvent.FAULT, faultHandler);
        service.addEventListener(LoadEvent.LOAD, loadHandler);
        service.loadWSDL(wsdl);
      }
      protected function loadHandler(event:LoadEvent):void
      {
        responder.token = service.getAllContacts();
      }
      protected function resultHandler(event:ResultEvent):void
      {
        contactData = event.result as ArrayCollection;
      }
      protected function faultHandler(event:FaultEvent):void
      {
        Alert.show(event.fault.faultString, event.fault.faultCode);
      }
    ]]>
  </fx:Script>
  <s:layout>
    <s:VerticalLayout horizontalAlign="center" paddingTop="20"/>
  </s:layout>
  <mx:DataGrid dataProvider="{contactData}">
    <mx:columns>
      <mx:DataGridColumn dataField="firstname" headerText="First Name"/>
      <mx:DataGridColumn dataField="lastname" headerText="Last Name"/>
    </mx:columns>
  </mx:DataGrid>
</s:Application>
```

On the Web

The code in Listing 25.5 is available in the Web site files as `WebServiceWithActionScript.mxml` in the `src` folder of the `chapter25` project. ∎

Passing parameters to Web service operations

You can pass parameters to Web service operations by using either explicit parameters or bound parameters. Explicit parameters are passed in the order in which they're declared in the service's WSDL description; bound parameters are set up in an MXML `<mx:WebService>` declaration.

Using explicit parameters

To pass explicit parameters to a Web service operation, you must know the order in which they're declared in the server-side code. If you don't have explicit documentation, you can find this information in the Web service's WSDL metadata description.

For example, the ColdFusion Web service has an operation named getFilteredContacts() that enables you to search for data by the data set's firstname and lastname columns. In a Web service's WSDL description, each incoming and outgoing packet is described as a "message." The incoming message for the getFilteredContacts() operation looks like this in the service's WSDL description:

```
<wsdl:message name="getFilteredContactsRequest">
  <wsdl:part name="firstname" type="xsd:string"/>
  <wsdl:part name="lastname" type="xsd:string"/>
</wsdl:message>
```

To pass explicit parameters, call the Web service operation just as you would call an ActionScript function. Match the order of the parameters exactly as you see them in the WSDL description. This code passes two values taken directly from the text properties of two TextInput controls as parameters of the getFilteredContacts() operation:

```
myService.getFilteredContacts(fnameInput.text, lnameInput.text);
```

The Web service will use the parameter values as needed to perform its functionality. In this case, the values are examined, and if they're not blank strings, the service filters the data before returning it to the Flex client.

Using bound parameters

You set up bound parameters by name and nest them within a pair of <s:request> tags, which in turn are nested in a pair of <s:operation> tags. Each parameter is expressed as an XML tag set where the element name matches the name of the parameter, as shown in the WSDL. This declaration includes a set of bindings that pass values directly from the TextInput controls to the Web service operations as parameters:

```
<s:WebService id="myService"
  wsdl="http://localhost:8500/flex4bible/SoapService.cfc?wsdl"
  result="resultHandler(event)">
  <s:operation name="getFilteredContacts">
    <s:request>
      <firstname>{fnameInput.text}</firstname>
      <lastname>{lnameInput.text}</lastname>
    </s:request>
  </s:operation>
</s:WebService>
```

When you call the Web service operation, you now must treat it as an operation object. Instead of calling the method directly, call the operation's send() method:

```
myService.getFilteredContacts.send();
```

Tip

Either explicit or bound parameters can be used effectively in Flex applications. I tend to use explicit parameters because, especially when calling an operation from different parts of an application, it makes it obvious where the parameters' values are coming from. ■

Figure 25.3 shows an application that uses server-side filtering through a call to a Web service.

On the Web

Applications that pass parameters to a Web service operation are available in the Web site files as
`WebServiceExplicitParams.mxml` **and** `WebServiceBoundParams.mxml` **in the** `src` **folder of the**
`chapter25` **project.** ∎

FIGURE 25.3

Passing parameters to a Web service operation

Using Web Service Data Connections

Flash Builder 4 includes a new feature that enables you to generate *proxy* classes that represent a Web service's API in the Flex application. When you use this feature, you're allowing Flash Builder to help you create a more maintainable coding pattern that has these benefits:

- Your code makes calls to local proxy methods instead of calling operations directly from the Web service. As a result, Flash Builder and the Flex compiler can do a better job with code completion and compile-time syntax checking.

- Local proxy methods are structured with required arguments. As a result, you get better code hints and completion as you write the code.

Once you've created the data connection, Flash Builder also provides tools to return data as automatically generated custom data types (also known as *value objects*), generate service calls, and bind returned data to visual controls.

Caution

If the Web service operation names or their input and output parameters change, you'll need to regenerate the proxy classes from within Flash Builder. ■

Defining a data connection

When you import a Web service data connection, Flash Builder creates a set of ActionScript proxy classes that you call instead of the native `WebService` object. In order to create the data connection, you must know its `WSDL` location.

To find the `WSDL` location and define a data connection, follow these steps:

1. **From the Flash Builder menu, choose Data ⇨ Connect to Web Service.**

2. **Set the WSDL URI (the location of the WSDL content on the server), as shown in Figure 25.4.** You can also set a custom service name and designate the package where the proxy classes will be created.

3. **Click Next.**

FIGURE 25.4

Selecting the Web service WSDL and designating the service name and package

Note

The option to use an LCDS/BlazeDS "destination" is enabled only if you create a Flex project that's configured to work with LiveCycle Data Services or BlazeDS. ■

    4. In the Configure Code Generation screen, shown in Figure 25.5, select the operations you want to call with the generated proxy class.

FIGURE 25.5

Selecting Web service operations

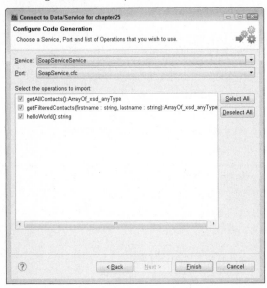

    5. **Click Finish to generate the proxy code.** As shown in Figure 25.6, the Data/Services view should now display the new data connection, along with all of the operations you selected.

Tip

When a Web service already has the word `Service` in its name, you'll see something like `SoapServiceService` as the default. If you like, you can remove the extra `Service` and set the proxy class's name to match the Web service's name. Alternatively, you can replace the last `Service` with the word `Proxy` to create an ActionScript class named; in this case, `SoapServiceProxy`. In the following examples, the generated ActionScript proxy class for the ColdFusion SoapService is `SoapServiceProxy`, located in the default package and subfolder structure `generated.webservices`. ■

FIGURE 25.6

The Data/Services view

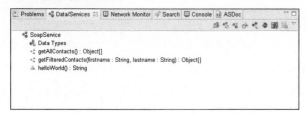

Managing Web service data connections

After generating a Web service data connection, your Flex project source root has a new subfolder structure matching the package you selected for code generation. As shown in Figure 25.7, the package contains the primary proxy class, such as `SoapService.as`, and a superclass from which it's extended.

FIGURE 25.7

The Package Explorer view displays the generated ActionScript proxy classes

Note

The inheritance model used in the generated classes enables you to customize the primary proxy class as needed. If you later regenerate the data connection from the Web service, the superclass will be regenerated, but the subclass that is called directly in your application is left alone. ■

Configuring a return type

When you configure a data connection's return type, you're generating a strongly typed value object class that has properties matching the data returned from a Web service operation. Follow these steps to generate the class and assign it to the operation:

1. **Locate the operation for which you want to configure a return type in the Data/Services view.**

2. **Right-click the operation.**

3. **Select Configure Return Type from the context menu.** As shown in Figure 25.8, you can either auto-detect the structure of the return type or select an existing ActionScript class.

FIGURE 25.8

Selecting either auto-detection of the return type or using an existing ActionScript class

4. **If this is the first time you've used this feature, select Auto-detect the return type from sample data and then click Next.**

   If you chose auto-detection, you'll see an additional screen (shown in Figure 25.9) that displays the structure of the returned data and enables you to set the name of the value object class you want to create.

5. **Click Finish to generate the class (if necessary) and configure it as the operation's return type.** In the Data/Services view, you should see that the selected return type is reflected in the operation signature, as in this example:

```
getAllContacts(): Contact[]
```

FIGURE 25.9

Reviewing the data structure and setting the name of a new value object class

Binding data to visual controls

Once you've defined the data connection and configured an operation's return type, you can then generate all of the code you need to make a call to an operation and display its returned data. Always start by creating the data control you want to populate with data. For example, you could start with a simple DataGrid placed in a specific location in your application or custom component:

```
<mx:DataGrid horizontalCenter="0" paddingTop="20"/>
```

Follow these steps to bind data to the control:

1. **Place the cursor anywhere in the DataGrid reference.** You can also select the control in Design mode if you prefer.

2. **Choose Data ➪ Bind to Data from the Flash Builder menu.**

3. **In the Bind to Data dialog box, shown in Figure 25.10, choose a Service and an Operation, and then click OK.**

Listing 25.6 demonstrates the resulting application after the required code has been generated. The SoapService class that's declared with MXML code references the generated ActionScript proxy class. When you run the application, it executes a call to the Web service operation upon startup, and the returned data is displayed in the DataGrid control as a result of a binding to the CallResponder object's lastResult property.

FIGURE 25.10

Binding data to a visual control

LISTING 25.6

An application with Web service generated code

```xml
<?xml version="1.0" encoding="utf-8"?>
<s:Application xmlns:fx="http://ns.adobe.com/mxml/2009"
  xmlns:s="library://ns.adobe.com/flex/spark"
  xmlns:mx="library://ns.adobe.com/flex/mx"
  xmlns:soapservice="services.soapservice.*">
  <fx:Script>
    <![CDATA[
      import mx.events.FlexEvent;
      import mx.controls.Alert;
      protected function dataGrid_creationCompleteHandler(
        event:FlexEvent):void
      {
        getAllContactsResult.token = soapService.getAllContacts();
      }
    ]]>
  </fx:Script>
  <fx:Declarations>
    <s:CallResponder id="getAllContactsResult"/>
    <soapservice:SoapService id="soapService"
      fault="Alert.show(event.fault.faultString + '\n' +
             event.fault.faultDetail)" showBusyCursor="true"/>
  </fx:Declarations>
  <mx:DataGrid horizontalCenter="0" paddingTop="20" id="dataGrid"
    creationComplete="dataGrid_creationCompleteHandler(event)"
    dataProvider="{getAllContactsResult.lastResult}">
    <mx:columns>
      <mx:DataGridColumn headerText="contactId" dataField="contactId"/>
      <mx:DataGridColumn headerText="lastname" dataField="lastname"/>
      <mx:DataGridColumn headerText="firstname" dataField="firstname"/>
```

```
        <mx:DataGridColumn headerText="city" dataField="city"/>
      </mx:columns>
    </mx:DataGrid>
  </s:Application>
```

On the Web

The code in Listing 25.6 is available in the Web site files as `WebServiceWithDataConnection.mxml` **in the** `src` **folder of the** `chapter25` **project.** ∎

Summary

In this chapter, I described how to integrate Flex applications with SOAP-based Web services. You learned the following:

- SOAP is an XML-based industry-standard messaging format used in RPC-style applications.

- SOAP client and server software is designed to be interoperable across operating systems and programming languages.

- The Flex SDK's `WebService` component encapsulates the process of sending and receiving SOAP-based messages.

- Like the other RPC components, the `WebService` component uses asynchronous communications.

- You can create and configure `WebService` objects in either MXML or ActionScript code.

- The new `CallResponder` class can be used to bind calls to responders at runtime.

- Flash Builder 4 includes new data-centric development features that enable you to quickly generate code to call Web service operations and display returned data in visual controls.

Integrating Flex Applications with BlazeDS and Java

F lex was originally created by Macromedia in 2004 as a server-based product. The Flex server incorporated the Flash Remoting technology that had been pioneered in ColdFusion and adapted its capabilities to work with Java-based classes stored in the server. Flex applications in their earliest incarnation were stored as source code on the server and compiled on demand when a browser made a request for the application's source code (its MXML file). A command-line compiler was included for those developers who wanted to pre-build their applications prior to deployment. (Flex Builder 1 was a completely different product than the integrated development environment [IDE] used today and was based on the Dreamweaver code base. It was provided to developers as part of the Flex server license.)

When Flex 2 was released in 2006, the product line's client-side and server-side capabilities were separated. The server-side functionality, including the Flash Remoting technology (now known as the *Remoting Service*) was packaged as Flex Data Services 2. Flex Data Services added support for server-pushed communications for messaging and distributed database applications.

In 2007, Flex Data Services was renamed as LiveCycle Data Services, with the intent of strong integration with Adobe's existing LiveCycle product line. Some new features were added, such as server-side PDF generation, but the product's licensing and intended usage didn't change enormously. LiveCycle Data Services (referred to in this chapter as LCDS) remained the primary server-side solution for Flex developers who wanted to integrate their applications with Java-based application servers.

In February 2008, Adobe released BlazeDS, a free open-source implementation of many of LCDS's features. BlazeDS includes support for the Remoting Service, plus two of LCDS's other popular features: the Message Service and the Proxy Service. Unlike LCDS, which remains an enterprise-level product both in terms of scalability and pricing, BlazeDS can be used freely without any license fees or registration.

IN THIS CHAPTER

Understanding the history of Flex with Java

Understanding BlazeDS

Getting and installing BlazeDS

Creating Flex projects for use with BlazeDS

Using the Proxy Service

Understanding the Remoting Service

Creating and placing Java classes on the server

Using the `RemoteObject` **component**

Setting up RDS with BlazeDS

Using BlazeDS data connections in Flash Builder 4

New Feature

The most recent version, BlazeDS 4.0, supports integration with Flash Builder 4 through the use of the Remote Development Service (RDS) protocol. ■

The point of this history is that features that were available only in an enterprise-level server product upon the initial release of Flex are now available at zero cost to any organization or individual who wants to learn how to use them. In this chapter, I describe how to get and install BlazeDS and how to use two of its features: the Proxy Service and the Remoting Service. In Chapter 27, I describe how to use the Message Service to share data between Flex applications and other messaging clients in real time.

On the Web

To use the sample code for this chapter, download `chapter26.zip` **from the Web site. This file is not built as a Flex project archive; it contains application and class files that you can copy into a Flex project after creating it in Flash Builder. Follow the instructions later in this chapter to create a Flex project for use with BlazeDS and install the project assets to the client and server.** ■

Using BlazeDS

BlazeDS is an open-source, freely available implementation of Java-based server-side functionality that's designed to deliver data and process messages from Flex applications at runtime. It includes the following features that are shared with LiveCycle Data Services:

- **The Message Service.** This service supports collaboration between Flex applications through a hub-and-spokes messaging architecture. Flex applications send messages to BlazeDS, and BlazeDS broadcasts the messages to other connected clients.

- **The Proxy Service.** This service supports proxying of HTTP requests and responses between Flex applications and remote servers. Typically it is used when direct communication between clients and servers is restricted due to cross-domain security issues.

- **The Remoting Service.** This service is a server-side gateway that allows Flex applications to call methods of server-side Java classes using binary Action Message Format (AMF).

Understanding supported platforms

BlazeDS is supported on the following operating systems:

- Windows
- Linux
- Solaris

Note

Although not officially supported or noted in the product documentation, BlazeDS appears to work just fine on Mac OS X. ■

LiveCycle Data Services Features

LiveCycle Data Services includes many other features that aren't part of BlazeDS:

- The Data Management Service enables you to create applications with distributed data that's synchronized in real time between multiple clients and servers. This service also supports automated data paging, enabling you to use Flex data visualization components with large data sets without overloading Flash Player memory.

- RTMP (Real Time Messaging Protocol) enables you to build applications with highly scaled server-push messaging and distributed data.

- An agent process for Mercury QuickTestPro 9.1 enables Flex applications to be tested with Mercury QuickTest Professional, also known as HP QuickTest Professional since Mercury's acquisition by HP in 2006.

- Software clustering when using stateful services and non-HTTP channels, such as RTMP, ensures that Flex applications continue running in the event of server failure.

- You can generate template-driven PDF documents that include graphical assets from Flex applications, such as graphs and charts.

- If you are an AIR developer, the local data cache enables you to cache client data requests and data changes to the local file system for later retrieval when an application resumes.

LiveCycle Data Services, in fact, is worthy of much more coverage than is possible in this book. For more information, see Adobe's Web site:

`www.adobe.com/products/livecycle/dataservices`

BlazeDS can be installed on and hosted with many Java Enterprise Edition application servers, including:

- Apache Tomcat 6 (included in the BlazeDS turnkey distribution)
- JBoss
- IBM WebSphere
- BEA WebLogic

BlazeDS requires a Java Development Kit (JDK) installation, with a minimum required version of JDK 5. The turnkey distribution that includes Tomcat 6 does not include a JDK. On a Windows-based development or server system, you must download and install the JDK (most likely from Sun Microsystems) before running Tomcat.

Getting started with BlazeDS

BlazeDS is hosted at Adobe's Open Source Web site and can be downloaded from `http://opensource.adobe.com/blazeds`. In addition to product downloads, this page includes links to the product's release notes, bug database, support forums, and developer documentation. As an open-source project, Adobe welcomes submissions of proposed patches for the product.

The End of JRun

In late 2007, Adobe announced that it would discontinue new feature development for JRun, its own Java Enterprise Edition application server. The packaging of BlazeDS with Tomcat instead of JRun represented Adobe's first move away from JRun, which had been the default application server for Flex/ LiveCycle Data Services, ColdFusion, and many other server-based products.

While JRun was one of the first Java servlet container applications, its lack of market share and the availability of free Java-based application servers such as Tomcat and JBoss drove the decision to move to other products. If you already use and are happy with JRun, there's no reason to stop using it, but as the Java-based application server market continues to evolve, JRun will eventually become a less compelling choice.

Downloading BlazeDS

Multiple download options are available for BlazeDS:

- The release builds are binary distributions that have been tested and declared stable and ready for production use.
- The nightly builds are binary distributions that are built with all the latest features and source code but haven't been fully tested.
- The product source code for the most recent release build is available for download as an archive file in .zip format.
- The latest product source code can be checked out from the source repository using any Subversion client. This source code is not tested or certified. As the product page says:

  "The Subversion repository should only be used if you want to be on the bleeding-edge of the development effort. The code contained in them may fail to work, or it may even eat your hard drive."

Two versions of BlazeDS are available for download:

- **A binary distribution.** This distribution includes Web Application Archive (WAR) files that can be deployed on any supported application server.
- **A turnkey distribution.** This distribution includes a preconfigured copy of Apache Tomcat 6.

To download the turnkey distribution, follow these steps:

1. **In any Web browser, navigate to** `http://opensource.adobe.com/blazeds`.
2. **Click Download BlazeDS now.**
3. **Review the Terms of Use.**
4. **If you accept the Terms of Use, locate and download the most recent BlazeDS turnkey distribution.** If the release build isn't at least version 4.0.0.7548, use a recent nightly build instead.

Note

To create BlazeDS data connections with Flash Builder 4, you must install BlazeDS 4, beta 1 (build 4.0.0.7548) or later. ■

The turnkey distribution is delivered in a ZIP file, the BlazeDS 4 beta 1 build, which was the most recent stable build available as of this writing. The downloaded turnkey installation file was named `blazeds_turnkey_4.0.0.7548.zip`. This ZIP file can be extracted to any folder on your hard disk. If you want to match the Windows configuration used in this chapter's sample code, extract the files to a new folder named `C:\blazeds`. If you're working on Mac OS X or another operating system, extract the files to any location and then adapt the instructions throughout this chapter to your custom BlazeDS location.

The turnkey installation includes three complete instances of BlazeDS. Each BlazeDS instance is included as a WAR file in the installation folder root and also is extracted as a working application in the Tomcat server's `webapps` folder:

- `blazeds.war`. Contains a starting copy of BlazeDS. To start a new BlazeDS installation, deploy `blazeds.war` to your application server. The same application is included in the turnkey installation in the `webapps/blazeds` folder.

- `ds-console.war`. Contains a management console application that makes calls to a Remoting Service destination to provide runtime information about various service activities. The same application is included in the turnkey installation in the `webapps/ds-console` folder.

- `samples.war`. Contains a completed BlazeDS instance with deployed release builds of the sample applications, required configurations, and documentation. The same application is included in the turnkey installation in the `webapps/samples` folder.

To create a new BlazeDS installation on Tomcat, copy `blazeds.war` to a filename of your choosing, such as `myblazeds.war`. Then copy the new version of the file to Tomcat's `webapps` folder. Tomcat detects the presence of the new file and extracts it to a new context root with the same name.

Starting BlazeDS in Windows

To start the Tomcat server in Windows, you first must have installed a Java Development Kit (JDK). The server requires an environment variable named `JAVA_HOME` that points to the root folder of the JDK.

Web Resource

You can download a free copy of the Java Development Kit from Sun Microsystems at `http://java.sun.com`. ■

Assuming you have a release of Sun's JDK 5 installed on your system, follow these steps to start Tomcat in Windows:

1. **Open a command window.**
   - In Windows XP, click Start and choose Run. Then type **cmd**, and click OK.
   - In Windows Vista or Windows 7, open the Windows Start menu. Click into Start Search, type **cmd**, and press Enter.

2. **Switch to the BlazeDS folder's** `tomcat/bin` **subfolder:**
   ```
   cd \blazeds\tomcat\bin
   ```

3. **Set the** `JAVA_HOME` **environment variable to point to your JDK's root folder.** This command assumes that JDK version 1.5.15 is installed on your system in the default location:
   ```
   set JAVA_HOME=\Program Files\Java\jdk1.5.0_15
   ```

4. **Type** `startup`, **and press Enter to run** `Startup.bat` **from the current folder.**

As shown in Figure 26.1, Tomcat starts in a separate command window.

To shut down Tomcat in Windows, use either of these methods:

- Close the command window in which it's running as an application.
- Return to the original command window, and run the `shutdown.bat` batch file.

FIGURE 26.1

The Tomcat server running in a separate command window

Starting BlazeDS on Mac OS X

As mentioned previously, BlazeDS and LCDS aren't officially supported on Mac OS X, but many developers use Mac systems as their primary development platform. Mac OS X comes equipped with an instance of the Java Development Kit, so unless your system has been otherwise configured, you shouldn't have to download and install the JDK. Just extract the turnkey distribution into any folder on your hard disk, and you should be ready to get started.

Follow these steps to start the version of Tomcat included with the turnkey distribution of BlazeDS on Mac OS X:

1. Open Terminal from `/Applications/Utilities`.

2. Switch to `tomcat/bin` in the folder in which you extracted the turnkey distribution. Assuming you extracted the distribution into `/Applications/blazeds`, this command would switch to the Tomcat server's `bin` folder:

   `cd /Applications/blazeds/tomcat/bin`

3. Start Tomcat with this command:

   `./startup.sh`

4. To stop Tomcat when you're finished, use this command in Terminal:

   `./shutdown.sh`

Starting the sample database

The turnkey distribution of BlazeDS includes an HSQLDB database that's designed to run as a separate process. Before using any of the sample applications that are included with BlazeDS, you must start the database process.

In Windows, follow these steps to start the sample database:

1. Open a separate command window.

2. Switch to the `sampledb` folder under the BlazeDS root folder, and run the `startdb.bat` batch file:

   ```
   cd \blazeds\sampledb
   startdb
   ```

The database runs as long as you keep the command window open. When you close the command window, the database shuts down.

On Mac OS X, follow these steps:

1. Open a new Terminal window.

2. Switch to the `sampledb` folder under the BlazeDS root folder, and run `startdb.sh` from the current folder:

   ```
   cd /Applications/blazeds/sampledb
   ./startdb.sh
   ```

As with Windows, the database runs only as long as you keep the window open. To shut down the database, press Ctrl+C on Windows or shut down the Terminal application on Mac OS X.

Using the samples application

The turnkey distribution includes a complete instance of BlazeDS that contains many sample applications. Each sample application includes complete source code to communicate with the sample database where necessary.

The copy of Tomcat that's included with the turnkey distribution is configured to run on port 8400 (not on port 8080 as a version of Tomcat downloaded directly from Apache might be). The samples application is stored in the Tomcat server's webapps folder under context root of /samples. To explore the sample applications from a browser, navigate to this URL in any Web browser:

```
http://localhost:8400/samples
```

As shown in Figure 26.2, the samples application's home page includes links to each of the applications. They include excellent examples of using the Message Service and Remoting Service to build complete Internet-enabled Flex applications with Java-based server resources.

Note
The sample applications are delivered as release builds; the folders from which they're executed don't contain Flex application source code. Instead, the Flex source code for all sample applications is delivered in a ZIP file in the samples application as WEB-INF/flex-src/ flex-src.zip. ■

FIGURE 26.2

The BlazeDS `samples` application's home page

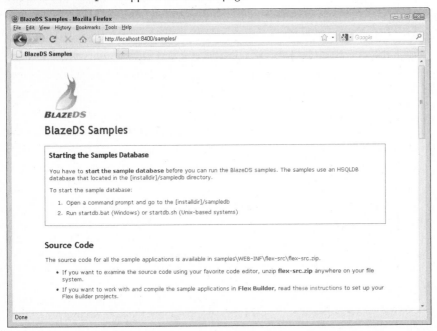

Creating Flex Projects for Use with BlazeDS

When you create a new Flex project that will communicate with resources hosted by BlazeDS at runtime, Flash Builder enables you to add special configuration options that automate much of the creation and deployment of the Flex application.

New Feature

In contrast to Flex Builder 3, which only directly supported LiveCycle Data Services, Flash Builder 4 now includes special options for applications that are integrated with BlazeDS. ∎

On the Web

The sample files for this chapter are in `chapter26.zip` on the Web. Unlike the sample files for other chapters, this is not a Flex project archive but rather a simple archive designed to be extracted after the project has been created. ∎

Follow these steps to create a new Flex project for deployment with BlazeDS:

1. Choose File ➪ New ➪ Flex Project from the Flash Builder menu.

2. Set the project name to chapter26. Use the default project location, which should be a folder named `chapter26` under the current workspace.

3. Set the Application type to Web application.

4. Set the Application server type to J2EE.

5. Select Use remote object access service and BlazeDS.

6. Click Next.

7. Set the Server location options to the physical location of the BlazeDS Web application (shown in Figure 26.3). For example, for a default installation in Windows, set the properties as follows:

   ● Root folder: `C:\blazeds\tomcat\webapps\blazeds`

   ● Root URL: `http://localhost:8400/blazeds`

   ● Context root: `/blazeds`

8. Verify that the Output folder is set to a location under the BlazeDS root folder.

9. Check to be sure that BlazeDS is currently running, then click Validate Configuration to verify that the Web root folder and root URL are valid.

10. Click Next.

11. Set the Main application filename to `HelloFromBlazeDS.mxml`.

12. Add a `Label` control with its text property set to Hello from BlazeDS.

13. Click Finish to create the application and project.

14. If you want to use the sample files from the Web site, extract `chapter26.zip` into the new project folder. Doing this overwrites your default Main application file and adds other required MXML and ActionScript source files.

15. Return to Flash Builder, and run the main application. The application should load from the BlazeDS URL `http://localhost:8400/blazeds/HelloFromBlazeDS.html`.

To use the server-side samples for this chapter, locate the `blazedsfiles` folder in the `chapter26` project. This folder contains Java classes, updated configuration files, and other required resources for this chapter.

FIGURE 26.3

Setting the location of BlazeDS

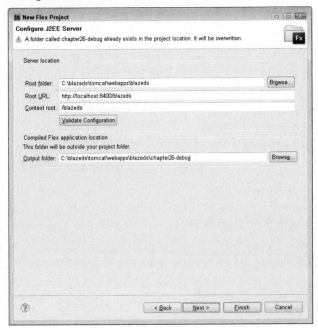

Follow these steps to install the files before trying any of the chapter's applications:

1. **If the application server that's hosting BlazeDS is currently running, shut it down.**

2. **Make backup copies of the files in the BlazeDS** `WEB-INF/flex` **folder.**

3. **Copy all of the file and folders from the** `blazedsfiles` **folder to the BlazeDS context root folder.** If you're using the turnkey distribution in Windows with the recommended installation location, copy the files to:

    `C:\blazeds\tomcat\webapps\blazeds`

    If prompted to overwrite existing files, confirm the operation.

4. **Restart Tomcat or whichever application server you're using.**

5. **Open a Web browser and navigate to this URL:**

    `http://localhost:8400/blazeds/flex4bible/data/contacts.xml`

    You should see an XML data file loaded into the browser from the Web server. This verifies that the files were copied into the correct location in the BlazeDS application.

Using the Proxy Service

The Proxy Service is one of BlazeDS's primary features. It enables you to use BlazeDS as a proxy for requests to servers in remote domains that would otherwise require the creation and placement of a cross-domain policy file.

When a Flex application (or, for that matter, any Flash document) makes an HTTP request, Flash Player first determines whether the domain of the request matches the domain from which the Flash document was downloaded. If the two domains don't match in any way, Flash Player makes a preliminary request for a file named `crossdomain.xml` that must be stored in the remote domain's Web root folder.

In many cases, it's difficult or impossible to get the cross-domain policy file placed where you need it. For example, if the content comes from a data syndication vendor, the vendor may be unaware of the need for, or unwilling to create and place, the cross-domain policy file. In this scenario, BlazeDS can help.

As shown in Figure 26.4, when you use the Proxy Service, requests from the `WebService` or `HTTPService` components are routed from the Flex application to BlazeDS at runtime. BlazeDS forwards the request to the remote domain. When the response from the remote domain is received, BlazeDS forwards the response back to the Flex client application.

Configuring the Proxy Service

The Proxy Service can proxy requests from the Flex framework's `WebService` and `HTTPService` components. You configure the service in nearly the same manner when creating a proxy for SOAP-based Web services or REST-style resources stored on a remote domain.

The configuration files for LCDS and BlazeDS are stored in a folder under the application's context root folder named `WEB-INF/flex`. The turnkey installation's BlazeDS context root, the folder `WEB-INF/flex`, contains these files:

- `services-config.xml` is the primary configuration file that contains basic configurations and instructions to include all other files listed here.
- `remoting-config.xml` contains configurations for the Remoting Service.
- `messaging-config.xml` contains configurations for the Message Service.
- `proxy-config.xml` contains configurations for the Proxy Service.

Note

The configuration folder for LCDS also includes the `data-management-config.xml` **file with configurations for the Data Management Service.** ■

The default `services-config.xml` file in a new BlazeDS installation contains these `<service-include>` elements, which include the individual configuration files for each service:

```
<service-include file-path="remoting-config.xml" />
<service-include file-path="proxy-config.xml" />
<service-include file-path="messaging-config.xml" />
```

All configuration options for the Proxy Service should be placed in `proxy-config.xml`.

FIGURE 26.4

The request to a remote domain is sent from the Flex application to BlazeDS when using the Proxy Service

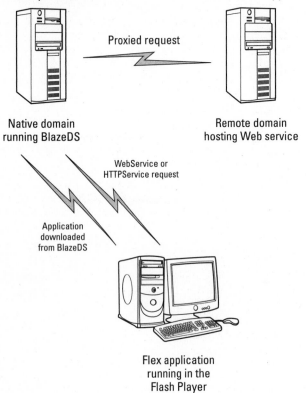

Native domain
running BlazeDS

Remote domain
hosting Web service

Proxied request

WebService or
HTTPService request

Application
downloaded
from BlazeDS

Flex application
running in the
Flash Player

Note

After making changes to any of the configuration files, you typically have to redeploy the BlazeDS instance.
The deployment method differs between application servers. In Tomcat, you can force redeployment by making any small change to the context root's `web.xml` file (located in the `WEB-INF` folder) and saving it to disk.
Tomcat is configured by default to listen for changes to this file and redeploy the context root when it notices
that the file has been updated. ■

Using the default destination

A *destination* in the world of LCDS and BlazeDS is a resource hosted by the application server to
which requests can be sent from a Flex application. A Proxy Service destination gives permission to
BlazeDS to proxy a request and, in some cases, defines an alias that can be used in the Flex application instead of the actual URL where the Web resource is stored.

There are two kinds of Proxy Service destinations:

- **The default destination.** The default destination supports proxying `HTTPService` requests to multiple resources through the use of dynamic URL declarations and wildcard characters.

- **Named destinations.** Named destinations create aliases that can be used by both `HTTPService` and `WebService` in a Flex application instead of the actual resource `url` or `wsdl` settings.

The default destination is defined by a reserved `id` of `DefaultHTTP`. The initial contents of `proxy-config.xml`, shown in Listing 26.1, includes the default destination but doesn't attach it to any URL patterns.

LISTING 26.1

The default contents of proxy-config.xml

```xml
<?xml version="1.0" encoding="UTF-8"?>
<service id="proxy-service"
  class="flex.messaging.services.HTTPProxyService">
  <properties>
    <connection-manager>
      <max-total-connections>100</max-total-connections>
      <default-max-connections-per-host>2</default-max-connections-per-host>
    </connection-manager>
    <allow-lax-ssl>true</allow-lax-ssl>
  </properties>
  <adapters>
    <adapter-definition id="http-proxy"
      class="flex.messaging.services.http.HTTPProxyAdapter" default="true"/>
    <adapter-definition id="soap-proxy"
      class="flex.messaging.services.http.SOAPProxyAdapter"/>
  </adapters>
  <default-channels>
    <channel ref="my-amf"/>
  </default-channels>
  <destination id="DefaultHTTP">
  </destination>
</service>
```

Caution

The default destination's `id` of `DefaultHTTP` is case-sensitive. If you spell it in the configuration file with all uppercase or lowercase letters, or with a different mixed case, it isn't recognized by BlazeDS. ■

The default destination can include one or more <dynamic-url> elements nested within a <properties> element. Each <dynamic-url> element declares a URL pattern that gives permission for requests that match the pattern to use the Proxy Service.

The following version of the default destination allows proxying of requests to resources on two different Web sites:

```
<destination id="DefaultHTTP">
  <properties>
    <dynamic-url>http://www.remotedomain.com/*</dynamic-url>
    <dynamic-url>http://www.anotherdomain.com/*</dynamic-url>
  </properties>
</destination>
```

You also can give global permission to the Proxy Service to proxy requests to any site with a <dynamic-url> element set to the * wildcard character:

```
<destination id="DefaultHTTP">
  <properties>
    <dynamic-url>*</dynamic-url>
  <properties>
</destination>
```

Caution

You should give global Proxy Service permission only in an environment where you're sure that only your applications can make requests to BlazeDS. The default destination is delivered without any <dynamic-url> **permissions, because this sort of declaration can create a security risk.** ■

After you've declared the default destination, any HTTPService component can use the Proxy Service by setting its useProxy property to true. As long as the component's url or wsdl value matches at least one of the <dynamic-url> declarations, the Proxy Service will route the request as needed.

This HTTPService component, for example, uses a proxy to make a request for an XML file on a remote domain that's been given permission in the default destination:

```
<s:HTTPService id="myHTTPService"
  url="http://www.remotedomain.com/somedata.xml"
  result="resultHandler(event)"
  fault="faultHandler(event)"
  useProxy="true"/>
```

Note

To use the Proxy Service with the default configuration, a Web-based Flex application should be downloaded from BlazeDS at runtime. The application then automatically sends its requests back to the server from which it was downloaded. ■

Note

Desktop Flex applications deployed with Adobe AIR don't need to use the Proxy Service. These applications aren't downloaded from the Web at runtime, so they aren't subject to the rules of the Web security sandbox and can make runtime requests directly to any domain. ■

The application in Listing 26.2 uses a proxied request for data in an XML file stored on the server.

LISTING 26.2

A Flex application using the Proxy Service

```xml
<?xml version="1.0" encoding="utf-8"?>
<s:Application xmlns:fx="http://ns.adobe.com/mxml/2009"
  xmlns:s="library://ns.adobe.com/flex/spark"
  xmlns:mx="library://ns.adobe.com/flex/mx">
  <fx:Declarations>
    <s:HTTPService id="contactService"
      useProxy="true"
      url="http://127.0.0.1:8400/blazeds/flex4bible/data/contacts.xml"
      result="resultHandler(event)"
      fault="faultHandler(event)"/>
  </fx:Declarations>
  <s:layout>
    <s:VerticalLayout horizontalAlign="center" paddingTop="20"/>
  </s:layout>
  <fx:Script>
    <![CDATA[
      import mx.collections.ArrayCollection;
      import mx.controls.Alert;
      import mx.rpc.events.FaultEvent;
      import mx.rpc.events.ResultEvent;
      [Bindable]
      private var myData:ArrayCollection
      private function resultHandler(event:ResultEvent):void
      {
        myData = event.result.contacts.row;
      }
      private function faultHandler(event:FaultEvent):void
      {
        Alert.show(event.fault.faultString, event.fault.faultCode);
      }
    ]]>
  </fx:Script>

  <s:Button label="Get Data" click="contactService.send()"/>
  <mx:DataGrid dataProvider="{myData}"/>
</s:Application>
```

On the Web

The code in Listing 26.2 is available in the Web site files as `DefaultProxyDestination.mxml` in the `src` folder of the `chapter26` project. ∎

When you run the application in its current state, it correctly downloads and displays the requested data. If you remove the `HTTPService` component's `useProxy` property or set it to `false`, the request fails because the domain of the XML file and the domain from which the application is downloaded don't match. The result is a security fault, as shown in Figure 26.5.

FIGURE 26.5

A Flex application displaying a security fault

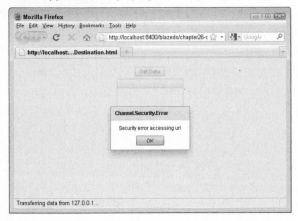

Note

In the example shown in Listing 26.2, the `HTTPService` request triggers a cross-domain security violation, because the application is downloaded from `http://localhost`, while the `HTTPService` component's `url` property refers to `http://127.0.0.1`. While these two ways of representing the `localhost` domain are technically the same, Flash Player doesn't have any way of knowing it. Flash Player cannot match Internet Protocol (IP) addresses to their Domain Name Service (DNS) equivalents and doesn't even try. ∎

Using named destinations

A named Proxy Service destination uses an `id` other than `DefaultHTTP`. You can use a named destination in two ways:

- When the named destination contains a nested `<url>` element, it represents an alias for a single Web resource. The destination `id` can then be referred to in the Flex application instead of the actual `url`.

- When the named destination contains one or more nested `<dynamic-url>` elements, it can proxy multiple Web resources.

To create a named destination for `HTTPService` that serves as an alias for a single Web resource, add a single `<url>` element nested within the destination's `<properties>` element. Set the `<url>` element's text value to the explicit address of the Web resource. The following declaration creates a destination with an `id` of `contactsXML` that points to the location of the data in the remote domain:

```
<destination id="contactsXML">
  <properties>
    <url>
    http://127.0.0.1:8400/blazeds/flex4bible/data/contacts.xml
    </url>
  </properties>
</destination>
```

In the Flex application, set the `HTTPService` object's `destination` property to the `id` you configured in BlazeDS:

```
<mx:HTTPService id="contactService"
  destination="contactsXML"
  result="resultHandler(event)"
  fault="faultHandler(event)"/>
```

Tip

When you set the `destination` property of a `WebService` or `HTTPService` object, its `useProxy` property is set to `true` automatically. Setting a `destination` and then setting `useProxy` to `false` wouldn't make any sense, because the `destination` refers to a Proxy Service resource on the server. ■

Try these steps to use a destination that's already been created in `proxy-config.xml`:

1. Open `DefaultProxyDestination.mxml`.

2. Choose File ➪ Save As from the Flash Builder menu, and name the new file `NamedProxyDestination.mxml`.

3. Locate the `<mx:HTTPService>` tag.

4. Remove the `url` and `useProxy` properties.

5. Add a destination property set to `contactsXML`. The `HTTPService` declaration should look like this:

   ```
   <mx:HTTPService id="contactService"
     destination="contactsXML"
     result="resultHandler(event)"
     fault="faultHandler(event)"/>
   ```

6. Run the new version of the application, and test retrieving data from the server.

The proxied request should be completed successfully.

On the Web

The completed code for this exercise is available in the Web site files as `NamedProxyDestinationComplete.mxml` in the `src` folder of the `chapter26` project. ■

You also can include <dynamic-url> elements in a named destination, either along with or instead of the <url> element. This declaration uses the same destination and a dynamic url:

```
<destination id="contactsXML">
  <properties>
    <dynamic-url>http://localhost:8400/blazeds/*</dynamic-url>
  </properties>
</destination>
```

To use a dynamic url in a named destination, set the HTTPService or WebService object's destination and url properties. The url should match the pattern in the dynamic url in the destination that's defined on the server:

```
<mx:HTTPService id="contactService"
  destination="contactsXML"
  url="http://127.0.0.1:8400/blazeds/flex4bible/data/contacts.xml"
  result="resultHandler(event)"
  fault="faultHandler(event)"/>
```

To use the Proxy Service with the Flex framework's WebService component, declare a named destination that uses an adapter named soap-proxy. Declare a nested <soap> property that points to the endpoint Uniform Resource Identifier (URI) where service requests should be sent and, optionally, a <wsdl> element that indicates the location of the service's Web Services Description Language (WSDL) service description:

```
<destination id="contactsWS">
  <adapter ref="soap-proxy"/>
  <properties>
    <wsdl>/myapp/services/contactService?wsdl</wsdl>
    <soap>/myapp/services/contactService</soap>
  </properties>
</destination>
```

The WebService object in the Flex application then declares just the destination and sends requests to execute service operations to BlazeDS:

```
<s:WebService id="myService"
  destination="contactsWS"
  result="resultHandler(event)"
  fault="faultHandler(event)"/>
```

Using the Remoting Service

The Remoting Service enables you to execute public methods of server-side Java classes hosted by LCDS or BlazeDS. The Flex application uses the RemoteObject component to execute the calls and handle results returned from the remote server.

AMF Documentation

In the past, a number of individuals and organizations reverse-engineered AMF to create open-source or commercial server implementations that are compatible with Flex applications. OpenAMF (`http://sourceforge.net/projects/openamf/`), Red5 (`http://osflash.org/red5`), AMFPHP (`www.amfphp.org`), and WebORB (`www.themidnightcoders.com/weborb/java/`) all represent potential alternatives to Adobe's own products for providing AMF-based messaging with Java-based application servers.

In February 2008, Adobe Systems publicly documented both AMF0 and AMF3 so that organizations that had previously implemented AMF-capable servers could verify that their work matched the protocol exactly and to allow new participants in the world of Flex development to get it right the first time.

The AMF documentation is currently available from these links:

AMF0:
```
http://opensource.adobe.com/wiki/download/attachments/1114283/amf0_
spec_121207.pdf?version=1
```

AMF3:
```
http://opensource.adobe.com/wiki/download/attachments/1114283/amf3_
spec_121207.pdf?version=1
```

The `RemoteObject` component is one of the Flex framework's three Remote Procedure Call (RPC) components. The other two, the `WebService` and `HTTPService` components, have been described previously. Like these two, the `RemoteObject` component makes calls asynchronously and handles returned results with either binding expressions or event handlers.

The Remoting Service on the server and the `RemoteObject` component on the client use a binary format to transfer data back and forth. This format, AMF (Action Message Format), was originally created for ColdFusion's Flash Remoting technology and was then adapted for use with Java classes in Flex Data Services, LiveCycle Data Services, and now BlazeDS. Because this format is binary, the result is smaller data bundles, and there is no need for resource-intensive XML parsing. In most cases, the result is better speed and performance.

Note

There are two versions of AMF. The first version, now known as AMF0, was originally supported in earlier versions of ColdFusion and Flex 1.x. The newer version, known as AMF3, is supported by the current versions of ColdFusion, LiveCycle Data Services, and BlazeDS. Flex 3 and Flex 4 applications make requests in AMF3 by default, but they can be configured to communicate in AMF0 when required. ■

Creating and exposing Java classes

The `RemoteObject` component can call public methods of any basic Java class that's been hosted and configured in LCDS or BlazeDS. (For convenience, I'll refer exclusively to BlazeDS for the rest of this chapter, but the functionality and techniques are exactly the same for LiveCycle Data Services.)

You need to follow two steps when making the Java methods available:

1. **Create and compile a Java class, and place in the BlazeDS classpath.**
2. **Create a destination that points to the Java class on the server**.

Any plain old Java Object (sometimes known as a POJO) can be used through the Remoting Service. Classes written in other common Java design patterns, such as servlets and Enterprise Java Beans (EJBs), can't be called directly through the Remoting Service. If you have existing functionality already built in these formats, though, it's a fairly easy task to create a POJO to call from Flex that in turn makes calls on the server to existing functions.

Follow these rules for creating Java classes for use with the Remoting Service:

- **All classes must be in the BlazeDS classpath.**
  - For individual classes, you can accomplish this by placing them in BlazeDS's WEB-INF/classes folder. As with all Java Enterprise Edition applications, classes placed in this folder are automatically available to the application.
  - For classes stored in JAR (Java Archive) files, the JAR file can be placed in BlazeDS's WEB-INF/lib folder. As with all Java Enterprise Edition applications, archive files placed in this folder are automatically added to the classpath when the application qis started.

- **The Java class must have a no-arguments constructor method or no explicit constructor methods at all.** At runtime, the Remoting Service gateway creates an instance of the Java class (static methods aren't supported). It assumes the presence of a constructor method that can be called with no arguments:

```
public ROService()
{
   System.out.println("constructor method called");
}
```

If you create a class with no explicit constructor method, the Java compiler adds the no-arguments constructor for you. If there's at least one constructor method with arguments, though, you're responsible for creating the alternative constructor method with no arguments.

- **All methods must be explicitly marked as** public. Java enables you to drop the access modifier from a method declaration, but these methods aren't available to the Remoting Service. This simple Java-based method is suitable for use by the Remoting Service:

```
public String helloWorld()
{
   return "Hello from the world of Java!";
}
```

- **You can't use a small set of reserved method names.** These methods are used by the gateway library at runtime; if your class implements any of these method names, conflicts can result:
  - addHeader()
  - addProperty()

- clearUsernamePassword()
- deleteHeader()
- hasOwnProperty()
- isPropertyEnumerable()
- isPrototypeOf()
- registerClass()
- setUsernamePassword()
- toLocaleString()
- toString()
- unwatch()
- valueOf()
- watch()

- **Method names should not start with an underscore (_) character.**

Listing 26.3 shows the source code for a Java class named ROService in the flex4bible package. It has an explicit no-arguments constructor method and a single method that returns a String value.

LISTING 26.3

A Java class suitable for use with the Remoting Service

```
package flex4Bible;
public class ROService
{
  public ROService() {
  }
  public String helloWorld() {
    return "Hello from the world of Java";
  }
  public List getArray() {
    Map stateObj;
    List ar = new ArrayList();
    stateObj = new HashMap();
    stateObj.put("capital", "Sacramento");
    stateObj.put("name", "California");
    ar.add(stateObj);
    stateObj = new HashMap();
    stateObj.put("capital", "Olympia");
    stateObj.put("name", "Washington");
    ar.add(stateObj);
    stateObj = new HashMap();
```

continued

LISTING 26.3 *(continued)*

```
        stateObj.put("capital", "Salem");
        stateObj.put("name", "Oregon");
        ar.add(stateObj);
        return ar;
    }
    public String concatValues(String val1, String val2) {
        return "You passed values " + val1 +
            " and " + val2;
    }
    public String setContact(Contact myContact) {
        return "Contact sent from server: " + myContact.getFirstName() + " " +
            myContact.getLastName();
    }
    public Contact getContact(String val1, String val2) {
        Contact myContact = new Contact();
        myContact.setFirstName(val1);
        myContact.setLastName(val2);
        return myContact;
    }
}
```

On the Web

The source code in Listing 26.3 is available in the Web site files as `ROService.java` in the BlazeDS `WEB-INF/src` folder. The compiled version of the class is stored in BlazeDS `WEB-INF/classes` folder. ■

Note

The no-arguments constructor method in Listing 26.3 isn't required as long as the class doesn't have any other constructor methods. ■

Configuring Remoting Service destinations

Each Java class you want to call from a Flex application with the Remoting Service must be configured as a destination in the BlazeDS configuration files. Remoting Service destinations are defined in `remoting-config.xml` in the BlazeDS `WEB-INF/flex` folder.

The default `remoting-config.xml` that's delivered with a fresh BlazeDS installation looks like this:

```
<?xml version="1.0" encoding="UTF-8"?>
<service id="remoting-service"
  class="flex.messaging.services.RemotingService">
  <adapters>
    <adapter-definition id="java-object"
      class=»flex.messaging.services.remoting.adapters.JavaAdapter»
      default=»true»/>
```

```
    </adapters>
    <default-channels>
      <channel ref=»my-amf»/>
    </default-channels>
  </service>
```

The `<channel>` element toward the bottom of the file indicates that Remoting Service communications are handled by default with AMF. The my-amf channel is defined in services-config.xml in the same folder and looks like this:

```
<channel-definition id="my-amf"
  class="mx.messaging.channels.AMFChannel">
  <endpoint url="http://{server.name}:{server.port}/
    {context.root}/messagebroker/amf"
    class="flex.messaging.endpoints.AMFEndpoint"/>
</channel-definition>
```

Notice that the `<endpoint>` element includes dynamic expressions (wrapped in curly braces) that refer to the server, port, and context root from which the application is downloaded at runtime. This is how the Flex application knows which server should receive requests for remote object method calls.

Each Java class you want to call from Flex should be configured as a destination. Each destination is declared as a child of the configuration file's `<service>` root element and looks like this in its simplest form:

```
<destination id="helloService">
  <properties>
    <source>flex4bible.ROService</source>
    <scope>application</scope>
  </properties>
</destination>
```

The `<destination>` element's id property is an arbitrary value that you use in the Flex application to refer to this class as a remote object. Within the `<properties>` element, you declare these two values:

- **The `<source>` element.** This element is required and is set to the fully qualified name and package of the Java class that contains methods you want to call.
- **The `<scope>` element.** This element is optional and is set to one these three values:
  - **application** means that a single instance of the Java class is constructed as BlazeDS starts up and is shared by all users and requests.
  - **session** means that a new instance of the Java class is constructed for each new browser session. As each user sends new requests, the session instances are tracked (via the host application server's session management) with cookies that are automatically generated and tracked by BlazeDS and the hosting application server.
  - **request** (the default) means that a new instance of the Java class is constructed for each call to any of the class's methods.

Tip

All other things being equal, you achieve the best performance and most efficient memory usage on the server with `<scope>` set to `application`. The only reason to use the default setting of `request` is if the Java class has code that can't be called safely by concurrent requests from multiple clients. ■

Using the RemoteObject Component

You use the Flex SDK's `RemoteObject` component to make calls to a server-side Java class's public methods. Just as the `HTTPService` component sends and receives requests with generic XML-formatted messages and the `WebService` component does with SOAP-based Web services, the `RemoteObject` component makes requests and handles responses using the HTTP communication protocol.

The big difference with `RemoteObject` is the message format: Because AMF is binary, instead of the text-based XML languages used by the `WebService` and `HTTPService` components, messages formatted in AMF are a fraction of the size generated by the other RPC components. As a result, communication is faster, less network bandwidth is used, and larger data packets can be transferred between client and server.

Instantiating the RemoteObject component

As with the `HTTPService` and `WebService` components, you can instantiate `RemoteObject` in MXML or ActionScript code. When used with BlazeDS, you instantiate the object and set its destination property.

This MXML code creates an instance of the `RemoteObject` component that points to a server-side destination:

```
<s:RemoteObject id="roHello" destination="helloService"/>
```

The equivalent code in ActionScript looks like this:

```
import mx.rpc.remoting.RemoteObject;
private var roHello:RemoteObject = new RemoteObject("roHello");
```

Alternatively, you can first declare the object and then set its `destination`:

```
var roHello:RemoteObject = new RemoteObject();
roHello.destination = "roHello";
```

Calling remote methods

You call public methods of server-side Java classes as though they were local methods of the `RemoteObject`. For example, the Java class in Listing 26.3 has a public method named `helloWorld()` that returns a simple `String`. As with local functions, you can call the remote method upon any application event. For example, this code calls the server-side `helloWorld()` method upon a `Button` component's `click` event:

```
<s:Button label="Click to say hello"
  click="roHello.helloWorld()"/>
```

You also can call a remote method by calling the `RemoteObject` object's `getOperation()` method to create an instance of the `Operation` class. The following code creates the `Operation` object and then calls its `send()` method to call the remote method:

```
import mx.rpc.remoting.mxml.Operation;
private function callIt():void
{
  var op:Operation = roHello.getOperation("helloWorld") as Operation;
  op.send();
}
```

This technique enables you to determine which remote method will be called at runtime, instead of having to hard code the method name.

Handling RemoteObject results

As with the other RPC components, you can handle data returned from a call to a remote method with binding expressions or event handlers. Binding expressions take less code and are easy to create, while an event handler gives you much more flexibility in how you receive, process, and save data to application memory.

Using binding expressions

A binding expression used to pass returned data to application components consists of three parts, separated with dots:

- The `RemoteObject` instance's `id`
- The remote method name
- The `lastResult` property

At runtime, the method is created as an `Operation` object that's a member of the `RemoteObject` instance with an `id` that matches the method's name. The `Operation` object's `lastResult` property is populated with data when it's received from the server.

The `lastResult` property is typed as an ActionScript `Object`, but at runtime its native type is determined by what type of data was returned from the server. A `String` returned from Java is translated into an ActionScript `String` value, so a binding expression that handles the value returned from the simple `helloWorld()` method can be used to pass the returned value to a `Label` or other text display control.

The application in Listing 26.4 calls the remote `helloWorld()` method and displays its returned data in a `Label` control with a binding expression in its text property.

LISTING 26.4

Handling returned data with a binding expression

```xml
<?xml version="1.0" encoding="utf-8"?>
<s:Application xmlns:fx="http://ns.adobe.com/mxml/2009"
  xmlns:s="library://ns.adobe.com/flex/spark"
  xmlns:mx="library://ns.adobe.com/flex/mx">
  <fx:Declarations>
    <s:RemoteObject id="roHello" destination="helloService"/>
  </fx:Declarations>
  <s:layout>
    <s:VerticalLayout horizontalAlign="center" paddingTop="20"/>
  </s:layout>
  <s:Label text="Hello from BlazeDS!" fontSize="14" fontWeight="bold"/>
  <s:Button label="Click to say hello" click="roHello.helloWorld()"/>
  <s:Label text="{roHello.helloWorld.lastResult}"
    fontSize="14" fontWeight="bold"/>
</s:Application>
```

On the Web

The code in Listing 26.4 is available in the Web site files as `ROWithBindings.mxml` in the `src` folder of the `chapter26` project. ∎

Using the result event

As with the other RPC components, you can handle results of a call to a remote method with the `RemoteObject` component's `result` event in an identical fashion. This event dispatches an event object typed as `mx.rpc.events.ResultEvent`, the same event object that's used by the other RPC components: `HTTPService` and `RemoteObject`. The event object's `result` property references the returned data.

To handle and save data using the `result` event, follow these steps:

1. **Declare a bindable variable outside of any functions that acts as a persistent reference to the returned data.**

2. **Cast the variable's type depending on what you expect to be returned by the remote method.** For example, if the data returned by the remote Java-based method is typed as a primitive array or an implementation of the Java `List` interface, the `RemoteObject` component casts the returned data as an `ArrayCollection`:

    ```
    import mx.collections.ArrayCollection;
    [Bindable]
    private var myData:ArrayCollection
    ```

3. **Create an event handler function that will be called when the event is dispatched.** The function should receive a single event argument typed as `ResultEvent` and return `void`:

```
private function resultHandler(event:ResultEvent):void
{
}
```

4. **Within the event handler function, use the event.result expression to refer to the data that's returned from the server.** Just as with the `WebService` component, `Result Event.result` is typed as an `Object`. Because the expression's native type differs depending on what's returned by the remote method, you typically have to explicitly cast the returned data. This code expects the remote method to return an `ArrayCollection`:

```
myData = event.result as ArrayCollection;
```

You can listen for the `result` event with either an MXML attribute-based event listener or a call to the ActionScript `addEventListener()` method. The attribute-based event listener looks like this:

```
<s:RemoteObject id="roHello" destination="helloService"
  result="resultHandler(event)"/>
```

When using `addEventListener()` to create an event listener, you can designate the event name with the `String` value result or with the `ResultEvent` class's RESULT constant:

```
var roHello:RemoteObject = new RemoteObject("helloService");
roHello.addEventListener(ResultEvent.RESULT, resultHandler);
roHello.helloWorld();
```

Listing 26.5 uses a `result` event handler function to capture and save data that's been returned from a remote method.

LISTING 26.5

Handling returned data with the result event

```
<?xml version="1.0" encoding="utf-8"?>
<s:Application xmlns:fx="http://ns.adobe.com/mxml/2009"
  xmlns:s="library://ns.adobe.com/flex/spark"
  xmlns:mx="library://ns.adobe.com/flex/mx">
  <fx:Declarations>
    <s:RemoteObject id="roHello" destination="helloService"
      result="resultHandler(event)"/>
  </fx:Declarations>
  <fx:Script>
    <![CDATA[
      import mx.collections.ArrayCollection;
      import mx.rpc.events.ResultEvent;
      [Bindable]
      private var statesData:ArrayCollection;
      private function resultHandler(event:ResultEvent):void
      {
        statesData = event.result as ArrayCollection;
      }
```

continued

LISTING 26.5 *(continued)*

```
      ]]>
  </fx:Script>
  <s:layout>
    <s:VerticalLayout horizontalAlign="center" paddingTop="20"/>
  </s:layout>
  <s:Button label="Get Array" click="roHello.getArray()"/>
  <mx:DataGrid dataProvider="{statesData}"/>
</s:Application>
```

On the Web

The code in Listing 26.5 is available in the Web site files as `ROResultEvent.mxml` in the `src` folder of the `chapter26` project. ∎

Note

As with the other RPC components, exceptions that occur during execution of remote methods generate a `fault` event. The code to handle faults is exactly the same as with the other RPC components. For a full description and some code examples, see Chapter 21 and Chapter 23. ∎

Note

As with the `HTTPService` and `WebService` components, you can pass `result` and `fault` event objects to ActionScript event handler functions using the `ItemResponder` and `AsyncToken` classes. See Chapter 21 for details. ∎

Working with multiple methods

When you need to call more than one method of a Java class on the server, you have to distinguish which event handler function should be called for each of them. You do this in MXML with the `<mx:method >` compiler tag, which is nested within a `<mx:RemoteObject>` tag set. Each `<mx:method >` tag represents a remote Java method and can declare its own distinct result and event handlers.

The Java class in Listing 26.6 has a number of different methods. Its `helloWorld()` method returns a `String`, `getArray()` returns a `List`, and so on.

LISTING 26.6

The Java class with methods being called from Flex

```
package flex4Bible;
import java.util.ArrayList;
import java.util.HashMap;
import java.util.List;
import java.util.Map;
```

```java
public class ROService {
  public String helloWorld()
  {
    return "Hello from the world of Java";
  }
  public List getArray()
  {
    Map stateObj;
    List ar = new ArrayList();
    stateObj = new HashMap();
    stateObj.put("capital", "Sacramento");
    stateObj.put("name", "California");
    ar.add(stateObj);
    stateObj = new HashMap();
    stateObj.put("capital", "Olympia");
    stateObj.put("name", "Washington");
    ar.add(stateObj);
    stateObj = new HashMap();
    stateObj.put("capital", "Salem");
    stateObj.put("name", "Oregon");
    ar.add(stateObj);
    return ar;
  }
  public String concatValues(String val1, String val2)
  {
    return "You passed values " + val1 +
      " and " + val2;
  }
  public String handleObject(Contact myContact)
  {
    return "You Contact # " + myContact.getContactId() + ": " +
      myContact.getFirstName() + " " + myContact.getLastName();
  }
}
```

On the Web

The code in Listing 26.6 is available in the Web site files as `ROService.java` in the BlazeDS application's `WEB-INF/src/flex4Bible` folder. The compiled version of the class is stored in `WEB-INF/classes`. ∎

A Flex application that needs to call more than one of these methods would use the `<s:method>` tag as in the following example:

```xml
<s:RemoteObject id="roHello" destination="helloService"
  result="arrayHandler(event)">
  <s:method name="helloWorld" result="helloHandler(event)"/>
  <s:method name="getArray" result="arrayHandler(event)"/>
</s:RemoteObject>
```

Each method's custom event handler function would then expect the appropriate type of data to be returned from its remote method.

The application in Listing 26.7 handles the `result` events of multiple remote methods using an MXML declaration.

LISTING 26.7

Handling multiple remote methods' result events

```xml
<?xml version="1.0" encoding="utf-8"?>
<s:Application xmlns:fx="http://ns.adobe.com/mxml/2009"
  xmlns:s="library://ns.adobe.com/flex/spark"
  xmlns:mx="library://ns.adobe.com/flex/mx">
  <fx:Declarations>
    <s:RemoteObject id="roHello" destination="helloService"
      result="arrayHandler(event)">
      <s:method name="helloWorld" result="helloHandler(event)"/>
      <s:method name="getArray" result="arrayHandler(event)"/>
    </s:RemoteObject>
  </fx:Declarations>
  <fx:Script>
    <![CDATA[
      import mx.collections.ArrayCollection;
      import mx.rpc.events.ResultEvent;

      [Bindable]
      private var statesData:ArrayCollection;
      [Bindable]
      private var helloString:String;
      private function arrayHandler(event:ResultEvent):void
      {
        statesData = event.result as ArrayCollection;
      }
      private function helloHandler(event:ResultEvent):void
      {
        helloString = event.result as String;
      }
    ]]>
  </fx:Script>
  <s:layout>
    <s:VerticalLayout horizontalAlign="center" paddingTop="20"/>
  </s:layout>
  <s:Button label="Get String" click="roHello.helloWorld()"/>
  <s:Label text="{helloString}" fontSize="14"/>
  <s:Button label="Get Array" click="roHello.getArray()"/>
  <mx:DataGrid dataProvider="{statesData}"/>
</s:Application>
```

On the Web

The code in Listing 26.7 is available as `ROMultipleMethods.mxml` in the `src` folder of the `chapter26.zip` file. ∎

Using the CallResponder class

The `CallResponder` class enables you to define unique responses to method calls. In contrast to using the `<s:method>` tag, which defines responses in a way that makes it difficult to modify at runtime, the `CallResponder` enables you to hook up method calls to particular responses using ActionScript code. You can wrap the calls with whatever logic you deem necessary to implement your application's required logic.

If you'll be calling multiple methods from a single Java class that's been exposed as a Remoting Service destination, you can declare one instance of the `RemoteObject` class and one or more instances of `CallResponder`. Each `CallResponder` can define its own `result` and `fault` event handlers:

```
<fx:Declarations>
  <s:RemoteObject id="roHello" destination="helloService"/>
  <s:CallResponder id="helloResponder" result="helloHandler(event)"/>
  <s:CallResponder id="arrayResponder" result="arrayHandler(event)"/>
</fx:Declarations>
```

When you call a remote method, you receive an instance of the AsyncToken class. By assigning a `CallResponder` object's token property to that `AsyncToken` object, you connect the responder to the method call:

```
arrayResponder.token=roHello.getArray()
```

Now when the data is returned from the server, the responder's `result` event is dispatched and your custom event handler method is called to process the returned data.

The application in Listing 26.8 shows the use of the `CallResponder` class to handle results from multiple method calls.

LISTING 26.8

Handling multiple remote methods with CallResponder

```
<?xml version="1.0" encoding="utf-8"?>
<s:Application xmlns:fx="http://ns.adobe.com/mxml/2009"
  xmlns:s="library://ns.adobe.com/flex/spark"
  xmlns:mx="library://ns.adobe.com/flex/mx">
  <fx:Declarations>
    <s:RemoteObject id="roHello" destination="helloService"/>
    <s:CallResponder id="helloResponder" result="helloHandler(event)"/>
    <s:CallResponder id="arrayResponder" result="arrayHandler(event)"/>
```

continued

837

LISTING 26.8   *(continued)*

```
    </fx:Declarations>
    <fx:Script>
      <![CDATA[
        import mx.collections.ArrayCollection;
        import mx.rpc.events.ResultEvent;
        [Bindable]
        private var statesData:ArrayCollection;
        [Bindable]
        private var helloString:String;
        private function arrayHandler(event:ResultEvent):void
        {
          statesData = event.result as ArrayCollection;
        }
        private function helloHandler(event:ResultEvent):void
        {
          helloString = event.result as String;
        }
      ]]>
    </fx:Script>
    <s:layout>
      <s:VerticalLayout horizontalAlign="center" paddingTop="20"/>
    </s:layout>
    <s:Button label="Get String"
      click="helloResponder.token=roHello.helloWorld()"/>
    <s:Label text="{helloString}" fontSize="14"/>
    <s:Button label="Get Array"
      click="arrayResponder.token=roHello.getArray()"/>
    <mx:DataGrid dataProvider="{statesData}"/>
  </s:Application>
```

On the Web

The code in Listing 26.8 is available as `ROCallResponder.mxml` in the `src` folder of the `chapter26.zip` file. ∎

Passing arguments to remote methods

As with `WebService` operation parameters, you can pass arguments to remote methods using either explicit or bound argument notation. Explicit notation means that arguments are passed in the same order in which they're declared in the Java method.

This Java method, for example, requires two `String` arguments and returns a concatenated `String`:

```
public String concatValues(String val1, String val2)
{
  return "You passed values " + val1 + " and " + val2;
}
```

The following ActionScript code passes arguments to this remote method with explicit syntax:

```
roHello.concatValues(fnameInput.text, lnameInput.text);
```

You also can use bound argument notation with XML elements for each argument wrapped in an `<mx:arguments>` tag set. This code binds the `concatValues()` method's two arguments to values gathered from `TextInput` controls:

```
<mx:RemoteObject id="roHello" destination="helloService">
  <mx:method name="concatValues">
    <mx:arguments>
      <val1>{fnameInput.text}</val1>
      <val2>{lnameInput.text}</val2>
    </mx:arguments>
  </mx:method>
</mx:RemoteObject>
```

To call the method with the bound arguments, call the operation's `send()` method without any explicit arguments:

```
roHello.concatValues.send()
```

Caution

You cannot pass arguments by name to Java-based remote methods using the Remoting Service. Although the bound arguments syntax makes it look like arguments are being matched by their names, in fact they're passed and received in the order of declaration in the Flex application and the Java method. It may seem odd, but in bound notation with Java, the names of the argument elements don't matter at all. ∎

The application in Listing 26.9 passes explicit arguments to a remote method on the server and displays the returned result with a binding expression.

LISTING 26.9

Passing arguments using explicit notation

```
<?xml version="1.0" encoding="utf-8"?>
<s:Application xmlns:fx="http://ns.adobe.com/mxml/2009"
  xmlns:s="library://ns.adobe.com/flex/spark"
  xmlns:mx="library://ns.adobe.com/flex/mx">
  <fx:Declarations>
    <s:RemoteObject id="roHello" destination="helloService"/>
  </fx:Declarations>
  <s:layout>
    <s:VerticalLayout horizontalAlign="center" paddingTop="20"/>
  </s:layout>
  <mx:Form>
    <mx:FormItem label="First Name:">
```

continued

LISTING 26.9 *(continued)*

```
      <mx:TextInput id="fnameInput"/>
    </mx:FormItem>
    <mx:FormItem label="Last Name:">
      <mx:TextInput id="lnameInput"/>
      <mx:Button label="Send Args"
        click="roHello.concatValues(fnameInput.text, lnameInput.text)"/>
    </mx:FormItem>
  </mx:Form>
  <s:Label text="{roHello.concatValues.lastResult}"
    fontSize="14" fontWeight="bold"/>
</s:Application>
```

On the Web

The code in Listing 26.9 is available as ROExplicitArgs.mxml in the src folder of the chapter26.zip file. Another file named ROBoundArgs.mxml, not shown here, demonstrates the use of bound arguments. ■

Passing data between ActionScript and Java

Data passed from a Flex application to a Java class with the Remoting Service is serialized, or transformed, from ActionScript data types to their equivalent types in Java. When data is returned from Java to Flex, a similar serialization occur"s.

Table 26.1 describes how data is serialized from ActionScript to Java and back again.

TABLE 26.1

ActionScript to Java Data Serialization

ActionScript	To Java	Back to ActionScript
Array (dense, meaning there are no "holes" in the indexing)	List	ArrayCollection
Array (sparse, meaning there is at least one gap in the indexing, or associative with non-numeric keys)	Map	Object
ArrayCollection	List	ArrayCollection
Boolean	java.lang.Boolean	Boolean
Date	java.util.Date	Date
Int/uint	java.lang.Integer	Int
Null	Null	Null

ActionScript	To Java	Back to ActionScript
Number	java.lang.Double	Number
Object	java.util.Map	Object
String	java.lang.String	String
Undefined	Null	Null
XML	org.w3c.dom.Document	XML

Notice that data moved in both directions doesn't always survive the round trip with the same data type as it had at the beginning. For example, a "sparse" ActionScript Array is serialized as a Java implementation of the Map interface. When the same data is returned from Java to ActionScript, it arrives as an ActionScript Object instead of an Array.

There are additional data conversions when returning data from Java to a Flex application. For example, both the Java Calendar and Date objects become instances of an ActionScript Date. All non-integer Java data types, such as Double, Long, and Float, are mapped to an ActionScript Number. And numeric Java types that don't fit the precision limitations of the ActionScript Number type, such as BigInteger and BigDecimal, are mapped to an ActionScript String.

Using value object classes

When passing data between a Flex client application and a Java-based server, data objects are typically built using the Value Object design pattern. This pattern ensures that data is serialized in a precise manner and avoids the uncertainties of automatic object serialization described in the previous section.

Note

The Value Object design pattern is known in various Flex and Java documentation sources as the Transfer Object and Data Transfer Object pattern. The different names are all used to refer to the same pattern: a class that contains data for a single instance of a data entity. ∎

The Java version of the value object is written with classic bean-style syntax. Each value is declared as a private field of the class and has its values set at runtime with public set and get accessor methods.

The Java class in Listing 26.10 has three private fields with matching accessor methods and is suitable for use in a Flex application.

LISTING 26.10

A Java-based value object class

```java
package flex4Bible;
public class Contact {
  private int contactId;
  private String firstName;
  private String lastName;
  public int getContactId() {
    return contactId;
  }
  public void setContactId(int contactId) {
    this.contactId = contactId;
  }
  public String getFirstName() {
    return firstName;
  }
  public void setFirstName(String firstName) {
    this.firstName = firstName;
  }
  public String getLastName() {
    return lastName;
  }
  public void setLastName(String lastName) {
    this.lastName = lastName;
  }
}
```

On the Web

The code in Listing 26.10 is available in the Web site files as `Contact.java` in the BlazeDS application's `WEB-INF/src/flex4bible` folder. The compiled version of the class is stored in `WEB-INF/classes`. ∎

To pass this object to a Java-based remote method, create a matching ActionScript class. The ActionScript version's properties must match the Java class in both name and data type.

Tip

Although this example uses public properties for brevity, you also can choose to use private properties with explicit `set` and `get` accessor methods. ∎

The ActionScript class requires a `[RemoteClass]` metadata tag with an alias attribute describing the fully qualified name and package of the matching Java class:

```
[RemoteClass(alias="flex4Bible.Contact")]
```

This is a two-way mapping: When an ActionScript version of the object is sent to the server, the Remoting Service gateway creates a Java-based version and passes the received object's property values to the server-side version. Similarly, if a Java-based remote method returns instances of the server-side version, client-side versions are created automatically and their property values set to the values received from the server.

The ActionScript class in Listing 26.11 declares the same set of values as public properties and maps itself to the server's version with the [RemoteClass] metadata tag.

LISTING 26.11

An ActionScript value object class for use with the Remoting Service

```
package vo
{
  [Bindable]
  [RemoteClass(alias="flex4bible.Contact")]
  public class ContactVO
  {
    public var contactId:int;
    public var firstName:String;
    public var lastName:String;
    public function ContactVO()
    {
    }
  }
}
```

On the Web

The code in Listing 26.11 is available as `ContactVO.as` in the `src/vo` folder of the `chapter26.zip` file. ■

Note

Both the Java and ActionScript versions of the value object class must have either a no-arguments constructor method or none at all. In both cases, if the compiler doesn't find an explicit constructor method, it creates a no-arguments version in the compiled class automatically. Both the client and server assume the presence of the no-arguments constructor method when instantiating the matching value objects. ■

Cross-Reference

If you're a Java developer who has a congenital distrust of public properties, you can define your ActionScript value object classes with implicit getter and setter accessor methods and private properties. In Chapter 2, I describe how Flash Builder 4 can generate the required getter and setter code for you based on existing public property declarations. ■

The Flex application in Listing 26.12 sends and receives instances of value object classes. When it sends an ActionScript value object to the server, the Java method extracts the received object's properties and returns a concatenated value. When the Flex application sends two `String` values, the server's method builds a strongly typed value object and returns it to Flex.

LISTING 26.12

Sending and receiving strongly typed value object classes

```
<?xml version="1.0" encoding="utf-8"?>
<s:Application xmlns:fx="http://ns.adobe.com/mxml/2009"
  xmlns:s="library://ns.adobe.com/flex/spark"
  xmlns:mx="library://ns.adobe.com/flex/mx">
  <fx:Declarations>
    <s:RemoteObject id="roHello" destination="helloService"/>
    <s:CallResponder id="getResponder" result="getHandler(event)"
      fault="faultHandler(event)"/>
    <s:CallResponder id="setResponder" result="setHandler(event)"
      fault="faultHandler(event)"/>
  </fx:Declarations>
  <fx:Script>
    <![CDATA[
      import mx.controls.Alert;
      import mx.rpc.events.ResultEvent;

      import valueObjects.Contact;

      [Bindable]
      private var myContact:Contact;

      private function setContact():void
      {
        myContact = new Contact();
        myContact.firstName = fnameInput.text;
        myContact.lastName = lnameInput.text;
        setResponder.token = roHello.setContact(myContact);
      }
      private function getContact():void
      {
        getResponder.token = roHello.getContact(
          fnameInput.text, lnameInput.text);
      }
      private function setHandler(event:ResultEvent):void
      {
        Alert.show(event.result as String, "Received String");
      }
      private function getHandler(event:ResultEvent):void
      {
        myContact = event.result as Contact;
        Alert.show("Contact VO received from server: " +
          myContact.firstName + " " + myContact.lastName,
          "Received Contact value object");
      }
```

```
      private function faultHandler(event:FaultEvent):void
      {
        Alert.show(event.fault.faultString, event.fault.faultCode);
      }    ]]>
  </fx:Script>
  <s:layout>
    <s:VerticalLayout horizontalAlign="center" paddingTop="20"/>
  </s:layout>
  <s:Panel title="Set or Get Contact">
    <mx:Form>
      <mx:FormItem label="First Name:">
        <s:TextInput id="fnameInput"/>
      </mx:FormItem>
      <mx:FormItem label="Last Name:">
        <s:TextInput id="lnameInput"/>
      </mx:FormItem>
    </mx:Form>
    <s:controlBarContent>
      <s:Button label="Send Object" click="setContact()"/>
      <s:Button label="Receive Object" click="getContact()"/>
    </s:controlBarContent>
  </s:Panel>
</s:Application>
```

On the Web

The code in Listing 26.12 is available as `ROPassVO.mxml` in the `src` folder of the `chapter26.zip` file. ∎

Note

The source code for the Java service class called from the Flex application in Listing 26.12 is shown in Listing 26.3. ∎

Working with BlazeDS Data Connections in Flash Builder 4

Flash Builder 4 includes tools for data centric development that introspect server-side components and then generate client-side ActionScript proxy classes. These classes make it easy to get started integrating application servers into your Flex applications. In this section I describe how to set up BlazeDS to take advantage of these tools and then how to introspect and generate proxy classes for your Remoting Service destinations.

Enabling RDS with BlazeDS

BlazeDS 4.0 uses the RDS (Remote Development Service) protocol to communicate with Flash Builder 4. RDS has been a part of development tools for ColdFusion for many years, but this is the first time it's been applied to other development platforms and languages.

Each copy of BlazeDS includes a Java archive named `flex-rds-server.jar` in its `WEB-INF/lib` folder. This file contains the classes you need to communicate with Flash Builder during development. However, the classes aren't initially enabled in a new BlazeDS installation. You must first add or uncomment a section in the BlazeDS application's `web.xml` file (stored in the `WEB-INF` folder).

Follow these steps to enable RDS in a BlazeDS application:

1. Open `web.xml` from the application's `WEB-INF` folder in any text editor.

2. Remove the comment tokens that are wrapped around this section of the file:

```
<servlet>
  <servlet-name>RDSDispatchServlet</servlet-name>
  <display-name>RDSDispatchServlet</display-name>
  <servlet-class>flex.rds.server.servlet.FrontEndServlet
  </servlet-class>
  <init-param>
    <param-name>useAppserverSecurity</param-name>
    <param-value>true</param-value>
  </init-param>
  <load-on-startup>10</load-on-startup>
</servlet>
<servlet-mapping id="RDS_DISPATCH_MAPPING">
  <servlet-name>RDSDispatchServlet</servlet-name>
  <url-pattern>/CFIDE/main/ide.cfm</url-pattern>
</servlet-mapping>
```

3. To allow introspection of your Remoting Service destinations from Flash Builder without having to deal with user authentication, change the value of the `useAppserverSecurity` parameter to `false`:

```
<init-param>
  <param-name>useAppserverSecurity</param-name>
  <param-value>false</param-value>
</init-param>
```

4. Save your changes.

5. Restart the application server.

Caution

You should only enable RDS without user authentication on instances of BlazeDS that you use during development. Because RDS enables introspection of your Java classes over the Web, it represents a security risk on a production server. ■

Defining BlazeDS data connections

Once you've enabled RDS, you can define a data connection in Flash Builder that references a Java class that's exposed as a Remoting Service destination. To define a data connection, follow these steps:

1. **Make sure you're working in a project that's been enabled for use with BlazeDS.**

2. **Choose Data ⇨ Connect to BlazeDS from the Flash Builder menu.**

3. **In the Connect to BlazeDS/LCDS Service dialog box, select one or more destinations for which you want to generate ActionScript proxy classes.**

4. **Configure the Service name, Service package, and Data type package as you like.** The default values for these options normally work fine for a simple application.

5. **Click Finish to generate the ActionScript classes.**

As shown in Figure 26.6, the Data/Services view now displays the new data connection. Each connection incorporates a list of the methods and return types. By default, if a Java class's public method returns an instance of a strongly typed value object class, the connection wizard creates a matching ActionScript value object class. The conversion of the server-side data to the ActionScript value object happens at runtime and is managed by the generated code.

FIGURE 26.6

The Data/Services view displaying the details of a BlazeDS data connection

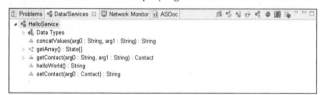

Once you've created the data connection, you can do everything with it that you do with data connections for other application server architectures such as HTTP and Web services:

- Bind data to visual controls

- Generate data entry forms

- Generate detail forms

- Reconfigure return data types for particular methods

Cross-Reference
See Chapter 25 for more information about tasks you can accomplish with Flash Builder data connections. ■

Summary

In this chapter, I described how to integrate Flex client applications with Java Enterprise Edition application servers using BlazeDS. You learned the following:

- BlazeDS is a freely available, open-source implementation of the most popular features of LiveCycle Data Services.

- BlazeDS supports the Proxy Service, Remoting Service, and Message Service.

- The Proxy Service routes HTTP requests to remote domains, eliminating the need for cross-domain policy files.

- The Remoting Service enables Flex client applications to call remote methods of a Java-based class hosted by BlazeDS.

- The Remoting Service sends and receives messages in AMF, a binary format that results in much smaller messages than those that are encoded in XML and SOAP.

- The Flex SDK's `RemoteObject` component is one of the three RPC components, along with `WebService` and `HTTPService`.

- Data can be sent and received between client and server as simple values or as strongly typed value objects.

- You can enable RDS with BlazeDS to support the definition of data connections in Flash Builder 4.

Using the Message Service with BlazeDS

When Flex Data Services 2 was first released, one of its most compelling new features was known as the Flex Message Service. This service enabled developers to create applications in which data and information could be shared instantly between multiple connected client applications without having to program with low-level socket-style application programming interfaces (APIs).

When Flex Data Services was renamed LiveCycle Data Services, this server-based function became known simply as the Message Service (or, when referred to in the context of BlazeDS, the BlazeDS Message Service). Using this service, Flex client applications send messages to a destination on the server. The server then distributes the messages to other connected clients over a supported communication protocol.

LiveCycle Data Services (referred to here simply as LCDS) supports the Real Time Messaging Protocol (RTMP), a protocol that implements true server-push capability. When LCDS Message Service destinations use an RTMP channel, data is pushed from the server to connected clients instantly (or as close as possible, given available network and server resources). BlazeDS, the free open-source implementation of LCDS features, doesn't include the RTMP protocol but adds the capability to define long-polling and streaming channels based on HTTP that enable you to create a messaging architecture that's very close to real time.

IN THIS CHAPTER

Understanding the Message Service

Configuring messaging on the server

Using adapters, channels, and destinations

Creating Flex messaging applications

Using producers and consumers

Sending and receiving simple messages

Working with complex messages

Filtering messages on the server

Debugging message traffic

In this chapter, I describe how to use the Flex framework and BlazeDS to create and deploy an application that shares messages between multiple connected clients.

On the Web

To use the sample code for this chapter, download `chapter27.zip` from the Web site. Follow the instructions later in this chapter to create a Flex project for use with BlazeDS and install the project components to the client and server. ■

Cross-Reference

BlazeDS installation and setup is described in Chapter 26. ■

Understanding the Message Service

The Message Service implements "publish/subscribe" messaging. Each client application that wants to participate in a messaging system can act as a *producer* that can publish messages and as a *consumer* that subscribes to a server-based destination. Messages are then distributed from the server to multiple connected clients using AMF-based encoding.

Cross-Reference

For more about AMF (Action Message Format), see Chapter 26. ■

Client applications that participate in a messaging system aren't always built in Flex. The Message Service includes Java classes that serve as *adapters*. In addition to its default ActionScript adapter that allows sharing of messages between multiple connected Flex-based applications, BlazeDS includes these two specialized adapters:

- **The ColdFusion Event Gateway Adapter.** This adapter supports integration between Flex client applications and Web applications hosted by Adobe ColdFusion Enterprise.

- **The JMS Adapter.** This adapter supports integration between Flex client applications and Java-based environments that use the Java Message Service (JMS).

The diagram in Figure 27.1 shows how messages travel between clients, using a BlazeDS or LCDS application running on a Java Enterprise Edition application server.

Note

Unlike messaging systems that allow clients to create peer-to-peer connections, the Message Service always uses the server as a messaging hub. Clients always send messages to the server, and the server distributes messages as configured. As a result, you can achieve a high level of security through server-based configuration. ■

FIGURE 27.1

Messages traveling between Flex client applications using the Message Service

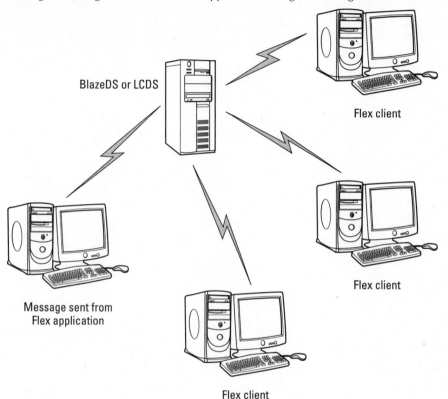

BlazeDS or LCDS

Flex client

Flex client

Message sent from
Flex application

Flex client

Configuring Messaging on the Server

Applications send and receive messages through server-based destinations. As with the Proxy
Service and the Remoting Service that were described in Chapter 26, you configure the Message
Service by defining adapters, channels, and destinations in the server application's configuration
files. As delivered in the starting BlazeDS application, `blazeds.war`, the primary configuration
file, named `services-config.xml`, contains channel definitions. An included file named
`messaging-config.xml` contains adapter and destination definitions for messaging.

Configuring channels for messaging

A channel definition includes information about the communication protocol, how messages are
formatted, the location where messages are sent from the client at runtime (the endpoint), and
whether messages are encrypted with SSL. BlazeDS supports the following types of channels for
use with the Message Service:

- **AMF with simple polling.** In this approach, the client makes a periodic request to the server for pending messages. The period between requests is configurable in the channel definition. The default services configuration file includes a channel with an `id` of `my-polling-amf` that looks like this:

```
<channel-definition id="my-polling-amf"
    class="mx.messaging.channels.AMFChannel">
  <endpoint url="http://{server.name}:{server.port}/{context.root}/
      messagebroker/amfpolling"
    class="flex.messaging.endpoints.AMFEndpoint"/>
  <properties>
    <polling-enabled>true</polling-enabled>
    <polling-interval-seconds>4</polling-interval-seconds>
  </properties>
</channel-definition>
```

  The polling interval in this channel is set to 4 seconds; as a result, each client application makes a request every 4 seconds for pending messages, regardless of whether messaging activity has occurred.

- **AMF with simple polling and piggybacking enabled.** Piggybacking means that when the client sends a message to the server between poll requests, the channel adds a poll request along with the message being sent. The server also piggybacks any pending messages for the client along with the response. To use this feature, add the `piggybacking-enabled` property to the channel definition:

```
<properties>
  <polling-enabled>true</polling-enabled>
  <polling-interval-seconds>4</polling-interval-seconds>
  <piggybacking-enabled>true</piggybacking-enabled>
</properties>
```

- **AMF with long polling.** This approach is similar to simple polling, but by setting the `wait-interval-mills` property to `-1`, you're telling the server to wait for requests indefinitely. With `polling-interval-millis` set to 0, the result is "almost real-time" behavior. A channel that implements this sort of behavior looks like this:

```
<channel-definition id="my-long-polling-amf"
  class="mx.messaging.channels.AMFChannel">
  <endpoint
    url="http://servername:8100/contextroot/messagebroker/amf"
    class="flex.messaging.endpoints.AMFEndpoint"/>
  <properties>
    <polling-enabled>true</polling-enabled>
    <polling-interval-millis>0</polling-interval-millis>
    <wait-interval-millis>-1</wait-interval-millis>
    <max-waiting-poll-requests>0</max-waiting-poll-requests>
  </properties>
</channel-definition>
```

  This strategy significantly reduces client wait times to receive messages, but scalability is limited by the number of available threads on the server. Each time a message is sent from the server to the client, the connection is closed to complete the communication. The client then immediately opens a new connection to wait for the next message.

- **AMF with streaming.** A streaming channel uses different server-side Java classes than the polling channels and results in true "real-time" messaging. A simple streaming channel looks like this in the configuration file:

```
<channel-definition id="my-streaming-amf"
  class="mx.messaging.channels.StreamingAMFChannel">
  <endpoint url="http://{server.name}:{server.port}/{context.root}/
      messagebroker/streamingamf"
    class="flex.messaging.endpoints.StreamingAMFEndpoint"/>
</channel-definition>
```

With this approach the client and server keep the HTTP connection open persistently, rather than closing and reopening it after every message. The result is instant message delivery to all connected clients, but there are some significant limitations.

All the AMF channel types used for messaging send and receive data between client and server as simple HTTP requests from the client. In the background, the server's servlet API uses *blocking I/O*, also known as *synchronous input/output*, so with long polling and streaming you have to explicitly manage the number of concurrent connections to avoid overwhelming the server's available threads.

For example, when using an AMF streaming channel, each browser session can have only a single concurrent connection. (You can change this in the channel configuration.) If you try to test a messaging application with multiple browser windows from a single browser application (for example, Firefox) on the same system, only the first copy of the application will successfully connect to the server. Application instances in additional browser windows will fail to connect because the maximum number of connections per browser session has been exceeded. You can solve this during testing by using multiple browser products (for example, both Internet Explorer and Firefox) or multiple computer systems.

Note

One of the benefits of moving to LiveCycle Data Services from BlazeDS is support for RTMP (Real Time Messaging Protocol). This protocol, originally developed and delivered with Flash Media Server, supports true server-push and streaming communications using nonblocking, or asynchronous, I/O channels. Unlike the HTTP streaming channel supported by BlazeDS, both RTMP and the LCDS implementation of HTTP streaming are capable of supporting thousands of concurrent connections and are limited only by available network and server resources. ∎

The default services configuration file delivered with BlazeDS doesn't contain a streaming channel definition. If you'd like to use one in your development and testing, follow these steps:

1. Open `services-config.xml` from the BlazeDS `WEB-INF/flex` folder in any text editor.

2. Locate the `<channels>` start tag, placed by default just after the `</security>` end tag.

3. Add this `<channel>` element as a child of the `<channels>` tag set:

```
<channel-definition id="my-streaming-amf"
  class="mx.messaging.channels.StreamingAMFChannel">
  <endpoint url="http://{server.name}:{server.port}/{context.
    root}/
      messagebroker/streamingamf"
    class="flex.messaging.endpoints.StreamingAMFEndpoint"/>
</channel-definition>
```

4. Save your changes and restart BlazeDS.

Note

The value of the `<endpoint>` element's `url` attribute should be an unbroken string without any spaces or line feeds. ∎

Tip

You can copy existing channel definitions from the version of `services-config.xml` that's included in the `samples` application. ∎

Configuring messaging adaptors and destinations

You configure messaging destinations in the `messaging-config.xml` file in the BlazeDS `WEB-INF/flex` folder. The default version of this file in the starting BlazeDS application (delivered as `blazeds.war`) looks like this:

```
<?xml version="1.0" encoding="UTF-8"?>
<service id="message-service"
  class="flex.messaging.services.MessageService">
  <adapters>
    <adapter-definition id="actionscript"
      class="flex.messaging.services.messaging.
        adapters.ActionScriptAdapter" default="true" />
    <!--
    <adapter-definition id="jms"
      class="flex.messaging.services.messaging.adapters.JMSAdapter"/>
    -->
  </adapters>
  <default-channels>
    <channel ref=»my-polling-amf»/>
  </default-channels>
</service>
```

Configuring adaptors

An adaptor is a server-side Java class that manages how requests from a client are handled at runtime. The default `messaging-config.xml` file declares one adaptor with an `id` of `actionscript` that manages messaging between Flex applications. It also includes a `jms` adaptor declaration that's used for integration with Java-based clients and is commented out in the default file.

Notice that the `actionscript` adaptor's `default` attribute is set to `true`. As a result, all messaging destinations without an explicit adapter use the `actionscript` adapter:

```
<adapter-definition id="actionscript"
  class="flex.messaging.services.messaging.
    adapters.ActionScriptAdapter" default="true" />
```

Note

If you want to integrate a messaging application with ColdFusion Enterprise, you must add this adaptor declaration:

```
<adapter-definition id="cfgateway"
  class="coldfusion.flex.CFEventGatewayAdapter"/>
```

The required Java class is included in the BlazeDS distribution, so this declaration just configures its use. ■

Configuring destinations

Each destination you configure is a hub for messages shared between multiple connected clients. To create a destination, add a `<destination>` child element of the `<service>` root with a unique `id`. To accept the default values for the adapter, channels, and all other properties, the destination configuration can be as simple as this:

```
<destination id="chat"/>
```

If you want to assign a particular channel to a destination, add a `<channels>` tag set and then declare one or more `<channel>` elements. If you declare more than one channel, they're used as a list in order of preference. The client always tries to use the first declared channel; in the event of any failure, it falls back to the second declared channel.

This destination uses the `my-streaming-amf` channel that was created in the preceding section as its first preference and adds the default `my-polling-amf` channel as a backup:

```
<destination id="chat">
  <channels>
    <channel ref="my-streaming-amf"/>
    <channel ref="my-polling-amf"/>
  </channels>
</destination>
```

If you're following the exercises in this chapter, follow these steps to configure three messaging destinations:

1. **Open** `messaging-config.xml` **from the BlazeDS** `WEB-INF/flex` **folder in any text editor.**

2. **Add these destination definitions:**
   ```
   <destination id="chat"/>
   <destination id="dashboard"/>
   ```

3. If you'd like to use the streaming channel described in the preceding section as your first default choice for all destinations, change the `<default-channels>` element as follows:

```
<default-channels>
  <channel ref="my-streaming-amf"/>
  <channel ref="my-polling-amf"/>
</default-channels>
```

4. Save your changes, and restart BlazeDS.

Creating a Flex Messaging Application

A Flex application can participate in messaging both as a producer, sending messages, and as a consumer, receiving and processing them. In this section, I describe how to create a simple application that exchanges messages using a server-side messaging destination.

Creating a Flex project

When you create a project in Flash Builder that uses the Message Service, you can integrate the project with LiveCycle Data Services or BlazeDS. The steps are the same as when you use the Remoting Service; the project properties include the location of the server, the location of the output folder where generated files are placed during the compilation process, and the URL where requests are made to download the application from the server for testing.

Follow these steps to create a Flex project for use with BlazeDS and the Message Service:

1. Choose File ➪ New ➪ Flex Project from the Flash Builder menu.
2. Set the project name to chapter27.
3. Use the default project location, which should be a folder named `chapter27` under the current workspace.
4. Select Web application in the Application type drop-down menu.
5. Select J2EE in the Application server type drop-down menu.
6. Select Use remote object access service and BlazeDS.
7. Click Next.
8. Set the server location properties as follows:
   - Root folder: **C:\blazeds\tomcat\webapps\blazeds**
   - Root URL: **http://localhost:8400/blazeds**
   - Context root: **/blazeds**
9. Confirm that the Output folder is set to a location under the BlazeDS root folder.
10. **Confirm that BlazeDS is currently running.** Then click Validate Configuration to verify that the Web root folder and root URL are valid.

11. **Click Next.**

12. **Accept the default Main application filename of** `chapter27.mxml`.

13. **Click Finish to create the application and project.**

14. **If you want to use the sample files from the Web site, extract** `chapter27.zip` **into the new project folder.** This ZIP file will overwrite your default Main application file and add other required MXML and ActionScript source files.

15. **Return to Flash Builder, and run the main application.** The application should load from the BlazeDS URL: `http://localhost:8400/blazeds/chapter27.html`.

Sending messages

A Flex application sends messages using the Flex framework's `Producer` component. You can create an instance of a `Producer` using either MXML or ActionScript code. The most important property of the `Producer` is the `destination`, which is set to a server-side destination as configured in the services configuration files.

The MXML code to create an instance of a `Producer` and set its `destination` looks like this:

```
<s:Producer id="myProducer" destination="chat"/>
```

Caution

The value of the `destination` property must be set exactly to the `id` of the destination, as declared in the server's configuration file, and is case-sensitive. ■

If you prefer to create the `Producer` using ActionScript, be sure to declare the object outside any functions so it persists for the duration of the user's application session. Then set the `destination` property inside a function that you call upon application startup:

```
import mx.messaging.Producer;
private var myProducer:Producer = new Producer();
private function initApp():void
{
   myProducer.destination = "chat";
}
```

To send a message to the destination at runtime, create an instance of the `AsyncMessage` class. This class is designed to serve as a message envelope that contains data you want to transfer between clients.

You start by instantiating the object:

```
var message:AsyncMessage = new AsyncMessage();
```

The message object has two properties that can contain data:

- `body`. The `body` property is the primary message data and can refer to any ActionScript object, including complex collection objects such as `ArrayCollection` and `XMLListCollection`.

- headers. The headers property is a dynamic Object that can contain arbitrary named header values that serve as message metadata. The Message Service automatically adds certain headers that have a prefix of DS; to be sure you're avoiding any naming collisions, be sure that any headers you add have your own unique prefix.

For example, in a simple chat application where you want to send both a message and the user name of the person who sent it, you might use the body as the primary message container and then create a chatUser header with the user's information:

```
message.body = messageToSend;
message.headers.chatUser = userWhoSentIt;
```

A complete function that sends a message using data from a set of TextInput controls might look like this:

```
private function sendMessage():void
{
   var message:AsyncMessage = new AsyncMessage();
   message.body = msgInput.text;
   message.headers.chatUser = userInput.text;
   myProducer.send(message);
}
```

Receiving and processing messages

A Flex application uses the Flex framework's Consumer component to receive and process messages sent through the Message Service. As with the Producer, you can instantiate a Consumer using either MXML or ActionScript code. These steps are required in order to receive messages:

1. Set the Consumer object's destination property to a destination that's been configured on the server.

2. Call the Consumer object's subscribe() method upon application startup or whenever you want to start receiving messages.

3. Handle the Consumer object's message event to receive and process each message when it comes in.

The code to create a Consumer object, set its destination, and add an event listener in MXML looks like this:

```
<s:Consumer id="myConsumer" destination="chat"
 message="messageHandler(event)"
```

If you prefer to create the Consumer in ActionScript, be sure to declare the object outside any functions so it persists for the lifetime of the user's application session. Then set its destination and add an event listener in a function that's called upon application startup or whenever you want to start receiving messages:

```
import mx.messaging.Consumer;
private var myConsumer:Consumer = new Consumer();
private function initApp():void
{
  myConsumer.destination = "chat";
  myConsumer.addEventListener(MessageEvent.MESSAGE, messageHandler);
}
```

Regardless of how you create a `Consumer`, it must explicitly subscribe to the messaging destination by calling its `subscribe()` method:

```
myConsumer.subscribe();
```

You can call `subscribe()` at application startup or whenever you want to start receiving messages.

When a message is received from the server, the `Consumer` dispatches a `message` event. The event object is typed as `mx.messaging.events.MessageEvent`. This event class has a `message` property that refers to an `AsyncMessage` object. This is essentially the same object that was created and sent by the `Producer` in the sending application.

To process the message, extract data as needed from the `AsyncMessage` object's `body` and `headers` properties. This event handler function extracts the `chatUser` header and the main message, stored in the object's `body`:

```
private function messageHandler(event:MessageEvent):void
{
  var chatUser:String = event.message.headers.chatUser;
  var msg:String = event.body as String;
  ... save or present data as needed ...
}
```

Note

Notice in the preceding code that the event object's `body` property is explicitly cast as `String`, while the `headers` item is referenced without explicit casting. This is because the compiler expects `body` to be an `Object`, and to assign its value to a variable typed as `String` it must be explicitly cast. In contrast, the arbitrarily named properties of the `headers` object don't have implict typing, so you can pass their values to variables of any type without explicit casting. ■

The application in Listing 27.1 uses `Producer` and `Consumer` components to send and receive messages. The body of each message is a simple String value, and the `chatUser` header value is created from a value entered by the user. When the message arrives, the `messageHandler()` function presents its contents by formatting and adding it to a `TextArea` control.

LISTING 27.1

Sending and receiving simple messages

```
<?xml version="1.0" encoding="utf-8"?>
<s:Application xmlns:fx="http://ns.adobe.com/mxml/2009"
  xmlns:s="library://ns.adobe.com/flex/spark"
  xmlns:mx="library://ns.adobe.com/flex/halo"
  creationComplete="myConsumer.subscribe()">
  <fx:Declarations>
    <s:Producer id="myProducer" destination="chat"
      acknowledge="myProducer_acknowledgeHandler(event)"/>
    <s:Consumer id="myConsumer" destination="chat"
      message="messageHandler(event)"/>
  </fx:Declarations>
  <fx:Script>
    <![CDATA[
      import mx.messaging.events.MessageAckEvent;
      import mx.controls.Alert;
      import mx.messaging.events.MessageEvent;
      import mx.messaging.messages.AsyncMessage;
      private function sendMessage():void
      {
        if (msgInput.text.length == 0 || userInput.text.length == 0)
        {
          Alert.show("Enter user name and message");
          return;
        }
        sendButton.enabled = false;
        var message:AsyncMessage = new AsyncMessage();
        message.body = msgInput.text;
        message.headers.chatUser = userInput.text;
        myProducer.send(message);
        msgInput.text="";
        msgInput.setFocus();
      }
      private function messageHandler(event:MessageEvent):void
      {
        msgLog.text += event.message.headers.chatUser + ": " +
          event.message.body + "\n";
      }
      protected function myProducer_acknowledgeHandler(
        event:MessageAckEvent):void
      {
        sendButton.enabled = true;
      }
    ]]>
  </fx:Script>
  <s:layout>
    <s:VerticalLayout paddingTop="20" horizontalAlign="center"/>
```

```
    </s:layout>
    <s:Panel title="Simple Chat" id="sendPanel">
      <mx:Form width="100%">
        <mx:FormItem label="User Name:">
          <s:TextInput id="userInput"/>
        </mx:FormItem>
        <mx:FormItem label="Message:">
          <s:TextInput id="msgInput" enter="sendMessage()"/>
        </mx:FormItem>
        <mx:FormItem>
          <s:Button id="sendButton" label="Send Message"
            click="sendMessage()"/>
        </mx:FormItem>
      </mx:Form>
    </s:Panel>
    <s:Panel title="Message Log" width="{sendPanel.width}">
      <s:TextArea id="msgLog" editable="false" height="200" width="100%"/>
    </s:Panel>
  </s:Application>
```

On the Web

The code in Listing 27.1 is available in the Web site files as `SimpleChat.mxml` **in the** `src` **folder of the** `chapter27` **project.** ■

Figure 27.2 shows the finished application sending and receiving simple strings as messages.

FIGURE 27.2

A simple chat application using the Message Service

Caution

If you want to test the application in more than one browser window and are using the `my-amf-streaming` channel, be sure to use a different browser product or different client system for each application session. If you have two copies of the application in different windows of the same browser product, and on the same client system, the second will fail to connect to the server.

Also, always completely close all browser windows between testing sessions to be sure you're starting a new browser session each time you test. ■

Sending and Receiving Complex Data

If you're using the Message Service's `actionscript` adapter and sharing data only between Flex client applications, the `AysncMessage` object's `body` property can refer to an instance of any ActionScript object. Unlike Java, where objects that can be serialized must be marked as such, in ActionScript all objects can be serialized. As long as both the sending and receiving application have included at least one reference to the class definition being used, the object can be deserialized upon receipt and made available to the receiving application in its native form.

The process for sending a complex message is exactly the same as for sending a simple value. After creating an `AsyncMessage` object, assign its `body` property to the object you want to send. Then, after assigning any headers you might need, send the message:

```
var message:AsyncMessage = new AsyncMessage();
message.body = acSales;
... assign headers if necessary ...
myProducer.send(message);
```

In the receiving application, the only difference in processing the message lies in how you typecast the received data. This version of the handler function for the `message` event assumes that the message object's `body` property refers to an `ArrayCollection` and explicitly casts it as such upon receipt:

```
private function messageHandler(event:MessageEvent):void
{
   acSales = event.message.body as ArrayCollection;
}
```

The application in Listing 27.2 uses an editable `DataGrid` to allow modifications to an `ArrayCollection` that in turn drives the presentation of a pie chart. Each time a user on any connected client makes a change to his copy of the data, the `ArrayCollection` dispatches a `collectionChange` event. The application reacts by transmitting a message to all other connected clients containing the updated data object.

Note

The code in the `messageHandler()` function removes the `ArrayCollection` object's event listener, updates the data, and sets the event listener again. This ensures that the receiving application doesn't send a message when its data changes, causing a potential infinite loop between two copies of the application. ∎

LISTING 27.2

Sending and receiving complex data

```
<?xml version="1.0" encoding="utf-8"?>
<s:Application xmlns:fx="http://ns.adobe.com/mxml/2009"
  xmlns:s="library://ns.adobe.com/flex/spark"
  xmlns:mx="library://ns.adobe.com/flex/halo"
  creationComplete="app_CreationCompleteHandler()">
  <fx:Declarations>
    <mx:CurrencyFormatter id="cf" precision="2"/>
    <mx:NumberFormatter id="nf" precision="1"/>
    <mx:Producer id="myProducer" destination="dashboard"/>
    <mx:Consumer id="myConsumer" destination="dashboard"
      message="messageHandler(event)"/>
  </fx:Declarations>
  <fx:Script>
    <![CDATA[
      import mx.collections.ArrayCollection;
      import mx.events.CollectionEvent;
      import mx.messaging.events.MessageEvent;
      import mx.messaging.messages.AsyncMessage;
      [Bindable]
      private var acSales:ArrayCollection = new ArrayCollection(
        [{name:"Popcorn", sales:65.00},
          {name:"Soda", sales:78.00},
          {name:"Candy", sales:32.00}]);
      private function app_CreationCompleteHandler():void
      {
        myConsumer.subscribe();
        acSales.addEventListener(CollectionEvent.COLLECTION_CHANGE,
          syncClients);
      }
      private function messageHandler(event:MessageEvent):void
      {
        acSales.removeEventListener(CollectionEvent.COLLECTION_CHANGE,
          syncClients);
        acSales = event.message.body as ArrayCollection;
        acSales.addEventListener(CollectionEvent.COLLECTION_CHANGE,
          syncClients);
```

continued

LISTING 27.2   *(continued)*

```
      }
      private function syncClients(event:Event):void
      {
        var message:AsyncMessage = new AsyncMessage();
        message.body = acSales;
        myProducer.send(message);
      }
      private function formatLabel(data:Object, field:String,
        index:Number, percentValue:Number):String
      {
        return data.name + "\n" +
          cf.format(data.sales) + "\n(" +
          nf.format(percentValue) + "%)";
      }
    ]]>
  </fx:Script>
  <s:layout>
    <s:VerticalLayout paddingTop="20" paddingBottom="20"
      horizontalAlign="center"/>
  </s:layout>
  <s:Label text="Concession Sales" fontWeight="bold" fontSize="14"/>
  <mx:PieChart id="chart" dataProvider="{acSales}"
    width="100%" height="100%">
    <mx:series>
      <mx:PieSeries field="sales" explodeRadius=".05"
        labelPosition="callout" labelFunction="formatLabel"
        fontSize="12" fontWeight="bold"/>
    </mx:series>
  </mx:PieChart>
  <mx:DataGrid dataProvider="{acSales}" editable="true"
    rowCount="{acSales.length}">
    <mx:columns>
      <mx:DataGridColumn dataField="name" headerText="Product Name"
        editable="false"/>
      <mx:DataGridColumn dataField="sales" headerText="Sales"/>
    </mx:columns>
  </mx:DataGrid>
</s:Application>
```

On the Web

The code in Listing 27.2 is available in the Web site files as `Dashboard.mxml` **in the** `src` **folder of the** `chapter27` **project.** ■

Figure 27.3 shows the resulting application, with a pie chart that's synchronized across multiple clients.

FIGURE 27.3

Synchronizing complex data with the Message Service

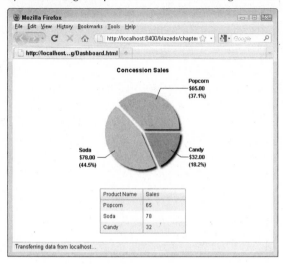

Filtering Messages on the Server

The Message Service supports these strategies for filtering messages on the server, so that a consumer application includes in its subscription information instructions to receive only messages that are of interest:

- The Consumer component's selector property filters messages based on values in message headers.

- The Producer and Consumer components implement a subtopic property that can be used to filter messages based on arbitrary topic names.

- The MultiTopicProducer and MultiTopicConsumer components enable you to send and receive messages that are filtered for multiple arbitrarily named topics.

In this section, I describe the use of the selector property and of subtopics with the Producer and Consumer components.

Note

When you filter messages either with the Consumer components selector property or with subtopics, the filtering always happens at the server. ■

Using the selector property

The selector property enables the Consumer to determine which messages are sent based on a Boolean evaluation. The syntax for a selector is based on SQL-style comparisons of header values to literal strings. This `Consumer`, for example, instructs the server to send messages only where their headers have a `chatroom` header with a value of `'Room1'`:

```
<s:Consumer id="myConsumer" destination="chat"
  message="messageHandler(event)"
  selector="chatRoom='Room1'"/>
```

Using a selector to filter messages has these advantages:

- **All Message Service destinations support the use of the selector property without any required additional configurations.** In contrast, a destination must be specifically configured to support the use of subtopics.

- **Complex Boolean expressions can be used with SQL-style syntax.** For example, this selector examines two header values to determine whether messages should be shared with the current application:

  ```
  selector="chatRoom='Room1' AND chatUser='Joe'"
  ```

On the downside, selectors don't perform on the server as well as subtopics.

Note

If a `Consumer` has already subscribed and you change its `selector` property at runtime, it automatically unsubscribes and resubscribes with the new `selector` data. ■

Using subtopics

In order for a Flex application to use subtopics to filter messages, the server-side destination must be specifically configured to support the feature. In the services configuration file, you add an `<allow-subtopics>` element as a child of a `<server>` element within `<properties>` and set its value to `true`. This destination supports subtopics:

```
<destination id="chatrooms">
  <properties>
    <server>
      <allow-subtopics>true</allow-subtopics>
    </server>
  </properties>
</destination>
```

The `subtopic` property is set in both the `Producer` and the `Consumer`. When you set a subtopic in a `Producer`, the message that's sent to the server includes the subtopic information. When a `Consumer` subscribes to a destination, its `subtopic` is sent along with the subscription information. The server then sends messages to a `Consumer` only where the `subtopic` matches what the `Consumer` requested. If the `Consumer` doesn't define a subtopic, any messages sent from `Producer` objects with subtopics are not passed to that `Consumer`.

Note

If a `Consumer` has already subscribed and you change its `subtopic` at runtime, it automatically unsubscribes and resubscribes with the new `subtopic` value. ■

Follow these steps to modify your services configuration file and add a destination that supports subtopics:

1. Open `messaging-config.xml` from the BlazeDS `WEB-INF/flex` folder in any text editor.

2. Add this destination before the closing `</service>` tag:

```
<destination id="chatrooms">
  <properties>
    <server>
      <allow-subtopics>true</allow-subtopics>
    </server>
  </properties>
</destination>
```

3. Save your changes, and restart BlazeDS.

The application in Listing 27.3 (the MXML code) and Listing 27.4 (the ActionScript code) uses subtopics to filter messages on the server, allowing sending applications to send messages only to a subset of connected clients.

Note

This application uses a separate ActionScript file to demonstrate the use of scripting to implement all nonvisual controls and event listeners. You could implement the same application with more MXML code and less ActionScript if you prefer. ■

LISTING 27.3

An application that filters messages with subtopics

```
<?xml version="1.0" encoding="utf-8"?>
<s:Application xmlns:fx="http://ns.adobe.com/mxml/2009"
  xmlns:s="library://ns.adobe.com/flex/spark"
  xmlns:mx="library://ns.adobe.com/flex/halo"
  creationComplete="initApp()"
  currentState="loggedOut">
<fx:Script source="chatRooms.as"/>
<s:states>
  <s:State name="loggedOut"/>
  <s:State name="loggedIn"/>
</s:states>
<s:controlBarContent>
  <s:Label text="My Chat Rooms" fontSize="24"/>
```

continued

LISTING 27.3 *(continued)*

```
    <mx:Spacer width="100%"/>
    <s:HGroup id="loginBox" includeIn="loggedOut" verticalAlign="middle">
      <mx:Label text="User name:"/>
      <mx:TextInput id="userInput" enter="login()" width="200"/>
      <mx:Button label="Log In" click="login()"/>
    </s:HGroup>
    <s:HGroup includeIn="loggedIn" verticalAlign="middle">
      <s:Label text="Room: {currentRoom==null?'None':currentRoom}"/>
      <s:Label text="User: {user}"/>
      <s:Button label="Log Out" click="logout()"/>
    </s:HGroup>
  </s:controlBarContent>
  <mx:HDividedBox width="100%" height="100%">
    <mx:VBox width="100%" height="100%">
      <s:Panel height="100%" width="100%" title="Rooms">
        <mx:List id="roomList" dataProvider="{acRooms}"
          width="100%" height="100%"/>
        <s:controlBarContent>
          <s:Button label="Change Room" click="changeChatRoom()"
            enabled="{roomList.selectedIndex != -1}"/>
        </s:controlBarContent>
      </s:Panel>
    </mx:VBox>
    <s:Panel width="100%" height="100%" id="chatPanel" title="Chat">
      <s:TextArea id="msgLog" width="100%"  height="100%"
        editable="false"/>
      <s:controlBarContent>
        <s:TextInput id="msgInput" enter="send()" width="100%"/>
        <s:Button label="Send" click="send()"/>
        <s:Button label="Log Out" click="logout()"/>
      </s:controlBarContent>
    </s:Panel>
  </mx:HDividedBox>
</s:Application>
```

On the Web

The code in Listing 27.3 is available in the Web site files as `ChatRooms.mxml` in the `src` folder of the `chapter27` project. ∎

Note

The following binding expression in Listing 27.3 uses a ternary expression, a syntax that's common to languages such as ActionScript, Java, and JavaScript:

```
<s:Label
    text="Room: {currentRoom==null?'None':currentRoom}"/>
```

A ternary expression is a shortened form of an `if` statement that includes three parts. The first part, before the `?` character, is a Boolean expression, frequently comparing two values. If the first part returns `true`, the ternary expression returns the second part of the expression (the part between the `?` and `:` characters). If the first part returns `false`, the ternary expression returns the third part (after the `:` character). ∎

LISTING 27.4

The ActionScript code for the Chat Rooms application

```
// ActionScript file
import mx.collections.ArrayCollection;
import mx.controls.Alert;
import mx.messaging.Consumer;
import mx.messaging.Producer;
import mx.messaging.events.MessageEvent;
import mx.messaging.events.MessageFaultEvent;
import mx.messaging.messages.AsyncMessage;
[Bindable]
private var user:String;
[Bindable]
private var currentRoom:String;
[Bindable]
private var acRooms:ArrayCollection =
  new ArrayCollection(["Room 1", "Room 2"]);
private var myConsumer:Consumer = new Consumer();
private var myProducer:Producer = new Producer();
private function initApp():void
{
  myProducer.destination = "chatrooms";
  myProducer.addEventListener(MessageFaultEvent.FAULT, faultHandler);
  myConsumer.destination = "chatrooms";
  myConsumer.addEventListener(MessageEvent.MESSAGE, messageHandler);
  myConsumer.addEventListener(MessageFaultEvent.FAULT, faultHandler);
}
private function send():void
{
  var message:AsyncMessage = new AsyncMessage();
  message.body = msgInput.text;
  message.headers.user = user;
  myProducer.send(message);
  msgInput.text="";
  msgInput.setFocus();
```

continued

LISTING 27.4   *(continued)*

```
}
private function messageHandler(event:MessageEvent):void
{
  msgLog.text += event.message.headers.user + ": " +
    event.message.body + "\n";
}
private function login():void
{
  user = userInput.text;
  myConsumer.subscribe();
  currentState = "loggedIn";
}
private function logout():void
{
  myConsumer.unsubscribe();
  msgLog.text="";
  currentState = "";
  currentRoom="";
  roomList.selectedIndex=-1;
}
private function changeChatRoom():void
{
  currentRoom = roomList.selectedItem as String;
  myProducer.subtopic = currentRoom;
  myConsumer.subtopic = currentRoom;
}
private function faultHandler(event:MessageFaultEvent):void
{
  Alert.show(event.faultString, event.faultCode);
}
```

On the Web

The code in Listing 27.4 is available in the Web site files as `chatRooms.as` **in the** `src` **folder of the** `chapter27` **project.** ∎

Figure 27.4 shows the resulting application sharing data only within a selected subtopic.

Caution

If you're using a streaming channel for this application, remember to use multiple browser products or client systems to successfully test messaging between multiple clients. ∎

FIGURE 27.4

An application sending and receiving filtered messages using subtopics

Tracing Messaging Traffic

As with all network communications between Flex clients and application servers, you can use the `TraceTarget` component to enable tracing of messaging traffic. Follow these steps to trace messaging:

1. **Open any Flex application that uses the Message Service.**

2. **Add an `<s:TraceTarget/>` tag as a child of the application's `<fx:Declarations>` element.**

3. **Set any optional values that determine what metadata is included with each tracing message.** For example, this declaration of the `TraceTarget` object would cause tracing messages to display date and time information:

   ```
   <fx:Declarations>
     <s:TraceTarget includeDate="true" includeTime="true"/>
   </fx:Declarations>
   ```

4. **Run the application in debug mode.**

5. **Watch Flash Builder's Console view to see the tracing output.**

Figure 27.5 shows the resulting output in Flash Builder's Console view.

FIGURE 27.5

Tracing output from a messaging application

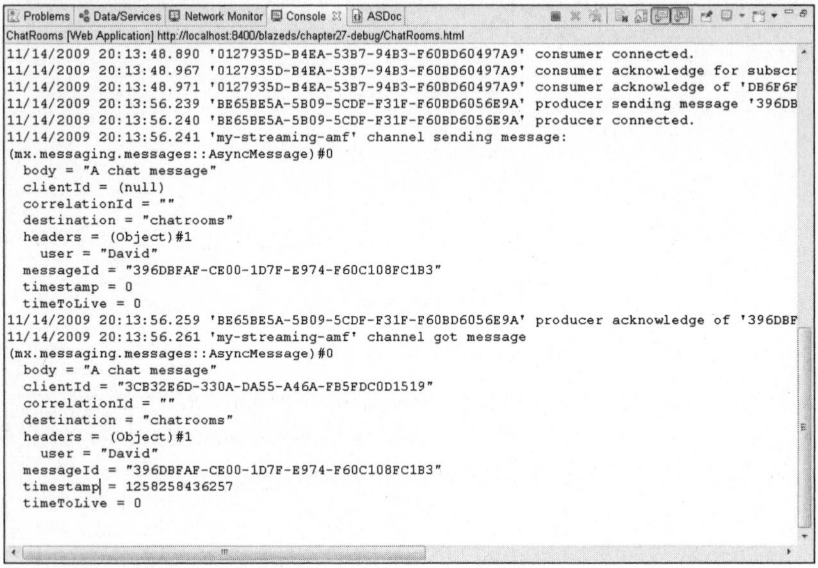

```
 Problems   Data/Services   Network Monitor   Console    ASDoc
ChatRooms [Web Application] http://localhost:8400/blazeds/chapter27-debug/ChatRooms.html
11/14/2009 20:13:48.890 '0127935D-B4EA-53B7-94B3-F60BD60497A9' consumer connected.
11/14/2009 20:13:48.967 '0127935D-B4EA-53B7-94B3-F60BD60497A9' consumer acknowledge for subscr
11/14/2009 20:13:48.971 '0127935D-B4EA-53B7-94B3-F60BD60497A9' consumer acknowledge of 'DB6F6F
11/14/2009 20:13:56.239 'BE65BE5A-5B09-5CDF-F31F-F60BD6056E9A' producer sending message '396DB
11/14/2009 20:13:56.240 'BE65BE5A-5B09-5CDF-F31F-F60BD6056E9A' producer connected.
11/14/2009 20:13:56.241 'my-streaming-amf' channel sending message:
(mx.messaging.messages::AsyncMessage)#0
  body = "A chat message"
  clientId = (null)
  correlationId = ""
  destination = "chatrooms"
  headers = (Object)#1
    user = "David"
  messageId = "396DBFAF-CE00-1D7F-E974-F60C108FC1B3"
  timestamp = 0
  timeToLive = 0
11/14/2009 20:13:56.259 'BE65BE5A-5B09-5CDF-F31F-F60BD6056E9A' producer acknowledge of '396DBF
11/14/2009 20:13:56.261 'my-streaming-amf' channel got message
(mx.messaging.messages::AsyncMessage)#0
  body = "A chat message"
  clientId = "3CB32E6D-330A-DA55-A46A-FB5FDC0D1519"
  correlationId = ""
  destination = "chatrooms"
  headers = (Object)#1
    user = "David"
  messageId = "396DBFAF-CE00-1D7F-E974-F60C108FC1B3"
  timestamp = 1258258436257
  timeToLive = 0
```

Summary

In this chapter, I described how to create and deploy Flex client applications that use the Message Service with BlazeDS. You learned the following:

- The Message Service is implemented in both LiveCycle Data Services and BlazeDS.

- The Message Service enables you to share data between multiple connected Flex applications in real time or "almost real time."

- Flex applications that use the Message Service can be integrated with other applications that are built in Java and ColdFusion.

- A Flex application sends messages using the Flex framework's `Producer` component.

- A Flex application receives and processes messages using the Flex framework's `Consumer` component.

- You can send and receive both simple and complex data.

- Messages can be filtered at the server with the `Consumer` component's `selector` property or with subtopics.

- You can use the `TraceTarget` logger target to turn on tracing of message traffic during debugging sessions.

Integrating Flex Applications with ColdFusion

Flash Remoting, the technology that enables Flash-based documents to communicate with Web-based resources over a high-speed, binary protocol, was first introduced with ColdFusion MX (also known as ColdFusion version 6). In the early days of the technology, before the introduction of Flex, applications built in Flash MX and subsequent releases had the ability to make remote procedure calls to functions of ColdFusion Components (CFCs) over a standard Web connection.

When Flex 1.0 was released, Flash Remoting was adapted for use with Java-based application servers that hosted Java-based classes. Flex client applications could make calls to Java-based methods just as easily as with ColdFusion using the feature first known as Remote Object Services, now known as the Remoting Service.

Cross-Reference
The Java-based Remoting Service is described in Chapter 26. ∎

Adobe ColdFusion 9 (the most recent version at the time that Flash Builder 4 and Flex 4 were released) continues to offer built-in support for Flash Remoting with Flex-based and Flash-based client applications, and it adds the capability to integrate tightly with features that are unique to LiveCycle Data Services or BlazeDS. When ColdFusion is integrated with these Adobe products, you can build and deploy Flex applications that share messages in real time or near real time with ColdFusion-based resources using the Message Service, and you can use LiveCycle Data Services' Data Management Service to create applications that synchronize data between multiple connected clients and servers.

IN THIS CHAPTER

Understanding Flash Remoting and ColdFusion

Creating a Flex project for use with ColdFusion

Configuring Flash Remoting on the server

Creating CFCs for Flex

Calling CFC functions and handling CFC function results

Passing arguments to CFC functions

Using value object classes

Using ColdFusion data connections in Flash Builder

Working with ColdFusion 9 Services

New Feature

BlazeDS is automatically installed with ColdFusion 9, so the features described in Chapters 26 and 27, such as the Message Service, are also available to ColdFusion 9 developers. ■

Note

All of the currently available ColdFusion features that support integration with Flex client applications were first introduced in ColdFusion version 7.02. With the exception of the event gateway used to integrate Flex applications with the Message Service, all of the features described in this chapter work equally well with ColdFusion 7.02 or later. ■

In this chapter, I describe how to use Flash Remoting to call ColdFusion component functions from Flex applications.

On the Web

To use the sample code for this chapter, download `chapter28.zip` from the Web site. Follow the instructions later in this chapter to create a Flex project for use with ColdFusion and install the various project components to the client and server. ■

Understanding Flash Remoting and ColdFusion

The feature known as the Remoting Service in LiveCycle Data Services and BlazeDS is known as Flash Remoting in ColdFusion. Flash Remoting enables you to directly make calls to functions of ColdFusion Components using the Flex SDK's `RemoteObject` component.

Calls from a Flex client application are sent directly to the ColdFusion server as HTTP requests encoded in Action Message Format (AMF), and responses are returned from ColdFusion to the Flex application without any intermediate proxy or additional software. As shown in Figure 28.1, when using the `RemoteObject` component to call CFC methods, you don't need to install or integrate LiveCycle Data Services or BlazeDS.

FIGURE 28.1

Flash Remoting requests and responses travel directly from the Flex application to ColdFusion and back again.

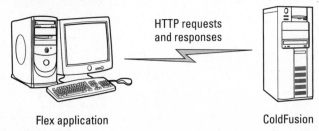

HTTP requests
and responses

Flex application   ColdFusion

To call CFC functions from a Flex application, follow these steps:

1. **Install Adobe ColdFusion or obtain access to a ColdFusion server.** You can use either the Standard or Enterprise edition, or, if you don't have a license, you can install ColdFusion locally as the Developer edition. This edition is free for development and testing and has some limitations, including allowing connections from only two browser clients during any particular session.

2. **Create ColdFusion Components on the server with code you can call from a Flex application.**

3. **If using Flash Builder, create a Flex project that's integrated with your ColdFusion server installation.**

4. **Create and test Flex client code to call the CFC functions.**

Note

The sample code and instructions in this chapter assume that ColdFusion 9 has been installed on a Windows-based development system using the development Web server running on port 8500. If your ColdFusion installation differs, adapt the instructions as needed. ■

Creating a Flex project for use with ColdFusion

When you create a new Flex project, you can add project properties that enable you to easily test your Flex application with the ColdFusion server. Follow these steps to create a new Flex project:

1. **Choose File ➪ New ➪ Flex Project from the Flex Builder menu.**

2. **On the first screen, set these properties, as shown in Figure 28.2:**
   - Project name: **chapter28**
   - Use default location: **selected**
   - Application type: **Web application**
   - Application server type: **ColdFusion**
   - Use remote object access service: **selected**
   - ColdFusion Flash Remoting: **selected**

3. **Click Next.**

4. **On the Configure ColdFusion Server screen, shown in Figure 28.3, set the ColdFusion installation type and location.** If you installed the server configuration to the default location in Windows, for the ColdFusion installation type, select Standalone.

5. **Set the ColdFusion root folder to the installation folder.** For example, if you are using the default stand-alone installation on Windows, the root folder is `C:\ColdFusion9`.

6. **Set the Web server root folder and URL.** If you are using the default stand-alone installation on Windows, the root folder is `C:\ColdFusion9\wwwroot`, and the Root URL is `http://localhost:8500`.

FIGURE 28.2

Creating a new Flex project

7. Click Validate Configuration to verify that your ColdFusion configuration settings are accurate.

Note

ColdFusion must be running in order to validate the configuration at this point. Flex Builder sends a test request to the ColdFusion server's Root URL to ensure that the server is reachable. ∎

8. Click Next.

9. Accept the Main application filename of `chapter28.mxml`.

10. **Set the Output folder to a location under the ColdFusion Root URL.** This is the folder where the application's debug output files will be generated during the compilation process and from which you retrieve documents in the browser during testing. The default setting is a subfolder under the ColdFusion Web root whose name starts with the project name and ends with -debug.

11. **Click Finish to create the project and application.**

12. **Run the application.**

You should see that the application is retrieved from the folder on the ColdFusion server using the server's root URL and the subfolder in which the output files are generated.

FIGURE 28.3

Configuring the ColdFusion server location

On the Web

If you want to use the sample applications for this chapter from the Web site, follow these instructions: Extract the contents of `chapter28.zip` to the new project's root folder, locate `ColdFusionFiles folder` in the project files, and copy its files to the ColdFusion server's Web root folder, such as `C:\ColdFusion9\www root`. This creates a new subfolder named `flex4bible/chapter28` under the ColdFusion Web root. ■

Configuring Flash Remoting on the server

Just as with the Remoting Service on LiveCycle Data Services or BlazeDS, to use Flash Remoting from a Flex application, it must be configured on the server. When you install ColdFusion, a folder named `WEB-INF/flex` is created that contains a default set of configuration files.

Note

The `WEB-INF` folder is located under the ColdFusion Web root, as defined during the ColdFusion installation process. The actual location differs depending on ColdFusion's configuration.

The "server" configuration that includes a limited JRun server places `WEB-INF` under the installation folder's `wwwroot` subfolder. When the server configuration of ColdFusion is installed on Windows with the default location, the Flex configuration files are stored in `C:\ColdFusion9\wwwroot\WEB-INF\flex`. For the J2EE or multi-server configurations, `WEB-INF` is located under the ColdFusion "context root" folder. For example, when installed with the default location on Windows, the Flex configuration files are stored in `C:\JRun4\servers\cfusion\cfusion-ear\cfusion-war\WEB-INF\flex`. ■

Flash Remoting access is configured in the primary services configuration file, `services-config.xml`, which includes a file named `remoting-config.xml` that declares Flash Remoting configuration options.

ColdFusion 9 includes a predefined Flash Remoting destination with an `id` of `ColdFusion` in `remoting-config.xml` that looks like this:

```
<destination id="ColdFusion">
  <channels>
    <channel ref="my-cfamf"/>
  </channels>
  <properties>
    <source>*</source>
  </properties>
</destination>
```

The following key destination properties are worth a detailed description:

- The `<channel>` is set to `my-cfamf`. This channel is defined in `services.config.xml` and uses the `AMFChannel` class on the server to serialize and deserialize AMF-formatted messages between client and server. The services configuration file also defines a channel named `my-cfamf-secure` that can be used for encrypted communications over SSL.

- The `<source>` property is set to a wildcard value of `*`, meaning that the predefined `ColdFusion` destination can be used to call any CFC on the server. This is in contrast to the use of the Java-based Remoting Service with LCDS and BlazeDS, where each Java class must be configured with its own unique destination.

The default `ColdFusion` destination is designed to be usable with its default property settings. In most cases, you can start calling CFC functions from a Flex client application without changing any of the server-side configuration options.

Creating ColdFusion Components for Flex

The rules for creating ColdFusion components for use with a Flex application are very similar to those CFCs used as SOAP-based Web services:

- **CFCs should be placed in a folder under the Web root.** With additional configuration, you also can place CFCs in folders that are mapped through the ColdFusion administrator.

- **CFC functions should have their access attribute set to remote.** With additional configuration, you also can expose functions with their `access` set to `public`.

- **Functions should return values with data types that are compatible with Flex applications.**

Web Resource

A complete description of how to create and deploy ColdFusion components is beyond the scope of this chapter. For a good starting tutorial on this subject, see Ben Forta's article on the Adobe Developer Center Web site at:

www.adobe.com/devnet/coldfusion/articles/intro_cfcs.html. ■

Table 26.1 describes the data types that can be returned from a CFC to a Flex application and how each value is translated into an ActionScript variable when it's returned from a CFC function to a Flex client application.

TABLE 26.1

Data Conversion from ColdFusion to ActionScript

ColdFusion Data Type	ActionScript Data Type
String	String
Array	Array
Query	ArrayCollection
Struct	Object
CFC instance	Strongly typed value object
Date	Date
Numeric	Number
XML object	XML object

The returned data type is determined in a ColdFusion function by its returntype property. The CFC in Listing 28.1 shows a ColdFusion component with a helloWorld() function that declares a returntype of string:

LISTING 28.1

A simple ColdFusion component

```
<cfcomponent name="HelloService" output="false"
  hint="A ColdFusion Component for use in Flash Remoting">
  <cffunction name="helloWorld" returntype="string" access="remote">
    <cfreturn "Hello from a ColdFusion Component!"/>
  </cffunction>
</cfcomponent>
```

On the Web

The code in Listing 28.1 is available in the Web site files as HelloService.cfc in the ColdFusion files of the chapter28 project. ■

Note

Unlike the worlds of Java and ActionScript, ColdFusion Markup Language is mostly case-insensitive. As a result, returntype **values of** string **and** String **mean the same thing.** ∎

The returntype attribute is also used by ColdFusion to verify that data being returned by a function is of the correct type. ColdFusion Markup Language (CFML) is a very loosely typed language, where simple values are generally stored as String values until being cast appropriately at runtime (a process sometimes known as "lazy evaluation"). But at runtime, ColdFusion can detect discrepancies between a declared returntype and the actual value being returned. This function, for example, would generate a server-side runtime error, because the value being returned can't be parsed as a number:

```
<cffunction name="getNumber" returntype="numeric" access="remote">
  <cfreturn "This is not a numeric value"/>
</cffunction>
```

This resulting server-side error would be exposed in the Flex client application as a fault event dispatched by the RemoteObject that made the remote call to the function.

New Feature

In ColdFusion 9, you can write CFCs with the pure scripting style known as CFScript. Using the new scripting syntax, the CFC in Listing 28.1 would look like this:

```
component hint="A CFC written in script" output="false"
{
  remote string function helloWorld()
  {
    return "Hello from a ColdFusion Component!";
  }
}
```

You can choose either tag- or scripting-based syntax in ColdFusion 9; in either case, the CFC is available to the Flex application using either Flash Remoting or SOAP-based Web services. ∎

Using CFCs with the RemoteObject Component

To call a CFC function from a Flex client application, you start by creating an instance of the RemoteObject component. This is the same RPC component that's used to integrate Flex applications with LiveCycle Data Services and BlazeDS, and the client-side code that's used to communicate with ColdFusion is almost exactly the same. If the source of the component is set to a wildcard in the server-side destination, you set the component's source property in the client-side RemoteObject declaration.

Setting the source property

The CFC is known to the Flex client application by its fully qualified name and location, declared with dot notation. This `String` value is passed to the `RemoteObject` component's `source` property to determine which component will be called on the server.

ColdFusion uses a naming pattern whereby CFCs are known by the name of the file in which the component is defined (without the file extension), prefixed with the names of the folders in which it's stored, starting at the Web root folder. Folder and component names are separated with dot characters, just like packages in Java. So, for example, a CFC that's defined in a file named `MyComponent.cfc` and stored in a subfolder under the ColdFusion Web root named `flex4bible/cfc` would be referred to from Flex as:

```
flex4bible.cfc.MyComponent
```

If you're working on a development server that has RDS enabled, you can generate a CFC's documentation by navigating to the component from a Web browser. The documentation includes the exact string you need to set the component's source accurately in Flex. For example, you can browse to the `HelloService.cfc` file stored in the Web root folder's `flex3bible/chapter28` folder with this URL:

```
http://localhost:8500/flex4bible/chapter28/HelloService.cfc
```

Tip
If you have RDS security turned on in ColdFusion Administrator, you'll need to enter your RDS password to view the CFC's documentation. ■

Figure 28.4 shows the resulting CFC documentation. The string value you use as the source attribute in Flex is displayed twice: once at the top of the documentation page and again in the hierarchy section.

Creating a RemoteObject instance

You can create an instance of the `RemoteObject` component that works with the `ColdFusion` destination in either MXML or ActionScript. In addition to the object's unique `id`, you set object's `destination` to the `id` of the destination on the server, named by default `ColdFusion`. The object's `source` attribute is set to the fully qualified name and location of the CFC in dot notation, as described in the preceding section.

The code to create a `RemoteObject` and set its required properties in MXML looks like this:

```
<s:RemoteObject id="helloService"
    destination="ColdFusion"
    source="flex4bible.chapter28.HelloService"/>
```

The code to create the same object in ActionScript looks like this:

```
import mx.rpc.remoting.RemoteObject;
var helloService:RemoteObject = new RemoteObject("ColdFusion");
helloService.source = "flex4bible.chapter28.HelloService";
```

After you've declared the `RemoteObject` and set its `source` and `destination` properties, you're ready to make runtime calls to remote CFC functions.

FIGURE 28.4

Automatically generated CFC documentation, including the component's fully qualified name and location

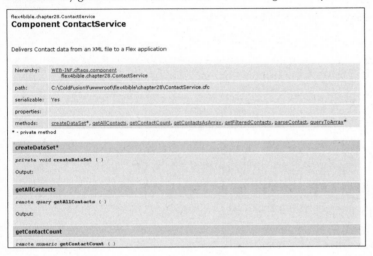

Calling CFC functions

You call CFC functions as though they were local methods of the `RemoteObject`. For example, the CFC in Listing 28.1 has a public method named `helloWorld()` that returns a simple `String`. As with local functions, you can call the remote method upon any application event. For example, the following code calls the server-side `helloWorld()` method upon a `Button` component's `click` event:

```
<s:Button label="Click to say hello"
    click="helloService.helloWorld()"/>
```

You also can call a CFC function by calling the `RemoteObject` component's `getOperation()` method to create an instance of the `Operation` class. The following code creates the `Operation` object and then calls its `send()` method to call the remote method:

```
import mx.rpc.remoting.mxml.Operation;
private function callIt():void
{
  var op:Operation = helloService.getOperation("helloWorld")
    as Operation;
  op.send();
}
```

This technique enables you to determine which remote method will be called at runtime, instead of having to hard code the method name.

Handling CFC Function Results

Calls to remote CFC functions are made asynchronously in Flex, so a call to a CFC function doesn't return data directly. Instead, as with the other RPC components, you handle the response with binding expressions or event handlers. Binding expressions require less code and are easy to create, while event handlers offer much more power and flexibility in how you receive, process, and save data to application memory.

Using binding expressions

A binding expression used to pass returned data to application components consists of three parts, separated with dots:

- The RemoteObject instance's id
- The CFC function name
- The lastResult property

At runtime, the method is created as an Operation object that's a member of the RemoteObject instance. The Operation object's lastResult property is populated with data when it's received from the server.

The lastResult property is explicitly typed as an ActionScript Object, but at runtime its native type is determined by the type of data that's returned from the server. A String returned from ColdFusion is translated into an ActionScript String value, so a binding expression that handles the value returned from the simple helloWorld() method can be used to pass the returned value to a Label or other text display control.

The application in Listing 28.2 calls the remote helloWorld() CFC function and displays its returned data in a Label control with a binding expression in its text property.

LISTING 28.2

Handling returned data with a binding expression

```xml
<?xml version="1.0" encoding="utf-8"?>
<s:Application xmlns:fx="http://ns.adobe.com/mxml/2009"
  xmlns:s="library://ns.adobe.com/flex/spark"
  xmlns:mx="library://ns.adobe.com/flex/halo">
  <fx:Declarations>
    <s:RemoteObject id="helloService"
      destination="ColdFusion"
      source="flex4bible.chapter28.HelloService"/>
  </fx:Declarations>
  <s:layout>
    <s:VerticalLayout paddingTop="20" horizontalAlign="center"/>
  </s:layout>
  <s:Button label="Hello World" click="helloService.helloWorld()"/>
  <s:Label text="{helloService.helloWorld.lastResult}"/>
</s:Application>
```

On the Web

The code in Listing 28.2 is available in the Web site files as `ROWithBinding.mxml` in the `src` folder of the `chapter28` project. ∎

Using the result event

As with other RPC components, you can handle results of a call to a CFC function with the `RemoteObject` component's `result` event. This event dispatches an event object typed as `mx.rpc.events.ResultEvent`, the same event object that's used by the other RPC components `HTTPService` and `RemoteObject`. The event object's `result` property references the returned data.

To handle and save data using the `result` event, follow these steps:

1. **Declare a bindable variable outside of any function that acts as a persistent reference to the returned data.** Cast the variable's type depending on what you expect to be returned by the remote method. For example, if the data returned by the CFC function is typed as a query object, the `RemoteObject` component casts the returned data as an `ArrayCollection`. The following code declares a bindable `ArrayCollection` variable:

   ```
   import mx.collections.ArrayCollection;
   [Bindable]
   private var myData:ArrayCollection
   ```

2. **Create an event handler function that will be called when the event is dispatched.** The function should receive a single event argument typed as `ResultEvent` and return `void`:

```
private function resultHandler(event:ResultEvent):void
{
}
```

3. **Within the event handler function, use the** `event.result` **expression to refer to the data that's returned from the server.** Just as with the `WebService` component, `ResultEvent.result` is typed as an `Object`. Because the expression's native type differs depending on what's returned by the CFC function, you typically have to explicitly cast the returned data. This code expects the CFC function to return an `ArrayCollection`:

```
myData = event.result as ArrayCollection;
```

You can listen for the `result` event with either an MXML attribute-based event listener or a call to the ActionScript `addEventListener()` method. The attribute-based event listener looks like this:

```
<s:RemoteObject id="myService" destination="helloClass"
  source="flex4bible.chapter28.ContactService"
  result="resultHandler(event)"/>
```

When using `addEventListener()` to create an event listener, you can designate the event name with the `String` value result, or with the `ResultEvent` class's `RESULT` static constant:

```
var contactService:RemoteObject = new RemoteObject("ColdFusion");
contactService.source = "flex4bible.chapter28.ContactService";
contactService.addEventListener(ResultEvent.RESULT, resultHandler);
contactService.getAllContacts();
```

Listing 28.3 uses a `result` event handler function to capture and present data that's been returned from a CFC function.

LISTING 28.3

Handling results from a CFC function with a result event handler

```
<?xml version="1.0" encoding="utf-8"?>
<s:Application xmlns:fx="http://ns.adobe.com/mxml/2009"
  xmlns:s="library://ns.adobe.com/flex/spark"
  xmlns:mx="library://ns.adobe.com/flex/halo"
  creationComplete="app_creationCompleteHandler()">
  <fx:Script>
    <![CDATA[
      import mx.collections.ArrayCollection;
      import mx.rpc.events.ResultEvent;
      import mx.rpc.remoting.RemoteObject;
```

continued

LISTING 28.3   *(continued)*

```
      [Bindable]
      private var contactData:ArrayCollection;
      private var contactService:RemoteObject;
      private function app_creationCompleteHandler():void
      {
        contactService = new RemoteObject("ColdFusion");
        contactService.source = "flex4bible.chapter28.ContactService";
        contactService.addEventListener(ResultEvent.RESULT, resultHandler);
      }
      private function resultHandler(event:ResultEvent):void
      {
        contactData = event.result as ArrayCollection;
      }
    ]]>
  </fx:Script>
  <s:layout>
    <s:VerticalLayout paddingTop="20" horizontalAlign="center"/>
  </s:layout>
  <s:Button label="Hello World" click="contactService.getAllContacts()"/>
  <mx:DataGrid dataProvider="{contactData}"/>
</s:Application>
```

On the Web

The code in Listing 28.3 is available in the Web site files as `ROResultHandler.mxml` in the `src` folder of the `chapter28` project. ∎

Listing 28.4 shows the code for the CFC that's called by this and other applications in this section. Notice that the query object is created manually in ColdFusion code, rather than being generated with a `<cfquery>` command. As a result, the case of the column names is controlled by this call to the ColdFusion `QueryNew()` function, rather than being derived from a database query's metadata:

```
<cfset var qContacts=queryNew('contactId,firstname,lastname,city')>
```

LISTING 28.4

A CFC returning a Query object

```
<cfcomponent name="ContactService" hint="Delivers Contact data from an XML
    file to a Flex application">

  <!--- Initialize data set in memory if it doesn't already exist --->
  <cfif not structKeyExists(session, "qContacts")>
    <cfset createDataSet()>
  </cfif>
  <!--- Creates a query object from an XML file --->
```

```
<cffunction name="createDataSet" returntype="void" access="private">
  <cfset var strContacts="">
  <cfset var xContacts="">
  <cfset var i="">
  <cfset var qContacts=queryNew('contactId,firstname,lastname,city')>

  <cffile action="read" file="#expandPath('data/contacts.xml')#"
  variable="strContacts">
  <cfset xContacts=xmlParse(strContacts)>

  <cfloop from="1" to="#arrayLen(xContacts.contacts.row)#" index="i">
    <cfset QueryAddRow(qContacts)>
    <cfset qContacts.firstname[i]=xContacts.contacts.row[i].firstname.
  xmltext>
    <cfset qContacts.lastname[i] =
      xContacts.contacts.row[i].lastname.xmltext>
    <cfset qContacts.contactId[i] =
      xContacts.contacts.row[i].contactId.xmltext>
    <cfset qContacts.city[i]=xContacts.contacts.row[i].city.xmltext>
  </cfloop>
  <cfset session.qContacts=qContacts>
</cffunction>

<!--- Returns all data as a query object --->
<cffunction name="getAllContacts" returntype="query" access="remote">
  <cfreturn session.qContacts>
</cffunction>

<!--- Returns all data as an array of value objects --->
<cffunction name="getContactsAsArray"
  returntype="flex4bible.chapter28.Contact[]">
  <cfreturn queryToArray(session.qContacts)>
</cffunction>
<!--- Returns filtered data as array --->
<cffunction name="getFilteredContacts"
  returnType="Contact[]" access="remote">
  <cfargument name="firstname" type="string" required="true">
  <cfargument name="lastname" type="string" required="true">

  <cfset var qFiltered="">
  <cfquery dbtype="query" name="qFiltered">
    SELECT * FROM session.qContacts
    WHERE 0=0
    <cfif len(trim(firstname))>
      AND firstname LIKE '%#trim(arguments.firstname)#%'
    </cfif>
    <cfif len(trim(lastname))>
      AND lastname LIKE '%#trim(arguments.lastname)#%'
    </cfif>
  </cfquery>
  <cfreturn queryToArray(qFiltered)>
```

continued

LISTING 28.4 *(continued)*

```
    </cffunction>
    <!--- Returns the total count of Contacts --->
    <cffunction name="getContactCount" returntype="numeric" access="remote">
      <cfreturn session.qContacts.recordCount>
    </cffunction>
      <!--- Returns all data from a query object --->
    <cffunction name="queryToArray" access="private"
      returntype="flex4bible.chapter28.Contact[]">
     <cfargument name="qData" type="query" required="true">
      <cfset var contact="">
      <cfset var arReturn=arrayNew(1)>

      <cfloop query="qData">
        <cfset contact=createObject("component",
          "flex4bible.chapter28.Contact")>
        <cfset contact.contactId = qData.contactId>
        <cfset contact.firstname = qData.firstname>
        <cfset contact.lastname = qData.lastname>
        <cfset contact.city = qData.city>
        <cfset arrayAppend(arReturn, contact)>
      </cfloop>
      <cfreturn arReturn>
    </cffunction>
    <!--- Receives a value object and returns a string --->
    <cffunction name="parseContact" access="remote" returntype="String">
      <cfargument name="contactVO" type="Contact" required="true">
      <cfreturn "Contact received: " & contactVO.firstname &
        " " & contactVO.lastname>
    </cffunction>
  </cfcomponent>
```

On the Web

The code in Listing 28.4 is available in the Web site files as `ContactService.cfc` in the ColdFusion files of the `chapter28` project. ∎

Handling results from multiple CFC functions

When you need to call more than one function from a CFC, you have to distinguish which event handler function should be called for each one. You do this in MXML with the `<s:method>` compiler tag, which is nested within a `<mx:RemoteObject>` tag set. Each `<s:method>` tag represents a CFC function and can declare its own distinct `result` and `fault` event handlers.

The CFC in Listing 28.4, for example, has a function named getContactCount() that returns a numeric value and a function named getAllContacts() that returns a Query object (translated to an `ArrayCollection` in the Flex application). To handle each function's `result` event with its own distinct event handler function, you create the functions and then declare the `<s:method>` tags as follows:

```
<s:RemoteObject id="contactService"
  destination="ColdFusion"
  source="flex4bible.chapter28.ContactService">
  <s:method name="getContactCount" result="countHandler(event)"/>
  <s:method name="getAllContacts" result="dataHandler(event)"/>
</s:RemoteObject>
```

The application in Listing 28.5 calls `getContactCount()` upon application startup to inform the user how many data items are available on the server. The call to `getAllContacts()` to actually retrieve the data is made only when the user clicks Get Contact Data.

LISTING 28.5

Handling result events from multiple CFC functions

```
<?xml version="1.0" encoding="utf-8"?>
<s:Application xmlns:fx="http://ns.adobe.com/mxml/2009"
  xmlns:s="library://ns.adobe.com/flex/spark"
  xmlns:mx="library://ns.adobe.com/flex/halo"
  creationComplete="contactService.getContactCount()">
  <fx:Declarations>
    <s:RemoteObject id="contactService"
      destination="ColdFusion"
      source="flex4bible.chapter28.ContactService">
      <s:method name="getContactCount" result="countHandler(event)"/>
      <s:method name="getAllContacts" result="dataHandler(event)"/>
    </s:RemoteObject>
  </fx:Declarations>
  <fx:Script>
    <![CDATA[
      import mx.collections.ArrayCollection;
      import mx.rpc.events.ResultEvent;
      [Bindable]
      private var recordCount:Number;
      [Bindable]
      private var contactData:ArrayCollection;
      private function countHandler(event:ResultEvent):void
      {
        recordCount = event.result as Number;
      }
      private function dataHandler(event:ResultEvent):void
      {
        contactData = event.result as ArrayCollection;
      }
    ]]>
```

continued

LISTING 28.5 *(continued)*

```
  </fx:Script>
  <s:layout>
    <s:VerticalLayout paddingTop="20" horizontalAlign="center"/>
  </s:layout>
  <s:Label text="There are {recordCount} Contacts"/>
  <s:Button label="Get Contact Data"
    click="contactService.getAllContacts()"/>
  <mx:DataGrid dataProvider="{contactData}"/>
</s:Application>
```

On the Web

The code in Listing 28.5 is available in the Web site files as ROMultipleFunctions.mxml **in the** src **folder of the** chapter28 **project.** ■

Figure 28.5 shows the resulting application. The Label at the top of the application displays the getContactCount() results immediately upon application startup, while the actual data is displayed only when the user requests it from the server.

FIGURE 28.5

An application using two different functions of a single CFC

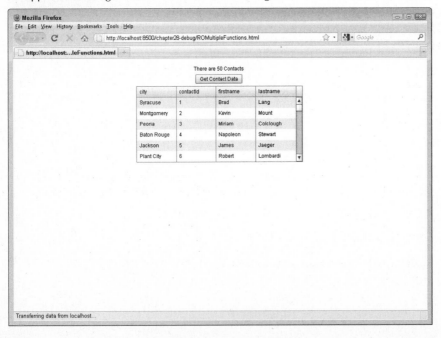

Cross-Reference

As with other RPC components, you can also handle `result` and `fault` events using the `CallResponder`, `ItemResponder`, and `AsyncToken` classes. For a description of these patterns and sample code, see Chapter 26. ■

Passing Arguments to CFC Functions

You can pass arguments to CFC functions in three different ways:

- **Explicit arguments.** These arguments are passed in the order in which they're declared in the CFC function.

- **Bound arguments.** These arguments are declared with MXML code and bound to data sources in the Flex application.

- **Named arguments.** These arguments are wrapped in an ActionScript Object and are passed as though the CFC function expects only a single argument.

Using explicit arguments

Explicit arguments are passed in the same order in which they're declared in the CFC function. The CFC's `getFilteredContacts()` function declares two required arguments:

```
<cffunction name="getFilteredContacts" returnType="query"
    access="remote">
  <cfargument name="firstname" type="string" required="true">
  <cfargument name="lastname" type="string" required="true">
  ... function body ...
</cffunction>
```

Using explicit arguments, you pass values that match the expected data types. This code sends the data in the same order in which they're declared:

```
contactService.getFilteredContacts(fnameInput.text, lnameInput.text);
```

Tip

It's also possible to pass arguments explicitly with the `Operation` class's `send()` method. The following syntax enables you to pass remote CFC function names as strings or variables, passed into the `RemoteObject` component's `getOperation()` method:

```
contactService.getOperation("getFilteredContacts").send(
   fnameInput.text, lnameInput.text);
```

This calling syntax also works with the `WebService` component. ■

Using bound arguments

Bound arguments are declared in MXML and then passed through a call to the `RemoteObject` component's `send()` method. Just as when using the `RemoteObject` component to call Java-based methods in classes hosted by BlazeDS, you use bound argument notation with XML elements for each argument wrapped in an `<s:arguments>` tag set. This code binds the `getFiltered Contacts()` method's two arguments to values gathered from `TextInput` controls:

```
<s:RemoteObject id="contactService" destination="ColdFusion"
  source="flex4bible.chapter28.ContactService">
  <s:method name="getFilteredContacts">
    <s:arguments>
      <firstname>{fnameInput.text}</firstname>
      <lastname>{lnameInput.text}</lastname>
    </s:arguments>
  </s:method>
</s:RemoteObject>
```

To call the method with the bound arguments, call the operation's `send()` method without any explicit arguments:

```
contactService.getFilteredContacts.send()
```

Note

When using bound arguments with CFC functions, the arguments are matched by name, not by the order of declaration in the client-side code. This behavior is different from Java-based methods and arguments, where bound arguments are sent in the order in which they're declared, and the XML element names are ignored. ■

Using named arguments

You can match CFC function arguments by name by wrapping them in an ActionScript `Object`. Each property has a name and a value; the name of the `Object` property must match the name of the CFC function argument.

This code creates an `Object` and attaches argument values by name:

```
var args:Object = new Object();
args.firstname = fnameInput.text;
args.lastname = lnameInput.text;
contactService.getFilteredContacts(args);
```

You also can write the same code using shorthand `Object` notation:

```
contactService.getFilteredContacts(
  {firstname:fnameInput.text, lastname:lnameInput.text});
```

This behavior is sometimes confusing to ColdFusion developers who first encounter it, because it means that you can't pass an anonymous `Object` as an argument to a CFC function and expect it to arrive intact as a ColdFusion structure. The `Object` is always broken down into its named properties, and then the individual properties are passed to the CFC function. If you need to pass a structure argument to a CFC function, you have to wrap it in another `Object` and pass it by name:

```
myService.myFunction({myArgumentName:myObject});
```

The named arguments behavior in Flex is very similar to ColdFusion's own `argumentCollection` attribute, which can be used to pass a structure of named arguments to functions from CFML code. This CFML code calls a CFC function and passes a structure in very much the same way:

```
<cfset stArgs=structNew()>
<cfset stArgs.firstname="firstnameValue">
<cfset stArgs.lastname="lastnameValue">
<cfinvoke component="flex4bible.chapter28.ContactService"
```

`argumentCollection="#stArgs#" returnVariable="qContacts"/>`

The application in Listing 28.6 uses named arguments wrapped in an ActionScript `Object`.

LISTING 28.6

An application passing named arguments to a CFC function

```
<?xml version="1.0" encoding="utf-8"?>
<s:Application xmlns:fx="http://ns.adobe.com/mxml/2009"
  xmlns:s="library://ns.adobe.com/flex/spark"
  xmlns:mx="library://ns.adobe.com/flex/halo">
  <fx:Declarations>
    <s:RemoteObject id="contactService" destination="ColdFusion"
      source="flex4bible.chapter28.ContactService"/>
  </fx:Declarations>
  <fx:Script>
    <![CDATA[
      private function getContacts():void
      {
        var args:Object = new Object();
        args.firstname = fnameInput.text;
        args.lastname = lnameInput.text;
        contactService.getFilteredContacts(args);
      }
    ]]>
  </fx:Script>
  <s:layout>
    <s:VerticalLayout paddingTop="20" horizontalAlign="center"/>
  </s:layout>
  <mx:Form>
    <mx:FormItem label="First Name:">
      <s:TextInput id="fnameInput"/>
    </mx:FormItem>
  <mx:FormItem label="Last Name:">
```

continued

LISTING 28.6 *(continued)*

```
        <s:TextInput id="lnameInput"/>
        <s:Button label="Get Filtered Data" click="getContacts()"/>
    </mx:FormItem>
  </mx:Form>
  <mx:DataGrid
    dataProvider="{contactService.getFilteredContacts.lastResult}"/>
</s:Application>
```

On the Web

The code in Listing 28.6 is available in the Web site files as `RONamedArgs.mxml` in the `src` folder of the `chapter28` project. Examples of the same application using explicit and bound arguments are in `ROExplicitArgs.mxml` and `ROBoundArgs.mxml`, respectively. ■

Using Value Object Classes

When passing data between a Flex client application and ColdFusion, you can build both client-side and server-side data objects using the Value Object design pattern. The Flex version is built as an ActionScript class, while the ColdFusion version is built as a CFC. At runtime, you can pass strongly typed value objects between the client and server tiers of your application, and the Flex application and the Flash Remoting gateway automatically transfer data between the objects based on a mapping that you provide in the code.

Note

The Value Object design pattern is also known in various industry documentation sources as the Transfer Object pattern and Data Transfer Object pattern. The different names are all used to refer to the same pattern: a class that contains data for a single instance of a data entity. ■

Creating a ColdFusion value object

The ColdFusion version of a value object is written as a simple CFC. The `<cfcomponent>` start tag requires an `alias` attribute that's set to the fully qualified name and location of the CFC:

```
<cfcomponent output="false" alias="flex4bible.chapter28.Contact">
    ... component body ...
</cfcomponent>
```

Each named property is declared after the `<cfcomponent>` start tag using the `<cfproperty>` tag. Each property has a name and a type to indicate how it will be exchanged with Flex. The following `<cfproperty>` tags declare one `numeric` and two `string` properties:

```
<cfproperty name="contactId" type="numeric" default="0">
<cfproperty name="firstname" type="string" default="">
<cfproperty name="lastname" type="string" default="">
```

Note

The `<cfproperty>` tag, which in conventional ColdFusion code is used only to generate CFC documentation, controls the name and case of the property name when it's exchanged with the Flex application at runtime. This overrides the settings in the configuration files that control the case of property names. ∎

The `<cfproperty>` tag's `default` attribute is used to generate CFC documentation and doesn't actually set default values when the CFC is instantiated in ColdFusion. Instead, you typically add code outside any function definitions that set the properties' default values upon instantiation:

```
<cfscript>
  this.contactId = 0;
  this.firstname = "";
  this.lastname = "";
</cfscript>
```

The CFC in Listing 28.7 is a value object that declares four properties of a `Contact` value object and sets their initial values upon instantiation.

LISTING 28.7

A simple value object CFC

```
<cfcomponent output="false" alias="flex4bible.chapter28.Contact">
  <cfproperty name="contactId" type="numeric" default="0">
  <cfproperty name="firstname" type="string" default="">
  <cfproperty name="lastname" type="string" default="">
  <cfproperty name="city" type="string" default="">
  <cfscript>
    this.contactId = 0;
    this.firstname = "";
    this.lastname = "";
    this.city = ""
  </cfscript>
</cfcomponent>
```

On the Web

The code in Listing 28.7 is available in the Web site files as `Contact.cfc` in the ColdFusion files of the `chapter28` project. ∎

Creating an ActionScript value object

The Flex client application uses an ActionScript version of the value object built as an ActionScript class. The class requires a `[RemoteClass]` metadata tag with an `alias` attribute that describes the fully qualified name and location of the matching CFC:

```
[RemoteClass(alias="flex4bible.chapter28.Contact")]
```

This is a two-way mapping: When an ActionScript version of the object is sent to ColdFusion, the Flash Remoting gateway creates an instance of the CFC and passes the received object's property values to the server-side version. Similarly, if a CFC function returns instances of the server-side version, client-side versions are created automatically and their property values set to the values received from the server.

Caution

The `alias` **attributes of the** `[RemoteClass]` **metadata tag on the client and the** `<cfcomponent>` **tag on the server must match exactly and are case-sensitive.** ■

The ActionScript class in Listing 28.8 declares the same set of values as public properties and maps itself to the server's version with the `[RemoteClass]` metadata tag.

LISTING 28.8

An ActionScript value object class

```
package valueObjects
{
  [Bindable]
  [RemoteClass(alias="flex4bible.chapter28.ContactVO")]
  public class Contact
  {
    public var contactId:int;
    public var firstname:String;
    public var lastname:String;
    public var city:String;
    public function ContactVO()
    {
    }
  }
}
```

On the Web

The code in Listing 28.8 is available in the Web site files as `ContactVO.as` **in the** `src/valueObjects` **folder in the** `chapter28` **project.** ■

Returning value objects from ColdFusion to Flex

After you've built versions of the value object in both ColdFusion and ActionScript and provided the appropriate mappings, a CFC function has the capability to return either individual value object instances or collections of value objects wrapped into arrays. This CFC function creates an instance of the `Contact` value object and returns it to Flex:

```
<cffunction name="getContactVO" access="remote"
  returntype="flex4bible.chapter28.Contact">
  <cfset contact=createObject("component",
    "flex4bible.chapter28.Contact")>
  <cfset contact.contactId = 1 >
  <cfset contact.firstname = "David">
  <cfset contact.lastname = "Gassner">
  <cfset contact.city = "Seattle">
  <cfreturn contact>
</cffunction>
```

Notice that the function's `returntype` attribute is set to the fully qualified name and location of the value object CFC.

New Feature

In ColdFusion 9, you can now use the `new` keyword and a constructor method call to instantiate the value object CFC:

```
<cfset contact = new flex4bible.chapter28.Contact()> ∎
```

Receiving value objects from ColdFusion

In order to receive value objects from a CFC function and have them automatically transformed into instances of the ActionScript value object, the Flex application must contain at least one reference to the ActionScript class. The reference can be a declared instance of the class or a call to any static properties or methods. This ensures that the class, which contains the `[RemoteClass]` metadata tag, is compiled into the application and is available at runtime.

Caution

It isn't enough to just import the value object class in the Flex application; you have to declare at least one instance. The purpose of importing a class is to inform the Flex compiler of the class's existence, but the compiler doesn't include the class definition in the binary version of the application unless at least one instance of the class is declared, or there's a reference to one of its static members. ∎

The Flex application in Listing 28.9 receives the `Array` of value objects and processes them in an event handler. Notice the declaration of the `ContactVO` class that ensures that the class is included in the compiled application even though it's never explicitly used.

Note

When a CFC function returns a ColdFusion `array`, it's received in Flex as an ActionScript `Array`, not an `ArrayCollection`. In this application, the `result` event handler expects an `Array` and assigns it to the `source` of the already-instantiated `ArrayCollection`:

```
contactData.source = event.result as Array; ∎
```

LISTING 28.9

Receiving an Array of strongly typed value objects

```xml
<?xml version="1.0" encoding="utf-8"?>
<s:Application xmlns:fx="http://ns.adobe.com/mxml/2009"
  xmlns:s="library://ns.adobe.com/flex/spark"
  xmlns:mx="library://ns.adobe.com/flex/halo"
  creationComplete="app_creationCompleteHandler()">
  <fx:Script>
    <![CDATA[
      import mx.collections.ArrayCollection;
      import mx.controls.Alert;
      import mx.rpc.events.FaultEvent;
      import mx.rpc.events.ResultEvent;
      import mx.rpc.remoting.RemoteObject;

      import valueObjects.ContactVO;

      [Bindable]
      private var contactData:ArrayCollection = new ArrayCollection();
      private var contactService:RemoteObject;
      private var contactVO:ContactVO;
      private function app_creationCompleteHandler():void
      {
        contactService = new RemoteObject("ColdFusion");
        contactService.source = "flex4bible.chapter28.ContactService";
        contactService.addEventListener(ResultEvent.RESULT, resultHandler);
        contactService.addEventListener(FaultEvent.FAULT, faultHandler);
      }
      private function resultHandler(event:ResultEvent):void
      {
        contactData.source = event.result as Array;
      }
      private function faultHandler(event:FaultEvent):void
      {
        var errorMessage:String = event.fault.faultString;
        errorMessage = errorMessage.substring(22, errorMessage.length);
        Alert.show(errorMessage, event.fault.faultCode);
      }
    ]]>
  </fx:Script>
  <s:layout>
    <s:VerticalLayout paddingTop="20" horizontalAlign="center"/>
  </s:layout>
  <s:Button label="Get Contacts"
    click="contactService.getContactsAsArray()"/>
  <mx:DataGrid dataProvider="{contactData}"/>
</s:Application>
```

On the Web

The code in Listing 28.9 is available in the Web site files as `ROReceiveValueObjects.mxml` in the `src` folder of the `chapter28` project. ■

Passing value object arguments to CFC functions

Value objects also can be passed from a Flex client application to a CFC function. The CFC function should have declared an argument typed as the ColdFusion version of the value object. This CFC function receives an instance of the `Contact` value object CFC and returns a concatenated string built from its properties:

```
<cffunction name="parseContact" access="remote">'
  <cfargument name="contactVO" type="flex4bible.chapter28.Contact"
    required="true">
  <cfreturn "Contact received: " + contactVO.firstname +
    " " + contactVO.lastname>
</cffunction>
```

To pass a value object argument to the CFC function from Flex, create an instance of the ActionScript version of the object and set its properties. Then pass the value object to the function using any of the argument-passing strategies described previously.

The application in Listing 28.10 passes an instance of the ActionScript value object to a CFC function that extracts its properties and returns a concatenated string.

LISTING 28.10

Passing a value object to a CFC function

```
<?xml version="1.0" encoding="utf-8"?>
<s:Application xmlns:fx="http://ns.adobe.com/mxml/2009"
  xmlns:s="library://ns.adobe.com/flex/spark"
  xmlns:mx="library://ns.adobe.com/flex/halo">
  <fx:Declarations>
    <s:RemoteObject id="contactService" destination="ColdFusion"
      source="flex4bible.chapter28.ContactService"
      result="contactService_resultHandler(event)"/>
  </fx:Declarations>
  <fx:Script>
    <![CDATA[
      import mx.controls.Alert;
      import mx.rpc.events.ResultEvent;

      import valueObjects.ContactVO;
      private function passArgument():void
      {
        var newContact:ContactVO = new ContactVO();
```

continued

LISTING 28.10 *(continued)*

```
      newContact.firstname = fnameInput.text;
       newContact.lastname = lnameInput.text;
       contactService.parseContact(newContact);
    }
    private function contactService_resultHandler(event:ResultEvent):void
    {
       Alert.show(event.result as String, "Returned Value");
    }
  ]]>
</fx:Script>
<s:Panel title="Enter Contact Information" top="20" horizontalCenter="0">
  <mx:Form>
    <mx:FormItem label="First Name:">
      <s:TextInput id="fnameInput"/>
    </mx:FormItem>
    <mx:FormItem label="Last Name:">
      <s:TextInput id="lnameInput"/>
    </mx:FormItem>
  </mx:Form>
  <s:controlBarContent>
    <s:Button label="Pass Argument" click="passArgument()"/>
  </s:controlBarContent>
</s:Panel>
</s:Application>
```

On the Web

The code in Listing 28.10 is available in the Web site files as `ROPassVOArg.mxml` in the `src` folder of the `chapter28` project. ∎

Working with RemoteObject Faults

When an exception occurs during a call to a CFC function, the `RemoteObject` dispatches a `fault` event. The event object is typed as `mx.rpc.events.FaultEvent` and contains a fault property typed as `mx.rpc.Fault`. This object in turn has `String` properties named `faultCode`, `fault-String`, and `faultDetail`. The values of these properties differ depending on the nature of the error, and in the case of `faultDetail` they sometimes don't contain useful information.

Handling the fault event

As with all events, you can create an event listener with either MXML or ActionScript code. The MXML attribute-based event listener looks like this:

```
<s:RemoteObject id="contactService" destination="ColdFusion"
  source="flex4bible.chapter28.ContactServiceWithVO"
```

```
fault="faultHandler(event)"/>
```

To create an event listener in ActionScript code, call the `RemoteObject` component's `addEvent Listener()` method and declare the event name using the `FaultEvent.FAULT` constant:

```
contactService.addEventListener(FaultEvent.FAULT, faultHandler);
```

When the event handler function receives the event object, you can handle it in any way you like. Minimally, you might display the fault information to the user with a pop-up dialog box generated by the `Alert` class:

```
private function faultHandler(event:FaultEvent):void
{
    Alert.show(event.fault.faultString, event.fault.faultCode);
}
```

Note

In ColdFusion 8 and 9, the value of the error message always has a prefix of "Unable to invoke CFC –". If you don't want to display this prefix, you have to parse the original error message from the value of the `faultString` **property:**

```
var errorMessage:String = event.fault.faultString;
errorMessage = errorMessage.substring(22, errorMessage.length);
Alert.show(errorMessage, event.fault.faultCode); ∎
```

Generating custom exceptions from a CFC function

On the server, you can generate your own faults from a CFC function by calling the ColdFusion `<cfthrow>` command. These `<cfthrow>` commands' attributes are exposed in the Flex application's `FaultEvent.fault` object:

- The `message` attribute appears in the `fault` object's `faultString` property.
- The `errorcode` attribute appears in the `fault` object's `faultCode` property.

The CFC in Listing 28.11 implements a `throwCFCFault()` function that always generates a fault with `message` and `errorcode` attributes.

LISTING 28.11

A CFC function generating a server-side fault

```
<cfcomponent output="false">
  <cffunction name="throwCFCFault" returntype="String">
    <cfthrow message="An error message generated by a CFC function"
      errorcode="CFC Function Error">
    <cfreturn "A String">
  </cffunction>
</cfcomponent>
```

On the Web

The code in Listing 28.11 is available in the Web site files as `FaultService.cfc` in the ColdFusion files of the `chapter28` project. ■

The Flex application in Listing 28.12 calls the CFC function to intentionally generate a fault and display its information in an `Alert` pop-up dialog box.

LISTING 28.12

A Flex application handling a server-side fault from a CFC function

```
<?xml version="1.0" encoding="utf-8"?>
<s:Application xmlns:fx="http://ns.adobe.com/mxml/2009"
  xmlns:s="library://ns.adobe.com/flex/spark"
  xmlns:mx="library://ns.adobe.com/flex/halo"
  creationComplete="app_creationCompleteHandler()">
  <fx:Script>
    <![CDATA[
      import mx.controls.Alert;
      import mx.rpc.events.FaultEvent;
      import mx.rpc.remoting.RemoteObject;
      private var contactService:RemoteObject;
      private function app_creationCompleteHandler():void
      {
        contactService = new RemoteObject("ColdFusion");
        contactService.source = "flex4bible.chapter28.FaultService";
        contactService.addEventListener(FaultEvent.FAULT, faultHandler);
      }
      private function faultHandler(event:FaultEvent):void
      {
        var errorMessage:String = event.fault.faultString;
        errorMessage = errorMessage.substring(22, errorMessage.length);
        Alert.show(errorMessage, event.fault.faultCode);
      }
    ]]>
  </fx:Script>
  <s:layout>
    <s:VerticalLayout paddingTop="20" horizontalAlign="center"/>
  </s:layout>
  <s:Button label="Throw Fault" click="contactService.throwCFCFault()"/>
</s:Application>
```

On the Web

The code in Listing 28.12 is available in the Web site files as `ROFaultHandler.mxml` in the `src` folder of the `chapter28` project. ■

Working with Data Connections in Flash Builder

As described in Chapters 25 and 26, Flash Builder 4 includes tools for data-centric development that introspect server-side components and then generate client-side ActionScript proxy classes. These classes make it easy to get started integrating application servers into your Flex applications.

The first step is to define a data connection for use with ColdFusion. There are some requirements you'll need to satisfy to use these tools in Flash Builder:

- You must be working with a Flex project that's connected to a ColdFusion server, and the server's root folder and URL must be defined.

- RDS (Remote Development Service) must be enabled in the ColdFusion server.

Follow these steps to define a ColdFusion data connection in Flash Builder 4:

1. **Choose Data ⇨ Connect to ColdFusion from the Flash Builder menu.**

2. **In the Configure ColdFusion Service screen, shown in Figure 28.6, provide the name and location of the CFC that you want to connect to.** You'll also need to provide the Service name as it will be known to the Flex application, and the packages in which you want to create ActionScript proxy and value object classes.

FIGURE 28.6

Selecting a ColdFusion Component for use as a data connection

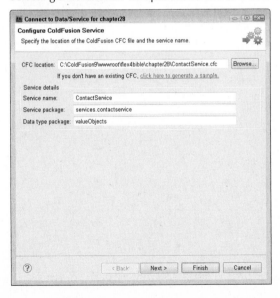

---

3. **Click Next.**

4. **If prompted for authentication credentials, enter the RDS user name and password for your ColdFusion server and click OK.** The Service Operations screen appears, displaying the CFC's remote functions (see Figure 28.7).

5. **Click Finish to create proxy and value object classes for the CFC's functions.**

FIGURE 28.7

The data connection wizard displaying the CFC's remote functions

Only those functions that are marked in the CFC with `access="remote"` are displayed. Also, if the CFC extends another CFC, the code generation tool shows only those functions that are defined in the CFC you selected (and not those defined in the CFC on which it's based). Flash Builder's Data/Services view should now display the new data connection. Once you've created the data connection, you can do everything with it that you do with data connections for other application server architectures such as HTTP and Web services:

- Bind data to visual controls
- Generate data entry forms
- Generate detail forms
- Reconfigure return data types for particular functions

Cross-Reference

See Chapter 25 for more information about tasks you can accomplish with Flash Builder data connections. ∎

Calling ColdFusion 9 Services

ColdFusion 9 provides a set of services that you can call directly from Flex applications without having to create custom server-side code. These functions are included:

- **Chart Service**. Generates Flash-based charts, using functionality traditionally provided by ColdFusion's `<cfchart>` command.

- **Document Service**. Generates PDF documents, using functionality traditionally provided by ColdFusion's `<cfdocument>` command.

- **Image Service**. Manages images on the server, using functionality traditionally provided by ColdFusion's `<cfimage>` command.

- **Mail Service**. Sends e-mail from a Flex application, using the functionality traditionally provided by ColdFusion's `<cfmail>` command.

- **PDF Service**. PDF document management, using functionality traditionally provided by ColdFusion's `<cfpdf>` command.

- **Pop Service**. Retrieves e-mails from POP-based e-mail services, using functionality traditionally provided by ColdFusion's `<cfpop>` command.

- **Upload Service**. Receives and manages files uploaded from the client hard disk, using functionality traditionally provided by ColdFusion's `<cffile>` command.

To use these features, you must first create authenticated user profiles in ColdFusion and grant them permission to call the services from client applications. Then, you use ActionScript classes from a component library that's included with ColdFusion to call the services from your Flex application.

Configuring ColdFusion security

Before calling services from a Flex application, you first must configure ColdFusion to accept service calls from external client applications. There are two critical steps:

- Create a user profile in ColdFusion Administrator and grant permissions to the user to call the required services.

- Provide IP addresses of the client applications that will call the services.

Creating a user profile

Follow these steps to create a ColdFusion user and grant permission to call services from external clients:

1. **In ColdFusion Administrator, select Security ⇨ User Manager.**

2. **In the User Manager screen, click Add User.**

3. **Set the User name and Password, as shown in Figure 28.8.**

4. **Scroll down to the bottom of the User Manager screen.** As shown in Figure 28.9, select each service in the Prohibited Services list for which you want to grant permission.

FIGURE 28.8

FIGURE 28.8

Add a User name and Password in the User Manager screen.

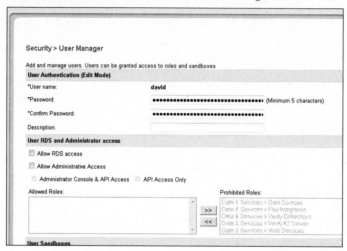

5. Click the << button to move the service to the Allowed Services list.

6. Click Add User.

FIGURE 28.9

Select allowed services.

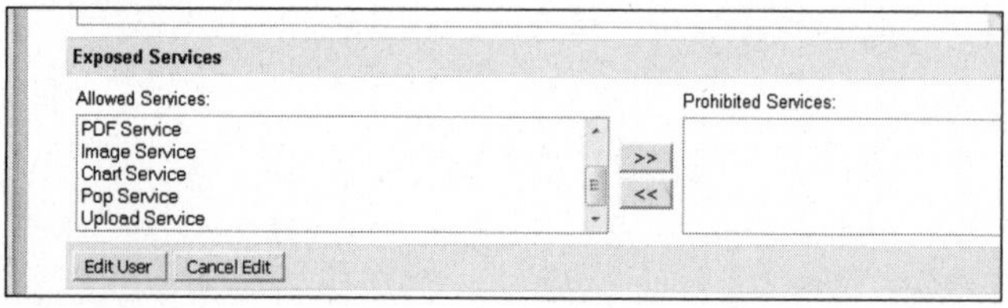

Specifying IP addresses

In the next step, you add IP addresses that have permission to make service calls. Both IPv4 and IPv6 addresses are support. Follow these steps to add your client's IP address:

1. **In ColdFusion Administrator, select Security ⇨ Allowed IP Addresses.**

2. **In the Allowed IP Addresses screen, type the IP Address of your client system and click Add.** On my system, I'm loading the Flex application from the local hard disk and making calls to my local copy of ColdFusion, so I've added two IP addresses: 127.0.0.1 (IPv4) and 0:0:0:0:0:0:0:1 (IPv6).

Using ColdFusion 9 client-side service components

In order to call services from your Flex application, you first must include a precompiled component library named `cfservices.swc` in the Flex project's library path. You'll then be able to use the ColdFusion 9 service components in your Flex applications.

Adding cfservices.swc to a Flex project

The `cfservices.swc` file is included in the ColdFusion 9 installation under the Web root folder, in a subfolder named `CFIDE/scripts/AIR`. You can either link directly to the file in that physical location using the Flex project's properties, or you can copy the SWC file into the Flex project's `libs` folder.

Follow these steps to include the required SWC file in the project's build path:

1. **Open Windows Explorer (Windows) or Finder (Mac) and navigate to the ColdFusion Web root folder.**

2. **Navigate to the `CFIDE/scripts/AIR` subfolder.** If you're using the server configuration on Windows with the development Web server, the folder is `C:\ColdFusion9\wwwroot\CFIDE\scripts\AIR`.

3. **Locate the `cfservices.swc` file and copy it to the clipboard.**

4. **Go to Flash Builder's Package Explorer view and locate the Flex project's `libs` folder.**

5. **Paste `cfservices.swc` into the `libs` folder.** SWC files that are placed in the `libs` folder automatically become part of the project's library path. Note that the SWC file is already included in the Web site's files for this chapter to ensure that the sample application shown in Listing 28.13 compiles correctly.

Calling services

Each client-side ColdFusion service component is exposed as an ActionScript class that can be instantiated with MXML or ActionScript code. The following is an example of the `Mail` component, which you use to send e-mails from a Flex application using ColdFusion's e-mail server interface.

Note

The `Mail` component uses ColdFusion's e-mail server integration features. You must configure ColdFusion to communicate with an SMTP (Simple Mail Transfer Protocol) server, which actually sends the e-mails to recipients designated by your application's users. To find this configuration option in ColdFusion Administrator, navigate to Server Settings ⇨ Mail. ∎

When declared with MXML code, the `Mail` component closely mimics the attribute names of ColdFusion's `<cfmail>` tag:

```
<cf:Mail xmlns:cf="coldfusion.service.mxml.*"
    id="cfMail"
    cfServer="localhost" cfPort="8500"
    serviceUserName="david"
    servicePassword="password"
```

```
            type="html"
            from="david@bardotech.com"
            to="{toInput.text}"
            subject="{subjectInput.text}"
            content="{contentInput.htmlText}">
```

You set `cfServer` to the IP address or DNS name of your ColdFusion server, and `cfPort` to the port on which the server listens. If you're using ColdFusion's J2EE configuration, you also need to set `cfContextRoot` to the server's context root.

The `serviceUserName` and `servicePassword` properties must match the authentication credentials of a user to whom you granted service permissions in ColdFusion Administrator. The `from`, `to`, `subject`, and `content` properties determine who sends and receives the message, and what content is sent. There are additional properties for attaching files, setting the e-mail type (`text` or `html`), and using other features of the `<cfmail>` command.

As with RPC components such as `WebService` and `RemoteObject`, the `Mail` component dispatches `result` and `fault` events that indicate the success or failure of the attempt to send mail. In both cases, the event object is an instance of `ColdFusionServiceResultEvent`, another class that's included in the ColdFusion services component library.

In the application in Listing 28.13, most of the `Mail` object's properties are filled in with binding expressions. When the user clicks Send Mail, the application sends the e-mail with the `Mail` object's `execute()` method:

```
            cfMail.execute();
```

LISTING 28.13

A Flex application sending e-mail through the ColdFusion 9 service layer

```xml
<?xml version="1.0" encoding="utf-8"?>
<s:Application xmlns:fx="http://ns.adobe.com/mxml/2009"
  xmlns:s="library://ns.adobe.com/flex/spark"
  xmlns:mx="library://ns.adobe.com/flex/mx"
  xmlns:cf="coldfusion.service.mxml.*">
  <fx:Declarations>
    <cf:Mail id="cfMail"
      cfServer="localhost" cfPort="8500"
      serviceUserName="david"
      servicePassword="password"
      type="html"
      from="david@bardotech.com"
      to="{toInput.text}"
      subject="{subjectInput.text}"
      content="{contentInput.htmlText}"
      result="cfMail_resultHandler(event)"
      fault="cfMail_faultHandler(event)">
```

```
      </cf:Mail>
    </fx:Declarations>
    <fx:Script>
      <![CDATA[
        import coldfusion.service.events.ColdFusionServiceFaultEvent;
        import coldfusion.service.events.ColdFusionServiceResultEvent;

        import mx.controls.Alert;

        protected function cfMail_resultHandler(
          event:ColdFusionServiceResultEvent):void
        {
          toInput.text="";
          subjectInput.text="";
          contentInput.text="";
          Alert.show("Your message was sent", "ColdFusion Mail");
        }
        protected function cfMail_faultHandler(
          event:ColdFusionServiceFaultEvent):void
        {
          Alert.show(event.fault.faultString, event.fault.faultCode);
        }
      ]]>
    </fx:Script>
    <s:Panel title="Send an Email" horizontalCenter="0" top="20">
      <mx:Form>
        <mx:FormItem label="To:">
          <s:TextInput id="toInput" width="300"/>
        </mx:FormItem>
        <mx:FormItem label="Subject">
          <s:TextInput id="subjectInput" width="300"/>
        </mx:FormItem>
        <mx:FormItem label="Content">
          <mx:RichTextEditor id="contentInput"
            title="Enter Content"
            width="300" height="300"/>
        </mx:FormItem>
      </mx:Form>
      <s:controlBarContent>
        <s:Button label="Send Mail" click="cfMail.execute()"/>
      </s:controlBarContent>
    </s:Panel>
  </s:Application>
```

On the Web

The code in Listing 28.13 is available in the Web site files as `FlexEmailClient.mxml` in the `src` folder of the `chapter28` project. ∎

The details of using all of the services exposed by ColdFusion 9 are beyond the scope of this book, but you can learn more about them from the services component library's API documentation at:

```
http://help.adobe.com/en_US/AS3LCR/ColdFusion_9.0/
```

Summary

In this chapter, I described how to integrate Flex client applications with Adobe ColdFusion 8 using Flash Remoting and the Flex framework's RemoteObject component. You learned the following:

- Flash Remoting was originally introduced with ColdFusion MX and was adapted for use in LiveCycle Data Services and Blaze as the Remoting Service.

- Flash Remoting enables you to call functions of ColdFusion components (CFCs) from a ColdFusion server.

- Remote function calls and responses are encrypted in AMF, a binary message format that's significantly smaller and faster than XML.

- Data can be exchanged between the Flex client and a CFC function based on documented data type mappings.

- Calls to CFC functions are asynchronous.

- CFC function results can be handled with binding expressions or by handling the RemoteObject component's result event.

- Arguments can be passed to CFC functions using explicit, named, or bound argument syntax.

- Strongly typed value objects can be created in both ActionScript and ColdFusion and exchanged automatically between client and server at runtime.

- Exceptions are handled as Flex application faults using the RemoteObject component's fault event.

- Custom exceptions can be generated in ColdFusion and handled in a Flex client application.

- Flash Builder 4 supports generation of data connections that call CFC functions marked as remote.

- ColdFusion 9 supports services that can be called from Flex applications without creating explicit server-side code.

Integrating Flex Applications with PHP

P HP has become one of the most widely used application scripting
frameworks on the Web. Originally standing for *Personal Home Page,*
PHP has evolved into a high-performance application server technology that's used both to dynamically generate Web pages and to provide a
middleware layer for rich client applications such as those built with Flex.

Tip

**The term PHP is used to refer to both the server technology and the program-
ming language used to create dynamic Web functionality.** ■

In addition to its core feature set, PHP has extensibility features that enable
developers to create and add modules as needed. PEAR (PHP Extension and
Application Repository), in the words of its creators, offers both a "structured
library of open-source code for PHP users" and a "system for code distribution
and package maintenance." It also encourages a standardized approach to formatting PHP code, including recommendations for indentation, identifier naming, and other issues that sometimes invite controversy between developers.

PHP is portable between operating systems. Binary distributions of PHP are
available for these operating systems:

- AS/400
- Mac OS X
- Novell NetWare
- OS/2
- RISC OS
- SGI IRIX 6.5.x
- Solaris (SPARC, INTEL)
- Windows

IN THIS CHAPTER

Understanding PHP

**Installing PHP with
WampServer and MAMP**

**Creating a Flex project for
use with PHP**

Returning simple XML to Flex

**Creating a Flex/PHP
application with
Flash Builder 4**

**Working with generated
PHP services**

Using `RemoteObject` **and
AMF with Flex and Zend AMF**

PHP is also included in most distributions of Linux and is available in source-code format that enables you to customize and build your own PHP distributions.

In addition to all of these benefits, PHP is completely free. Because it's a free, open-source project managed by the PHP Group (`www.php.net`), you can download and use PHP on as many servers as you like without any registration or license fees.

There are many ways to integrate Flex applications with PHP, including these strategies:

- You can send and receive generic XML-formatted data using a RESTful architecture.
- You can use XML-RPC libraries that are delivered with PEAR (`http://pear.php.net/package/XML_RPC`).
- You can use a PHP implementation of SOAP-based Web services, such NuSOAP (`http://dietrich.ganx4.com/nusoap`) or PEAR (`http://pear.php.net/package/SOAP`).
- You can choose from a variety of Remoting and binary AMF implementations, such as AMFPHP, SabreAMF, and Zend AMF.

New Feature

Flash Builder 4 includes tools to get started using Zend AMF, which is a part of the Zend Framework, an open-source object-oriented application framework implemented in PHP 5. ■

In this chapter, I describe how to integrate PHP with Flex applications, first using RESTful XML with `HTTPService` and then AMF with `RemoteObject` in the Flex application and Zend AMF on the server.

On the Web

To use the sample code for this chapter, download `chapter29.zip` **from the Web site. This is not a Flex project archive file. Its use and installation are described later in this chapter. ■**

Installing PHP

You can install PHP in a number of ways. Developers who are new to PHP typically select from one of these options:

- If you already have a Web server and database installed, you can download the core PHP binary distribution for your operating system and then install it as a Web server module.
- If you don't have a Web server or database installed, you can download and install a free integrated software bundle package that includes the Apache Web server, PHP, and the MySQL database. Software bundles of note include:

- **MAMP.** A free bundle for Mac OS X.

- **WampServer.** A free bundle for Windows.

- **XAMPP.** A free bundle for Linux, Solaris, Windows, and Mac OS X. In addition to the usual bundle of Apache, MySQL, and PHP, this bundle includes support for Perl and an FTP server. XAMPP is available at `http://sourceforge.net/projects/xampp/`.

- **Zend Server.** A commercial bundle for Windows and Linux from Zend. It is available at `www.zend.com`.

The easiest way to get started with PHP on Windows or Mac OS X is to select one of the integrated software bundles. Both WampServer and MAMP are free and install quickly and easily so you can get started with development work with as little delay. In this section, I describe how to download and install WampServer for Windows and MAMP for Mac OS X.

Installing WampServer on Windows

WampServer is a free integrated software bundle for the Windows operating system that includes the Apache Web server, PHP, and the MySQL database. You can download the WampServer installer from:

```
www.wampserver.com/en
```

Follow these steps to download the WampServer installer application:

1. **Click Downloads from the WampServer home page:** `www.wampserver.com/en`.

2. **Click Download on the Downloads page, as shown in Figure 29.1.** The installer application is in .exe format and can be run from any folder after downloading. When you start the installer application, you first see a warning indicating that if you have an older version of WampServer installed you should first uninstall it.

3. **Follow the installer application's prompts to complete the installation.** As shown in Figure 29.2, the installer sets the default destination folder to `c:\wamp` on your system's hard disk.

4. **After installing the software, click on the Windows start men and choose WampServer.**

Note

The instructions in this chapter assume that you are using WampServer and you've accepted the default folder location of `c:\wamp`. If you've selected a different installation folder or are using PHP with a different configuration, adapt the instructions as necessary. ∎

FIGURE 29.1

Selecting the latest release from the WampServer downloads page

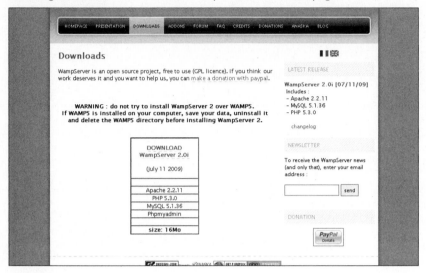

FIGURE 29.2

Setting the WampServer destination folder

Managing WampServer

The WampServer installer creates an icon in the system tray that enables you to start and stop the Apache and MySQL servers and to navigate to key Web pages. The system tray icon is shown in Figure 29.3.

Click the system tray icon to see the WampServer menu, as shown in Figure 29.4.

FIGURE 29.3

The WampServer system tray icon

WAMP icon

FIGURE 29.4

The WampServer system menu

The WampServer menu offers the following options under the Quick Admin heading (toward the bottom of the menu):

- Start All Services (includes both Apache and MySQL)
- Stop All Services
- Restart All Services

Tip

You also can start and stop Apache and MySQL individually by navigating to the appropriate section of the menu. For example, to restart the Apache Web server, choose Apache ➪ Service ➪ Restart Service from the WampServer menu. ∎

The menu also offers quick links to these key Web pages:

- **Localhost.** This link opens a Web browser to `http://localhost/` to view the WampServer server's home page, as shown in Figure 29.5.
- **phpMyAdmin.** This link opens a Web browser to a Web-based application that manages MySQL databases.
- **SQLiteManager.** This link opens a Web browser to a Web-based application that manages SQLite databases.
- **www directory.** This link opens Windows Explorer to the WampServer Web root folder, which defaults to `c:\wamp\www`.

FIGURE 29.5

WampServer's home page

Installing MAMP on Mac OS X

MAMP offers the same integrated server functionality as WampServer, but it's designed for Mac OS X. You can download the MAMP installer from www.mamp.info/en/downloads/ and get more information about MAMP at www.mamp.info/en. The installer is delivered as a DMG file (in a compressed ZIP file) that you mount as a virtual drive on your Mac development system.

When you open the DMG file, you're first prompted with the MAMP server's license agreement. Just as with WampServer, MAMP can be used freely according to the license terms. After accepting the license the installation screen appears, as shown in Figure 29.6.

Drag the MAMP folder icon to the Applications folder to complete the installation. The server installs into a folder on your Mac hard disk named /Applications/MAMP.

Note

The MAMP Pro folder installs the professional version of MAMP that includes additional enterprise-level features. This version of MAMP is installed with a fee-based license. ∎

Note

The How to upgrade.rtf link opens a document describing how to upgrade from one version of MAMP to another. ∎

FIGURE 29.6

The MAMP server's installation screen

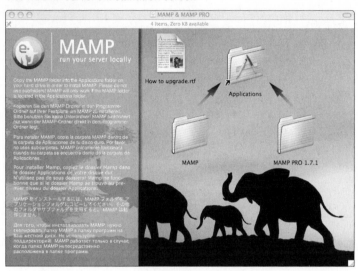

Managing MAMP servers

To start MAMP servers, open the /Applications/MAMP folder and run the MAMP application. Because starting servers requires administrative access, you're prompted for your Mac administrative user name and password.

After entering your administrative credentials, the MAMP server starts and two windows open:

- The MAMP application window, shown in Figure 29.7, includes tools for starting, stopping, and configuring Apache, PHP, and MySQL.

- A browser window opens to the MAMP server's home page, as shown in Figure 29.8. This page includes links to phpMyAdmin and SQLLiteManager.

Tip

When you close the MAMP application window, the Apache and MySQL servers both shut down by default. There is an option on the Preferences screen that enables you to override this behavior. ■

When you first install MAMP, the Apache and MySQL servers run on custom ports rather than their respective default ports of 80 and 3306. If you don't have other copies of Apache or MySQL running on your Mac development system, you can switch to the default ports.

FIGURE 29.7

The MAMP application window

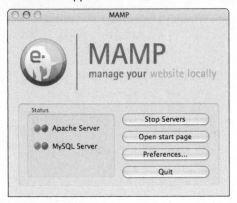

FIGURE 29.8

The MAMP home page

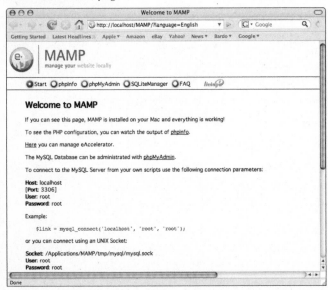

If you're not sure whether the Apache Web server that's included with Mac OS X is currently running, follow these steps:

1. **Open the Mac OS X System Preferences application.**

2. **Click Sharing.**

3. **Make sure the Web Sharing option is unchecked. If it's checked, uncheck it.**

Then follow these steps to configure the MAMP ports:

1. **Click Preferences in the MAMP application window.**

2. **Click Ports in the Preferences toolbar.**

3. **Click the Set to default Apache and MySQL ports option, as shown in Figure 29.9.**

FIGURE 29.9

Changing Apache and MySQL ports

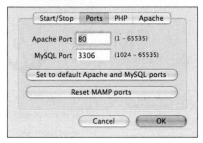

4. **Click OK to accept the new port settings.**

5. **When prompted, enter your administrative password again to restart both servers.**

You also can change the Apache Web root folder, which defaults to a subfolder name `htdocs` under the MAMP installation folder. For example, on a system that's used by more than one developer, you may want to set the document root folder to a new subfolder under your home directory, such as `/[UserName]/htdocs`.

Follow these steps to set the Apache document root folder:

1. **Click Preferences in the MAMP application window.**

2. **Click Apache in the Preferences toolbar.**

3. **Select a new document root folder, and click OK.**

4. **When prompted, enter your administrative password again to restart Apache.**

Creating a Flex Project for Use with PHP

When you create a Flex project, you have the option to integrate the project with PHP and its hosting Web server. The steps are similar to those for integrating ColdFusion, described in Chapter 28. The project includes properties that designate the disk location and testing URL for the PHP Web root folder. The debug version of the application is created in a folder under the PHP Web root. To test the Flex application, you download the application's HTML wrapper from the Web server, resulting in running the application from the Web server rather than from the local hard disk.

Follow these steps to create a Flex application that's integrated with your PHP installation:

1. **Choose File ⇨ New ⇨ Flex Project from the Flash Builder menu.**
2. **On the first screen of the New Flex Project wizard, shown in Figure 29.10, use these property settings:**
   - Project name: **chapter29**
   - Project location: **Use default location**
   - Application type: **Web application**
   - Flex SDK version: **Use default SDK**
   - Server technology: **PHP**
3. **Click Next.**
4. **On the Configure PHP Server screen, shown in Figure 29.11, set the PHP server's Web root and Root URL.** If you're using WampServer with the default installation settings, these properties are:
   - Web root: **C:\wamp\www**
   - Root URL: **http://localhost**

The New Flex Project wizard creating a project for use with PHP

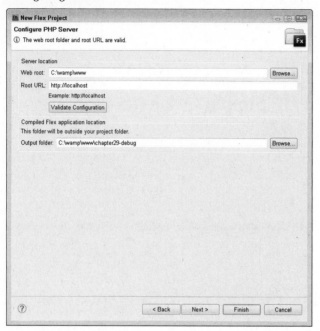

FIGURE 29.11

Configuring the PHP server

5. **Make sure the Web server that hosts PHP is running, and then click Validate Configuration to ensure that Flash Builder can reach the Web server.** The output folder can be set to any location within the Web server's document root. The default output folder name starts with the project name and ends with -debug to indicate that the output folder contains the debug version of the application. For example, the default output folder in the chapter29 project is placed under the PHP Web root with a name of chapter29-debug.

6. **Click Next.**

7. **Select a Main application filename, and click Finish to create the project and main application.**

When you create your PHP pages, they can be placed in the project's source root folder. During the compilation process, the PHP pages are recognized as application resources and copied to the project output folder from which they're called at runtime.

On the Web

If you want to try the sample applications from this chapter, extract the files from the Web site's chapter29.zip file into the new Flex project's root folder. ■

Using PHP with HTTPService and XML

You can integrate Flex applications with PHP using the Flex SDK's HTTPService component and PHP pages that generate structured XML-based content on the server. To return structured data from a PHP page, you can either generate your own XML content with conventional text concatenation or you can use a more reliable approach that requires an external library to serialize XML packets.

Using the PHP SimpleXML extension

The PHP page in Listing 29.1 uses a PHP5 extension named SimpleXML to generate and return an XML-formatted response with literal values in each of the XML elements. The header() function is used to inform the client application that the content is being delivered with the xml/text content type.

Web Resource

The documentation for the PHP SimpleXML extension is available on the Web at http://us3.php.net/ simplexml. ∎

LISTING 29.1

A PHP page that returns simple XML

```
<?php
$xmlstr = <<<XML
<?xml version='1.0'?>
<vendors>
 <vendor>
  <name>You Grow ,em, We Mow ,em</name>
  <service>Lawn Mowing</service>
 </vendor>
 <vendor>
  <name>How High the Shingle</name>
  <service>Roofing</service>
 </vendor>
 <vendor>
  <name>Ma &amp; Pa Kettle</name>
  <service>Cooking Supplies</service>
 </vendor>
</vendors>
XML;
header("Content-type: text/xml");
echo $xmlstr;
?>
```

On the Web

The code in Listing 29.1 is available in the Web site files as `ReturnSimpleXML.php` in the `src` folder of the `chapter29` project. ∎

To request this XML-formatted content in a Flex application, use the Flex framework's `HTTPService` component. Set the `HTTPService` object's `url` property to the location of the PHP page:

```
<s:HTTPService id="phpService"
  url="ReturnSimpleXML.php"/>
```

Retrieving XML data with HTTPService

Retrieving the data from the server is a simple matter of calling the `HTTPService` object's `send()` method and handling the returned results with a binding expression or a `result` event handler. The Flex application in Listing 29.2 retrieves the data in XML format from the PHP page and displays it in a `DataGrid` control.

LISTING 29.2

Retrieving XML-formatted data from PHP

```
<?xml version="1.0" encoding="utf-8"?>
<s:Application xmlns:fx="http://ns.adobe.com/mxml/2009"
  xmlns:s="library://ns.adobe.com/flex/spark"
  xmlns:mx="library://ns.adobe.com/flex/mx">
  <fx:Declarations>
    <s:HTTPService id="phpService"
      url="ReturnSimpleXML.php"
      result="resultHandler(event)"/>
  </fx:Declarations>
  <fx:Script>
    <![CDATA[
      import mx.collections.ArrayCollection;
      import mx.controls.Alert;
      import mx.rpc.events.ResultEvent;
      [Bindable]
      private var vendorData:ArrayCollection;

      private function resultHandler(event:ResultEvent):void
      {
        vendorData = event.result.vendors.vendor as ArrayCollection;
      }
    ]]>
  </fx:Script>
```

continued

LISTING 29.2 *(continued)*

```
  <s:layout>
    <s:VerticalLayout paddingTop="20" horizontalAlign="center"/>
  </s:layout>
  <s:Button label="Get XML" click="phpService.send()"/>
  <mx:DataGrid dataProvider="{vendorData}" width="400"/>
</s:Application>
```

On the Web

The code in Listing 29.2 is available in the Web site files as `GetSimpleXML.mxml` in the default package in the `src` folder of the `chapter29` project. ■

Tip

If you prefer to parse the returned XML with E4X syntax, set the `HTTPService` component's `resultFormat` property to a value of `e4x`. ■

Cross-Reference

See Chapter 22 for more information on working with data using the HTTPService component. ■

Using PHP and Remoting with Zend AMF

There are a number of PHP implementations of the technology that are variously known as the Remoting Service (in BlazeDS and LiveCycle Data Services) or Flash Remoting (in ColdFusion). They include:

- **AMFPHP.** A free, open-source project available at www.amfphp.org.

- **SabreAMF.** A free, open-source project available at http://osflash.org/sabreamf.

- **WebOrb.** A commercial implementation of Remoting for PHP, Java, ASP.NET, and Ruby on Rails that's available at www.themidnightcoders.com.

- **Zend AMF.** A part of the free, open-source Zend Framework available at http://framework.zend.com/download/amf.

Developers typically switch from using the `HTTPService` component and generic XML to an implementation of AMF when they want better performance in applications that exchange data with a server at runtime. As with Flash Remoting in ColdFusion, described in Chapter 28, and the Java-based Remoting Service in LiveCycle Data Services and BlazeDS, described in Chapter 26, messages that use binary AMF are significantly smaller than an equivalent message formatted in SOAP or generic XML. The result is faster exchange of data and decreased use of network resources.

The details of implementation on the server are different for each of these server-based software packages. In order to support PHP AMF services, Flash Builder 4 automatically installs a version of Zend AMF into your PHP server. From that point, it's very easy to create server-side PHP code that exchanges data with your Flex application using the binary AMF protocol.

Note

The effort to provide AMF support for the Zend Framework was sponsored by Adobe starting in 2008 and was based on the existing codebase of AMFPHP. Because Zend AMF is now approved for use by Adobe Systems and support for it included in Flash Builder 4, upgrades and maintenance of other open-source implementations of AMF for PHP have either slowed down or completely ceased. WebOrb for PHP from The Midnight Coders remains a robust commercial option. ■

Installing Zend AMF

The easiest way to install Zend AMF into your PHP server is to ask Flash Builder 4 to generate a PHP data connection. As described in Chapters 22, 26, and 28, a data connection is built as a set of ActionScript proxy and value object classes that you call from your Flex application. The resulting ActionScript code uses the Flex SDK's RemoteObject class to exchange messages in the binary AMF format.

Follow these steps to trigger the installation of Zend AMF:

1. **Make sure you have a currently active Flex project that's integrated with PHP.**

2. **Choose Data ➪ Connect to PHP from the Flash Builder menu.**

3. **In the Configure PHP Service dialog box, shown in Figure 29.12, click the link to generate a sample service.**

FIGURE 29.12

The Configure PHP Service dialog box

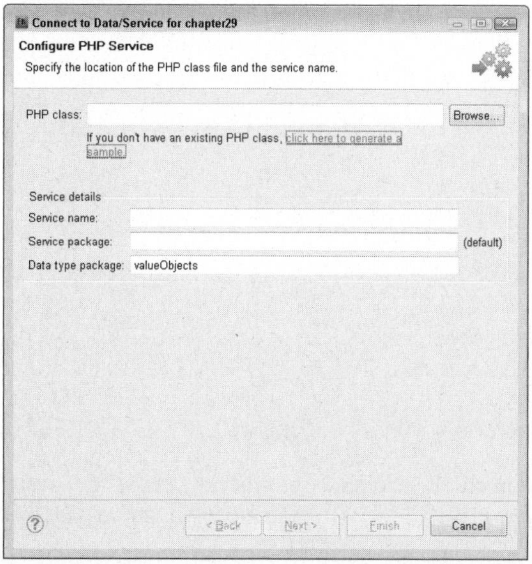

4. In the Generate Sample PHP Service dialog box, shown in Figure 29.13, select Generate from template.

FIGURE 29.13

The Generate Sample PHP Service dialog box

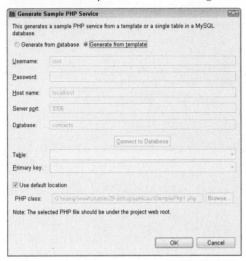

5. Click OK.

As shown in Figure 29.14, a message dialog box tells you that a file named `SamplePhp.php` will be created in your project's output folder under a subfolder named services.

6. Click OK.

FIGURE 29.14

A message indicating the name and location of the sample PHP service file

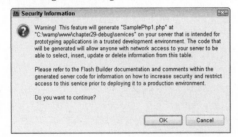

As shown in Figure 29.15, the next message tells you that Flash Builder will install Zend AMF as a PHP library.

7. **Click OK.** The installation of the Zend Framework now proceeds and takes a few minutes.

8. **When you see the dialog box indicating that the installation is complete, click OK.**

FIGURE 29.15

A message indicating that Zend AMF will be installed into your PHP server

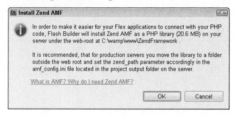

9. **If you see a message indicating the version of the installed software, click OK again.**

10. **When the Configure PHP Service screen appears, click Cancel for now.**

Web Resource

The Zend AMF library is installed in a `ZendFramework` subfolder under the Web server's document root folder. For security and maintenance reasons, you might want to move the Zend Framework out of the Web server's document root folder. The following Web page has a good discussion of various options and their pros and cons:

`http://devzone.zend.com/article/4683` ■

Creating a service class in PHP

Zend AMF services are built as basic PHP classes. Functions declared as class members return values that are encoded in binary AMF for exchange with a client Flex application. Just as with any PHP file, you don't need to compile or otherwise prepare a PHP class to be called as a service. You just create the file in the correct location, and it's immediately ready for use.

The file must conform to these requirements:

- The file must have an extension of `.php`.

- It must be placed in a folder named `services`. The location of the services folder can be anywhere within the PHP server's document root but typically is placed in the project's output folder.

The PHP class in Listing 29.3 implements a single `sayHello()` function that returns a string value to the client application.

LISTING 29.3

A simple Hello World PHP class that's compatible with Zend AMF

```php
<?php
class HelloWorld {
  function sayHello()
  {
    return "Hello Flex from PHP!";
  }
}
?>
```

On the Web

The code in Listing 29.3 is available in the Web site files as `HelloWorld.php` in the `services` package of the `chapter29` project. ∎

Tip

If you try to open a PHP file from Flash Builder's Package Explorer view by double-clicking it, it will open in whatever software application the current operating system has registered for the .php file extension. If you want to open the file directly within Flash Builder, right-click the file and choose Open With ⇨ Text Editor from the context menu. ∎

Calling a PHP class with RemoteObject

You call an AMF service's methods using the `RemoteObject` component. The behavior and functionality of the `RemoteObject` component on the client is exactly the same as when you use it with Java or ColdFusion.

Cross-Reference

Because the client-side code for using the `RemoteObject` component is pretty much the same regardless of the language or platform on the server, many details of the client-side code aren't covered in this chapter. See Chapters 24 and 26 for more client-side code samples. ∎

Whether you declare your `RemoteObject` instance in MXML or ActionScript, you set the object's `endpoint` property to a file named `gateway.php`. The object's `destination` and `source` properties are then set to the name of the PHP service file, without the `.php` extension. For example, the file HelloWorld.php is referenced with the following `RemoteObject` declaration:

```
<s:RemoteObject id="helloService" source="HelloWorld"
    destination="HelloWorld" endpoint="gateway.php"/>
```

The application in Listing 29.4 declares a `RemoteObject` component instance in MXML code and sets its source to the location of the `HelloWorld` service installed previously. When the user clicks the button labeled Say Hello, a call is made to the PHP class's `sayHello()` function. The returned string is then displayed in the `Label` control using a binding expression.

LISTING 29.4

A Flex application calling a Zend AMF service

```
<?xml version="1.0" encoding="utf-8"?>
<s:Application xmlns:fx="http://ns.adobe.com/mxml/2009"
  xmlns:s="library://ns.adobe.com/flex/spark"
  xmlns:mx="library://ns.adobe.com/flex/mx">
  <fx:Declarations>
    <s:RemoteObject id="helloService"  endpoint="gateway.php"
      source="HelloWorld" destination="HelloWorld"/>
  </fx:Declarations>
  <s:layout>
    <s:VerticalLayout paddingTop="20" horizontalAlign="center"/>
  </s:layout>
  <s:Button label="Say Hello" click="helloService.sayHello()"/>
  <s:Label text="{helloService.sayHello.lastResult}"/>
</s:Application>
```

On the Web

The code in Listing 29.4 is available in the Web site files as `HelloWorld.mxml` in the default package in the `src` folder of the `chapter29` project. ∎

Returning complex data from Zend AMF

You can return complex data from PHP either by manually constructing an array to return or by generating and returning a simple data set.

On the Web

The PHP classes used in this section and in a later one on Flash Builder data connections depend on a database named `contacts`. You can import the structure and data for this database into your copy of MySQL using the `contacts.sql` file that's included in the `database` folder included in `chapter29.zip`. ∎

The PHP service class in Listing 29.5 executes a simple query and returns its data.

LISTING 29.5

Returning a simple data set from a PHP class

```
<?php
class DataManager {
  function getData()
  {
    mysql_connect('localhost', 'root', '');
    mysql_select_db('contacts');
```

continued

LISTING 29.5 *(continued)*

```
    return mysql_query(sprintf(
      "SELECT personid, firstname, lastname
      FROM person
      ORDER BY lastname, firstname"));
  }
}
?>
```

On the Web

The code in Listing 29.5 is available in the Web site files as `DataManager.php` **in the** `services` **package in the** `chapter29` **project.** ■

When you call the service function, the query result is received in Flex as an `ArrayCollection`. The Flex application in Listing 29.6 calls the service function and uses debugging code to determine how much time elapses between sending the request and receiving the result. When you run the application in debug mode and send the request, a tracing message reports the time elapsed in Flash Builder's Console view.

LISTING 29.6

A Flex application receiving complex data

```
<?xml version="1.0" encoding="utf-8"?>
<s:Application xmlns:fx="http://ns.adobe.com/mxml/2009"
  xmlns:s="library://ns.adobe.com/flex/spark"
  xmlns:mx="library://ns.adobe.com/flex/mx">
  <fx:Script>
    <![CDATA[
      import mx.collections.ArrayCollection;
      import mx.rpc.events.ResultEvent;
      [Bindable]
      private var myData:ArrayCollection;
      [Bindable]
      private var elapsedTime:Number;
      private var startTime:Number;
      private function sendRequest():void
      {
        startTime = (new Date()).getTime();
        dataResponder.token = dataService.getData();
      }
      protected function dataResponder_resultHandler(event:ResultEvent):void
      {
```

```
        var endTime:Number = (new Date()).getTime();
        elapsedTime = endTime - startTime;
        myData = event.result as ArrayCollection;
      }
    ]]>
  </fx:Script>
  <fx:Declarations>
    <s:RemoteObject id="dataService" endpoint="gateway.php"
      source="DataManager" destination="DataManager"/>
    <s:CallResponder id="dataResponder"
      result="dataResponder_resultHandler(event)"/>
  </fx:Declarations>
  <s:layout>
    <s:VerticalLayout paddingTop="20" horizontalAlign="center"/>
  </s:layout>
  <s:Button label="Get Data" click="sendRequest()"/>
  <mx:DataGrid dataProvider="{dataService.getData.lastResult}"/>
  <s:Label text="Time elapsed: {elapsedTime}ms"
    visible="{!isNaN(elapsedTime)}"/>
</s:Application>
```

On the Web

The code in Listing 29.6 is available in the Web site files as `GetComplexData.php` in the default package in the src file of the `chapter29` project. ∎

Figure 29.16 shows the resulting application, displaying data returned from the MySQL database.

FIGURE 29.16

Data returned from PHP and MySQL

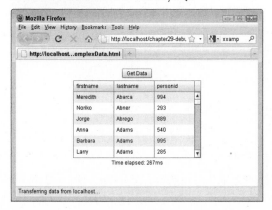

Understanding ActionScript to PHP data serialization

The PHP `mysql_query()` function returns a PHP `resource`, which is serialized to an ArrayCollection when returned to Flex. Table 29.1 describes how other PHP data types are serialized from ActionScript to PHP and back again.

TABLE 29.1

ActionScript to PHP Data Serialization

ActionScript	To PHP	Back to ActionScript
Null	Null	Null
Boolean	Boolean	Boolean
String	String	String
Date	Float	Number
Array	Array	Array
Object	Associative array	Object
XML	String	String

Web Resource

The documentation for Zend AMF is available at `http://framework.zend.com/manual/en/zend.amf.html.` ∎

Using PHP Data Connections in Flash Builder

As described in Chapters 26 and 28, and as referred to earlier in this chapter, Flash Builder 4 includes the capability to generate client-side proxy classes that can be used to make calls to PHP service classes on the server. In this section I describe both how to build data connections for existing PHP classes and how to generate new classes based on the structure of MySQL database tables.

Defining data connections

The steps for creating a PHP data connection in Flash Builder 4 are nearly identical to those for connecting to a ColdFusion CFC as described in Chapter 28:

1. **Choose Data ➪ Connect to PHP from the Flash Builder menu.**

2. **Select the PHP class you want to call from your Flex application.** As shown in Figure 29.17, also set the Service name as it will be known in Flex, and the packages in which you want to generate your proxy and value object classes.

Configuring a data connection for an existing PHP class

3. **Click Next.** As shown in Figure 29.18, the Service Operations screen displays the PHP service class's functions.

4. **Click Finish to generate the proxy service.**

If you're working with a PHP page that returns a simple result set, the function's return data type is set to an array of ActionScript Object by default. Follow these steps to generate a custom value object ActionScript class and use it as the function's return type:

1. **Open the Data/Services view and locate the new class.**

2. **Right-click on the function and select Configure Return Type.**

3. **In the Configure Return Type dialog box, shown in Figure 29.19, click Next to auto-detect the return type.** As shown in Figure 29.20, the Configure Return Type dialog box shows the structure of the returned data.

4. **Enter the name of the ActionScript class you want to create and click Finish.** The return type of the function is changed in the Data/Services view.

FIGURE 29.18

The Service Operations screen

FIGURE 29.19

The Configure Return Type screen

FIGURE 29.20

The Service Operations screen

Generating a service based on a database table structure

Flash Builder 4 also can create complete service classes based on an existing database table structure. The resulting PHP class implements functions that retrieve data (as either an entire table's worth of data or as a paged data set); insert, update, and delete data; and retrieve single objects based on primary key identifiers.

Follow these steps to generate a PHP class that supports a single database table:

1. **Make sure you're working in a currently active Flex project that's integrated with PHP.**

2. **Choose Data ⇨ Connect to PHP from the Flash Builder menu.**

3. **In the Connect to Data Services dialog box, click the link to generate a sample service.**

4. **In the Generate Sample PHP Service dialog box, select Generate from database.**

5. **As shown in Figure 29.21, enter the Username and Password for your MySQL database.** If you're using WampServer or MAMP, the default user name is `root`. The password is a blank string for WampServer and `root` for MAMP.

6. **Enter the DNS name or IP address of your MySQL server.** If it's installed on your local system, use `localhost` or `127.0.0.1`.

7. **Set the Server port.** The default for MySQL is 3306.

8. **Set the database name.**

FIGURE 29.21

Setting the database credentials to generate a PHP service class

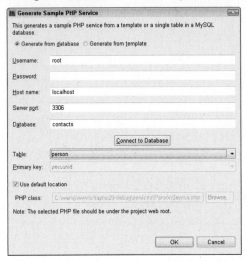

9. **Click Connect to Database.**

10. **Select the name of the table for which you want to generate a PHP service class.**

11. **Set the location and name of the PHP service class.** The class must be placed within the Web server's document root folder.

12. **Click OK.** As shown in Figure 29.22, you're warned that the PHP file is intended for prototyping applications in a trusted development environment.

13. **Click OK to continue.**

14. **In the Connect to Data/Service dialog box, select the name of the ActionScript class you want to create.** Also select the Service name and the packages in which you want to create the proxy and value object classes, and then click Next.

FIGURE 29.22

A warning that the generated PHP file is intended for application prototyping only

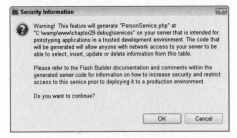

As shown in Figure 29.23, the Service Operations screen displays the list of functions in the generate class.

15. Click Finish to complete the operation.

A list of the generated data access functions

The PHP class and its generated ActionScript proxy class implement the following functions that you can call from your Flex application (note that the name of the database table is incorporated into many of the function names and will depend on your database table names):

- `count()`. Returns the number of rows in the table.

- `createPerson($item)`. Creates the item in the database and returns the value of the object's new primary key (in the case of an auto-incrementing primary key column).

- `deletePerson($itemID)`. Deletes the item in the database based on the primary value.

- `getAllPerson()`. Returns all the rows from the table.

- `getPersonByID($itemID)`. Returns the item corresponding to the value specified for the primary key.

- `getPerson_paged($startIndex, $numItems)`. Returns $numItems rows starting from the $startIndex row from the table.

- `updatePerson($item)`. Updates the item in the database.

Note

The generated PHP code is intended only as a starting point. You'll need to modify the PHP code to implement the specific data management features that are required by your application. ■

Flash Builder's Data/Services view should now display the new data connection. Once you've created the data connection, you can do everything with it that you do with data connections for other application server architectures such as HTTP and Web services:

- Bind data to visual controls
- Generate data entry forms
- Generate detail forms
- Reconfigure return data types for particular functions

Cross-Reference

See Chapter 25 for more information about tasks you can accomplish with Flash Builder data connections and Chapter 26 for more information about working with the RemoteObject component. ■

Summary

In this chapter, I described how to build Flex applications that are integrated with server-side code managed by PHP. You learned the following:

- PHP is an open-source, freely available application server that is compatible with many operating systems.
- PHP's scripting language doesn't require any compilation prior to being requested from a client application.
- To get started quickly with PHP, you can download and use free integrated software bundles named WampServer (for Windows) and MAMP (for Mac OS X) that include the Apache Web server, PHP, and MySQL.
- When you create a Flex project, you can associate it with your PHP installation.
- The PHP5 SimpleXML extension can create XML packets to return to a Flex application.
- Flash Builder 4 can generate complete client and server code to manage a MySQL database table with PHP code on the server.
- You can build your own client Flex application to work with the generated PHP code using the HTTPService component.
- Better network and data exchange performance can be achieved by using the RemoteObject component and PHP classes hosted by Zend AMF, a free, open-source project that's included with Flash Builder 4.

Part V

Additional Subjects

IN THIS PART

Chapter 30
Localizing Flex 4 Applications

Chapter 31
Deploying Desktop Applications
with Adobe AIR

Localizing Flex 4 Applications

When you localize an application, you create a pattern that enables you to easily publish and run an application in multiple languages. The Flex 4 SDK includes a number of tools that support localization, including compiler tools that support selecting a *locale* at compilation time or runtime, and *resource bundles* that represent strings, images, and other resources used in specific locales.

Using these tools, you can create an application that's localized either during compilation or while the application is running. The localization architecture works the same with both MX and Spark components, and with both Web applications and desktop applications deployed with Adobe AIR.

In this chapter, I describe how to develop resource bundles for localized applications and how to select locales for a compiled application and at runtime.

On the Web

To use the sample code for this chapter, download `chapter30.zip` from the Web site. This is not a Flex project archive file. Its use and installation are described later in this chapter. ■

IN THIS CHAPTER

Understanding Flex application localization

Understanding locales

Defining resource bundles at runtime

Binding text controls to string-based localization properties

Defining external resource bundle files

Setting Flex project compiler arguments for localization

Embedding graphics in external resource bundle files

Using Locales to Select Application Resources

A *locale* is a way of designating a specific set of strings, images, fonts, and other resources that are used in an application's user interface. In the version of Flash Builder that's sold by Adobe Systems in North America, the default locale is named en_US for the U.S. version of the English language.

Follow these steps to create a new Flex project and look at its default locale setting:

1. Choose File ➪ New ➪ Flex Project from the Flash Builder menu.

2. **Set the project name as** chapter30, **confirm that no application server is selected, and click Finish.**

3. **After the project has been created, right-click the project in the Package Explorer view and select Properties.**

4. **Click Flex Compiler in the category list in the Properties dialog box.**

5. **Look at the Additional compiler arguments.** As shown in Figure 30.1, the default compiler arguments for a new Flex project in North America look like this:

   ```
   -locale en_US
   ```

6. **Click Cancel to close the Properties dialog box without making any changes.**

FIGURE 30.1

The compiler additional arguments for a new Flex project

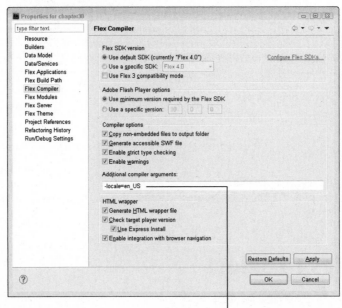

Setting the default locale

Next, follow these steps to look at the list of available locales that are installed by default with Flash Builder 4:

1. **Open Windows Explorer or Finder and navigate to the Flash Builder installation folder.**

2. **Navigate to the following subfolder:**

   `/sdks/4.0/frameworks/locale`

3. **Look at the list of subfolders under locale.** You'll see many locales listed for some of the most commonly used countries and languages in which Flash Builder and the Flex 4 SDK are used.

New Feature

Flash Builder 4 includes many more pre-built locales than were included with Flex Builder 3. ∎

On the Web

If you want to review the sample applications described in this chapter, extract the contents of the `chapter30.zip` file into the root folder of the `chapter30` Flex project. You might see a compiler error if you try to run any of the ZIP file's applications immediately. The error will be resolved when you add compiler arguments to the project properties as described later in this chapter. ∎

Changing locales at compile time

To change locales for a compiled application, just set the locale property in the Flex project's compilation arguments. Follow these steps to create a simple application that demonstrates use of two of Flash Builder's pre-built locales:

1. **With the chapter30 project active, choose File ➪ New ➪ MXML Application.**

2. **Name the new application** `SimpleLocaleUse.mxml` **and click Finish.**

3. **Declare a new DateFormatter object in the** `<fx:Declarations>` **section with an ID of df:**

   ```
   <mx:DateFormatter id="df"/>
   ```

4. **Declare a Label object below the <fx:Declarations> section and set its properties as follows:**

   - `horizontalCenter="0"`
   - `top="20"`
   - `fontSize="24"`

5. **Set the Label object's text property to a binding expression that outputs the current date, formatted with the DateFormatter object.** The binding expression might look like this:

   ```
   Today's date: {df.format(new Date())}
   ```

The completed application is shown in Listing 30.1.

LISTING 30.1

An application that outputs a formatted date

```
<?xml version="1.0" encoding="utf-8"?>
<s:Application xmlns:fx="http://ns.adobe.com/mxml/2009"
  xmlns:s="library://ns.adobe.com/flex/spark"
  xmlns:mx="library://ns.adobe.com/flex/mx">
  <fx:Declarations>
    <mx:DateFormatter id="df"/>
  </fx:Declarations>
  <s:Label text="Today's date: {df.format(new Date())}"
    horizontalCenter="0" top="20" fontSize="24"/>
</s:Application>
```

On the Web

The code in Listing 30.1 is available in the Web site files in the `chapter30` **project as**
`SimpleLocalUseComplete.mxml.` ∎

When you run the application, it displays the current date in the locale designated by the project's locale property. When using the en_US locale, the application displays the current date with "long" date formatting:

```
Today's date: 12/07/2009
```

Next, follow these steps to change the locale in the project's properties to use the fr_FR locale (the French language as it's spoken in France):

1. **Right-click the Flex project in the Package Explorer view and select Properties.**
2. **Click Flex Compiler in the category list in the Properties dialog box.**
3. **Change the Additional compiler arguments to:**
   ```
   -locale fr_FR
   ```
4. **Click OK to save the new locale setting.**
5. **Run the application.**

The application now displays the current date using the default date setting for the fr_FR locale:

```
Today's date: 7 Déc 2009
```

Changing locales at runtime

You change locales at runtime by modifying an application's `resourceManager` object. The application's `resourceManager` is a singleton object that manages all of the application's localization resources. It implements the `IResourceManager` interface and includes many methods for managing resource selection and presentation at runtime.

To change the current locale at runtime, you modify the value of the `resourceManager` object's `localeChain` property. The `localeChain` is an array that lists locales in the order of preference. For example, the following code sets `localeChain` to an array of three locales:

```
resourceManager.localeChain = ["fr_FR","es_ES","en_US"];
```

Any references to objects that use locales first tries to use the `fr_FR` locale (French). If the required resource doesn't exist in that locale, the resource manager tries to use `es_ES` (Spanish). If neither locale includes the required resource, the resource manager then uses the version in `en_US` (English).

Before you can refer to multiple locales in the application's code, you must ensure that they're all compiled into the application. The simplest way to do this is by setting the application's initial `localeChain` in the compiler arguments with the `locales` property. For example, the following compiler argument ensures that locale resource bundles for English, French, and Japanese are compiled into the application:

```
-locale=en_US,fr_FR,ja_JP
```

Follow these steps to configure a Flex project to use multiple locales, and then select a locale at runtime:

1. **Right-click the current project in the Package Explorer view and choose Project ⇨ Properties.**

2. **Select the Flex Compiler category.**

3. **Set Additional compiler arguments to:**

   ```
   -locale=en_US,fr_FR,ja_JP
   ```

4. **Click OK.**

5. **Open** `ChangeLocaleAtRuntime.mxml`.

The application declares instances of the `Date` and `DateFormatter` classes in its `<fx:Declarations>` section. It also declares an `ArrayList` with an `id` of `locales` that contains strings representing each of the compiled locales:

```
<fx:Declarations>
  <fx:Date id="currentDate"/>
  <mx:DateFormatter id="df"/>
  <s:ArrayList id="locales">
    <fx:String>en_US</fx:String>
    <fx:String>fr_FR</fx:String>
    <fx:String>ja_JP</fx:String>
  </s:ArrayList>
</fx:Declarations>
```

In the visual presentation section of the application, a `Label` control displays the formatted date:

```
<s:Label id="dateLabel"
  text="Today's date: {df.format(currentDate)}" fontSize="24"/>
```

A `DropDownList` lets the user select from the three locales. When the user makes a selection, a change event handler is triggered:

```
<s:DropDownList dataProvider="{locales}"
  change="dropdownlist1_changeHandler(event)"
  selectedIndex="0"/>
```

The event handler function changes the `localeChain` to the selected locale and then executes the `Label` control's binding to update its display:

```
protected function dropdownlist1_changeHandler(
  event:IndexChangeEvent):void
{
  resourceManager.localeChain = [locales.getItemAt(event.newIndex)];
  dateLabel.executeBindings();
}
```

The resulting application, shown in its entirety in Listing 30.2, enables the user to select a locale and see the display updated immediately.

LISTING 30.2

An application that updates its locale at runtime

```xml
<?xml version="1.0" encoding="utf-8"?>
<s:Application xmlns:fx="http://ns.adobe.com/mxml/2009"
  xmlns:s="library://ns.adobe.com/flex/spark"
  xmlns:mx="library://ns.adobe.com/flex/mx">
  <fx:Declarations>
    <fx:Date id="currentDate"/>
    <mx:DateFormatter id="df"/>
    <s:ArrayList id="locales">
      <fx:String>en_US</fx:String>
      <fx:String>fr_FR</fx:String>
      <fx:String>ja_JP</fx:String>
    </s:ArrayList>
  </fx:Declarations>
  <fx:Script>
    <![CDATA[
      import spark.events.IndexChangeEvent;

      protected function dropdownlist1_changeHandler(
        event:IndexChangeEvent):void
      {
        resourceManager.localeChain = [ locales.getItemAt(event.newIndex) ];
        dateLabel.executeBindings();
      }
    ]]>
```

```
    </fx:Script>
    <s:layout>
      <s:VerticalLayout horizontalAlign="center" paddingTop="20"/>
    </s:layout>
    <s:DropDownList dataProvider="{locales}"
      change="dropdownlist1_changeHandler(event)"
      selectedIndex="0"/>
    <s:Label id="dateLabel"
      text="Today's date: {df.format(currentDate)}" fontSize="24"/>
  </s:Application>
```

On the Web

The code in Listing 30.2 is available in the Web site files in the chapter30 project as
ChangeLocaleAtRuntime.mxml. ■

Note

The application in Listing 30.2 only works as intended if the requested locales are compiled into the application as described earlier in this section. ■

Using Custom Resource Bundles

You can create your own resource bundles that represent strings and other resources. Typically you create a custom resource bundle for each locale that you want to support. Resource bundles that include only replaceable strings can be created either at runtime or as compiled bundles; if you need to include fonts, images, and other binary resources, you should use compiled resource bundles.

Creating resource bundles at runtime

To create a resource bundle at runtime, declare a variable that's an instance of the ResourceBundle class. This class has two key properties you'll need to set so you can reference the bundle's resources in binding expressions and ActionScript statements:

- bundleName. This is a string that you'll refer to in your code.
- locale. This is the name of the locale with which the resource bundle is associated.

You can set the locale and bundleName properties when you instantiate the bundle object with its constructor method. The following code creates a resource bundle named customStrings that's associated with the fr_FR locale:

```
var frBundle:ResourceBundle =
  new ResourceBundle("fr_FR", "customStrings");
```

Tip
The name of the resource bundle is arbitrary and should describe what's contained in the bundle. You can create a single bundle for each locale that includes all replaceable strings for the entire application or create smaller bundles that group strings by their purpose. ∎

The ResourceBundle class has a content property that's defined as a dynamic object to which you can assign your own name/value pairs. The name of each property is a key by which you refer to the associated value in the selected locale. You can add new properties to the bundle by setting the name/value pair as a property of the content object:

```
frBundle.content.helloWorld = "Bonjour tout le Monde";
```

After adding as many properties as you need, you then add the resource bundle to the application with the resourceManager object's addResourceBundle() method:

```
resourceManager.addResourceBundle(frBundle);
```

Finally, after creating and adding all resource bundles, you call the resourceManager object's update() method:

```
resourceManager.update();
```

To use any of the properties of the resource bundle in a binding expression, call the resourceManager object's getString() method and pass in the name of the resource bundle and the key of the name/value pair that you want to display. The following Label object displays the value of the helloWorld property for the current locale:

```
<s:Label
   text="{resourceManager.getString('customStrings','helloWorld')}"/>
```

The application in Listing 30.3 creates two resource bundles at runtime. They share a name of customStrings but are associated with distinct locales of en_US and fr_FR. When the user switches locales, the strings displayed by the Label objects are updated immediately.

LISTING 30.3

An application using resource bundles declared at runtime

```
<?xml version="1.0" encoding="utf-8"?>
<s:Application xmlns:fx="http://ns.adobe.com/mxml/2009"
   xmlns:s="library://ns.adobe.com/flex/spark"
   xmlns:mx="library://ns.adobe.com/flex/mx"
   creationComplete="app_creationCompleteHandler(event)">
   <fx:Declarations>
     <fx:Date id="currentDate"/>
     <mx:DateFormatter id="df"/>
     <s:ArrayList id="locales">
```

```
        <fx:String>en_US</fx:String>
        <fx:String>fr_FR</fx:String>
      </s:ArrayList>
    </fx:Declarations>
  <fx:Style>
    @namespace s "library://ns.adobe.com/flex/spark";
    s|Label { font-size:18; }
  </fx:Style>
  <fx:Script>
    <![CDATA[
      import mx.events.FlexEvent;
      import mx.resources.ResourceBundle;

      import spark.events.IndexChangeEvent;

      protected function dropdownlist1_changeHandler(
        event:IndexChangeEvent):void
      {
        resourceManager.localeChain = [locales.getItemAt(event.newIndex)];
        dateLabel.executeBindings();
      }
      protected function app_creationCompleteHandler(event:FlexEvent):void
      {
        var enBundle:ResourceBundle =
          new ResourceBundle("en_US", "customStrings");
        enBundle.content.helloWorld = "Hello World";
        enBundle.content.todayItIs = "Today it's";
        resourceManager.addResourceBundle(enBundle);
        var frBundle:ResourceBundle =
          new ResourceBundle("fr_FR", "customStrings");
        frBundle.content.helloWorld = "Bonjour tout le Monde";
        frBundle.content.todayItIs = "Aujourd'hui, il est";
        resourceManager.addResourceBundle(frBundle);
        resourceManager.update();
      }
    ]]>
  </fx:Script>
  <s:layout>
    <s:VerticalLayout horizontalAlign="center" paddingTop="20"/>
  </s:layout>
  <s:DropDownList dataProvider="{locales}"
    change="dropdownlist1_changeHandler(event)"
    selectedIndex="0"/>
  <s:Label id="dateLabel"
    text="{resourceManager.getString('customStrings','todayItIs')}
          {df.format(currentDate)}"/>
  <s:Label id="helloLabel"
    text="{resourceManager.getString('customStrings','helloWorld')}"/>
</s:Application>
```

On the Web

The code in Listing 30.3 is available in the Web site files in the `chapter30` project as `RuntimeResourceBundles.mxml`. ∎

Using external resource bundles

External resource bundles are created as UTF-8 formatted text files with a file extension of `.properties`. As with the `ResourceBundle` class, you define an external resource bundle as a collection of name/value pairs.

Tip

When building localized applications, it's common to work with translators who are native speakers in each language you support. Using external resource bundles makes it much easier to send the files with keys already in place to the translators. Because the resource bundles are simple text files, the translators can edit them with any text editor application. ∎

String-based properties are declared in external resource files with the key name, an equals (=) operator, and the property value without any quotes or other delimiting characters:

```
helloWorld=Bonjour tout le Monde
```

Once you've included the resource bundle in an application as described later in this section, you can refer to the property with the `resourceManager` object's `getString()` method:

```
<s:Label
  text="{resourceManager.getString('customStrings','helloWorld')}"/>
```

You can also embed graphic files in external resource bundle files. The graphic files should be placed in a subfolder inside the Flex project's source-code root folder. Figure 30.2 shows two graphic files placed within the project's `src/images` folder named `helloworld_en_US.png` and `helloworld_fr_FR.png`.

FIGURE 30.2

Two graphics designed for use in the `fr_FR` and `en_US` locales

In the external resource bundle file, you declare the embedded graphic with a key (just like a string), and associate it with the graphic filename wrapped in the `Embed()` compiler directive. As with string-based properties, you do not include a semicolon or other line-ending character:

```
helloFlag=Embed("images/helloworld_fr_FR.png")
```

In the application, you can now display the graphic for the currently selected locale with the Spark `BitmapImage` control, setting its `source` property to the resource using the `resourceManager` object's `getClass()` method:

```
<s:BitmapImage
   source="{resourceManager.getClass('customStrings','helloFlag')}"/>
```

This same concept can be used to store style information, such as colors (stored as `uint`) and fonts (stored as strings), or formatter properties. The process is the same: declare the properties in the properties file, then use the relevant get method of the `resourceBundle` object in the MXML binding or in your ActionScript to retrieve the appropriate value at runtime.

The file shown in Listing 30.4 is a resource bundle that defines the same string-based properties that were used in the runtime version in Listing 30.3 and a new graphic image property named `helloFlag`.

LISTING 30.4

A simple resource bundle

```
#resource file for fr_FR
helloWorld=Bonjour tout le Monde
todayItIs=Aujourd'hui, il est
helloFlag=Embed("images/helloworld_fr_FR.png")
```

On the Web

The resource bundle file in Listing 30.4 is available in the Web site files in the `chapter30` project as `locale/fr_FR/customStrings.properties`. A matching file for the `en_US` locale is included as `locale/en_US/customStrings.properties`. ∎

To use external resource bundles in your Flex application, modify the project's compiler arguments to indicate the location of the resource bundle files. First set the `source-path` compiler argument to point to the folder where the properties file is created. Assuming that you've created a subfolder named `locale` under the Flex project's source-code root folder (usually named `src`), the following compiler argument indicates that the referenced resource bundles are available in a subfolder named for the currently selected locale:

```
-source-path=locale/{locale}
```

Next, add another compiler argument that indicates that the Flex project has overlapping source-code folders. Because the project's default source-code root folder is a parent of the `locale` folder, you must set `allow-source-path` as follows to avoid any compiler errors:

```
-allow-source-path-overlap=true
```

The following complete compiler arguments string supports custom resource bundles named in two locales (`en_US` and `fr_FR`):

```
-locale=en_US,fr_FR -source-path=locale/{locale}
    -allow-source-path-overlap=true
```

Caution

If you include locales for which there are no resource bundles, you will see compiler errors and won't be able to compile or run the application. ■

In the application, you indicate which resource bundles will be used with the `[ResourceBundle]` metadata tag. The following code indicates that the application will use the `customStrings` bundle, which in turn will be found in the `customStrings.properties` files in the source path for each locale:

```
<fx:Metadata>
    [ResourceBundle("customStrings")]
</fx:Metadata>
```

Your application can now reference the bundle properties using binding expressions, using the same syntax as when using resource bundles that were created at runtime:

```
<s:Label id="helloLabel"
    text="{resourceManager.getString('customStrings','helloWorld')}"/>
```

The application in Listing 30.5 uses custom strings that are stored in the two resource bundle files named `customStrings.properties` (one for each of the two supported locales for this project and application).

LISTING 30.5

An application using external resource bundles

```xml
<?xml version="1.0" encoding="utf-8"?>
<s:Application xmlns:fx="http://ns.adobe.com/mxml/2009"
  xmlns:s="library://ns.adobe.com/flex/spark"
  xmlns:mx="library://ns.adobe.com/flex/mx">
  <fx:Declarations>
    <fx:Date id="currentDate"/>
    <mx:DateFormatter id="df"/>
    <s:ArrayList id="locales">
```

```
        <fx:String>en_US</fx:String>
        <fx:String>fr_FR</fx:String>
      </s:ArrayList>
    </fx:Declarations>
    <fx:Style>
      @namespace s "library://ns.adobe.com/flex/spark";
      s|Label { font-size:18; }
    </fx:Style>
    <fx:Metadata>
      [ResourceBundle("customStrings")]
    </fx:Metadata>
    <fx:Script>
      <![CDATA[
        import spark.events.IndexChangeEvent;

        protected function dropdownlist1_changeHandler(
          event:IndexChangeEvent):void
        {
          resourceManager.localeChain = [ locales.getItemAt(event.newIndex) ];
          dateLabel.executeBindings();
        }
      ]]>
    </fx:Script>
    <s:layout>
      <s:VerticalLayout horizontalAlign="center" paddingTop="20"/>
    </s:layout>
    <s:DropDownList dataProvider="{locales}"
      change="dropdownlist1_changeHandler(event)"
      selectedIndex="0"/>
    <s:Label id="dateLabel"
      text="{resourceManager.getString('customStrings','todayItIs')}
        {df.format(currentDate)}"/>
    <s:Label id="helloLabel"
      text="{resourceManager.getString('customStrings','helloWorld')}"/>
    <s:BitmapImage
      source="{resourceManager.getClass('customStrings','helloFlag')}"/>
</s:Application>
```

On the Web

The code in Listing 30.5 is available in the Web site files in the `chapter30` project as
`UseExternalResourceBundles.mxml`. ∎

Caution

When you change property values in external resource bundle files and save the changes, it does not necessarily result in rebuilding a Flex project in Flash Builder. To ensure that the changes are reflected in the application, choose Project ⇨ Clean from the Flash Builder menu and rebuild the entire project. ∎

Summary

In this chapter, I described how to add localization to Flex applications so that they can support multiple languages and cultures. You learned the following:

- You can declare resource bundles for localized Flex applications at runtime or in external resource bundle files.

- Every Flex application has a `resourceManager` object that manages resources and locales.

- The `ResourceBundle` class is used to define resource bundles at runtime.

- External resource bundle files are created as UTF-8 formatted text files with as many property declarations as are needed for the application's localized properties.

- You can define localized graphic files using the `Embed()` function within external resource bundle files.

- The `resourceManager` object's `getString()`, `getClass()`, and other related methods are used in binding expressions to output a resource for the currently selected locale.

Deploying Desktop Applications with Adobe AIR

IN THIS CHAPTER

Understanding Adobe AIR

Creating desktop application projects with Flash Builder 4

Using the application descriptor file

Packaging an AIR application for deployment

Debugging AIR applications with Flash Builder 4

Incorporating HTML and PDF documents

Creating RPC channels at runtime

A dobe's release of Flex 3 in February 2008 was tightly integrated with the release of Adobe AIR. Formerly known as the Adobe Integrated Runtime (and before that by its public code name, Apollo), AIR is Adobe's strategy for offering a universal runtime client that can run local applications on a variety of personal computer systems and other computing devices.

With AIR 1.0, Adobe delivered the capability to deploy applications on Windows, Mac OS X, and Linux client systems. With the release of Flash CS5 Professional, Adobe is extending support for AIR to the Apple iPhone. The roadmap for AIR includes future versions for other cell phones and mobile devices, which eventually would allow AIR desktop applications to be deployed on a more truly universal basis.

AIR applications can be built from many different kinds of assets, but each application's core asset is made up of either Flash-based content, built in either Flash Professional (starting with Flash CS3) or Flex, or HTML-based content. Regardless of which kind of asset is used as the application's core element, any AIR application can use and present HTML, Flash, Flex, or Acrobat PDF content.

Tip

Adobe AIR's capability to present and manipulate Acrobat PDF content is dependent on the user having Acrobat Reader 8.1 or higher installed on her client system. ∎

The Adobe AIR 2.0 SDK, which includes many new features for integration with local clients, isn't included in the initial release of Flash Builder 4, but it can be downloaded from the Adobe Web site at: `www.adobe.com/go/ air`. In this chapter, I describe the basics of creating and deploying a Flex-based desktop application with Flash Builder 4 and Adobe AIR.

On the Web

To use the sample code for this chapter, download `chapter31.zip` from the Web site. This is not a Flex project archive file. Its use and installation are described later in this chapter. ■

Understanding AIR Architecture

Adobe AIR is installed as a runtime library on your client system. Its purpose is to provide core runtime functionality that's needed by all AIR-based desktop applications, regardless of whether they're built in Flash, Flex, or HTML.

As shown in Figure 31.1, Adobe AIR includes a copy of both the Flash Player and a Web browser. AIR 2.0 includes Flash Player 10.1, while the Web browser is an implementation of WebKit 4.0, an open-source Web browser engine.

FIGURE 31.1

Adobe AIR architecture with Flex applications

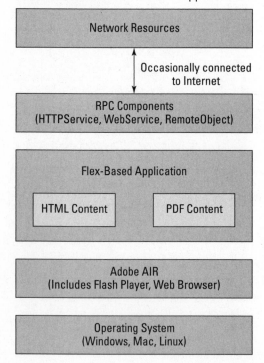

New Features in Adobe AIR 2.0

Version 2 of Adobe AIR includes many new features that provide better performance and improved integration with local client resources:

- New version of WebKit
- Microphone Access API
- Opens with default application
- Mass storage device detection
- New networking support
- Database transaction savepoints
- Creates native installers
- Launches and interacts with native processes
- Screen reader support (Windows only)
- Mac vector printing support
- Idle time-out settings
- Linux installers available as native DEB and RPM files
- IPv6 support
- Increased maximum size of NativeWindow
- File promises
- Multi-touch events
- Print Job Enhancements
- IME API and IME text input enhancement
- Global Exception Handler

Adobe AIR 2.0 no longer supports Mac OS X for PowerPC. Future versions of Adobe AIR will only work on Intel platform Macs.

Tip

The WebKit Web browser engine is used as the kernel for the Safari browser on Mac OS X, Google's Chrome browser on Windows, and the Konqueror browser that's available with the K desktop environment on Linux. The version that's used in AIR is derived from the open-source version of WebKit that's available at http:// webkit.org. ■

A desktop application deployed on AIR is delivered as an installable archive file with a file extension of .air. After installation, it runs as a local application that's native to the operating system, rather than as a Web-based application. As a result, desktop applications deployed on AIR aren't subject to the same security sandbox restrictions as a Web-based application that's downloaded and run on request from within a Web browser.

Because an AIR application's assets are made up of content that runs equally well on multiple operating systems without having to be rebuilt (Flash documents, HTML pages, JavaScript, CSS code, and Acrobat PDF documents), a single application can run on all supported operating systems without having to be recompiled.

Installing Adobe AIR

If you're using Flash Builder 4 to develop Flex applications, you don't necessarily have to install AIR on your development system because Flash Builder includes all the tools you need to compile, test, and debug an AIR application. But to fully install a completed application, the runtime must be installed.

You can install the runtime in two ways:

- If you know you need AIR on your system, you can download the AIR installer from Adobe's Web site and install it on your system prior to installing any applications.
- When you install an AIR application that uses a seamless installation badge, the application installer detects whether the runtime is already installed and, if not, offers to include the runtime installation along with the application.

I describe the seamless installation badge experience in a section near the end of this chapter. In this section, I describe how to download and install the correct version of AIR for your operating system.

Downloading the AIR installer

To download the AIR installer directly from Adobe, navigate to this URL:

```
http://get.adobe.com/air/
```

The Adobe Web page detects which operating system the request comes from and offers a download link for the appropriate version of the AIR installer.

Web Resource

You can download versions of AIR for other operating systems from `http://get.adobe.com/air/otherversions.` ∎

Installing and uninstalling AIR on Windows

The AIR installer for Windows is delivered as an executable application that's approximately 11.2MB.

Tip

You must be logged into Windows as an administrative user to successfully install or uninstall AIR. ■

After downloading the installer application, run the installer application and follow the prompts to complete the installation process.

No configuration options are available, so the installation completes from that point without any further requests for information. On a typical Windows installation, the runtime is installed into the following folder:

```
C:\Program Files\Common Files\Adobe AIR
```

To uninstall AIR on Windows, use the Control Panel's Add or Remove Programs tool on Windows XP or Uninstall a program on Windows Vista or Windows 7.

Caution

When you uninstall AIR from your system, any installed AIR applications are disabled. You can no longer run them or perform a clean uninstall process. If you want to permanently remove AIR and any dependent applications, you should uninstall the applications first and run the AIR uninstaller afterward. ■

Installing and uninstalling AIR on Mac OS X

The Adobe AIR installer for Mac OS X is delivered as a DMG file. After downloading the installer file, follow these steps to install AIR:

1. **Open the DMG file.**
2. **Double-click the Adobe AIR Installer application.**
3. **After accepting the license agreement, enter your Mac administrator password and click OK to complete the installation.**

As with installation on Windows, no configuration options are available, so the installation completes from that point with no further requests for information.

Follow these steps to uninstall AIR on Mac OS X:

1. **Navigate to the /Applications/Utilities folder.**
2. **Locate and run the Adobe AIR Uninstaller application.**
3. **When the Adobe AIR Setup dialog box appears, click Uninstall to remove AIR from your system.**
4. **Enter your Mac administrator password, and click OK to uninstall AIR.**

Creating a Flex Desktop Application

You can create and deploy a desktop application with Flex using one of these strategies:

- If you're using the free Flex SDK to build your Flex applications, you can use the free AIR SDK to package your applications for deployment.

- If you're using Flash Builder to create your Flex applications, everything you need to package an AIR application is already included.

In this section, I describe the steps for building a Flex desktop application project with Flash Builder.

Creating a Flex desktop application project

When you create a new Flex project in Flash Builder, you have the option of setting the Application type to Desktop. All MXML applications in such a project are designated as desktop applications and are tested and deployed with AIR.

Tip

In Flash Builder 4, you can't deploy a single application to both the desktop and the Web. The selection of AIR-based or Web-based deployment is made at the project level, and after a project is configured as such, you can't change it without going back and rebuilding the project from scratch.

If you do need to create a Flex application that's deployed with both architectures, consider creating three projects: one for the Web, one for the desktop, and one that's created as a Flex library project. The first two projects would have applications that are bare skeletons and get all their real functionality from components in the library project. Then, as you code and compile the library project, its assets are shared with the "real" projects that contain and are responsible for building the Web and desktop applications. ■

Follow these steps to create a Flex project in Flash Builder 4 that's designed for the desktop:

1. Choose File ➪ New ➪ Flex Project from the Flash Builder menu.

2. On the first screen of the New Flex Project wizard, shown in Figure 31.2, set these project properties:
   - Project name: **chapter31**
   - Project location: **Use default location**
   - Application type: **Desktop**
   - Flex SDK version: **Use default SDK**
   - Application server type: **None**

3. Click Next.

4. On the Configure Output screen, accept the default Output folder location and click Next.

FIGURE 31.2

Creating a new Flex desktop application project

5. On the final screen, shown in Figure 31.3, set the Main application filename to `MyDesktopApp`.

6. Set the Application ID to `com.mycompany.MyDesktopApp`.

7. Click Finish to create the project and application.

   You should see a starting Flex application open in the Flash Builder editor with a root element of `<s:WindowedApplication>`. In the Package Explorer view, you should see both the main application file and the XML-based application descriptor file `MyDesktopApp-app.xml`.

8. Delete the default `<fx:Declarations>` element from the new application.

9. Add a `Label` control to the application with a `text` property of `Hello from AIR!` and a `fontSize` style of `24`. Place it 20 pixels from the top of the application and center it horizontally:

   ```
   <s:Label text="Hello from AIR!" fontSize="24"
     top="20" horizontalCenter="0"/>
   ```

10. Save and run the application.

FIGURE 31.3

Setting the main application filename and the application `id`

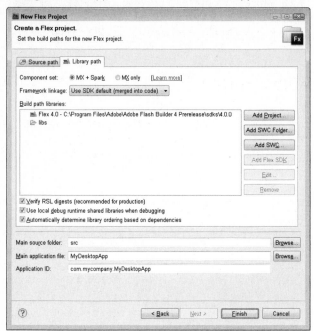

As shown in Figure 31.4, the application runs in a native window, rather than within a Web browser.

FIGURE 31.4

The resulting "Hello World" AIR application

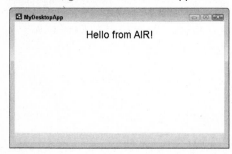

Note

The appearance of a basic Flex application differs depending on the hosting operating system. This screen shot was taken on Windows Vista, so the window title bar, borders, and control icons have the look of a standard Windows Vista window. The magic of AIR is that you don't have to recompile the application for different operating systems. When packaged with default settings in the application descriptor file, the version of AIR that's currently hosting the application at runtime controls the application window's look and feel. ■

Using the application descriptor file

The application descriptor file is in XML format and contains settings that are used by the AIR Developers Tool (ADT) and the AIR Debug Launcher (ADL) during packaging and testing of the application. When you create a new MXML application in a Flex desktop project, Flash Builder prompts you for both an application filename and an application id, and it creates both the application file and the application descriptor file at the same time.

Note

A clean starting copy of an application descriptor file with all available options is included in the Flex SDK as `descriptor-template.xml` in the Flash Builder installation folder's `sdks\4.0.0\templates\air` subfolder. ■

When you create a new Flex application in a desktop project, the following required properties are set in the default descriptor file:

- `filename`. This is the name of the packaged application's installer file, without a file extension. When the application is packaged for installation, this value is appended with the `.air` file extension.

- `id`. The application `id` is a string that uniquely identifies each AIR desktop application. To ensure that each application has an `id` that's globally unique, the `id` should start with a package-style reference based on your organization's reversed domain name, with the domain parts separated with dots. For example, if an organization's Web domain name is `coolstuff.com`, the `id` for its desktop applications would always start with `com.coolstuff`.

- `initialWindow/content`. This is the primary asset that's presented in the application's primary window. When working with the AIR SDK, this can be either a Flash SWF file or an HTML file. When working in Flash Builder, the `<content>` element initially contains a comment and is filled in during compilation and testing with the Flex application's compiled `.swf` filename.

- `name`. This is the name of the application as known to its users. This can be any string and can include spaces and special characters.

- `version`. This is the version number of the application.

The following starting application descriptor file contains only the required elements after commented-out elements and strings have been removed from the starting file you get in Flash Builder.

```
<?xml version="1.0" encoding="UTF-8"?>
<application xmlns="http://ns.adobe.com/air/application/1.5.3">
  <id>com.mycompany.MyDesktopApp</id>
```

```
      <filename>MyDesktopApp</filename>
      <name>MyDesktopApp</name>
      <version>v1</version>
      <initialWindow>
        <content>[This value will be overwritten by Flash Builder
          in the output app.xml]</content>
      </initialWindow>
    </application>
```

Note

The `<application>` element's `xmlns` namespace declaration is used to determine which version of AIR is required to run the application. The namespace shown in Listing 31.1 is for the version of AIR that was included in the initial release of Flash Builder 4. You can recognize application descriptor files that were created for the various public beta releases of AIR by their namespace declaration. For example, the namespace for the AIR 2.0 public beta looked like this:

```
<application
  xmlns="http://ns.adobe.com/air/application/2.0beta">
</application> ∎
```

You can include many other optional elements in the application descriptor file that affect the installation experience or the behavior and appearance of the application at runtime. As shown in Listing 31.1, the default application descriptor file includes comments above each element describing its purpose.

LISTING 31.1

The default application descriptor file with comments describing the purpose of each element

```
<?xml version="1.0" encoding="utf-8" standalone="no"?>
<application xmlns="http://ns.adobe.com/air/application/1.5.3">
<!-- Adobe AIR Application Descriptor File Template.
    Specifies parameters for identifying, installing, and launching AIR
    applications.
      xmlns - The Adobe AIR namespace: http://ns.adobe.com/air/
    application/1.5.3
                The last segment of the namespace specifies the version
                of the AIR runtime required for this application to run.
      minimumPatchLevel - The minimum patch level of the AIR runtime required
    to run the application. Optional.-->
    <!-- The application identifier string, unique to this application.
    Required. -->
    <id>AIRWebBrowser</id>
    <!-- Used as the filename for the application. Required. -->
    <filename>AIRWebBrowser</filename>
    <!-- The name that is displayed in the AIR application installer.
        May have multiple values for each language. See samples or xsd
    schema file. Optional. -->
    <name>AIRWebBrowser</name>
```

```
<!-- An application version designator (such as "v1", "2.5", or "Alpha
1"). Required. -->
<version>v1</version>
<!-- Description, displayed in the AIR application installer.
     May have multiple values for each language. See samples or xsd
schema file. Optional. -->
<!-- <description></description> -->
<!-- Copyright information. Optional -->
<!-- <copyright></copyright> -->
<!-- Settings for the application's initial window. Required. -->
<initialWindow>
     <!-- The main SWF or HTML file of the application. Required. -->
     <!-- Note: In Flash Builder, the SWF reference is set
automatically. -->
     <content>[This value will be overwritten by Flash Builder in the
output app.xml]</content>
     <!-- The title of the main window. Optional. -->
     <!-- <title></title> -->
     <!-- The type of system chrome to use (either "standard" or
"none"). Optional. Default standard. -->
     <!-- <systemChrome></systemChrome> -->
     <!-- Whether the window is transparent. Only applicable when
systemChrome is none. Optional. Default false. -->
     <!-- <transparent></transparent> -->
     <!-- Whether the window is initially visible. Optional. Default
false. -->
     <!-- <visible></visible> -->
     <!-- Whether the user can minimize the window. Optional. Default
true. -->
     <!-- <minimizable></minimizable> -->
     <!-- Whether the user can maximize the window. Optional. Default
true. -->
     <!-- <maximizable></maximizable> -->
     <!-- Whether the user can resize the window. Optional. Default
true. -->
     <!-- <resizable></resizable> -->
     <!-- The window's initial width. Optional. -->
     <!-- <width></width> -->
     <!-- The window's initial height. Optional. -->
     <!-- <height></height> -->
     <!-- The window's initial x position. Optional. -->
     <!-- <x></x> -->
     <!-- The window's initial y position. Optional. -->
     <!-- <y></y> -->
     <!-- The window's minimum size, specified as a width/height pair,
such as "400 200". Optional. -->
     <!-- <minSize></minSize> -->
     <!-- The window's initial maximum size, specified as a width/
height pair, such as "1600 1200". Optional. -->
```

continued

LISTING 31.1 *(continued)*

```
        <!-- <maxSize></maxSize> -->
   </initialWindow>
   <!-- The subpath of the standard default installation location to use.
Optional. -->
   <!-- <installFolder></installFolder> -->
   <!-- The subpath of the Programs menu to use. (Ignored on operating
systems without a Programs menu.) Optional. -->
   <!-- <programMenuFolder></programMenuFolder> -->
   <!-- The icon the system uses for the application. For at least one
resolution,
        specify the path to a PNG file included in the AIR package.
Optional. -->
   <!-- <icon
   <image16x16></image16x16>
        <image32x32></image32x32>
        <image48x48></image48x48>
        <image128x128></image128x128>
   </icon> -->
   <!-- Whether the application handles the update when a user double-
clicks an update version
   of the AIR file (true), or the default AIR application installer
handles the update (false).
   Optional. Default false. -->
   <!-- <customUpdateUI></customUpdateUI> -->
   <!-- Whether the application can be launched when the user clicks a
link in a web browser.
   Optional. Default false. -->
   <!-- <allowBrowserInvocation></allowBrowserInvocation> -->
   <!-- Listing of file types for which the application can register.
Optional. -->
   <!-- <fileTypes> -->
        <!-- Defines one file type. Optional. -->
        <!-- <fileType> -->
            <!-- The name that the system displays for the registered
file type. Required. -->
            <!-- <name></name> -->
            <!-- The extension to register. Required. -->
            <!-- <extension></extension> -->
            <!-- The description of the file type. Optional. -->
            <!-- <description></description> -->
            <!-- The MIME content type. -->
            <!-- <contentType></contentType> -->
            <!-- The icon to display for the file type. Optional. -->
            <!-- <icon>
                <image16x16></image16x16>
                <image32x32></image32x32>
                <image48x48></image48x48>
                <image128x128></image128x128>
```

```
            </icon> -->
        <!-- </fileType> -->
    <!-- </fileTypes> -->
</application>
```

Packaging a release version of an AIR application

When you package a release version of an AIR application, you create an AIR file (with a file extension of `.air`) that's delivered to the user as the application installer. When the user opens the AIR file on a system where Adobe AIR has already been installed, the application installer is executed.

Follow these steps to package the application for installation and deployment:

1. **With the application open in the Flash Builder editor, choose Project ➪ Export Release Build from the menu.**

2. **In the Export Release Build wizard, shown in Figure 31.5, set these properties:**

   - Project: **The selected project.**

   - Application: **The MXML application you want to package.**

   - View source: **Whether you want to allow the user to view the application's source code** (available when the user right-clicks on the application at runtime).

   - Export to file: **The name of the generated AIR file you want to build.** By default, this file is placed in the Flex project's root folder, but you can browse and select any other location within a currently open Eclipse project.

FIGURE 31.5

The Export Release Build wizard's initial screen

3. **Click Next.**

   On the Digital Signature screen, shown in Figure 31.6, you can either export and sign the generated AIR file with a digital certificate or create an intermediate file with a file extension of `.air` that can be signed and completed in a secondary step.

Selecting a security certificate

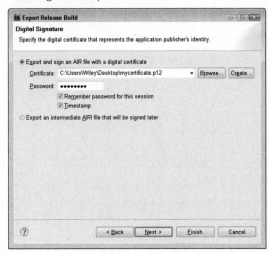

Tip

To package any AIR application, you must provide a security certificate that certifies to the user who developed the application. For applications that are in testing or that are only deployed within an organization, you can generate a self-signed certificate from within Flash Builder. This certificate enables you to package and deploy the application, but because no recognized certificate authority will have authenticated your organization's identity, the resulting installer application indicates that the author of the application is "Unknown."

For an application that will be deployed to a public audience, you should always purchase a security certificate from a recognized certificate authority such as VeriSign (www.verisign.com) or Thawte (www.thawte. com). When you use this sort of publicly recognized certificate to package your AIR application, the resulting installer correctly displays your organization name as the application author. ■

Caution

Even an application that reports an unknown author has unrestricted access to the user's system. The purpose of the security certificate is to give the user an opportunity to accept or reject installation based on the author's identity and doesn't stop bad applications from doing bad things. ■

If you don't have a security certificate, follow these steps to create a self-signed certificate for testing or internal use:

1. **Click Create on the Digital Signature screen.**

2. **Enter the requested values on the Create Self-Signed Digital Certificate screen, shown in Figure 31.7.** Items marked with an asterisk are required. In particular, you must provide a password that will then be required each time the certificate is used.

FIGURE 31.7

Creating a self-signed digital certificate

3. **Select the name of your certificate file with a file extension of** `.p12`, **and click OK to create the certificate file.** When you return to the Digital Signature screen, the certificate filename and password will are already filled in. If you already have a digital certificate file, just select the file and enter the certificate password.

4. **Click Finish in the Digital Signature screen to create the AIR installer file.** You should see that the application's AIR file is available in the project root folder and can be seen in the Package Explorer view,

Installing AIR applications

To install an AIR application on a desktop system that already has the runtime installed, just open the AIR file that was generated in Flash Builder. From within Flash Builder, you can open the file by double-clicking it in the Project Explorer view.

As shown in Figure 31.8, the initial installation screen displays the application's Publisher (displayed as UNKNOWN when the AIR file is built with a self-signed certificate) and the application's name as configured in the descriptor file.

FIGURE 31.8

An AIR installer's initial screen

After clicking Install on the initial screen, the confirmation screen, shown in Figure 31.9, displays the application name and the description as provided in the descriptor file. The installer also offers the user these options:

- Whether to include a shortcut icon for the application on the desktop
- Whether to start the application after installation is complete
- The application installation location, which defaults to `C:\Program Files` on Windows and `/Applications` on Mac OS X

Note

On Windows, the application is installed in a subfolder of the selected location named for the application name. For example, the default location `MyDesktopApp` on Windows is a folder named `C:\Program Files\MyDesktopApp`. On Mac OS X, the application is installed as a single application package file in the selected location folder with a file extension of `.app`. For example, the default location of `MyDeskTopApp` on Mac is a single application file named `/Applications/MyDesktopApp.app`. ∎

When the user clicks Continue, the application is installed on his system. If the user selects the option to start the application after installation is complete, the application opens.

Note

If a user downloads an AIR file from a site and doesn't have AIR installed, there is no way to prompt AIR is missing like one can do with JavaScript and SWF files. It's up to you to ensure that the user understands the runtime requirement. ∎

FIGURE 31.9

An AIR installer's confirmation screen

Uninstalling AIR applications

You uninstall an AIR desktop application in the same manner as most other native applications. Follow these steps to uninstall AIR applications in Windows:

1. Go to the Windows Control Panel.

2. Select Add or Remove Programs on Windows XP or Uninstall a program on Windows Vista or Windows 7.

3. Select the application entry.

4. Click Remove on Windows XP or Uninstall on Windows Vista or Windows 7.

5. When the Adobe AIR Setup dialog box appears, click Uninstall to remove AIR from your system.

To uninstall an AIR application on Mac OS X, just delete the application package file from the /Applications folder by dragging it into the trash.

Note
Running the AIR installation package file after the application is installed also results in displaying the setup dialog box and displays the uninstall option. ■

Flex Application Tips and Tricks with AIR

As described earlier in this chapter, the subject of developing Flex applications for desktop deployment with AIR is too large for a single chapter. There are, however, a few specific things you do a bit differently in a desktop application, and there are many Flex SDK features that are available only when you're developing for AIR. These include:

- Debugging AIR applications in Flash Builder
- Rendering and managing HTML-based and PDF-based content
- Using the `WindowedApplication` component as the application's root element
- Creating channels at runtime for communicating with Remoting gateways

In this section, I briefly describe some of these programming and development techniques.

On the Web

If you want to review the sample applications described in this section, extract the contents of the `chapter31.zip` **file into the root folder of the** `chapter30` **Flex desktop application project. Each sample application includes both an application file and an application descriptor file.** ∎

Debugging AIR applications in Flash Builder

For the most part, debugging an AIR application in Flash Builder is just like debugging a Web-based Flex application. You have access to all the same debugging tools, including the `trace()` function, breakpoints, and the capability to inspect the values of application variables when the application is suspended.

When you run a Flex application from within Flash Builder in either standard or debug mode, Flash Builder uses ADL (AIR Debug Launcher) in the background. In some cases, ADL can stay in system memory with hidden windows even after an AIR application session has apparently been closed.

The symptom for this condition is that when you try to run or debug that or another application, Flash Builder simply does nothing. Because a debugging session is still in memory, Flash Builder can't start a new one.

Follow these steps to recover from this condition in Windows:

1. **Open the Windows Task Manager.**
2. **In the Processes pane, locate and select the entry for** `adl.exe`.
3. **Click End Process to force ADL to shut down.**
4. **Close Task Manager, and return to Flash Builder.**

Follow these steps to recover from this condition on the Mac:

1. **In the Apple menu, select Force Quit.**
2. **In the Force Quit dialog box, select adl and click the Force Quit button.**
3. **Close the Force Quit dialog box, and return to Flash Builder.**

You should now be able to start your next AIR application session successfully. One common scenario that can result in this problem is when a runtime error occurs during execution of startup code. For example, if you make a call to a server-based resource from an application-level `creation`

`Complete` event handler and an unhandled fault occurs, the application window might never become visible. If you're running the application in debug mode, you can commonly clear the ADL from memory by terminating the debugging session from within Flash Builder. When running in standard mode, however, the ADL can be left in memory with the window not yet visible.

To solve this issue, it's a good idea to explicitly set the application's initial windows as visible. In the application descriptor file, the `<initialWindow>` element's child `<visible>` property is commented out by default. Because this value defaults to `false`, if the window construction code never succeeds to a runtime error, you're left with an invisible window and ADL still in memory. To solve this, open the application's descriptor file, uncomment the `<visible>` element, and set its value to `true`:

```
<visible>true</visible>
```

Working with HTML-based content

The Flex framework offers two ways of creating a Web browser object within any application:

- **The `HTMLLoader` class is extended from the Sprite class and can be used in any Flash or Flex application.** Because this class doesn't extend from `UIComponent`, you can't add it to a Flex container with simple MXML code or by using the `addChild()` or `addElement()` methods.

- **The `HTML` control is extended from `UIComponent` and can be instantiated with either MXML or ActionScript code.**

The `HTML` control is quite a bit easier to use and provides the same functionality as `HTMLLoader`. Declaring an instance of the control results in a Web browser instance that can freely navigate to any location on the Web (assuming the client system is currently connected).

Instantiating the HTML control

As with all visual controls, the `HTML` control can be instantiated in MXML or ActionScript code. After it's been instantiated, its `location` property determines which Web page is displayed. This `HTML` object, for example, displays Adobe's home page and expands to fill all available space within the application:

```
<mx:HTML id="myHTML" width="100%" height="100%"
    location="http://www.adobe.com"/>
```

When you assign the `HTML` control's `id` property, you can then reset its location as needed from any ActionScript code. This statement resets the `HTML` control's `location` to the Wiley home page:

```
myHTML.location = "http://www.wiley.com";
```

The application in Listing 31.2 uses an `HTTPService` object to retrieve an RSS listing from a URL. When the user selects an item from the `ComboBox` that presents the RSS items, a bit of ActionScript code causes the `HTML` object to navigate to the selected Web page.

Note

Because the structure of an RSS feed is consistent regardless of the data provider, this application should work with any RSS feed from any data provider. ∎

LISTING 31.2

A Flex desktop application displaying Web pages from an RSS feed

```
<?xml version="1.0" encoding="utf-8"?>
<s:WindowedApplication xmlns:fx="http://ns.adobe.com/mxml/2009"
  xmlns:s="library://ns.adobe.com/flex/spark"
  xmlns:mx="library://ns.adobe.com/flex/mx"
  width="900" height="600"
  creationComplete="app_creationCompleteHandler(event)">
  <fx:Declarations>
    <s:HTTPService id="photosXML" url="{feedURL}"
      result="resultHandler(event)" fault="faultHandler(event)"/>
  </fx:Declarations>
  <fx:Script>
    <![CDATA[
      import mx.collections.ArrayCollection;
      import mx.controls.Alert;
      import mx.events.FlexEvent;
      import mx.rpc.events.FaultEvent;
      import mx.rpc.events.ResultEvent;
      private const feedURL:String =
        "http://www.wiley.com/WileyCDA/feed/RSS_WILEY2_ALLNEWTITLES.xml";
      [Bindable]
      private var feed:ArrayCollection;
      private function resultHandler(event:ResultEvent):void
      {
        feed = event.result.rss.channel.item as ArrayCollection;
        feedSelector.selectedIndex = 0;
        updateHTML();
      }
      private function faultHandler(event:FaultEvent):void
      {
        Alert.show(event.fault.faultString, event.fault.faultCode);
      }
      private function updateHTML():void
      {
        myHTML.location = feedSelector.selectedItem.link;
      }
      protected function app_creationCompleteHandler(event:FlexEvent):void
      {
        photosXML.send();
      }
```

```
      ]]>
    </fx:Script>
    <s:layout>
      <s:VerticalLayout paddingTop="20" paddingLeft="10" paddingRight="10"/>
    </s:layout>
    <s:HGroup>
      <s:Label text="Select a title:"/>
      <s:DropDownList id="feedSelector"
        width="700"
        dataProvider="{feed}"
        labelField="title"
        change="updateHTML()"/>
    </s:HGroup>
    <mx:HTML id="myHTML" width="100%" height="100%"/>
</s:WindowedApplication>
```

On the Web

The code in Listing 31.2 is available in the Web site files in the `chapter31` **project as** `NewTitlesReader.`
`mxml.` ∎

Figure 31.10 shows the completed application, displaying the contents of the RSS feed in the
`DropDownList` and a currently selected Web page in the `HTML` component.

FIGURE 31.10

A simple RSS feed application displaying Web pages in an HTML component instance

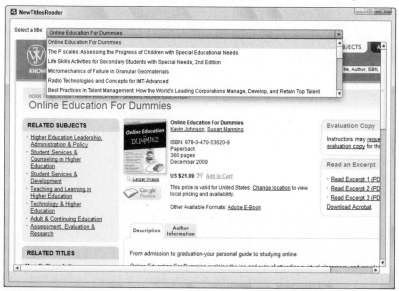

Navigating with the HTML control

In addition to the location property, the HTML control implements these methods that enable you to control navigation with ActionScript code:

- `historyBack()`. Navigates back one step in the control's history list.

- `historyForward()`. Navigates back one step in the control's history list.

- `historyGo(steps:int)`. Navigates the number of steps. The value of the `steps` argument can be positive to move forward or negative to move back.

As described earlier, the runtime doesn't include a copy of Acrobat Reader but instead requires that this software package is already installed on the client system. You can find out whether the current client system is capable of displaying Acrobat PDF documents by evaluating the HTML control's static `pdfCapability` property. The property's value is matched to constants in a `PDFCapability` class with these values and meanings:

- `ERROR_INSTALLED_READER_NOT_FOUND`. No version of Acrobat Reader is installed.

- `ERROR_INSTALLED_READER_TOO_OLD`. Acrobat Reader is installed, but it's older than version 8.1.

- `ERROR_PREFERED_READER_TOO_OLD`. Acrobat Reader 8.1 or later is installed, but another older version is viewed by the operating system as the preferred application for PDF documents.

- `STATUS_OK`. Acrobat Reader 8.1 or later is installed.

The application in Listing 31.3 is a simple Web browser application. The application's `navigate()` function examines the file extension of a document requested by a client application. If the file extension is `.pdf` and Acrobat Reader 8.1 or later isn't detected, the application displays an error to the user.

LISTING 31.3

A browser application reading PDF content

```
<?xml version="1.0" encoding="utf-8"?>
<s:WindowedApplication xmlns:fx="http://ns.adobe.com/mxml/2009"
  xmlns:s="library://ns.adobe.com/flex/spark"
  xmlns:mx="library://ns.adobe.com/flex/mx"
  width="1024" height="768">
  <fx:Script>
    <![CDATA[
      import mx.controls.Alert;
      [Bindable]
      private var myURL:String = "http://";
      private function navigate():void
      {
```

```
        myURL = urlInput.text;
        if (myURL.substr(0,4) != "http")
        {
          myURL = "http://" + myURL;
        }
        var fileExtension:String = myURL.substr(myURL.length-3, 3);
        if (fileExtension.toLowerCase() == "pdf" &&
          HTML.pdfCapability != HTMLPDFCapability.STATUS_OK)
        {
          Alert.show("This request requires Acrobat Reader 8.1 or later",
            "Acrobat Error");
        }
        else
        {
          myHTML.location = myURL;
          status = myURL;
        }
      }
    ]]>
  </fx:Script>
  <s:layout>
    <s:VerticalLayout paddingTop="20" paddingLeft="10" paddingRight="10"/>
  </s:layout>
  <s:HGroup verticalAlign="middle">
    <s:Label text="My AIR Web Browser" fontWeight="bold" fontSize="14"/>
    <mx:Spacer width="25"/>
    <s:Label text="New URL:" fontWeight="bold" fontSize="10"/>
    <s:TextInput id="urlInput" text="{myURL}" enter="navigate()"/>
    <s:Button label="Go" click="navigate()"/>
  </s:HGroup>
  <mx:HTML id="myHTML" width="100%" height="100%"/>
</s:WindowedApplication>
```

On the Web

The code in Listing 31.3 is available in the Web site files in the `chapter31` project as `AIRWebBrowser.mxml`. ■

Using the WindowedApplication component

Flex applications designed for desktop deployment typically use `<s:WindowedApplication>` as the application root element. A beginning desktop application's code looks like this:

```
<?xml version="1.0" encoding="utf-8"?>
<s:WindowedApplication xmlns:fx="http://ns.adobe.com/mxml/2009"
  xmlns:s="library://ns.adobe.com/flex/spark"
  xmlns:mx="library://ns.adobe.com/flex/mx">
```

```
      <fx:Declarations>
        <!-- Place non-visual elements
           (e.g., services, value objects) here -->
      </fx:Declarations>
    </s:WindowedApplication>
```

The `WindowedApplication` component is extended from `Application` and provides all the application-level functionality you expect from a typical Flex application. It also adds these capabilities that are unique to Flex desktop applications:

- Native menus can be displayed and integrated into the overall application look and feel.
- The application can be integrated with a dock or system tray icon to provide easy access to common application functions.
- The application can display operating system-specific "chrome" (the graphics in the application window's border, title bar, and control icons).
- A status bar can be displayed at the bottom of the application window for string-based status messages.

Here's one example: The `WindowedApplication` component can display a status bar at the bottom of the application window. This display is controlled by two of the `WindowedApplication` component's properties:

- `showStatusBar:Boolean`. When this property is `true` (the default), the application window displays a status bar.
- `status:String`. The string value displayed in the status bar.

The following modified custom `updateHTML()` function from the `NewTitlesReader` application updates the application's status bar with the title of the currently selected RSS item:

```
    private function updateHTML():void
    {
      myHTML.location = feedSelector.selectedItem.link;
      status = "Current Title: " + feedSelector.selectedItem.title;
    }
```

Creating Remoting channels at runtime

When a Web-based Flex application communicates with an application server that supports Flash Remoting (known as the Remoting Service in LiveCycle Data Services and BlazeDS), it typically uses a channel definition with dynamic expressions that evaluate at runtime to the location of the server from which the application was downloaded. This is the default my-amf channel delivered with BlazeDS:

```
    <channel-definition id="my-amf"
        class="mx.messaging.channels.AMFChannel">
      <endpoint
```

```
        url="http://{server.name}:{server.port}/{context.root}/
        messagebroker/amf" class="flex.messaging.endpoints.AMFEndpoint"/>
</channel-definition>
```

The `<endpoint>` element's `url` attribute uses dynamic expressions to evaluate the server name and port and the context root of the hosting instance of BlazeDS.

This approach doesn't work with desktop applications deployed with AIR, because the concept of "the current application server" doesn't have any meaning in a desktop application. Instead, you must provide the explicit location of the server-based application to which Remoting requests should be sent at runtime.

You can solve this in one of two ways:

- If the location of the server providing Remoting Services is always the same, you can define a custom channel in the application's services configuration file with a hard-coded `url`:

```
<endpoint url="http://www.mycompany.com/messagebroker/amf"
    class="flex.messaging.endpoints.AMFEndpoint"/>
```

- For flexibility and the capability to set a `url` at runtime, declare a channel in either MXML or ActionScript code.

The `RemoteObject` component has a `channelSet` property, cast as a class named `ChannelSet`, that contains one or more instances of the `AMFChannel` component. To declare a runtime channel in MXML, nest the `<mx:ChannelSet>` tag inside a `<mx:RemoteObject>` tag pair's `<mx:channelSet>` property. Then nest one or more `<mx:AMFChannel>` tags, and assign each a `uri` property pointing to the selected server and its Remoting `url`.

Note

If you declare more than one `AMFChannel` tag inside the `channelSet`, they're treated as a list in order of preference. The client application always tries to use the first channel; if there's a communication failure, it goes to the next one, and so on. ∎

The following `RemoteObject` instance declares a single `AMFChannel` at runtime:

```
<s:RemoteObject id="myRO" destination="myRemotingDestination">
  <s:channelSet>
    <s:ChannelSet>
      <s:channels>
        <s:AMFChannel uri="http://myserver/messagebroker/amf"/>
      </s:channels>
    </s:ChannelSet>
  </s:channelSet>
</s:RemoteObject>
```

You can accomplish the same result with ActionScript. The following ActionScript code creates a ChannelSet object, populates it with a single AMFChannel object, and adds it to the RemoteObject component:

```
var endpointURL:String = "http://myserver/messagebroker/amf";
var cs:ChannelSet = new ChannelSet();
var customChannel:Channel =
  new AMFChannel("myCustomAMF", endpointURL);
cs.addChannel(customChannel);
myRemoteObject.channelSet = cs;
```

Tip

You also can create channels at runtime for use with the Message Service, Proxy Service, and Data Management Service when using LiveCycle Data Services or BlazeDS. ∎

Note

When communicating with remote servers using the HTTPService or WebService components in a desktop application, you don't have to deal with the cross-domain security constraint as you do with Web-based Flex applications. Because the application loads locally, it isn't subject to the restrictions of the Web browser's security sandbox and can make connections freely over the Web just like any other local application. ∎

A Conclusion about Adobe AIR

In addition to the features described in this chapter, AIR applications can accomplish the following tasks that aren't possible with Flex Web applications:

- Full screen and spanned monitor display
- Integration with native visual components such the operating system's window and menu systems
- Creation of applications with transparency that serve as widgets
- Reading and writing files and folders on the local file system
- Persisting data in SQLite, a local database embedded in the runtime
- Interacting with the system clipboard, including drag-and-drop to and from AIR applications and the OS
- Synchronization of data managed on the server by LiveCycle Data Services
- Access to all network services supported by the Flex framework

The subject of building and deploying AIR-based desktop applications is worthy of an entire book, and in fact there are many such books available. In particular, check out the *Adobe AIR Bible* (from Wiley, of course!).

Summary

In this chapter, I described how to build and deploy desktop Flex applications with the Adobe Integrated Runtime. You learned the following:

- Adobe AIR enables you to build and deploy cross-operating system desktop applications with Flex, Flash, or HTML.

- Users can download and install AIR freely from Adobe Systems.

- Flash Builder 4 includes everything you need to build and deploy AIR applications.

- Each AIR application requires an application descriptor file that determines how an application is packaged and delivered.

- You must provide a security certificate to create an AIR application installer file.

- Flash Builder 4 enables you to create a self-signed security certificate suitable for testing or deployment within an organization.

- For public deployment of AIR applications, a security certificate issued by a recognized certificate authority is strongly recommended.

- Flex applications built for AIR commonly use `<s:WindowedApplication>` as the application's root element.

- The Flex framework's `HTML` control displays both HTML and PDF content.

- You can declare channels at runtime for use with Remoting destinations called from a Flex-based desktop application.

Index

A

absolute address, 724
absolute layout, 78, 133, 253, 311, 330
absolute sizing, 333, 334
absolute-layout properties, `Canvas` container, 315
abstraction layer, SOAP-based Web service, 779
`acceptDragDrop()` method, 395
`access` attribute, CFCs, 878
access modifiers, 115–116, 153, 543, 582
accessor methods, 539, 545–549
`Accordion` container, 472, 497, 500–502
acompc command-line tool, 28
Acrobat PDF, 809, 955, 976–977
Acrobat Reader, 976
Action Message Format. *See* AMF Zend AMF
ActionScript 2, 99
ActionScript 3. *See also* E4X effects; value objects
   ActionScript Virtual Machine, 99
   arguments, passing to remote methods, 839
   classes, 48, 139–140, 440–441, 897
   combining MXML and, 120–128
   complex data objects, selecting with, 607–610
   component methods, calling with statements, 154–155
   conditional statements, 117–119
   `Consumer` component, 858–859
   control properties and styles, setting with, 251
   controlling styles with, 366–369
   controls, instantiating with, 250–251
   custom classes, 237–242, 534, 698
   data collections, 554, 578
   data conversion from ColdFusion to, 879
   defined, 5
   effects, declaring in, 375–377
   embedded fonts, declaring, 302
   event listener, executing single statement in, 210
   `fault` event, 901
   `formatter` objects, 306
   functions, handling events with, 211–213
   handling events of multiple operations, 791
   `HTTPService` object, creating, 723
   and Java, passing data between, 840–841
   looping, 119
   `Menu` control, 494
   menu events, handling, 493
   versus MXML, 6–8
   MXML and, 101–103
   named parameters, passing, 744
   navigator containers, working with, 477–482
   objects, declaring in, 7–8
   overview, 114
   package declarations in, 541
   percentage sizing, 334
   to PHP data serialization, 932
   pie chart, 651
   populating value object data with, 699
   `Producer` component, 857
   `RemoteObject`, 830, 882
   reverse domain package names, 141
   runtime channel, declaring in, 980
   serialized objects in, 862
   subtopics, filtering messages with, 869–870
   syntax, 114
   `text` property, 255
   `TextFlow` class, 256
   validating data entry with, 691–695
   validator object, 688
   value objects, 551–552, 842–845, 895–896, 899
   variables, declaring, 114–117
   `WebService`, 784, 795–796
   XML structure, hard-coded, 752
   `XMLListCollection`, 755
ActionScript 3.0 Language Reference, 29
`actionscript` adapter, 854–855, 862
ActionScript class option, 238
ActionScript Class Warning dialog box, 67
ActionScript editor, Flash Builder, 50–51, 125–128, 180–181, 191–192
ActionScript File option, 121
ActionScript Virtual Machine (AVM), 99, 727, 786
adapters, Message Service, 850, 854–855
Add or Remove Programs option, 971

Index

Add Watch Expression dialog box, 191–192

AddAction class, 415

AddChild element, 408

addChild() method, 148, 483

addChildAt() method, 483

addData() method, 392, 393

addElement() method, 112, 148, 252

addElementAt() method, 112

addEventListener() method
  custom event class, 245
  event name constants, 226–227, 240
  fault event, 734–735
  menu events, 493
  overview, 223
  PopUpManager, 525
  PopUpMenuButton, 518
  RemoteObject component, 901
  removing event listener, 227
  result event, 732, 833, 885
  setting up event listener, 223–225
  for single method, 791–792
  void return type, 213
  WebService, 785, 788

addItem() method, 555, 576

addItemAt() method, 555

Additional compiler arguments section, Properties dialog
  box, 942, 944, 945

addPopUp() method, 524, 525

addResourceBundle() method, 948

addResponder() method, 740

AddressRenderer.mxml file, 624

ADL (AIR Debug Launcher), 972–973

adl command-line tool, 27

Adobe Acrobat PDF, 809, 955, 976–977

Adobe Acrobat Reader, 976

Adobe AIR
  architecture of, 956–958
  debugging applications, 972–973
  desktop application, creating
    application descriptor file, 963–967
    Flex project for, 960–963
    installing, 969–971
    overview, 960
    packaging release version of, 967–969
    uninstalling, 971
  drag-and-drop in, 389
  versus Flash Player, 18
  HTML-based content, 973–977
  HTTPService component method property, 725
  image types, 282

  installing, 958–959
  list controls for, 573
  LiveCycle Data Services features, 809
  local data, retrieving in applications, 578
  overview, 11, 955–956, 980–981
  Proxy Service, 821
  remoting channels at runtime, creating, 978–980
  Version 2, 957
  WindowedApplication component, 977–978

Adobe AIR Installer application, 959

Adobe AIR Setup dialog box, 959, 971

Adobe AIR Uninstaller application, 959

Adobe ColdFusion. *See* ColdFusion

Adobe Community Help application, 29, 55–57

Adobe Creative Suite, 19, 420, 432–439. *See also specific*
    programs by name

Adobe Developer Center Web site, 879

Adobe Dreamweaver, 93–96

Adobe Fireworks, 437–439

Adobe Flash Builder 4. *See* Flash Builder 4

Adobe Flash Catalyst, 4, 5, 10

Adobe Flash Player. *See* Flash Player

Adobe Flex 4. *See* Flex 4

Adobe Flex 4 SDK Command Prompt option, 28

Adobe Illustrator, 433–437, 439

Adobe Integrated Runtime. *See* Adobe AIR

Adobe Labs Web page, 25

Adobe Open Source Web site, 809, 810

Adobe Photoshop, 432–433

Adobe Web site
  AIR installer, 958
  Flash Player installation from, 24–26
  Flex themes, 342
  FXG specifications, 420
  getting help from, 29
  LiveCycle Data Services features, 809

adt command-line tool, 27

advanced text layout, 288–294

AdvancedDataGrid control, 572, 641–645. *See also* list
    controls

AdvancedDataGridColumn control, 642

AdvDataGridDemo.mxml file, 643

AdvDataGridFlatData.mxml file, 645

AeonGraphical theme, 342

afterLast property, 562

AIR, Adobe. *See* Adobe AIR

AIR Debug Launcher (ADL), 972–973

AIR file, 967, 969

airfare search application, 402–406

AIRWebBrowser.mxml file, 977

AJAX (Asynchronous JavaScript and XML), 470
`Alert` class
    buttons, managing, 506–508
    CSS selectors, using with, 512–514
    custom graphical icon, 509–512
    events, handling, 508–509
    `fault` event, 734–735, 790, 791, 792
    modality, controlling, 504–506
    overview, 503, 504
    `Panel` container, 327
    `RadioButton` controls, 270–271
    `show()` method, 504
`AlertDemos.mxml` file, 512
`Alert.NONMODAL` constant, 505, 506
`AlertWithStyles.mxml` file, 514
`alias` attribute, 894, 895, 896
aliases, constants as, 152
`all` value, `creationPolicy` property, 483
`<allow-access-from>` element, 747
`allowDisjointSelection` property, 273
Allowed IP Addresses screen, ColdFusion Administrator, 906
Allowed Services list, User Manager screen, 906
`allowMultipleSelection` property, 273, 635
`allowMultipleSelections` property, 584, 585
`allowScriptAccess` parameter, 86
`allow-source-path` compiler argument, 952
`<allow-subtopics>` element, 866
alpha styles, 133, 316
`alphaFrom` property, 379
`alphaTo` property, 379
`alternatingItemColors` style, 614
`altKey` property, 220, 222
AMF (Action Message Format). *See also* Zend AMF
    documentation, 825
    Message Service channels, 852–853
    overview, 825
    PHP, services for, 924–925
    `RemoteObject` class, 205, 578, 830
    value object classes, 539
AMF0, 825
AMF3, 825
`AMFChannel` component, 878, 979–980
AMFPHP, 825, 924, 929–931
amxmlc command-line tool, 28
anchors, Constraints interface, 331–332
`angleBy` property, 381
`angleFrom` property, 381
`angleTo` property, 381
`angleXFrom` property, 382
`angleXTo` property, 382

`angleYFrom` property, 382
`angleYTo` property, 382
`angleZFrom` property, 382
`angleZTo` property, 382
`Animate` effect, 372, 377–379
`AnimateColor` effect, 372
`AnimateDemo.mxml` file, 378–379
`AnimateFilter` effect, 372
`AnimateProperty` effect, 377
`AnimateShaderTransition` effect, 372
`AnimateTransform` effect, 372
animation, 9, 10, 371. *See also* effects; transitions
anonymous class, 594
anti-aliasing, 297, 303
Apache Axis, 779, 780
Apache document root folder, 919
Apache Tomcat 6. *See* Tomcat 6, Apache
Apache Web server, 917, 918
API (application programming interface). *See also* Logging API
    `ArrayList` class, modifying data with, 576–577
    classes, 208
    controls, 250
    encapsulation, 13–14
    events, 221
`app_creationCompleteHandler()` function, 224–225
Appearance view, Flash Builder, 54, 355
applets, 91–92
`Application` component
    calling Web services from, 785
    containership, 111–112
    `contentGroup` property, 148
    custom skin for
        applying with style sheet declaration, 453
        assigning skin, 451–452
        associating with host component, 446–447
        creating, 444–446
        FXG graphics, adding to, 449–451
        loading at runtime, 454–455
        overview, 444
        skin parts, adding required, 448–449
        skin states, declaring required, 447–448
    dimensions, controlling, 130–131
    `layout` property, setting, 131–134
    `MenuBar` control, 496
    overview, 8, 128–129
    passing parameters, 130
    view states, 399
application descriptor file, 963–967, 973
application location, 282
application programming interface. *See* API; Logging API

Index

`application` property, 129
Application server type drop-down menu, 75, 197, 815, 856
application servers. *See also specific servers by name*
    configuring messaging on, 851–856
    filtering messages on, 865–871
    Flash Remoting, configuring on, 877–878
    `HTTPService`, 707, 709, 744–745
    supported, 46–48
Application type drop-down menu, 46, 75, 815, 856
`application` value, `<scope>` element, 829–830
application window, MAMP, 917–918, 919
`<application>` element, 964
`Application.cfc` file, 783
applications, Flex. *See* Flex applications
`AppLoadStyleAtRunting.mxml` file, 455
`AppWithButtonsComplete.mxml` file, 462
`AppWithButtons.mxml` file, 455, 461, 466
`AppWithCustomSkin.mxml` file, 452
`AppWithSkinStyleSheet.mxml` file, 453
area charts, 649, 666–667, 670–672
`AreaChart` component, 649
`AreaSeries` series class, 649, 672
`argumentCollection` attribute, 893
arguments. *See also specific arguments by name*
    event object, 213–214
    instantiating value objects with default values, 552
    passing to CFC functions, 891–900
    passing to remote methods, 838–840
`Array` class
    adding new test expressions to helper class, 770
    `ArrayUtil.toArray()` method, 538–539
    data collection object `source` property, 554
    menu data providers, 492
    navigator bar container, 485
    receiving value objects from ColdFusion, 897–898
    `trace()` function, 172
array notation, extracting data from XML objects with, 759–760
`array` value, `resultFormat` property, 726
`ArrayCollection` class
    accessing data at runtime, 555–556
    bindable variable as, 731–732
    charting controls, 649
    data collection, declaring for, 553
    data cursors, 562–569
    as data provider for `PopUpMenuButton`, 515
    `DataGrid` control, 614
    flat data, 644
    `HTTPService` responses, handling, 728
    list controls, 578

    managing data at runtime, 556–562
    navigator bar container, 485
    overview, 552–553
    receiving complex messages, 862–863
    `source` property, 554
    value objects, working with, 742
    `WebService result` event, 788
`ArrayList` class
    charting controls, 649
    `DataGrid` control, 614
    `getItemAt()` method, 585
    `itemRenderer` property, 629
    `label` property, 579
    list controls, 575, 577
    modifying data with API, 576–577
    navigator bar container, 485–486
    overview, 552–553
    RPC components, 578
    `source` property, 554
`ArrayUtil.toArray()` method, 538–539
`arrowKeysWrapFocus` property, 613
`as` ActionScript operator, 788
`.as` extension, 120–121
asdoc command-line tool, 28
ASP.NET, Microsoft, 470, 779, 781
assets, Flex Library Project, 156
`assets` folder, 164–165, 437
Assets tab, New Flex Library Project wizard, 156
asynchronous (nonblocking) I/O channels, 853
asynchronous communications, 727
Asynchronous JavaScript and XML (AJAX), 470
`AsyncMessage` class, 857, 859, 862
`AsyncToken` class, 736–741, 794, 837
`attribute()` function, 756
attributes. *See also specific attributes by name*
    adding to objects, 765–766
    deleting, 766–770
    filtering XML data with predicate expressions, 761
    modifying values of, 765
    order of declaration in MXML, 345
    value object properties, 549–550
    values, in MXML, 104
    XML, versus child elements, 109
    XML object, modifying, 765–770
`auto` value, `creationPolicy` property, 482
`autoCenter Transform` property, 381, 382
Auto-detect the return type from sample data option, 802
auto-detecting return type, 714
automatic garbage collection, 116

986

automatic validation, 688–690
AVM (ActionScript Virtual Machine), 99, 727, 786
Axis, Apache, 779, 780

B

backgroundAlpha setting, 316
backgroundColor style, 128, 276, 343
backgroundFill property, 324
backgrounds, pie chart, 660–662
backward navigation, 478–481
bar charts, 649, 666–670
BarAndColumnDemo.mxml file, 670
BarChart component, 647–648, 649, 668
BarSeries series class, 649
Basic Latin character set, 301
basic layout, 78, 133–134, 311, 320, 331
BasicLayout layout class, 131, 133
beans. *See* value objects
beforeFirst property, 562
bgcolor parameter, 86
bidirectional text, 292–294
binary distribution, BlazeDS, 810
binary files, 9
Bind to Data dialog box, 719–720, 803–804
bindable properties
    complex data objects, 588–589
    <fx:Binding/> tag, 137–139
    MXML component, 150–151
    result event, 731, 884
    value objects, 544–545
    XML structure, 752
[Bindable] metadata tag
    accessor method properties, 548
    ArrayCollection class, 553
    complex data objects, 588, 589
    making properties bindable, 138, 150
    value objects, 544, 551
bin-debug folder, 47, 76, 169
binding expressions
    bound parameters, 745
    ColdFusion Component results, 883–884
    component methods, calling with, 154
    external resource bundles, 952
    formatter classes in, 307–308
    <fx:binding> tag, 137
    HTTPService responses, 728–730
    making expressions bindable, 137–139
    Model object, 535–536, 537
    outputting current date, 944

overview, 135–136
    RemoteObject results, 831–832
    shorthand MXML, 136–137
    value object properties, 549, 550
    view state, controlling with, 407
    ViewStack, setting as dataProvider, 487
    WebService results, 786–787
BindingUtils class, 136
bitmap graphics, 430, 432–433, 437, 440
BitMapAsset object, 394
BitMapClass object, 394
BitMapFill class, 660
<BitmapGraphic> element, 433
BitmapImage control
    changing images at runtime, 285–286
    defined, 421
    effects, 385
    embedding images, 284–285
    external resource bundles, 951
    overview, 281–283
    resizing images, 283–284
Blank State option, 402
BlazeDS. *See also* Message Service; Remoting Service
    data connections, 845–847
    downloading, 810–811
    Flex projects, creating for use with, 814–816
    included in ColdFusion 9, 874
    messaging architecture, 849
    overview, 807–808
    Proxy Service, 817–824
    RemoteObject component
        instantiating, 830
        overview, 830
        passing arguments to remote methods, 838–840
        passing data between ActionScript and Java, 840–841
        remote methods, calling, 830–831
        results, handling, 831–838
        value object classes, 841–845
    sample applications, 813–814
    sample database, starting, 813
    starting, 811–813
    supported platforms, 808–809
BlazeDS context root folder, 816
BlazeDS WEB-INF/flex folder, 816
blazedsfiles folder, 816
blazeds.war BlazeDS instance, 811
blocking I/O, 853
body property, 857, 859, 862
bookItem format, 393
bookmark property, 567

Index

bookmarking data, with cursors, 567–569

`BookmarkingData.mxml` file, 569

`Books.mxml` file, 473

`BookStoreAccordion.mxml` file, 501

`BookStoreIndexNavigation.mxml` file, 480

`BookStoreMenuBar.mxml` file, 497

`BookStore.mxml` file, 474

`BookStoreNavBar.mxml` file, 488

`BookStoreReferenceNavigation.mxml` file, 482

`BookStoreTabNav.mxml` file, 499

`BookStoreVerticalButtonBar.mxml` file, 491

`BookStoreVerticalNav.mxml` file, 490

Boolean expressions, 114, 117, 557

border styles, 512

`BorderContainer` component, 323–325

`BorderContainerDemo.mxml` file, 324

`borderStroke` property, 324

bottom property, 332, 423

`Bounce` class, 387–388

bound argument notation, 839, 840

bound arguments, passing to CFC functions, 891, 892

bound CSS declarations, 368–369

bound parameters, 745, 797–798

Box, Don, 778

box model, CSS, 319

`Box` superclass, 312–313

`BreakElement` class, 289

Breakpoint Properties dialog box, 182

breakpoints

    Breakpoints view, 183–185

    clearing, 180

    conditional, 181–183

    Debug view, controlling application execution with, 192–194

    debugging event object, 220

    debugging session, using in, 185–187

    defined, 167

    inspecting variables and expressions

        adding expression, 191–192

        Expressions view, 191

        Variables view, 187–188

        watchpoints, setting, 188–191

    removing, 180–181

    setting, 180–181

Breakpoints view, Flash Builder, 55, 183–185

"A Brief History of SOAP," 778

`bringToFront()` method, 524, 525

brittle applications, 12

browser, Web. *See* Web browser

bubble charts, 649

`BubbleChart` component, 649

bubbles property, 228, 237, 240, 699

`BubbleSeries` series class, 649

bubbling, event, 227–229

Build Automatically feature, 54, 81

build path, Flex Project, 159

`bundleName` property, 947

`Button` class, 208–209, 210

Button control

    `addEventListener()`, 225

    custom skin, 461–467

    default button, 682

    descendant selector in, 354

    event bubbling, 227–228

    event handler for, 214, 215–216, 223

    exporting existing styles, 359–361

    `Form` component, adding to, 686

    overview, 266–267

    `selectedIndex` property, 478–479

    skin, creating new by copying default skin, 455–460

    trigger events, controlling validation with, 689

button controls, 266–271. *See also specific controls by name*

Button portion, `PopUpMenuButton`, 515–517

`ButtonBar` control. *See also* list controls

    defined, 484, 571, 572

    generating using `dataProvider`, 485–486

    Spark, use of, 611–613

    Spark versus MX, 488

    vertical, 490–491

`ButtonBarDemo.mxml` file, 612

`buttonDown` property, 220

`buttonMode` property, 440

buttons. *See also specific button controls by name*

    default, 507–508, 681–683

    pop-up window, 506–508

`buttonWidth` property, 507

C

C command, 424

caching, 708, 809

Cairngorm microarchitecture, 741

`calculator.as` file, 123–124

`Calculator.mxml` application, 122–123

`CalculatorWithScript.mxml` file, 122

calendar, for date controls, 273–274

Call Trace option, 173

`CallAction` class, 415

`CallComponentMethodWithAS.mxml` file, 155

callout value, `labelPosition` style, 652

CallResponder class, 736–739, 794–795, 837–838
CallResponderDemo.mxml file, 739
camel case, 345, 347
cancel event, 523
cancelable property, 240
cancelLabel property, 506
candlestick charts, 650, 663–666
CandleStickChart component, 650
CandleStickSeries series class, 650
Canvas container, 312, 315–317, 318, 328, 330
CanvasDemo.mxml file, 316
Cascading Style Sheets. See CSS, selectors, CSS
case sensitivity, 104, 114, 260, 346
caseInsensitive property, 560
casting, explicit, 859
catalog.xml file, 158
CategoryAxis component, 667, 668
CDATA blocks, 109–110, 120
centerPopUp() method, 525
centerRadius property, 657
certificate, packaged AIR application, 968–969
certificate authority, 968
<cfchart> command, 905
<cfcomponent> tag, 894, 896
cfContextRoot property, 908
CFCs. See ColdFusion Components
<cfdocument> command, 905
CFEclipse, 34
<cffile> command, 905
<cfhttp> command, 727
CFIDE/scripts/AIR folder, 907
<cfimage> command, 905
<cfmail> command, 905, 907, 908
CFML (ColdFusion Markup Language), 778, 880, 893
<cfpdf> command, 905
<cfpop> command, 905
cfPort property, 908
<cfproperty> tag, 894–895
CFScript, 880
<cfselect> command, 607
cfServer property, 908
cfservices.swc file, 907
<cfthrow> command, 901
change event
    ButtonBar control, 611
    ColorPicker control, 276
    HorizontalList control, 635
    list controls, 584, 585, 586
    navigator bar container, 487

    PopUpMenuButton, 518
    RadioButtonGroup control, 271
    ScrollBar controls, 278–279
    Slider control, 280, 281
    TileList control, 635
Change Font Size button, 366–367
ChangeEventDemo.mxml file, 586
ChangeLocaleAtRuntime.mxml application, 945–947
changing event, 584
ChangingSelectors.mxml file, 369
<channel> tag, 829, 878
channels, 851–854, 878, 978–980
<channels> tag, 853–854, 855
ChannelSet object, 980
channelSet property, 979
characters, embedding ranges of, 300–302
Chart Service, ColdFusion, 905
chartable values, 666
charting controls
    area charts, 666–667, 670–672
    bar charts, 666–670
    column charts, 666–670
    declaring, 650–652
    financial charts, 663–666
    line charts, 666–667, 670–672
    overview, 647–650
    pie charts, 652–662
Chat Rooms application, 867–871
chatRooms.as file, 870
ChatRooms.mxml file, 868
CheckBox control, 268–269, 629–632
child class, 15
child objects
    Accordion navigator container, 500
    adding to container, 148
    layout of, 78
    TabNavigator navigator container, 498
    value object properties, 549–550
    XML, 109
childList argument, 525
childrenField property, 642
chrome, operating system, 978
chromeColor style, 355
class selectors, 346, 351
Class variable, 284, 302, 509
Class view, Flash Builder, 124
classes. See also effects; specific classes by name; value objects
    ActionScript, 48, 139–140, 440–441, 897
    API documentation for, 208

Index

classes *(continued)*
  custom, to handle unique RPC requests, 741
  custom event, 237–246
  easing, 387–388
  encapsulation, 13–14
  formatter, 305–310
  names, 48, 67–68
  nonvisual, in MXML, 112–113
  XML, 750–756
ClassReference() compiler directive, 453
Clean all projects option, 85
Clean dialog box, 199
Clean option, 953
click event
  addEventListener(), 225
  Button control, 209, 210, 215–216, 266–267
  documentation for, 221, 222
  event bubbling, 228
  event listener, setting up, 223
  LinkButton control, 268
  transitions, 416
click XML attribute, 210
clickHandler() method, 212, 213, 225, 228, 700–701
client-side service components, ColdFusion, 907–910
clone() method, 238, 240–242, 699
close button, TitleWindow container, 527–529
close event, 508, 509, 527
close() method, 518
closeField property, 663
code
  generating using Flash Builder 4, 64–66
  managing with Flash Builder, 124–128
  searching for, 58–64
code completion tool
  camel case or hyphenated syntax in, 347
  event name constants, 226–227
  external style sheets, 357
  overview, 79
  selecting custom component, 145
  triggering, 244
code folding, 125–127
code management, Flex versus Flash, 11
code model search tools, Flash Builder
  moving existing source-code files, 63–64
  refactoring source-code files, 63
  refactoring variable names, 61–62
  searching for declaration, 60–61
  searching for references, 60
code points, Unicode, 301
code refactoring tool, 61–62

ColdFusion. *See also* ColdFusion Components
  <cfhttp> command, 727
  <cfselect> command, 607
  data connections, 903–904
  download page, 783
  Flash Remoting, 874–878
  Flex project, configuring for use with, 197–201
  installing, 783
  Network Monitor, 196–197
  overview, 873–875
  RemoteObject fault events, 900–902
  services, calling, 905–910
  SOAP-based Web services, 778, 779–780
  support site for, 47
  value objects, 894–900
  WSDL page generated by, 781–782
ColdFusion Administrator, 905, 906
ColdFusion Builder, 34
ColdFusion Components (CFCs)
  calling from Flex application, 875
  creating, 878–880
  passing arguments to, 891–894
  RemoteObject component, using with, 880–883
  results, handling, 883–891
  SOAP-based Web services, 780
ColdFusion destination, 878, 881
ColdFusion Enterprise, 855
ColdFusion Event Gateway Adapter, 850
ColdFusion installation type option, 197, 875
ColdFusion Markup Language (CFML), 778, 880, 893
ColdFusion Web root, 876, 877
ColdFusionFiles folder, 877
ColdFusionServiceResultEvent class, 908
Collapse Functions option, 126
collapse value, whiteSpaceCollapse style, 258
collectionChange event, 862
color style, 294, 353
color values, style, 362
ColorPicker control, 275–277, 573
ColorPickerDemo.mxml file, 276
Colors and Fonts section, Preferences dialog box, 43–44
column charts, 650, 666–670
ColumnChart component, 650, 668
columnCount property, 292
ColumnDemo.mxml file, 292
columnGap property, 292
columns
  DataGrid control, 614–619
  presenting text in, 292, 293
columns property, 614, 617–618, 642

ColumnSeries series class, 650
columnWidth property, 292
ComboBase class, 573
ComboBox control. *See also* list controls
    complex data objects, selecting, 607–610
    defined, 571, 572
    overview, 603
    prompt property, 604–605
    properties, 585
    selectedIndex property, 588
    Spark ButtonBar control, 611–613
    using, 605–607
ComboBoxDemo.mxml file, 607
command button, 267
Command design pattern, 741
command window, Windows, 812
commandKey property, 220
comments, in default application descriptor file, 964–967
communications, asynchronous, 727
Community Help application, Adobe, 29
compareFunction property, 562
compc command-line tool, 28
Compile CSS to SWF option, 363–364
compile time, changing locales at, 943–944
Compiled Flex application location option, 47, 198
compiled style sheets, 344, 363–365
compiledStyles.css file, 363
compiledstyles.swf file, 363
compiler tags, MXML, 106
complex data, 862–865, 929–931
complex data objects, selecting, 588–590, 607–610
component folder, creating, 141
component item editors, 632–634
component item renderers, 597–600
component libraries, 155–161
component renderers, 591, 623
components. *See also* custom components; MX components;
        MXML components; programmatic skins; Spark
        components
    custom pop-up window, 521–522
    view states, adding to and removing from, 408–409
    in view states, managing, 412–413
Components view, Flash Builder, 54, 146–147, 162
composite effects, 383–387
CompWithBindableProp.mxml file, 151
CompWithPublicMethod.mxml file, 154
concatValues() method, 839
concurrency property, 723, 724, 726
concurrent connections, 853
conditional statements, 117–119

Configure Code Generation screen, 800
Configure ColdFusion Server screen, 875, 877
Configure ColdFusion Service screen, 903
Configure Columns dialog box, 720
Configure Output screen, 76–77, 960
Configure PHP Server screen, 920–921
Configure PHP Service dialog box, 925
Configure Return Type wizard, 714–716, 802–803, 933,
    934–935
Confirm Perspective Switch dialog box, 185–186
Connect to BlazeDS/LCDS Service dialog box, 847
Connect to ColdFusion option, 903
Connect to Database button, 936
Connect to Data/Service dialog box, 711, 799–800, 903–904,
    933–937
Connect to HTTP option, 711
connections, concurrent, 853. *See also* data connections
Console view, Flash Builder
    DataGrid trace() statements, 622
    debug mode, 169–170
    managing during debug session, 170–171
    overview, 54
    trace() function messages in, 173
    tracing messaging traffic, 871–872
constants
    defined, 149
    encapsulation, 14
    event name, 226–227, 240
    use of, 152
    whiteSpaceCollapse style, 259
constraint-based layout, 330–332
constraint-based sizing, 333, 335–336
Constraints interface, 331–332
ConstraintSizing.mxml file, 336
constructor method, 551–552, 560, 826, 843
Consumer component, 858–861, 865–871
Contact value object class, 545, 550, 744, 899
Contact[] return type, 717
Contact.as file, 540, 543, 544, 546, 717–718
Contact.as value object class, 717
Contact.cfc file, 895
ContactComplete.as file, 545
_ContactEntityMetadata class, 717
Contact.java file, 842
ContactPrivateVars.as file, 548
contacts database, 929
ContactService class, 711
ContactService.as file, 712
ContactService.cfc file, 888
contacts.xml file, 714, 728

Index

ContactVO class, 632–633, 897

ContactVO.as file, 843, 896

Container class, 315, 483, 498

containers, 249, 290–291, 311, 380. *See also* layout containers; navigator containers; *specific containers by name*

containership
    descendant selectors, 350
    event bubbling, 228–229
    MXML, 110–112
    overlapping element tag, 104
    type selector inheritance, 349

Containership.mxml file, 111

content, component, 112

Content Debugger Player, 21

content property
    ResourceBundle class, 948
    richly formatted text, 288
    RichText control, 289
    Spark text control, 255
    versus textFlow property, 256
    whiteSpaceCollapse style, 258–259

contentBackgroundAlpha style, 355

contentBackgroundColor style, 355, 512

content-based sizing, 333–334

contentGroup container, 112, 148, 252

contentGroup skin part, 448, 449, 450

contract-based programming, 17

control bars, Panel containers with, 329–330

Control Panel, Windows, 971

ControlBar container, 311, 328–329

controlBarContent property, 129, 311, 329–330, 496, 527

ControlBarDemo.mxml file, 328

controller, in model-view-controller architecture, 139

controls, 249, 311, 333–336. *See also* layout controls; *specific controls by name*; visual controls

Convert to CSS option, 360

Convert to Desktop/Adobe AIR Project option, 46

cookies, 470

copy() method, 756

Copy non-embedded files to output folder setting, 82

Copy Settings section, Workspace Launcher dialog box, 37

Correct Indentation feature, 50

count() function, 937

counter variable, 119

Create a Flex project screen, 76–78, 961–962

Create as copy of option, 528

Create Self-Signed Digital Certificate screen, 969

Create Skin option, 455–456, 528

Create Watch Expression option, 191

createComponentsFromDescriptors() method, 483, 484

createCursor() method, 556, 562

createMenu() method, 494

createPerson() method, 937

createPopUp() method, 524

creation policy, navigator containers, 482–484

creationComplete event, 225, 479, 727

creationPolicy property, 482–484

Creative Suite, Adobe, 19, 420, 432–439. *See also specific programs by name*

CreditCardValidator class, 687

cross-domain policy, 724, 746–747, 817

crossdomain.xml file, 747, 817

CrossFade effect, 372

CSS (Cascading Style Sheets). *See also* selectors, CSS
    ActionScript, controlling styles with, 366–369
    compiled style sheets, 363–365
    custom pop-up window skin, 529
    custom skins, 453, 461–462
    embedded style sheets, 353–355
    external style sheets, 356–362
    Flex-based, 319
    fonts, controlling with, 294–302
    <fx:Style>, declaring style sheets with, 345
    HTML wrapper template, 83
    inline style declarations, 344–345
    overview, 341–343
    style sheet, defined, 343–344

CSS File option, 356

CSS Namespaces Module, 347

CSSStyleDeclaration class, 367–368

Ctrl key, 585, 586

ctrlKey property, 220

CurrencyFormatter class, 305, 307

CurrencyValidator class, 687

current property, 562, 564

current view state, 399

currentState property, 399, 400, 406–407, 410, 412

currentTarget property, 228–229

CursorBookmark class, 567

cursors, data, 562–569

curve value, form property, 672

CurvedArrow graphic, 428–430

custom classes, 741

custom component item renderer, 597–600

custom components
    CSS type selectors, applying to, 348
    dataChange event, 623–624

inheritance, 349
managing view states in, 412–413
in navigator containers, 472–473
custom constructor methods, 551–552
custom drag-and-drop operations, 391–398
custom event classes
creating in ActionScript, 238–242
dispatching, 242–244
handling event using, 244–246
overview, 237–238
custom events
declaring, 231–233
dispatching, 233–235, 699–704
handling, 235–237
overview, 230–231
custom Form components, 683–687
custom function, 211–212
custom graphical icon, pop-up window, 509–512
custom item renderers
component, 597–600
drop-in, 591–593
inline, 593–597
overview, 590–591
Spark, customizing with view states, 600–602
custom label function, 653–654
custom namespace prefix, 144, 549
custom perspective, Eclipse, 42
custom pop-up windows, 503, 521–529
custom resource bundles, 947–953
Custom section, Components view, 146, 162
custom skins
binding to component, 451–455
for other Spark components
assigning with CSS, 461–462
creating new skin, 455–460
customizing skin, 462–467
overview, 444
for Spark Application component
associating with host component, 446–447
creating, 444–446
FXG graphics, adding to, 449–451
overview, 444
skin parts, adding required, 448–449
skin states, declaring required, 447–448
CustomAppSkinComplete.mxml file, 451
CustomAppSkin.mxml file, 448, 449
CustomButton component, 348
CustomButton.mxml file, 348
CustomButtonSkinComplete.mxml file, 460

CustomButtonSkin.mxml file, 462
CustomDragAndDrop.mxml file, 397
CustomEventAppComplete.mxml file, 237
CustomEventApp.mxml application, 232, 236

D

dashboard applications, 647
Dashboard.mxml file, 864
data
conversion from ColdFusion to ActionScript, 879
passing to component property, 151–152
persistence of in Web applications, 470
working with in Flex versus Flash, 10
data collections
accessing data at runtime, 555–556
ArrayCollection, declaring, 553
cursors, 562–569
dynamic data providers, 577–578
managing data at runtime, 556–562
overview, 533, 552–553
source property, setting, 554
using as dataProvider, 485–486
data connections
BlazeDS, 845–847
ColdFusion, 903–904
defined, 707
PHP, 925, 932–938
Web service, 798–805
Data Controls section, Components view, 719
data elements, in custom event classes, 237, 240
data entry controls, 271–277
data entry forms
custom Form components, 683–687
Form container, 676–683
overview, 675–676
sharing data with application, 697–704
validating data entry, 687–697
data folder, 783
Data Management Service, 614, 631, 809
data model, 533–539
data points, pie chart, 652
data property
item renderer, 623
list controls, 595, 597, 598
Path class, 423–424, 425
data providers
dynamic, 577–578
hard-coded, 575–577

Index

data providers *(continued)*
menu controls, 492–493
overview, 574
PopUpMenuButton control, creating for, 514–515
data serialization, 840–841, 932
data series, for charts, 649, 652, 659–660, 666
data set, returning from PHP class, 929–930
Data Transfer Object pattern, 841
data transfer objects. *See* value objects
data types, 362, 539
Data Visualization components, 4, 27, 641, 648
databases, 534, 813, 935–938
data-centric applications
binding returned data to visual controls, 719–722
data connections, 710–714
overview, 707, 710
return data type, defining, 714–719
dataChange event, 623–625
data/contacts.xml expression, 724
dataField property, 617, 619, 621
dataForFormat() method, 395
DataGrid control. *See also* list controls
binding data to, 803–804
binding returned data to visual controls, 719–720
custom components in navigator container, 473
custom labels, displaying, 619–622
customizing display, 614–619
dataChange event, 623–625
defined, 572
drag-and-drop support, 390
financial charts, 664–666
handling HTTPService responses, 728, 729–730
item editors, 627–628
itemRenderer property, 629–632
numeric data, 647–648
overview, 613–614
Spark item renderers, 626
DataGridColumn control
controlling column display, 617–619
displaying custom labels, 619–621
drop-in item editors, 628–629
dynamic data field, 621
item renderers and editors, 622–623
label properties, 583
Spark item renderers, 626–627
DataGridCustomRenderer.mxml file, 625
DataGridDefaultColumns.mxml file, 616
DataGridDropinEditor.mxml file, 631
DataGridExplicitColumns.mxml file, 618

DataGridFormatLabels.mxml file, 621
DataGridInlineEditor.mxml file, 634
DataGroup control, 392, 395
data-management-config.xml file, 817
DataManager.php file, 930
dataProvider property
AdvancedDataGrid control, 644
data collection, using as, 485–486
DataGrid control, 615, 616
menu control, 493, 494
overview, 571
pie charts, 649
PieSeries series class, 659
ViewStack, using as, 487–488
DataSeries class, 652
Data/Services view, Flash Builder, 712, 714, 715, 847, 933
date application, 943–944
Date class, 945
date controls, 273–275
DateChooser control, 273–275, 307–308, 518–520
DateField control, 273–274, 275, 405, 573, 632–634
DateFormatter class, 305–309, 944, 945
DateFormatterDemo.mxml file, 308
DateFormatterWithStaticMethod.mxml file, 310
DateTimeAxis component, 667, 668
DateValidator class, 687
"Dave's History of SOAP," 778
dayNames property, 275
Debug button, 169–170
Debug Current Instruction Pointer, 186–187
Debug menu option, 169
debug() method, 176
debug mode, Flash Builder, 169–172
debug version
Flash Player, 21–22, 24, 25–26, 168
Flex application, 88, 169
Debug view, Flash Builder, 54, 190
Debugger menu item, 168
debugging. *See also* breakpoints
Adobe AIR applications, 972–973
custom formatting function, 622
debug mode, running application in, 169–172
debug version of application, 169
event objects, 220–221
logging, 172–180
Network Monitor, 196–206
overview, 167–169
profiling tools, 194–196
debugging views, Flash Builder, 54–55
Declarations tag, 178

declarative instantiation, 250

deep linking, 87–88

default application descriptor file, 964–967

default argument values, instantiating value objects with, 552

default attribute, 855, 895

default button, 507–508, 681–683

default columns display, DataGrid control, 615–616

default destination, Proxy Service, 818–822

default dimensions, content-based sizing, 333

default skin, creating custom skin by copying, 455–460

default values, value object class properties, 539

defaultButton property, 682, 683

<default-channels> tag, 856

DefaultHTTP id, 819

DefaultProxyDestination.mxml file, 822, 823

deferred instantiation, 483, 614

DELETE method, 725

delete operator, 766–767

deletePerson() function, 937

deploying Flex applications

    creating release build, 88–90

    deploying release build, 91

    integrating into existing Web page, 91–92

    integrating with Dreamweaver, 93–96

    testing release build, 90–91

deployment, BlazeDS, 818

derived class, 15

descendant accessor operator, 760

descendant selectors, CSS, 346, 350–351, 354

DescendantSelectorDemo.mxml file, 351

descending property, 560

descriptor-template.xml file, 963

design, with Flex versus Flash, 10

Design view

    constraint properties, 332

    constraint-based layout, 331–332

    event handler function, generating, 215–216

    Flash components, 162–163, 165

    inserting custom component instance in, 146–149

    MXML editor, 49–50

    view states, defining in, 401–406

    views used in, 54

Desktop application option, 46

desktop applications. *See* Adobe AIR

desktop deployment, Flash Player, 18

destination, binding expression, 136

destination property

    Consumer component, 858

    Producer component, 857

RemoteObject component, 830, 881, 928

    WebService or HTTPService object, 823, 824

<destination> tag, 829, 855

destinationLabel control, 138

destinations

    Flash Remoting, 878

    Message Service, 855–856

    Proxy Service, 818–824

    Remoting Service, 828–830

detached view, Eclipse, 39–40

detail property, 508

Developer edition, ColdFusion, 875

development, Flex versus Flash, 8–11

development tools, 26–28

device fonts, 295–296

DHTML (Dynamic HTML), 210

Digital Signature screen, Export Release Build wizard, 968–969

dimensions. *See also* sizing containers and controls

    controlling application, 130–131

    navigator containers, 484

    ViewStack, 477

direction property

    bidirectional text, 293

    Box superclass, 312

    FormItem container, 681

    LinearGradient class, 426

    navigator bar container, 488

    Spark ButtonBar component, 490

disabled skin state, 448

disabledDays property, 275

disabledRanges property, 275

disabling validation trigger events, 691–692

Disconnect tool, 193

dispatchEvent() method, 234, 238

displayAsPassword property, 260

DisplayBookCollection.mxml file, 556

distribution, Eclipse, 35

div element, textFlow property, 256

<div> tag, 83, 85, 92

DivElement class, 289

docked view, Eclipse, 39–40

Document Class feature, 66, 70

Document Object Model (DOM), 750–751, 785

document property, 785

Document Service, ColdFusion, 905

documentation

    CFC, 881, 882

    ColdFusion, 910

Index

documentation *(continued)*
event object, 221
Flash Builder 4, 29, 55–57, 125, 126
Flex 4, 29
Zend AMF, 932
doDrag() method, 392, 393, 394
DOM (Document Object Model), 750–751, 785
dot notation, 588, 758–759
doubleClickEnabled property, 584
doughnut charts, 657–658
DoughnutDemo.mxml file, 658
Download BlazeDS now option, 810
downloading
AIR installer, 958
BlazeDS, 810–811
debug version of Flash Player, 25–26
Eclipse, 34
production Flash Player, 24–25
Downloads page, WampServer Web site, 913
drag proxy, 390, 393–394
drag-and-drop operations
custom, 391–398
List controls, implementing with, 389–391
overview, 371, 388–389
dragDrop event, 395–398
dragEnabled property, 389–390, 393
dragEnter event, 394–395
DragEvent class, 395
dragInitiator property, 395
DragManager class, 391
dragMoveEnabled property, 389
DragSource class, 391–393, 395
dragSource property, 395
drawing. *See* FXG
Dreamweaver, Adobe, 93–96
DropDownDemo.mxml file, 605
DropDownList control. *See also* list controls
ArrayCollection class filtering, 558
ChangeLocaleAtRuntime.mxml application, 946
complex data objects, selecting, 607–610
defined, 571, 572
overview, 603
prompt property, 604–605
properties, 585
Spark ButtonBar control, 611–613
dropEnabled property, 389–390, 392
drop-in item editors, 628
drop-in item renderers, 591–593, 623
ds-console.war BlazeDS instance, 811
Duplicate of option, 402

duration property, 374, 380
dynamic data field, DataGrid control, 621
dynamic data providers, 577–578
dynamic help, Flash Builder, 57
Dynamic HTML (DHTML), 210
dynamic url, 824
<dynamic-url> tag, 820, 822–824

E

E4X (EcmaScript for XML)
expressions
extracting data from XML objects, 758–764
modifying data in XML objects, 765–770
overview, 756–757
namespaces, working with, 770–773
overview, 749–750
XML classes
object, creating, 751–754
overview, 750–751
XMLList class, 754–755
XMLListCollection class, 755–756
e4x value
format property, 753
resultFormat property, 726, 753
E4XChangingHelper class, 767
E4XChanging.mxml file, 768
E4XParser component, 758
E4XParsingHelper class, 763–764
E4XParsingHelper.as file, 764
E4XParsing.xml file, 763
E4XPChangingHelper.as file, 770
E4XWithNamespaces.mxml file, 773
easer property, 387
easing classes, 387–388
EasingDemo.mxml file, 387–388
Eclipse
configuring, 43–45
distribution, selecting, 35
downloading, 34
Flash Builder plug-in, installing, 36
installing, 35–36
overview, 32, 33–34, 36
preparing to install, 34
search tools, 58–60
workspace, 37–43
Eclipse Classic, 35
Eclipse IDE for Java Developers, 35
Eclipse IDE for Java EE Developers, 35
Eclipse Public License version 1.0 (EPL), 34

ECMAScript 4th Edition standard, 114
EcmaScript for XML. *See* E4X
Edit ActionScript 3.0 Class dialog box, 68
`editable` property
    ComboBox control, 588, 605, 606
    DataGrid control, 627–628
    DateField component, 274, 632, 634
    `TextInput/TextArea` controls, 260
    `whiteSpaceCollapse` style, 259
`editorDataField` property, 629
editors, Eclipse, 41
`effectEnd` event, 386
effects. *See also* transitions
    ActionScript, declaring in, 375–377
    composite, 383–387
    declaring, 373–377
    defined, 399
    easing classes, 387–388
    overview, 372–373
    playing, 373–375
    Spark, 377–383
`Ellipse` class, 421, 422, 426–427
elliptical shapes, drawing with FXG, 422–423
`EllipticalButtonSkin.mxml` file, 466
`else` clause, 117–118
`else if` clause, 117–118
em measurement, 262
e-mail application, 907–909
`email` property, 703
`EmailValidator` class, 687, 689, 694
`@Embed()` compiler directive, 440
`Embed()` compiler directive, 951
`[Embed]` metadata tag, 284, 302, 394, 509
embedded fonts
    declaring with ActionScript, 302
    declaring with CSS
        embedding by font file location, 298
        embedding font variations, 298–300
        embedding ranges of characters, 300–302
        overview, 297–298
    versus device fonts, 295–296
    overview, 297
embedded style sheets, 344, 353–355
`EmbeddedStyles.mxml` file, 354
embedding
    FXG graphics, with `<s:BitmapImage>`, 440
    images, 284–285
`EmbedFontByFileName.mxml` file, 299–300
empty tag syntax, 104

en_US locale, 942, 944
`Enable Condition` property, 182
Enable integration with Web browsers option, 88
Enable Monitor icon, 201
`enabled` property, 110, 182, 252, 478–479
enabling Network Monitor, 201–202
encapsulation, 13–14, 135
end tag, 104
`endpoint` property, 928
`<endpoint>` tag, 829, 979
Enter a sample XML/JSON response option, 714
`enterPopUp()` method, 524
entities, XML, 110
entries, 362
`entries` property, 422
`<Envelope>` tag, 778
EPL (Eclipse Public License version 1.0), 34
error messages, validation rules and, 695–697
`errorcode` attribute, 901
`errorString` property, 704
`evalE4X()` method, 763, 764, 770
event argument, 220, 221–222, 244
event bubbling, 227–229
`Event` class, 213–214, 216–217, 219–220, 224, 237–238
event listeners
    ActionScript functions, 211–212
    `ChangeLocaleAtRuntime.mxml` application, 946
    event handler function, using, 212–213
    executing single ActionScript statement in, 210
    generating, 66
    handling specific event objects, 221–222
    `ItemResponder` class, 739–740
    overriding in view state, 409–412
    overview, 210
    removing, 227
    `result` event, 731–732, 832–833, 885
    setting up, 223–225
    simple event handling application, 211
    watchpoints, 190–191
    working with multiple Java class methods, 834, 836
event objects
    arguments, 213–214
    for custom event, 233–234
    debugging, 220–221
    defined, 207
    documentation, reading, 221
    `Event` class inheritance, 219–220
    event handler function, generating, 214–216
    handling specific, 221–223
    overview, 213

event objects *(continued)*
    properties, 216–219
    variable name, 213
`[Event]` metadata tag, 231, 234
`EventBubbling.mxml` file, 228–229
`EventDispatcher` class, 223
`event.item` expression, 487, 493, 516
`EventObjectProperties.mxml` file, 218–219
`event.result` expression, 732, 753, 758, 788, 833, 885
events. *See also specific events by name*
    `addEventListener()`, handling with, 223–227
    `Alert` window, handling, 508–509
    bubbling, 227–229
    custom, 230–237, 699–704
    custom event classes, 237–246
    defined, 149
    encapsulation, 14
    event-driven applications, 207
    Flex architecture for, 208–209
    `List` control, 584
    menu control, handling, 493
    MXML, handling in
        event listeners, declaring, 210–213
        event objects, working with, 213–223
        overview, 210
    navigator bar container, handling, 487
    overview, 207
    `PopUpButton` control, handling, 518–520
    `PopUpMenuButton` control, handling, 515–517
    sharing data with, in custom pop-up window, 522–524
    `Slider` controls, 281
events folder, 238
Events link, API documentation, 208–209, 221
Events section, help page, 209
`event.target` expression, 217
`event.target.data` expression, 393
`EventWithFunction.mxml` file, 212–213
`excludeFrom` property, 408, 448
`execute()` method, 908
`executeBindings()` method, 479
`executeFilter()` method, 558
Existing Projects into Workspace option, 74
explicit arguments, 891
explicit casting, 859
explicit notation, 838–840
explicit parameters, 796–797
`explodeRadius` property, 651, 654–657
exploding pie charts, 654–657
Export Breakpoints dialog box, 184
`export()` method, 256

Export Release Build wizard, 89, 93, 967–969
Export to FXG option, Fireworks, 437
`ExportStylesComplete.mxml` file, 361
`ExportStyles.mxml` file, 359
`expressInstall.swf` file, 96
expression tools, 167
expressions. *See also specific expressions by name*
    E4X
        extracting data from XML objects, 758–764
        modifying data in XML objects, 765–770
        overview, 756–757
    inspecting with breakpoints
        adding expression, 191–192
        Expressions view, 191
        Variables view, 187–188
        watchpoints, setting, 188–191
    predicate, filtering data with, 760–764
Expressions tab, Flex Debugging perspective, 191
Expressions view, Flash Builder, 55, 191–192
Extensible Application Markup Language (XAML), 105
Extensible Stylesheet Language Transformations (XSLT), 105
external ActionScript files, 120–124
external resource bundles, 950–953
external style sheets
    creating blank style sheet, 356–359
    exporting existing styles, 359–362
    overview, 356
    referencing with `<fx:Style>` element, 345
`externalStyles.css` file, 358
`ExternalStyles.mxml` file, 359

F

faceless components, 113
`Fade` effect, 372, 374–376, 379, 414–416
Fake Name Generator Web site, 615
`false` value, `ArrayCollection` filtering function, 557
`fault` event
    `CallResponder`, 794
    `HTTPService` component, 733–736
    `ItemResponder` class, 739–740
    `Mail` component, 908
    `RemoteObject` component, 834, 900–902
    `token` property, 737
    `WebService` component, 790–792
`faultCode` property, 733, 790
`faultDetail` property, 733, 790
`FaultEvent` argument, 734
`FaultEvent.fault` object, 901
`FaultService.cfc` file, 902

`faultString` property, 733, 790

`fb` prefix, 460

fcsh (Flex Compiler Shell) command-line tool, 28

fdb command-line tool, 28

`field` argument, 653

Fielding, Roy, 708

`fields` property, 560

`fieldSeparator` property, 177

File Search tool, 58–59

filename, application, 48

`filename` property, 963

`FileSystemDataGrid` control, 613

fill colors, pie chart, 660–662

`fill` property, 422, 425–428

`fillColors` style, 362

fills, gradient, 425–428

`fills` property, 660–661

`FilterDemo.mxml` file, 560

`filterFunction` property, 557–558

filtering

    data, 556, 760–764

    data collections, 557–560

    FXG, 431–432

    messages on server, 865–871

financial charts, 663–666

`FinancialCharts.mxml` file, 665

Find in Files dialog box, 58–60

Find Next option, 58

Find Previous option, 58

`findAny()` method, 564

`findFirst()` method, 564

finding data, with cursors, 564–566

`findLast()` method, 564

Find/Replace dialog box, 58

Fireworks, Adobe, 437–439

`FireworksFXGDemo.mxml` file, 441

Fixed width console option, 170

FLA file, 9, 164

flags, 505–506

Flash Builder 4. *See also* data-centric applications

    Adobe AIR applications, debugging in, 972–973

    data connections

        BlazeDS, 845–847

        ColdFusion, 903–904

        PHP, 932–938

    documentation feature, 125, 126

    Eclipse

        configuring, 43–45

        overview, 36

        workspace, 37–43

    Flash Player installation with, 24

Flash Professional CS5, integrating with, 66–71

Flex project, creating, 45

versus Flex SDK, 4, 7

generating code, 64–66

getter functions in, generating, 546–549

Help application, 55–57

importing FXP files into, 100

indentation in, 50–51

installing, 32–36

licenses, 31–32

managing ActionScript code with, 124–128

overview, 26

searching for code, 58–64

setter functions in, generating, 546–549

user interface, 49–55

Flash Builder 4 Premium Edition, 4, 32

Flash Builder 4 Standard Edition, 31

Flash Builder Premium license, 648

Flash Catalyst, Adobe, 4, 5, 10

Flash CS5 Professional, 20

Flash Lite, 20

Flash perspective, Flash Builder, 75

Flash Player. *See also* Proxy Service

    ActionScript Virtual Machine, 99

    advanced text layout, 288

    application dimensions, controlling, 130–131

    asynchronous communications, 727

    configuring with `mm.cfg`, 174

    cross-domain policy issues, 746–747

    debug version, 21–22, 168

    Dreamweaver detection of version, 96

    generic device font names, 296

    history of, 19–20

    HTML wrapper template evaluation of version, 83–85

    `HTTPService` component `method` property, 725

    image types, 282

    installation, 22–26

    overview, 18

    penetration statistics, 21

    rich text in, 255

Flash Player 10.1, 20

Flash Player Support Center, Adobe, 25–26

Flash presentation, creating in Flash Builder, 67–71

Flash Professional

    versus Flex development, 8–11

    integrating with Flash Builder 4, 66–71

Flash Profile perspective, Flash Builder, 194

Flash Remoting. *See also* Remoting Service; Zend AMF

    ColdFusion, 873–874

    ColdFusion code, 200

    configuring on server, 877–878

Index

Flash Remoting (*continued*)
    creating channels at runtime with, 978–980
    Flex project, creating, 875–877
    overview, 807, 874–875
    packet size, 205
    PHP, 924
Flash Text Engine (FTE), 255, 288
Flash XML Graphics. *See* FXG
FlashApp.mxml file, 165
Flash-based components, creating, 161–165
flashContent id selector, 83, 85
flash.events.Event class, 213–214, 237, 239
flash.events.Event event object, 281
flash.events.TextEvent event object, 232, 234
flashlog.txt, sending tracing messages to, 173–175
FlashPlayer.exe file, 24
flash-unicode-table.xml file, 302
flashvars variable, 130, 726
flat data, grouping, 644–645
flat presentation, Package Explorer view, 52
Flex 1.x, 106
Flex 2, 105, 106–107
Flex 3, 105, 106–107
Flex 3.4 projects, 46
Flex 4
    development tools, 26–28
    documentation, 29
    versus Flash Builder, 4, 7
    Flash Player, 18–26
    versus Flash Professional development, 8–11
    Flex applications, 4–8
    namespace prefixes, 107
    namespaces, 105–106
    object-oriented programming, 11–18
    as open-source project, 5
Flex 4.0 projects, 46
Flex applications. *See also* data-centric applications;
        debugging; *specific application files by name*
    ActionScript 3, 6–8, 101–103, 114–119
    Application component, 128–134
    combining MXML and ActionScript, 120–128
    deploying, 88–96
    FXG files in, 439–441
    Hello World, 74–81
    html-template folder, 81–88
    messaging, 856–862
    MXML, 6–8, 104–113
    overview, 4, 73, 99–101
    programming languages, 5–6
    sharing data with, 697–704

Flex Build Path screen, 90, 93
Flex Builder. *See* Flash Builder 4
Flex Compiler section, Properties dialog box, 84, 88, 101–102
Flex Compiler Shell (fcsh) command-line tool, 28
Flex Data Services 2, 807
Flex Debugging perspective, Flash Builder, 183, 185–186,
        190, 191, 220
Flex Library Project
    component libraries
        adding to project build path, 159
        creating project, 156–157
        folder structure, creating for project, 157–158
        libs folder, 159–161
        overview, 155
    defined, 46
Flex Message Service, 849
Flex Mobile SDK, 20
Flex Project (FXP) format, 100, 158
Flex Project option, 75
Flex projects
    for Adobe AIR application, 960–963
    BlazeDS, creating for use with, 814–816
    cfservices.swc file, adding to, 907
    ColdFusion, creating for use with, 197–201, 875–877
    component libraries, adding to build path, 159
    creating in Flash Builder, 45
    for Hello World application, 75–78
    for messaging application, 856–857
    PHP, creating for use with, 919–921
Flex Properties view, Flash Builder, 331–332, 359–360, 404
Flex Server option, 47
Flex Theme option, 342
Flex Web Tier Compiler, 3
flex-config.xml file, 85, 107
FlexEmailClient.mxml file, 909
FlexGlobals class, 129
flex-rds-server.jar file, 846
focalPointRatio property, 426
focusColor style, 355
folder structure, Library Project, 157–158
folding, code, 125–127
font styles, 512
fontAntiAliasType style, 294
@font-face style selector, 297–299
fontFamily style, 294, 295, 296–297, 298–299, 353
fontGridType style, 294
fontName attribute, 302
fonts
    configuring Eclipse, 43–44
    controlling with CSS, 294–302

`fontSharpness` style, 294

`fontSize` style, 294, 344–345, 362, 413, 678

`fontStyle` style, 294, 299, 350

`fontThickness` style, 294

`fontWeight` style, 294, 299, 362, 678

`for` loop, 119

Force Quit dialog box, 972

Form container
    custom, 683–687
    default button, setting, 681–683
    dispatching custom event, 242–244, 700, 703–704
    `FormHeading` control, 678–680
    `FormItem` container, 680–681
    modeling data with value object, 697–699
    overview, 676–677
    triggering individual validator objects with ActionScript, 692
    value object, modeling data with, 697

`form` property, 672

`<form>` tag, 676

`format()` method, 305, 307, 620

`format` property, 753

`formatDate()` method, 309

`formatString` property, 306–307, 309

formatter classes
    in binding expressions, 307–308
    objects, creating, 305–306
    overview, 305
    properties, setting, 306–307
    in static methods, 308–310

formatting function, debugging custom, 622

`FormatUtil.as` file, 309

`FormComponentDemoComplete.mxml` file, 704

`FormComponentDemo.mxml` file, 702

`FormDefaultButton.mxml` file, 683

`FormHeading` control, 676–680

`FormInPanel.mxml` file, 680

`FormItem` container
    adding controls to `Form` component, 685, 686
    `FormHeading` control, 678
    label alignment, controlling, 680–681
    layout, controlling, 681
    `NumericStepper` control, 272
    overview, 676–677
    `TextInput` control, 259

Forta, Ben, 879

forward navigation, 478–481

`fr_FR` locale, 944

`frameRate` property, 129

Framework linkage drop-down menu, 90, 93

`frameworks` folder, 107

`fromState` property, 414

FTE (Flash Text Engine), 255, 288

functions. *See also* ColdFusion Components; methods; *specific functions by name*
    ActionScript 3, handling events with, 211–213
    code folding, 126
    declaring variables within, 116
    event handler, generating, 214–216

Future Splash Animator, 19, 371

FutureWave Software, 19

`fx` prefix, 106, 108

`<fx:binding>` tag, 137

`<fx:Component>` tag, 408, 593, 594, 597

`<fx:Declarations>` tag
    declaring separate data objects, 577
    easing classes, 387
    `<fx:Model>` tag within, 534
    nonvisual classes, 113, 230, 306, 374, 492
    public properties, declaring, 151
    validator objects, 688
    value object class, 549

`<fx:Definition>` tag, 285, 428–430

FXG (Flash XML Graphics)
    custom skin, adding to, 449–451
    defined, 5–6
    FXG files
        Creative Suite software, creating with, 432–439
        in Flex applications, 439–441
        overview, 432
    MXML, declaring in
        arbitrary shapes, drawing with `Path` class, 423–425
        elliptical shapes, drawing, 422–423
        filters, applying, 431–432
        gradient fills, 425–428
        gradient strokes, 421–422
        lines, drawing, 421
        overview, 101, 420–432
        rectangular shapes, drawing, 422–423
        reusing graphic elements, 428–430
        scaling graphic elements, 430
    overview, 419–420

FXG 1.0 specification, 420

FXG 2 specification, 420

FXG files
    Creative Suite software, creating with, 432–439
    in Flex applications, 439–441
    overview, 420, 432

FXG Options dialog box, 433–434

`<fx:Library>` tag, 285, 428–430

`<fx:Metadata>` tag, 231, 232

Index

`<fx:Model>` tag
  benefits of, 537
  data collection `source` property, 554
  `DataGrid` control, 615
  drawbacks of, 537
  importing data with, 538–539
  overview, 534, 535–537
  versus value objects, 539
`<fx:Object>` tag, 486, 575
FXP (Flex Project) format, 100, 158
`<fx:Script>` tag
  `[Embed]` metadata tag, 302
  CDATA blocks, 109
  code folding, 125
  external ActionScript files, 121
  `fb` prefix, 460
  use of, 120
`<fx:Style>` tag, 345, 347, 353, 358, 680

G

`gap` property, 321
gap settings, 80
garbage collection, automatic, 116
Generate Click Handler prompt, 214–215
Generate constructor from superclass option, 239
Generate Event Handler option, 216
Generate from database option, 935
Generate from template option, 926
Generate Getter/Setter dialog box, 65, 546, 547
Generate ItemClick Handler prompt, 234
Generate Sample PHP Service dialog box, 926, 935–936
Generated SizeSelected Handler prompt, 236
`generated` subfolder, 101–103
generic device font names, 296
gestures, user, 207
get accessor method, 545–546
Get Data option, 199–200, 729
Get Font Size button, 366–367
`GET` method, 725, 744
`getAllContacts()` method, 786, 791, 888–889
`getAllPerson()` function, 937
`getClass()` method, 951
`GetComplexData.php` file, 931
`getContactCount()` function, 888–889, 890
`getContacts()` operation, 717
`getExpressionsArray()` method, 764, 770
`getFilteredContacts()` method, 797, 891, 892
`getFullName()` method, 154
`getItemAt()` method, 555, 585

`getLogger()` method, 175
`getOperation()` method, 831, 882, 891
`getPerson_paged()` function, 937
`getPersonByID()` function, 937
`GetSimpleXML.mxml` file, 924
`getStateLabel()` method, 582, 611
`getString()` method, 948, 950
`getStyle()` method, 454
getter methods, 64–66, 546–549
global Proxy Service permission, 820
global search and replace, 61
`global` selector, CSS, 346, 352–353, 355, 360
globally unique package name, 141
Go to File for Breakpoint button, 183
gradient fills, 425–428, 435–437, 438–439
gradient strokes, 421–422
`GradientDemos.mxml` file, 427
`GradientEntry` class, 422, 427–428
`GradientStroke` class, 421–422
`Graphic` class, 421
graphic design, with Flash Builder, 10
`<Graphic>` root element, 433
graphical icon, pop-up window, 509–512
`GraphicElement` class, 251–253
graphics, 950–951. *See also* FXG
`Group` component, 111–112, 320–321, 322–323, 385
`Group` components, Spark, 319–325. *See also specific components by name*
`GroupBase` class, 319
`GroupDemo.mxml` file, 320–321
grouping flat data, 644–645
`GroupingCollection` class, 644
`GroupingCollection2` class, 644
`GroupingField` objects, 644
`groupName` property, 269–270

H

H command, 424
Halo theme, 342
hard-coded data providers, 575–577
hard-coded XML structure, declaring, 752
`hasFormat()` method, 395
HBox container, 312–313, 314–315, 317–318, 488–489
`HBoxDemo.mxml` file, 314
`HEAD` method, 725
`<head>` section, applets, 92
`Header` component, 474
`header()` function, 922
headers, Accordion navigator container, 500

headers property, 731–732, 858, 859
headerText property, 617
height property
  charting controls, 650
  containers/controls, 252, 333–334
  DataGrid control, 614
  HRule/VRule controls, 263
  Image control, 283
  Line class, 421
  MX containers, 312
  percentage sizing, 334
  <s:Application> tag, 92
  shape classes, 423
  Spacer control, 265
Hello World application
  for AIR, 960–962
  deploying, 88–96
  displaying message, 78–81
  Flex project, creating for, 75–78
  MXML and ActionScript 3, 103
  switching workspaces, 74–75
HelloService.cfc file, 879
helloWorld() method, 781–782, 786, 831–832, 879, 882–884
helloworld_en_US.png graphic file, 950
helloworld_fr_FR.png graphic file, 950
HelloWorld.mxml file, 929
HelloWorld.php file, 928
Help application, Flash Builder, 55–57, 209, 221
helper class, 763–764, 767, 768–770
Hex view, Network Monitor, 202
hexadecimal code, 362
HGroup component, 259, 319–320, 321–323
HGroupDemo.mxml file, 323
hidden setting, overflow style, 83
Hide Non-Public Members option, 124
Hide Static Functions and Variables option, 124
hierarchical data display, 641–643
hierarchical presentation, Package Explorer view, 52
HierarchicalData class, 642
highField property, 663
HighLowOpenClose (HLOC) charts, 650, 663–666
history management files, 87–88
history subfolder, 82, 87–88
historyBack() method, 976
history.css file, 82, 83
historyForward() method, 976
historyFrame.html file, 82
historyGo() method, 976

history.js file, 82, 83
Hit Count property, 182
HLOC (HighLowOpenClose) charts, 650, 663–666
HLOCChart component, 650
HLOCseries series class, 650
horizontal Accordion, 500
horizontal layout, 131–133, 635–641
horizontal layout container, 312–315
horizontal value, form property, 672
horizontalAlign style, 132, 317, 321
horizontalAxis declaration, 668, 670
horizontalCenter property, 332, 423
horizontalGap style, 317
HorizontalLayout class, 80, 131, 132–133
HorizontalList control, 573, 635–641
HorizontalListDemo.mxml file, 639
hostComponent id, 447
[HostComponent] metadata tag, 446
hovered view state, 600
How to upgrade.rtf link, MAMP server installation screen, 916
HRule control, 263–264
HRuleDemo.mxml file, 264
HScrollBar control, 277–279
HSlider control, 279–281
HSQLDB database, BlazeDS, 813
htdocs subfolder, 919
HTML control, 973–977
HTML wrapper file, 90, 130–131
HTML wrapper template (index.template.html)
  <head> section, 83–86
  <noscript> section, 86–87
  flashvars parameter, 86
  overview, 81, 82
  running application, 86
HTML-based content, Adobe AIR, 973–977
HTMLLoader class, 973
html-template folder, 81–88
htmlText property, 258, 262
HTTP (Hypertext Transfer Protocol). See also RemoteObject component
  data connection code, 721–722
  requests, 747, 817, 818
  service, remote, 710–714
HTTPFaultEvent.mxml file, 736
HTTPMultiService class, 714
HTTPRequest class, 202–203, 727
HTTPRequestDemo application, 198–199, 202–203
HTTPResultEvent.mxml file, 733

Index

HTTPService component
    cross-domain policy, 746–747, 980
    data-centric applications
        binding returned data to visual controls, 719–722
        data connections, creating and managing, 710–714
        overview, 710
        return data type, defining, 714–719
    defined, 578
    dot notation, 758
    HTML control, 973
    HTTPServiceDemo application, 198
    object, creating, 722–723
    overview, 707–708
    passing parameters to server pages, 744–745
    PHP with, 922–924
    properties, 723–726
    Proxy Service
        default destination, 820, 822
        named destinations, 823, 824
    REST architecture, 708–709
    RPC architecture, 709–710
    sending and receiving data
        asynchronous communications, 727
        CallResponder and AsyncToken, 736–739
        ItemResponder and AsyncToken, 739–741
        overview, 727
        responses, handling, 727–736
    value objects, working with, 741–744
    XML, importing with, 753
HTTPServiceDemo.mxml file, 198–199, 202–203
HTTPServiceWithBindings.mxml application, 729
HTTPValueObjects.mxml file, 744
HTTPWithBindingsComplete.mxml file, 730
Hypertext Transfer Protocol. See HTTP; RemoteObject
        component
hyphenated syntax, 347

I

ICollectionView interface, 556
icon, custom, for pop-up window, 509–512
iconClass argument, 509
id (unique identifier)
    <fx:Model> tag, 537, 538
    application descriptor file, 963
    binding expression syntax, 136
    CSS ID selector, 344, 346, 352
    FormItem container, 687
    HTML control, 973

HTTPService object, 722
Parallel effect, 384
Proxy Service default destination, 819
RemoteObject instance, 831
UIComponent class/GraphicElement class, 252
ViewStack nested containers, 480–482
ID selectors, CSS, 344, 346, 352
IDE (integrated development environment), 26
IDropInListItemRenderer interface, 591, 628
if statement, 117–118
IFill interface, 422
IFlexDisplayObject interface, 394, 521
ignoreComments property, 754
ignoreProcessingInstructions property, 754
ignoreWhitespace property, 754
IList interface, 555, 556, 574, 611
Illustrator, Adobe, 433–437, 439
ILogger interface, 175, 176
image, proxy, 393–394
Image control, 281–286
Image Service, ColdFusion, 905
imageAlpha argument, 394
ImageRenderer.mxml file, 598
imageSource property, 596
Import Breakpoints dialog box, 185, 186
Import dialog box, 74
Import Flex Project dialog box, 100
import statement, 127–128, 144, 148, 244, 504
Import Theme button, 342
importFromText() method, 256
importFromXML() method, 256
importing FXP files into Flash Builder 4, 100
INavigatorContent interface, 472
includeCategory property, 177
includeDate property, 178
includeIn property, 408, 448
includeLevel property, 178
includeTime property, 178
indentation, in Flash Builder 4, 50–51
index argument, 653
index.template.html file. See HTML wrapper template
        (index.template.html)
inheritance
    CSS type selectors, 348–349
    DataGrid control, 613
    Event class, 219–220, 224
    MXML components, 140–141
    navigator containers, 472
    overview, 15–16

`inherited` branch, Variables view, 187
`initApp()` method, 629
`initialized()` method, 723
`<initialWindow>` element, 973
`initialWindow/content` property, 963
`initiateDrag()` method, 392, 393
inline item editors, 593–597, 632–634
inline renderers, 591, 593–597, 623
inline style declarations, 344–345, 451–452
`InlineGraphicElement` class, 289
`InlineRendererComplexObjects.mxml` file, 597
`InlineRenderer.mxml` file, 595
input/output, Message Service, 853
Insert CDATA Block option, 120
Insert Pane dialog box, 475–476
`inside` value, `labelPosition` style, 652
`insideWithCallout` value, `labelPosition` style, 652
Install Flash Player 10 Plugin.exe file, 24
Install Flash Player 10ActiveX.exe file, 24
Install Options screen, 33
installation files, Flash Builder, 24
installer, Flash Player upgrade, 83
installing
    Adobe AIR, 958–959
    `blazedsfiles` folder files, 816
    ColdFusion, 783
    desktop application, 969–971
    Eclipse, 35–36
    Flash Builder, 32–36
    Flash Player, 22–26
    PHP, 912–919
    Zend AMF, 925–927
instance class, equivalent to effect class, 374
instantiation, deferred, 483, 614
integrated development environment (IDE), 26
interactive controls
    overview, 250
    `ScrollBar`, 277–279
    `Slider`, 279–281
`InteractiveObject` superclass, 209
interface. *See also specific interfaces by name*
    ActionScript 3, 175
    polymorphism, 16–17
    user, Flash Builder, 49–55
`internal` access modifier, 115–116, 543
introspection of Remoting Service destinations, 846
`INVALID` constant, 692
`invoice` element, 759
`<invoices>` tag, 758

`invoices.xml` file
    array notation, 759
    descendant accessor operator, 760
    dot notation, 758–759
    filtering XML data with predicate expressions, 760–762
    modifying data in XML objects, 765–770
    overview, 756–757
IP address, configuring, 906–908
`IResourceManager` interface, 944
`Iris` effect, 373
`IStroke` interface, 421, 422
`isValid()` method, 694, 700–701
item editors
    component, 632–634
    drop-in, 628
    `editorDataField` property, 629
    inline, 593–597, 632–634
    versus item renderers, 590
    `itemEditor` property, 629
    overview, 627–628
    `rendererIsEditor` property, 629–632
`item` property, 487, 493, 653
Item Renderer for MX DataGrid template, 626
item renderers
    custom
        component, 597–600
        drop-in, 591–593
        inline, 593–597
        overview, 590–591
        Spark, customizing, 600–602
    `dataChange` event, 623–625
    `HorizontalList` control, 635
    overview, 622–623
    Spark, 626–627
    `TileList` control, 635
`item[column.dataField]` expression, 621
`itemClick` event, 271, 487, 493, 515–517
`ItemClickEvent` event object, 234
`itemEditor` property, 591–593, 599, 628, 629
`ItemRenderer` class, 594, 598, 600
`itemRenderer` property, 591–593, 599, 628, 629, 639
`ItemResponder` class, 739–741
`ItemResponderDemo.mxml` file, 741
`IViewCursor` interface
    bookmarking data, 567–569
    finding data, 564–566
    overview, 556, 562
    traversing data, 562–564
`IVisualElement` interface, 251–252

Index

J

JAR (Java Archive) files, 826
Java. *See also* BlazeDS
    adapters, Message service, 854
    classes, creating and exposing with Remoting Service, 825–828
    passing data between ActionScript and, 840–841
    reverse domain package names, 141
    value object classes, 841–845
Java Development Kit (JDK), 809, 811–812
Java Development Tools (JDT), 34
Java Enterprise Edition (JEE) application servers, 539, 809, 810
Java Message Service (JMS), 850
Java Runtime Environment (JRE), 34
JAVA_HOME environment variable, 811, 812
JavaScript, 86–87, 114
JMS Adapter, 850, 854
JRun, 810

K

kerning style, 294
keyboard shortcuts, 501, 612–613
keyframes property, 377

L

L command, 424
Label control
    ActionScript 3, declaring objects in, 78
    Canvas container, 316
    customizing skin, 462–463
    embedded font, 298, 299–300
    <fx:Binding> tag, 137
    MX versus Spark, 253
    MXML, declaring objects in, 6
    NumericStepper control, 272
    overview, 80
    rotation property, 303–305
    styleManager object, 365
    TextInput control, 259
label property
    Button control, 354
    CheckBox control, 268
    FormItem container, 676, 680, 685
    labelField property, 579
    LinkButton control, 268
    navigator bar container, 486
    navigator container, 472, 481, 487
    RadioButton controls, 269

Label type selector, 350
labelDisplay skin part, 448
labelField property
    ButtonBar control, 611
    drop-in item renderers, 593
    List control, 579–582
    menu control, 493
    navigator bar container, 486
    pie chart wedge labels, 652
labelFunction property
    ButtonBar control, 611
    DataGrid control, 628
    DataGridColumn control, 619
    drop-in item renderers, 593
    List control, 579, 582–584
    pie chart wedge labels, 652–653
labelPosition style, 652, 659
labels
    alignment, FormItem container, 680–681
    button, 506–507
    custom DataGrid control, displaying, 619–622
    List item, controlling, 579–584
    pie chart wedge, 652–654, 655
labelStyleName style, 680
Labriola, Michael, 758
last value, concurrency property, 726
lastResult property
    binding expressions, 786
    CallResponder class, 737, 795, 803
    HTTPService component, 728
    Operation class, 831, 883
Latin alphabet, 301
layout. *See also* layout containers; layout controls
    advanced text, 288–294
    child object, 78
    FormItem container, 681
Layout class, 78
layout containers
    constraint-based layout, 330–332
    creationPolicy property, 484
    MX basic, 312–319
    overview, 311–312
    Panel, 325–330
    scrolling region, creating, 337–338
    sizing, 333–336
    Spark Group components, 319–325
layout controls
    HRule, 263–264
    overview, 263

Spacer, 265–266
VRule, 263–264
layout property
    basic layout, 133–134
    ButtonBar component, 490
    ComboBox and DropDownList controls, 603
    container, 330
    <mx:Application> component, 78
    overview, 131
    Panel containers, 326–327
    vertical and horizontal layout, 131–133
LayoutBase class, 131, 326
lazy evaluation, 880
LCDS (LiveCycle Data Services), 807, 809, 849. *See also*
    BlazeDS; Message Service
left property, 332, 335, 423
left to right (ltr) value, direction property, 490
legacy classes, 751
length() method, 760
length property, 555
level property, 178
levels, logging, 175–176
library definition, 428–429
library path, 159
Library path tab, Properties dialog box, 159–160
Library Project. *See* Flex Library Project
library.swf file, 158
libs folder, 159–161, 164–165, 907
line charts, 650, 666–667, 670–672
Line class, 421
LineAndAreaDemo.mxml file, 671
LinearAxis component, 667
LinearGradient class, 425–427, 660
LinearGradientStroke class, 421–422
LineChart component, 650
LineFormDemo.mxml file, 672
<lineitem> tag, 750
lines
    drawing with FXG, 421
    HRule and VRule controls, 263
LineSeries series class, 650, 672
<link> tag, 83
LinkBar navigator bar container, 484, 488–490
LinkButton control, 268
LinkElement class, 289
linking, deep, 87–88
Linux, 174
List control. *See also* list controls
    defined, 571, 573
    events, 584

labels, controlling, 579–584
properties, 584
user data selections, handling, 585–590
list controls
    AdvancedDataGrid
        grouping flat data, 644–645
        hierarchical data display, 641–643
        overview, 641
    ComboBox
        complex data objects, selecting with ActionScript,
            607–610
        overview, 603
        prompt property, 604–605
        Spark ButtonBar control, 611–613
        using, 605–607
    custom item renderers
        component, 597–600
        drop-in, 591–593
        inline renderers and editors, 593–597
        overview, 590–591
        Spark, customizing with view states, 600–602
    data providers
        dynamic, 577–578
        hard-coded, 575–577
        overview, 574
    DataGrid
        custom labels, displaying, 619–622
        customizing display, 614–619
        overview, 613–614
    drag-and-drop operations, 389–391, 392, 393
    DropDownList
        complex data objects, selecting with ActionScript,
            607–610
        overview, 603
        prompt property, 604–605
        Spark ButtonBar control, 611–613
    events, 584
    with horizontal and tile layout, 635–641
    item renderers and editors
        dataChange event, 623–625
        item editors, 627–634
        overview, 622–623
        Spark item renderers, 626–627
    labels, controlling
        labelField property, 579–582
        labelFunction property, 582–584
        overview, 579
    overview, 571–574, 603
    properties, 584

list controls (*continued*)
    user data selections, handling
        change event, 585
        complex data objects, selecting, 588–590
        overview, 585
        `selectedIndex` property, 587–588
        `selectedItem` property, 585–586
`ListBase` class, 613
`ListCollectionView` superclass, 755, 756
`ListControls.mxml` file, 573
`ListDragAndDrop.mxml` file, 391
`ListWithBoundData.mxml` file, 577
`ListWithHardCodedData.mxml` file, 577
literal characters, 109–110
literal numeric expressions, 761–762, 765
Live Objects view, 195–196
Live View, Dreamweaver, 95–96
LiveCycle Data Services (LCDS), 807, 809, 849. *See also*
        BlazeDS; Message Service
`load` event, 785
`load()` method, 286
`LoadEvent` class, 785
`loadStyleDeclarations()` method, 364
`loadWSDL()` method, 784, 795
local data cache, LCDS, 809
local data, retrieving in AIR applications, 578
`locale` folder, 943, 952
`locale` property, 947
`localeChain` property, 945, 946
`locale/en_US/customStrings.properties` file, 951
`locale/fr_FR/customStrings.properties` file, 951
locales
    changing at compile time, 943–944
    changing at runtime, 944–947
    overview, 941–943
`locales` property, 945
`Localhost` link, WampServer menu, 915
localizing applications
    custom resource bundles, 947–953
    locales, 941–947
    overview, 941
`localX` property, 220
`localY` property, 220
`location` property, 973
Log class, 175–176
`log()` method, 176
`LogAxis` component, 667
`LogEventLevel` class, 176, 179
Logger objects, 175, 176

logging
    Logging API, 175–180
    overview, 172
    `trace()` function, 172–175
Logging API
    Log class, 175–176
    Logger objects, 176
    overview, 175
    self-logging components, 176–177
    tracing targets, 177–180
`LoggingButton.mxml` file, 177
login data entry form, 238, 409–410
`login` event, 240, 242, 700
`login` property, 699, 701
`LoginApp.mxml` file, 246
`LoginEvent` class, 238–240, 241, 242
`LoginEvent.as` file, 240, 522, 700
`LoginEventComplete.as` file, 241–242
`LoginForm` component, 689–690, 694, 697, 702, 703
`LoginFormAutoValidation.mxml` file, 690
`LoginFormComplete.mxml` file, 244, 702
`LoginForm.mxml` file, 685, 689, 694, 697, 700
`LoginFormSingleValidation.mxml` file, 693
`loginHandler()` method, 245, 703
`LoginTitleWindow.mxml` file, 524
`LoginVO` class, 699, 703
`LoginVO.as` file, 698
`LoginWindow` component, 521–522, 525–526
`LogLogger` class, 175
long polling, 852–853
looping, in ActionScript 3, 119
loose type declaration, 115
`lowField` property, 663
`ltr` (left to right) value, `direction` property, 490
Luhn mod10 algorithm, 687

M

M command, 424
Mac OS X
    Adobe AIR, installing, 959
    AIR applications, 970, 971
    AIR Debug Launcher, quitting, 972
    BlazeDS, 812–813
    Eclipse, 35–37
    Flash Player, uninstalling, 23
    `flashlog.txt` file location, 174
    MAMP, installing on, 916–917
    `mm.cfg` file location, 174

Macromedia Flash 1.0, 19
Mail component, 907–909
Mail Service, ColdFusion, 905
maintainAspectRatio property, 283
MAMP, 913, 916–919
managed data, 555
manifests, MXML, 107–109
manipulating text, 303–305
margin styles, 319
Mark Occurrences feature, 61
Markers view, 38
maxChars property, 260, 272
maxHeight property, 252, 333
maximizing view, Eclipse, 40
maximum dimensions, content-based sizing, 333–334
maximum property, 272–273, 278, 280
maxWidth property, 252, 333
maxYear property, 275
measurement, units of, 344
member objects, 149
members, object, 13–14
Memory Usage view, 195
menu capability, WindowedApplication, 978
Menu control, 491–495
menu controls
    data providers, 492–493
    handling events, 493
    Menu control, 494–495
    MenuBar control, 495–497
    overview, 491–492
menu_ClickHandler() function, 493
MenuBar control, 491–493, 495–497
MenuDemo.mxml file, 495
MenuEvent.ITEM_CLICK constant, 493
Mercury QuickTestPro 9.1, 809
Merged into code option, 93
message event, 858, 859, 862
message property, 695, 733, 790, 859, 901
Message Service
    complex data, sending and receiving, 862–865
    configuring messaging on server, 851–856
    filtering messages on server, 865–871
    Flex application, creating, 856–862
    overview, 808, 849–851
    tracing messaging traffic, 871–872
messageHandler() function, 859, 863
messages, logging, 176
messaging-config.xml file, 817, 851, 854, 855–856, 867
.metadata subfolder, 74
method overloading, 551

method property, 724, 725, 744–745
methods. See also specific methods by name
    accessor, 539, 545–549
    binding expressions, calling with, 154
    constructor, 551–552, 560, 826, 843
    customized constructor, 551–552
    date entry, 275
    defined, 149, 152
    encapsulation, 14
    getter, 64–66, 546–549
    Java class, 834, 836
    MXML component, 149, 152–155
    public access modifier, 153
    remote, 830–831, 838–840
    setter, 64–66, 546–549
    static, formatter classes in, 308–310
Microsoft ASP.NET, 470, 779, 781
Microsoft Windows. See Windows operating systems
middleware application servers, 707
mimeType attribute, 302
minHeight property, 79, 131, 252, 333
minimum dimensions, content-based sizing, 333–334
minimum property, 272–273, 278, 280
minWidth property, 79, 131, 253, 333
minYear property, 275
mm.cfg file, 174
modal argument, 525
modality, pop-up window, 504–506
model components, 139
Model object, 535–536, 538
ModelDemo.mxml file, 537
modeling data
    data collections
        accessing data at runtime, 555–556
        ArrayCollection, declaring, 553
        cursors, 562–569
        managing data at runtime, 556–562
        overview, 552–553
        source property, setting, 554
    data model, creating, 534–539
    overview, 533
    value objects
        instantiating, 549–552
        New ActionScript Class wizard, 540–541
        overview, 539
        syntax, 541–549
model-view-controller architecture, 139, 469
modularity, 12–13, 135, 139
monolithic applications, 12–13
motionPaths property, 377

Index

mouseDown event, 392, 393, 416

mouseEnabled property, 228

MouseEvent class, 219–220, 221–223, 224, 226, 393

MouseEventObjectProperties.mxml file, 223

MouseEvent.stageX property, 416

MouseEvent.stageY property, 416

Move dialog box, 63–64

Move effect, 372, 379–381, 384, 385–386, 415

Move option, 63

Move3D effect, 372, 379–381

Move3DDemo.mxml file, 381

MoveDemo.mxml file, 380–381

moveNext() method, 563

movePrevious() method, 563

MovieClip class, 69

Mozilla Public License (MPL), version 1.1, 5

multiple data series, in pie charts, 659–660

multiple value, concurrency property, 726

MultipleFormHeadings.mxml file, 678

MultiTopicConsumer component, 865

MultiTopicProducer component, 865

MX components. *See also* list controls; *specific components by name*

  button controls, 266

  constraint-based layout, 330

  containers, 312–319

  CSS namespaces, 347

  data entry controls, 272

  defined, 249

  effects, 372–373, 375

  Flex themes, 342

  formatter classes, 305–310

  GraphicElement class, 251–253

  navigator containers, 472–473

  overview, 6

  scrollbars, 337

  text controls, 253

  UIComponent class, 251–253

mx prefix, 106–107, 108

mx|Alert type selector, 512, 514

mx-2009-manifest.xml file, 108

<mx:Accordion> tag, 500

<mx:arguments> tag, 839

mx.binding.utils.BindingUtils class, 136

<mx:ChannelSet> tag, 979

mx.collections.Sort class, 560, 562

mx.collections.SortField class, 560

mx.controls package, 504

mx.core.ClassFactory class, 591

mx.core.Container class, 472

<mx:dataProvider> tag, 576

mx.effects package, 372, 385

mx.events.CalendarLayoutChangeEvent event object, 518

mx.events.CloseEvent event object, 508–509, 527

mx.events.ItemClickEvent event object, 487

mx.events.MenuEvent event object, 493, 516

mx.events.ScrollEvent class, 278

<mx:fills> tag, 661

<mx:Form/> tag, 683

<mx:HTTPService> tag, 823

mx.logging.LogEventLevel class, 176

mx.logging.LogLogger class, 175

mx.messaging.events.MessageEvent event object, 859

<mx:method > tag, 834

MXML. *See also* FXG; MXML components

  Accordion navigator container, 500

  versus ActionScript 3, 6–8

  and ActionScript 3, 104–113

  ArrayCollection class, declaring, 553

  binding expressions, 136–137

  chart data series, 666–667

  code folding, 125–126

  combining ActionScript and, 120–128

  Consumer component, 858

  containership, 110–112

  content property, 255

  control properties and styles, setting with attributes, 251

  controls, instantiating with, 250–251

  custom event, handling with, 235–237

  data collection object source property, 554

  data collections, declaring, 578

  data objects, declaring separate with tags, 577

  declaring objects in, 6–7

  defined, 5

  event listeners, declaring, 210–213

  event objects, working with, 213–223

  fault event, 900–901

  Form component, integrating into new application, 702–704

  formatter objects, 305–306

  grouping flat data, 644

  HTTPService object, creating, 722–723

  inline style declarations, 344–345

  load event, handling, 785

  Mail component, 907–908

  menu events, handling, 493

  MenuBar control, 495

  multiple operations, handling, 792

nonvisual classes, 112–113

Organize Imports feature, 128

Outline view, using with, 124

overview, 99

pie chart, 651

populating value object data with, 698

`Producer` component, 857

public properties, declaring with, 151

`RemoteObject` component, 830, 881

runtime channel, declaring in, 979

subtopics, filtering messages with, 867–868

`TabNavigator` navigator container, 498

`text` property, 254–255

value objects, 549–551

view states, 399, 407–412

`ViewStack`, 477

`WebService` object, creating, 784

as XML, 104–110, 770

XML object, declaring in, 753

`XMLList` object, declaring, 754

`XMLListCollection`, declaring in, 755

MXML components

    component folder, creating, 141

    component item renderers, 598

    component libraries, 155–161

    creating new, 142–143

    custom, 598

    for custom pop-up window, 521

    for custom skin, 444–445

    Flash-based components, creating, 161–165

    inheritance, 140–141

    instantiating, 144–149

    methods, 149, 152–155

    overview, 135, 139–140

    properties, 149–152

    self-logging, 176–177

MXML editor, Flash Builder, 49–50, 180–181, 191–192

MXML Item Renderer option, 626

`mxmlc` command-line compiler, 28

`<mx:Parallel>` tag, 384

`mx.rpc.events.FaultEvent` event object, 733, 790, 900

`mx.rpc.events.ResultEvent` event object, 730, 787, 832, 884

`mx.rpc.Fault` property, 900

`mx.rpc.http` package, 723

`mx.rpc.http.mxml` package, 108, 723

`<mx:SetStyle>` tag, 412

`<mx:SolidColor>` tag, 661

`<mx:Spacer>` control, 322

`<mx:State>` tag, 408

`mx.states` package, 414

`<mx:TabNavigator>` tag, 498

`MXTileList.mxml` file, 637

`mx.validators` package, 687

`<mx:verticalAxis>` tag, 667

`<mx:ViewStack>` tag, 472

`<mx:WebService>` tag, 792, 796

`<mx:XML>` tag, 753

my-amf channel, 829, 978–979

my-amf-streaming channel, 862

my-cfamf channel, 878

my-cfamf-secure channel, 878

`MyComponent` component, 349

`MyComponent_Complete.mxml` file, 143

`MyFlashLibrary.fla` file, 165

`MyFlashLibrary.swc` file, 165

`MyFlashLibrary.swf` file, 165

my-polling-amf channel, 855

myService.lastResult expression, 728

MySQL server, 917

my-streaming-amf channel, 855

`myStrictVar` variable, 115

`myVar` variable, 137, 138, 188–189

N

name, style, 343, 344

name property, 231, 400, 429, 963

named arguments, passing to CFC functions, 891, 892–894

named colors, 362

named destinations, Proxy Service, 819, 822–824

named parameters, `HTTPService`, 744–745

`NamedProxyDestinationComplete.mxml` file, 823

Namespace class, 771

@namespace declaration, 347

namespace keyword, ActionScript, 771

`namespace()` method, 771

namespace object, 770–771

namespaces

    Adobe AIR, 964

    CSS, 347–348

    custom component prefix, 148

    custom prefix, 144, 549

    E4X, 770–773

    MXML components, 140

    prefixes, XML, 106–107

    s prefix, 7

    value object class prefix, 549

    XML, 105–106

Index

Namespaces in XML recommendation, W3C, 347

<namespaces> tag, 107

native class type, 224

native menu capability, WindowedApplication, 978

NavBarWithArrayData.mxml file, 486

navigate() function, 976

navigation, application. *See also* navigator bar containers; navigator containers

    Accordion container, 497, 500–502

    classic Web, 470–471

    Flex, 471

    with HTML control, 976–977

    menu controls, 491–497

    overview, 469

    TabNavigator container, 497–502

navigator bar containers

    data collection, using as dataProvider, 485–486

    handling events, 487

    overview, 484–485

    presentation, managing, 488–491

    ViewStack, using as dataProvider, 487–488

navigator containers

    ActionScript, working with in, 477–482

    creation policy, 482–484

    custom components in, 472–473

    defined, 471

    dimensions, 484

    overview, 471

    ViewStack, 472–477

NavigatorContent container, 472, 473, 498

Navigators section, Components view, 475

NetConnection Debugger, 196

Network Monitor, Flash Builder

    ColdFusion, configuring Flex project for use with, 197–201

    overview, 55, 167, 196–197

    tracing network traffic, 201–206

network traffic, tracing, 201–206

New ActionScript Class wizard, 238–240, 540–541, 542

New ActionScript File dialog box, 121

New Adobe Flash Component dialog box, 162–163

New CSS File dialog box, 356, 360

New Document dialog box, 67

New Editor option, 41

New Flash Professional Component option, 162

New Flex Library Project wizard, 156–157

New Flex Project wizard

    BlazeDS, 815–816

    ColdFusion, 875–877

    desktop application, 960–962

    Hello World application, 75–78

    messaging application, 856–857

    PHP, 920–921

    project creation process, 45–49

new keyword, ColdFusion, 897

New MXML Component wizard, 141–142, 445–446, 598, 684

New MXML Skin dialog box, 455–456, 528

New Package wizard, 157–158, 444–445

New State dialog box, 401–403

New Style Rule dialog box, 360–361

newIndex property, 487, 585

newStyleSheetComplete.css file, 361

NewTitlesReader.mxml application, 975, 978

nightly builds, BlazeDS, 810

no-arguments constructor method, 148

noLabel property, 506

nonblocking (asynchronous) I/O channels, 853

none value

    creationPolicy property, 483

    labelPosition style, 652

non-modal dialog boxes, 505–506

nonvisual classes, in MXML, 112–113

normal skin state, 448

normal view state, 600

null value

    filterFunction property, 558

    Model property, 536

    restrict property, 260

NumberFormatter class, 305, 307, 653

NumberValidator class, 687

numChildren property, 478, 479

numeric data, 647–648. *See also* charting controls

numeric expressions, literal, 761–762, 765

numeric property, 560

numeric values, style, 362

NumericStepper control, 272–273

O

Object class, 217, 741–742, 744, 759–760, 892–894

Object Tag Accessibility Attributes dialog box, 94

object value, resultFormat property, 726

object-oriented programming (OOP). *See also* ActionScript 3

    encapsulation, 13–14

    inheritance, 15–16

    modularity, 12–13

    overview, 11

    polymorphism, 16–18

ObjectProxy class, 728
objects. *See also* value objects
    ActionScript 3, declaring in, 7–8
    data, declaring separate with MXML tags, 577
    declaration, jumping to, 125
    formatter class, 305–306
    HTTPService component, 722–723
    members, and encapsulation, 13–14
    MXML, declaring in, 6–7
    WebService, 784–785
    XML classes, 751–754
okLabel property, 506
OlapDataGrid control, 573. *See also* list controls
oldIndex property, 487
On click prompt, Properties view, 216
onClick event, 210
oneway state, 405, 406
online help, 55
OOP. *See* ActionScript 3; object-oriented programming
openAlways property, 520
OpenAMF, 825
openDuration property, 500
OpenFace fonts, 297
openField property, 663
open-source project, Flex SDK as, 5
operating systems, Adobe AIR and, 963. *See also* specific
    operating systems by name
Operation class, 786, 831, 882–883, 891
Operation Name column, Connect to Data/Service dialog
    box, 711
operators, ActionScript, 116–117
optimizer command-line tool, 28
<option> tag, 607–608
OPTIONS method, 725
Organize Imports feature, 128
Other Views option, 38
outbound script, 86
Outline view, Flash Builder, 53, 124–125
output folder, 82, 169, 198, 921
outside value, labelPosition style, 652
overflow style, 83
overlapping objects, 133, 316–317
override keyword, 241
overrides
    clone() method, 240–242
    defined, 401
    view state, 404–412

P

<p> tags, 290
Package Explorer view, Flash Builder, 51–52
Package Presentation option, 52
packages, 48, 141, 157–158, 541–542. *See also specific*
    packages by name
packaging release version, 967–969
padding settings, 80, 132, 322
paddingBottom style, 318, 319
paddingLeft style, 317, 319
paddingRight style, 318, 319
paddingTop style, 318, 319
pageSize property, 278
pageTitle property, 83, 128
Pan tool, 404
Panel containers
    with control bars, 329–330
    custom pop-up window, 521
    Form container in, 679–680
    layout property, 326–327
    MX ControlBar, 328–329
    MX versus Spark, 311
    overview, 325
    Scroller object, 337–338
    title property, 327
    windowStyles selector, 513
<Panel> tags, 325
paragraph element, 256
ParagraphElement class, 289
Parallel effect, 383, 384–385, 415
ParallelDemo.mxml file, 385
parameters
    HTTPService, passing to server pages, 744–745
    passing application, 130
    passing to Web service operations, 796–798
    polymorphism, 16
parameters property, 86, 130, 727
params object, 86
parent argument, 525
parsers, E4X, 758
parsing, 752–754
password property, 240, 703
passwordInput property, 243
passwordValidator object, 694
Path class, 421, 423–425, 427–428, 431
Pause effect, 373, 385
PDF, Acrobat, 809, 955, 976–977
PDF Service, ColdFusion, 905

Index

`PDFCapability` class, 976

`pdfCapability` property, 976

PDPhoto.org Web site, 641

PEAR (PHP Extension and Application Repository), 911, 912

pencil icon, 67

penetration statistics, Flash Player, 21

percentage ratios, 334–335

percentage sizing, 333–335

`percentHeight` property, 252, 253, 334

`percentValue` argument, 653

`percentWidth` property, 253, 334

permission, global Proxy Service, 820

perspective selection tool, 42

perspectives, Eclipse, 41–43

`PhoneFormatter` class, 305, 307, 619–620

`PhoneNumberValidator` class, 687

Photoshop, Adobe, 432–433

PHP
    data connections, 932–938
    Flex project, creating for use with, 919–921
    with `HTTPService` and XML, 922–924
    installing, 912–919
    overview, 911–912
    Zend AMF, 924–932

PHP Extension and Application Repository (PEAR), 911, 912

PHP Group, 912

`phpMyAdmin` link, 915

pie charts
    backgrounds, controlling, 660–662
    doughnut chart, 657–658
    exploding pie, 654–657
    fill colors, controlling, 660–662
    multiple data series, using, 659–660
    overview, 650, 652
    wedge labels, setting, 652–654

`PieChart` component, 650

`PieChartCustomLabel.mxml` file, 654

`PieExplode.mxml` file, 657

`PieMultipleSeries.mxml` file, 660

`PieSeries` series class, 650, 653, 659, 660–661

`PieSetFillColors.mxml` file, 662

piggybacking, 852

`piggybackingenabled` property, 852

pixilated graphics, 430

plain old Java Object (POJO), 826

Play button, Dreamweaver, 95

`play()` method, 374, 376–377, 384

`PlayEffectWithAS.mxml` file, 376

`playerProductInstall.swf` file, 82, 83

`PlayingEffects.mxml` file, 375

`PlotChart` component, 650

`PlotSeries` series class, 650

plug-ins, Eclipse, 33–36

POJO (plain old Java Object), 826

polling, AMF and, 852–853

`polling-interval-millis` property, 852

polymorphism, 16–18, 214, 224

Pop Service, ColdFusion, 905

`popUp` property, 518

pop-up windows. *See also* `Alert` class
    custom, 521–529
    overview, 327, 503
    `PopUpButton` control, 517–520
    `PopUpMenuButton` control, 514–517

`PopUpButton` control, 503, 517–520

`PopUpButtonDemo.mxml` file, 520

`PopUpManager` class, 505, 524–529

`PopUpMenuButton` control, 491, 503, 514–517

`PopUpMenuButtonDemo.mxml` file, 517

ports, MAMP, 919

`position` property, 278

POST method, 725, 745

post-colon data typing syntax, 115

predicate expressions, filtering data with, 760–764

Preferences dialog box, 43–45, 170–171

prefixes, 106–107, 144, 148, 549, 771. *See also specific prefixes by name*

presentation, navigator bar container, 488–491

`preserve` value, `whiteSpaceCollapse` style, 258

Preview button, 62

primitives, 249, 252, 282

`PrintDataGrid` control, 613

private access modifier, 65–66, 115, 543, 545–548

private classes, 542–543

private properties, 545–546

Problems view, Flash Builder, 53–54

Processes pane, Windows Task Manager, 972

processing messages, Message Service, 858–862

`Producer` component, 857–858, 859–861, 865, 866–871

production Flash Player, downloading, 24–25

professional version, MAMP, 916

Profile option, 195

profiling Flex applications, 194–196

profiling tools, 167

programmatic instantiation, 251

programmatic skins
    `Application` component, 148
    `ButtonBar` component, 491

custom
    binding to component, 451–455
    overview, 444
    for Spark Application component, 444–451
custom pop-up window, 528–529
FXG graphics, 419
overview, 443–444
skinning other Spark components
    assigning with CSS, 461–462
    creating new skin, 455–460
    customizing skin, 462–467
versus style data types, 362
programmatic validation, 692–694
programming. *See* object-oriented programming
programming languages, 5–6, 11, 104–105
Prohibited Services list, 905–906
Project properties dialog box, 93
projects, Eclipse, 38. *See also* Flex projects
prompt property, 604–606
properties. *See also specific properties by name*
    constraint, 332
    control, setting, 251
    data connection, 710–712
    date entry, 275
    defined, 149
    encapsulation, 14
    event object, 216–219
    formatter classes, 306–307
    GraphicElement class, 252–253
    HTTPService component, 723–726
    List control, 584
    MXML component, 149–152
    overriding in view state, 409–412
    Panel containers, 326–327
    public, 151, 240
    ScrollBar controls, 278
    Slider controls, 280–281
    Spark text control, 254–259
    versus styles, 343–344
    TextArea control, 260
    TextInput control, 260
    UIComponent class, 252–253
    value object, 539, 543–551
Properties dialog box
    breakpoints, 182
    ColdFusion, configuring Flex project for, 197–198
    component library, adding to build path, 159–160
    data connection properties, 712
    deep linking, disabling, 88

Flash Player version parameters, 84
Flex Compiler section, 101–102
Flex themes, 342
history management, disabling, 88
locale information, 942, 944, 945
.properties file extension, 950
Properties panel, Flash Professional CS5, 67–68
Properties view, Flash Builder, 54, 162–163, 216
<properties> element, 829
property property, validator object, 704
protected access modifier, 115, 215, 543
proxy classes, 798–801
proxy image, 393–394
Proxy Service
    configuring, 817–818
    default destination, 818–822
    named destinations, 822–824
    overview, 808, 817
proxy-config.xml file, 817, 818, 819, 823
public access modifier
    ActionScript class properties, 543–544
    converting to private, 65–66
    Java class, 826
    methods, 153
    overview, 115–116
    properties, setting, 150
public class, 542–543
public properties, 151, 240
Publish settings, Flash component, 164
"publish/subscribe" messaging, 850
purpose attribute, 460
PUT method, 725

Q

Q command, 424
quality parameter, 86
quantity property, 564
query object, CFC returning, 886–888
QueryNew() function, 886
questionicon.png file, 512
queued value, creationPolicy property, 484
Quick Admin heading, WampServer menu, 915
quotation marks
    in ActionScript 3, 210
    in E4X expressions, 761–762, 765
    in MXML, 104
    when designating typeface, 295
    in XML structure, 752

R

RadialGradient class, 425–428, 661
RadialGradientStroke class, 421–422
RadioButton controls, 230, 269–271, 285–286, 406–407
RadioButtonDemo.mxml file, 271, 279
RadioButtonGroup control, 230, 235, 269–270, 407
ranges of characters, embedding, 300–302
ratio value, GradientEntry object, 427
ratios, percentage, 334–335
Raw view, Network Monitor, 202
RDS (Remote Development Service), 808, 846, 881, 903
read-only properties, TextInput control, 261
Real Time Messaging Protocol (RTMP), 809, 849, 853
Rect class, 111–112, 421, 422–423
rectangular shapes, drawing with FXG, 422–423
red, green, blue (RGB) percentage values, 362
redeployment, BlazeDS, 818
redFont selector, 352
refactoring
    source-code files, 63
    variable names, 61–62
references, searching for, 60
refresh() method, 557–558, 560, 644
RegExpValidator class, 687
register state, 410
relational databases, 534
relative address, 724
relative depth (z-index), 133
release builds
    application, 88–91, 967–969
    BlazeDS, 810, 814
Remote Development Service (RDS), 808, 846, 881, 903
remote HTTP service, 710–714
remote methods, 830–831, 838–840
Remote Procedure Call (RPC) components, 578, 631, 707, 709–710. See also HTTPService component; RemoteObject component; WebService component
[RemoteClass] metadata tag, 842, 843, 895, 896, 897
RemoteObject component
    channels, creating at runtime, 979–980
    ColdFusion Components, 880–883
    defined, 578
    fault events, 900–902
    Flash Remoting, 874
    instantiating, 830
    overview, 830
    passing arguments to remote methods, 838–840
    passing data between ActionScript and Java, 840–841

remote methods, calling, 830–831
    in Remoting Service, 824–825
    result event, 736, 884–888, 889
    results, handling, 831–838
    in RPC architecture, 709–710
    send() method, 892
    versus SOAP, 780
    testing Flex applications, 200
    tracing data, 204–206
    value object classes, 841–845
    Zend AMF class, calling with, 928–929
RemoteObjectDemo.mxml file, 200, 204–205
Remoting Service. See also Zend AMF
    destinations, configuring, 828–830
    Java classes, creating and exposing, 825–828
    overview, 807, 808, 824–825
    PHP, 924
remoting-config.xml file, 817, 828–829, 878
Remove ActionScript styling code option, 456
Remove All button, 183
Remove button, 183
RemoveAction class, 415
removeAll() method, 555
RemoveChild element, 408
removeChild() method, 483
removeEventListener() method, 227
removeItemAt() method, 555
removePopUp() method, 524, 525–527
Rename Class dialog box, 63
Rename Variable dialog box, 62
rendererIsEditor property, 629–632
renderers package, 598
RendererWithViewStates.mxml file, 601
Representational State Transfer (REST), 708–709, 777
request value, <scope> element, 829–830
requestTimeout property, 736
Required Flash Player version option, 84
required validation rule, 695
requiredFieldError property, 695, 697
reserved characters, 110
Resize effect, 372
resizeToContent property, 484
resizing images, 283–284
resource bundles, custom, 947–953
ResourceBundle class, 947–948
[ResourceBundle] metadata tag, 952
resourceManager object, 944–946, 950, 951
responder classes, 210
Response tab, Network Monitor, 202, 204, 205
REST (Representational State Transfer), 708–709, 777

RESTful pattern, Ruby on Rails, 725
resthttpservice library, 725
Restore button, 40
restrict property, 260
RESULT constant, 788
result event
    CallResponder object, 837
    ColdFusion Component, 884–888
    versus fault event, 736
    HTTPService component, 730–733
    ItemResponder class, 739–740
    Mail component, 908
    RemoteObject component, 832–834, 836, 889
    WebService component, 787–789, 792
ResultEvent class, 730–731, 758, 788
resultFormat property, 724, 726, 728, 753, 924
resultHandler() method, 791
Resume tool, 192
return type
    HTTPService component, 714–719
    PHP service class functions, 933
    Web service data connection, 801–803
ReturnSimpleXML.php file, 923
returntype property, 879, 880, 897
reusable graphic elements, 428–430
reverse domain package names, 141
reverseStep value, form property, 672
RGB (red, green, blue) percentage values, 362
rgb key word, 362
Rhino, 750
rich internet applications (RIAs), 19
rich text, 256, 258–259, 288–291
RichEditableText control, 254, 259
RichText control
    bidirectional text, 293–294
    columnar display, 292
    content property, 255
    embedded font, 298
    fontFamily style, 295
    richly formatted text, 289–290
    Spark components, 254
    text justification and indentation, 291
    TextFlowUtil class, 257
    whiteSpaceCollapse style, 258–259
RichTextDemo.mxml file, 289–290
RichTextEditor control, 253
right property, 332, 335, 423
right to left (rtl) value, direction property, 293, 490–491
ROBoundArgs.mxml file, 840, 894

ROCallResponder.mxml file, 838
ROExplicitArgs.mxml file, 840, 894
ROFaultHandler.mxml file, 902
rollOut event, 412
rollOver event, 412
rollOverColor style, 355
rollOverState view state, 412
RollOverText.mxml file, 413
ROMultipleFunctions.mxml file, 890
ROMultipleMethods.mxml file, 837
RONamedArgs.mxml file, 894
root element
    custom namespace prefix in, 144
    MXML, 104, 106–107
    MXML component, 140
    XML document, 752
root folder location, ColdFusion, 197
ROPassVOArg.mxml file, 900
ROPassVO.mxml file, 845
ROReceiveValueObjects.mxml file, 899
ROResultEvent.mxml file, 834
ROResultHandler.mxml file, 886
ROService Java class, 827–828
ROService.java file, 828, 835
Rotate effect, 372, 381–383, 384
Rotate3D effect, 372, 381–383
Rotate3DDemo.mxml file, 383
RotateDemo.mxml file, 382
RotatingFonts.mxml file, 303
RotatingFontsWithSlider.mxml file, 304
rotation, text control, 297, 303–304
rotation property, 303–305, 426
<row> tag, 728
rowCount property, 614
ROWithBinding.mxml file, 884
ROWithBindings.mxml file, 832
RPC (Remote Procedure Call) components, 578, 631, 707,
           709–710. See also HTTPService component;
           RemoteObject component; WebService
           component
RSL (Runtime Shared Library) files, 90
RSS feed, 973–975
rtl (right to left) value, direction property, 293, 490–491
RTLDemo.mxml file, 293
RTMP (Real Time Messaging Protocol), 809, 849, 853
Ruby on Rails, 725
rules, validation, 695–697
Run menu, 193–194
Run to Line feature, 194

Index

runtime. *See also* ActionScript 3
   Adobe AIR, 958
   custom resource bundles, creating at, 947–950
   data collections, 555–562
   E4X parsers, 758
   images at, changing, 285–286
   loading custom skin at, 454–455
   locales, changing at, 944–947
   remoting channels, creating at, 978–980
   view states, switching at, 406–407
runtime library. *See* Adobe AIR
Runtime Shared Library (RSL) files, 90
`RuntimeResourceBundles.mxml` file, 950
`RuntimeStylesComplete.mxml` file, 365
`RuntimeStyles.mxml` application, 365

S

s prefix, 106, 108
`<s:a>` tag, 289
SabreAMF, 924
sample applications, BlazeDS, 813–814
`samples.war` BlazeDS instance, 811
_sans font family, 296
`<s:Application>` tag
   applets, 92
   `currentState` property, 407
   `CustomEventApp.mxml` application, 232
   HTML wrapper template, 83
   integrating applications with Dreamweaver, 93
   layout, 78–79
   MXML components, instantiating, 146
   as XML document root, 104
`<s:ArrayCollection>` tag, 553
`<s:ArrayList>` tag, 576, 577
Save As dialog box, 432, 433
Save Perspective As option, 42
`sayHello()` function, 927, 928
`<s:BitmapImage>` tag, 440
`<s:br>` tag, 289
`<s:Button>` tag, 218, 729
scalability, Web application, 470
Scalable Vector Graphics (SVG), 6
`Scale` effect, 373
`Scale3D` effect, 373
`scaleX` property, 378, 428
`scaleY` property, 378, 428
scaling graphic elements, 430
`ScalingGraphics.mxml` file, 429

`<s:content>` tag, 256
`<scope>` tag, 829–830
`<script>` tag, 83
`<Script>` tag, 120–121
`scroll` event, 278
scroll setting, `overflow` style, 83
scrollbar, `TextArea` control, 262
`ScrollBar` controls, 277–279
`Scroller` component, 277, 337–338
`ScrollerDemo.mxml` file, 338
scrolling
   `DataGrid` control, 614, 622
   `HorizontalList` control, 635
   `TileList` control, 635
scrolling region, creating, 337–338
`scrollPosition` property, 277–279
`<s:dataProvider>` tag, 575
`<s:div>` tag, 256, 289
SDK (Software Developers Kit). *See* Flex 4
searching Flash Builder, 56–64
`SearchingData.mxml` file, 566
security, ColdFusion, 905–908
security certificate, 968–969
`seek()` method, 567
segment value, `form` property, 672
Select Folder dialog box, 437
Select root selector drop-down list, 714
`<select>` tag, 607–608
selectable property, 260, 624, 630
`SelectableDropDown.as` file, 609, 610
`SelectableDropDownDemo.mxml` file, 610
`selectableRange` property, 275
`selected` property, 267, 268–269, 629, 631
selected text, working with, 261
selected view state, 600
`selectedChild` property, 477, 480–482
`selectedColor` property, 275
`selectedDate` property, 275, 307–308, 518
`selectedImage` variable, 282
`selectedIndex` property
   `ButtonBar` control, 611
   `ComboBox` control, 588, 605, 606
   conditional statements, 117
   `DropDownList` control, 605
   `List` control, 587–588
   list controls, 584
   navigator containers, 477–478
   `ViewStack`, 477, 478–479
`selectedIndices` property, 584, 585

selectedItem property
  ButtonBar control, 611
  ComboBox control, 606
  DataGrid control, 618
  HorizontalList control, 635
  List control, 585–586
  list controls, 584, 588
  TileList control, 635
selectedItems property, 584, 585
selectedState variable, 589
selectedValue property, 271
selectField property, 608, 609
selectFieldValue property, 608
SelectingComplexObjects.mxml file, 590
selectionActivePosition property, 261
selectionAnchorPosition property, 261
selectionBeginIndex property, 261
selectionColor style, 355
selectionEndIndex property, 261
selection.value property, 235
selector property, 865–866
selectors, CSS
  Alert class, using with, 512–514
  applying skin with style sheet declaration, 453
  defined, 343
  descendant, 346, 350–351, 354
  global, 346, 352–353, 355, 360
  ID, 344, 346, 352
  modifying at runtime with ActionScript, 367–369
  overview, 345, 346
  style name, 346, 351–352
  type, 346–349
selectRange() method, 261
self-logging components, 176–177, 179
send() method
  bound argument notation, 839
  calling remote method with, 831
  HTTPRequest object, 727
  HTTPService component, 738, 745, 923
  Operation class, 882–883, 891
  properties object, 744
  RemoteObject component, 892
  Web service operation, 797
Sequence effect, 383, 385–387, 415–418
SequenceDemo.mxml file, 387
serialization, 840–841, 862, 932
series class, 648
_serif font family, 296
server configuration, ColdFusion, 877
servers, 91, 917–919. See also application servers

server-side fault, from CFC function, 901–902
server-side proxy, 725
service class, 927–928, 935–938
Service Details section, Connect to Data/Service dialog box, 711
Service Operations screen, 904, 933–934, 937
<service> root element, 829, 855
<serviceinclude> element, 817
servicePassword property, 908
services, ColdFusion, 905–910
services folder, 927
services-config.xml file, 817, 829, 851–854, 878
serviceUserName property, 908
session value, <scope> element, 829
set accessor method, 545–546
Set to default Apache and MySQL ports option, 919
SetAction class, 415
setElementIndex() method, 112
setFocus() method, 261
setItemAt() method, 555, 742
setStyle() method, 251, 344, 366, 368–369, 454
setStyleDeclaration() method, 368
setter methods, generating, 64–66, 546–549
SettingAndGettingStyles.mxml file, 367
shadowColor property, 263
Shape tween, 164
shapes, drawing with FXG, 422–425
shiftKey property, 220
ShoppingCart.mxml file, 473
shortcuts, 501, 612–613
shorthand MXML binding expressions, 136–137
Show Breakpoints button, 183
Show class view icon, 53, 124, 125
Show Inherited Events link, 209
Show Inherited Skin States option, 447
show() method, 494, 504–508, 510
Show View dialog box, 39
showBusyCursor property, 723, 724
showStatusBar property, 978
showToday property, 275
<s:HTTPService> tag, 723, 729
shutdown.bat batch file, 812
<s:img> tag, 289
simple data set, returning from PHP class, 929–930
Simple Object Access Protocol. See SOAP-based Web services
simple polling, 852
SimpleChat.mxml file, 861
SimpleEvent.mxml file, 211
SimpleForm.mxml file, 677
SimpleLocaleUseComplete.mxml file, 944
SimpleLocaleUse.mxml application, 943

SimpleMotionPath class, 377
SimpleText control, 405
SimpleXML extension, PHP, 922–923
Sine class, 387
single value, concurrency property, 726
single-column controls, 593
size partial event attribute, 232
sizeChanged event, 234
sizeGroup_itemClickHandler() event handler
          function, 234
sizeMessage object, 236
sizeSelected event, 232, 236
SizeSelectorComplete.mxml file, 235
SizeSelectorStart.mxml file, 230, 232, 234
sizing containers and controls
    absolute, 334
    constraint-based, 335–336
    content-based, 333–334
    overview, 333
    percentage, 334–335
skin parts, 14, 252, 448–449
skin states, 14, 447–448
Skin States page, Flex help system, 447
skinClass style, 451, 453, 460, 461, 529
SkinnableComponent class, 444, 451
SkinnableContainer class, 148, 323
skinning, 249. *See also* programmatic skins
skins package, 444–445
Skip All Breakpoints button, 183
<s:Label> tag, 80
<s:layout> tag, 78, 79
Slider controls, 279–281, 303–305
SliderDemo.mxml file, 280–281
SmartSketch, 19
<s:method > tag, 835, 888–889
snapInterval property, 279, 280
SOAP language, 204, 778–780
<soap> tag, 824
SOAP-based Web services. *See also* WebService component
    data connections, 798–805
    overview, 777–778
    PHP implementation of, 912
    SOAP language, 778–780
    WSDL, 780–782
soap-proxy adapter, 824
SoapService.cfc file, 783
SoapServiceProxy class, 800
SocialSecurityValidator class, 687
software bundle packages, 912–913
software clustering, 809

Software Developers Kit (SDK). *See* Flex 4
SolidColor class, 425, 661
SolidColorStroke instance, stroke property, 421
<s:operation> tag, 792, 797
Sort class, 560, 562
Sort option, 124
sort property, 560–561
SortDemo.mxml file, 562
SortField class, 560–561
sorting data collections, 560–562
SoundEffect effect, 373
source, binding expression, 136
Source button, 142
source code, 10, 63–64, 810
Source mode, Flash Builder, 49–50, 76–78, 476–477
source path, adding component library to, 159
source property
    [Embed] metadata tag, 302
    BitmapImage control, 284
    data collection, setting for, 554
    external ActionScript files, 120, 121
    external style sheets, 358
    Image control, 285
    image controls, 282
    RemoteObject component, 881, 928
    validator object, 695
    XMLListCollection class, 755
Source view, Flash Builder, 221, 359–360
<source> tag, 829, 878
source-code root (src) folder, 48, 157–158
source-path compiler argument, 951
<s:p> tag, 256, 289
Spacer control, 263, 265–266, 329
SpacerDemo.mxml file, 265
spaghetti code, 12
span element, 256
SpanElement class, 289
<s:Parallel> tag, 384
Spark components. *See also* list controls; programmatic skins;
        specific components by name; visual controls
    button controls, 266
    constraint-based layout, 330–331
    CSS namespaces, 347
    defined, 249
    effects, 372–373, 377–383
    Group, 319–325
    item renderers, 600–602, 626–627
    layout, 263, 311
    MX effects, 375
    MXML manifests, 108

namespace, 106
overview, 6
scrollbars, 337–338
text, 253–262
visual presentation, 312
Spark theme, 342
SparkAddressRenderer.mxml file, 627
Spark-based themes, 342
spark.components.Application class, 128
SparkControlBarDemo.mxml file, 330
spark.effects package, 372
spark.effects.easing package, 387
spark.events.IndexChangeEvent event object, 487, 585
spark.events.TrackBaseEvent event object, 281
spark.filters package, 431
spark-manifest.xml file, 108
SparkPanelDemo.mxml file, 327
spark.primitives package, 420–421
SparkSkin class, 443, 444
SparkTileList.mxml file, 641
specialized fonts, 300
Specific component option, 360–361
SpiderMonkey, 750
Sprite class, 69
SpriteVisualElement class, 440
SQLite database, 631
SQLiteManager link, 915
src (source-code root) folder, 48, 157–158
src:local style, 298
src:url style, 298
<s:request> tag, 745, 797
<s:source> tag, 554
<s:span> tag, 256, 289
<s:State> tag, 407
<s:states> tag, 407–408, 414
<s:States> tag, 600
<s:tab> tag, 289
stageX:int property, 220
stageY:int property, 220
stand-alone installer, Flash Builder, 32–34
startdb.bat batch file, 813
startdb.sh file, 813
Startup.bat file, 812
State class, 400, 414
State selector, Design view, 404–405
stateful applications, 533, 556
stateGroups attribute, 462
stateless requests, REST architecture, 708
states, skin, 447–448. *See also* view states
states property, 400

States view, Flash Builder, 54, 401, 402–403, 404–405
StateVO class, 588
StateVO.as file, 610
static data, 115, 538
static event name constants, 240
static keyword, 150
static methods, formatter classes in, 308–310
static properties, MXML component, 150
status bar, WindowedApplication, 978
status property, 978
<s:tcy> tag, 289
Step Into tool, 193
Step Over tool, 193
Step Return tool, 193
step value, form property, 672
stepSize property, 272–273
<s:text> tag, 254
<s:TitleWindow> tag, 529
stopPropagation() method, 228
<s:TraceTarget/> tag, 167, 178, 871
<s:Transition> tag, 414
<s:transitions> tag, 414
streaming channel, 853–854
String value
    parsing XML-formatted, 752
    selection.value property, 235
    TextEvent class, 232
    trace() function, 172
stringData variable, 752
StringValidator class, 687, 689
stroke property, 421, 422, 424
strokeColor property, 263
strokeWidth property, 263
style name selectors, CSS, 346, 351–352
style name, style sheet, 343, 344
style sheet, 343–344, 453. *See also* CSS
style sheet file, 356
style value, style sheet, 343, 344
StyleManager class, 364, 365, 367–368, 454
styleManager object, 364–365, 368–369
styleManager property, 364
StyleManager2 interface, 364
styleName property, 253, 346, 352
styles
    control, setting, 251
    data types, 362
    defined, 149
    encapsulation, 14
    MX basic containers, 317–319

styles *(continued)*
    overriding in view state, 409–412
    versus properties, 343–344
    text, 290–291
subclass, 15
subscribe() method, 858, 859
subString() method, 261
subtopic property, 865, 866–871
subtopics, filtering messages with, 866–871
Sun Microsystems Web site, 811
super() method, 237, 240, 699
_Super_Contact.as class, 717, 718–719
_Super_ContactService class, 712
superclass, 15, 224. *See also specific superclasses by name*
Superclass dialog box, 239
Suspend tool, 193
<s:VerticalLayout> tag, 79, 702
SVG (Scalable Vector Graphics), 6
SWC files, 158, 164, 342
<s:WebService> tag, 784, 792
SWF files, 90, 164, 282, 344, 363
SWFObject JavaScript library, 82
swfobject_modified.js file, 96
swfobject.createCSS() method, 85
swfobject.embedSWF() method, 85, 130
swfobject.js file, 82, 83
<s:WindowedApplication> root element, 104, 977–978
switch statement, 118
Switch Workspace option, 37, 74
switching view states at runtime, 406–407
switching workspaces, in Flash Builder, 74–75
symbolColor style, 355
synchronous input/output, 853
system events, 207
system menu, WampServer, 915
System Preferences application, 918
system tray icon, 914–915
systemFont attribute, 302

T

Tab component, 485
TabBar container, 485
TabElement class, 289
table structure, database, 534, 935–938
TabNavigator container, 472, 497–500, 501–502
tags. *See also specific tags by name*
    compiler, 106
    data objects, declaring separate with, 577

    in MXML, 104
    Text Layout Framework, 288–289
target property, 217, 228–229
<target-player> tag, 85
targets property, 377
Task Manager, Windows, 972
TCYElement class, 289
template, HTML wrapper. *See* HTML wrapper template (index.template.html)
template-driven PDF documents, 809
Terminal application, Mac OS X, 813
Terminate tool, 193
Terms of Use, BlazeDS, 810
ternary expressions, 869–870
ternary operator, ActionScript 3, 119
Test Movie option, 70
testing
    E4X expressions, 762–763
    event declaration, 232–233
    Flex applications for ColdFusion, 198–201
    messaging application, 862
    release build, 90–91
TestPage.cfm ColdFusion page, 783
TestRollover.mxml file, 413
text
    advanced layout of, 288–294
    fonts, 294–302
    formatter classes, 305–310
    manipulating, 303–305
    overview, 287
Text control, 253
text controls
    formatters in binding expressions, 307–308
    properties of, 254–259
    rotation of, 297, 303–304
    text entry, 259–262
    transparency, 297
text files, 10
Text Font option, 44
Text Layout Framework (TLF), 255, 288–289
text nodes, filtering with predicate expressions, 761
text property
    binding expression, 136–137
    ComboBox control, 606
    custom event handler, 236
    Spark text control, 254–255
    TextArea control, 262
    TextEvent class, 232
text value, resultFormat property, 726

TextArea control, 129, 253, 254, 259, 262
TextBase selector, 348–349
text-decoration setting, 350
textDecoration style, 294
TextEvent class, 232, 234, 235
TextFlow class, 256
textFlow property, 256–257
TextFlowUtil class, 256–258
TextFlowXMLDemo.mxml file, 258
TextIndentDemo.mxml file, 291
TextInput control
    ComboBox control, nested in, 605, 606
    Form component, adding to, 685
    frameRate, 129
    as item editor for DataGrid control, 627–628
    MX, 253
    overview, 259–260
    restrict property, 260
    selected text, working with, 261
    Spark, 254
    validator object, creating, 688
textLayout.swc file, 288
Thawte certificate authority, 968
themes, Flex, 342
this item, 8, 187, 412, 552, 594
throwCFCFault() function, 901
thumb icon, Slider control, 279
thumbDrag event, 281
thumbPress event, 281
thumbRelease event, 281
tile layout, list controls with, 635–641
TileLayout layout class, 131, 326–327
TileList control, 573, 635–641
timeline, Flash, 9, 10, 69, 371
timeout value, 736
title property, 327, 564
<title> tag, HTML wrapper template, 83
TitleWindow container, 327, 505, 513, 521, 527–529
TLF (Text Layout Framework), 255, 288–289
TODO comment, 218
Toggle Breakpoint option, 180–181
toggle property, 267, 268
Toggle Watchpoint option, 190
ToggleButton control, 267
ToggleButtonBar container, 485, 487–488, 489
token property, 737, 794
Tomcat 6, Apache
    configuring Proxy Service, 817–818
    overview, 809

sample applications, using, 813–814
    starting, 811–813
tooltip property, 253
top property, 332, 423
topLevelApplication property, 129
toState property, 414
toString() method, 761
trace() function, 167, 172–175, 622
TRACE method, 725
TraceTarget component, 175, 177–179, 871
tracing
    messaging traffic, 871–872
    network traffic, 201–206
    targets, 177–180
Transfer Object design pattern, 539, 841
transfer objects. See value objects
Transition class, 414, 416
TransitionDemo.mxml file, 417
transitions
    declaring, 414–415
    defined, 399
    overview, 414–418
    Parallel effect, using in, 415
    Sequence effect, using in, 415–418
transitions property, 414
transparency, 297, 316, 379
traversing data, with cursors, 562–564
TraversingData.mxml file, 564
Tree control, 573
Tree view, Network Monitor, 202
trigger events, 373, 688–692
trigger property, 689, 691, 694
triggerEvent property, 689, 691, 694
triggering validator objects, 692–695
true value, ArrayCollection class filtering function, 557
TrueType fonts, 297
turnkey distribution, BlazeDS
    configuring Proxy Service, 817–818
    downloading, 810–811
    JDK, 809
    sample applications, using, 813–814
    sample database, starting, 813
    starting, 811–813
tweening, 371, 379
two-way bindings, 137
type property, 217, 231, 233, 234, 241, 692
type selectors, CSS, 346–349
typecasting literal values, 761–762
_typewriter font family, 297

Index

U

UIComponent class, 251–253, 368, 444, 517, 521
UML (Unified Modeling Language) diagram
    class with data structure, 535
    Event class inheritance, 219
    event object properties, 216–217
    inheritance, 15
    MXML components, 140
    vertical and horizontal layout containers, 312–313
Unexpected character error, 347
Unicode, 301–302
unicodeRange attribute, 301, 302
Uniform Resource Identifier (URI), 105–106, 771
uninstalling
    Adobe AIR, 958–959
    desktop application, 971
    Flash Player, 23
unique identifier. See id
units of measurement, 344
update() method, 948
updateHTML() function, 978
updatePerson() function, 937
updateSelection() method, 608, 609
upgrade installer, Flash Player, 83
Upload Service, ColdFusion, 905
URI (Uniform Resource Identifier), 105–106, 771
URI Reference, 105
URL column, Connect to Data/Service dialog box, 711
url property
    Application component, 129
    <endpoint> element, 979
    HTTPService component, 722, 723, 724, 923
    navigator bar container, 486
    WebService or HTTPService object, 824
<url> tag, 822–824
URLs, 91, 708
useAppserverSecurity parameter, 846
UseComponent.mxml file, 146
UseComponentWithAS.mxml file, 149
UseComponentWithMethod.mxml file, 154
UseCustomPopUp.mxml file, 527
UseDataConnection.mxml application, 711, 719
UseExternalResourceBundles.mxml file, 953
-use-network compiler argument, 730, 731
useProxy property, 820, 822, 823
user data selections, handling, 585–590
user events, 207
user interface, Flash Builder, 49–55
User Manager screen, 905–906

user profile, ColdFusion, 905–906
username property, 240
userNameInput property, 243
UseValueObject.mxml file, 551
UseWatchpoint.mxml file, 190
Using Flash Builder 4 heading, 55
UsingAddEventListener.mxml file, 225
UsingComponentRenderers.mxml file, 600
UsingConstraintsComplete.mxml file, 331
UsingLabelField.mxml file, 582
UsingLabelFunction.mxml file, 583
UsingOverridesBegin.mxml file, 410
UsingOverridesComplete.mxml file, 412
UsingRenderersWithViewStates.mxml file, 601

V

V command, 424
VALID constant, 692
Validate Configuration button, 198, 815, 856, 876, 921
validate() method, 692, 693
validateAll() method, 693, 694
validating data entry
    ActionScript, controlling with, 691–695
    error messages, 695–697
    overview, 687–688
    rules, 695–697
    trigger events, controlling with, 688–691
    validator object, creating, 688
validation interface, visual components, 704
ValidationDemo.mxml file, 690
ValidationResultEvent class, 692, 693, 694
Validator class, 694
validator objects, 688, 692–695
ValidatorDemo.mxml file, 694, 697
value, style, 343, 344
Value Object design pattern, 588, 698, 841, 894
value objects
    ColdFusion, 894–900
    Form container, modeling data with, 697–699
    generating, 714–717
    HTTPService component, 741–744
    instantiating, 549–552
    New ActionScript Class wizard, 540–541
    overview, 539
    RemoteObject component, 841–845
    reviewing code, 717–719
    syntax, 541–549
value property, 272, 273, 278, 280, 596
valueCommitted event, 689, 692

`valueObjects` package, 540
`valueToDisplay` variable, 150–151
`var` keyword, 114–115, 150
`variableRowHeight` property, 592, 624
variables. *See also specific variables by name*
    access modifiers, 115–116
    counter, in `for` loop, 119
    data collection, 553
    debugging tools, 167
    declaring in ActionScript 3, 114–117
    inspecting with breakpoints, 187–192
    names, event object, 213
    refactoring names, 61–62
Variables view, Flash Builder, 55, 187–188, 189, 220–221,
        733–734
variations, font, 298–300
VBox container, 227–228, 312–314, 316–319, 328, 334–335
`VBoxDemo.mxml` file, 313
`VBoxGapAndPadding.mxml` file, 318
vector graphics, 430, 433–434, 437–438. *See also* FXG
VeriSign certificate authority, 968
version, Flash Player, 83–85, 96
`version` property, 963
`version_major` parameter, 84
`version_minor` parameter, 84
`version_revision` parameter, 84
vertical layout, 78, 131–133
vertical layout container, 312–315
vertical navigator bars, 488–491
vertical scrollbar, `TextArea` control, 262
`vertical` value, `form` property, 672
`verticalAlign` style, 132, 317, 321
`verticalAxis` declaration, 667
`verticalCenter` property, 332, 423
`verticalGap` style, 317, 319
`VerticalLayout` class, 80, 131–133, 143, 146
`VGroup` component, 111, 113, 228, 319–323, 337–338
`VGroupDemo.mxml` file, 323
`view` attribute, XML node, 493
View Menu button, 52
View source option, 967
view states
    components, managing in, 412–413
    Design view, defining in, 401–406
    for Flex navigation, 471
    item renderers, customizing with, 600–602
    MXML, declaring in, 407–412
    overview, 399–401
    skin states, matching required, 447

switching at runtime, 406–407
    transitions, 414–418
`viewport`, `Scroller` object, 337, 338
views. *See also* MXML components; navigation, application
    defined, 469
    Eclipse, 38–40
    Flash Builder, 51–55
    in model-view-controller architecture, 139
`views/Authors.mxml` file, 473
`ViewStack` container
    in ActionScript, 477–482
    `ButtonBar` control, 613
    creating in Design mode, 473–477
    declaring in MXML, 472
    handling menu events, 493
    menu data providers, 492
    overview, 471
    using as `dataProvider`, 487–488
`ViewState` architecture, ASP.NET, 470
`ViewStatesBegin.mxml` file, 402, 404
`ViewStatesComplete.mxml` file, 406
`visible` property, 253, 373
`<visible>` tag, 973
visual controls. *See also* custom item renderers; *specific
        controls by name*
    binding returned data to, 719–722
    binding Web service data connection data to, 803–805
    `BitmapImage`, 281–286
    button, 266–271
    `Canvas` container, 315
    data entry, 271–277
    `GraphicElement`, 251–253
    `Image`, 281–286
    instantiating, 250–251
    interactive, 277–281
    layout, 263–266
    overview, 249–250
    properties, setting, 251
    styles, setting, 251
    text, 253–262
    `UIComponent`, 251–253
visual effects, FXG
    filters, applying, 431–432
    gradient fills, 425–428
    overview, 425
    reusing graphic elements, 428–430
    scaling graphic elements, 430
visual objects, 110–112, 133, 449–451
`void` return datatype, 213

Index

`VRule` control, 263–264
`VScrollBar` control, 277, 278
`VSlider` control, 279, 280, 281

W

W3C (World Wide Web Consortium), 105, 341, 347, 778
`wait-interval-mills` property, 852
WampServer, 913–916
watchpoints, setting, 188–191
Web browser
    Adobe AIR, 956
    classic Web navigation, 470–471
    configuring Eclipse, 44–45
    CSS implementation, 341
    debugging session, terminating, 171
    testing release build in, 90
Web Browser section, Preferences dialog box, 44–45
Web deployment, Flash Player, 18
Web navigation, 470–471
Web page, integrating Flex application into, 91–92
Web Premium software bundle, 9
Web server, testing release build with, 91
Web services. *See* SOAP-based Web services
Web Services Description Language (WSDL), 777, 780–782,
    784–785
Web Sharing option, 918
Web Tier Compiler, Flex, 3
Web Tools Platform All-in-One, 35
Web Tools Project, 34
`WEB-INF` folder, 846, 877–878
`WEB-INF/classes` folder, 826, 835
`WEB-INF/flex` folder, 817, 828, 877
`WEB-INF/lib` folder, 826, 846
WebKit Web browser engine, 957
WebORB, 825, 924, 925
`WebService` component
    ColdFusion, installing, 783
    creating object, 784–785
    cross-domain security constraint, 980
    defined, 578
    overview, 779, 783
    passing parameters to Web service operations, 796–798
    Proxy Service, 817, 818, 824
    `result` event, 736
    results, handling
        binding expressions, 786–787
        `CallResponder` class, 794–795
        fault events, 790–791
        multiple operations, handling events of, 791–794
        overview, 786
        processing Web service operations with ActionScript,
          795–796
        `result` event, 787–789
    in RPC architecture, 709–710
    tracing data, 203–204
`WebServiceBoundParams.mxml` file, 798
`WebServiceDemo.mxml` file, 199–200, 203–204
`WebServiceExplicitParams.mxml` file, 798
`WebServiceFaultEvent.mxml` file, 791
`WebServiceMultipleOperations.mxml` file, 794
`WebServiceResultEvent.mxml` file, 789
`WebServiceWithActionScript.mxml` file, 796
`WebServiceWithBindings.mxml` file, 786
`WebServiceWithDataConnection.mxml` file, 805
Webster, Steven, 741
`web.xml` file, 846
wedges, pie chart, 652–657
`while` statement, 119
white space, 425, 754
`whiteSpaceCollapse` style, 258–259
`width` property
    charting controls, 650
    components, 253
    containers/controls, 333–334
    `DataGrid` control, 614
    `HRule`/`VRule` controls, 263
    `Image` control, 283
    `Line` class, 421
    MX containers, 312
    percentage sizing, 334
    shape classes, 423
    `Spacer` control, 265
`width` setting, `<s:Application>` tag, 92
`widthInChars` property, 262
`window` argument, 525
window styles, 512
`WindowedApplication` component, 977–978
Windows operating systems
    Adobe Flex 4 SDK Command Prompt option, 28
    AIR, 958–959, 970–972
    BlazeDS, 811–813
    Eclipse, 35, 37
    Flash Player, uninstalling, 23
    `flashlog.txt` file location, 174
    `mm.cfg` file location, 174
    WampServer, installing on, 913–914
`.windowStyles` style name selector, 512, 513, 514

Winer, Dave, 778
Wipe effect, 373
WipeDown effect, 373
WipeLeft effect, 373
WipeRight effect, 373, 375
WipeUp effect, 373
Wireframe theme, 342
Wischusen, Derek, 725
workbench, 33
workspace
    Eclipse, 37–43
    Flash Builder, switching in, 74–75
Workspace Launcher dialog box, 37–38
World Wide Web Consortium (W3C), 105, 341, 347, 778
wrapper template, HTML. *See* HTML wrapper template
      (index.template.html)
WSDL (Web Services Description Language), 777, 780–782,
      784–785
WSDL location, 799
wsdl property, WebService object, 784
wsdl query string parameter, 780
<wsdl> element, 824
www directory link, WampServer menu, 915

X

x property, 253, 315, 423
XAML (Extensible Application Markup Language), 105
XAMPP, 913
xBy property, 380
xField property, 668
xFrom property, 379–380
XML. *See also* HTTPService component; SOAP-based Web
      services
    classes, 750–756
    data-centric applications
        binding returned data to visual controls, 719–722
        data connections, creating and managing, 710–714
        overview, 710
        return data type, defining, 714–719
    DataGrid control, 615
    E4X expressions
        extracting data from XML objects, 758–764
        modifying data in XML objects, 765–770
        overview, 756–757
    event handling strategy, 210
    <fx:Model> tag, 538
    HTTPService responses, handling with binding
        expression, 728–730

menu data providers, 492–493
MXML as
    CDATA blocks, 109–110
    child elements, 109
    entities, 110
    manifests, 107–109
    namespace prefixes, 106–107
    namespaces, 105–106
    overview, 104–105
    programming with, 104–105
namespaces, working with, 770–773
overview, 707–708, 749–750
PHP with, 922–924
REST architecture, 708–709
RPC architecture, 709–710
value object code, generating, 714–717
XML class
    array notation, 759
    defined, 751
    extracting data from objects, 758–764
    filtering XML data with predicate expressions, 761
    modifying data in objects, 765–770
    object, creating, 751–754
xml property value, 726, 753
XML User Interface Language (XUL), 105
xmlData.item expression, E4X, 754–755
XMLDocument class, 750, 751
XMLHttpRequest object, 727
XMLList class
    as data provider for PopUpMenuButton, 514–515
    defined, 751
    descendant accessor operator, 760
    dot notation, 758–759
    filtering with predicate expressions, 761–762
    Menu control, 494–495
    menu data providers, 492–493
    use of, 754–755
XMLListCollection class, 553, 751, 755–756
XMLNode class, 750, 751
xmlns attribute, 106, 964
xOffset argument, 394
XSLT (Extensible Stylesheet Language Transformations), 105
xTo property, 379–380
XUL (XML User Interface Language), 105

Y

y property, 253, 315, 423
yBy property, 380

yesLabel property, 506
yField property, 668
yFrom property, 379–380
yOffset argument, 394
yTo property, 379–380

Z

Z command, 424
zBy property, 380
Zend AMF
    ActionScript to PHP data serialization, 932
    calling class with RemoteObject, 928–929
    installing, 925–927
    overview, 924–925
    returning complex data from AMFPHP, 929–931
    service class, creating, 927–928
Zend Server, 913
ZendFramework subfolder, 927
zFrom property, 380
z-index (relative depth), 133
ZipCodeFormatter class, 305, 307
ZipCodeValidator class, 687
Zoom effect, 373, 415
Zoom tool, 404